Protect and Investment
Extended Warranty available

Savings to 50% off Dealer's Extended Warranty Prices!

Edmunds Teams up with Warranty Gold to offer You the Best Deal on Peace of Mind when Owning, Buying, or Selling Your Vehicle!

FREE QUOTE

http://edmunds.com/warranty
1-800-580-9889

Most people have three things in common when they buy a car.

They pay too much.

They waste time.

They hate the experience.

Which is exactly why you should call the Consumers Car Club, a nationwide auto buying service. We offer the quickest and most convenient way to save time and money when you buy a new car or truck. Simple as that. Just tell us the vehicle and options you want (any make or model-foreign or domestic) and we'll get you a lower price than you can get on your own. Guaranteed in writing. We can factory order any domestic vehicle and usually save you even more. No haggling. No hassles. No games.

Don't forget to ask about our loans, leases and extended service contracts. It's a terrific way to save even more money on the purchase of your new car. For more information, call the Consumers Car Club at 1-800-CAR-CLUB (1-800-227-2582).

The Smart New Way to Buy Your Car™

All new cars arranged for sale are subject to price & availability from the selling franchised new car dealer.

"Car dealers take advantage of their knowledge and the customer's lack of knowledge... Edmund's New Car Prices... provides standard costs for cars and optional items."

— Steve Ross, **Successful Car Buying**
(Harrisburg, PA: Stackpole Books, 1990)

"Never pay retail. Buy only at wholesale or below. When buying a car, it is <u>imperative</u> that you know the dealer's cost. Refer to Edmund's ...price guides for current dealer cost information. Armed with this information, you can determine the price that provides the dealer with a <u>minimum</u> 'win' profit."

— Lisa Murr Chapman, **The Savvy Woman's Guide to Cars**
(New York, NY: Bantam Books, 1995)

"How much should you pay for a new car?...Your goal is to buy the car for the lowest price at which the dealer will sell it... To be accurate about profit margins, you should use the most recent edition of Edmund's New Car Prices."

— Dr. Leslie R. Sachs, **How to Buy Your Next Car
For a Rock Bottom Price** (New York: Signet, 1986)

"Edmund's publishes a variety of useful guides... buy the guide that deals specifically with the type of car you need. Wouldn't it be nice if you could know beforehand the dealer's cost for the new vehicle you just fell in love with? Wouldn't it be even nicer if you knew how much to offer him over his costs, a price he would just barely be able to accept? Well you are in luck. You can find out exactly what the car cost the dealership ...in Edmund's auto books."

— Burke Leon, **The Insider's Guide to Buying A New
or Used Car** (Cincinnati, OH: Betterway Books, 1993)

"Obtain a copy of Edmund's New Car Prices... and be certain you have the current copy since they are revised regularly during a year. Edmund's will provide you with the dealer's cost prices for all makes and models along with corresponding prices for the available factory options. These prices will be listed alongside the sticker prices. Match the sticker information of the car you want to buy to the cost prices in Edmund's and add these up... to provide you with a useable answer to "what should I pay for the car?"... It will furnish you with a very reliable figure. This, in turn, will enable you to successfully negotiate with confidence because ultimately you will be able to pay a price that you know is realistic and fair."
—Edward Roop, **Best Deals for New Wheels: How to Save Money When Buying or Leasing a Car** (New York: Berkley Books, 1992)

"Using the percent factor to figure dealer cost is not as accurate as using specific information published in Edmund's New Car Prices."
—Mark Eskeldson, **What Car Dealers Don't Want You to Know** (Fair Oaks, CA: Technews Publishing, 1995)

"If you really want the nitty-gritty, you're going to have to... (get) ...Edmund's New Car Prices. This little book is a gold mine for the curious car buyer... It is an automobile fancier's delight, a straightforward, meaty compendium of raw facts... Buy the book, follow the steps outlined... and you will determine the exact cost of just about any car."
—Demar Sutton, **Don't Get Taken Every Time** (New York: Penguin Books, 1994)

Edmund's — Perfect Partners

USED CARS: PRICES & RATINGS

For 30 years, Edmund's has guided smart consumers through the complex used car marketplace. By providing you with the latest trade-in and market value, you are able to determine a fair price for your car before negotiations begin.

Whether buying, selling, or trading, Edmund's *Used Cars: Prices & Ratings* gives all the information you need to get your very best deal.

- Prices Most American and Imported Used Cars, Pickup Trucks, Vans, and Sport Utilities

- Shows Summary Ratings Graphs for Most Used Vehicles

- Listings Cover Models Over Last 10 Years

- Price any Vehicle Quickly and Accurately

- Adjust Value for Optional Engines, Equipment and Mileage

$8.99
CANADA $12.99

For information on all Edmund's Automotive Books, call 914-962-6297

1998

Edmund's

NEW TRUCKS

PRICES & REVIEWS

"THE ORIGINAL CONSUMER PRICE AUTHORITY"

NEW TRUCKS

TABLE OF CONTENTS
WINTER 1998   **VOL S3103-9803**

Publisher: Peter Steinlauf

Cover photo:
1998 Mercedes-Benz ML320

Published by:
Edmund Publications Corp.
P.O. Box 18327
Beverly Hills, CA 90209-4827

ISBN: 0-87759-623-9
ISSN: 1089-8735

Editor-in-Chief:
Christian J. Wardlaw

Managing Editor:
B. Grant Whitmore

Automotive Editor:
Greg Anderson

Copy Editor:
Wendy Logston

Contributing Editor:
James Flammang

Production Manager:
Lev Stark

Creative Design:
John H. Davis
Lynette R. Archbold

Cover Design:
Karen Ross

© 1997 by Edmund Publications Corporation. All rights reserved. No reproduction in whole or in part may be made without explicit written permission from the publisher.

Introduction 11
Understanding the Language of Auto Buying 14
How to Buy Your Next New Automobile 15
Step-by-Step Costing Form 17
Abbreviations 18
Editor's Picks for 1997 21
Cars without De-powered Airbags 24
Specifications 476
Crash Test Data 514
Leasing Tips 520
Warranties and Roadside Assistance 526
Dealer Holdbacks 528
Payment Table 531
Automaker Customer Assistance Numbers 532
Frequently Asked Questions 534
Road Test - Mercedes-Benz ML320 544
Road Test - Isuzu Rodeo 548
Notes 554

ACURA
'97 SLX 27

CHEVROLET
'98 Astro 29
'98 Blazer 35
'98 Chevy Van 42
'98 C/K 1500 Pickup 47
'98 C/K 2500 Pickup 57
'98 C/K 3500 Pickup 63
'98 Express Van 80
'98 S-10 Pickup 85
'98 Suburban 91
'98 Tahoe 101
'98 Tracker 108
'98 Venture 113

CHRYSLER
'98 Town & Country 119

DODGE
'98 Caravan 125
'98 Dakota 133
'98 Durango 149
'98 Grand Caravan 153
'98 Ram BR1500 Pickup 163
'98 Ram BR2500 Pickup 172
'97 Ram BR3500 Pickup 181
'97 Ram Van / Wagon 188

FORD
'98 Club Wagon 197
'98 Econoline 202
'98 Expedition 205
'98 Explorer 211
'98 F150 Pickup 220
'98 F250 Pickup 228
'97 F350 Pickup 234
'98 Ranger 240
'98 Windstar 249

GMC
'98 Jimmy 255
'98 Safari 261
'98 Savana 266

Special offer from 1-800-CAR-CLUB - details on page 3

'98 Sierra 1500 273
'98 Sierra 2500 284
'97 Sierra 3500 292
'97 Sonoma 299
'98 Suburban 307
'98 Yukon 318

HONDA
'97 CR-V 322
'97 Odyssey 324
'97 Passport 326

INFINITI
'97 QX4 328

ISUZU
'97 Hombre 330
'97 Oasis 333
'98 Rodeo 335
'97 Trooper 338

JEEP
'98 Cherokee 341
'98 Grand Cherokee 352
'98 Wrangler 360

KIA
'97 Sportage 369

LAND ROVER
'97 Defender 90 372
'97 Discovery 374
'97 Range Rover 376

LEXUS
'97 LX 450 379

LINCOLN
'98 Navigator 381

MAZDA
'98 B-Series Pickup 384
'98 MPV 389

MERCEDES-BENZ
'98 ML320 392

MERCURY
'98 Mountaineer 395
'98 Villager 399

MITSUBISHI
'97 Montero 404
'98 Montero Sport 407

NISSAN
'98 Pathfinder 411

'97 Quest 414
'97 Truck 416

OLDSMOBILE
'98 Bravada 419
'98 Silhouette 422

PLYMOUTH
'98 Grand Voyager 426
'98 Voyager 434

PONTIAC
'98 Trans Sport 441

SUBARU
'98 Forester 448

SUZUKI
'97 Sidekick 452
'97 X-90 454

TOYOTA
'98 4Runner 456
'97 Land Cruiser 460
'98 RAV4 462
'98 Sienna 464
'97 T100 467
'98 Tacoma 470

1998 Mitsubishi Montero Sport

EDMUND'S 1998 NEW TRUCKS

Buying a car is a GAME of NUMBERS!

These two numbers could SAVE YOU THOUSANDS OF DOLLARS the next time you BUY A NEW CAR OR TRUCK!

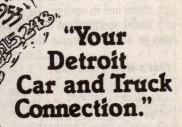

"Your Detroit Car and Truck Connection."

Auto Quote Line:
1-800-521-7257

9 am - 7 pm EST Mon.-Fri.

Obtain a printed computer quote on the make and model of your choice. Your quote contains all factory equipment available in an easy to read format. Instructions and pricing (both "**MSRP**" and dealer "**INVOICE**") make it simple to price your own vehicle.

First Quote $11.95, each additional quote $9.95. Add $6.95 for faxes.

Auto Hot Line:
1-900-884-6800

9 am - 5 pm EST Mon.-Fri.

Talk live to one of our sales staff for information on an "**IMMEDIATE QUOTE**", options, rebates, dealer incentives, used vehicle fair market value and plain old good advice!
$2.00 per minute. 6-10 min. avg. per call. You must be 18 or older to use this service.

We're **NATIONWIDE AUTO BROKERS**. For nearly thirty years, we have provided our customers with the lowest vehicle prices and best service because **we do the shopping for them**! Once you approve our low, low price (as little as $50-$125 over dealer invoice*) on the domestic or import vehicle of your choice, **NATIONWIDE** can order your domestic vehicle and have it delivered direct to a dealership near you. Factory-authorized service is then handled by the local dealership, and you rest easy knowing you've received a truly remarkable deal! Of course, if you choose, you can pick up your domestic or import vehicle at our offices here in Detroit. **NATIONWIDE** can handle all the arrangements.

Let us give you a quote on the make, model and options you want. In any numbers game, it's always great to have the winning combination!

VISIT OUR INTERNET WEB SITE AT
http://www.car-connect.com

---

*Some vehicles may be higher. Some specialty imports and limited production models and vehicles may not be available for delivery to your area or through our pricing service. A message on your printout will advise you of this. You will still be able to use the printout in negotiating the best deal with the dealer of your choice. New car pricing and purchasing services not available where prohibited by law.

NATIONWIDE Auto Brokers
29623 Northwestern Hwy., Southfield, MI 48034 • (810) 354-3400 • FAX (810) 223-1770

INTRODUCTION

Since 1966, Edmund's has been providing consumers with the information they need to get the best price on a new car. This edition of New Truck Prices continues the tradition of listing most of the trucks available on the market today, including pricing data for dealer invoice price and Manufacturer's Suggested Retail Price (MSRP) on each model and its options. We also provide detailed lists of standard equipment for each model, specifications for each model, and helpful articles that will allow you to make an educated decision about your purchase.

What's New For 1998?

We've changed our look to provide a cleaner and crisper appearance to the pages, making things easier to find and read. We also tell you which 1998 models have those new de-powered airbags for front passengers, and which ones do not. You might also notice that we've started to standardize equipment language for better consistency between models.

Why Are Some 1997 Models Included in This Book?

Some of you might be chagrined to discover that certain vehicles contained herein are 1997 models, with 1997 pricing. Let us explain why this has occurred. Our deadline for this book was mid October. At that time, pricing for a few models was unavailable to us, forcing us to run final 1997 pricing. For those of you looking for deep discounts on leftover 1997 models, this is not a problem. For those of you looking for a 1998 model, this is a bit more than an inconvenience.

We have this problem each year, and haven't found a solution that will allow us to get the book out in a timely manner and have complete information all at the same time. One place you can find price updates is on our world wide web Internet site; the address is http://www.edmunds.com. The very nature of the online medium allows us to quickly update prices, while the nature of publishing printed materials results in some lag time between completion of the project and the on-sale publication date.

How Do I Use This Guide?

If you're new to Edmund's, or are new to the car buying experience, we should explain how to use this book effectively. Your first step should be to visit a car dealership. Take a pad of paper with you, and write down all pertinent information from the window sticker of the car you like. Then, go home, or go to Mc Donald's, or go have an espresso at the local coffeehouse. Snuggle up with Edmund's New Truck Prices, and start figuring out how to get the best deal on the car of your dreams.

INTRODUCTION

Read the articles on **dealer holdbacks**, **buying your next new automobile**, and **leasing tips**. Then study the make and model that you're interested in. You'll find a representative photo of the vehicle, followed by a synopsis of what's new for 1998, where applicable. Then, a short review provides our opinion of the car, followed by safety data. An extensive listing of standard equipment for each trim level comes next, telling you what items are included in the base price of the vehicle. The first paragraph pertains to the base model, and if more than one trim level is available, successive paragraphs will explain what additional features the additional trim levels include over the base model.

Next is the meat of this guide: the pricing data. Each vehicle has base invoice price and base MSRP listed for each trim level, and the destination charge, which is the cost of shipping the vehicle from the factory to the dealer. Don't forget to add the destination charge, which is non-negotiable, when pricing a vehicle. Following the base prices and destination charge is a listing of all the optional equipment available on the vehicle from the factory. Along the left margin you'll find a factory code for each option. The dealer invoice price and the MSRP are listed near the right margin. Some option listings have short descriptions that tell you, for example, what might be included in a particular option package, or what trim level the option is available on, or that you must purchase the power lock group to get the power sunroof.

You'll notice that some imported makes do not have options listings. This is because the automaker includes the most popular accessories as standard equipment on a particular trim level, and any additional items that you might like to add to the vehicle will have to be purchased from and installed by the dealer, or are installed at the port of entry. For example, the Honda CRV comes with power door locks and power windows standard from the factory. A cassette player is a dealer add-on, and each dealer may price the item differently. Generally, you can haggle about 25% off dealer-installed accessories with little effort.

Supply and Demand

Now that you've priced the vehicle you're interested in, and you've read the articles about how to get the best deal, you're ready to go back to the dealership and buy your new car armed with the knowledge and information that is crucial to getting a good deal. Keep in mind that the laws of supply and demand apply to auto sales as much as they apply to any other material commodity. If a vehicle is in great demand and short supply, don't expect to get much of a discount. On the other hand, inflated inventories and tough competition mean that deals are readily available on models

INTRODUCTION

that aren't selling well. If you've got to be the first on your block with a hot new model, you'll pay for the privilege. In fact, dealers sometimes demand profit above the MSRP on ultra hot models, and they expect to get it. Meanwhile, it is not uncommon for older, stale models to sell below invoice thanks to hefty incentive programs and rebates, particularly at year-end clearance time. All things considered equal, Edmund's feels that a 5% profit to the dealer is fair on a new vehicle. After all, the sales staff has bills to pay just like you do.

Looking for the exact specifications of your dream car? Check the back of this book, where you'll find charts displaying the length of the vehicle, the curb weight of the vehicle, and how much horsepower the base engine makes, among others. This format allows you to easily locate and compare specifications between different models and trim levels.

Write to Us

New Car Prices has even more to offer, from step-by-step costing forms that you can use right at the dealership, to lists of warranty coverage, to pages of crash test data. Edmund's strives to give you precise, accurate information so that you can make your very best deal, and we invite your comments. Please send correspondence to:

Edmund Publications Corporation
P.O. Box 18827
Beverly Hills, CA 90209-4827
Attn: Automotive Editors

or send e-mail to:
editor@edmund.com

We wish you luck in your hunt for a new vehicle. Use the information contained within to your advantage!

> NOTE: All information and prices published herein are gathered from sources which, in the editor's opinion, are considered reliable, but under no circumstances is the reader to assume that this information is official or final. All prices are represented as approximations only, in US dollars, and are rounded to the highest whole dollar amount over 50 cents. Unless otherwise noted, all prices are effective as of 10/15/97, but are subject to change without notice. The publisher does not assume responsibility for errors of omission or interpretation. The computerized consumer pricing services advertised herein are not operated by nor are they are the responsibility of the publisher. The publisher assumes no responsibility for claims made by advertisers regarding their products or services.

UNDERSTANDING THE LANGUAGE OF AUTO BUYING

Many consumers are justifiably confused by the language and terms used by automobile manufacturers and dealers. To assist you, here are some basic definitions:

Advertising Fee The amount you are charged to cover the cost of national and local advertising. This fee should be no more than 1-3% of the MSRP.

Dealer Charges These are highly profitable extras that dealers try to sell in addition to the vehicle itself. Items such as rustproofing, undercoating and extended warranties fall into this category. Most consumer experts do not recommend the purchase of these extras. These extras are also known as "Dealer Pack."

Dealer Holdback Many manufacturers provide dealers with a *holdback allowance* (usually 2 or 3% of MSRP) which is eventually credited to the dealer's account. That way, the dealer can end up paying the manufacturer less than the invoiced amount — meaning that they could sell you the vehicle at cost and still make a small profit.

Dealer Invoice The amount that dealers are invoiced or billed by the manufacturer for a vehicle and each of its optional accessories.

Destination Charge The fee charged for shipping, freight, or delivery of the vehicle to the dealer from the manufacturer or Port of Entry. This charge is passed on to the buyer without any mark-up.

Manufacturer's Rebate/Dealer Incentives Programs offered by the manufacturers to increase the sales of slow-selling models or to reduce excess inventories. While manufacturer's rebates are passed directly on to the buyer, dealer incentives are passed on only to the dealer — who may or may not elect to pass the savings on to the customer.

MSRP — Manufacturer's Suggested Retail Price The manufacturer's recommended selling price for a vehicle and each of its optional accessories.

Preparation Charges These are dealer-imposed charges for getting the new car ready to drive away including a full tank of gas, checking and filling the fluid levels, making sure the interior and exterior is clean, etc. Preparation Charges masquerade at many dealerships as D&H (delivery and handling) fees. Most D&H fees are negotiable.

Trade-in Value The amount that the dealership will give you for the vehicle you trade in. The trade-in value will be deducted from the price of the new vehicle.

Upside-down When you owe more on your car loan than your trade-in is worth, you are *upside-down* on your trade. When this happens, the dealer will add the difference between the trade-in value and what you owe to the price of the new vehicle.

Note: Occasionally there will appear in the "Dealer Invoice" and "MSRP" columns, prices enclosed in parenthesis, example: (90), which indicate a credit or refunded amount is involved.

HOW TO BUY YOUR NEXT NEW AUTOMOBILE

Every automobile buyer has but one thought in mind — to save money by getting a good deal. Your goal should be to pay 5% over the dealer's true cost, not the 10-15% the dealer wants you to pay. Use the following guide to help you plan your purchase:

Step 1 Know what type of vehicle you need, and study the different models available.

Step 2 Test drive, as extensively as possible, each model you're interested in. Pay special attention to safety features, design, comfort, braking, handling, acceleration, ride quality, ease of entry and exit, etc.

Step 3 Check insurance rates on the models you're interested in, to make sure the premiums fall within your budget.

Step 4 Contact several financial institutions to obtain loan rate information. Later on, you can compare their arrangement with the dealer's financing plan.

Step 5 Find the exact vehicle you want, and copy all the contents of the window sticker onto a pad of paper. Then, use the information in this book to determine actual dealer cost (if ordering the vehicle from the factory, just use the book to determine what the order will cost when you place it):

a) Total the dealer invoice column for the model and equipment you want using the costing form on page 17.

b) Find the holdback amount on page 528, and subtract this from the invoice amount, along with any applicable customer rebates and dealer incentives. The resulting figure is true dealer cost.

c) Add 5% fair profit. Keep in mind that hot-selling models that are in high demand and short supply will command additional profit.

d) Add the destination charge, which is non-negotiable. Also expect non-negotiable advertising fees ranging in value from 1-3% of the sticker price to be added to the total.

HOW TO BUY YOUR NEXT NEW AUTOMOBILE

e) Some dealers charge a D&H fee. This stands for Delivery and Handling. Pay half, if any at all. It's just added profit.

Step 6 Shop this price around to several different dealerships. The dealer who meets or comes closest to your target price should get your business. Be sure that the dealer's price quote will be your final cost. Get it in writing!

Step 7 If your present vehicle will be used as a trade-in, negotiate the highest possible value for it. Try not to accept a value that is less Edmund's trade-in value for your car (consult Edmund's *Used Cars; Prices and Ratings* book). When trading in your vehicle, you should deduct the trade value from the cost of the new vehicle. If you owe the bank more money than the trade-in is worth to the dealer, you are upside-down on your trade and must add the difference between what you owe and the trade value to the cost of the new vehicle. If you're making a cash down payment, either with or without a trade-in, be sure to deduct this amount from the cost of the new vehicle as well.

Step 8 Add dealer preparation charges (a.k.a. D&H), documentation fees, applicable state and/or local sales taxes and, in some areas, license plate charges to the final vehicle cost.

Step 9 When talking to the finance manager as you close the deal, he or she will try to sell you rustproofing, undercoating, protection packages, dealer-added options, and an extended warranty or service contract. Forget about this stuff. Dealers charge a substantial markup on these usually useless items to fatten the profit margin on your deal.

Step 10 Enjoy your new vehicle, knowing that you did everything possible to get the best deal.

See our Frequently Asked Questions section on Page 534 for more information on cars and car buying.

STEP-BY-STEP COSTING FORM

MAKE: \
MODEL: \
TRIM LEVEL:

EXTERIOR COLOR: \
INTERIOR COLOR: \
ENGINE SIZE/TYPE:

ITEMS	MSRP	INVOICE
Basic Vehicle Price:		
Optional Equipment		
1.		
2.		
3.		
4.		
5.		
6.		
7.		
8.		
9.		
10.		
11.		
12.		
13.		
14.		
TOTAL		
SUBTRACT Holdback Amount		
SUBTRACT Rebates and/or Incentives		
ADD 5% Fair Profit to New Total		
ADD Destination Charge		
ADD Advertising Fees (1-3% of MSRP)		
SUBTRACT Trade-In Value or Cash Down Payment		
or		
ADD Difference Between Trade Value and Loan Balance		
FINAL PRICE		
ADD Sales Taxes, Documentation/Prep Fees, and License Plates		
TOTAL COST		

ABBREVIATIONS

16V	16-valve	**Cyl**	Cylinder
24V	24-valve	**DC**	Direct Current
32V	32-valve	**DFRS**	Dual Facing Rear Seats
2WD	Two-wheel Drive		
3A/4A/5A	3-speed/4-speed/5-speed Automatic Transmission	**DME**	Digital Motor Electronics
		DOHC	Dual Overhead Cam Engine
4M/5M/6M	4-speed/5-speed/6-speed Manual Transmission	**Dr**	Door
		DRLs	Daytime Running Lights
4WD	Four-wheel Drive	**DRW**	Dual Rear Wheels
4WS	Four-wheel Steering	**Dsl**	Diesel Engine
A/S	All-season Tires	**ECT**	Electronically Controlled Transmission
A/T	All-terrain Tires		
A/C	Air Conditioning		
A/M	Auto-manual Transmission	**EEC**	Electronic Engine Control
ABS	Anti-lock Braking System	**EFI**	Electronic Fuel Injection
ALR	Automatic Locking Retractor Seat Belt	**ELR**	Emergency Locking Retractor Seat Belt
Amp	Ampere(s)		
AS	All-season Tires	**ETR**	Electronically Tuned Radio
AT	Automatic Transmission		
		ETS	Electronically Tuned Stereo
Auto	Automatic		
AWD	All-wheel Drive	**Ext**	Extended
BSW	Black Sidewall Tires	**FI**	Fuel Injection
BW	Blackwall Tires	**Ft**	Foot (Feet)
Cass	Cassette	**FWD**	Front-wheel Drive
CD	Compact Disc	**Gal**	Gallon
CFC	Chloroflorocarbon	**GVW**	Gross Vehicle Weight
Cntry	Country		
Conv	Convertible	**GVWR**	Gross Vehicle Weight Rating
Cpe	Coupe		
Cu Ft	Cubic Foot (Feet)		
Cu In	Cubic Inch(es)		
CVT	Continuously Variable Transmission	**H4**	Horizontally-opposed, Four-cylinder Engine

ABBREVIATIONS

H6	Horizontally-opposed, Six-cylinder Engine	**MT**	Manual Transmission
Hbk	Hatchback	**N/A**	Not Available or Not Applicable
HD	Heavy Duty	**NA**	Not Available or Not Applicable
HO	High Output		
HP	Horsepower	**Nbk**	Notchback
HUD	Heads Up Display	**N/C**	No Charge
HVAC	Heating/Ventilation/Air Conditioning	**NC**	No Charge
		OBD II	On-board Diagnostic System
I4	Inline Type, Four-cylinder Engine	**OD**	Overdrive
I5	Inline Type, Five-cylinder Engine	**OHC**	Overhead Camshaft Engine
I6	Inline Type, Six-cylinder Engine	**OHV**	Overhead Valve Engine
Kw	Kilowatt	**Opt**	Optional
L	Liter	**OS**	Outside
L/R	Left and Right	**OWL**	Outline White-letter Tires
LB	Longbed		
Lbk	Liftback	**P/U**	Pickup Truck
Lbs/ft	Pounds/Feet (measurement of engine torque)	**Pass**	Passenger
		PEG	Preferred Equipment Group
Lb(s)	Pound(s)		
LCD	Liquid Crystal Display	**PEP**	Preferred Equipment Package
LD	Light Duty		
LED	Light Emitting Diode	**PGM-FI**	Programmed Fuel Injection
LH	Left Hand		
Ltd	Limited	**Pkg**	Package
LWB	Long Wheelbase	**Pkup**	Pickup Truck
M+S	Mud and Snow Tires	**PS**	Power Steering
Max	Maximum	**Psngr**	Passenger
Mm	Millimeter	**Reg**	Regular
MPFI	Multi-point Fuel Injection	**RH**	Right Hand
		Rpm	Revolutions Per Minute
Mpg	Miles Per Gallon		
Mph	Miles Per Hour	**RWD**	Rear-wheel Drive
MPI	Multi-point Fuel Injection	**RWL**	Raised White-letter Tires

ABBREVIATIONS

SB	Shortbed
SBR	Steel-belted Radial Tires
Sdn	Sedan
SEFI	Sequential Fuel Injection
SFI	Sequential Fuel Injection
SLA	Short/Long Arm Suspension
SOHC	Single Overhead Camshaft Engine
Spd	Speed
SPFI	Sequential Port Fuel Injection
SRS	Supplemental Restraint System (Airbag)
SRW	Single Rear Wheels
Std	Standard
SUV	Sport/Utility Vehicle
S/W	Station Wagon
SWB	Short Wheelbase
Tach	Tachometer
TBI	Throttle Body Fuel Injection
TCS	Traction Control System
TD	Turbo-diesel Engine
Temp	Temperature
TPI	Tuned Port Fuel Injection
TrbDsl	Turbo-diesel Engine
V6	V-type, Six-cylinder Engine
V8	V-type, Eight-cylinder Engine
V10	V-type, Ten-cylinder Engine
V12	V-type, Twelve-cylinder Engine
VTEC	Variable Valve Timing and Lift Electronic Control
W/	With
W/O	Without
W/T	Work Truck
WB	Wheelbase
Wgn	Wagon
WS	Wideside
WSW	White Sidewall Tires
X-Cab	Extended Cab Pickup

EDITORS' PICKS FOR 1998

**by Christian Wardlaw, B. Grant Whitmore and Greg Anderson
Automotive Editors, Edmund Publications**

Each year, consumers are bombarded with sound and text bites in advertising proclaiming their car worthy of recommendation by top automotive publications. These accolades are usually culled from top ten lists of this or that published by enthusiast magazines and consumer publications. We don't want to miss out on the fun this year, so we've compiled our own list of recommended vehicles for 1998.

Edmund's has decided to take a different tack than other buyer's guides and magazines. We've broken the car and truck markets into size/class segments, and then price segments, resulting in 37 categories. So, instead of giving consumers a list of ten recommended vehicles, Edmund's provides nearly 40 models that you ought to consider. Any model within a given category has a base price, including destination charge, which falls under the price threshold. As a bonus, we recommend six additional car models that cost more than $50,000. Enjoy our picks for 1998!

photo by Greg Anderson

EDITORS' PICKS FOR 1998

Size Category	Recommended Vehicle

CARS
$0-20,000:
Subcompact	Hyundai Accent
Compact	Honda Civic
Mid-size	Honda Accord LX
Station Wagon	Subaru Impreza Outback
Sport Sedan	Mazda Protégé ES
Sport Coupe	Nissan 200SX SE-R
Convertible	Chevrolet Cavalier Z24
Sports Car	Mazda Miata (based on final 1997 pricing)

$20,001-35,000:
Compact	Audi A4
Mid-size	Oldsmobile Intrigue
Full-size	Chrysler Concorde
Station Wagon	Subaru Legacy Outback
Sport Sedan	Ford Contour SVT
Sport Coupe	Honda Prelude Type SH
Convertible	Ford Mustang Cobra
Sports Car	Pontiac Firebird Formula

$35,001-50,000
Mid-size	Cadillac Seville
Full-size	Buick Park Avenue Ultra
Station Wagon	Volvo V70 T5
Sport Sedan	BMW 528i
Sport Coupe	BMW M3
Convertible	BMW Z3 2.8
Sports Car	Chevrolet Corvette

ULTIMATE CARS ($50,000 and up)
Mid-size	Jaguar XJR
Full-size	BMW 750iL
Sport Sedan	BMW 540i
Sport Coupe	Jaguar XK8
Convertible	Porsche 911 Carrera Cabriolet
Sports Car	Acura NSX-T

EDITORS' PICKS FOR 1998

TRUCKS (because the truck market is narrower with less price variation, we will not separate by price classes in most categories)

Compact Pickup	Dodge Dakota
Full-size Pickup	Dodge Ram Quad Cab
Minivan	Toyota Sienna
Full-size Van	Ford Club Wagon
Mini-SUV	Jeep Wrangler
Compact SUV (under $25,000)	Isuzu Rodeo S 4WD
Compact SUV (over $25,000)	Mercedes-Benz ML320
Full-size SUV	Toyota Land Cruiser

Cars Without De-powered Airbags

During the summer of 1997, after many children and small adults had been killed or seriously injured by front airbags in passenger vehicles, the National Highway and Traffic Safety Administration (NHTSA) ruled that automakers could begin installing lower-powered airbags in 1998 models. The lower-powered airbags (known as de-powered airbags, Next Generation airbags, Second Generation airbags, or Generation II airbags depending on whom you're discussing the topic with) inflate at a slower speed than previous airbags. This means that the lower-powered airbags protect small belted passengers better, while unbelted passengers will be taking even greater risks than before.

The following list contains 1998 vehicles that **will not** offer lower-powered airbags to consumers. Some models, like certain Audis, Jaguars, and Volkswagens, are getting the lower-powered airbags sometime during the course of the model year.

Audi A6 Wagon	
Audi A8	*November 1 production*
Audi Cabriolet	*November 1 production*
BMW 3-series	*January 1 production*
BMW 5-series	
BMW 7-series	
BMW Z3	
Chevrolet Astro	
Chevrolet Chevy Van	
Chevrolet Corvette	*Phased in during model year*
Chevrolet Express	
Chrysler Sebring Coupe	*Phased in during model year*
Dodge Avenger	*Phased in during model year*
Eagle Talon	*Phased in during model year*
GMC Safari	
GMC Savana	
Hyundai Accent	
Hyundai Elantra	
Hyundai Sonata	
Hyundai Tiburon	

Cars Without De-powered Airbags

Jaguar XJ-Series — January 1 production
Jaguar XK8 — January 1 production
Kia Sephia
Kia Sportage
Land Rover Discovery
Land Rover Range Rover
Mazda MPV
Mazda Millenia
Mazda Protégé
Mercedes-Benz C-Class
Mercedes-Benz CL-Class
Mercedes-Benz CLK320
Mercedes-Benz E-Class
Mercedes-Benz ML320
Mercedes-Benz S-Class
Mercedes-Benz SL-Class
Mercedes-Benz SLK230
Mitsubishi 3000GT
Mitsubishi Diamante
Mitsubishi Eclipse
Mitsubishi Galant
Mitsubishi Mirage
Saab 900
Saab 9-5
Subaru Forester
Subaru Impreza
Subaru Legacy
Suzuki Esteem
Suzuki Sidekick
Suzuki Swift
Suzuki X-90
Volkswagen Cabrio — Added during model year
Volkswagen Golf — Added during model year
Volkswagen Jetta — Added during model year
Volvo S90
Volvo V90

http://edmunds.com

AUTO-BY-TEL. The **ONLY** place on the Internet where you can buy or lease any new car or truck, **Edmund's way.**
NO FEES. NO CLUBS TO JOIN.
Not just a "shoppers" guide or directory. You will be able to purchase directly from a subscribing Auto-by-Tel dealer near you. Visit us today on Edmund's Internet site (http://edmunds.com).

SLX
ACURA

CODE   DESCRIPTION   INVOICE   MSRP

1997 SLX

1997 Acura SLX

What's New?

No changes for this 1-year-old Isuzu Trooper twin.

Review

Corporate sharing is reaching a fever pitch. Manufacturers are scrambling to fill the holes in their line ups by slapping their badges on vehicles they buy from other makers. Even highly regarded firms like Acura are not above climbing into a cozy relationship with a lesser marque; witness the Acura SLX. Based on Isuzu's competent Trooper, the Acura is a marginally spruced up version of the same truck. This isn't a bad thing since we have always thought the Trooper to be attractive, but it does seem dishonest. Imagine the embarrassment of SLX owners who think they got something special only to find that they are driving an Isuzu?

The SLX has a 3.2-liter dual-overhead-cam engine that produces 190 horsepower. It delivers capable acceleration in a vehicle this large, and this vehicle is definitely large. Markedly wider and taller than most of its competitors, the SLX has a rear cargo capacity capable of hauling several sheets of plywood.

The Acura SLX is priced the same as the top-of-the-line Isuzu Trooper Limited. Offering similar levels of luxury as the Trooper, the SLX has a softer ride that results in improved on-road manners. Off-road capability is equal to the ground-pounding Trooper but large bumps may cause the suspension to bottom out: the price you pay for that luxurious highway ride. Of course, very few SLXs will ever find their way off-road, unless the gravel driveway of the local polo club counts.

We know that luxurious sport-utes of today are like the sports cars so prevalent in the mid-Eighties. Designed for function but purchased for prestige, they are seldom driven to their capabilities. With this in mind, the SLX is a fine vehicle delivering the prestige and comfort that Acura owners have come to expect. Infiniti, Mercedes, and Lincoln have released luxury sport-utes this year; most of them are based on vehicles that are already in existence. This, and the bad press that the Acura SUV received as a result of an independent consumer group's roll-over test, has made the SLX somewhat vulnerable in the highly competitive luxury sport-ute marketplace. As a result, we've seen great lease deals and attractive financing to move these trucks out of

ACURA SLX

showrooms. If you are looking for a large, luxurious sport-utility vehicle and aren't prone to whip-sawing the steering wheel back and forth during your daily commute, this truck might just be perfect for you.

Safety Data

Driver Airbag: *Standard*
Side Airbag: *Not Available*
Traction Control: *Not Available*
Driver Crash Test Grade: *Average*

Passenger Airbag: *Standard*
4-Wheel ABS: *Standard*
Integrated Child Seat(s): *Not Available*
Passenger Crash Test Grade: *Average*

Standard Equipment

SLX w/o PREMIUM PKG: 3.2 liter 24-valve SOHC EFI V6 engine, 4-speed automatic transmission, speed sensitive power steering, cruise control, anti-lock power 4-wheel disc brakes, driver and front passenger air bags, power windows w/driver side express down feature, air conditioning, power door locks, alarm system, conventional spare tire, P245/70R16 SBR mud and snow tires, 5-spoke aluminum wheels, console, electric rear window defroster, AM/FM ETR stereo radio with cassette and 6 speakers, front and rear stabilizer bars, digital clock, privacy glass, tachometer, 22.5 gallon fuel tank, trip odometer, voltmeter: oil pressure gauge, dual heated power mirrors, rear window wiper/washer, intermittent windshield wipers, leather-wrapped tilt steering wheel, power antenna, skid plates (transmission, transfer case, fuel tank, radiator, exhaust), front and rear wheel flares, front and rear mud guards, rear step bumper, cloth reclining front bucket seats, 60/40 split folding rear seat, cut-pile carpeting, rear air deflector, vinyl spare tire cover, outside spare tire carrier, passenger assist grips, and 80 amp battery.

SLX w/PREMIUM PKG (in addition to or instead of SLX w/o PREMIUM PKG equipment): Power moonroof, halogen fog lights, limited slip differential, 6-spoke aluminum alloy wheels with locks, leather seating surfaces, heated front bucket seats with 8-way power driver's seat and 4-way power passenger seat, woodgrain door trim inserts.

Base Prices

Code	Description	Invoice	MSRP
9C326V	SLX	30833	35300
9C327V	SLX Premium	33453	38300
Destination Charge:		435	435

Accessories

NOTE: Accessories are dealer installed. Contact a dealer for accessory availability.

ASTRO / CHEVROLET

| CODE | DESCRIPTION | INVOICE | MSRP |

1998 ASTRO

1998 Chevrolet Astro LT

What's New?

New colors, etch-resistant clearcoating, a standard theft deterrent system (like anybody wants to steal one of these), and the addition of composite headlights and an uplevel grille to base models are all that's different on this year's Astro. Full-power airbags continue for 1998.

Review

Models that have been around for a while can still deliver impressive value—and valor. That's true of the long-lived Astro van, a staple in Chevy's lineup since 1985. This hard-working passenger/cargo hauler, sporting a conventionally boxy shape, has, if anything, mellowed with age.

No, you don't get the curvaceous contours of a Caravan/Voyager or a Windstar. What you do acquire is a highly practical carrier that can be equipped to suit just about any family, trimmed in any of three levels. Depending on configuration, Astros can seat up to eight passengers and haul as much as three tons.

Out on the road, rolling hour after hour, is where the Astro demonstrates its true worth. Taller than its likely rivals, Astros are admittedly more truck-like in temperament, but deliver a pleasant highway ride with competent handling for long journeys. Seats are a little short, but comfortable, in both the front and center positions. Unfortunately, overly small front foot wells drop the comfort level a notch. A 190-horsepower 4.3-liter V-6 is standard, driving a smooth shifting 4-speed electronically controlled automatic transmission.

Dual airbags and anti-lock brakes are standard. This year, Chevy adds a standard theft deterrent system, just in case there might be some thieves around dying to get their hands on an Astro. Base models come equipped with the same composite headlights and uplevel grille of LS and LT versions for 1998. Three new paint colors are available, and clearcoats are etch-resistant for better longevity.

You get only one body choice: the extended-length version. The lower-priced rear-drive rendition is the ticket for hauling plenty of weight. All-wheel drive costs more and delivers improved wet-pavement traction, but slurps up more fuel along the route.

CHEVROLET ASTRO

Solid and substantial, Astros remain tempting if dated choices, whether in passenger or cargo form. If you need a small van with big van capacity, the Astro should be on your shopping list.

Safety Data

Driver Airbag: *Standard*
Side Airbag: *Not Available*
Traction Control: *Not Available*
Driver Crash Test Grade: *Average*

Passenger Airbag: *Standard*
4-Wheel ABS: *Standard*
Integrated Child Seat(s): *Opt. (Psgr. Van); N/A (Cargo Van)*
Passenger Crash Test Grade: *Average*

Standard Equipment

RWD CARGO VAN: 4.3L V-6 OHV SMPI 12-valve engine; 4-speed electronic overdrive automatic transmission with lock-up; 600-amp battery; engine oil cooler, HD radiator; 100-amp alternator; transmission oil cooler; rear wheel drive, 3.23 axle ratio; partial stainless steel exhaust; front independent suspension with anti-roll bar, front coil springs, front shocks, suspension with rear leaf springs, rear shocks; power steering with engine speed-sensing assist; front disc/rear drum brakes with 4 wheel anti-lock braking system; 25 gal capacity fuel tank; front license plate bracket; 3 doors with sliding right rear passenger door, split swing-out rear cargo door; front colored bumper, rear colored step bumper; sealed beam headlights with daytime running lights; additional exterior lights include center high mounted stop light; front and rear 15" x 6" painted styled steel wheels with partial wheel covers; P215/75SR15 BSW AS front and rear tires; underbody mounted compact steel spare wheel; air conditioning; AM/FM stereo with clock, seek-scan, 2 speakers and fixed antenna; 3 power accessory outlets; analog instrumentation display includes oil pressure gauge, water temp gauge, volt gauge, trip odometer; warning indicators include lights on; dual airbags; fixed rear door glass; variable intermittent front windshield wipers; seating capacity of 2, front bucket seats, driver seat includes 4-way direction control, passenger seat includes 4-way direction control; vinyl seats; front cloth headliner, front vinyl floor covering; interior lights include dome light; day-night rearview mirror; engine cover console with storage, locking glove box, driver and passenger door bins; cargo light; colored grille.

AWD CARGO VAN (in addition to or instead of RWD equipment): Full-time 4 wheel drive, 3.42 axle ratio; front torsion suspension with front torsion springs and front torsion bar.

RWD PASSENGER VAN (in addition to or instead of CARGO VAN equipment): HD transmission oil cooler; trailer harness; front and rear body-colored bumpers; monotone paint; rear heat ducts; 6 stereo speakers; child safety rear door locks; 4 power accessory outlets; PRNDL in instrument panel; warning indicators include battery, key in ignition; vented rear windows, fixed 1/4 vent windows; seating capacity of 5; removeable 2nd row bench seat with adjustable rear outboard mounted headrests; front height adjustable seatbelts; cloth door trim insert, full headliner, full carpet floor covering, deluxe sound insulation; vanity mirrors, dual auxiliary visors; carpeted cargo floor, plastic trunk lid; black side window moldings, black front windshield molding, black rear window molding, black door handles.

AWD PASSENGER VAN (in addition to or instead of RWD equipment): Engine oil cooler; full-time 4 wheel drive, 3.42 axle ratio; front torsion suspension with front torsion springs and front torsion bar.

ASTRO — CHEVROLET

CODE	DESCRIPTION	INVOICE	MSRP

Base Prices

Code	Description	Invoice	MSRP
CM11005	RWD Cargo Van	17503	19340
CM11006	RWD Passenger Van	18167	20074
CL11005	AWD Cargo Van	19675	21740
CL11006	AWD Passenger Van	20248	22374
	Destination Charge:	585	585

Accessories

Code	Description	Invoice	MSRP
UG1	3-Channel Garage Door Opener (Passenger)	99	115
	NOT AVAILABLE with (1SA) Preferred Equipment Group 1SA, (1SB) Preferred Equipment Group 1SB.		
GU6	3.42 Axle Ratio (RWD)	NC	NC
	NOT AVAILABLE with (GT4) 3.73 axle ratio.		
GT4	3.73 Axle Ratio	NC	NC
	NOT AVAILABLE with (GU6) 3.42 axle ratio.		
AG1	6-Way Power Driver's Seat (Passenger)	206	240
	REQUIRES (1SB) Preferred Equipment Group 1SB or (1SC) Preferred Equipment Group 1SC. NOT AVAILABLE with 1SA, 1SD, or 1SE.		
AG2	6-Way Power Passenger's Seat (Passenger)	206	240
	REQUIRES (1SB or 1SC and AG1) or 1SD or 1SE. NOT AVAILABLE with 1SA.		
ZP7	7-Passenger Seating (Passenger)	273	318
	Includes 4 high back buckets with seat back recliners and 3-passenger 3rd row bench, seat map pockets. NOT AVAILABLE with 1SA, 1SB, 1SE, AN5, ZP8.		
ZP7	7-Passenger Seating (Passenger)	NC	NC
	Includes 4 high back buckets with seat back recliners and 3-passenger 3rd row bench, seat map pockets. REQUIRES 1SE. NOT AVAILABLE with AN5, ZP8.		
ZP7	7-Passenger Seating (Passenger)	833	969
	Includes 4 high back buckets with seat back recliners and 3-passenger 3rd row bench, seat map pockets. REQUIRES 1SA. NOT AVAILABLE with AN5, ZP8.		
ZP7	7-Passenger Seating (Passenger)	349	406
	Includes 4 high back buckets with seat back recliners and 3-passenger 3rd row bench, seat map pockets. REQUIRES 1SB. NOT AVAILABLE with AN5, ZP8.		
ZP8	8-Passenger Seating (Passenger)	340	395
	Includes 2 front buckets and 2 rear bench seats. NOT AVAILABLE with (ZP7) 7-passenger seating, (AN6) seat lumbar support.		
YG6	Air Conditioning Not Desired (Cargo)	(727)	(845)
NP5	Black Leather Wrapped Steering Wheel (Passenger)	46	54
	NOT AVAILABLE with 1SA, 1SB, 1SE.		
V54	Black Luggage Carrier (Passenger)	108	126
B74	Body Side Molding	104	121
	NOT AVAILABLE with 1SB, 1SC, 1SD, 1SE.		
YF5	California Emissions	146	170
	Automatically added to vehicles shipped to and/or sold to retailers in California. Out-of-state retailers must order on vehicles to be registered or leased in California. NOT AVAILABLE with (NG1) MA/NY/CT Emissions.		

CHEVROLET ASTRO

CODE	DESCRIPTION	INVOICE	MSRP
E54	Cargo Dutch Doors (Passenger)	262	305
	Includes flip-up rear window with wiper/washer, rear doors with electric release. REQUIRES 1SC or 1SD or 1SE. NOT AVAILABLE with A18.		
E54	Cargo Dutch Doors (Passenger)	313	364
	Includes flip-up rear window with wiper/washer, rear doors with electric release. REQUIRES (1SA or 1SB) and AU3. NOT AVAILABLE with 1SC, 1SD, 1SE, A18, ZW2.		
V10	Cold Climate Package	40	46
	Includes coolant protection, engine block heater.		
ZW6	Complete Body Glass Arrangement (Cargo)	316	368
	Includes rear panel doors.		
ZQ2	Convenience Group (Cargo)	408	474
	Includes power windows, power door lock system.		
ZQ3	Convenience Group (Cargo)	329	383
	Includes manual tilt steering wheel, speed control.		
—	Custom Cloth Seat Trim	NC	NC
AJ1	Deep Tinted Glass (Cargo)	92	107
	REQUIRES 1SL. NOT AVAILABLE with ZW2.		
AJ1	Deep Tinted Glass (Cargo)	225	262
	REQUIRES 1SL and ZW6. NOT AVAILABLE with ZW2, ZW3.		
AJ1	Deep Tinted Glass (Cargo)	46	54
	REQUIRES 1SL and ZW2. NOT AVAILABLE with ZW3, ZW6.		
AJ1	Deep Tinted Glass (Passenger)	249	290
C95	Dome & Reading Lamps (Cargo)	28	33
AN5	Dual Integrated Child Safety Seats (Passenger)	206	240
	REQUIRES 1SA or 1SB or 1SC or 1SD or 1SE. NOT AVAILABLE with ZP7.		
C49	Electric rear window defogger	132	154
	REQUIRES (E54) dutch doors. NOT AVAILABLE with (A18) sliding side and rear doors glass, (ZW2) rear panel doors glass.		
D48	Electric Remote Black Mirrors (Passenger)	84	98
	NOT AVAILABLE with (1SA) Preferred Equipment Group 1SA.		
B37	Front & Rear Color-Keyed Floor Mats (Passenger)	40	47
	REQUIRES (1SA) Preferred Equipment Group 1SA. NOT AVAILABLE with (ZP7) 7-passenger seating, (ZP8) 8-passenger seating.		
B37	Front & Rear Color-Keyed Floor Mats (Passenger)	59	69
	REQUIRES (ZP7) 7-passenger seating or (ZP8) 8-passenger seating.		
—	Leather Seat Trim (Passenger)	817	950
	NOT AVAILABLE with AN5, 1SA, 1SB, 1SC, 1SD.		
G80	Locking Differential	217	252
NG1	MA/NY/CT Emissions	146	170
	Automatically added to vehicles shipped to and/or sold to retailers in Massachusetts, New York or Connecticut. Out-of-state retailers must order on vehicles to be registered or leased in Massachusetts, New York or Connecticut. NOT AVAILABLE with (YF5) California Emissions.		
AU3	Power Door Lock System	192	223

ASTRO — CHEVROLET

CODE	DESCRIPTION	INVOICE	MSRP
1SA	Preferred Equipment Group 1SA (Passenger)	NC	NC
	Includes base decor package. NOT AVAILABLE with AG1, AG2, AN6, D48, NP5, UG1, UK6, UPO, ZY2, ULO, UNO, ANO, FE2.		
1SB	Preferred Equipment Group 1SB (Passenger)	1767	2055
	Manufacturer Discount	(516)	(600)
	Net Price	1251	1455
	Includes base decor package, power windows, power door lock system, deep tinted glass, 8 passenger seats, front and rear color-keyed floor mats, body side molding, styled steel painted silver wheels, seat map pockets, tilt steering wheel, cruise control, cargo net, reading lamps. NOT AVAILABLE with NP5, UG1, UK6, ZY2, AN6, FE2.		
1SC	Preferred Equipment Group 1SC (Passenger)	2843	3306
	Manufacturer Discount	(602)	(700)
	Net Price	2241	2606
	Includes LS Decor package, power windows, power door lock system, deep tinted glass, 8 passenger seats, front and rear color-keyed floor mats, body side molding, styled steel painted silver wheels, seat map pockets, tilt steering wheel, cruise control, cargo net, reading lamps, chrome wheels, power exterior mirrors, roof console, illuminated visor vanity mirrors, front seat passenger storage compartment. NOT AVAILABLE with FE2, AN6, PA6, B74.		
1SD	Preferred Equipment Group 1SD (Passenger)	3308	3847
	Manufacturer Discount	(602)	(700)
	Net Price	2706	3147
	Includes LS Decor package, power windows, power door lock system, deep tinted glass, 8 passenger seats, front and rear color-keyed floor mats, body side molding, styled steel painted silver wheels, seat map pockets, tilt steering wheel, cruise control, cargo net, reading lamps, aluminum wheels, power exterior mirrors, roof console, illuminated visor vanity mirrors, front seat passenger storage compartment, luggage rack, remote keyless entry, 6-way power driver's seat. NOT AVAILABLE with TL1, B74, AN6, FE2, PA6.		
1SE	Preferred Equipment Group 1SE (Passenger)	4740	5512
	Manufacturer Discount	(688)	(800)
	Net Price	4052	4712
	Includes LT Decor package, power windows, power door lock system, deep tinted glass, 8 passenger seats, front and rear color-keyed floor mats, body side molding, styled steel painted silver wheels, seat map pockets, tilt steering wheel, cruise control, cargo net, reading lamps, aluminum wheels, power exterior mirrors, roof console, illuminated visor vanity mirrors, front seat passenger storage compartment, luggage rack, remote keyless entry, 6-way power driver's seat. NOT AVAILABLE with TL1, B74, PA6, FE2.		
1SL	Preferred Equipment Group 1SL (Cargo)	NC	NC
	Includes vehicle with standard equipment.		
ULO	Radio: AM/FM Stereo with Cassette	264	307
	Includes digital clock, automatic tone control, theft lock and speed compensated volume. REQUIRES ZQ2. NOT AVAILABLE with 1SA, UPO, UNO, UL5.		

CHEVROLET ASTRO

CODE	DESCRIPTION	INVOICE	MSRP
UM6	Radio: AM/FM Stereo with Cassette	126	147
	Includes digital clock. NOT AVAILABLE with UPO, UK6, ULO, UNO, UL5.		
UN0	Radio: AM/FM Stereo with CD	350	407
	Includes seek and scan, automatic tone control, digital clock, theft lock and speed compensated volume. REQUIRES ZQ2. NOT AVAILABLE with 1SA, UPO, UK6, ULO, UL5.		
UP0	Radio: AM/FM Stereo with CD & Cassette	436	507
	Includes seek and scan, search and repeat, theft lock, speed compensated volume, automatic tone control and digital clock. REQUIRES ZQ2. NOT AVAILABLE with 1SA, ULO, UNO, UL5.		
UL5	Radio: Delete (Cargo)	(164)	(191)
	NOT AVAILABLE with (ULO) radio, (UNO) radio, (UPO) radio.		
C69	Rear Air Conditioning (Passenger)	450	523
	Includes 105-amp alternator.		
C36	Rear Heater	176	205
ZW2	Rear Panel Doors Glass (Cargo)	75	87
	NOT AVAILABLE with E54, ZW3, ZW6, A18, A19, C49.		
UK6	Rear Seat Radio Control with Jack (Passenger)	136	158
	REQUIRES ULO or UPO. NOT AVAILABLE with 1SA, 1SB, UNO.		
AU0	Remote Keyless Entry	129	150
	REQUIRES (AU3 and 1SA) or 1SB or 1SC or ZQ2.		
AN6	Seat Lumbar Support (Passenger)	86	100
	REQUIRES ZP7. NOT AVAILABLE with ZP8, 1SA, 1SB, 1SC, 1SD.		
AN0	Seat Package	144	168
	Includes inboard/outboard armrests, manually adjustable lumbar support and seat map pockets. NOT AVAILABLE with (1SA) Preferred Equipment Group 1SA.		
A19	Side Door Swing Out Glass (Cargo)	66	77
	REQUIRES E54. NOT AVAILABLE with A18, ZW2.		
ZW3	Sliding Side & Rear Doors Glass (Cargo)	133	155
	Includes rear panel doors. NOT AVAILABLE with (ZW2) rear panel doors glass, (ZW6) complete body glass arrangement.		
A18	Sliding Side & Rear Doors Glass (Cargo)	117	136
	Includes swing-out rear door glass. REQUIRES ZW3 or ZW6. NOT AVAILABLE with ZW2, E54, A19, C49.		
QCM	Tires: P215/75R15 AS WOL	76	88
	NOT AVAILABLE with (FE2) Touring Suspension Package.		
FE2	Touring Suspension Package (RWD Passenger)	263	306
	Includes front and rear gas shock absorbers, rear stabilizer bar, P235/65R15 touring WOL tires. REQUIRES PF3. NOT AVAILABLE with QCM, 1SA, 1SB, 1SC, 1SD, PC2, PA6.		
Z82	Trailering Special Equipment	266	309
	Includes platform trailer hitch and 8-lead wiring harness.		
ZY2	Two-Tone Paint (Passenger)	NC	NC
	NOT AVAILABLE with (1SA) Preferred Equipment Group 1SA, (1SB) Preferred Equipment Group 1SB.		
TL1	Uplevel Grille (Passenger)	129	150
	REQUIRES 1SA OR 1SB. NOT AVAILABLE with 1SD, 1SE, 1SC.		

ASTRO / BLAZER — CHEVROLET

CODE	DESCRIPTION	INVOICE	MSRP
PF3	Wheels: Aluminum Brushed (Passenger)	235	273
	REQUIRES 1SB. NOT AVAILABLE with 1SA, 1SC, 1SD, 1SE, PC2, PA6.		
PF3	Wheels: Aluminum Brushed (Passenger)	22	25
	REQUIRES 1SC. NOT AVAILABLE with 1SA, 1SB, 1SD, 1SE, PA6, PC2.		
PF3	Wheels: Aluminum Brushed (Passenger)	314	365
	REQUIRES 1SA. NOT AVAILABLE with 1SB, 1SC, 1SD, 1SE, PA6, PC2.		
PC2	Wheels: Styled Steel Chrome Appearance (Passenger)	(22)	(25)
	REQUIRES 1SD or 1SE. NOT AVAILABLE with PA6, FE2, PF3.		
PC2	Wheels: Styled Steel Chrome Appearance (Passenger)	292	340
	REQUIRES 1SA. NOT AVAILABLE with PA6, FE2, PF3, 1SB, 1SC, 1SD, 1SE.		
PC2	Wheels: Styled Steel Chrome Appearance (Passenger)	213	248
	REQUIRES 1SB. NOT AVAILABLE with PA6, FE2, PF3, 1SA, 1SC, 1SD, 1SE.		
PA6	Wheels: Styled Steel Painted Silver	79	92
	NOT AVAILABLE with PC2, FE2, 1SE, PF3, 1SD, 1SC.		

1998 BLAZER

1998 Chevrolet Blazer LT 4-Door

What's New?

Blazer gets a nose job and an interior redesign. New standard equipment includes a theft deterrent system, automatic headlight control, 4-wheel disc brakes, and dual airbags incorporating second-generation technology to reduce the bags' inflation force. New radios, colors, and a column-mounted automatic shift selector round out the major changes.

Review

Back in 1982, Chevrolet rolled out the S-10 Blazer, the first modern compact sport-utility vehicle. Sixteen years later, the Blazer remains a bestseller in one of the hottest automotive markets. It's not hard to understand the Blazer's appeal.

CHEVROLET BLAZER

Powered by a strong 4.3-liter, 190-horsepower, V6 engine and offering several suspension choices, the Blazer can be tailored to specific needs, with either 2-wheel or 4-wheel drive, two doors or four. The four-door is the most popular by far: the model of choice with families on the go.

There are accommodations for as many as six passengers in the bigger Blazer, but four would most likely be more comfortable. There's lots of cargo space too, with the spare tire mounted underneath the cargo floor on four-door models. Chevy claims that, with the rear seat folded, a washing machine box will fit into the cargo bay. We tried it with a test vehicle, and they aren't fibbing. Sadly, the Blazer's interior is marred by acres of chintzy plastic and little rear foot room in front of a somewhat low and mushy seat. Adult rear seat riders will complain loudly.

Off-road is not where the Blazer shines, though a ZR2 super-duty suspension package is optional. Available only on 2-door 4WD models, the ZR2 Blazer has a special chassis with four-inch wider track, huge 31-inch tires, specially-tuned Bilstein 46mm shocks, drivetrain refinements, an underbody shield package, and LS trim. Regular Blazers are capable enough for two-track dirt, but serious off-road adventures would be better handled by something with more wheel travel. However, most families don't spend much, if any, time off-road in their sport-utes, so this is not a large shortcoming. As a road going hauler, the Blazer is quite capable. An all-wheel drive option is available on 4-door models with LT decor, making the Blazer even more sure-footed.

For 1998, Chevrolet has updated the Blazer nicely. The exterior gets new front styling that provides a more familial look to help tie the Blazer to other truck models in the Chevrolet stable. The interior is new, featuring a redesigned dashboard and dual airbags. The automatic shifter is located on the steering column rather than the center console, lending the interior a more airy and open appearance. A theft-deterrent system, automatic headlight control, and four-wheel disc brakes are all standard. Heated exterior mirrors and an electrochromic rearview mirror are standard on LT models and optional on the LS. Two new colors debut: Light Pewter Metallic and Dark Copper Metallic.

When the current Blazer debuted for the 1995 model year, it won the North American Truck of the Year award. Smart styling, a powerful drivetrain, and reasonable pricing made it a hit with the public. Lately, however, the competition has caught up with the Blazer. A new V6 engine went into the more refined Ford Explorer for 1997, and it is more powerful than the Blazer's motor. Jeep updated the Cherokee last year, offering nearly as much interior space as the Blazer and four-wheel drive for around $20,000. Simply put, this Chevy isn't the value it used to be.

Safety Data

Driver Airbag: *Standard*
Side Airbag: *Not Available*
Traction Control: *Not Available*
Driver Crash Test Grade: *Not Available*

Passenger Airbag: *Standard*
4-Wheel ABS: *Standard*
Integrated Child Seat(s): *Not Available*
Passenger Crash Test Grade: *Not Available*

Standard Equipment

BASE 2WD 2-DOOR: 4.3L V-6 OHV SMPI 12-valve engine; 4-speed electronic overdrive automatic transmission with lock-up; 525-amp battery; engine oil cooler; 100-amp alternator; transmission oil cooler; rear wheel drive, 3.08 axle ratio; stainless steel exhaust; front independent suspension with anti-roll bar, front coil springs, front shocks, rear suspension with anti-roll bar, rear leaf springs, rear shocks; power re-circulating ball steering; 4 wheel disc brakes with 4 wheel anti-lock braking system; 19 gal capacity fuel tank; front license plate bracket; rear tailgate cargo door; trailer harness; rear body-colored bumper with rear step; monotone paint; aero-composite halogen fully automatic headlamps with daytime running lights; additional exterior lights include center high mounted stop light, underhood light; driver and passenger manual black folding outside mirrors; front and rear 15" x 7" painted styled steel wheels with hub wheel

BLAZER

CHEVROLET

CODE	DESCRIPTION	INVOICE	MSRP

covers and trim rings; P205/75SR15 RWL AS front and rear tires; inside mounted compact steel spare wheel; air conditioning, rear heat ducts; AM/FM stereo with clock, seek-scan, 4 speakers and fixed antenna; power rear window remote release; 1 power accessory outlet; analog instrumentation display includes oil pressure gauge, water temp gauge, volt gauge, trip odometer; warning indicators include battery, lights on, key in ignition; dual airbags; ignition disable; deep tinted windows, vented rear windows, fixed 1/4 vent windows; variable intermittent front windshield wipers, flip-up rear window; seating capacity of 2, front bucket seats with tilt adjustable headrests, center armrest with storage, driver seat includes 4-way direction control with lumbar support, passenger seat includes 4-way direction control with lumbar support and easy entry feature; cloth seats, cloth door trim insert, full cloth headliner, full carpet floor covering with carpeted floor mats; interior lights include dome light; passenger side vanity mirror; day-night rearview mirror; partial floor console, glove box with light, front and rear cupholders, instrument panel bin, driver and passenger door bins; carpeted cargo floor, cargo tie downs, cargo light; chrome grille, black side window moldings, black front windshield molding, black rear window molding, black door handles.

BASE 4WD 2-DOOR (in addition to or instead of BASE 2WD 2-DOOR equipment): Part-time 4 wheel drive, auto locking hub control and electronic shift; front torsion springs, front torsion bar.

BASE 2WD 4-DOOR (in addition to or instead of BASE 2WD 2-DOOR equipment): Battery with run down protection; 18 gal capacity fuel tank; underbody mounted spare wheel; child safety rear door locks, power rear window remote release; 1 power accessory outlet; manual rear windows; seating capacity of 3, 60-40 split-bench front seat; 2 seat back storage pockets.

BASE 4WD 4-DOOR (in addition to or instead of BASE 2WD 4-DOOR equipment): Part-time 4 wheel drive, auto locking hub control and electronic shift; front torsion springs, front torsion bar, seating capacity of 6, 60-40 split-bench front seat,; 60-40 folding rear split-bench seat; 2 seat back storage pockets.

Base Prices

CS10516-E55	2WD 2-door	19605	21663
CS10506-E55	2WD 4-door	20985	23188
CT10516-E55	4WD 2-door	21404	23651
CT10506-E55	4WD 4-door	22784	25176
Destination Charge:		515	515

Accessories

GU6	3.42 Axle Ratio	NC	NC
GT4	3.73 Axle Ratio (4WD)	NC	NC
	REQUIRES (G80) locking differential.		
M50	5-Speed Manual Transmission (2-door)	(765)	(890)
AG1	6-Way Power Driver's Seat	206	240
	NOT AVAILABLE with 1SA, 1SB, or 1SD (4-door).		
UA1	690 CCA HD Battery	48	56
	NOT AVAILABLE with (V10) Cold Climate Package.		
ANL	Air Dam with Fog Lamps (All except 4WD 2-door)	99	115
	NOT AVAILABLE with 1SA, 1SB, 1SD (4-door).		
V54	Black Luggage Carrier	108	126
	REQUIRES 1SA.		

CHEVROLET BLAZER

Code	Description	Invoice	MSRP
YF5	California Emissions	146	170

Automatically added to vehicles shipped to and/or sold to retailers in California. Out-of-state retailers must order on vehicles to be registered or leased in California. NOT AVAILABLE with (NG1) CT/MA/NY Emissions.

V10	Cold Climate Package	77	89

Includes 690 CCA HD battery, engine block heater.

ZQ3	Convenience Group	340	395

Includes manual tilt steering wheel, speed control. NOT AVAILABLE with 1SB, 1SC, or 1SD.

NG1	CT/MA/NY Emissions	146	170

Automatically added to vehicles shipped to and/or sold to retailers in Connecticut, Massachusetts, or New York. Out-of-state retailers must order on vehicles to be registered or leased in Connecticut, Massachusetts, or New York. NOT AVAILABLE with (YF5) California Emissions.

ZQ6	Driver's Convenience (2-door)	460	535

Includes power windows with driver's one-touch down, power door locks, power exterior mirrors. NOT AVAILABLE with 1SC or 1SD.

ZQ6	Driver's Convenience (4-door)	611	710

Includes power windows with driver's one-touch down, power door locks, power exterior mirrors. NOT AVAILABLE with 1SC or 1SD.

CF5	Electric Glass Sunroof	598	695

REQUIRES (DK6) roof console.

KA1	Heated Seats (4-door)	194	225

REQUIRES (1SD) Preferred Equipment Group 1SD.

AV5	High Back Reclining Bucket Seats	NC	NC

Includes floor console. NOT AVAILABLE with 1SA or 1SB on 4-door models.

UG1	Homelink Transmitter	112	130

Homelink system operates garage doors, lights and other devices. Includes enhanced electronic display, compass/temperature display, trip computer. REQUIRES (DK6) roof console. NOT AVAILABLE with (1SD) Preferred Equipment Group 1SD.

TB4	Liftgate (4-door)	NC	NC

Rear liftgate with flip-up window. REQUIRES (ZQ6) Driver's Convenience and (ZM8) Rear Window Convenience Package. NOT AVAILABLE with (1SC) Preferred Equipment Group 1SC, (1SD) Preferred Equipment Group 1SD.

G80	Locking Differential	217	252

REQUIRES GT4 or GU6 axle ratio.

ZM6	Off-Road Suspension Package (4WD 2-door)	545	634

Includes upsized torsion bar, jounce bumpers, stabilizer bar, full-size spare tire, firm ride suspension, HD/LD trailering equipment, GVWR: 4850 lbs., GAWR: 2500/2700, special yellow Bilstein gas shocks. REQUIRES QEB. NOT AVAILABLE with 1SC, 1SD, Z85, QBF, QBG, ZCE, ZBF, ZBG, PNV, M50, ZM6.

ZM6	Off-Road Suspension Package (4WD 2-door)	211	245

Includes upsized torsion bar, jounce bumpers, stabilizer bar, full-size spare tire, firm ride suspension, HD/LD trailering equipment, GVWR: 4850 lbs., GAWR: 2500/2700, special yellow Bilstein gas shocks. REQUIRES QEB. NOT AVAILABLE with Z83, QCE, QBG, ZCE, ZBF, ZBG, PNV, ZM6, 1SA, 1SB.

BLAZER — CHEVROLET

CODE	DESCRIPTION	INVOICE	MSRP
1SA	Preferred Equipment Group 1SA (4WD 4-door)	NC	NC
	Includes vehicle with standard equipment.		
1SA	Preferred Equipment Group 1SA (All except 4WD 4-door)	NC	NC
	Includes vehicle with standard equipment and folding rear bench seat.		
1SB	Preferred Equipment Group 1SB	553	643

Includes folding rear bench seat, Convenience Group: tilt steering wheel, cruise control; luggage carrier, ETR AM/FM stereo with seek-scan, cassette, and clock.

| 1SC | Preferred Equipment Group 1SC (2-door) .... | 2455 | 2855 |

Includes folding rear bench seat, Convenience Group: tilt steering wheel, cruise control; luggage carrier, ETR AM/FM stereo with seek-scan, automatic tone control, theft lock, speed compensated volume, cassette, and clock; overhead console with compass and external temperature display, Convenience Group: power windows, power locks, power exterior mirrors; exterior mirror defoggers, electrochromic inside rearview mirror, Touring Suspension Package, tachometer, P235/70R15 tires, LS Decor: custom cloth interior, deep tinted glass, dual front reading lights, illuminated visor mirrors, cargo net, two auxiliary power outlets, leather-wrapped steering wheel, uplevel interior door trim.

| 1SC | Preferred Equipment Group 1SC (4-door) .... | 3058 | 3556 |

Includes folding rear bench seat, Convenience Group: tilt steering wheel, cruise control; luggage carrier, ETR AM/FM stereo with seek-scan, automatic tone control, theft lock, speed compensated volume, cassette, and clock; rear liftgate with flip-up glass, bucket seats with center console, overhead console with compass and external temperature display, Convenience Group: power windows, power locks, power exterior mirrors; exterior mirror defoggers, electrochromic inside rearview mirror, Premium Suspension Package, tachometer, P235/70R15 tires, LS Decor: custom cloth interior, deep tinted glass, dual front reading lights, illuminated visor mirrors, cargo net, two auxiliary power outlets, leather-wrapped steering wheel, uplevel interior door trim.

| 1SD | Preferred Equipment Group 1SD (2-door) .... | 3001 | 3490 |

Includes folding rear bench seat, Convenience Group: tilt steering wheel, cruise control; luggage carrier, ETR AM/FM stereo with seek-scan, automatic tone control, theft lock, speed compensated volume, cassette, and clock; overhead console with compass and external temperature display, Convenience Group: power windows, power locks, power exterior mirrors; exterior mirror defoggers, electrochromic inside rearview mirror, Touring Suspension Package, tachometer, P235/70R15 tires, LS Decor: custom cloth interior, deep tinted glass, dual front reading lights, illuminated visor mirrors, cargo net, two auxiliary power outlets, leather-wrapped steering wheel, uplevel interior door trim; remote keyless entry, 6-way power driver's seat, Homelink 3-channel transmitter.

| 1SD | Preferred Equipment Group 1SD (4-door) .... | 4755 | 5529 |

Includes folding rear bench seat, Convenience Group: tilt steering wheel, cruise control; luggage carrier, ETR AM/FM stereo with seek-scan, automatic tone control, theft lock, speed compensated volume, cassette, and clock; rear liftgate with flip-up glass, bucket seats with center console, overhead console with compass and external temperature display, Convenience Group: power windows, power locks, power exterior mirrors; exterior mirror defoggers, electrochromic inside rearview mirror, Premium Suspension Package, tachometer, P235/70R15 tires, LS Decor: custom cloth

CHEVROLET BLAZER

CODE	DESCRIPTION	INVOICE	MSRP

interior, deep tinted glass, dual front reading lights, illuminated visor mirrors, cargo net, two auxiliary power outlets, leather-wrapped steering wheel, uplevel interior door trim; LT Decor: leather seats, 8-way power driver's seat, remote keyless entry, Homelink 3-channel transmitter, front air dam with fog lights, body-color grille, body striping, electronic climate control.

ZW7 — **Premium Ride Suspension Package (4-door)** 169 197
Includes smooth ride suspension, HD/LD trailering equipment, special yellow Bilstein gas shocks, GAWR: 2500/2700. REQUIRES (1SA or 1SB) and (QBF or QBG). NOT AVAILABLE with QCE, QCA, ZCE, ZCA, 1SC, 1SD.

UL5 — **Radio Delete** .... (194) (226)
REQUIRES 1SA.

UM6 — **Radio: AM/FM Stereo with Cassette** 105 122
Includes digital clock. REQUIRES 1SA.

UN0 — **Radio: AM/FM Stereo with CD** 86 100
Includes digital clock, theft lock, speed compensated volume and enhanced performance speaker system.

UP0 — **Radio: AM/FM Stereo with CD & Cassette** 172 200
Includes auto tone control, digital clock, theft lock, enhanced performance speaker system and speed compensated volume.

RYJ — **Rear Compartment Shade (4WD 2-door)** 59 69
REQUIRES (P16) spare tire and wheel carrier. NOT AVAILABLE with (1SA) Preferred Equipment Group 1SA, (1SB) Preferred Equipment Group 1SB.

ZM8 — **Rear Window Convenience Package** 277 322
Includes electric tailgate release, rear window defogger and rear wiper/washer. NOT AVAILABLE with 1SC or 1SD.

AU0 — **Remote Keyless Entry** 129 150
REQUIRES (AG1) 6-way power driver's seat. NOT AVAILABLE with 1SA, 1SB, or 1SD (4-door).

DK6 — **Roof Console** 126 147
Includes lighting, compass/temperature display. REQUIRES (1SA and CF5) or (1SB and CF5).

ZM5 — **Shield Package (4WD)** 108 126
Includes transfer case, front differential skid plates, fuel tank and steering linkage shield. NOT AVAILABLE with (ZR2) Wide Stance Sport Performance Package.

Z83 — **Smooth Ride Suspension Package (2-door)** .... (236) (275)
Includes smooth ride suspension, light-duty trailering equipment, GAWR 2200/2600. REQUIRES 1SC or 1SD. NOT AVAILABLE with QBG, 1SA, 1SB, M50, ZM6, QEB, GT4.

ZQ1 — **Smooth Ride Suspension Package (4-door)** .... (236) (275)
Includes GAWR: 2500/2700, sporty/firm ride suspension, light-duty trailering equipment. REQUIRES QCE or QCA. NOT AVAILABLE with 1SA, 1SB.

P16 — **Spare Tire & Wheel Carrier (4WD 2-door)** 137 159
Includes cover. NOT AVAILABLE with (PNV) spare tire carrier not desired.

PNV — **Spare Tire Carrier Not Desired (4WD 2-door)** .... NC NC
NOT AVAILABLE with (QEB) tires, (ZM6) Off-Road Suspension Package, (P16) spare tire and wheel carrier.

BLAZER — CHEVROLET

CODE	DESCRIPTION	INVOICE	MSRP
U16	Tachometer (2-door)	51	59
	REQUIRES (M50) transmission. NOT AVAILABLE with (1SD) Preferred Equipment Group 1SD.		
QCE	Tires: P205/75R15 AS BSW	NC	NC
	NOT AVAILABLE with ZM6, 1SC, 1SD.		
QCA	Tires: P205/75R15 AS WOL (2WD)	104	121
	REQUIRES 1SA or 1SB. NOT AVAILABLE with 1SC, 1SD.		
QBF	Tires: P235/70R15 AS BSW	165	192
	NOT AVAILABLE with (1SC) Preferred Equipment Group 1SC, (1SD) Preferred Equipment Group 1SD.		
QBG	Tires: P235/70R15 M&S WOL	114	133
	REQUIRES 1SC or 1SD. NOT AVAILABLE with ZM6, Z83.		
QBG	Tires: P235/70R15 M&S WOL	280	325
	NOT AVAILABLE with ZM6, Z83, 1SC, 1SD.		
QEB	Tires: P235/75R15 AT WOL (4WD 2-door)	288	335
	REQUIRES (1SA or 1SB) and P16 and Z85. NOT AVAILABLE with ZM6, PNV, Z83.		
QEB	Tires: P235/75R15 AT WOL (4WD 2-door)	123	143
	REQUIRES (1SC or 1SD) and P16 and Z85. NOT AVAILABLE with ZM6, PNV, Z83.		
QEB	Tires: P235/75R15 AT WOL (4WD 2-door)	NC	NC
	REQUIRES ZM6 and P16. NOT AVAILABLE with PNV, Z83, Z85.		
Z85	Touring Suspension Package	NC	NC
	Includes special yellow Bilstein gas shocks, GAWR: 2200/2600, firm ride suspension, HD/LD trailering equipment. REQUIRES 1SC or 1SD. NOT AVAILABLE with QCE, QCA, ZCE, ZCA, ZQ1, 1SA, 1SB.		
Z85	Touring Suspension Package	169	197
	Includes special yellow Bilstein gas shocks, GAWR: 2200/2600, firm ride suspension, HD/LD trailering equipment. REQUIRES (1SA and QBF or QBG) or (1SB and QBF or QBG). NOT AVAILABLE with ZM6, QCE, QCA, ZCE, ZCA, ZW7, ZQ1, 1SC, 1SD.		
Z82	Trailering Special Equipment (2WD)	181	210
	Includes 7-lead wiring harness, weight distributing hitch platform and heavy duty flasher. REQUIRES (GU6) 3.42 axle ratio or (GT4) 3.73 axle ratio. NOT AVAILABLE with (M50) transmission.		
Z82	Trailering Special Equipment (4WD)	181	210
	Includes 7-lead trailering harness, weight distribution hitch platform and heavy-duty flasher.		
ZY7	Two-Tone Sport Paint (4-door)	169	197
	Includes chrome grille. NOT AVAILABLE with (1SA) Preferred Equipment Group 1SA, (1SB) Preferred Equipment Group 1SB.		
N90	Wheels: Aluminum (4WD 4-door)	241	280
	NOT AVAILABLE with 1SC or 1SD.		
N60	Wheels: Aluminum Argent (2WD)	241	280
	NOT AVAILABLE with 1SC or 1SD.		
PA3	Wheels: Bright Aluminum (4WD 2-door)	NC	NC
	Includes medium gray accent. NOT AVAILABLE with 5P2, 1SC, and 1SD.		

CHEVROLET BLAZER / CHEVY VAN

CODE	DESCRIPTION	INVOICE	MSRP
5P2	Wheels: Special Aluminum (4WD)	NC	NC
	NOT AVAILABLE with (PA3) wheels, (1SA) Preferred Equipment Group 1SA, (1SB) Preferred Equipment Group 1SB.		
ZR2	Wide Stance Sport Performance Package (4WD 2-door)	1591	1850
	Includes unique revised frame for wider front and rear track, unique strengthened front differential gears and drive axles, unique rear axle with 8.5" ring gear, larger wheel bearings, longer and larger axle shafts, unique rear suspension with revised multi-leaf springs and added rear axle track bar, unique 28mm front stabilizer bar, 46mm Bilstein gas shocks, underbody shields, 3" higher ride height. REQUIRES (1SC or 1SD) and GT4 and G80. NOT AVAILABLE with 1SA, 1SB, or Z82.		

1998 CHEVY VAN

1998 Chevrolet Chevy Van

What's New?

All vans equipped with airbags switch to mini-module bag designs for the driver, but they still deploy with more force than second generation types. A theft deterrent system is standard, and three new colors debut.

Review

For the first time in 25 years, Chevy dealers received a brand new, completely redesigned, full-size van to sell in 1996. The Chevy Van (the cargo hauler) and the Express Van (the people hauler) come equipped with powerful optional engines, lots of cargo space, dual airbags and four-wheel anti-lock brakes. With this modern new design, Chevrolet is stealing some of Ford's thunder in the full-size van market.

Converters prefer rugged full-frame construction, because it allows for improved stability, ride and handling. Since most full-size vans are bought for conversion into rolling motel rooms, the new van employs this type of platform. Regular-length models carry 267 cubic feet of cargo, and extended-length vans can haul 317 cubic feet of stuff. Trick rear doors open 180 degrees to

CHEVY VAN   CHEVROLET

make loading and unloading the van easier. Up to 15 passengers can ride in the extended-length Express, making it perfect for use as an airport shuttle. Other seating options include five-, eight- and 12-passenger arrangements. G3500's can tow up to 10,000 pounds when properly equipped.

For convenience, the full-size spare is stored underneath the cargo floor. A 31-gallon fuel tank keeps this thirsty vehicle from frequent fill-ups, but topping off an empty tank will quickly empty your wallet. Engine choices are sourced from the Chevrolet family of Vortec gasoline motors, and a turbocharged diesel can be installed under the hood. Available are the Vortec 4300 V6, the 5000, 5700, and 7400 V8's, and a 6.5-liter Turbo-diesel V8. Standard side cargo doors are a 60/40 panel arrangement, but a traditional slider is a no-cost option on 135-inch wheelbase vans.

Child safety locks are standard on the rear and side doors of the Express. Assist handles help passengers into and out of the van. Front and rear air conditioning is optional. For 1998, all vans have a standard theft deterrent system, and Express models get new seat belt comfort guides. Airbags switch to a new mini-module design.

Exterior styling is an interesting mix of corporate Chevrolet, Astro Van and Lumina Minivan. The high, pillar-mounted taillights are odd, but functional. They can easily be seen if the van is operated with the rear doors open. Low-mounted bumpers and moldings make the Express look taller than it is. An attractively sculpted body side gives the van's smooth, slab-sided flanks a dose of character. Three new colors arrive for 1998, in shades of gray, blue, and copper.

Overall, Chevrolet's thoughtful rendition of the traditional full-size van appears to be right on target, giving Ford's Econoline/Club Wagon the first real competition it has faced in years.

Safety Data

Driver Airbag: *Standard*
Side Airbag: *Not Available*
Traction Control: *Not Available*
Driver Crash Test Grade: *Not Available*

Passenger Airbag: *Standard*
4-Wheel ABS: *Standard*
Integrated Child Seat(s): *Not Available*
Passenger Crash Test Grade: *Not Available*

Standard Equipment

CHEVY VAN G1500: 4.3L V-6 OHV SMPI 12-valve engine; 4-speed electronic overdrive automatic transmission with lock-up; 600-amp HD battery; 100-amp alternator; rear wheel drive, 3.42 axle ratio; stainless steel exhaust; front independent suspension with anti-roll bar, front coil springs, front shocks, suspension with rear leaf springs, rear shocks; power steering with vehicle speed-sensing assist; front disc/rear drum brakes with 4 wheel anti-lock braking system; 31 gal capacity fuel tank; 3 doors with split swing-out right rear passenger door, split swing-out rear cargo door; front and rear argent bumpers, rear step bumper; sealed beam halogen headlamps with daytime running lights; additional exterior lights include center high mounted stop light, underhood light; folding passenger convex outside mirror; front and rear 15" x 6" silver styled steel wheels with hub wheel covers; P215/75SR15 BSW AS front and rear tires; underbody mounted full-size conventional steel spare wheel; AM/FM stereo with clock, seek-scan, 4 speakers and fixed antenna; child safety rear door locks; 2 power accessory outlets; analog instrumentation display includes oil pressure gauge, water temp gauge, volt gauge, trip odometer; warning indicators include lights on; dual airbags; tinted windows; variable intermittent front windshield wipers; seating capacity of 2, front bucket seats with fixed adjustable headrests, driver seat includes 4-way direction control, passenger seat includes 4-way direction control; vinyl seats, front vinyl headliner, full vinyl floor covering; day-night rearview mirror; engine cover console with storage; vinyl cargo floor, plastic trunk lid, cargo light; colored grille.

G2500 (in addition to or instead of G1500 equipment): Front and rear 16" x 6.5" wheels.

G3500 (in addition to or instead of G2500 equipment): 5.7L V-8 engine; 3.73 axle ratio.

CHEVROLET — CHEVY VAN

CODE	DESCRIPTION	INVOICE	MSRP

Base Prices

CODE	DESCRIPTION	INVOICE	MSRP
CG11405	G1500 Regular Length	17073	19512
CG21405	G2500 Regular Length	17445	19937
CG21705	G2500 Extended Length	18232	20837
CG31405	G3500 Regular Length	18784	21471
CG31705	G3500 Extended Length	19571	22371
Destination Charge:		615	615

Accessories

CODE	DESCRIPTION	INVOICE	MSRP
KW2	124-amp Alternator (G1500/G2500)	52	60
GU6	3.42 Axle Ratio	NC	NC
	REQUIRES (L29) engine on G3500 models. NOT AVAILABLE with (G80) locking differential on G3500 models.		
GT4	3.73 Axle Ratio	NC	NC
	REQUIRES C5Y or C6P on G1500/G2500. NOT AVAILABLE with L30, L31.		
GT5	4.10 Axle Ratio (G2500/G3500)	NC	NC
	REQUIRES (C6P) GVWR: 8600 lbs. on G2500 models NOT AVAILABLE with (L30) engine.		
AG1	6-Way Power Driver's Seat	206	240
C60	Air Conditioning	838	975
	NOT AVAILABLE with R6G, C69, 1SB.		
R6G	Air Conditioning Not Desired	NC	NC
	NOT AVAILABLE with 1SB, C60, C69.		
KL5	Alternative Fuel Conversion (G2500/G3500)	108	125
	REQUIRES MT1 and C6P on G2500 models. NOT AVAILABLE with L30, L65, L29.		
ZR7	Appearance Package	272	316
	Includes chrome grille, composite headlamps, front and rear chrome bumpers.		
TR9	Auxiliary Lighting	138	160
	Includes retractable underhood lamp, reading lamps, front and side door step well lights. NOT AVAILABLE with (1SB) Preferred Equipment Group 1SB.		
B31	Black Vinyl Floor Covering	NC	NC
	Front seating area only (rear delete).		
YF5	California Emissions	146	170
	Automatically added to vehicles shipped to and/or sold to retailers in California. Out-of-state retailers must order on vehicles to be registered or leased in California. NOT AVAILABLE with (MT1) transmission.		
V10	Cold Climate Package	41	48
	Includes engine block heater. NOT AVAILABLE with (L65) engine.		
ZQ2	Convenience Group	408	474
	Includes power door locks, power windows with driver's one touch down.		
ZQ3	Convenience Group	331	385
	Includes cruise control, tilt steering.		
ZX2	Driver's & Passenger's Highback Buckets	NC	NC
	NOT AVAILABLE with (ZX1) driver's side highback bucket.		

CHEVY VAN — CHEVROLET

CODE	DESCRIPTION	INVOICE	MSRP
ZX1	Driver's Side Highback Bucket	(350)	(407)
	Passenger seat cannot be added later. Includes passenger's airbag delete. NOT AVAILABLE with (ZX2) driver's and passenger's highback buckets; (AJ3) driver's side only airbag.		
AJ3	Driver's Side Only Airbag (G2500/G3500)	(189)	(220)
	Deletes passenger side. REQUIRES ZX2. REQUIRES C6P on G2500. NOT AVAILABLE with ZX1.		
DE5	Electric Remote Fold-Away Mirrors	97	113
	Includes defog feature. REQUIRES C60 and ZQ2.		
L30	Engine: 5.0L V8 SFI (G1500/G2500)	426	495
	NOT AVAILABLE with GT4, MT1, GT5, C6P, XHF, KL5.		
L31	Engine: 5.7L V8 Vortec (G1500/G2500)	830	965
	REQUIRES C5Y on G1500 models. NOT AVAILABLE with C6P, XHF, KL5.		
L65	Engine: 6.5L V8 Turbo Diesel (G2500)	3290	3825
	Includes dual batteries. REQUIRES GT4 or GT5 and C6P and XHF. NOT AVAILABLE with V10, KL5.		
L65	Engine: 6.5L V8 Turbo Diesel (G3500)	2460	2860
	Includes dual batteries. NOT AVAILABLE with (V10) Cold Climate Package, (KL5) alternative fuel conversion.		
L29	Engine: 7.4L V8 Vortec (G3500)	516	600
	NOT AVAILABLE with (KL5) alternative fuel conversion.		
ZW4	Fixed Rear & Right Side Door Glass	122	142
	NOT AVAILABLE with ZW2, ZW3, ZW6, A18.		
ZW3	Fixed Rear & Side Door Glass	86	100
	NOT AVAILABLE with ZW2, ZW4, ZW6, A18.		
ZW2	Fixed Rear Door Glass	52	60
	NOT AVAILABLE with ZW3, ZW4, ZW6, A19.		
ZW6	Full Body Glass	267	311
	NOT AVAILABLE with ZW2, ZW3, ZW4, A18.		
C5Y	GVWR: 7100 lbs. (G1500)	129	150
	REQUIRES (XHA) tires or (XHB) tires or (XHM) tires.		
C6P	GVWR: 8600 lbs. (G2500)	284	330
	REQUIRES (XHF) tires. NOT AVAILABLE with (L30) engine, (L31) engine.		
G80	Locking Differential	217	252
	NOT AVAILABLE with (GU6) 3.42 axle ratio on G3500.		
U75	Power Antenna	73	85
	NOT AVAILABLE with (UL5) radio delete.		
1SA	Preferred Equipment Group 1SA	NC	NC
	Includes vehicle with standard equipment. REQUIRES (R6G or C60) and (ZX1 or ZX2).		
1SB	Preferred Equipment Group 1SB	1307	1520
	Includes air conditioning, Auxiliary Lighting: reading lamps, front and side door step well lights; Convenience Group: cruise control, tilt steering. REQUIRES ZX1 or ZX2. NOT AVAILABLE with R6G, C69.		
UL5	Radio Delete	(264)	(307)
	Deletes antenna and speakers. NOT AVAILABLE with (UM6) radio, (U75) power antenna.		

CHEVROLET — CHEVY VAN

CODE	DESCRIPTION	INVOICE	MSRP
UM6	Radio: AM/FM Stereo with Cassette	126	147
	Includes digital clock. NOT AVAILABLE with (UL5) radio delete.		
P06	Rally Wheel Trim	52	60
C69	Rear Air Conditioning (G1500/G2500)	1578	1835
	Includes front and rear air conditioning, 124-amp alternator, rear heater. NOT AVAILABLE with (R6G) air conditioning not desired, (1SB) Preferred Equipment Group 1SB.		
C69	Rear Air Conditioning (G1500/G2500)	740	860
	Includes front and rear air conditioning, 124-amp alternator, rear heater. NOT AVAILABLE with (R6G) air conditioning not desired, (1SA) Preferred Equipment Group 1SA.		
C69	Rear Air Conditioning (G3500)	691	804
	Includes front and rear air conditioning, 124-amp alternator, rear heater. NOT AVAILABLE with (R6G) air conditioning not desired, (1SA) Preferred Equipment Group 1SA.		
C69	Rear Air Conditioning (G3500)	1530	1779
	Includes front and air conditioning, 124-amp alternator, rear heater. NOT AVAILABLE with (R6G) air conditioning not desired, (1SB) Preferred Equipment Group 1SB Preferred Equipment Group 1SB		
A18	Rear Door Swing-Out Window	69	80
	REQUIRES ZW2. NOT AVAILABLE with ZW3, ZW4, ZW6.		
C36	Rear Heater	206	240
	NOT AVAILABLE with (C69) front and rear air conditioning.		
A19	Rear Side Door Swing-Out Window	135	157
	REQUIRES ZW3 or ZW4 or ZW6. NOT AVAILABLE with ZW2.		
PNF	Side Rear and Rear Doors Panel Delete	(26)	(30)
YA2	Sliding Side Rear Door	NC	NC
XHF	Tires: LT225/75R16E AS BSW (G2500)	73	85
	NOT AVAILABLE with (L30) engine, (L31) engine.		
XHA	Tires: P235/75R15X AS BSW (G1500)	138	160
	NOT AVAILABLE with (XHB) tires, (XHM) tires.		
XHB	Tires: P235/75R15X AS WSW (G1500)	224	260
	NOT AVAILABLE with (XHA) tires, (XHM) tires.		
XHM	Tires: P235/75R15XL AS WOL (G1500)	245	285
	NOT AVAILABLE with (XHA) tires, (XHB) tires.		
ZX9	Tires: Spare Delete w/XCU (G1500)	(95)	(110)
	Also deletes jack.		
ZX9	Tires: Spare Delete w/XHA (G1500)	(122)	(142)
	Also deletes jack.		
ZX9	Tires: Spare Delete w/XHB (G1500)	(139)	(162)
	Also deletes jack.		
ZX9	Tires: Spare Delete w/XHF (G2500)	(232)	(270)
	Also deletes jack.		
ZX9	Tires: Spare Delete w/XHH (G3500)	(256)	(298)
	Also deletes jack.		
ZX9	Tires: Spare Delete w/XHM (G1500)	(144)	(167)
	Also deletes jack.		

CHEVY VAN / C/K 1500 PICKUP CHEVROLET

CODE	DESCRIPTION	INVOICE	MSRP
ZX9	Tires: Spare Delete w/XHP (G2500)	(217)	(252)
	Also deletes jack.		
Z82	Trailering Special Equipment	267	310
	Includes trailer hitch and 8-wire harness.		
MT1	Transmission: 4 Speed HD Automatic (G2500/G3500)	NC	NC
	REQUIRES GT4 or GT5. NOT AVAILABLE with L30, L31, L65, YF5.		

1998 CHEVROLET C/K PICKUP

1998 Chevrolet K1500 4x4 Silverado X-Cab Short Box

What's New?

This year's big news is a standard theft-deterrent system, revised color choices, and fresh tailgate lettering. The Sport package has been dropped from the option list. Second-generation airbags are standard on models under 8,600 GVWR.

Review

General Motors' best-selling vehicles, as truck loyalists know full well, are the full-size pickups: half-, 3/4, and one-tonners with a reputation as reliable workhorses. Ford's similar-sized F-Series grabs the higher sales totals each year, but faithful Chevrolet buyers are seldom swayed. The pickup that feels right at home to a Chevy fan tends to send prickles up the spine of a Ford fan, and vice versa. Each is likely to declare the other's truck to be harder riding or anemic in acceleration, even if an impartial observer discerns little difference between the two.

Most truck fans know by now that an all-new Chevrolet pickup is due in showrooms within months. Dubbed Silverado, this 1999 model will be available as 1500 and 2500 light-duty models initially, with the heavy-duty 2500 and 3500 trucks following a year or two later. So, it's not surprising that few changes are on tap for the 1998 C/K pickup. A theft-deterrent system is now standard, tailgate badging is updated, the Sport model is dropped, and colors are shuffled.

CHEVROLET C/K 1500 PICKUP

Four-wheel anti-lock braking is standard fare, and models under 8,600 lbs. GVWR have an airbag installed in the steering wheel hub. Correctly fitted, a C/K pickup can tow as much as 10,000 pounds. Long-life engine components extend service intervals up to 100,000 miles on some items. For luxury-oriented truckers, a C/K can be trimmed in leather when the top Silverado trim package is specified.

When selecting a full-size Chevy truck, you have to face the usual bewildering selection of models, which vary by wheelbase, cargo-bed size, cab design, and Sportside or Fleetside bed styling. Don't stop yet: you also have to choose from five engine sizes (including two diesels), and decide whether you want two- or four-wheel drive. Then, you still have the dizzying single-option list to ponder.

We get tired just thinking about all those possibilities, but they come with the territory when you're heading into big-pickup range. Truck customers don't want the same hauler that everybody else is buying. They want one tailored to their own specific needs, and Chevrolet provides these customers with myriad possibilities to create that special, one-of-a-kind truck.

Safety Data

Driver Airbag: *Standard*
Side Airbag: *Not Available*
Traction Control: *Not Available*
Driver Crash Test Grade: *Excellent*

Passenger Airbag: *Standard*
4-Wheel ABS: *Standard*
Integrated Child Seat(s): *Not Available*
Passenger Crash Test Grade: *Good*

Standard Equipment

C/K1500 REGULAR CAB: Vortec 4300 V-6 engine, heavy-duty 600 CCA battery, 4-wheel antilock power front disc/rear drum brakes, 25 gallon fuel tank (34 gallon on Longbed models), 100-amp generator, speed-sensitive power steering, 5-speed manual transmission, dual front airbags with passenger side deactivation switch, dual in-dash cupholders, full black rubber floor covering, trip odometer, tachometer, oil pressure gauge, voltmeter, engine temperature gauge, solar-ray tinted windows, cloth headliner, dome light with delayed entry feature, reading light, ashtray light, glovebox light, underhood lamp, cargo box lamp, 2 accessory power outlets, AM/FM stereo with seek-scan and clock, vinyl bench seat, theft deterrent system, right-side vanity mirror, chrome front bumper, dark argent air dam, painted rear bumper, argent grille, halogen headlights, daytime running lights, black breakaway exterior mirrors, full-size spare tire, front tow hooks (K1500 only), silver painted wheels with dark center caps, intermittent windshield wipers, 8-lead trailer harness.

C/K 1500 EXTENDED CAB: Vortec 5000 V-8 engine (Extended Cab Longbed only), 60/40 split bench front seat, rear quarter swing out windows.

Base Prices

CODE	DESCRIPTION	INVOICE	MSRP
CC10703	C1500 Fleetside W/T Reg. Cab Shortbed	13512	14930
CC10903	C1500 Fleetside W/T Reg. Cab Longbed	13801	15250
CC10703	C1500 Fleetside Reg. Cab Shortbed	14311	16355
CC10903	C1500 Fleetside Reg. Cab Longbed	14573	16655
CC10703	C1500 Sportside Reg. Cab Shrobed	14814	16930
CC10753	C1500 Fleetside X-cab Shortbed	16061	18355
CC10953	C1500 Fleetside X-cab Longbed	16756	19150

C/K 1500 PICKUP — CHEVROLET

CODE	DESCRIPTION	INVOICE	MSRP
CC10753	C1500 Sportside X-cab Shortbed	20212	23099
CK10703	K1500 Fleetside W/T Reg. Cab Shortbed	16860	18630
CK10903	K1500 Fleetside W/T Reg. Cab Longbed	17150	18950
CK10703	K1500 Fleetside Reg. Cab Shortbed	16936	19355
CK10903	K1500 Fleetside Reg. Cab Longbed	17198	19655
CK10703	K1500 Sportside Reg. Cab Shortbed	17439	19930
CK10753	K1500 Fleetside X-cab Shortbed	18686	21355
CK10953	K1500 Fleetside X-cab Longbed	19381	22150
CK10753	K1500 Sportside X-cab Shortbed	22837	26099
	Destination Charge:	625	625

Accessories

CODE	DESCRIPTION	INVOICE	MSRP
GU4	3.08 Axle Ratio (C1500)	NC	NC
	REQUIRES L30 or L31. NOT AVAILABLE with G80, KNP, Z82.		
GU6	3.42 Axle Ratio	NC	NC
	NOT AVAILABLE with (Z82) HD trailering special equipment.		
GT4	3.73 Axle Ratio (All except W/T)	116	135
	Includes engine oil cooler. REQUIRES L30 or L31 and M30. NOT AVAILABLE with KC4, Z82, M50.		
GT4	3.73 Rear Axle Ratio (W/T)	NC	NC
FG5	46mm Bilstein Shocks (C1500)	194	225
	NOT AVAILABLE with (F51) HD front and rear shock absorbers; or (Z82) HD trailering special equipment on extended cab.		
YG6	Air Conditioning Not Desired	NC	NC
	NOT AVAILABLE with C60, R9A, 1SB, 1SC.		
V22	Appearance Package (All except W/T)	164	191
	Includes chrome grille, composite halogen headlamps. REQUIRES 1SA.		
R9B	Bright Appearance Package (Fleetside except W/T)	415	483
	Includes bright bodyside moldings, Appearance Package: chrome grille, composite halogen headlamps, rear chrome step bumper with rub strip, front chrome deluxe bumper with rub strip, rally wheel trim. REQUIRES 1SA.		
R9B	Bright Appearance Package (Sportside)	389	452
	Includes Appearance Package: chrome grille, composite halogen headlamps, rear chrome step bumper with rub strip, front chrome deluxe bumper with rub strip, rally wheel trim, bright bodyside moldings. REQUIRES 1SA.		
B85	Bright Bodyside Moldings (Fleetside except W/T)	92	107
	Includes bright wheel openings. REQUIRES 1SA. NOT AVAILABLE with R9B.		
B85	Bright Bodyside Moldings (Sportside Reg Cab)	65	76
	REQUIRES 1SA. NOT AVAILABLE with R9B.		
YF5	California Emissions	146	170
	Automatically added to vehicles shipped to and/or sold to retailers in California. Out-of-state retailers must order on vehicles to be registered or leased in California.		
B30	Carpet Floor Covering (Reg Cab except W/T)	30	35
	REQUIRES 1SA.		

CHEVROLET C/K 1500 PICKUP

CODE	DESCRIPTION	INVOICE	MSRP
B30	Carpet Floor Covering (X-cab)	44	51
	REQUIRES 1SA.		
VG3	Chrome Front Bumper with Rub Strip (All except W/T)	22	26
	NOT AVAILABLE with 1SB, 1SC.		
VB3	Chrome Rear Step Bumper with Rub Strip (All except W/T)	85	99
	Vehicles registered in certain states must have a rear bumper to be operated on their roads. Consult your local laws. Cheyenne does not include a rear bumper. REQUIRES (VG3) chrome front bumper with rub strip. NOT AVAILABLE with 1SB, 1SC.		
C	Cloth Seat Trim (All except W/T)	NC	NC
V10	Cold Climate Package	28	33
	Includes engine block heater.		
R9A	Comfort & Convenience Package (All except W/T)	1150	1337
	Includes air conditioning, tilt steering wheel, cruise control, AM/FM stereo with seek-scan, digital clock, and cassette player. REQUIRES 1SA.		
ZQ3	Convenience Group	331	385
	Includes tilt steering wheel, speed control. NOT AVAILABLE with 1SB, 1SC.		
ZY2	Conventional Two-Tone Paint (All except W/T)	163	190
	REQUIRES 1SB or 1SC.		
AJ1	Deep Tinted Solar Ray Glass (Reg Cab except W/T)	30	35
	REQUIRES (A28) sliding rear window.		
AJ1	Deep Tinted Solar Ray Glass (X-cab)	92	107
	NOT AVAILABLE with (C49) electric rear window defogger.		
AJ1	Deep Tinted Solar Ray Glass w/C49 (X-cab)	62	72
	REQUIRES (C49) electric rear window defogger.		
C49	Electric rear window defogger (X-cab)	132	154
	NOT AVAILABLE with (A28) sliding rear window.		
DD7	Electrochromic Rearview Mirror (All except W/T)	125	145
	Includes 8-point compass. REQUIRES 1SB.		
NP1	Electronic Shift Transfer Case (K1500)	129	150
KC4	Engine Oil Cooler	116	135
	NOT AVAILABLE with (GT4) 3.73 Axle Ratio, (Z82) HD special trailering equipment.		
L56	Engine: 6.5-liter Turbo Diesel V-8 (X-cab Longbed)	3062	3560
L56	Engine: 6.5-liter Turbo Diesel V-8 (X-cab Shortbed)	3487	4055
L30	Engine: Vortec 5000 V8 SFI (Reg Cab except W/T)	426	495
L30	Engine: Vortec 5000 V8 SFI (X-cab)	NC	NC
L31	Engine: Vortec 5700 V8 SFI (Reg Cab except W/T)	1028	1195
L31	Engine: Vortec 5700 V8 SFI (X-cab)	602	700
C60	Front Air Conditioning	692	805
	NOT AVAILABLE with YG6. R9A, 1SB, 1SC.		
V76	Front Tow Hooks (C1500)	33	38
B32	Front Vinyl Floor Mats (All except W/T)	17	20
	REQUIRES B30 AND 1SA.		
BG9	Full Rubber Color-Keyed Flooring (Reg Cab except W/T)	(30)	(35)
	Replaces carpeting and floor mats with full floor rubber.		

C/K 1500 PICKUP — CHEVROLET

CODE	DESCRIPTION	INVOICE	MSRP
BG9	Full Rubber Color-Keyed Flooring (X-cab)	(44)	(51)
	Replaces carpeting and floor mats with full floor rubber. NOT AVAILABLE with (E24) third door.		
TP2	HD Auxiliary Battery (All except W/T)	115	134
	REQUIRES (L30) engine or (L31) engine.		
KNP	HD Auxiliary Transmission Cooler (All except W/T)	83	96
	REQUIRES L31 and M30 and GU6 or GT4. NOT AVAILABLE with L30, GU4, MT1, M30, Z82.		
F44	HD Chassis Equipment (K1500 X-cab)	198	230
	NOT AVAILABLE with L56.		
F51	HD Front & Rear Shock Absorbers	34	40
	NOT AVAILABLE with FG5, VYU, Z82.		
F60	HD Front Springs (K1500 Reg Cab)	54	63
	NOT AVAILABLE with VYU.		
Z82	HD Special Trailering Equipment with Z71 or VYU (K1500)	257	299
	Includes trailer hitch platform, HD shocks, and engine oil cooler. REQUIRES GU4 or GT4. NOT AVAILABLE with L56.		
Z82	HD Special Trailering Equipment with Z71 or VYU (K1500)	141	164
	Includes trailer hitch platform, HD shocks, and engine oil cooler. REQUIRES L56 or GT4.		
Z82	HD Trailering Special Equipment	175	204
	Includes trailer hitch platform, HD shocks, and engine oil cooler. NOT AVAILABLE with Z71 or VYU. REQUIRES L56 or GT4.		
Z82	HD Trailering Special Equipment	292	339
	Includes trailer hitch platform, HD shocks, engine oil cooler. REQUIRES GU4 or GU6. NOT AVAILABLE with Z71, VYU, GT4, L56.		
K47	High Capacity Air Cleaner	22	25
—	Leather Seat Trim (All except W/T)	860	1000
	REQUIRES 1SB.		
G80	Locking Differential	217	252
Z71	Off-Road Package (K1500 except W/T)	232	270
	Includes skid plates, HD shocks front and rear. REQUIRES 1SB or 1SC.		
AU3	Power Door Locks (All except W/T)	134	156
	REQUIRES 1SA.		
AG9	Power Driver's Seat (X-cab)	206	240
	REQUIRES 1SB.		
1SA	Preferred Equip. Group 1SA with M30 or MT1 and R9A and R9B (All except W/T)	NC	NC
	Manufacturer Discount	(602)	(700)
	Net Price	(602)	(700)
	Includes standard Cheyenne Decor. REQUIRES M30 or MT1 and R9A and R9B.		
1SA	Preferred Equipment Group 1SA with M30 or MT1 and R9B (All except W/T)	NC	NC
	Manufacturer Discount	(172)	(200)
	Net Price	(172)	(200)
	Includes standard Cheyenne Decor. REQUIRES M30 or MT1 and R9B.		

CHEVROLET C/K 1500 PICKUP

CODE	DESCRIPTION	INVOICE	MSRP
1SA	Preferred Equipment Group 1SA with MG5 or M50 and R9A (All except W/T)	NC	NC
	Manufacturer Discount	(860)	(1000)
	Net Price	(860)	(1000)

Includes standard Cheyenne Decor. REQUIRES MG5 or M50 and R9A.

1SA	Preferred Equip Grp 1SA w/MG5 or M50 and R9A and R9B. (All except W/T)	NC	NC
	Manufacturer Discount	(1032)	(1200)
	Net Price	(1032)	(1200)

Includes standard Cheyenne Decor. REQUIRES MG5 or M50 and R9A and R9B.

1SA	Preferred Equipment Group 1SA with MG5 or M50 and R9B (All except W/T)	NC	NC
	Manufacturer Discount	(602)	(700)
	Net Price	(602)	(700)

Includes standard Cheyenne Decor. REQUIRES MG5 or M50 and R9B.

1SA	Preferred Equipment Group 1SA with R9A (All except W/T)	NC	NC
	Manufacturer Discount	(430)	(500)
	Net Price	(430)	(500)

Includes standard Cheyenne Decor. REQUIRES R9A.

1SB	Preferred Equip Grp 1SB w/ M30 or MT1 (All except W/T & Sportside X-cab)	2611	3036
	Manufacturer Discount	(645)	(750)
	Net Price	1966	2286

Includes Silverado Decor: front air conditioning, power windows, power door locks, tilt steering wheel, cruise control, full floor carpet with rubber floor mats, AM/FM stereo with seek-scan, digital clock, and cassette player; cloth bench seat with Scotchgard protectant (60/40 split bench on X-cab), leather-wrapped steering wheel, behind seat storage tray, chrome front bumper with rub strip, chrome rear bumper with step pad, chrome deluxe grille, composite halogen headlamps, power exterior mirrors, chrome wheel opening trim, rally wheel trim: chrome trim rings and bright center caps. REQUIRES M30.

1SB	Preferred Equip Grp 1SB w/ MG5 & M50 (All except W/T & Sportside X-cab)	2611	3036
	Manufacturer Discount	(1075)	(1250)
	Net Price	1536	1786

Includes Silverado Decor: front air conditioning, power windows, power door locks, tilt steering wheel, cruise control, full floor carpet with rubber floor mats, AM/FM stereo with seek-scan, digital clock, and cassette player; cloth bench seat with Scotchgard protectant (60/40 split bench on X-cab), leather-wrapped steering wheel, behind seat storage tray, chrome front bumper with rub strip, chrome rear bumper with step pad, chrome deluxe grille, composite halogen headlamps, power exterior mirrors, chrome wheel opening trim, rally wheel trim: chrome trim rings and bright center caps. REQUIRES MG5 or M50.

1SB	Preferred Equipment Group 1SB with MG5 or M50 (Sportside X-cab)	NC	NC
	Manufacturer Discount	(1075)	(1250)
	Net Price	(1075)	(1250)

Includes Silverado Decor: front air conditioning, power windows, power door locks, tilt steering wheel, cruise control, full floor carpet with rubber floor mats, AM/FM stereo with seek-scan, digital clock, and cassette player; cloth 60/40 split bench seat with Scotchgard protectant, leather-wrapped steering wheel, behind seat storage tray,

C/K 1500 PICKUP — CHEVROLET

CODE	DESCRIPTION	INVOICE	MSRP

chrome front bumper with rub strip, chrome rear bumper with step pad, chrome deluxe grille, composite halogen headlamps, power exterior mirrors, chrome wheel opening trim, rally wheel trim: chrome trim rings and bright center caps. *REQUIRES MG5 or M50.*

1SC	Preferred Equipment Group 1SC with M30 or MT1 (Fleetside X-cab)	3931	4571
	Manufacturer Discount	(645)	(750)
	Net Price	3286	3821

Includes Silverado Decor: front air conditioning, power windows, power door locks, tilt steering wheel, cruise control, full floor carpet with rubber floor mats, AM/FM stereo with seek-scan, digital clock, and cassette player; 60/40 split bench seat, leather-wrapped steering wheel, behind seat storage tray, chrome front bumper with rub strip, chrome rear bumper with step pad, chrome deluxe grille, composite halogen headlamps, power exterior mirrors, chrome wheel opening trim, rally wheel trim: chrome trim rings and bright center caps; remote keyless entry, electrochromic rearview mirror with 8-point compass, power driver's seat, leather seats.

1SC	Preferred Equipment Group 1SC with M30 or MT1 (Reg Cab except W/T)	3874	4505
	Manufacturer Discount	(645)	(750)
	Net Price	3229	3755

Includes Silverado Decor: front air conditioning, power windows, power door locks, tilt steering wheel, cruise control, full floor carpet with rubber floor mats, AM/FM stereo with seek-scan, digital clock, and cassette player; leather-wrapped steering wheel, behind seat storage tray, chrome front bumper with rub strip, chrome rear bumper with step pad, chrome deluxe grille, composite halogen headlamps, power exterior mirrors, chrome wheel opening trim, rally wheel trim: chrome trim rings and bright center caps; remote keyless entry, electrochromic rearview mirror with 8-point compass, leather bench seat.

1SC	Preferred Equipment Group 1SC with M30 or MT1 (Sportside X-cab)	1320	1535
	Manufacturer Discount	(645)	(750)
	Net Price	675	785

Includes Silverado Decor: front air conditioning, power windows, power door locks, tilt steering wheel, cruise control, full floor carpet with rubber floor mats, AM/FM stereo with seek-scan, digital clock, and cassette player; 60/40 split bench seat, leather-wrapped steering wheel, behind seat storage tray, chrome front bumper with rub strip, chrome rear bumper with step pad, chrome deluxe grille, composite halogen headlamps, power exterior mirrors, chrome wheel opening trim, rally wheel trim: chrome trim rings and bright center caps; remote keyless entry, electrochromic rearview mirror with 8-point compass, power driver's seat, leather seats.

1SC	Preferred Equipment Group 1SC with MG5 or M50 (Fleetside X-cab)	3931	4571
	Manufacturer Discount	(1075)	(1250)
	Net Price	2856	3321

Includes Silverado Decor: front air conditioning, power windows, power door locks, tilt steering wheel, cruise control, full floor carpet with rubber floor mats, AM/FM stereo with seek-scan, digital clock, and cassette player; 60/40 split bench seat, leather-wrapped steering wheel, behind seat storage tray, chrome front bumper with rub strip, chrome rear bumper with step pad, chrome deluxe grille, composite halogen

CHEVROLET C/K 1500 PICKUP

CODE	DESCRIPTION	INVOICE	MSRP

headlamps, power exterior mirrors, chrome wheel opening trim, rally wheel trim: chrome trim rings and bright center caps; remote keyless entry, electrochromic rearview mirror with 8-point compass, power driver's seat, leather seats.

1SC Preferred Equipment Group 1SC with MG5 or M50 (Reg Cab except W/T) 3931 4571
Manufacturer Discount .... (1075) (1250)
Net Price 2856 3321

Includes Silverado Decor: front air conditioning, power windows, power door locks, tilt steering wheel, cruise control, full floor carpet with rubber floor mats, AM/FM stereo with seek-scan, digital clock, and cassette player; leather-wrapped steering wheel, behind seat storage tray, chrome front bumper with rub strip, chrome rear bumper with step pad, chrome deluxe grille, composite halogen headlamps, power exterior mirrors, chrome wheel opening trim, rally wheel trim: chrome trim rings and bright center caps; remote keyless entry, electrochromic rearview mirror with 8-point compass, leather bench seat.

1SC Preferred Equipment Group 1SC with MG5 or M50 (Sportside X-cab) 1320 1535
Manufacturer Discount .... (1075) (1250)
Net Price 245 285

Includes Silverado Decor: front air conditioning, power windows, power door locks, tilt steering wheel, cruise control, full floor carpet with rubber floor mats, AM/FM stereo with seek-scan, digital clock, and cassette player; 60/40 split bench seat, leather-wrapped steering wheel, behind seat storage tray, chrome front bumper with rub strip, chrome rear bumper with step pad, chrome deluxe grille, composite halogen headlamps, power exterior mirrors, chrome wheel opening trim, rally wheel trim: chrome trim rings and bright center caps; remote keyless entry, electrochromic rearview mirror with 8-point compass, power driver's seat, leather seats.

1SW Preferred Equipment Group 1SW (W/T) .... NC NC
Manufacturer Discount .... (430) (500)
Net Price .... (430) (500)

Includes vehicle with standard equipment.

1SB Preferred Equipment Package 1SB with M30 or MT1 (Sportside X-cab) .... NC NC
Manufacturer Discount .... (645) (750)
Net Price .... (645) (750)

Includes Silverado Decor: front air conditioning, power windows, power door locks, tilt steering wheel, cruise control, full floor carpet with rubber floor mats, AM/FM stereo with seek-scan, digital clock, and cassette player; cloth 60/40 split bench seat with Scotchgard protectant, leather-wrapped steering wheel, behind seat storage tray, chrome front bumper with rub strip, chrome rear bumper with step pad, chrome deluxe grille, composite halogen headlamps, power exterior mirrors, chrome wheel opening trim, rally wheel trim: chrome trim rings and bright center caps. REQUIRES M30 or MT1.

UL5 Radio Delete .... (247) (287)
REQUIRES 1SA.

UM6 Radio: AM/FM Stereo with Cassette 126 147
Includes seek-scan and digital clock. NOT AVAILABLE with R9A, 1SB, 1SC.

C/K 1500 PICKUP — CHEVROLET

CODE	DESCRIPTION	INVOICE	MSRP
UL0	**Radio: AM/FM Stereo with Cassette (All except W/T)**	77	90
	Includes digital clock, theft lock, automatic tone control, speed compensated volume and enhanced performance speaker system. NOT AVAILABLE with 1SA, UNO, UP0, UL5.		
UN0	**Radio: AM/FM Stereo with CD (All except W/T)**	163	190
	Includes digital clock, theft lock, automatic tone control, speed compensated volume and enhanced performance speaker system. NOT AVAILABLE with 1SA, UL0, UP0, UL5.		
UP0	**Radio: AM/FM Stereo with CD & Cassette (All except W/T)**	249	290
	Includes digital clock, search and repeat cassette player, CD player, theft lock, speed compensated volume and enhanced performance speaker system. REQUIRES M30 or MT1. NOT AVAILABLE with 1SA, UL0, UNO, UL5.		
P06	**Rally Wheel Trim**	52	60
	REQUIRES 1SA or 1SW.		
EF1	**Rear Bumper Delete**	(112)	(130)
	Vehicles registered in certain states must have a rear bumper to be operated on their roads. Consult your local laws. NOT AVAILABLE with (Z82) HD trailering special equipment.		
EF1	**Rear Bumper Delete (All except W/T)**	(172)	(200)
	Vehicles registered in certain states must have a rear bumper to be operated on their roads. Consult your local laws. REQUIRES 1SB or 1SC. NOT AVAILABLE with (Z82) HD trailering special equipment.		
B33	**Rear Floor Mats (X-cab)**	14	16
	REQUIRES B30 and B32. NOT AVAILABLE with (YG4) seats.		
AU0	**Remote Keyless Entry (All except W/T)**	129	150
	REQUIRES 1SB.		
AE7	**Seat: Reclining 60/40 Split Bench (Reg Cab except W/T)**	150	174
	Includes storage armrest and power lumbar supports. REQUIRES 1SB.		
A95	**Seats: Reclining High-Back Buckets (Reg Cab except W/T)**	332	386
	Includes power lumbar supports, floor console. REQUIRES 1SA or 1SB.		
A95	**Seats: Reclining High-Back Buckets (X-cab)**	232	270
	Includes power lumbar supports, floor console. REQUIRES 1SA or 1SB.		
NZZ	**Skid Plate Package (K1500)**	82	95
	NOT AVAILABLE with Z71.		
A28	**Sliding Rear Window**	99	115
	NOT AVAILABLE with (C49) electric rear window defogger.		
VYU	**Snow Plow Prep Package (K1500)**	136	158
	Includes HD front springs and HD shock absorbers. NOT AVAILABLE with Z71.		
VYU	**Snow Plow Prep Package with Z71 (K1500)**	47	55
	Includes HD front springs and HD shock absorbers. REQUIRES Z71.		
DF2	**Stainless Steel Camper Type Mirrors (All except W/T)**	46	53
	7.5"x 10.5." REQUIRES 1SA.		
DF2	**Stainless Steel Camper Type Mirrors (All except W/T)**	(39)	(45)
	7.5"x 10.5." REQUIRES 1SB or 1SC.		

CHEVROLET C/K 1500 PICKUP

CODE	DESCRIPTION	INVOICE	MSRP
E24	Third Door (Fleetside X-cab)	361	420
	Door lock latch is non-electric. REQUIRES L30 or L31 and 1SB or 1SC and M30. NOT AVAILABLE with BG9.		
E24	Third Door (Sportside X-cab)	NC	NC
	Door lock latch is non-electric. REQUIRES L30 or L31 and M30. NOT AVAILABLE with BG9.		
XBN	Tires: Front LT245/75R16 On-Off Road BSW (K1500)	19	22
XBX	Tires: Front LT245/75R16 On-Off WOL (K1500)	62	72
XFN	Tires: Front P235/75R15 AS White Lettered (C1500 except W/T)	43	50
XGB	Tires: Front P245/75R16 All Terrain WOL (K1500)	43	50
XGC	Tires: Front P265/75R16 All Terrain BSW (K1500)	46	54
XGD	Tires: Front P265/75R16 All Terrain WOL (K1500)	89	104
ZFN	Tires: P235/75R15 AS White Lettered Spare (C1500 except W/T)	22	25
ZGB	Tires: P245/75R16 All Terrain WOL (K1500)	22	25
YBN	Tires: Rear LT245/75R16 On-Off Road BSW (K1500)	19	22
YBX	Tires: Rear LT245/75R16 On-Off WOL (K1500)	62	72
YFN	Tires: Rear P235/75R15 AS White Lettered (C1500 except W/T)	43	50
YGB	Tires: Rear P245/75R16 All Terrain WOL (K1500)	43	50
YGC	Tires: Rear P265/75R16 All Terrain BSW (K1500)	46	54
YGD	Tires: Rear P265/75R16 All Terrain WOL (K1500)	89	104
ZBN	Tires: Spare LT245/75R16 On-Off Road BSW (K1500)	9	11
ZBX	Tires: Spare LT245/75R16 On-Off Road WOL (K1500)	31	36
ZGC	Tires: Spare P265/75R16 All Terrain BSW (K1500)	23	27
ZGD	Tires: Spare P265/75R16 All Terrain WOL (K1500)	45	52
M30	Transmission: 4-Speed Automatic (All except X-cab Sportside)	834	970
M30	Transmission: 4-Speed Automatic (X-cab Sportside)	NC	NC
MT1	Transmission: 4-Speed HD Automatic Transmission (All except W/T)	834	970
MG5	Transmission: 5-Speed Manual	NC	NC
M50	Transmission: 5-Speed Manual (All except W/T)	NC	NC
	REQUIRES L31.		
BZY	Under Rail Bedliner (All except Sportside)	194	225
N90	Wheels: Aluminum (C1500 except W/T)	344	400
	Includes spare wheel not matching. REQUIRES 1SA. NOT AVAILABLE with R9B.		
N90	Wheels: Aluminum (C1500 except W/T)	292	340
	Includes spare wheel not matching. REQUIRES 1SB or 1SC or R9B.		
PF4	Wheels: Aluminum (K1500 except W/T)	344	400
	REQUIRES 1SA.		
PF4	Wheels: Aluminum (K1500 except W/T)	292	340
	REQUIRES 1SB or 1SC.		
N83	Wheels: Chrome (C1500)	267	310
	Includes spare wheel not matching. REQUIRES 1SA. NOT AVAILABLE with R9B.		
N83	Wheels: Chrome (C1500 except W/T)	215	250
	Includes spare wheel not matching. REQUIRES 1SB or 1SC or R9B.		

C/K 2500 PICKUP — CHEVROLET

1998 2500

Safety Data

Driver Airbag: *Std. (LD Models); N/A (HD Models)*
Side Airbag: *Not Available*
Traction Control: *Not Available*
Driver Crash Test Grade: *Excellent (LD Models); N/A (HD Models)*

Passenger Airbag: *Std. (LD Models); N/A (HD Models)*
4-Wheel ABS: *Standard*
Integrated Child Seat(s): *Not Available*
Passenger Crash Test Grade: *Good (LD Models); N/A (HD Models)*

Standard Equipment

C/K 2500 REGULAR CAB: Vortec 5000 V-8 engine (C2500 LD), Vortec 5700 V-8 engine (C2500 HD & K2500 models), heavy-duty 600 CCA battery, 4-wheel antilock power front disc/rear drum brakes, 25 gallon fuel tank (34 gallon on Longbed models), 100-amp generator, speed-sensitive power steering, 5-speed manual transmission, dual front airbags with passenger side deactivation switch (LD models), passenger assist handles, dual in-dash cupholders, full color-keyed rubber floor covering, trip odometer, tachometer, oil pressure gauge, voltmeter, engine temperature gauge, solar-ray tinted windows, cloth headliner, dome light with delayed entry feature, reading light, ashtray light, glovebox light, underhood lamp, cargo box lamp, 2 accessory power outlets, AM/FM stereo with seek-scan and clock, vinyl bench seat, theft deterrent system, right-side vanity mirror, chrome front bumper, dark argent air dam, painted rear bumper, argent grille, halogen headlights, daytime running lights, black breakaway exterior mirrors, full-size spare tire, front tow hooks (K2500 only), silver painted wheels with dark center caps, intermittent windshield wipers, 8-lead trailer harness.

C/K 2500 EXTENDED CAB: 60/40 split bench front seat, rear quarter swing out windows.

Base Prices

Code	Description	Invoice	MSRP
CC20903	LD Regular Cab Longbed	15603	17832
CC20903	HD Regular Cab Longbed	16516	18880
CC20753	LD X-cab Longbed	17892	20448
CC20953	HD X-cab Longbed	17920	20484
CK20903	Fleetside Reg Cab Longbed	18927	21635
CK20753	Fleetside X-cab Shortbed	20638	23590
CK20953	Fleetside X-cab Longbed	20749	23717
Destination Charge:		625	625

Accessories

Code	Description	Invoice	MSRP
GT4	3.73 Axle Ratio (LD models)	116	135
	Includes engine oil cooler. NOT AVAILABLE with (L56) engine, (Z82) HD trailering equipment, (KC4) engine oil cooler.		
GT5	4.10 Axle Ratio (HD models)	NC	NC
	Includes engine oil cooler. NOT AVAILABLE with (KL6) natural gas provisions.		

CHEVROLET C/K 2500 PICKUP

CODE	DESCRIPTION	INVOICE	MSRP
AE7	60/40 Reclining Split-Bench Seat (Reg Cab)	150	174
	Includes storage armrest and power lumbar supports with custom cloth or leather upholstery. NOT AVAILABLE with 1SA, A95.		
C60	Air Conditioning	692	805
	REQUIRES 1SA. NOT AVAILABLE with (YG6) air conditioning not desired.		
YG6	Air Conditioning Not Desired	NC	NC
	NOT AVAILABLE with 1SB, 1SC, R9A, C60.		
KL5	Alternative Fuel Conversion (All except LD X-cab)	108	125
	LPG and CNG conversion ready. REQUIRES (MT1) transmission. NOT AVAILABLE with (L29) engine, (L65) engine.		
V22	Appearance Package	164	191
	Includes aero-composite halogen headlamps, chrome grille. REQUIRES 1SA.		
TP2	Auxiliary Battery	115	134
	NOT AVAILABLE with (L56) engine, (L65) engine.		
R9B	Bright Appearance Package (C2500)	415	483
	Includes bright bodyside and wheel opening moldings, Appearance Package: aero-composite halogen headlamps, chrome grille, rear chrome step bumper with rub strip, chrome deluxe front bumper with rub strip, rally wheel trim. REQUIRES 1SA. NOT AVAILABLE with 1SB, 1SC, R9C.		
R9B	Bright Appearance Package (K2500)	389	452
	Includes chrome grille, chrome bumpers, body side moldings, and rally wheel trim. REQUIRES 1SA.		
B85	Bright Bodyside & Wheel Opening Moldings (C2500)	92	107
	REQUIRES 1SA.		
B85	Bright Exterior Moldings (K2500)	65	76
	NOT AVAILABLE with 1SB, 1SC, R9B.		
YF5	California Emissions	146	170
	Automatically added to vehicles shipped to and/or sold to retailers in California. Out-of-state retailers must order on vehicles to be registered or leased in California. REQUIRES M50 or M30 or L65 or L31. NOT AVAILABLE with L56, U01.		
B30	Carpet Floor Covering (Reg Cab)	30	35
B30	Carpet Floor Covering (X-cab)	44	51
VG3	Chrome Deluxe Front Bumper with Rub Strip	22	26
	REQUIRES 1SA.		
VB3	Chrome Rear Step Bumper with Rub Strip	85	99
	REQUIRES VG3 and 1SA. NOT AVAILABLE with (EF1) rear bumper delete provisions.		
—	Cloth Seat Trim	NC	NC
	NOT AVAILABLE with 1SB, 1SC, A95.		
V10	Cold Climate Package	28	33
	Includes engine block heater. REQUIRES 1SA or 1SB or 1SC.		
R9C	Commercial Option Package (C2500)	325	378
	Includes under rail bedliner, front tow hooks, sliding rear window. REQUIRES 1SA. NOT AVAILABLE with 1SB, 1SC, R9B.		
R9C	Commercial Option Package (K2500)	428	498
	Includes bedliner, HD front springs, skid plates, sliding rear window. REQUIRES 1SA. NOT AVAILABLE with R9B, R9A.		

C/K 2500 PICKUP — CHEVROLET

CODE	DESCRIPTION	INVOICE	MSRP
ZQ3	**Convenience Group**	331	385
	Includes speed control, tilt steering wheel. NOT AVAILABLE with 1SB, 1SC, R9A.		
R9A	**Convenience Package**	1150	1337
	Includes air conditioning, AM/FM stereo with cassette player, seek-scan, and digital clock; Convenience Group: speed control, tilt steering wheel. REQUIRES 1SA. NOT AVAILABLE with YG6, UL5, R9C.		
ZY2	**Conventional Two-Tone Paint**	163	190
	NOT AVAILABLE with (1SA) Preferred Equipment Group 1SA.		
AJ1	**Deep Tinted Solar-Ray Glass (Reg Cab)**	30	35
	REQUIRES (A28) sliding rear window.		
AJ1	**Deep Tinted Solar-Ray Glass (X-cab)**	92	107
	REQUIRES 1SA or 1SB or 1SC. NOT AVAILABLE with C49.		
AJ1	**Deep Tinted Solar-Ray Glass with C49 (X-cab)**	62	72
	Includes light tint glass in rear window. REQUIRES (C49) electric rear window defogger.		
C49	**Electric rear window defogger (X-cab)**	132	154
	NOT AVAILABLE with (1SA) Preferred Equipment Group 1SA, (A28) sliding rear window.		
DD7	**Electrochromic Rearview Mirror**	125	145
	Includes 8-point compass. NOT AVAILABLE with 1SA, 1SC.		
NP1	**Electronic Shift Transfer Case (K2500)**	129	150
KC4	**Engine Oil Cooler (LD models)**	116	135
	NOT AVAILABLE with L56, MT1, GT4, Z82.		
L65	**Engine: 6.5L V8 Turbo Diesel (HD models)**	2460	2860
	Includes HD auxiliary battery. NOT AVAILABLE with KL5, KL6, TP2, V10.		
L56	**Engine: 6.5L V8 Turbo Diesel with GU6 (LD models)**	3062	3560
	Includes HD auxiliary battery. REQUIRES MT1 and GU6. NOT AVAILABLE with M50, M30, G80, K47, TP2, KC4, YF5, Z82, V10.		
L31	**Engine: Vortec 5700 V8 SFI (LD models)**	602	700
	REQUIRES M50 or M30. NOT AVAILABLE with MT1, Z82.		
L29	**Engine: Vortec 7400 V8 SFI (K1500 & C2500 HD X-cab)**	516	600
	NOT AVAILABLE with (KL5) alternative fuel conversion, (KL6) natural gas provisions.		
B32	**Front Floor Mats**	17	20
	REQUIRES (B30) carpet floor covering. REQUIRES 1SA.		
BG9	**Full Rubber Color-Keyed Flooring (Reg Cab)**	(30)	(35)
	Replaces carpeting and floor mats with full floor rubber. NOT AVAILABLE with (1SA) Preferred Equipment Group 1SA.		
BG9	**Full Rubber Color-Keyed Flooring (X-cab)**	(44)	(51)
	Replaces carpeting and floor mats with full floor rubber. NOT AVAILABLE with (1SA) Preferred Equipment Group 1SA.		
KNP	**HD Auxiliary Transmission Cooler**	83	96
	REQUIRES (L31) engine and (M30) transmission. NOT AVAILABLE with (M50) transmission.		
F60	**HD Front Springs**	54	63
	NOT AVAILABLE with VYU, R9C.		

CHEVROLET C/K 2500 PICKUP

CODE	DESCRIPTION	INVOICE	MSRP
Z82	HD Trailering Equipment	257	299
	Includes engine oil cooler, trailer hitch platform. REQUIRES M30 and L30 and GU6. NOT AVAILABLE with L56, MT1, GT4, Z82, M50, EF1.		
Z82	HD Trailering Equipment (HD models)	141	164
	Includes trailer hitch platform. REQUIRES GT4 or L65. NOT AVAILABLE with Z82, M50, EF1, L56.		
K47	High Capacity Air Cleaner	22	25
	NOT AVAILABLE with (L56) engine.		
—	Leather Seat Trim	860	1000
	NOT AVAILABLE with 1SA, A95.		
G80	Locking Differential	217	252
	REQUIRES (GT4) 3.73 axle ratio. NOT AVAILABLE with (L56) engine.		
KL6	Natural Gas Provisions (C2500 Reg Cab)	4988	5800
	Includes alternative fuel conversion. REQUIRES MT1. NOT AVAILABLE with L29, L65, GT5, BZY.		
AU3	Power Door Locks	134	156
	REQUIRES 1SA.		
AG9	Power Driver's Seat (X-cab)	206	240
	NOT AVAILABLE with 1SA.		
1SA	Preferred Equipment Group 1SA with R9A	NC	NC
	Manufacturer Discount	(430)	(500)
	Net Price	(430)	(500)
	Includes standard Cheyenne Decor. REQUIRES R9A.		
1SA	Preferred Equipment Group 1SA with R9A and R9B or R9C	NC	NC
	Manufacturer Discount	(602)	(700)
	Net Price	(602)	(700)
	Includes standard Cheyenne Decor. REQUIRES R9A and R9B or R9C.		
1SA	Preferred Equipment Group 1SA with R9B or R9C	NC	NC
	Manufacturer Discount	(172)	(200)
	Net Price	(172)	(200)
	Includes standard Cheyenne Decor. REQUIRES R9B or R9C.		
1SB	Preferred Equipment Group 1SB	2611	3036
	Manufacturer Discount	(645)	(750)
	Net Price	1966	2286
	Includes Silverado Decor: front air conditioning, power windows, power door locks, tilt steering wheel, cruise control, color-keyed carpet with rubber floor mats, AM/FM stereo with cassette player, seek-scan, and digital clock; cloth bench seat (regular cab models), cloth 60/40 split bench seat (extended cab models), leather-wrapped steering wheel, behind seat storage tray, chrome front bumper with black rub strip, chrome rear bumper with step pad, chrome deluxe grille, composite halogen headlights, power exterior mirrors, chrome wheel well openings (7,200 GVW models only), rally wheel trim with chrome trim rings and bright center caps.		
1SC	Preferred Equipment Group 1SC (Reg Cab)	3874	4505
	Manufacturer Discount	(645)	(750)
	Net Price	3229	3755
	Includes Silverado Decor: front air conditioning, power windows, power door locks, tilt steering wheel, cruise control, color-keyed carpet with rubber floor mats, AM/FM		

C/K 2500 PICKUP — CHEVROLET

CODE	DESCRIPTION	INVOICE	MSRP

stereo with cassette player, seek-scan, and digital clock; cloth bench seat (regular cab models), cloth 60/40 split bench seat (extended cab models), leather-wrapped steering wheel, behind seat storage tray, chrome front bumper with black rub strip, chrome rear bumper with step pad, chrome deluxe grille, composite halogen headlights, power exterior mirrors, chrome wheel well openings (7,200 GVW models only), rally wheel trim with chrome trim rings and bright center caps; remote keyless entry, electrochromic rearview mirror with 8-point compass, leather upholstery.

1SC   Preferred Equipment Group 1SC (X-cab) 3931   4571
     Manufacturer Discount .... (645)   (750)
     Net Price 3286   3821

Includes Silverado Decor: front air conditioning, power windows, power door locks, tilt steering wheel, cruise control, color-keyed carpet with rubber floor mats, AM/FM stereo with cassette player, seek-scan, and digital clock; cloth bench seat (regular cab models), cloth 60/40 split bench seat (extended cab models), leather-wrapped steering wheel, behind seat storage tray, chrome front bumper with black rub strip, chrome rear bumper with step pad, chrome deluxe grille, composite halogen headlights, power exterior mirrors, chrome wheel well openings (7,200 GVW models only), rally wheel trim with chrome trim rings and bright center caps; remote keyless entry, electrochromic rearview mirror with 8-point compass, power driver's seat, leather upholstery.

UL5   Radio Delete .... (247)   (287)
Includes clock delete. NOT AVAILABLE with 1SB, 1SC, R9A, UM6.

UM6   Radio: AM/FM Stereo with Cassette 126   147
Includes digital clock, seek-scan, and cassette player. REQUIRES 1SA. NOT AVAILABLE with (UL5) radio.

UL0   Radio: AM/FM Stereo with Cassette 77   90
Includes digital clock, automatic tone control, theft lock, speed compensated volume and enhanced performance speaker system. NOT AVAILABLE with (1SA) Preferred Equipment Group 1SA, (UN0) radio, (UP0) radio.

UN0   Radio: AM/FM Stereo with CD 163   190
Includes digital clock, automatic tone control, theft lock, speed compensated volume and enhanced performance speaker system. NOT AVAILABLE with (1SA) Preferred Equipment Group 1SA, (UL0) radio, (UP0) radio.

UP0   Radio: AM/FM Stereo with CD & Cassette 249   290
Includes digital clock, automatic tone control, search and repeat on cassette, theft lock, speed compensated volume and enhanced performance speaker system. REQUIRES M30 or MT1. NOT AVAILABLE with 1SA, UL0, UN0, M50.

P06   Rally Wheel Trim 52   60
Includes chrome trim rings and bright center caps. NOT AVAILABLE with 1SB, 1SC, R9B.

EF1   Rear Bumper Delete Provisions .... (112)   (130)
NOT AVAILABLE with 1SB, 1SC, Z82, EF1, VB3.

EF1   Rear Bumper Delete Provisions .... (172)   (200)
NOT AVAILABLE with 1SA, Z82, EF1, VB3.

B33   Rear Floor Mats (X-cab) 14   16
REQUIRES B30 and B32 and 1SA.

CHEVROLET C/K 2500 PICKUP

CODE	DESCRIPTION	INVOICE	MSRP
A95	Reclining High Back Bucket Seats (Reg Cab)	332	386
	Includes power lumbar supports, floor console. NOT AVAILABLE with 1SA, 1SC, AE7		
A95	Reclining High Back Bucket Seats (X-cab)	232	270
	Includes power lumbar supports, floor console. NOT AVAILABLE with 1SA, YG4.		
AU0	Remote Keyless Entry	129	150
	NOT AVAILABLE with 1SA, 1SC.		
U01	Roof Marker Lamps	47	55
	NOT AVAILABLE with (YF5) California Emissions.		
NZZ	Skid Plate Package (K2500)	82	95
	NOT AVAILABLE with R9C.		
A28	Sliding Rear Window	99	115
	NOT AVAILABLE with C49, R9C.		
VYU	Snow Plow Prep Package (K2500)	47	55
	REQUIRES R9C.		
VYU	Snow Plow Prep Package (K2500)	101	118
	NOT AVAILABLE with R9C.		
DF2	Stainless Steel Camper Mirrors With 1SA	46	53
	7.5"x 10.5." NOT AVAILABLE with (1SB) Preferred Equipment Group 1SB, (1SC) Preferred Equipment Group 1SC.		
DF2	Stainless Steel Camper Type Mirrors	(39)	(45)
	7.5"x 10.5." NOT AVAILABLE with (1SA) Preferred Equipment Group 1SA.		
ZHR	Tire: Spare LT225/75R16D AT BSW (LD models)	9	11
ZHH	Tire: Spare LT245/75R16E AS BSW (LD models)	39	46
ZGK	Tire: Spare LT245/75R16E AT BSW (HD models)	9	11
ZGK	Tire: Spare LT245/75R16E AT BSW (LD models)	48	57
XGK	Tires: Front LT245/75R16 On-Off Road (K2500)	19	22
XHH	Tires: Front LT245/75R16E AS BSW (LD models)	77	92
YHR	Tires: Rear LT225/75R16D AT BSW (LD models)	19	22
YHH	Tires: Rear LT245/75R16E AS BSW (LD models)	77	92
YGK	Tires: Rear LT245/75R16E AT BSW (HD models)	19	22
YGK	Tires: Rear LT245/75R16E AT BSW (LD models)	96	114
V76	Tow Hooks (C2500)	33	38
M30	Transmission: 4-Speed Automatic (LD models)	834	970
	NOT AVAILABLE with (L56) engine.		
MT1	Transmission: 4-Speed HD Automatic	834	970
	Includes HD auxiliary transmission cooler. NOT AVAILABLE with L31, KC4, Z82, YF5.		
M50	Transmission: 5-Speed Manual (LD models)	NC	NC
	NOT AVAILABLE with (L56) engine, (Z82) HD trailering equipment, (UP0) radio.		
MG5	Transmission: 5-Speed Manual (LD models)	NC	NC
MW3	Transmission: HD 5-Speed Manual with Deep Low (HD models)	NC	NC
BZY	Under Rail Bedliner	194	225
	NOT AVAILABLE with KL6, R9C.		
—	Vinyl Seat Trim	NC	NC
	Includes center armrest with storage delete, driver's and passenger's power lumbar delete, no seatback storage pockets. NOT AVAILABLE with 1SA, 1SC, AE7, A95.		

C/K 3500 PICKUP — CHEVROLET

1998 C3500

Safety Data

Driver Airbag: *Not Available*
Side Airbag: *Not Available*
Traction Control: *Not Available*
Driver Crash Test Grade: *Not Available*

Passenger Airbag: *Not Available*
4-Wheel ABS: *Standard*
Integrated Child Seat(s): *Not Available*
Passenger Crash Test Grade: *Not Available*

Standard Equipment

C3500 REGULAR CAB: 5.7L V-8 OHV SMPI 16-valve engine; 5-speed overdrive manual transmission; 600-amp HD battery; engine oil cooler; 100-amp alternator; rear wheel drive, power take-off, 4.1 axle ratio; stainless steel exhaust; front independent suspension with anti-roll bar, front coil springs, front shocks, rear suspension with rear leaf springs, rear shocks; power re-circulating ball steering with vehicle speed-sensing assist; front disc/rear drum brakes with 4 wheel anti-lock braking system; 34 gal capacity fuel tank; trailer harness; front chrome bumper; monotone paint; sealed beam halogen headlamps with daytime running lights; additional exterior lights include center high mounted stop light, pickup cargo box light, underhood light; driver and passenger manual black folding outside mirrors; front and rear 16" x 6.5" silver steel wheels with hub wheel covers; LT245/75SR16 BSW AS front and rear tires; underbody mounted full-size conventional steel spare wheel; AM/FM stereo with clock, seek-scan, 4 speakers and fixed antenna; 2 power accessory outlets; analog instrumentation display includes tachometer gauge, oil pressure gauge, water temp gauge, volt gauge, trip odometer; warning indicators include battery, lights on, key in ignition; dual airbags; ignition disable; tinted windows; variable intermittent front windshield wipers; seating capacity of 3, bench front seat with tilt adjustable headrests, driver seat includes 2-way direction control, passenger seat includes 2-way direction control; front height adjustable seatbelts; vinyl seats, full cloth headliner, full vinyl floor covering, cab-back insulator; interior lights include dome light, front reading lights; sport steering wheel; passenger side vanity mirror; day-night rearview mirror; glove box with light, front cupholder, dashboard storage, driver and passenger door bins; colored grille, black side window moldings, black front windshield molding, black rear window molding, black door handles.

CREW CAB (in addition to or instead of C3500 REGULAR CAB equipment): Rear heat ducts; manual rear windows; seating capacity of 6; rear bench seat with reclining adjustable rear headrest; rear door bins.

EXTENDED CAB (in addition to or instead of CREW CAB equipment): Additional exterior lights include cab clearance lights; vented rear windows; 60-40 split-bench front seat driver seat with 4-way direction control, passenger seat with 4-way direction control; full folding rear bench seat; vinyl cargo floor.

Base Prices

Code	Description	Invoice	MSRP
CC30903-E63	Regular Cab	16638	19019
CC30943-E63	Crew Cab	19377	22149
CC30953-E63	Extended Cab DRW	19637	22442
	Destination Charge:	625	625

CHEVROLET C/K 3500 PICKUP

CODE	DESCRIPTION	INVOICE	MSRP
	Accessories		
MT1	4-Speed HD Automatic Transmission	834	970
	Includes HD auxiliary transmission oil cooler.		
HC4	4.56 Axle Ratio	217	252
	Includes locking differential. REQUIRES C7A. NOT AVAILABLE with L65, YF5, R9B, ZGK.		
C60	Air Conditioning	692	805
	NOT AVAILABLE with (YG6) air conditioning not desired.		
YG6	Air Conditioning Not Desired	NC	NC
	NOT AVAILABLE with C60, R9A, 1SB, 1SC, C49.		
KL5	Alternative Fuel Conversion (Reg Cab/X-cab)	108	125
	LPG and CNG conversion ready. REQUIRES MT1. NOT AVAILABLE with L29, L65, C7A, R05.		
V22	Appearance Package	164	191
	Includes composite halogen headlamps, chrome grille.		
TP2	Auxiliary Battery	115	134
	NOT AVAILABLE with (L65) engine.		
R9B	Bright Appearance Package (Crew Cab)	301	350
	Includes Appearance Package: composite halogen headlamps, chrome grille, deluxe chrome rear step bumper, rally wheel trim. NOT AVAILABLE with 1SB, 1SC, R05, C7A, HC4, XHP, XYK, YHP, YHR, YYK, ZHP, ZHR, ZYK.		
R9B	Bright Appearance Package (Reg Cab)	415	483
	Includes Appearance Package: composite halogen headlamps, chrome grille, deluxe chrome front bumper, deluxe chrome rear step bumper, bright bodyside moldings, rally wheel trim. NOT AVAILABLE with 1SB, 1SC, R9C, R05, EF1.		
R9B	Bright Appearance Package with R05 (Reg Cab/X-cab)	323	376
	Includes Appearance Package: composite halogen headlamps, chrome grille, deluxe chrome front bumper, deluxe chrome rear step bumper, rally wheel trim. NOT AVAILABLE with 1SB, 1SC, R9C, EF1.		
B85	Bright Bodyside Moldings (Reg Cab)	92	107
	Includes wheel openings. NOT AVAILABLE with (R05) dual rear wheels.		
YF5	California Emissions	146	170
	Automatically added to vehicles shipped to and/or sold to retailers in California. Out-of-state retailers must order on vehicles to be registered or leased in California. REQUIRES MT1 or L65. NOT AVAILABLE with HC4, U01.		
DF2	Camper Type Mirrors	(39)	(45)
	Exterior stainless steel 7.5" x 10.5" mirrors. REQUIRES 1SB or 1SC. NOT AVAILABLE with 1SA, DF2.		
DF2	Camper Type Mirrors	46	53
	Exterior stainless steel 7.5" x 10.5" mirrors. REQUIRES 1SA. NOT AVAILABLE with 1SB, 1SC, DF2.		
B30	Carpet Floor Covering (Reg Cab)	30	35
B30	Carpet Floor Covering (X-cab)	44	51
—	Cloth Seat Trim (Reg Cab/X-cab)	NC	NC
	NOT AVAILABLE with (1SB) Preferred Equipment Group 1SB, (1SC) Preferred Equipment Group 1SC with R05, (A95) seats.		

C/K 3500 PICKUP — CHEVROLET

CODE	DESCRIPTION	INVOICE	MSRP
V10	Cold Climate Package	28	33

Includes engine block heater. NOT AVAILABLE with (L65) engine.

R9C	Commercial Option Package (Reg Cab/X-cab)	325	378

Includes under rail bedliner, tow hooks, sliding rear window. NOT AVAILABLE with 1SB, 1SC, R9B.

ZQ3	Convenience Group	331	385

Includes tilt wheel, cruise control.

R9A	Convenience Package	1150	1337

Includes air conditioning, AM/FM stereo with cassette and seek-scan, Convenience Group: tilt wheel, cruise control. NOT AVAILABLE with 1SB, 1SC, UL5, YG6.

ZY2	Conventional Two-Tone Paint (Reg Cab/X-cab)	163	190

NOT AVAILABLE with (1SA) Preferred Equipment Group 1SA with R9A and R9B or R9C.

AJ1	Deep Tinted Solar-Ray Glass (Crew Cab)	185	215

Includes light tinted rear window when A28 is specified. REQUIRES 1SA or 1SB or 1SC. NOT AVAILABLE with A28.

AJ1	Deep Tinted Solar-Ray Glass (Crew Cab)	155	180

Includes light tinted rear window when A28 is specified. REQUIRES (1SA or 1SB or 1SC) and A28.

AJ1	Deep Tinted Solar-Ray Glass (Reg Cab)	30	35

REQUIRES (A28) sliding rear window.

AJ1	Deep Tinted Solar-Ray Glass (X-cab)	62	72

REQUIRES (1SB) Preferred Equipment Group 1SB or (1SC) Preferred Equipment Group 1SC with R05 and (C49) electric rear window defogger.

AJ1	Deep Tinted Solar-Ray Glass (X-cab)	92	107

REQUIRES (1SA) Preferred Equipment Group 1SA with R9A and R9B or R9C, or (1SB) Preferred Equipment Group 1SB, or (1SC) Preferred Equipment Group 1SC with R05.

VG3	Deluxe Chrome Front Bumper (Reg Cab/X-cab)	22	26

Includes rubber strip.

VB3	Deluxe Chrome Rear Step Bumper	85	99

Includes rubber strip. REQUIRES (VG3) deluxe chrome front bumper. NOT AVAILABLE with (EF1) rear bumper delete.

C49	Electric rear window defogger (X-cab/Crew Cab)	132	154

REQUIRES C60 or R9A. NOT AVAILABLE with 1SA, A28, YG6.

DD7	Electrochromic Rearview Mirror (Reg Cab/X-cab)	125	145

Includes 8 point compass. NOT AVAILABLE with (1SA) Preferred Equipment Group 1SA with R9A and R9B or R9C.

L65	Engine: 6.5L V8 Turbo Diesel with 1SA	2460	2860

NOT AVAILABLE with HC4, TP2, KL5, 1SB, 1SC, L65, V10.

L29	Engine: 7.4L V8 Vortec	516	600

NOT AVAILABLE with (KL5) alternative fuel conversion.

NC7	Federal Emission Override	NC	NC

For vehicles that will be registered or leased in California/New York/Massachusetts/Connecticut, but sold by retailers outside those states. REQUIRES (YF5) California Emissions.

CHEVROLET C/K 3500 PICKUP

CODE	DESCRIPTION	INVOICE	MSRP
B32	Front Floor Mats (Reg Cab/X-cab)	17	20
	REQUIRES (B30) carpet floor covering.		
BG9	Full Rubber Color-Keyed Flooring (Reg Cab)	(30)	(35)
	Replaces carpet and floor mats. NOT AVAILABLE with (1SA) Preferred Equipment Group 1SA with R9A and R9B or R9C.		
BG9	Full Rubber Color-Keyed Flooring (X-cab)	(44)	(51)
	Replaces carpet and floor mats. NOT AVAILABLE with (1SA) Preferred Equipment Group 1SA with R9A and R9B or R9C.		
C7A	GVWR: 10000 Lbs. (Reg Cab/Crew Cab)	NC	NC
	REQUIRES R05. NOT AVAILABLE with YGK, ZGK, KL5, R9B.		
Z82	HD Trailering Equipment	141	164
	Includes trailer hitch platform. REQUIRES (VB3) deluxe chrome rear step bumper. NOT AVAILABLE with (EF1) rear bumper delete.		
A95	High Back Reclining Bucket Seats (Crew Cab)	364	423
	Includes power lumbar supports, seatback storage pockets, floor console. REQUIRES (1SB) Preferred Equipment Group 1SB. NOT AVAILABLE with (1SA) Preferred Equipment Group 1SA with R9A and R9B or R9C, (AE7) seats.		
A95	High Back Reclining Bucket Seats (Crew Cab)	278	323
	Includes power lumbar supports, seatback storage pockets, floor console. REQUIRES 1SC. NOT AVAILABLE with 1SA, 1SB, AE7.		
A95	High Back Reclining Bucket Seats (Reg Cab)	332	386
	Includes power lumbar supports, floor console. NOT AVAILABLE with (1SA) Preferred Equipment Group 1SA with R9A and R9B or R9C, (1SC) Preferred Equipment Group 1SC with R05, (AE7) seats.		
A95	High Back Reclining Bucket Seats (X-cab)	232	270
	Includes power lumbar supports, seatback storage pockets, floor console. NOT AVAILABLE with (1SA) Preferred Equipment Group 1SA with R9A and R9B or R9C, (YG4) rear seat delete with front bench.		
K47	High Capacity Air Cleaner	22	25
—	Leather Seat Trim (X-cab/Crew Cab)	860	1000
	Leather seating on surface only. NOT AVAILABLE with (1SA) Preferred Equipment Group, 1SA with R9A and R9B or R9C, (A95) seats.		
—	Leather Seat Trim with 1SB (Crew Cab)	946	1100
	Leather seating on surface only. REQUIRES (1SB) Preferred Equipment Group 1SB. NOT AVAILABLE with (1SA) Preferred Equipment Group, 1SA with R9A and R9B or R9C, (1SC) Preferred Equipment Group 1SC with R05.		
—	Leather Seat Trim with 1SC (Crew Cab)	860	1000
	Leather seating on surface only. REQUIRES 1SC. NOT AVAILABLE with 1SA, 1SB, AE7.		
G80	Locking Differential	217	252
AU3	Power Door Locks (Crew Cab)	192	223
	REQUIRES (1SA) Preferred Equipment Group 1SA with R9A and R9B or R9C.		
AU3	Power Door Locks (Reg Cab/X-cab)	134	156
AG9	Power Driver's Seat (X-cab/Crew Cab)	206	240
	REQUIRES (1SB and (AE7 or A95)) or 1SC. NOT AVAILABLE with 1SA.		

C/K 3500 PICKUP — CHEVROLET

CODE	DESCRIPTION	INVOICE	MSRP
1SA	**Preferred Equipment Group 1SA (Crew Cab)** .... *Includes Cheyenne decor package. REQUIRES YG6 or C60 or R9A. NOT AVAILABLE with A95, AG9, AUO, ULO, UNO, UPO, AE7, DF2.*	NC	NC
1SA	**Preferred Equipment Group 1SA (Reg Cab)** .... *Includes Cheyenne decor package. REQUIRES YG6 or C60. NOT AVAILABLE with L65, BG9, AUO, ULO, UNO, UPO, ZY2, DF2, A95, AE7, DD7, R05, R9A, R9B, R9C.*	NC	NC
1SA	**Preferred Equipment Group 1SA (X-cab)** .... *Includes Cheyenne decor package. REQUIRES YG6 or C60. NOT AVAILABLE with A95, AG9, BG9, C49, DD7, L65, ULO, UNO, UPO, ZY2, AUO, R9A, R9B, R9C, DF2.*	NC	NC
1SA	**Preferred Equipment Group 1SA with R9A (Reg Cab)** .... *Includes Cheyenne decor package. REQUIRES R9A. NOT AVAILABLE with L65, BG9, AUO, ZY2, DF2, A95, AE7, DD7, R05, R9B, R9C, ULO, UNO, UPO.*	(430)	(500)
1SA	**Preferred Equipment Group 1SA with R9A (X-cab)** .... *Includes cheyenne decor package. REQUIRES R9A. NOT AVAILABLE with A95, AG9, BG9, C49, DD7, L65, ULO, UNO, UPO, ZY2, AUO, R9B, R9C, DF2.*	(430)	(500)
1SA	**Preferred Equipment Group 1SA with R9A and R9B or R9C (Reg Cab)** .... *Includes Cheyenne decor package. REQUIRES R9A and R9B or R9C. NOT AVAILABLE with L65, BG9, AUO, ZY2, DF2, A95, AE7, DD7, R05, ULO, UNO, UPO.*	(602)	(700)
1SA	**Preferred Equipment Group 1SA with R9A and R9B or R9C (X-cab)** .... *Includes Cheyenne decor package. REQUIRES R9A and (R9B or R9C). NOT AVAILABLE with A95, AG9, BG9, C49, DD7, L65, ULO, UNO, UPO, ZY2, AUO, DF2.*	(602)	(700)
1SA	**Preferred Equipment Group 1SA with R9B or R9C (Reg Cab)** .... *Includes Cheyenne decor package. REQUIRES YG6 or C60 and R9B or R9C. NOT AVAILABLE with L65, BG9, AUO, ZY2, DF2, A95, AE7, DD7, R05, R9A, ULO, UNO, UPO.*	(172)	(200)
1SA	**Preferred Equipment Group 1SA with R9B or R9C (X-cab)** .... *Includes Cheyenne decor package. REQUIRES (YG6 or C60) and (R9B or R9C). NOT AVAILABLE with A95, AG9, BG9, C49, DD7, L65, ULO, UNO, UPO, ZY2, AUO, R9A, DF2.*	(172)	(200)
1SB	**Preferred Equipment Group 1SB (Crew Cab)** .... *Includes Silverado Decor Package: air conditioning, power door locks; Convenience Group: tilt wheel, cruise control; Appearance Package: composite halogen headlamps, chrome grille; AM/FM stereo with cassette and seek-scan, deluxe chrome rear step bumper, power windows, extra sound insulation, custom cloth seat trim. NOT AVAILABLE with A95, R9A, R9B, UL5, YG6, DF2, ULO, UNO, UPO.*	3156	3670
1SB	**Preferred Equipment Group 1SB (Reg Cab)** .... *Includes Silverado Decor Package: air conditioning, power door locks; Convenience Group: tilt wheel, cruise control; Appearance Package: composite halogen headlamps, chrome grille; AM/FM stereo with cassette and seek-scan, deluxe chrome rear step bumper, power windows, extra sound insulation, custom cloth seat trim. NOT AVAILABLE with L65, R9A, R9B, R9C, DF2, UL5, A95, YG6, R05, ULO, UNO, UPO.*	2611	3036
1SB	**Preferred Equipment Group 1SB (X-cab)** .... *Includes Silverado Decor Package: air conditioning, power door locks; Convenience Group: tilt wheel, cruise control; Appearance Package: composite halogen headlamps, chrome grille; AM/FM stereo with cassette and seek-scan, deluxe chrome rear step bumper, power windows, extra sound insulation, custom cloth seat trim. NOT AVAILABLE with A95, L65, R9A, R9B, R9C, UL5, YG4, YG6, DF2, ULO, UNO.*	2526	2937

CHEVROLET C/K 3500 PICKUP

CODE	DESCRIPTION	INVOICE	MSRP
1SB	**Preferred Equipment Group 1SB with R05 (Reg Cab)**	2526	2937

Includes Silverado Decor Package: air conditioning, power door locks; Convenience Group: tilt wheel, cruise control; Appearance Package: composite halogen headlamps, chrome grille; AM/FM stereo with cassette and seek-scan, deluxe chrome rear step bumper, power windows, extra sound insulation, custom cloth seat trim. REQUIRES R05. NOT AVAILABLE with L65, R9A, R9B, R9C, DF2, UL5, A95, YG6, ULO, UNO, UPO.

1SC	**Preferred Equipment Group 1SC (Crew Cab)**	4524	5260

Includes Silverado Decor Package with Leather: power door locks; Appearance Package: composite halogen headlamps, chrome grille; AM/FM stereo with cassette and seek-scan, deluxe chrome rear step bumper, power windows, extra sound insulation, remote keyless entry, power driver's seat, reclining 60/40 split-bench seat. NOT AVAILABLE with R9A, R9B, A95, UL5, YG6, DF2, ULO, UNO, UPO.

1SC	**Preferred Equipment Group 1SC (Reg Cab)**	3874	4505

Includes Silverado Decor Package with Leather: power door locks; Appearance Package: composite halogen headlamps, chrome grille; AM/FM stereo with cassette and seek-scan, deluxe chrome rear step bumper, power windows, extra sound insulation, remote keyless entry, electrochromic rearview mirror with 8 point compass, reclining 60/40 split-bench seat. NOT AVAILABLE with L65, R9A, R9B, R9C, DF2, A95, UL5, YG6, R05, ULO, UNO, UPO.

1SC	**Preferred Equipment Group 1SC (X-cab)**	3846	4472

Includes Silverado Decor Package with Leather: power door locks, carpet floor covering, front floor mats; deluxe chrome front bumper, Appearance Package: composite halogen headlamps, chrome grille; AM/FM stereo with cassette and seek-scan, deluxe chrome rear step bumper, power windows, up-level door trim panels, extra sound insulation, rally wheel trim, reclining 60/40 split-bench seat, remote keyless entry, electrochromic rearview mirror with 8 point compass, reclining 60/40 split-bench seat, power driver's seat. NOT AVAILABLE with A95, L65, R9A, R9B, R9C, UL5, YG6, YG4, DF2, ULO, UNO.

1SC	**Preferred Equipment Group 1SC with R05 (Reg Cab)**	3789	4406

Includes Silverado Decor Package with Leather: power door locks; Appearance Package: composite halogen headlamps, chrome grille; AM/FM stereo with cassette and seek-scan, deluxe chrome rear step bumper, power windows, extra sound insulation, remote keyless entry, electrochromic rearview mirror with 8 point compass, reclining 60/40 split-bench seat. REQUIRES R05. NOT AVAILABLE with L65, R9A, R9B, R9C, DF2, A95, UL5, YG6, ULO, UNO, UPO.

UL5	**Radio Delete**	(247)	(287)

Includes clock delete. NOT AVAILABLE with 1SB, 1SC, R9A, UM6, ULO, UNO, UPO.

UM6	**Radio: AM/FM Stereo with Cassette**	126	147

Includes digital clock and 4 speakers. NOT AVAILABLE with (UL5) radio.

ULO	**Radio: AM/FM Stereo with Cassette**	77	90

Includes digital clock, automatic tone control, speed compensated volume, and theft lock. REQUIRES 1SB or 1SC. NOT AVAILABLE with 1SA, UL5, UNO, UPO.

ULO	**Radio: AM/FM Stereo with Cassette**	174	202

Includes digital clock, automatic tone control, speed compensated volume, theft lock, and enhanced performance speaker system. REQUIRES 1SA. NOT AVAILABLE with 1SB, 1SC, UL5, UNO, UPO.

C/K 3500 PICKUP — CHEVROLET

CODE	DESCRIPTION	INVOICE	MSRP
UP0	Radio: AM/FM Stereo with Cassette & CD	346	402
	Includes seek-scan, digital clock, automatic tone control, theft lock, and speed compensated volume. REQUIRES MT1 or 1SA. NOT AVAILABLE with 1SB, 1SC, UL5, ULO, UNO.		
UP0	Radio: AM/FM Stereo with Cassette & CD	249	290
	Includes seek-scan, digital clock, automatic tone control, theft lock, speed compensated volume and enhanced performance speaker system. REQUIRES 1SB or 1SC and MT1. NOT AVAILABLE with 1SA, UL5, ULO, UNO.		
UN0	Radio: AM/FM Stereo with CD	163	190
	Includes digital clock, automatic tone control, theft lock, speed compensated volume and enhanced performance speaker system. REQUIRES 1SB or 1SC. NOT AVAILABLE with 1SA, UL5, ULO, UP0.		
UN0	Radio: AM/FM Stereo with CD	260	302
	Includes digital clock, automatic tone control, theft lock, and speed compensated volume. REQUIRES 1SA. NOT AVAILABLE with 1SB, 1SC, UL5, ULO, UP0.		
P06	Rally Wheel Trim	52	60
EF1	Rear Bumper Delete	(112)	(130)
	REQUIRES 1SA. NOT AVAILABLE with R9B, Z82.		
EF1	Rear Bumper Delete	(172)	(200)
	REQUIRES 1SB or 1SC. NOT AVAILABLE with R9B, Z82, VB3.		
B33	Rear Floor Mats (X-cab)	14	16
	REQUIRES (B30) carpet floor covering and (B32) front floor mats. NOT AVAILABLE with (YG4) rear seat delete.		
YG4	Rear Seat Delete (X-cab)	(374)	(435)
	NOT AVAILABLE with 1SB, 1SC, B33, A95.		
AE7	Reclining 60/40 Split-Bench Seat (Crew Cab)	86	100
	Includes storage armrest and power lumbars. NOT AVAILABLE with (1SA) Preferred Equipment Group 1SA with R9A and R9B or R9C, (A95) seats.		
AE7	Reclining 60/40 Split-Bench Seat (Reg Cab)	150	174
	Includes storage armrest and power lumbars. NOT AVAILABLE with (1SA) Preferred Equipment Group 1SA with R9A and R9B or R9C, (A95) seats.		
AU0	Remote Keyless Entry	129	150
	NOT AVAILABLE with (1SA) Preferred Equipment Group 1SA with R9A and R9B or R9C.		
U01	Roof Marker & Tailgate Lamps (Reg Cab/Crew Cab)	47	55
	NOT AVAILABLE with (YF5) California Emissions.		
A28	Sliding Rear Window	99	115
	NOT AVAILABLE with (C49) electric rear window defogger, (AJ1) deep tinted solar-ray glass.		
XYK	Tires: Front LT215/85R16D Highway BSW (Reg Cab/Crew Cab)	64	72
	REQUIRES YYK and ZYK and R05. NOT AVAILABLE with XHP, YGK, ZGK, YHP, ZHP, YHR, ZHR, R9B.		
XYK	Tires: Front LT215/85R16D Highway BSW (X-cab)	122	142
	REQUIRES YYK and ZYK. NOT AVAILABLE with YHR, ZHR.		
XHP	Tires: Front LT225/75R16D AS BSW (Reg Cab/Crew Cab)	(58)	(70)
	REQUIRES YHP or YHR and R05. NOT AVAILABLE with XYK, YGK, ZGK, YYK, ZYK, R9B.		

CHEVROLET C/K 3500 PICKUP

CODE	DESCRIPTION	INVOICE	MSRP
YYK	Tires: Rear LT215/85R16D Highway BSW (Reg Cab/Crew Cab)	614	712
	REQUIRES C7A and ZYK and R05. NOT AVAILABLE with YHP, YHR, YGK, XHP, ZHP, ZHR, ZGK, R9B.		
YYK	Tires: Rear LT215/85R16D Highway BSW (X-cab)	244	284
	REQUIRES (ZYK) tires. NOT AVAILABLE with (YHR) tires, (ZHR) tires.		
YHP	Tires: Rear LT225/75R16D AS BSW (Reg Cab/Crew Cab)	370	428
	REQUIRES C7A and ZHP and R05. NOT AVAILABLE with YYK, YHR, YGK, XYK, ZYK, ZGK, ZHR, R9B.		
YHR	Tires: Rear LT225/75R16D AT BSW (Reg Cab/Crew Cab)	408	472
	REQUIRES C7A and ZHR and R05. NOT AVAILABLE with YYK, YHP, YGK, XYK, ZYK, ZHP, ZGK, R9B.		
YHR	Tires: Rear LT225/75R16D AT BSW (X-cab)	38	44
	REQUIRES ZHR. NOT AVAILABLE with XYK, YYK, ZYK.		
YGK	Tires: Rear LT245/75R16E AT BSW (Reg Cab/Crew Cab)	19	22
	REQUIRES ZGK. NOT AVAILABLE with C7A, XYK, YYK, XHP, YHP, YHR, R05, ZYK, ZHP, ZHR.		
ZYK	Tires: Spare LT215/85R16D Highway BSW (Reg Cab/Crew Cab)	32	36
	NOT AVAILABLE with ZHP, ZHR, ZGK, XHP, YHP, YHR, YGK, R9B.		
ZYK	Tires: Spare LT215/85R16D Highway BSW (X-cab)	61	71
	NOT AVAILABLE with (YHR) tires, (ZHR) tires.		
ZHP	Tires: Spare LT225/75R16D AS BSW (Reg Cab/Crew Cab)	(29)	(35)
	NOT AVAILABLE with ZYK, ZHR, ZGK, XYK, YYK, YHR, YGK, R9B.		
ZHR	Tires: Spare LT225/75R16D AT BSW (Reg Cab/Crew Cab)	(20)	(24)
	NOT AVAILABLE with ZYK, ZHP, ZGK, XYK, YYK, YHP, YGK, R9B.		
ZHR	Tires: Spare LT225/75R16D AT BSW (X-cab)	9	11
	NOT AVAILABLE with (XYK) tires, (YYK) tires, (ZYK) tires.		
ZGK	Tires: Spare LT245/75R16/E BSW AT (Reg Cab/Crew Cab)	9	11
	NOT AVAILABLE with C7A, XYK, ZYK, XHP, ZHP, ZHR, R05, YYK, YHP, YHR, HC4.		
V76	Tow Hooks	33	38
BZY	Under Rail Bedliner	194	225
R05	Wheels: Dual Rear (Crew Cab)	737	857
	Includes roof marker and tailgate lamps. NOT AVAILABLE with (YGK) tires, (ZGK) tires, (R9B) Bright Appearance Package.		
R05	Wheels: Dual Rear with 1SA (Reg Cab)	821	955
	Includes roof marker and tailgate lamps. NOT AVAILABLE with 1SB, 1SC, KL5, YGK, ZGK, R9B, R05, B85.		

1998 K3500

Safety Data

Driver Airbag: *Not Available*
Side Airbag: *Not Available*
Traction Control: *Not Available*
Driver Crash Test Grade: *Not Available*

Passenger Airbag: *Not Available*
4-Wheel ABS: *Standard*
Integrated Child Seat(s): *Not Available*
Passenger Crash Test Grade: *Not Available*

C/K 3500 PICKUP — CHEVROLET

Standard Equipment

K3500 REGULAR CAB: 5.7L V-8 OHV SMPI 16-valve engine; 5-speed overdrive manual transmission; 600-amp HD battery; engine oil cooler; 100-amp alternator; part-time 4 wheel drive, auto locking hub control and manual shift, power take-off, 4.1 axle ratio; stainless steel exhaust; front independent torsion suspension with HD anti-roll bar, front torsion springs, front torsion bar, front shocks, rear suspension with rear leaf springs, rear shocks; power re-circulating ball steering with vehicle speed-sensing assist; front disc/rear drum brakes with 4 wheel anti-lock braking system; 34 gal capacity fuel tank; trailer harness; rear colored bumper with tow hooks; colored fender flares; monotone paint; sealed beam halogen headlamps with daytime running lights; additional exterior lights include center high mounted stop light, pickup cargo box light, underhood light; driver and passenger manual black folding outside mirrors; front and rear 16" x 6.5" painted steel wheels with hub wheel covers; LT245/75SR16 BSW AS front and rear tires; underbody mounted full-size conventional steel spare wheel; AM/FM stereo with clock, seek-scan, 4 speakers and fixed antenna; 2 power accessory outlets; analog instrumentation display includes tachometer gauge, oil pressure gauge, water temp gauge, volt gauge, trip odometer; warning indicators include battery, lights on, key in ignition, door ajar; dual airbags; ignition disable; tinted windows; variable intermittent front windshield wipers; seating capacity of 3, bench front seat with tilt adjustable headrests, driver seat includes 2-way direction control, passenger seat includes 2-way direction control; front height adjustable seatbelts; vinyl seats, full cloth headliner, full vinyl floor covering, cab-back insulator; interior lights include dome light, front reading lights; sport steering wheel; passenger side vanity mirror; day-night rearview mirror; glove box with light, front cupholder, dashboard storage, driver and passenger door bins; colored grille, black side window moldings, black front windshield molding, black rear window molding, black door handles.

EXTENDED CAB (in addition to or instead of REGULAR CAB equipment): Additional exterior lights include cab clearance lights; vented rear windows; seating capacity of 6, 60-40 split-bench front seat, driver seat includes 4-way direction control, passenger seat includes 4-way direction control; full folding rear bench seat with adjustable rear headrest; vinyl cargo floor.

CREW CAB (in addition to or instead of EXTENDED CAB equipment): Rear heat ducts; child safety rear door locks; manual rear windows; bench front seat; rear reclining bench seat, rear door bins.

Base Prices

Code	Description	Invoice	MSRP
CK30903-E63	Regular Cab	19263	22019
CK30953-E63	Extended Cab	22096	25253
CK30943-E63	Crew Cab	22154	25323
	Destination Charge:	625	625

Accessories

Code	Description	Invoice	MSRP
MT1	4-Speed HD Automatic Transmission	834	970
	Includes HD auxiliary transmission oil cooler.		
HC4	4.56 Axle Ratio	217	252
	Includes locking differential. REQUIRES C7A and L29. NOT AVAILABLE with L65, YF5, KL5, XGK, YGK, ZGK.		
AE7	60/40 Split-Bench Seat (Crew Cab)	86	100
	Includes storage armrest and power lumbar support. REQUIRES 1SB or 1SC. NOT AVAILABLE with 1SA.		

CHEVROLET C/K 3500 PICKUP

CODE	DESCRIPTION	INVOICE	MSRP
C60	Air Conditioning	692	805
	Includes R134A refrigerant. NOT AVAILABLE with (YG6) air conditioning not desired.		
YG6	Air Conditioning Not Desired	NC	NC
	NOT AVAILABLE with C60, R9A, 1SB, 1SC, C49.		
KL5	Alternative Fuel Compatible Engine (Reg Cab/X-cab)	108	125
	LPG and CNG conversion ready. REQUIRES MT1. NOT AVAILABLE with 1SB, L29, L65, HC4, XYK, YYK, ZYK, XYL, YYL, ZYL, XHR, YHR, ZHR, XHP, YHP, ZHP, R05.		
V22	Appearance Package	164	191
	Includes composite halogen headlamps, chrome grille.		
R9B	Bright Appearance Package (Regular Cab)	389	452
	Includes Appearance Package: composite halogen headlamps, chrome grille, chrome deluxe front bumper with rub strip, deluxe chrome rear step bumper, rally wheel trim, bright bodyside moldings. NOT AVAILABLE with R9C, R05, 1SB, 1SC.		
R9B	Bright Appearance Package with R05 (Crew Cab)	301	350
	Includes Appearance Package: composite halogen headlamps, chrome grille, deluxe chrome rear step bumper, rally wheel trim. NOT AVAILABLE with (1SB) Preferred Equipment Group 1SB, (1SC) Preferred Equipment Group 1SC with R05, (R9B) Bright Appearance Package.		
R9B	Bright Appearance Package with R05 (Reg Cab/X-cab)	323	376
	Includes Appearance Package: composite halogen headlamps, chrome grille, chrome deluxe front bumper with rub strip, deluxe chrome rear step bumper, rally wheel trim. REQUIRES R05. NOT AVAILABLE with 1SB, 1SC, R9C.		
B85	Bright Bodyside Moldings (Regular Cab)	65	76
	NOT AVAILABLE with (R05) wheels: dual rear.		
NB8	CA/NY/MA/CT Emission Override	NC	NC
	For vehicles sold by retailers in California, Massachusetts, Connecticut or New York for out-of-state registration. NOT AVAILABLE with (YF5) California Emissions.		
YF5	California Emissions	146	170
	Automatically added to vehicles shipped to and/or sold to retailers in California. Out-of-state retailers must order on vehicles to be registered or leased in California. REQUIRES MT1 or L65. NOT AVAILABLE with HC4, NB8.		
DF2	Camper Type Mirrors	46	53
	7.5" x 10.5" stainless steel. NOT AVAILABLE with (1SB) Preferred Equipment Group 1SB, (1SC) Preferred Equipment Group 1SC with R05.		
DF2	Camper Type Mirrors with Silverado Decor	(39)	(45)
	7.5" x 10.5" stainless steel. NOT AVAILABLE with (1SA) PEG 1SA with R9A and R9B or R9C.		
VG3	Chrome Deluxe Front Bumper with Rub Strip (Reg Cab/X-cab)	22	26
VB3	Chrome Deluxe Rear Step Bumper	85	99
	Includes rub strip. REQUIRES (VG3) chrome deluxe front bumper with rub strip.		
—	Cloth Seat Trim (Reg Cab/X-cab)	NC	NC
	NOT AVAILABLE with A95, 1SB, 1SC.		
V10	Cold Climate Package	28	33
	Includes engine block heater. NOT AVAILABLE with (L65) engine.		
R9C	Commercial Option Package (Reg Cab/X-cab)	428	498
	Includes under rail bedliner, HD front springs, off road skid plates, sliding rear window. NOT AVAILABLE with R9B, 1SB, 1SC, VYU.		

C/K 3500 PICKUP — CHEVROLET

CODE	DESCRIPTION	INVOICE	MSRP
ZQ3	Convenience Group	331	385
	Includes manual tilt steering wheel, speed control.		
R9A	Convenience Package	1150	1337
	Includes air conditioning, ETR AM/FM stereo with cassette, Convenience Group: manual tilt steering wheel, speed control. NOT AVAILABLE with 1SA, 1SB, 1SC, YG6, UL5.		
ZY2	Conventional Two-Tone Paint (Reg Cab/X-cab)	163	190
	NOT AVAILABLE with (1SA) PEG 1SA with R9A and R9B or R9C.		
AJ1	Deep Tinted Glass (Crew Cab)	185	215
AJ1	Deep Tinted Glass (Extended Cab)	92	107
	REQUIRES 1SA or 1SB or 1SC. NOT AVAILABLE with C49.		
AJ1	Deep Tinted Glass (Regular Cab)	30	35
	REQUIRES (A28) sliding rear window.		
AJ1	Deep Tinted Glass with A28 (Crew Cab)	155	180
	Includes light tinted rear window when (A28) sliding rear window is specified. REQUIRES (A28) sliding rear window.		
AJ1	Deep Tinted Glass with C49 (Extended Cab)	62	72
	(1SA or 1SB or 1SC) and C49.		
C49	Electric Rear Window Defogger (X-cab/Crew Cab)	132	154
	REQUIRES 1SB or 1SC or C60 or R9A. NOT AVAILABLE with AJ1, A28, YG6.		
DD7	Electrochromic Rearview Mirror (Reg Cab/X-cab)	125	145
	Includes 8 point compass. NOT AVAILABLE with (1SA) PEG 1SA with R9A and R9B or R9C.		
L65	Engine: 6.5L V8 Turbo Diesel	2460	2860
	NOT AVAILABLE with KL5, TP2, HC4, L29, V10.		
L29	Engine: Vortec 7400 V8 SFI	516	600
	NOT AVAILABLE with (KL5) alternative fuel compatible engine, (L65) engine.		
B32	Front Floor Mats (Reg Cab/X-cab)	17	20
B30	Full Carpeted Flooring (Extended Cab)	44	51
B30	Full Carpeted Flooring (Regular Cab)	30	35
BG9	Full Rubber Color Keyed Flooring (Extended Cab)	(44)	(51)
	Replaces carpeting and floor mats. NOT AVAILABLE with (1SA) PEG 1SA with R9A and R9B or R9C.		
BG9	Full Rubber Color-Keyed Flooring (Regular Cab)	(30)	(35)
	Replaces carpeting and floor mats. NOT AVAILABLE with (1SA) PEG 1SA with R9A and R9B or R9C.		
C7A	GVWR: 10000 Lbs	NC	NC
	Includes 4250 lb. front and 7500 lb. rear GAWR. REQUIRES R05 and (XYK or XYL or XHR or XHP). NOT AVAILABLE with 1SB, XGK, YGK, ZGK.		
TP2	HD Auxiliary Battery	115	134
	NOT AVAILABLE with (L65) engine.		
F60	HD Front Springs	54	63
K47	High Capacity Air Cleaner	22	25
—	Leather Seat Trim (Crew Cab)	946	1100
	NOT AVAILABLE with (1SA) PEG 1SA with R9A and R9B or R9C.		
—	Leather Seat Trim (Reg Cab/X-cab)	860	1000
	NOT AVAILABLE with (1SA) PEG 1SA with R9A and R9B or R9C, (A95) seats.		

CHEVROLET C/K 3500 PICKUP

CODE	DESCRIPTION	INVOICE	MSRP
G80	Locking Differential	217	252
NZZ	Off Road Skid Plates	82	95
	Includes fuel tank, front differential and transfer case shields.		
1SA	PEG 1SA with R9A (Extended Cab)	NC	NC
	Manufacturer Discount	(430)	(500)
	Net Price	(430)	(500)
	Includes Cheyenne Decor Package. REQUIRES R9A. NOT AVAILABLE with R9B, R9C, DF2, DD7, ZY2, UL0, UN0, UP0, L65, C49, BG9, AU0, AG9, A95, YG6.		
1SA	PEG 1SA with R9A (Regular Cab)	NC	NC
	Manufacturer Discount	(430)	(500)
	Net Price	(430)	(500)
	Includes Cheyenne Decor Package. REQUIRES R9A. NOT AVAILABLE with R05, R9B, R9C, L65, BG9, AU0, DD7, ZY2, UL0, UN0, UP0, DF2, AE7, A95, YG6.		
1SA	PEG 1SA with R9A and (R9B or R9C) (Extended Cab)	NC	NC
	Manufacturer Discount	(602)	(700)
	Net Price	(602)	(700)
	Includes Cheyenne Decor Package. REQUIRES R9A and (R9C OR R9B). NOT AVAILABLE with DF2, DD7, ZY2, UL0, UN0, UP0, L65, C49, BG9, AU0, AG9, A95, YG6.		
1SA	PEG 1SA with R9A and (R9B or R9C) (Regular Cab)	NC	NC
	Manufacturer Discount	(602)	(700)
	Net Price	(602)	(700)
	Includes Cheyenne Decor Package. REQUIRES R9A and (R9C or R9B). NOT AVAILABLE with R05, L65, BG9, AU0, DD7, ZY2, UL0, UN0, UP0, DF2, AE7, A95, YG6.		
1SA	PEG 1SA with R9A, R9B or R9C (Extended Cab)	NC	NC
	Includes Cheyenne Decor Package. REQUIRES YG6 or C60. NOT AVAILABLE with R9A, R9B, R9C, DF2, DD7, ZY2, UL0, UN0, UP0, L65, C49, BG9, AU0, AG9, A95.		
1SA	PEG 1SA with R9A, R9B or R9C (Regular Cab)	NC	NC
	Includes Cheyenne Decor Package. REQUIRES YG6 or C60. NOT AVAILABLE with R05, R9A, R9B, R9C, L65, BG9, AU0, DD7, ZY2, UL0, UN0, UP0, DF2, AE7, A95.		
1SA	PEG 1SA with R9B or R9C (Extended Cab)	NC	NC
	Manufacturer Discount	(172)	(200)
	Net Price	(172)	(200)
	Includes Cheyenne Decor Package. REQUIRES (R9B or R9C) and (YG6 or C60). NOT AVAILABLE with R9A, DF2, DD7, ZY2, UL0, UN0, UP0, L65, C49, BG9, AU0, AG9, A95.		
1SA	PEG 1SA with R9B or R9C (Regular Cab)	NC	NC
	Manufacturer Discount	(172)	(200)
	Net Price	(172)	(200)
	Includes Cheyenne Decor Package. REQUIRES (R9B or R9C) and (YG6 or C60). NOT AVAILABLE with R05, R9A, L65, BG9, AU0, DD7, ZY2, UL0, UN0, UP0, DF2, AE7, A95.		
AU3	Power Door Locks (Crew Cab)	192	223
AU3	Power Door Locks (Reg Cab/X-cab)	134	156
AG9	Power Driver's Seat (X-cab/Crew Cab)	206	240
	REQUIRES AE7 or A95. NOT AVAILABLE with 1SA.		

C/K 3500 PICKUP — CHEVROLET

CODE	DESCRIPTION	INVOICE	MSRP
1SA	Preferred Equipment Group 1SA (Crew Cab)	NC	NC
	Includes Cheyenne Decor Package. REQUIRES (YG6 or C60 or R9A) or (R9B and (YG6 or C60)). NOT AVAILABLE with EF1, AUO, ULO, UNO, UPO, AG9, A95, AE7, R05, DF2.		
1SB	Preferred Equipment Group 1SB (Crew Cab)	3156	3670
	Includes Silverado Decor Package (1SB): dual power remote mirrors, chrome deluxe front bumper with rub strip, Appearance Package: composite halogen headlamps, chrome grille, rally wheel trim; driver's and passenger's power lumbar, center armrest with storage, custom cloth seat trim, cloth with lower carpet door trim, carpet floor covering with rubber mats, deluxe sound insulation, seatback storage pockets, air conditioning, ETR AM/FM stereo with cassette, Convenience Group: manual tilt steering wheel, speed control; power door locks, leather wrapped steering wheel, power windows with driver's one touch down, deluxe chrome rear step bumper. NOT AVAILABLE with R9A, R9B, YG6, DF2, UL5, R05, A95.		
1SB	Preferred Equipment Group 1SB (Extended Cab)	2526	2937
	Manufacturer Discount	(645)	(750)
	Net Price	1881	2187
	Includes Silverado Decor Package (1SB): dual power remote mirrors, chrome deluxe front bumper with rub strip, Appearance Package: composite halogen headlamps, chrome grille, rally wheel trim; driver's and passenger's power lumbar, center armrest with storage, custom cloth seat trim, cloth with lower carpet door trim, carpet floor covering with rubber mats, deluxe sound insulation, seatback storage pockets, air conditioning, ETR AM/FM stereo with cassette, Convenience Group: manual tilt steering wheel, speed control; power door locks, leather wrapped steering wheel, power windows with driver's one touch down, deluxe chrome rear step bumper. NOT AVAILABLE with L65, R9A, R9B, R9C, YG6, DF2, UL5, YG4, A95.		
1SB	Preferred Equipment Group 1SB (Regular Cab)	2611	3036
	Manufacturer Discount	(645)	(750)
	Net Price	1966	2286
	Includes Silverado Decor Package (1SB): dual power remote mirrors, chrome deluxe front bumper with rub strip, Appearance Package: composite halogen headlamps, chrome grille, rally wheel trim; driver's and passenger's power lumbar, center armrest with storage, custom cloth seat trim, cloth with lower carpet door trim, carpet floor covering with rubber mats, deluxe sound insulation, seatback storage pockets, air conditioning, ETR AM/FM stereo with cassette, Convenience Group: manual tilt steering wheel, speed control; power door locks, leather wrapped steering wheel, power windows with driver's one touch down, deluxe chrome rear step bumper. NOT AVAILABLE with R05, C7A, XYK, YYK, ZYK, XYL, YYL, ZYL, XHR, YHR, ZHR, XHP, YHP, ZHP, L65, R9A, R9B, R9C, YG6, DF2, UL5, A95.		
1SB	Preferred Equipment Group 1SB with R05 (Regular Cab)	2526	2937
	Manufacturer Discount	(645)	(750)
	Net Price	1881	2187
	Includes Silverado Decor Package (1SB): dual power remote mirrors, chrome deluxe front bumper with rub strip, Appearance Package: composite halogen headlamps, chrome grille, rally wheel trim; driver's and passenger's power lumbar, center armrest with storage, custom cloth seat trim, cloth with lower carpet door trim, carpet floor		

CHEVROLET C/K 3500 PICKUP

CODE	DESCRIPTION	INVOICE	MSRP

covering with rubber mats, deluxe sound insulation, seatback storage pockets, air conditioning, ETR AM/FM stereo with cassette, Convenience Group: manual tilt steering wheel, speed control; power door locks, leather wrapped steering wheel, power windows with driver's one touch down, deluxe chrome rear step bumper. NOT AVAILABLE with L65, KL5, R9A, R9B, R9C, YG6, XGK, YGK, ZGK, DF2, UL5, A95.

1SC   **Preferred Equipment Group 1SC (Crew Cab)** 4524   5260

Includes Silverado Decor Package (1SB): dual power remote mirrors, chrome deluxe front bumper with rub strip, Appearance Package: composite halogen headlamps, chrome grille, rally wheel trim; driver's and passenger's power lumbar, center armrest with storage, custom cloth seat trim, cloth with lower carpet door trim, carpet floor covering with rubber mats, deluxe sound insulation, seatback storage pockets, air conditioning, ETR AM/FM stereo with cassette, Convenience Group: manual tilt steering wheel, speed control; power door locks, leather wrapped steering wheel, power windows with driver's one touch down, deluxe chrome rear step bumper, remote keyless entry, power driver's seat, 60/40 split-bench seat, leather seat trim. NOT AVAILABLE with R9A, R9B, YG6, DF2, UL5, R05, A95.

1SC   **Preferred Equipment Group 1SC (Extended Cab)** 3846   4472
        Manufacturer Discount .... (645)   (750)
        Net Price 3201   3722

Includes Silverado Decor Package (1SC): dual power remote mirrors, chrome deluxe front bumper with rub strip, Appearance Package: composite halogen headlamps, chrome grille, rally wheel trim; driver's and passenger's power lumbar, center armrest with storage, cloth with lower carpet door trim, carpet floor covering with rubber mats, deluxe sound insulation, 2 door curb/courtesy lights, seatback storage pockets, cargo area concealed storage, air conditioning, ETR AM/FM stereo with cassette, Convenience Group: manual tilt steering wheel, speed control; power door locks, leather wrapped steering wheel, power windows with driver's one touch down, deluxe chrome rear step bumper, front floor mats, remote keyless entry, electrochromic rearview mirror with 8 point compass, power driver's seat, 60/40 split-bench seat, leather seat trim.

1SC   **Preferred Equipment Group 1SC (Regular Cab)** 3874   4505
        Manufacturer Discount .... (645)   (750)
        Net Price 3229   3755

Includes Silverado Decor Package (1SC): dual power remote mirrors, chrome deluxe front bumper with rub strip, Appearance Package: composite halogen headlamps, chrome grille, rally wheel trim; driver's and passenger's power lumbar, center armrest with storage, cloth with lower carpet door trim, carpet floor covering with rubber mats, deluxe sound insulation, 2 door curb/courtesy lights, seatback storage pockets, cargo area concealed storage, air conditioning, ETR AM/FM stereo with cassette, Convenience Group: manual tilt steering wheel, speed control; power door locks, leather wrapped steering wheel, power windows with driver's one touch down, deluxe chrome rear step bumper, front floor mats, remote keyless entry, electrochromic rearview mirror with 8 point compass, 60/40 split-bench seat, leather seat trim. NOT AVAILABLE with R05, A95, L65, R9A, R9B, R9C, YG6, DF2, UL5.

C/K 3500 PICKUP — CHEVROLET

CODE	DESCRIPTION	INVOICE	MSRP
1SC	Preferred Equipment Group 1SC with R05 (Regular Cab)	3789	4406
	Manufacturer Discount	(645)	(750)
	Net Price	3144	3656
	Includes Silverado Decor Package (1SC): dual power remote mirrors, chrome deluxe front bumper with rub strip, Appearance Package: composite halogen headlamps, chrome grille, rally wheel trim; driver's and passenger's power lumbar, center armrest with storage, cloth with lower carpet door trim, carpet floor covering with rubber mats, deluxe sound insulation, 2 door curb/courtesy lights, seatback storage pockets, cargo area concealed storage, air conditioning, ETR AM/FM stereo with cassette, Convenience Group: manual tilt steering wheel, speed control; power door locks, leather wrapped steering wheel, power windows with driver's one touch down, deluxe chrome rear step bumper, front floor mats, remote keyless entry, electrochromic rearview mirror with 8 point compass, 60/40 split-bench seat, leather seat trim. NOT AVAILABLE with A95, L65, R9A, R9B, R9C, YG6, DF2, UL5.		
UL0	Radio: AM/FM Stereo with Cassette	77	90
	Includes seek scan, digital clock, automatic tone control, theft lock, speed compensated volume and enhanced performance speaker system. NOT AVAILABLE with (UNO) radio, (UPO) radio, (1SA) PEG 1SA with R9A and R9B or R9C.		
UM6	Radio: AM/FM Stereo with Cassette	126	147
	Includes seek scan and digital clock. NOT AVAILABLE with (UL5) radio.		
UP0	Radio: AM/FM Stereo with Cassette & CD	249	290
	Includes seek scan, digital clock, search and repeat cassette player, CD player, automatic tone control, theft lock, speed compensated volume and enhanced performance speaker system. REQUIRES MT1. NOT AVAILABLE with ULO, UNO, 1SA.		
UN0	Radio: AM/FM Stereo with CD	163	190
	Includes seek scan, digital clock, automatic tone control, theft lock, speed compensated volume and enhanced performance speaker system. NOT AVAILABLE with (ULO) radio, (UPO) radio, (1SA) PEG 1SA with R9A and R9B or R9C.		
UL5	Radio: Delete	(247)	(287)
	NOT AVAILABLE with UM6, 1SB, 1SC, R9A.		
P06	Rally Wheel Trim	52	60
EF1	Rear Bumper Delete Provisions	(112)	(130)
	Vehicles registered in certain states must have a rear bumper to be operated on their roads. Consult your local laws. NOT AVAILABLE with (Z82) HD trailering equipment.		
EF1	Rear Bumper Delete Provisions with Silverado Decor (Reg Cab/X-cab)	(172)	(200)
	Vehicles registered in certain states must have a rear bumper to be operated on their roads. Consult your local laws. REQUIRES 1SB or 1SC. NOT AVAILABLE with Z82.		
B33	Rear Floor Mats (Extended Cab)	14	16
	REQUIRES (B32) front floor mats.		
AE7	Reclining 60/40 Split-Bench Seat (Regular Cab)	150	174
	Includes storage armrest and power lumbar support. NOT AVAILABLE with (A95) seats, (1SA) PEG 1SA with R9A and R9B or R9C.		
A95	Reclining Bucket Seats (Crew Cab)	364	423
	Includes power lumbar support, floor console. REQUIRES 1SB or 1SC. NOT AVAILABLE with 1SA.		

CHEVROLET C/K 3500 PICKUP

CODE	DESCRIPTION	INVOICE	MSRP
A95	**Reclining Bucket Seats (Extended Cab)**	232	270
	Includes power lumbar support, floor and overhead consoles. NOT AVAILABLE with (1SA) PEG 1SA with R9A and R9B or R9C.		
A95	**Reclining High Back Bucket Seats (Regular Cab)**	332	386
	Includes power lumbar support, floor console. NOT AVAILABLE with 1SA, 1SC, AE7.		
AU0	**Remote Keyless Entry**	129	150
	NOT AVAILABLE with (1SA) PEG 1SA with R9A and R9B or R9C.		
U01	**Roof Marker Lamps (Reg Cab/Crew Cab)**	47	55
A28	**Sliding Rear Window**	99	115
	NOT AVAILABLE with (C49) electric rear window defogger.		
VYU	**Snow Plow Prep Package (Reg Cab)**	101	118
	Includes HD front springs. NOT AVAILABLE with (R9C) Commercial Option Package.		
VYU	**Snow Plow Prep Package with R9C (Reg Cab)**	47	55
	Includes HD front springs. REQUIRES (R9C) Commercial Option Package.		
ZYL	**Tire: Spare LT215/85R16D AT BSW (Reg Cab/Crew Cab)**	56	64
	Includes tire carrier. REQUIRES F60 and R05. NOT AVAILABLE with 1SB, XYK, YYK, ZYK, XHR, YHR, ZHR, XHP, YHP, ZHP, XGK, ZGK, YGK, KL5.		
ZYK	**Tire: Spare LT215/85R16D Highway BSW (Extended Cab)**	61	71
	Includes tire carrier. NOT AVAILABLE with XYL, YYL, ZYL, XHR, YHR, ZHR.		
ZYK	**Tire: Spare LT215/85R16D Highway BSW (Reg Cab/Crew Cab)**	32	36
	Includes tire carrier. REQUIRES R05. NOT AVAILABLE with 1SB, XYL, YYL, ZYL, XHR, YHR, ZHR, XHP, YHP, ZHP, XGK, YGK, ZGK, KL5.		
ZHP	**Tire: Spare LT225/75R16D AS BSW (Reg Cab/Crew Cab)**	(29)	(35)
	Includes tire carrier. REQUIRES R05. NOT AVAILABLE with 1SB, XYK, YYK, ZYK, XYL, YYL, ZYL, XHR, YHR, ZHR, XGK, YGK, ZGK, KL5.		
ZHR	**Tire: Spare LT225/75R16D AT BSW (Extended Cab)**	9	11
	Includes tire carrier. NOT AVAILABLE with XYK, YYK, ZYK, XYL, YYL, ZYL.		
ZHR	**Tire: Spare LT225/75R16D AT BSW (Reg Cab/Crew Cab)**	(20)	(24)
	Includes tire carrier. REQUIRES R05. NOT AVAILABLE with 1SB, XYK, YYK, ZYK, XYL, YYL, ZYL, XHP, YHP, ZHP, XGK, YGK, ZGK, KL5.		
ZGK	**Tire: Spare LT245/75R16-E BSW AT (Reg Cab/Crew Cab)**	9	11
	Includes tire carrier. NOT AVAILABLE with 1SB, XYK, YYK, ZYK, XYL, YYL, ZYL, XHR, YHR, ZHR, XHP, YHP, ZHP, R05, C7A, HC4.		
XYL	**Tires: Front LT215/85R16D AT BSW (Extended Cab)**	170	198
	REQUIRES F60 and YYL and ZYL. NOT AVAILABLE with XYK, YYK, ZYK, XHR, YHR, ZHR.		
XYL	**Tires: Front LT215/85R16D AT BSW (Reg Cab/Crew Cab)**	112	128
	REQUIRES F60 and YYL and R05 and ZYL. NOT AVAILABLE with 1SB, XYK, YYK, ZYK, XHR, YHR, ZHR, XHP, YHP, ZHP, XGK, YGK, ZGK, KL5.		
XYK	**Tires: Front LT215/85R16D Highway BSW (Extended Cab)**	122	142
	REQUIRES YYK and ZYK. NOT AVAILABLE with XYL, YYL, ZYL, XHR, YHR, ZHR.		
XYK	**Tires: Front LT215/85R16D Highway BSW (Reg Cab/Crew Cab)**	64	72
	REQUIRES YYK and R05 and ZYK. NOT AVAILABLE with 1SB, XYL, YYL, ZYL, XHR, YHR, ZHR, XHP, YHP, ZHP, XGK, YGK, ZGK, KL5.		

C/K 3500 PICKUP — CHEVROLET

CODE	DESCRIPTION	INVOICE	MSRP
XHP	Tires: Front LT225/75R16D AS BSW (Reg Cab/Crew Cab)	(58)	(70)
	REQUIRES YHP and R05 and ZHP. NOT AVAILABLE with 1SB, XYK, YYK, ZYK, XYL, YYL, ZYL, XHR, YHR, ZHR, XGK, YGK, ZGK, KL5.		
XHR	Tires: Front LT225/75R16D AT BSW (Extended Cab)	19	22
	REQUIRES YHR and ZHR. NOT AVAILABLE with XYK, YYK, ZYK, XYL, YYL, ZYL.		
XHR	Tires: Front LT225/75R16D AT BSW (Reg Cab/Crew Cab)	(40)	(48)
	REQUIRES YHR and R05 and ZHR. NOT AVAILABLE with 1SB, XYK, YYK, ZYK, XYL, YYL, ZYL, XHP, YHP, ZHP, XGK, YGK, ZGK, KL5.		
XGK	Tires: Front LT245/75R16E AT BSW (Reg Cab/Crew Cab)	19	22
	REQUIRES YGK and ZGK. NOT AVAILABLE with 1SB, XYK, YYK, ZYK, XYL, YYL, ZYL, XHR, YHR, ZHR, XHP, YHP, ZHP, R05, C7A, HC4.		
YYL	Tires: Rear LT215/85R16D AT BSW (Extended Cab)	341	396
	REQUIRES F60 and ZYL. NOT AVAILABLE with XYK, YYK, ZYK, XHR, YHR, ZHR.		
YYL	Tires: Rear LT215/85R16D AT BSW (Reg Cab/Crew Cab)	710	824
	REQUIRES F60 and R05 and ZYL. NOT AVAILABLE with 1SB, XYK, YYK, ZYK, XHR, YHR, ZHR, XHP, YHP, ZHP, XGK, ZGK, KL5, YGK.		
YYK	Tires: Rear LT215/85R16D Highway BSW (Extended Cab)	244	284
	REQUIRES ZYK. NOT AVAILABLE with XYL, YYL, ZYL, XHR, YHR, ZHR.		
YYK	Tires: Rear LT215/85R16D Highway BSW (Reg Cab/Crew Cab)	614	712
	REQUIRES R05 and ZYK. NOT AVAILABLE with 1SB, XYL, YYL, ZYL, XHR, YHR, ZHR, XHP, YHP, ZHP, XGK, YGK, ZGK, KL5.		
YHP	Tires: Rear LT225/75R16D AS BSW (Reg Cab/Crew Cab)	370	428
	REQUIRES R05 and ZHP. NOT AVAILABLE with 1SB, XYK, YYK, ZYK, XYL, YYL, ZYL, XHR, YHR, ZHR, XGK, YGK, ZGK, KL5.		
YHR	Tires: Rear LT225/75R16D AT BSW (Extended Cab)	38	44
	REQUIRES ZHR. NOT AVAILABLE with XYK, YYK, ZYK, XYL, YYL, ZYL.		
YHR	Tires: Rear LT225/75R16D AT BSW (Reg Cab/Crew Cab)	408	472
	REQUIRES R05 and ZHR. NOT AVAILABLE with 1SB, XYK, YYK, ZYK, XYL, YYL, ZYL, XHP, YHP, ZHP, XGK, YGK, ZGK, KL5.		
YGK	Tires: Rear LT245/75R16E AT BSW (Reg Cab/Crew Cab)	19	22
	REQUIRES ZGK. NOT AVAILABLE with 1SB, XYK, YYK, ZYK, XYL, YYL, ZYL, XHR, YHR, ZHR, XHP, YHP, ZHP, R05, C7A, HC4.		
ZYL	Tires: Spare LT215/85R16D AT BSW (Extended Cab)	85	99
	Includes tire carrier. REQUIRES F60. NOT AVAILABLE with XYK, YYK, ZYK, XHR, YHR, ZHR.		
Z82	Trailering Equipment	141	164
	Includes wiring harness and trailer hitch platform. REQUIRES (VB3) chrome deluxe rear step bumper. NOT AVAILABLE with (EF1) rear bumper delete provisions.		
BZY	Under Rail Bedliner	194	225
—	Vinyl Seat Trim	NC	NC
	NOT AVAILABLE with 1SA, 1SC, A95, AE7, AG9.		
R05	Wheels: Dual Rear (Crew Cab)	737	857
	Includes tailgate lamps, roof marker lamps. NOT AVAILABLE with XGK, YGK, ZGK, R9B.		
R05	Wheels: Dual Rear (Regular Cab)	821	955
	Includes tailgate lamps, roof marker lamps. NOT AVAILABLE with B85, KL5, XGK, YGK, ZGK, R9B.		

CHEVROLET EXPRESS VAN

1998 EXPRESS

1998 Chevrolet Express G3500 Extended

What's New?

All vans equipped with airbags switch to mini-module bag designs for the driver, but they still deploy with more force than second-generation types. A theft deterrent system is standard, and three new colors debut.

Review

For the first time in 25 years, Chevy dealers received a brand new, completely redesigned, full-size van to sell in 1996. The Chevy Van (the cargo hauler) and the Express Van (the people hauler) come equipped with powerful optional engines, lots of cargo space, dual airbags and four-wheel anti-lock brakes. With this modern new design, Chevrolet is stealing some of Ford's thunder in the full-size van market.

Converters prefer rugged full-frame construction, because it allows for improved stability, ride and handling. Since most full-size vans are bought for conversion into rolling motel rooms, the new van employs this type of platform. Regular-length models carry 267 cubic feet of cargo, and extended-length vans can haul 317 cubic feet of stuff. Trick rear doors open 180 degrees to make loading and unloading the van easier. Up to 15 passengers can ride in the extended-length Express, making it perfect for use as an airport shuttle. Other seating options include five-, eight- and 12-passenger arrangements. G3500's can tow up to 10,000 pounds when properly equipped.

For convenience, the full-size spare is stored underneath the cargo floor. A 31-gallon fuel tank keeps this thirsty vehicle from frequent fill-ups, but topping off an empty tank will quickly empty your wallet. Engine choices are sourced from the Chevrolet family of Vortec gasoline motors, and a turbocharged diesel can be installed under the hood. Available are the Vortec 4300 V6, the 5000, 5700, and 7400 V8's, and a 6.5-liter Turbo-diesel V8. Standard side cargo doors are a 60/40 panel arrangement, but a traditional slider is a no-cost option on 135-inch wheelbase vans.

Child safety locks are standard on the rear and side doors of the Express. Assist handles help passengers into and out of the van. Front and rear air conditioning is optional. For 1998, all vans have a standard theft deterrent system, and Express models get new seat belt comfort guides. Airbags switch to a new mini-module design.

EXPRESS VAN — CHEVROLET

CODE	DESCRIPTION	INVOICE	MSRP

Exterior styling is an interesting mix of corporate Chevrolet, Astro Van and Lumina Minivan. The high, pillar-mounted taillights are odd, but functional. They can easily be seen if the van is operated with the rear doors open. Low-mounted bumpers and moldings make the Express look taller than it is. An attractively sculpted body side gives the van's smooth, slab-sided flanks a dose of character. Three new colors arrive for 1998, in shades of gray, blue, and copper. Overall, Chevrolet's thoughtful rendition of the traditional full-size van appears to be right on target, giving Ford's Econoline/Club Wagon the first real competition it has faced in years.

Safety Data

Driver Airbag: *Standard*
Side Airbag: *Not Available*
Traction Control: *Not Available*
Driver Crash Test Grade: *Not Available*

Passenger Airbag: *Standard*
4-Wheel ABS: *Standard*
Integrated Child Seat(s): *Not Available*
Passenger Crash Test Grade: *Not Available*

Standard Equipment

EXPRESS G1500: 4.3L V-6 OHV SMPI 12-valve engine; 4-speed electronic overdrive automatic transmission with lock-up; 600-amp HD battery; 100-amp alternator; rear wheel drive, 3.42 axle ratio; stainless steel exhaust; front independent suspension with anti-roll bar, HD front coil springs, front shocks, rear suspension with HD rear leaf springs, rear shocks; power re-circulating ball steering with engine speed-sensing assist; front disc/rear drum brakes with 4 wheel anti-lock braking system; 31 gal capacity fuel tank; 3 doors with split swing-out right rear passenger door, split swing-out rear cargo door; trailer harness; front and rear argent bumpers with rear step; monotone paint; sealed beam halogen headlamps with daytime running lights; additional exterior lights include center high mounted stop light, underhood light; driver and passenger manual black folding outside mirrors; front and rear 15" x 6" silver styled steel wheels with hub wheel covers; P235/75SR15 BSW AS front and rear tires; underbody mounted full-size conventional steel spare wheel; air conditioning; AM/FM stereo with clock, seek-scan, 4 speakers and fixed antenna; child safety rear door locks; 2 power accessory outlets; analog instrumentation display includes oil pressure gauge, water temp gauge, volt gauge, PRNDL in instrument panel, trip odometer; warning indicators include battery, lights on, key in ignition; dual airbags; ignition disable; tinted windows, vented rear windows, fixed 1/4 vent windows; variable intermittent front windshield wipers, vented rear window; seating capacity of 8, front bucket seats with fixed adjustable headrests, driver seat includes 4-way direction control, passenger seat includes 4-way direction control; bench 2nd row seat with adjustable outboard rear headrests; 3rd row removeable bench seat with adjustable outboard headrests; vinyl seats, cloth door trim insert, full cloth headliner, full vinyl floor covering; interior lights include dome light; day-night rearview mirror; engine cover console with storage, glove box, front cupholder, instrument panel covered bin, 2 seat back storage pockets, driver and passenger door bins; vinyl cargo floor, plastic trunk lid, cargo light; black grille, black side window moldings, black front windshield molding, black rear window molding, black door handles.

G2500/G3500 HD (in addition to or instead of G1500 equipment): 5.7L V-8 engine; 124-amp alternator; 3.73 axle ratio; front and rear 16" x 6.5" wheels; seating capacity of 12, colored grille (G2500 extended models).

Base Prices

CODE	DESCRIPTION	INVOICE	MSRP
CG11406	G1500 Regular Length	19916	22761
CG21406	G2500 HD Regular Length	22103	25261
CG21706	G2500 HD Extended Length	22891	26161

CHEVROLET — EXPRESS VAN

CODE	DESCRIPTION	INVOICE	MSRP
CG31406	G3500 HD Regular Length	22353	25550
CG31706	G3500 HD Extended Length	23140	26450
	Destination Charge:	615	615

Accessories

CODE	DESCRIPTION	INVOICE	MSRP
KW2	124-amp Alternator (G1500 Regular)	52	60
ZP3	15 Passenger Seating (G3500 Extended)	319	371
GU6	3.42 Axle Ratio (G3500)	NC	NC
	REQUIRES (L29) engine. NOT AVAILABLE with (G80) locking differential, (L65) engine.		
GT4	3.73 Axle Ratio (G1500 Regular)	NC	NC
	NOT AVAILABLE with (L30) engine, (L31) engine.		
GT5	4.10 Axle Ratio (All except G1500 Regular)	NC	NC
ZP5	5 Passenger Seating (G1500 Regular)	(319)	(371)
AG1	6-Way Power Driver's Seat	206	240
	REQUIRES (AS5) seats.		
AG2	6-Way Power Passenger's Seat	206	240
	REQUIRES AG1 and AS5.		
ZP8	8 Passenger Seating (G2500 Regular/G3500 Regular)	(319)	(371)
KL5	Alternative Fuel Conversion (All except G1500 Regular)	108	125
	NOT AVAILABLE with (L65) engine, (L29) engine.		
TR9	Auxiliary Lighting	138	160
	Includes retractable underhood lamp. reading lamps, front and side door step well lights.		
YF5	California Emissions	146	170
	Automatically added to vehicles shipped to and/or sold to retailers in California. Out-of-state retailers must order on vehicles to be registered or leased in California.		
V10	Cold Climate Package	41	48
	Includes engine block heater. NOT AVAILABLE with (L65) engine.		
ZQ3	Convenience Group	331	385
	Includes tilt steering, speed control.		
ZQ2	Convenience Group	408	474
	Includes power door locks, power windows with driver's one-touch down.		
AJ1	Deep Tinted Glass	335	390
DH6	Dual Illuminated Visor Vanity Mirrors	64	75
	NOT AVAILABLE with (1SA) Preferred Equipment Group 1SA, (1SB) Preferred Equipment Group 1SB.		
DE5	Electric Remote Fold-Away Mirrors	97	113
	With defog feature. REQUIRES (ZQ2) Convenience Group.		
L30	Engine: 5.0L V8 SFI (G1500 Regular)	426	495
	NOT AVAILABLE with (GT4) 3.73 axle ratio.		
L31	Engine: 5.7L V8 SFI (G1500 Regular)	830	965
	NOT AVAILABLE with (GT4) 3.73 axle ratio.		
L65	Engine: 6.5L V8 Turbo Diesel (G2500 Regular/G3500 Regular/G3500 Extended)	2460	2860
	NOT AVAILABLE with (KL5) alternative fuel conversion, (V10) Cold Climate Package, (GU6) 3.42 axle ratio.		

EXPRESS VAN — CHEVROLET

CODE	DESCRIPTION	INVOICE	MSRP
L29	Engine: 7.4L V8 Vortec HD (G3500)	516	600
	NOT AVAILABLE with (KL5) alternative fuel conversion.		
NC7	Federal Emission Override	NC	NC
	For vehicles that will be registered or leased in California, New York, Massachusetts or Connecticut, but sold by retailers outside those states. REQUIRES YF5.		
C69	Front & Rear Air Conditioning (All except G1500 Regular)	691	804
	Includes rear heater.		
C69	Front & Rear Air Conditioning (G1500 Regular)	740	860
	Includes 124-amp alternator, rear heater.		
B30	Full Carpeted Flooring	126	147
	Includes front and rear vinyl mats.		
NP5	Leather Wrapped Steering Wheel	52	60
G80	Locking Differential	217	252
	NOT AVAILABLE with (GU6) 3.42 axle ratio.		
U75	Power Antenna	73	85
1SA	Preferred Equipment Group 1SA	NC	NC
	Includes vehicle with standard equipment. NOT AVAILABLE with AUO, DH6, ULO, UNO, UPO.		
1SB	Preferred Equipment Group 1SB	739	859
	Includes Convenience Group: power door locks, power windows with driver's one-touch down; Convenience Group: tilt steering, speed control. NOT AVAILABLE with (AUO) remote keyless entry, (DH6) dual illuminated visor vanity mirrors.		
1SC	Preferred Equipment Group 1SC	1423	1655
	Includes Convenience Group: power door locks, power windows with driver's one-touch down; Convenience Group: tilt steering, speed control; LS Decor Package: chrome bumpers, chrome grille, aero-composite headlamps, trim rings and bright center hub caps; front deluxe bucket seats with custom cloth seat trim, cloth door trim, Auxiliary Lighting: reading lamps, front and side door step well lights; carpeted cargo area, front floor mats, full carpeted flooring.		
1SD	Preferred Equipment Group 1SD (All except G1500 Regular)	2792	3247
	Includes Convenience Group: power door locks, power windows with driver's one-touch down; Convenience Group: tilt steering, speed control; LS Decor Package: chrome bumpers, chrome grille, aero-composite headlamps, trim rings and bright center hub caps; front deluxe bucket seats with custom cloth seat trim, cloth door trim, Auxiliary Lighting: reading lamps, front and side door step well lights; carpeted cargo area, front floor mats, full carpeted flooring, front and rear air conditioning, 124-amp alternator, rear heater, deep tinted glass, remote keyless entry, electric remote fold-away mirrors, dual illuminated visor vanity mirrors, leather wrapped steering wheel.		
1SD	Preferred Equipment Group 1SD (G1500 Regular)	2841	3303
	Includes Convenience Group: power door locks, power windows with driver's one-touch down; Convenience Group: tilt steering, speed control; LS Decor Package: chrome bumpers, chrome grille, aero-composite headlamps, trim rings and bright center hub caps; front deluxe bucket seats with custom cloth seat trim, cloth door trim, Auxiliary Lighting: reading lamps, front and side door step well lights; carpeted cargo area, front floor mats, full carpeted flooring, front and rear air conditioning, 124-amp alternator, rear heater, deep tinted glass, remote keyless entry, electric remote fold-away mirrors, dual illuminated visor vanity mirrors, leather wrapped steering wheel.		

CHEVROLET EXPRESS VAN

CODE	DESCRIPTION	INVOICE	MSRP
UL0	Radio: AM/FM Stereo with Cassette	380	442
	Includes automatic tone control, digital clock, theft lock, speed compensated volume, 8 speakers, and power antenna. NOT AVAILABLE with 1SA, UM6, UN0, UP0.		
UM6	Radio: AM/FM Stereo with Cassette	126	147
	Includes digital clock. NOT AVAILABLE with (UL0) radio, (UN0) radio, (UP0) radio.		
UN0	Radio: AM/FM Stereo with CD	466	542
	Includes auto tone control, digital clock, theft lock, seek and scan, speed compensated volume, 8 speakers, and power antenna. NOT AVAILABLE with 1SA, UM6, UL0, UP0.		
UP0	Radio: AM/FM Stereo with CD & Cassette	552	642
	Includes automatic tone control, digital clock, theft lock, search and repeat, speed compensated volume, 8 speakers, and power antenna. NOT AVAILABLE with 1SA, UM6, UL0, UN0.		
P06	Rally Wheel Trim	52	60
	NOT AVAILABLE with (N90) wheels, (N83) wheels.		
C36	Rear Heater	206	240
AU0	Remote Keyless Entry	129	150
	NOT AVAILABLE with (1SA) Preferred Equipment Group 1SA, (1SB) Preferred Equipment Group 1SB.		
YA2	Sliding Side Rear Door	NC	NC
XHB	Tires: P235/75R15X AS WSW (G1500 Regular)	86	100
	Includes front, rear and spare.		
XHM	Tires: P235/75R15XL AS WOL (G1500 Regular)	108	125
	Includes front, rear and spare.		
ZX9	Tires: Spare Delete (G1500 Regular)	(144)	(167)
	Also deletes jack. REQUIRES (XHM) tires.		
ZX9	Tires: Spare Delete (G1500 Regular)	(139)	(162)
	Also deletes jack. REQUIRES (XHB) tires.		
ZX9	Tires: Spare Delete (G1500 Regular)	(122)	(142)
	Also deletes jack. REQUIRES 1SA or 1SB or 1SC or 1SD. NOT AVAILABLE with XHB, XHM.		
ZX9	Tires: Spare Delete (G2500)	(232)	(270)
	Also deletes jack.		
ZX9	Tires: Spare Delete (G3500)	(256)	(298)
	Also deletes jack.		
Z82	Trailering Special Equipment	267	310
	Includes platform trailer hitch and 8-lead wiring harness.		
N90	Wheels: Aluminum (G1500 Regular)	215	250
	Spare is steel. REQUIRES (1SC) Preferred Equipment Group 1SC or (1SD) Preferred Equipment Group 1SD. NOT AVAILABLE with (N83) wheels.		
N90	Wheels: Aluminum (G1500 Regular)	267	310
	Spare is steel. REQUIRES 1SA or 1SB. NOT AVAILABLE with N83, P06.		
N83	Wheels: Chrome (G1500 Regular)	215	250
	Spare is steel. REQUIRES (1SC) Preferred Equipment Group 1SC or (1SD) Preferred Equipment Group 1SD. NOT AVAILABLE with (N90) wheels.		
N83	Wheels: Chrome (G1500 Regular)	267	310
	Spare is steel. REQUIRES 1SA or 1SB. NOT AVAILABLE with N90, P06.		

S-10   CHEVROLET

| CODE | DESCRIPTION | INVOICE | MSRP |

1998 S-10

1998 Chevrolet S-10

What's New?

The S-10 gets a sheetmetal makeover and a new interior with dual airbags that incorporate second-generation technology for reduced force deployments. The basic 4-cylinder engine benefits from Vortec technology this year, while 4WD models now have 4-wheel disc brakes and a more refined transfer case on trucks with an automatic transmission. New radios, automatic headlight control, and a standard theft deterrent system sum up the changes.

Review

Like most of today's compact trucks, Chevrolet's S-Series grew more car-like when it was redesigned for 1994. That's the trend, and Chevy has done a good job of transforming its small-scale pickups, without blurring their identity as practical machines. Riding smoother and handling better, they gained plenty in performance potential and overall refinement, ranking closer to their main competition, Ford's similar-size Ranger. Grasp the S-10's long manual-transmission gearshift lever and it's easy to imagine you're wielding a big rig, while enjoying the blissful comforts of a compact.

Four-cylinder models need that manual shift to derive top performance, but the two V6 engine options are strong with either manual or automatic transmissions. For maximum output, the optional 180-horsepower L35 Vortec 4300 V6 is the engine to select (190 horsepower in 4WD models). The slightly less energetic LF6 Vortec 4300 V6 is no slouch, nearly matching the L35 in power and torque.

Extended cab models can be equipped with a handy access panel that opens wide to allow for easier access to the rear of the cab. Located on the driver's side, the optional third door deletes one of the extended cab's jump seats, but makes it much easier to load cargo, a friend, or your pal Spot into the S-10. Be warned, the third door makes for aggravating rattles on broken pavement.

Two- and 4-wheel-drive trucks come in several configurations, with a short or long bed, fleetside box or sportside box, and a short or extended wheelbase available. Ride comfort varies from car-smooth to strictly firm, depending on the choice of suspensions and tires.

CHEVROLET S-10

Headroom is ample and seats are supportive, but the driver sits low, facing a tall steering wheel and cowl. In theory, three people fit across an S-Series bench seat, but it's hard to imagine an adult human being slim enough to squeeze into the space allotted. Surprisingly, the extended cab's rear jump seats are comfortable for short trips, as long as only one adult occupies the space behind the front seats.

Full gauges are excellent and easy to read, but the upright dashboard is constructed of cheap and brittle looking plastic. Despite a low-height windshield—not unlike the Ranger's—visibility is super, helped by huge mirrors. Dual airbags and daytime running lamps are standard. All models have 4-wheel anti-lock braking. Off-roaders will want the burly ZR2 package that makes the truck's body wider and taller, featuring special wheel flares, tough suspension components, and aggressive rubber.

For 1998, the S-10 gets a new front end and redesigned rear bumper. The new styling helps to associate the S-10 with the rest of the Chevy truck lineup thanks to a thick horizontal chrome bar and thin headlamps just below the edge of the hood. The interior is revised, and a new dashboard debuts with dual airbags. Ergonomics are very good, but the plastic used to construct the dash still looks like it belongs on a Tonka truck. Standard equipment now includes a theft deterrent system and automatic headlight control. On 4WD models, 4-wheel disc brakes have been added, and with an automatic transmission, the transfer case is refined for smoother and quieter operation. The standard 2.2-liter 4-cylinder benefits from the same Vortec technology Chevrolet bestows upon the optional V6 engines. There are also new radios and automatics have a column-mounted shifter instead of a space-robbing console stick.

Like many Chevrolets, the S-10 is loaded with value, but we've never warmed up to it. With the refinements made for 1998, perhaps this little pickup will prove to be likeable. A test drive later this year will tell the tale.

Safety Data

Driver Airbag: *Standard*
Side Airbag: *Not Available*
Traction Control: *Not Available*
Driver Crash Test Grade: *Not Available*

Passenger Airbag: *Standard*
4-Wheel ABS: *Standard*
Integrated Child Seat(s): *Not Available*
Passenger Crash Test Grade: *Not Available*

Standard Equipment

S-10 2WD BASE: 2.2L Vortec I4 SFI engine, 5-speed manual transmission, power front disc/rear drum 4-wheel anti-lock brakes, power recirculating ball steering, independent front coil spring suspension, semi-floating rear suspension with 2-stage multi-leaf springs, air dam, daytime running lights with automatic headlamp control, manual LH/RH exterior mirrors, P205/75R15 tires, 15"x 7" steel argent painted wheels with black center caps, dual front airbags with passenger disable switch, full color-keyed cloth headliner, gauges for fuel level, odometer, oil pressure, speedometer, temperature, trip odometer, voltmeter; delayed entry interior lighting, PassLock theft deterrent system, reatined accessory power, Scotchgard fabric protector, vinyl seats, deluxe 4-spoke steering wheel, padded color-keyed cloth sunvisors, headlamps-on warning tone, intermittent variable windshield wipers.

S-10 2WD LS (in addition to or instead of BASE equipment): 60/40 split bench front seat with custom cloth, storage armrest, cloth door trim panels, ETR AM/FM stereo with digital clock, sunvisor extensions, illuminated visor vanity mirrors, rear quarter swing-out windows (on X-cab), chrome grille, composite headlamps, rear color-keyed step bumper, chrome wheel trim rings.

S-10 4WD (in addition to or instead of 2WD LS equipment): 4.3L Vortec V-6 engine, 4-wheel disc brakes, manual shift transfer case, independent front torsion bar suspension, P235/70R15 tires (Longbed models only), front tow hooks.

S-10 CHEVROLET

CODE	DESCRIPTION	INVOICE	MSRP

Base Prices

CODE	DESCRIPTION	INVOICE	MSRP
CS10603	2WD Fleetside Reg. Cab Shortbed	11339	11998
CS10803	2WD Fleetside Reg. Cab Longbed	11966	12662
CS10603	LS 2WD Fleetside Reg. Cab Shortbed	11927	13179
CS10803	LS 2WD Fleetside Reg. Cab Longbed	12245	13530
CS10653	LS 2WD Fleetside Ext. Cab	13784	15230
CS10603	LS 2WD Reg. Cab Sportside	12358	13655
CS10653	LS 2WD Ext. Cab Sportside	14214	15705
CT10603	4WD Fleetside Reg. Cab Shortbed	15632	16541
CT10803	4WD Fleetside Reg. Cab Longbed	15945	16873
CT10603	LS 4WD Fleetside Reg. Cab Shortbed	16003	17682
CT10803	LS 4WD Fleetside Reg. Cab Longbed	16389	18109
CT10653	LS 4WD Fleetside Extended Cab	17722	19582
CT10603	LS 4WD Reg. Cab Sportside	16410	18132
CT10653	LS 4WD Ext. Cab Sportside	18129	20032
Destination Charge:		510	510

Accessories

CODE	DESCRIPTION	INVOICE	MSRP
C60	Air Conditioning	692	805
	NOT AVAILABLE with 1SS.		
ANL	Air Dam with Fog Lamps (2WD LS)	99	115
	NOT AVAILABLE with 1SA, B4U.		
YF5	California Emissions	146	170
V10	Cold Climate Package	77	89
	Includes HD battery and engine block heater.		
ZQ3	Convenience Group	340	395
	Includes cruise control and tilt steering wheel. NOT AVAILABLE with 1SR.		
NG1	CT/MA/NY Emissions	146	170
AJ1	Deep Tinted Glass (Reg Cab)	64	75
AJ1	Deep Tinted Glass (X-cab)	99	115
AJ1	Deep Tinted Glass with A28 (Reg Cab)	34	40
AJ1	Deep Tinted Glass with A28 (X-cab)	64	75
L35	Engine: Vortec 4300 High Output V-6 (2WD)	1160	1349
	Includes tachometer.		
L35	Engine: Vortec 4300 High Output V-6 (4WD)	223	259
	NOT AVAILABLE with 1SR.		
LF6	Engine: Vortec 4300 V-6 (2WD)	937	1090
	NOT AVAILABLE with 1SJ.		
B32	Floor Mats — Front	17	20
	NOT AVAILABLE with 1SA.		
UA1	HD Battery	48	56
	Includes 690 CCA battery. NOT AVAILABLE with V10.		
NP5	Leather-Wrapped Steering Wheel	46	54
	NOT AVAILABLE with 1SA, 1SR, B4U.		

CHEVROLET S-10

CODE	DESCRIPTION	INVOICE	MSRP
G80	Locking Differential	232	270
	REQUIRES LF6 OR L35. NOT AVAILABLE with B4U.		
YC5	LS Exterior Appearance Package (All LS except Reg Cab LB)	254	295
	Includes color-keyed bumpers, dark gray bodyside moldings with chrome insert, chrome wheel opening moldings, aluminum wheels. REQUIRES 1SH or 1SJ or 1SM.		
YC5	LS Exterior Appearance Package (All LS except Reg Cab LB)	494	575
	Includes color-keyed bumpers, dark gray bodyside moldings with chrome insert, chrome wheel opening moldings, aluminum wheels. REQUIRES 1SB.		
ZQ6	Power Convenience Group	460	535
	NOT AVAILABLE with 1SA, 1SR.		
1SA	Preferred Equipment Group 1SA (Base Reg Cab)	(194)	(226)
	Includes vehicle with standard equipment and radio delete.		
1SB	Preferred Equipment Group 1SB (LS)	NC	NC
	Includes standard LS Decor.		
1SH	Preferred Equipment Group 1SH (2WD Reg Cab except LB)	346	402
	Manufacturer Discount	(172)	(200)
	Net Price	174	202
	Includes AM/FM stereo with cassette, seek-scan, and digital clock; 60/40 reclining split bench seat, and aluminum wheels.		
1SH	Preferred Equipment Group 1SH (2WD X-cab)	346	402
	Manufacturer Discount	(215)	(250)
	Net Price	131	152
	Includes AM/FM stereo with cassette, seek-scan, and digital clock; 60/40 reclining split bench seat, and aluminum wheels.		
1SJ	Preferred Equipment Group 1SJ (2WD X-cab)	1490	1733
	Manufacturer Discount	(172)	(200)
	Net Price	1318	1533
	Includes AM/FM stereo with cassette, seek-scan, and digital clock; reclining highback bucket seats with deluxe cloth and manual lumbar support, center storage console, aluminum wheels, Vortec 4300 V-6 engine.		
1SM	Preferred Equipment Group 1SM (4WD X-cab)	566	658
	Manufacturer Discount	(473)	(550)
	Net Price	93	108
	Includes reclining highback bucket seats with deluxe cloth and manual lumbar support, center storage console, AM/FM stereo with cassette, seek-scan, and digital clock; HD front and rear shocks, HD rear springs, cast aluminum wheels, P235/70R15 AS BSW tires.		
UM7	Radio: AM/FM Stereo	194	226
	Includes seek-scan and digital clock. REQUIRES 1SA.		
UL0	Radio: AM/FM Stereo with Cassette	174	202
	Includes seek-scan, digital clock, automatic tone control, speed compensated volume, and enhanced speaker system. NOT AVAILABLE with 1SA, 1SR.		
UM6	Radio: AM/FM Stereo with Cassette	299	348
	Includes seek-scan and digital clock. REQUIRES 1SA.		
UM6	Radio: AM/FM Stereo with Cassette	105	122
	Includes seek-scan and digital clock. REQUIRES 1SB.		

S-10 CHEVROLET

CODE	DESCRIPTION	INVOICE	MSRP
UP0	Radio: AM/FM Stereo with Cassette & CD	346	402
	Includes seek-scan, digital clock, automatic tone control, speed compensated volume, and enhanced speaker system. NOT AVAILABLE with 1SA.		
UN0	Radio: AM/FM Stereo with CD	260	302
	Includes seek-scan, digital clock, automatic tone control, speed compensated volume, and enhanced speaker system. NOT AVAILABLE with 1SA.		
VF6	Rear Step Bumper (2WD Reg Cab SB)	47	55
	REQUIRES B4U.		
VF7	Rear Step Bumper Delete	NC	NC
	REQUIRES 1SA or 1SB. NOT AVAILABLE with B4U.		
AU0	Remote Keyless Entry	129	150
AM6	Seat: 60/40 Reclining Split Bench (X-cab)	(121)	(141)
	REQUIRES 1SJ or 1SM.		
AV5	Seat: Reclining Highback Buckets	83	96
	Includes center console storage, deluxe cloth, and manual lumbar supports. REQUIRES 1SA or 1SS or 1SB or 1SH. NOT AVAILABLE with LF6, L35, M30.		
AV5	Seat: Reclining Highback Buckets	207	241
	Includes center console storage, deluxe cloth, and manual lumbar supports. REQUIRES 1SA or 1SS or 1SB or 1SH and LF6 or L35 and M30.		
A28	Sliding Rear Window	103	120
1SS	Sport Bonus Package (2WD Base Reg Cab SB)	1297	1508
	Manufacturer Discount	(109)	(127)
	Net Price	1188	1381
	Includes air conditioning, 4.10 rear axle ratio, AM/FM stereo with seek-scan and digital clock, sport suspension: HD springs, P235/55R16 AS tires, 16" x 8" cast aluminum wheels; cloth bench seat.		
ZY7	Sport Two-Tone Paint (LS)	194	225
	NOT AVAILABLE with B4U.		
B4U	SS Package (2WD LS Reg Cab SB)	556	647
	Includes locking differential, air dam with fog lights, aluminum wheels with unique hub covers, body-color grille, leather-wrapped steering wheel, rear bumper delete. REQUIRES L35 and M30 and ZQ8.		
Z85	Suspension: Increased Capacity (2WD Reg Cab/4WD X-cab) ..	55	64
	NOT AVAILABLE with 1SH on X-cab models.		
ZM6	Suspension: Off-Road (4WD except Reg Cab LB)	598	695
	Includes Bilstein shocks, P235/75R15 on-off road tires, torsion bars, jounce bumpers.		
Z83	Suspension: Solid-Smooth (2WD X-cab)	(55)	(64)
ZQ8	Suspension: Sport (2WD LS Reg Cab SB)	605	703
	Includes HD springs, P235/55R16 AS tires, 16" x 8" cast aluminum wheels. NOT AVAILABLE with B4U.		
ZQ8	Suspension: Sport (2WD LS Reg Cab SB)	391	455
	Includes HD springs, P235/55R16 AS tires, 16" x 8" cast aluminum wheels. REQUIRES B4U.		
U16	Tachometer	51	59
	NOT AVAILABLE with L35.		
E24	Third Door (X-cab)	322	375

CHEVROLET S-10

CODE	DESCRIPTION	INVOICE	MSRP
QJJ	Tires: 31x10.5R15 On-Off Road BSW (4WD LS Reg Cab SB)	NC	NC
	REQUIRES ZR2 or 1SR.		
QCA	Tires: P205/75R15 AS WOL (All except 4WD Reg Cab LB)	104	121
	REQUIRES Z83 on 4WD models. NOT AVAILABLE with ZQ8.		
QBF	Tires: P235/70R15 AS BSW (4WD except Reg Cab Longbed)	165	192
	REQUIRES Z85.		
QEB	Tires: P235/75R15 On-Off Road WOL (4WD except Reg Cab LB)	335	390
	REQUIRES Z85. NOT AVAILABLE with ZM6, ZR2, Z83.		
QEB	Tires: P235/75R15 On-Off Road WOL (4WD Reg Cab LB)	123	143
	REQUIRES Z85. NOT AVAILABLE with ZM6, ZR2, Z83.		
—	Tires: Spare	64	75
	NOT AVAILABLE with ZM6.		
M30	Transmission: 4-Speed Automatic	920	1070
ZM5	Underbody Shield Package (4WD)	108	126
	NOT AVAILABLE with 1SR, ZR2.		
N60	Wheels: Aluminum (2WD)	241	280
	NOT AVAILABLE with 1SH, 1SS, B4U, YC5.		
N90	Wheels: Aluminum (4WD)	241	280
	NOT AVAILABLE with 1SH, 1SM, 1SR, ZR2, YC5.		
PA3	Wheels: Aluminum (4WD LS)	241	280
	NOT AVAILABLE with 1SH, 1SM, 1SR, ZR2, YC5.		
ZR2	Wide Stance Sport Perf. Package (4WD LS except Reg Cab LB/Sportside)	1544	1795
	Includes unique frame for wider track, unique rear axle, strengthened front differential gears, strengthened drive axles, larger wheel bearings, bigger axle shafts, unique rear suspension, thicker front stabilizer bar, Bilstein gas shock absorbers, extra wide wheel flares, 3" higher ride height. REQUIRES LF6 or L35 and AV5 and QJJ. NOT AVAILABLE with 1SR, ZY7.		
1SR	ZR2 4WD Bonus Package (4WD LS Reg Cab SB)	4098	4765
	Manufacturer Discount	(825)	(959)
	Net Price	3273	3806
	Includes cruise control, tilt steering wheel, power door locks, power windows, power exterior mirrors, remote keyless entry, floor mats, AM/FM stereo with cassette, seek-scan, digital clock, automatic tone control, speed compensated volume control, and enhanced speaker system; reclining highback bucket seats with deluxe cloth and manual lumbar supports, center storage console, underbody shield package, leather-wrapped steering wheel, aluminum wheels, P235/70R15 AS BSW tires, Vortec 4300 H.O. V-6 engine, ZR2 Sport Performance Package: unique frame for wider track, unique rear axle, strengthened front differential gears, strengthened drive axles, larger wheel bearings, bigger axle shafts, unique rear suspension, thicker front stabilizer bar, Bilstein gas shock absorbers, extra wide wheel flares, 3" higher ride height.		
1SR	ZR2 4WD Bonus Package (4WD LS X-cab)	4098	4765
	Manufacturer Discount	(997)	(1159)
	Net Price	3101	3606
	Includes cruise control, tilt steering wheel, power door locks, power windows, power exterior mirrors, remote keyless entry, floor mats, AM/FM stereo with cassette, seek-scan, digital clock, automatic tone control, speed compensated volume control, and enhanced speaker system; reclining highback bucket seats with deluxe cloth and		

S-10 / SUBURBAN CHEVROLET

| CODE | DESCRIPTION | INVOICE | MSRP |

manual lumbar supports, center storage console, underbody shield package, leather-wrapped steering wheel, aluminum wheels, P235/70R15 AS BSW tires, Vortec 4300 H.O. V-6 engine, ZR2 Sport Performance Package: unique frame for wider track, unique rear axle, strengthened front differential gears, strengthened drive axles, larger wheel bearings, bigger axle shafts, unique rear suspension, thicker front stabilizer bar, Bilstein gas shock absorbers, extra wide wheel flares, 3" higher ride height.

1998 SUBURBAN 1500

1998 Chevrolet Suburban 4x4

What's New?

New colors, a standard theft deterrent system, optional heated seats, second-generation airbags, and an automatic 4WD system improve the 1998 Suburban.

Review

In some sections of the country, wise middle-class folks have been tooling around for several years in mile-long Suburbans, whether or not they have great need for all that expanse behind the driver's seat. These days, throughout the suburban reaches of Houston and Dallas, among other spots, the Chevrolet and GMC Suburban have become de facto status-flaunting vehicles, pushing prices beyond the reach of the common man.

Yes, those who formerly wheeled about town in a Cadillac or Lincoln or Mercedes, and wouldn't feel quite right in a pickup truck, appear to have twirled their affections toward the biggest passenger vehicles in the General Motors repertoire. Chevrolet, in fact, considers the Suburban "as suited to the country club as to a roughneck oil field."

Mechanically, you get the same layout in the smaller Chevrolet Tahoe, but that vehicle is only available with Chevy's Vortec 5700 V8 engine. Select a Suburban and you can accept that motor, with 255 horsepower. Or, with the 3/4-ton C/K 2500 series you can go all the way, opting for the mammoth Vortec 7400 V8, whipping out 290 strutting horses and a mean 410 lbs.-ft. of ground-tromping torque. Oh, there's also an optional turbo-diesel. Both the half- and 3/4-ton versions come with either two- or four-wheel drive, and all have four-wheel anti-lock braking.

CHEVROLET SUBURBAN

| CODE | DESCRIPTION | INVOICE | MSRP |

This season brings a new optional four-wheel drive system. Called Autotrac, it automatically shifts from 2WD to 4WD when wheel slippage is detected, just like Ford's Control-Trac system in the similarly gargantuan Expedition. Also new is an Enhancement Package, which adds heated front seats, heated exterior mirrors, carpeted floor mats, a reversible rear cargo mat, an electrochromic rearview mirror with integrated compass and exterior temperature readout, a Homelink programmable 3-channel transmitter, and 46mm Bilstein shocks. New colors are available for 1998, and a theft deterrent system is standard this year.

Suburbans can seat up to nine occupants and tow as much as five tons when properly equipped. For families that need plenty of room for youngsters, or for retirees who need loads of power to haul a travel trailer, a Suburban can make good sense. Chevrolet is combating competition from Ford's new Expedition, but for heavy-duty use and maximum space, Chevrolet and GMC are still the only serious games in town for a mammoth "truck wagon."

Safety Data

Driver Airbag: *Standard*
Side Airbag: *Not Available*
Traction Control: *Not Available*
Driver Crash Test Grade: *Good*

Passenger Airbag: *Standard*
4-Wheel ABS: *Standard*
Integrated Child Seat(s): *Not Available*
Passenger Crash Test Grade: *Good*

Standard Equipment

SUBURBAN C1500: 5.7L V-8 OHV SMPI 16-valve engine; 4-speed electronic overdrive automatic transmission with lock-up; 600-amp HD battery; 100-amp alternator; rear wheel drive, 3.42 axle ratio; stainless steel exhaust; front independent suspension with HD anti-roll bar, front coil springs, HD front shocks, rear suspension with anti-roll bar, rear leaf springs, HD rear shocks; power re-circulating ball steering with vehicle speed-sensing assist; front disc/rear drum brakes with 4 wheel anti-lock braking system; 42 gal capacity fuel tank; split swing-out rear cargo door; trailer harness; front and rear chrome bumpers with black rub strip and chrome bumper insert, rear step bumper; black bodyside molding with chrome bodyside insert, chrome wheel well molding; monotone paint; sealed beam halogen headlamps with daytime running lights; additional exterior lights include center high mounted stop light, underhood light; driver and passenger manual black folding outside mirrors; front and rear 15" x 7" painted styled steel wheels with hub wheel covers; P235/75SR15 BSW AS front and rear tires; inside mounted full-size conventional steel spare wheel; rear heat ducts; AM/FM stereo, clock, with seek-scan, 4 speakers and fixed antenna; power door locks, child safety rear door locks, power remote tailgate release; 3 power accessory outlets; analog instrumentation display includes tachometer gauge, oil pressure gauge, water temp gauge, volt gauge, PRNDL in instrument panel, trip odometer; warning indicators include battery, lights on, key in ignition, door ajar; dual airbags; ignition disable; tinted windows, manual rear windows, fixed 1/4 vent windows; variable intermittent front windshield wipers; seating capacity of 3, bench front seat with tilt adjustable headrests, driver seat includes 2-way direction control, passenger seat includes 2-way direction control; front height adjustable seatbelts; vinyl seats, full cloth headliner, full vinyl floor covering; interior lights include dome light, front reading lights; sport steering wheel; passenger side vanity mirror; day-night rearview mirror; glove box with light, front cupholder, instrument panel bin, driver and passenger door bins, rear door bins; vinyl cargo floor, cargo net, cargo tie downs, cargo light; black grille, black side window moldings, black front windshield molding, black rear window molding, black door handles.

K1500 (in addition to or instead of C1500 equipment): Part-time 4 wheel drive, auto locking hub control and manual shift; front torsion suspension with front torsion springs and front torsion bar; tow hooks; front and rear 16" x 6.5" styled steel wheels; interior lights include illuminated entry.

SUBURBAN — CHEVROLET

CODE	DESCRIPTION	INVOICE	MSRP

Base Prices

CC10906	C1500	21932	25065
CK10906	K1500	24207	27665
	Destination Charge:	675	675

Accessories

Code	Description	Invoice	MSRP
GT4	3.73 Axle Ratio	116	135
	Includes engine oil cooler. NOT AVAILABLE with L65, MT1, Z82, KC4.		
MT1	4-Speed HD Automatic Transmission	NC	NC
	Includes HD auxiliary transmission oil cooler. REQUIRES B71. NOT AVAILABLE with YF5, GT4, KC4, N90, V10, Z82, QHM, PF4.		
AE7	60/40 Split-Bench Seat	NC	NC
	NOT AVAILABLE with (1SB) Preferred Equipment Group 1SB with L65, (1SC) Preferred Equipment Group 1SC, (A95) seats.		
C60	Air Conditioning	727	845
	NOT AVAILABLE with (YG6) air conditioning not desired.		
YG6	Air Conditioning Not Desired	NC	NC
	NOT AVAILABLE with C60, C69, 1SB, 1SC, ZP6.		
NP8	Autotrac Transfer Case (K1500)	344	400
	REQUIRES (ZQ3) Convenience Group.		
C36	Auxiliary Rear Passenger Heater	176	205
	Includes cloth covered rear quarter panel with 1SA.		
BVE	Black Side Step Running Boards	236	275
	Supports 600 lbs. and is dealer installed.		
YF5	California Emissions	146	170
	Automatically added to vehicles shipped to and/or sold to retailers in California. Out-of-state retailers must order on vehicles to be registered or leased in California. NOT AVAILABLE with (L65) engine, (MT1) transmission, (U01) roof marker lamps.		
DF2	Camper Type Exterior Mirrors	(39)	(45)
	7.5" x 10.5" stainless steel. REQUIRES 1SB or 1SC. NOT AVAILABLE with 1SA, DF2.		
DF2	Camper Type Exterior Mirrors	46	53
	7.5" x 10.5" stainless steel. REQUIRES 1SA. NOT AVAILABLE with DF2, 1SB, 1SC.		
AS3	Center and Rear Bench Seat	1017	1182
	Includes cloth covered rear quarter trim. NOT AVAILABLE with AS3, 1SA, 1SB, 1SC.		
AT5	Center Folding Bench Seat	544	632
	Includes adjustable shoulder belt system.		
V10	Cold Climate Package	28	33
	Includes engine block heater. NOT AVAILABLE with L65, MT1, QIZ, QIW.		
ZM9	Comfort & Security Package	989	1150
	Includes heated driver's and passenger's seats, power passenger's seat, carpeted floor mats, carpeted/vinyl reversible rear cargo mat, heated mirrors, Homelink 3 channel transmitter, 46 mm Bilstein shocks. REQUIRES 1SC and A95. NOT AVAILABLE with 1SA, 1SB.		

CHEVROLET SUBURBAN

CODE	DESCRIPTION	INVOICE	MSRP
ZQ3	Convenience Group	329	383
	Includes tilt steering wheel, cruise control.		
ZY2	Conventional Two-Tone Paint	172	200
AJ1	Deep Tinted Solar-Ray Glass	262	305
C49	Electric rear window defogger	132	154
	REQUIRES (C60) air conditioning.		
KC4	Engine Oil Cooler	116	135
	NOT AVAILABLE with L65, GT4, MT1, QIZ, QIW.		
L65	Engine: 6.5L V8 Turbo Diesel	2460	2860
	Includes front bumper guards. HD auxiliary battery, engine oil cooler. REQUIRES MT1. NOT AVAILABLE with GT4, YF5, V10, KC4, QHM, Z82, N90, QBN, QBX, QGB, PF4, F60.		
C5I	GVWR: 8050 Lbs. (K1500)	NC	NC
KNP	HD Auxiliary Transmission Oil Cooler	83	96
F60	HD Front Springs (K1500)	54	63
	NOT AVAILABLE with (L65) engine.		
Z82	HD Trailering Special Equipment	267	310
	Includes platform hitch, HD auxiliary transmission oil cooler. REQUIRES (GT4) 3.73 axle ratio. NOT AVAILABLE with (MT1) transmission, (L65) engine.		
Z82	HD Trailering Special Equipment	383	445
	Includes platform hitch, engine oil cooler, HD auxiliary transmission oil cooler. NOT AVAILABLE with (L65) engine, (MT1) transmission, (GT4) 3.73 axle ratio.		
Z82	HD Trailering Special Equipment	184	214
	Includes platform hitch, REQUIRES (L65) engine.		
K47	High Capacity Air Cleaner	22	25
A95	Highback Bucket Seats	249	290
	Includes floor console, roof console. NOT AVAILABLE with (1SA) Preferred Equipment Group 1SA, (AE7) seats, (A95) seats.		
G80	Locking Differential	217	252
1SA	Preferred Equipment Group 1SA (C1500)	NC	NC
	Includes vehicle with standard equipment. REQUIRES YG6 or C60 or C69. NOT AVAILABLE with DK6, D55, A95, UNO, UPO, ZM9, YG4, AS3, DF2.		
1SA	Preferred Equipment Group 1SA (K1500)	NC	NC
	Includes vehicle with standard equipment. REQUIRES YG6 or C60 or C69. NOT AVAILABLE with DK6, D55, A95, UNO, UPO, ZM9, YG4, AS3, DF2.		
1SB	Preferred Equipment Group 1SB (C1500)	6379	7418
	Includes LS Decor: Convenience Group: tilt steering wheel, cruise control, interior trim and storage, automatic dimming rearview mirror, compass, exterior temperature display, 60/40 split-bench seat, rear bench seats, color-keyed cloth spare tire cover, leather wrapped steering wheel, dual illuminated visor vanity mirrors, roof rack, chrome grille, aero-composite headlamps, exterior power remote mirrors, electric rear window defogger, rear window wiper/washer, deep tinted solar-ray glass, custom cloth seat trim, rear air conditioning, AM/FM stereo with seek, scan, automatic tone control, cassette; auxiliary rear passenger heater, remote keyless entry, power driver's seat. NOT AVAILABLE with L65, P06, UL5, UM6, AE7, YG6, A95, ZM9, YG4, AS3, DF2.		

SUBURBAN — CHEVROLET

CODE	DESCRIPTION	INVOICE	MSRP
1SB	**Preferred Equipment Group 1SB (K1500)**	6379	7418

Includes LS Decor: Convenience Group: tilt steering wheel, cruise control, interior trim and storage, automatic dimming rearview mirror, compass, exterior temperature display, 60/40 split-bench seat, rear bench seats, color-keyed cloth spare tire cover, leather wrapped steering wheel, dual illuminated visor vanity mirrors, roof rack, chrome grille, aero-composite headlamps, exterior power remote mirrors, electric rear window defogger, rear window wiper/washer, deep tinted solar-ray glass, custom cloth seat trim, rear air conditioning, AM/FM stereo with seek, scan, automatic tone control, cassette; auxiliary rear passenger heater, remote keyless entry; power driver's seat. NOT AVAILABLE with L65, P06, UL5, UM6, AE7, YG6, A95, ZM9, YG4, AS3, DF2.

| 1SB | **Preferred Equipment Group 1SB with L65 (C1500)** .... | 6164 | 7168 |

Includes LS Decor: Convenience Group: tilt steering wheel, cruise control, interior trim and storage, automatic dimming rearview mirror, compass, exterior temperature display, 60/40 split-bench seat, rear bench seats, color-keyed cloth spare tire cover, leather wrapped steering wheel, dual illuminated visor vanity mirrors, roof rack, chrome grille, aero-composite headlamps, exterior power remote mirrors, electric rear window defogger, rear window wiper/washer, deep tinted solar-ray glass, custom cloth seat trim, rear air conditioning, AM/FM stereo with seek, scan, automatic tone control, cassette; auxiliary rear passenger heater, remote keyless entry, power driver's seat. REQUIRES L65. NOT AVAILABLE with P06, UL5, UM6, AE7, YG6, A95, ZM9, YG4, AS3, DF2.

| 1SB | **Preferred Equipment Group 1SB with L65 (K1500)** .... | 6164 | 7168 |

Includes LS Decor: Convenience Group: tilt steering wheel, cruise control, interior trim and storage, automatic dimming rearview mirror, compass, exterior temperature display, 60/40 split-bench seat, rear bench seats, color-keyed cloth spare tire cover, leather wrapped steering wheel, dual illuminated visor vanity mirrors, roof rack, chrome grille, aero-composite headlamps, exterior power remote mirrors, electric rear window defogger, rear window wiper/washer, deep tinted solar-ray glass, custom cloth seat trim, rear air conditioning, AM/FM stereo with seek, scan, automatic tone control, cassette; auxiliary rear passenger heater, remote keyless entry, power driver's seat. REQUIRES L65. NOT AVAILABLE with P06, UL5, UM6, AE7, YG6, A95, ZM9, YG4, AS3, DF2.

| 1SC | **Preferred Equipment Group 1SC (C1500)** .... | 7687 | 8938 |

Includes rear air conditioning, auxiliary rear passenger heater, remote keyless entry, power driver's seat, LT Decor: Convenience Group: tilt steering wheel, cruise control, interior trim and storage, automatic dimming rearview mirror, compass, exterior temperature display, color-keyed cloth spare tire cover, leather wrapped steering wheel, dual illuminated visor vanity mirrors, roof rack, chrome grille, aero-composite headlamps, exterior power remote mirrors, electric rear window defogger, rear window wiper/washer, deep tinted solar-ray glass, leather seat trim, AM/FM stereo with seek-scan, CD, cassette; 60/40 split-bench seat, rear bench seats. NOT AVAILABLE with L65, P06, UL5, UM6, YG6, A95, AE7, UNO, YG4, AS3, DF2.

| 1SC | **Preferred Equipment Group 1SC (K1500)** .... | 7884 | 9168 |

Includes rear air conditioning, auxiliary rear passenger heater, remote keyless entry, power driver's seat, LT Decor: Convenience Group: tilt steering wheel, cruise control, interior trim and storage, automatic dimming rearview mirror, compass, exterior

CHEVROLET — SUBURBAN

CODE	DESCRIPTION	INVOICE	MSRP
	temperature display, color-keyed cloth spare tire cover, leather wrapped steering wheel, dual illuminated visor vanity mirrors, roof rack, chrome grille, aero-composite headlamps, exterior power remote mirrors, electric rear window defogger, rear window wiper/washer, deep tinted solar-ray glass, leather seat trim, AM/FM stereo with seek-scan, CD, cassette; 60/40 split-bench seat, rear bench seats. NOT AVAILABLE with L65, P06, UL5, UM6, YG6, A95, AE7, UNO, YG4, AS3, DF2.		
1SC	**Preferred Equipment Group 1SC with L65 (C1500)**	7687	8938
	Includes rear air conditioning, auxiliary rear passenger heater, remote keyless entry, power driver's seat, LT Decor: Convenience Group: tilt steering wheel, cruise control, interior trim and storage, automatic dimming rearview mirror, compass, exterior temperature display, color-keyed cloth spare tire cover, leather wrapped steering wheel, dual illuminated visor vanity mirrors, roof rack, chrome grille, aero-composite headlamps, exterior power remote mirrors, electric rear window defogger, rear window wiper/washer, deep tinted solar-ray glass, leather seat trim, AM/FM stereo with seek-scan, CD, cassette; 60/40 split-bench seat, rear bench seats. REQUIRES L65. NOT AVAILABLE with P06, UL5, UM6, YG6, A95, AE7, UNO, YG4, AS3, DF2.		
1SC	**Preferred Equipment Group 1SC with L65 (K1500)**	7669	8918
	Includes rear air conditioning, auxiliary rear passenger heater, remote keyless entry, power driver's seat, LT Decor: Convenience Group: tilt steering wheel, cruise control, interior trim and storage, automatic dimming rearview mirror, compass, exterior temperature display, color-keyed cloth spare tire cover, leather wrapped steering wheel, dual illuminated visor vanity mirrors, roof rack, chrome grille, aero-composite headlamps, exterior power remote mirrors, electric rear window defogger, rear window wiper/washer, deep tinted solar-ray glass, leather seat trim, AM/FM stereo with seek-scan, CD, cassette; 60/40 split-bench seat, rear bench seats. REQUIRES L65. NOT AVAILABLE with P06, UL5, UM6, YG6, A95, AE7, UNO, YG4, AS3, DF2.		
UL5	**Radio Delete**	(247)	(287)
	NOT AVAILABLE with UM6, UNO, UPO, 1SB, 1SC.		
UM6	**Radio: AM/FM Stereo with Cassette**	126	147
	Includes digital clock. NOT AVAILABLE with UL5, UNO, 1SB, 1SC, UPO.		
UNO	**Radio: AM/FM Stereo with CD**	86	100
	Includes automatic tone control, theft lock, speed compensated volume, digital clock and enhanced performance speaker system. NOT AVAILABLE with UPO, UM6, UL5, 1SA, 1SC.		
UPO	**Radio: AM/FM Stereo with CD & Cassette**	172	200
	Includes automatic tone control, theft lock, speed compensated volume, digital clock and enhanced performance speaker system. NOT AVAILABLE with UNO, UM6, UL5, 1SA.		
P06	**Rally Wheel Trim**	52	60
	NOT AVAILABLE with N90, 1SB, 1SC, PF4.		
C69	**Rear Air Conditioning**	1200	1395
	Includes dual controls. NOT AVAILABLE with (YG6) air conditioning not desired.		
ZP6	**Rear Window Equipment**	240	279
	Includes electric rear window defogger, rear window wiper/washer. REQUIRES (C60) air conditioning OR (C69) rear air conditioning. NOT AVAILABLE with (YG6) air conditioning not desired.		

SUBURBAN — CHEVROLET

CODE	DESCRIPTION	INVOICE	MSRP
U01	Roof Marker Lamps (5)	47	55
	NOT AVAILABLE with (YF5) California Emissions.		
NZZ	Skid Plate Package (K1500)	194	225
	Includes fuel tank shield, front differential and transfer case shields.		
YG4	Third Seat Delete	(531)	(618)
	REQUIRES (1SB) Preferred Equipment Group 1SB with L65 and (AS3) center and rear bench seat. NOT AVAILABLE with (1SA) Preferred Equipment Group 1SA.		
YG4	Third Seat Delete	(875)	(1018)
	REQUIRES AS3 and 1SC. NOT AVAILABLE with 1SA.		
QBN	Tires: LT245/75R16C MS BSW (K1500)	47	55
	NOT AVAILABLE with L65, QBX, QIW, QIZ, QGB.		
QBX	Tires: LT245/75R16C MS WOL SBR (K1500)	155	180
	NOT AVAILABLE with L65, QBN, QIW, QIZ, QGB.		
QIZ	Tires: LT245/75R16E AS BSW (C1500)	391	459
	Includes 16" wheels. REQUIRES L65. NOT AVAILABLE with QHM, V10, KC4, N90.		
QIZ	Tires: LT245/75R16E AS BSW (K1500)	146	174
	REQUIRES L65. NOT AVAILABLE with QBN, QBX, QIW, QGB, V10, KC4, PF4.		
QIW	Tires: LT245/75R16E AT BSW (K1500)	194	229
	REQUIRES L65. NOT AVAILABLE with QBN, QBX, QIZ, QGB, V10, KC4, PF4.		
QHM	Tires: P235/75R15 AS WOL (C1500)	155	180
	NOT AVAILABLE with (L65) engine, (QIZ) tires, (MT1) transmission.		
QGB	Tires: P245/75R16 AT WOL (K1500)	120	140
	NOT AVAILABLE with L65, QBN, QBX, QIW, QIZ.		
V76	Tow Hooks (front) (C1500)	33	38
V96	Trailering Hitch Ball & Mount	26	30
	REQUIRES (Z82) HD Trailering Special Equipment.		
B71	Wheel Flare Moldings (K1500)	155	180
N90	Wheels: Aluminum (C1500)	267	310
	NOT AVAILABLE with P06, L65, MT1, QIZ.		
PF4	Wheels: Aluminum (K1500)	267	310
	NOT AVAILABLE with P06, L65, MT1, QIZ, QIW.		

1998 SUBURBAN 2500

Standard Equipment

C2500: 5.7L V-8 OHV SMPI 16-valve engine; 4-speed electronic overdrive automatic transmission with lock-up; HD battery; transmission oil cooler; rear wheel drive, 3.73 axle ratio; stainless steel exhaust; front independent suspension with HD anti-roll bar, front coil springs, HD front shocks, rear suspension with anti-roll bar, rear leaf springs, HD rear shocks; power re-circulating ball steering with engine speed-sensing assist; front disc/rear drum brakes with 4 wheel anti-lock braking system; 42 gal capacity fuel tank; split swing-out rear cargo door; trailer harness; front and rear chrome bumpers with black rub strip and chrome bumper insert, rear step bumper; black bodyside molding with chrome bodyside insert, chrome wheel well molding; monotone paint; sealed beam halogen headlamps with daytime running lights; additional exterior lights

CHEVROLET SUBURBAN

| CODE | DESCRIPTION | INVOICE | MSRP |

include center high mounted stop light, underhood light; driver and passenger manual black folding outside mirrors; front and rear 16" x 6.5" painted styled steel wheels with hub wheel covers; LT245/75SR16 BSW AS front and rear tires; inside mounted full-size conventional steel spare wheel; rear heat ducts; AM/FM stereo with clock, seek-scan, 4 speakers and fixed antenna; power door locks, child safety rear door locks; 3 power accessory outlets; analog instrumentation display includes tachometer gauge, oil pressure gauge, water temp gauge, volt gauge, PRNDL in instrument panel, trip odometer; warning indicators include battery, lights on, key in ignition, door ajar; dual airbags; ignition disable; tinted windows, manual rear windows, fixed 1/4 vent windows; variable intermittent front windshield wipers; seating capacity of 3, bench front seat with tilt adjustable headrests, driver seat includes 2-way direction control, passenger seat includes 2-way direction control; front height adjustable seatbelts; vinyl seats, full cloth headliner, full vinyl floor covering; interior lights include dome light, front reading lights; sport steering wheel; passenger side vanity mirror; day-night rearview mirror; glove box with light, front cupholder, instrument panel bin, driver and passenger door bins, rear door bins; vinyl cargo floor, vinyl trunk lid, cargo net, cargo tie downs, cargo light; colored grille, black side window moldings, black front windshield molding, black rear window molding, black door handles.

K2500 (in addition to or instead of C2500 equipment): 600-amp battery; 100-amp alternator; part-time 4 wheel drive, auto locking hub control and manual shift, 4.1 axle ratio; front torsion springs, front torsion bar; tow hooks.

Base Prices

		Invoice	MSRP
CC20906	C2500	23314	26649
CK20906	K2500	25589	29249
Destination Charge:		675	675

Accessories

Code	Description	Invoice	MSRP
AE7	60/40 Split-Bench Seat	NC	NC
	Includes storage armrest and power lumbar. NOT AVAILABLE with (1SA) Preferred Equipment Group 1SA, (A95) seats.		
YG6	Air Conditioning Not Desired	NC	NC
	NOT AVAILABLE with (C60) Air Conditioning, (C69) Rear Air Conditioning, (V10) Cold Climate Package.		
NP8	Autotrac Transfer Case (K2500)	344	400
	REQUIRES (ZQ3) Convenience Group or (1SB) Preferred Equipment Group 1SB or (1SC) Preferred Equipment Group 1SC.		
C36	Auxiliary Rear Passenger Heater	176	205
	Includes cloth covered quarter panel trim.		
BVE	Black Side Step Running Boards	236	275
	Dealer installed. Supports 600 lbs.		
B39	Carpeted Floor Mats	133	155
AS3	Center & Rear Bench Seating	1017	1182
	Includes cloth covered rear quarter trim, center folding bench seat, adjustable rear seatbelts. NOT AVAILABLE with (1SB) Preferred Equipment Group 1SB, (1SC) Preferred Equipment Group 1SC.		

SUBURBAN   CHEVROLET

CODE	DESCRIPTION	INVOICE	MSRP
AT5	Center Folding Bench Seat	544	632

Includes headrests, center fold-down armrests, easy entry feature on passenger side for access to rear seat/cargo area, adjustable front and rear seatbelts, rear cupholders. NOT AVAILABLE with (1SB) Preferred Equipment Group 1SB, (1SC) Preferred Equipment Group 1SC.

V10	Cold Climate Package	28	33

Includes engine block heater. NOT AVAILABLE with (L29) engine, (L65) engine, (YG6) air conditioning not desired.

ZM9	Comfort & Security Package	989	1150

Includes heated front seats, power passenger's seat, carpeted floor mats, reversible rear cargo mat, dual heated mirrors, Homelink 3 channel transmitter, 46 mm Bilstein shocks. REQUIRES (1SC) Preferred Equipment Group 1SC and (A95) seats.

ZQ3	Convenience Group	329	383

Includes manual tilt steering wheel, cruise control.

ZY2	Conventional Two-Tone Paint	172	200
AJ1	Deep Tinted Solar Ray Glass	262	305
L29	Engine: 7.4L V8	516	600

NOT AVAILABLE with (V10) Cold Climate Package.

U01	Exterior Roof Marker Lamps (5)	47	55

NOT AVAILABLE with (YF5) California Emissions, (1SA) Preferred Equipment Group 1SA.

D55	Floor Console	143	166
F60	HD Front Springs (K2500)	54	63
A95	Highback Bucket Seats with Console	249	290

Includes center and roof console and power lumbar adjustment. NOT AVAILABLE with (1SA) Preferred Equipment Group 1SA, (AE7) seats.

1SA	Preferred Equipment Group 1SA (C2500)	NC	NC

Includes vehicle with standard equipment. REQUIRES C60 or C69 or YG6. NOT AVAILABLE with AE7, A95, U01, UNO, UPO.

1SA	Preferred Equipment Group 1SA (K2500)	NC	NC

Includes vehicle with standard equipment. REQUIRES C60 or C69 or YG6. NOT AVAILABLE with AE7, A95, U01, UNO, UPO.

1SB	Preferred Equipment Group 1SB (C2500)	6164	7168

Includes LS Decor: roof rack, dual exterior power remote mirrors, chrome grille, aero-composite headlamps, wheel trim rings, dual illuminated visor vanity mirrors, 9 passenger cloth seats, cloth door inserts with lower carpet, carpeting with rubber mats, deluxe sound insulation, 4 door curb/courtesy lights, rear cupholder storage, cargo net, compass, leather wrapped steering wheel, power windows front and rear, rear air conditioning, automatic tone control stereo with cassette, deep tinted solar ray glass, auxiliary rear passenger heater, electric rear window defogger, center and rear bench seating: center folding bench seat, Convenience Group: manual tilt steering wheel, cruise control; rally wheel trim. NOT AVAILABLE with (UM6) radio, (UL5) radio, (A95) seats.

1SB	Preferred Equipment Group 1SB (K2500)	6164	7168

Includes LS Decor: roof rack, dual exterior power remote mirrors, chrome grille, aero-composite headlamps, wheel trim rings, dual illuminated visor vanity mirrors, 9 passenger cloth seats, cloth door inserts with lower carpet, carpeting with rubber

CHEVROLET — SUBURBAN

CODE	DESCRIPTION	INVOICE	MSRP

mats, deluxe sound insulation, 4 door curb/courtesy lights, rear cupholder storage, cargo net, compass, leather wrapped steering wheel, power windows front and rear, rear air conditioning, automatic tone control stereo with cassette, deep tinted solar ray glass, auxiliary rear passenger heater, electric rear window defogger, Convenience Group: manual tilt steering wheel, cruise control; rally wheel trim. NOT AVAILABLE with (UM6) radio, (UL5) radio, (A95) seats.

1SC — **Preferred Equipment Group 1SC (C2500)** 7669   8918
Includes LT Decor: roof rack, dual exterior power remote mirrors, chrome grille, aero-composite headlamps, wheel trim rings, dual illuminated visor vanity mirrors, 9 passenger leather seats, cloth door inserts with lower carpet, carpeting with rubber mats, deluxe sound insulation, illuminated entry lights, rear cupholder storage, cargo net, compass, leather wrapped steering wheel, power windows front and rear, rear air conditioning, deep tinted solar ray glass, auxiliary rear passenger heater, electric rear window defogger, center and rear bench seating: center folding bench seat, Convenience Group: manual tilt steering wheel, cruise control; AM/FM stereo with CD and cassette, seek/scan; remote keyless entry, illuminated entry, 60/40 split-bench seat, rally wheel trim. NOT AVAILABLE with UM6, UNO, UL5, A95.

1SC — **Preferred Equipment Group 1SC (K2500)** 7669   8918
Includes LT Decor: roof rack, dual exterior power remote mirrors, chrome grille, aero-composite headlamps, wheel trim rings, dual illuminated visor vanity mirrors, 9 passenger leather seats, cloth door inserts with lower carpet, carpeting with rubber mats, deluxe sound insulation, illuminated entry lights, rear cupholder storage, cargo net, compass, leather wrapped steering wheel, power windows front and rear, rear air conditioning, deep tinted solar ray glass, auxiliary rear passenger heater, electric rear window defogger, Convenience Group: manual tilt steering wheel, cruise control; AM/FM stereo with CD and cassette, seek/scan, remote keyless entry, illuminated entry, rally wheel trim. NOT AVAILABLE with UM6, UNO, UL5, A95.

UL5 — **Radio Delete** .... (247)   (287)
NOT AVAILABLE with (1SB) Preferred Equipment Group 1SB, (1SC) Preferred Equipment Group 1SC, (UM6) radio.

UM6 — **Radio: AM/FM Stereo with Cassette** 126   147
Includes digital clock. NOT AVAILABLE with (1SB) Preferred Equipment Group 1SB, (1SC) Preferred Equipment Group 1SC, (UL5) radio.

UN0 — **Radio: AM/FM Stereo with CD** 86   100
Includes automatic tone control, theft lock, speed compensated volume, digital clock and enhanced speaker system. NOT AVAILABLE with (1SA) Preferred Equipment Group 1SA, (1SC) Preferred Equipment Group 1SC, (UP0) radio.

UP0 — **Radio: AM/FM Stereo with CD & Cassette** 172   200
Includes automatic tone control, theft lock, speed compensated volume, digital clock and enhanced speaker system. REQUIRES 1SB or 1SC. NOT AVAILABLE with UN0, 1SA.

P06 — **Rally Wheel Trim** 52   60
ZP6 — **Rear Window Equipment** 240   279
Includes electric rear window defogger, rear window wiper/washer. REQUIRES (1SA) Preferred Equipment Group 1SA and ((C60) air conditioning or (C69) rear air conditioning).

SUBURBAN / TAHOE — CHEVROLET

CODE	DESCRIPTION	INVOICE	MSRP
ZP6	Rear Window Equipment .... *Includes electric rear window defogger, rear window wiper/washer. REQUIRES (1SB) Preferred Equipment Group 1SB OR (1SC) Preferred Equipment Group 1SC.*	NC	NC
DK6	Roof Console .... *REQUIRES (A95) seats.*	43	50
NZZ	Skid Plate Package (K2500) .... *Includes fuel tank shield, front differential and transfer case shields.*	194	225
QIW	Tires: LT245/75R16E On/Off Road BSW SBR (K2500)	47	55

1998 TAHOE

1998 Chevrolet Tahoe LT 4x4

What's New?

Autotrac is a new optional automatic four-wheel drive system that switches from 2WD to 4WD automatically as conditions warrant. A new option package includes heated seats and heated exterior mirrors. Second generation airbags deploy with less force than last year. A theft deterrent system is standard, and color selections are modified.

Review

Compact sport-utility vehicles get most of the attention nowadays, but for folks with big families—or scads of goods to lug around—they're just not spacious enough inside. Chevrolet offers a solution to this problem with the Tahoe, based on the full-size C/K pickup platform but garageable in either two- or four-door body styles.

At a glance, the four-door Tahoe and larger Suburban look nearly identical, but a Tahoe measures 20 inches shorter. Beneath the hood sits a Vortec 5700 V8, rated for 255 horsepower. Two-door 4WD Tahoes with LS or LT trim can be equipped with a 6.5-liter turbodiesel V8 instead of the Vortec 5700.

From the driver's seat forward, Tahoes are virtually identical to Chevy's full-size pickups. Space is massive up front. Capable of towing as much as 7,000 pounds, four-door Tahoes seat either five or six passengers, and an underbody-mounted spare tire helps boost cargo space.

CHEVROLET TAHOE

On the Interstate, the Tahoe rides nicely, but the wide body takes some getting used to if you're accustomed to compacts. Turning onto smaller roads, it suddenly feels more like a truck. Easy to control either way, this sizeable machine is reasonably maneuverable, if driven with discretion. The V8 is strong, and the four-speed automatic transmission shifts neatly.

Think about the "entry assist" running boards if your regular riders aren't so nimble. They help. So do the robust grab bars that ease entry into the rear seats. Rear cargo doors are standard, but a lift glass version is available.

New for 1998 is an optional automatic four-wheel drive system that shifts between 2WD and 4WD as conditions warrant. No longer is it necessary to push a button on the dashboard to actively engage four-wheel traction. Also new is an option package that includes such goodies as heated front seats, heated exterior mirrors, carpeted floor mats, an electrochromic rearview mirror with integrated compass and outside temperature readout, a rear cargo mat, a programmable Homelink transmitter, and 46mm Bilstein shocks. A theft deterrent system is standard on all Tahoe models, and three new colors are available.

Because Chevrolet targets customers with an income of $85,000 a year, luxury conveniences such as these are part of upscale Tahoe packages. The typical prospect is an upscale 40-year-old man who currently drives a Chevy Blazer and is attracted to a vehicle's size and power. Those attributes, the Tahoe has in abundance, as does its little-different GMC Yukon counterpart.

With the introduction of the Ford Expedition, Chevrolet loses its dominance in the full-size SUV market. Further complicating matters, the Tahoe is based on a decade-old platform, while the slightly larger, slightly less expensive Expedition is derived from all-new F-Series underpinnings. While the Expedition is certainly the better off-road vehicle, we feel the Tahoe delivers superior urban performance due to its lower ride height, more maneuverable size, and zippy Vortec V8. But drive both before making a final decision, unless you're a dyed-in-the-wool Chevy fan.

Safety Data

Driver Airbag: *Standard*
Side Airbag: *Not Available*
Traction Control: *Not Available*
Driver Crash Test Grade: *Good*

Passenger Airbag: *Standard*
4-Wheel ABS: *Standard*
Integrated Child Seat(s): *Not Available*
Passenger Crash Test Grade: *Good*

Standard Equipment

TAHOE 2WD 2-DOOR: 5.7L V-8 OHV SMPI 16-valve engine; 4-speed electronic overdrive automatic transmission with lock-up; 600-amp HD battery; 100-amp alternator; rear wheel drive, 3.08 axle ratio; stainless steel exhaust; front independent suspension with HD anti-roll bar, front coil springs, front shocks, rear suspension with rear leaf springs, rear shocks; power re-circulating ball steering with vehicle speed-sensing assist; front disc/rear drum brakes with 4 wheel anti-lock braking system; 30 gal capacity fuel tank; split swing-out rear cargo door; trailer harness; front and rear chrome bumpers with black rub strip, chrome bumper insert, rear step bumper; black bodyside molding with chrome bodyside insert, chrome wheel well molding; monotone paint; sealed beam halogen headlamps with daytime running lights; additional exterior lights include center high mounted stop light, underhood light; driver and passenger manual black folding outside mirrors; front and rear 15" x 7" silver styled steel wheels with hub wheel covers; P235/75SR15 BSW AS front and rear tires; inside mounted full-size conventional steel spare wheel; rear heat ducts; AM/FM stereo with clock, seek-scan, 4 speakers and fixed antenna; power door locks; 3 power accessory outlets; analog instrumentation display includes tachometer gauge, oil pressure gauge, water temp gauge, volt gauge, PRNDL in instrument panel, trip odometer; warning indicators include battery, lights on, key in ignition, door ajar; dual airbags; ignition disable; tinted windows, fixed rear windows; variable intermittent front windshield wipers; seating capacity of 5, front bucket seats with tilt adjustable headrests, driver seat includes 4-way direction control with easy entry feature, passenger seat includes 4-way direction control with easy entry feature; full folding rear bench seat with adjustable rear headrest; front height adjustable seatbelts; vinyl seats, full cloth headliner, full vinyl floor covering; interior lights include dome light, front and rear reading lights; sport steering wheel; passenger side vanity

TAHOE — CHEVROLET

CODE	DESCRIPTION	INVOICE	MSRP

mirror; day-night rearview mirror; glove box with light, front cupholder, interior concealed storage, driver and passenger door bins; vinyl cargo floor, cargo net, cargo light; colored grille, black side window moldings, black front windshield molding, black rear window molding, black door handles.

4WD 2-DOOR (in addition to or instead of 2WD 2-DOOR equipment): Part-time 4 wheel drive, auto locking hub control and manual shift, 3.42 axle ratio; front suspension with anti-roll bar, front torsion springs, front torsion bar; tow hooks; front and rear 16" x 6.5" wheels.

2WD 4-DOOR (in addition to or instead of 2WD 2-DOOR equipment): Rear wheel drive; front coil springs; roof rack; aero-composite headlamps; front and rear 15" x 7" alloy wheels; underbody mounted full-size temporary spare wheel; air conditioning; AM/FM stereo with cassette, 8 performance speakers, automatic equalizer, theft deterrent; cruise control; child safety rear door locks; compass; deep tinted windows, power front windows with driver 1-touch down, power rear windows; rear window defroster; seating capacity of 6, 60-40 split-bench front seat with center armrest with storage, driver seat includes power lumbar support, passenger seat includes power lumbar support; 60-40 folding rear split-bench seat with center storage armrest; front and rear height adjustable seatbelts; premium cloth seats, cloth door trim insert, carpet floor covering with rubber floor mats, deluxe sound insulation; interior lights include 4 door curb lights; leather-wrapped steering wheel; illuminated driver's side vanity mirror; dual auxiliary visors; auto-dimming rearview mirror; 2 seat back storage pockets; carpeted cargo floor, cargo cover; chrome grille.

4WD 4-DOOR (in addition to or instead of 2WD 4-DOOR equipment): Part-time 4 wheel drive with auto locking hub control and manual shift; front torsion springs, front torsion bar, rear with anti-roll bar; tow hooks.

Base Prices

CC10516-ZW9 2WD 2-door		20637	23585
CK10516-ZW9 4WD 2-door		22912	26185
CC10706-ZW9 2WD 4-door		25712	29385
CK10706-ZW9 4WD 4-door		27987	31985
Destination Charge:		640	640

Accessories

Code	Description	Invoice	MSRP
GU6	3.42 Axle Ratio (2WD)	NC	NC
GT4	3.73 Axle Ratio	116	135
	NOT AVAILABLE with (KC4) engine oil cooler, (Z82) HD Trailering Equipment.		
AG9	6-Way Power Driver's Seat (2WD 2-door)	206	240
	REQUIRES A95. NOT AVAILABLE with 1SB, 1SC.		
C60	Air Conditioning (2-door)	727	845
	NOT AVAILABLE with (YG6) air conditioning not desired.		
YG6	Air Conditioning Not Desired (2-door)	NC	NC
	NOT AVAILABLE with 1SB, 1SC, C60, C49.		
NP8	Autotrac Transfer Case (4WD)	344	400
	REQUIRES (1SA and ZQ3) or 1SB or 1SC.		
BVE	Black Side Step Running Boards	236	275
	Supports 600 lbs. Dealer installed. REQUIRES (1SB) Preferred Equipment Group 1SB or (1SC) Preferred Equipment Group 1SC.		

CHEVROLET — TAHOE

CODE	DESCRIPTION	INVOICE	MSRP
YF5	**California Emissions**	146	170
	Required for all vehicles to be registered in the State of California. NOT AVAILABLE with (L56) engine.		
DF2	**Camper Type Mirrors (2-door)**	46	53
	7.5" x 10.5" stainless steel. NOT AVAILABLE with (1SB) Preferred Equipment Group 1SB, (1SC) Preferred Equipment Group 1SC.		
DF2	**Camper Type Mirrors (2-door)**	(39)	(45)
	7.5" x 10.5" stainless steel. NOT AVAILABLE with (1SA) Preferred Equipment Group 1SA, (BYP) Sport Package.		
V10	**Cold Climate Package**	28	33
	Includes engine block heater. NOT AVAILABLE with (L56) engine.		
ZM9	**Comfort & Convenience Package (2-door)**	783	910
	Includes carpeted floor mats, carpeted/vinyl reversible cargo mat, electrochromic rearview mirror, heated seats, Bilstein shocks with premium ride, integrated Homelink transmitter, heated mirrors. REQUIRES (A95) seats. NOT AVAILABLE with (1SA) Preferred Equipment Group 1SA, (1SB) Preferred Equipment Group 1SB.		
ZM9	**Comfort & Convenience Package (4-door)**	1462	1700
	Includes carpeted floor mats, carpeted/vinyl reversible cargo mat, electrochromic rearview mirror, heated seats, Bilstein shocks with premium ride, integrated Homelink transmitter, dual illuminated visor vanity mirrors, front and rear air conditioning. REQUIRES (A95) seats. NOT AVAILABLE with (1SB) Preferred Equipment Group 1SB.		
ZQ3	**Convenience Group (2-door)**	329	383
	Includes speed control, tilt steering.		
ZY2	**Conventional Two-Tone Paint**	172	200
	NOT AVAILABLE with (BYP) Sport Package on 2-door.		
A95	**Custom Cloth Highback Bucket Seats**	204	237
	Includes power lumbar, floor console and overhead console. NOT AVAILABLE with (1SA) Preferred Equipment Group 1SA, (1SC) Preferred Equipment Group 1SC, (1SB) Preferred Equipment Group 1SB.		
AJ1	**Deep Tinted Glass (2-door)**	185	215
	NOT AVAILABLE with (1SB) Preferred Equipment Group 1SB, (1SC) Preferred Equipment Group 1SC.		
AJ1	**Deep Tinted Glass (4-door)**	262	305
	Rear doors, quarter glass and cargo doors. NOT AVAILABLE with (1SB) Preferred Equipment Group 1SB, (1SC) Preferred Equipment Group 1SC.		
C49	**Electric rear window defogger (2-door)**	132	154
	REQUIRES 1SA and C60. NOT AVAILABLE with YG6.		
KC4	**Engine Oil Cooler**	116	135
	NOT AVAILABLE with (L56) engine, (GT4) 3.73 axle ratio, (Z82) HD Trailering Equipment.		
L56	**Engine: 6.5L V8 Turbo Diesel (4WD 2-door)**	2460	2860
	Includes 4-speed HD automatic transmission; HD auxiliary transmission cooler, GVWR 6450 lbs., HD auxiliary battery. NOT AVAILABLE with KC4, K47, V10, BYP, F60, Z82, YF5.		

TAHOE — CHEVROLET

CODE	DESCRIPTION	INVOICE	MSRP
NC7	**Federal Emission Override**	NC	NC
	For vehicles that will be registered or leased in California, New York, Massachusetts or Connecticut, but sold by retailers outside those states. REQUIRES (YF5) California Emissions.		
C69	**Front & Rear Air Conditioning (4-door)**	473	550
	Includes dual controls.		
KNP	**HD Auxiliary Transmission Cooler**	83	96
	REQUIRES (GU6) 3.42 axle ratio. NOT AVAILABLE with (Z82) Trailering Equipment.		
F60	**HD Front Springs (2-door)**	54	63
	NOT AVAILABLE with (1SA) Preferred Equipment Group 1SA, (L56) engine, (Z82) HD Trailering Equipment.		
Z82	**HD Trailering Equipment with GT4**	267	310
	Includes trailer hitch platform, wiring harness, HD auxiliary transmission cooler. REQUIRES GT4. NOT AVAILABLE with L56, KC4, Z82.		
Z82	**HD Trailering Equipment with GU4 (2WD 2-door)**	300	349
	Includes trailer hitch platform, wiring harness, engine oil cooler.		
Z82	**HD Trailering Equipment with GU6**	383	445
	Includes trailer hitch platform, wiring harness, engine oil cooler, HD auxiliary transmission cooler. REQUIRES GU6. NOT AVAILABLE with L56, GT4, Z82.		
Z82	**HD Trailering Equipment with L56 (4WD 2-door)**	184	214
	Includes trailer hitch platform and wiring harness. REQUIRES (L56) engine. NOT AVAILABLE with (F60) HD front springs.		
K47	**High Capacity Air Cleaner**	22	25
	NOT AVAILABLE with (L56) engine.		
G80	**Locking Differential**	217	252
	REQUIRES (GU6) 3.42 Axle Ratio.		
Z71	**On/Off Road Chassis Equipment (4WD 2-door)**	344	400
	Includes skid plate package, Bilstein shock absorbers. REQUIRES QBN or QBX or QGC or QGD. NOT AVAILABLE with 1SA.		
1SA	**Preferred Equipment Group 1SA (2WD)**	NC	NC
	Includes Base Decor Package. REQUIRES YG6 or C60. NOT AVAILABLE with UNO, UPO, A95, DF2, ZM9, F60.		
1SA	**Preferred Equipment Group 1SA (4WD)**	NC	NC
	Includes Base Decor Package. REQUIRES YG6 or C60. NOT AVAILABLE with Z71, UNO, UPO, A95, BYP, DF2, ZM9, F60.		
1SB	**Preferred Equipment Group 1SB (2WD 2-door)**	3757	4369
	Includes LS Decor Package, ETR AM/FM stereo with cassette, seek-scan; remote keyless entry, 6-way power driver's seat. NOT AVAILABLE with YG6, UM6, A95, P06, DF2, ZM9.		
1SB	**Preferred Equipment Group 1SB (2WD 4-door)**	NC	NC
	Includes LS Decor Package, AM/FM stereo with seek-scan and cassette, remote keyless entry, 6-way power driver's seat. NOT AVAILABLE with A95, ZM9, UM6, C69, AJ1, B85.		

CHEVROLET TAHOE

CODE	DESCRIPTION	INVOICE	MSRP
1SB	**Preferred Equipment Group 1SB (4WD 2-door)**	3757	4369
	Includes LS Decor Package, ETR AM/FM stereo with cassette, seek-scan; remote keyless entry, 6-way power driver's seat. NOT AVAILABLE with YG6, UM6, A95, P06, DF2, ZM9.		
1SB	**Preferred Equipment Group 1SB (4WD 4-door)**	NC	NC
	Includes LS Decor Package, AM/FM stereo with seek-scan and cassette, remote keyless entry, 6-way power driver's seat. NOT AVAILABLE with (A95) seats, (ZM9) Comfort and Convenience Package.		
1SC	**Preferred Equipment Group 1SC (2WD 2-door)**	4918	5719
	Includes remote keyless entry, 6-way power driver's seat, LT Decor Package: up-level door trim panels, leather seat trim, ETR AM/FM stereo with CD and cassette, 60/40 split-bench seat. NOT AVAILABLE with YG6, UM6, UNO, A95, P06, DF2.		
1SC	**Preferred Equipment Group 1SC (2WD 4-door)**	1161	1350
	Includes remote keyless entry, 6-way power driver's seat, LT Decor Package: up-level door trim panels, leather seat trim, ETR AM/FM stereo with CD and cassette, 60/40 split bench seat. NOT AVAILABLE with A95, UM6, UNO, C69, AJ1, B85.		
1SC	**Preferred Equipment Group 1SC (4WD 2-door)**	4918	5719
	Includes remote keyless entry, 6-way power driver's seat, LT Decor Package: up-level door trim panels, leather seat trim, ETR AM/FM stereo with CD and cassette, 60/40 split-bench seat. NOT AVAILABLE with YG6, UM6, UNO, A95, P06, DF2.		
1SC	**Preferred Equipment Group 1SC (4WD 4-door)**	1161	1350
	Includes remote keyless entry, 6-way power driver's seat, LT Decor Package: up-level door trim panels, leather seat trim, ETR AM/FM stereo with CD and cassette, 60/40 split bench seat. NOT AVAILABLE with (A95) seats, (UNO) radio.		
UM6	**Radio: AM/FM Stereo with Cassette (2-door)**	126	147
	Includes digital clock. NOT AVAILABLE with 1SB, 1SC.		
UN0	**Radio: AM/FM Stereo with CD**	86	100
	Includes digital clock, theft lock, automatic tone control, speed compensated volume and enhanced performance speaker system. NOT AVAILABLE with (1SA) Preferred Equipment Group 1SA, (1SC) Preferred Equipment Group 1SC, (UP0) radio.		
UP0	**Radio: AM/FM Stereo with CD & Cassette**	172	200
	Includes seek-scan, digital clock, theft lock, automatic tone control, speed compensated volume and enhanced performance speaker system. NOT AVAILABLE with (1SA) Preferred Equipment Group 1SA, (1SC) Preferred Equipment Group 1SC, (UNO) radio.		
P06	**Rally Wheel Trim (2-door)**	52	60
	NOT AVAILABLE with 1SB, 1SC, N90, PF4.		
ZP6	**Rear Window Equipment (2-door)**	240	279
	Includes rear window wiper/washer, electric rear window defogger. REQUIRES (1SA) Preferred Equipment Group 1SA.		
ZP6	**Rear Window Equipment (2-door)**	NC	NC
	Includes rear window wiper/washer, electric rear window defogger. REQUIRES (1SB) Preferred Equipment Group 1SB or (1SC) Preferred Equipment Group 1SC.		
NZZ	**Skid Plate Package (4WD 2-door)**	194	225
	Includes fuel tank, front differential and transfer case shields.		
NZZ	**Skid Plate Package (4WD 4-door)**	82	95
	Includes fuel tank, front differential and transfer case shields.		

TAHOE   CHEVROLET

CODE	DESCRIPTION	INVOICE	MSRP
BYP	Sport Package (4WD 2-door)	260	302
	Includes black front air dam, black mirrors, wheel flare moldings, dark argent grille, dark argent bumpers with rub strip, sport decals, conventional two-tone paint. NOT AVAILABLE with 1SA, L56, QBN, QBX, QGD, DF2.		
QFN	Tires: LT235/75R15 AS WOL SBR (2WD)	120	140
QBN	Tires: LT245/75R16C AT BSW SBR (4WD 2-door)	47	55
	NOT AVAILABLE with QBX, QGC, QGD, BYP.		
QBX	Tires: LT245/75R16C AT WOL SBR (4WD 2-door)	155	180
	NOT AVAILABLE with QBN, QGC, QGD, BYP.		
QGB	Tires: P245/75R16 AT WOL (4WD 4-door)	120	140
QGC	Tires: P265/75R16 AT BSW SBR (4WD 2-door)	163	190
	REQUIRES (1SA and PF4) or 1SB or 1SC. NOT AVAILABLE with QBN, QBX, QGD.		
QGD	Tires: P265/75R16 AT WOL SBR (4WD 2-door)	271	315
	REQUIRES (1SA and PF4) or 1SB or 1SC. NOT AVAILABLE with QBN, QBX, QGC, BYP.		
V76	Tow Hooks (front) (2WD)	33	38
B71	Wheel Flare Moldings (4WD 2-door)	155	180
	NOT AVAILABLE with (BYP) Sport Package.		
N90	Wheels: Aluminum (2WD 2-door)	267	310
	Includes steel spare. NOT AVAILABLE with (PO6) rally wheel trim.		
PF4	Wheels: Aluminum (4WD 2-door)	267	310
	Includes steel spare. NOT AVAILABLE with (PO6) rally wheel trim.		

For expert advice in selecting/buying/leasing a new car, call
1-900-AUTOPRO
($2.00 per minute)

CHEVROLET TRACKER

| CODE | DESCRIPTION | INVOICE | MSRP |

1998 TRACKER

1998 Chevrolet Tracker 2-Door 4x4

What's New?

Geo is gone, so all Trackers are now badged as Chevrolets. The LSi models are dropped, though an LSi equipment package is available on Base models. Two new colors are available. Second-generation airbags are standard.

Review

To the chagrin of Chevrolet dealers, the redesigned Tracker has been slightly delayed. As a result, the 1997 model is carried over until an all-new design arrives early next year. The new truck will be slightly larger and more powerful, but is not slated to get the V6 engine that will be optional in its twin, the Suzuki Sidekick. That's too bad, because the Tracker is quite underpowered, particularly in four-door guise.

Due to its carryover status, changes for 1997 are limited. Since General Motors decided to kill the import-oriented Geo brand, the Tracker now wears a Chevy bowtie on its bonnet. The uplevel LSi trim level has been dropped, though most of the items from that model are available on base Trackers for 1998. Purple Graphite and California Gold have been added to the color chart. Prices have been set at or near 1997 levels in an effort to make the Tracker more attractive to folks cross-shopping the hot-selling Kia Sportage, Toyota RAV4 and Honda CR-V.

Fun-in-the-sun takes on fresh meaning behind the wheel of a snug-but-cozy Tracker convertible, whether its engine is driving two wheels or four. A 16-valve engine powers all Tracker models, sending out 95 horsepower. Naturally, the optional automatic transmission saps much of that strength.

Short and stubby, these friendly little vehicles maneuver easily but handle with a very light, sometimes twitchy touch on both the highway and off-road. They're more solidly built than they appear at first glance—not at all like a toy—and deliver a passably pleasant ride most of the time. Differing little from the Suzuki Sidekick, Trackers look and feel substantial, though during off-road driving, the door frames on the four-door shudder just enough to let in a fine silt of dust that coats every plastic interior trim piece. Front seats are firm but lack leg support, and wear nice-looking upholstery. The rear seat of four-door models is surprisingly comfortable for two adults. Dual cupholders and a storage tray sit in the center console.

TRACKER   CHEVROLET

| CODE | DESCRIPTION | INVOICE | MSRP |

Convertibles have an "easy opening" top that folds in two ways: either the front half folds back like a sunroof, or the entire canvas top can be stowed for fully-open motoring. Though improved, putting the top up and down still isn't exactly a quickie operation. Several "expressions packages" feature color-keyed convertible tops and wheels, and a Tracker can be equipped to tow half a ton. Optional are automatic-locking hubs, which are nice to have if you switch often between two- and four-wheel drive.

Four-door models can be equipped with power windows, door locks and mirrors. Child security rear door locks are standard on the four-door, and daytime running lights are standard on all Trackers. The 1.6-liter engine provides barely enough power in convertibles; in the four-door the engine is severely overmatched. Interstate cruising requires putting the pedal nearly to the metal just to maintain speed.

Would you want the convertible as your sole vehicle? Probably not, but a soft top Tracker in the garage just might turn sunny summer days into a veritable binge of adventure. Practical-minded folks, on the other hand, might prefer the weather-tight construction of a hardtop model. Sadly, we can't recommend using a Tracker for anything but light duty in the flatlands. The 1.6-liter motor is zippy enough to keep up in city traffic, but a heavy load of passengers or cargo keeps the Tracker's breathless engine wound out tightly on slight inclines or at freeway speeds. With a bigger engine, lightly-equipped Trackers would certainly give the competition a run for the money.

Safety Data

Driver Airbag: *Standard*
Side Airbag: *Not Available*
Traction Control: *Not Available*
Driver Crash Test Grade: *Poor*

Passenger Airbag: *Standard*
4-Wheel ABS: *Optional*
Integrated Child Seat(s): *Not Available*
Passenger Crash Test Grade: *Average*

Standard Equipment

2WD CONVERTIBLE: 1.6L I-4 SOHC MPI 16-valve engine; 5-speed overdrive manual transmission; 390-amp battery; 55-amp alternator; rear wheel drive, 5.12 axle ratio; stainless steel exhaust; front independent strut suspension with anti-roll bar, front coil springs, front shocks, rear suspension with rear coil springs, rear shocks; manual re-circulating ball steering; front disc/rear drum brakes; 11.1 gal capacity fuel tank; skid plates; tailgate cargo door; manual convertible roof with roll-over protection; front and rear black bumpers with front and rear tow hooks, rear step bumper; monotone paint; aero-composite halogen headlamps with daytime running lights; additional exterior lights include center high mounted stop light; front and rear 15" x 5.5" silver styled steel wheels with hub wheel covers; P195/75SR15 BSW AS front and rear tires; outside rear mounted full-size conventional steel spare tire; radio prep and manual retractable antenna; fuel filler door; 1 power accessory outlet; analog instrumentation display includes tachometer gauge, water temp gauge, trip odometer; warning indicators include oil pressure, battery, lights on, key in ignition; dual airbags; tinted windows, fixed rear windows; fixed interval front windshield wipers; seating capacity of 4, front bucket seats with fixed adjustable headrests, driver seat includes 4-way direction control with easy entry feature, passenger seat includes 4-way direction control with easy entry feature; full folding rear bench seat; cloth seats, vinyl door trim insert, full carpet floor covering; interior lights include dome light; passenger side vanity mirror; day-night rearview mirror; partial floor console, locking glove box, front cupholder, instrument panel bin, driver and passenger door bins; carpeted cargo floor; body-colored grille, black front windshield molding, black door handles.

4WD CONVERTIBLE (in addition to or instead of 2WD CONVERTIBLE equipment): Part-time 4 wheel drive, manual locking hub control and manual shift; power steering.

2WD WAGON (in addition to or instead of 4WD CONVERTIBLE equipment): Rear wheel drive; 14.5 gal capacity fuel tank; conventional rear cargo door; child safety rear door locks; manual

CHEVROLET TRACKER

CODE	DESCRIPTION	INVOICE	MSRP

rear windows, fixed 1/4 vent windows; rear window defroster; tilt adjustable headrests; 60-40 folding rear bench seat; premium cloth seats, full cloth headliner; body-colored side window moldings, black rear window molding.

4WD WAGON (in addition to or instead of 2WD WAGON equipment): Part-time 4 wheel drive, manual locking hub control and manual shift.

Base Prices

Code	Description	Invoice	MSRP
CE10367	2WD Convertible	13000	13655
CJ10367	4WD Convertible	13952	14655
CE10305	2WD Wagon	14147	14860
CJ10305	4WD Wagon	14856	15605
	Destination Charge:	340	340

Accessories

Code	Description	Invoice	MSRP
MX1	3-Speed Automatic Transmission (Convertible)	556	625
	Includes 4.30 axle ratio.		
MX0	4-Speed Automatic Transmission (Wagon)	890	1000
JM4	4-Wheel Antilock Brakes	530	595
C60	Air Conditioning	832	935
	NOT AVAILABLE with (R6G) air conditioning not desired.		
R6G	Air Conditioning Not Desired	NC	NC
	NOT AVAILABLE with (1SB) Preferred Equipment Group 1SB, (C60) air conditioning, (1SC) Preferred Equipment Group 1SC.		
X6Z	Automatic Locking Hubs (4WD)	178	200
41T	Black Convertible Top (Convertible)	NC	NC
	NOT AVAILABLE with (WT3) Expressions Appearance Package, (10T) white convertible top.		
B84	Bodyside Moldings	76	85
YF5	California Emissions	151	170
	Automatically added to vehicles shipped to and/or sold to retailers in California. Out-of-state retailers must order on vehicles to be registered or leased in California. NOT AVAILABLE with (NG1) NY/MA/CT Emissions.		
K34	Cruise Control With Resume Speed	156	175
WT3	Expressions Appearance Package with 1SA (Convertible)	222	249
	Includes tan spare tire cover, tan decals, tan accents on styled wheel center caps or aluminum wheels, bodyside moldings, custom fabric seat trim, fold and stow bucket seats, tan convertible top. NOT AVAILABLE with 10T, 41T, WT3, 1SB.		
WT3	Expressions Appearance Package with 1SB (Convertible)	146	164
	Includes tan spare tire cover, tan decals, tan accents on styled wheel center caps or aluminum wheels, tan accents on bodyside and rocker moldings, custom fabric seat trim, fold and stow bucket seats, tan convertible top. NOT AVAILABLE with 10T, 41T, WT3, 1SA.		
B37	Front & Rear Color-Keyed Floor Mats (Convertible)	25	28
B58	Front & Rear Color-Keyed Floor Mats (Wagon)	36	40
NY7	Front Differential Skid Plate (4WD Convertible)	67	75

TRACKER — CHEVROLET

CODE	DESCRIPTION	INVOICE	MSRP
NG1	**NY/MA/CT Emissions**	151	170
	Automatically added to vehicles shipped to and/or sold to retailers in Massachusetts/New York/Connecticut. Out-of-state retailers must order on vehicles to be registered or leased in Massachusetts/New York/Connecticut. NOT AVAILABLE with (YF5) California Emissions.		
Z05	**Power Convenience Package (Wagon)**	516	580
	Includes power windows, power door locks, and power mirrors.		
N40	**Power Steering (2WD Convertible)**	258	290
	NOT AVAILABLE with (N51) power steering not desired.		
N51	**Power Steering Not Desired (2WD Convertible)**	NC	NC
	NOT AVAILABLE with (1SB) Preferred Equipment Group 1SB, (N40) power steering.		
1SA	**Preferred Equipment Group 1SA (2WD Convertible)**	NC	NC
	Includes vehicle with standard equipment. REQUIRES (10T or 41T) and (R6G or C60) and (N40 or N51). NOT AVAILABLE with ULO, UNO.		
1SA	**Preferred Equipment Group 1SA (2WD Wagon)**	NC	NC
	Includes vehicle with standard equipment. REQUIRES R6G or C60. NOT AVAILABLE with ULO, UNO.		
1SA	**Preferred Equipment Group 1SA (4WD Convertible)**	NC	NC
	Includes vehicle with standard equipment. REQUIRES (10T or 41T) and (R6G or C60). NOT AVAILABLE with ULO, UNO.		
1SA	**Preferred Equipment Group 1SA (4WD Wagon)**	NC	NC
	Includes vehicle with standard equipment. REQUIRES R6G or C60. NOT AVAILABLE with ULO, UNO.		
1SB	**Preferred Equipment Group 1SB (2WD Convertible)**	1463	1644
	Includes air conditioning, AM/FM stereo with seek-scan, clock; front and rear color-keyed floor mats, bodyside moldings, power steering. REQUIRES 10T or 41T. NOT AVAILABLE with R6G, N51, ULO, UNO.		
1SB	**Preferred Equipment Group 1SB (2WD Wagon)**	1216	1366
	Includes air conditioning, AM/FM stereo with seek-scan, clock; front and rear color-keyed floor mats, bodyside moldings. NOT AVAILABLE with (R6G) air conditioning not desired, (ULO) radio, (UNO) radio.		
1SB	**Preferred Equipment Group 1SB (4WD Convertible)**	1205	1354
	Includes air conditioning, AM/FM stereo with seek-scan, clock; front and rear color-keyed floor mats, bodyside moldings. REQUIRES 10T or 41T. NOT AVAILABLE with R6G, ULO, UNO.		
1SB	**Preferred Equipment Group 1SB (4WD Wagon)**	1216	1366
	Includes air conditioning, AM/FM stereo with seek-scan, clock; front and rear color-keyed floor mats, bodyside moldings. NOT AVAILABLE with (R6G) air conditioning not desired, (ULO) radio, (UNO) radio.		
1SC	**Preferred Equipment Group 1SC (2WD Wagon)**	1888	2121
	Includes air conditioning, AM/FM stereo with seek-scan, clock; front and rear color-keyed floor mats, bodyside moldings, cruise control with resume speed, Power Convenience Package. NOT AVAILABLE with (R6G) air conditioning not desired, (UNO) radio, (ULO) radio.		

CHEVROLET TRACKER

CODE	DESCRIPTION	INVOICE	MSRP
1SC	**Preferred Equipment Group 1SC (4WD Wagon)**	2066	2321
	Includes air conditioning, AM/FM stereo with seek-scan, clock; front and rear color-keyed floor mats, bodyside moldings, cruise control with resume speed, Power Convenience Package, automatic locking hubs. NOT AVAILABLE with (R6G) air conditioning not desired, (UN0) radio, (UL0) radio.		
UL1	**Radio: AM/FM Stereo**	272	306
	Includes 4 speakers. NOT AVAILABLE with (UL0) radio, (UN0) radio.		
UL0	**Radio: AM/FM Stereo with Cassette**	196	220
	Includes tone select, digital clock, and 4 speakers. NOT AVAILABLE with (UL0) radio, (UN0) radio, (1SA) Preferred Equipment Group 1SA.		
UL0	**Radio: AM/FM Stereo with Cassette**	468	526
	Includes tone select, digital clock, and 4 speakers. NOT AVAILABLE with UL1, UL0, UN0, 1SB, 1SC.		
UN0	**Radio: AM/FM Stereo with CD**	285	320
	Includes tone select and 4 speakers. NOT AVAILABLE with (UL0) radio, (UN0) radio, (1SA) Preferred Equipment Group 1SA.		
UN0	**Radio: AM/FM Stereo with CD**	557	626
	Includes tone select and 4 speakers. NOT AVAILABLE with UL1, UL0, UN0, 1SB, 1SC.		
C25	**Rear Window Wiper/Washer (Wagon)**	111	125
QA4	**Wheels: 15" Alloy**	325	365
	Includes tan-colored accents when ordered with WT3 Expressions Color Appearance Package.		
10T	**White Convertible Top (Convertible)**	NC	NC
	NOT AVAILABLE with (WT3) Expressions Appearance Package, (41T) black convertible top.		

Take Advantage of Warranty Gold!

Savings up to 50% off Dealer's Extended Warranty Prices. Protect and enhance YOUR investment with the best extended warranty available.

Call Toll Free 1-800-580-9889

VENTURE CHEVROLET

| CODE | DESCRIPTION | INVOICE | MSRP |

1998 VENTURE

1998 Chevrolet Venture

What's New?

Venture is the first minivan to get side-impact airbags. Other changes include the availability of a cargo van edition, a wider variety of dual door models, and an optional power sliding door on regular wheelbase vans. Power rear window vents are also added for 1998. Front airbags deploy with less force thanks to second-generation technology.

Review

If you think Chevrolet's minivan resembles a popular household mini-vac, think again. The hideous Lumina Minivan has gone to that plastic recycling center in car heaven, replaced by a conservative, steel-bodied family hauler that was developed in concert with GM's European Opel division. The Venture, as the van is so aptly monikered, is an outstanding entry in the minivan market, featuring an available driver's side sliding door, optional traction control, optional integrated child seats, standard anti-lock brakes, and enough power to make it fun to drive.

Two versions are available on two different wheelbases: base or LS trim on a 112-inch or 120-inch wheelbase. Choose between three- or four-door body styles, and all Ventures come equipped with a 180-horsepower 3.4-liter V6 engine. Designed to satisfy consumers on either side of the Atlantic Ocean, the Venture surprises with a communicative chassis, sharp steering, and nimble handling while providing room inside for up to seven passengers and a good amount of their belongings.

Like to drink and drive (soda, water, or juice, that is)? The Venture accommodates with cup and drink box holders galore. Don't worry too much about Junior spilling Hawaiian Punch either, because Chevrolet Scotchgards all fabrics at the factory. Several seating configurations are available, with the most user-friendly but least comfortable setup being the multiconfigurable modular buckets. Weighing just 38 pounds each, they're easy to install, remove, and re-arrange, but they're mighty uncomfortable for adults. Front buckets are much more soothing for elder backsides.

Cool stuff includes optional rear seat audio controls that allow rear passengers to listen to a CD via headphones while front passengers catch NPR on the radio. Also available are rear seat heat and air conditioning controls, a load-leveling suspension complete with auxiliary air

CHEVROLET VENTURE

hose, and daytime running lamps that illuminate parking lights instead of headlights. Uncool is the toothy chrome eggcrate grille up front that screams "MOMMOBILE." At least there's no fake wood siding, no body cladding, and no gold package.

Our main reservation about the Venture concerns crashworthiness. Last year, the Insurance Institute for Highway Safety conducted 40 mph offset crash tests of the Pontiac Trans Sport, which is essentially a clone of the Venture. The Trans Sport did not fare well in the test. True, there are no federal regulations in place regarding offset crashworthiness, but the Ford Windstar has performed wonderfully in both offset and head-on crash testing. The National Highway and Traffic Safety Administration crashed a Venture head-on into a fixed barrier later in the year, and the van performed well. Contradictory results mean consumers will have to weigh this van more carefully against the competition.

One new feature added to the Venture for 1998 might sway favor in Chevy's direction. This stylish minivan is the first of its ilk to receive standard side-impact airbags for both front passengers. Other changes include the addition of a cargo van model, and expanded availability of dual door and power sliding door versions. Rear vent windows are now power operated, and second row captain's chairs are newly available with seven-passenger seating.

We like the Venture, in case you hadn't already guessed. Pontiac and Oldsmobile serve up versions of the same van (Oldsmobile's is called Silhouette), and any of the three would make a dandy alternative to Chrysler and import minivans. In the case of the Chevy, though, we'll wait for stylists to offer an LTZ model with body-color grille (yeah, like that's gonna happen).

Safety Data

Driver Airbag: *Standard*
Side Airbag: *Standard*
Traction Control: *Optional*
Driver Crash Test Grade: *Good*

Passenger Airbag: *Standard*
4-Wheel ABS: *Standard*
Integrated Child Seat(s): *Optional*
Passenger Crash Test Grade: *Good*

Standard Equipment

VENTURE 3-DOOR: 3.4L V-6 OHV SMPI 12-valve engine; 4-speed electronic overdrive automatic transmission with lock-up; 600-amp battery with run down protection; 105-amp alternator; front wheel drive, 3.29 axle ratio; stainless steel exhaust; comfort ride suspension, front independent strut suspension with anti-roll bar, front coil springs, front shocks, rear non-independent suspension with anti-roll bar, rear coil springs, rear shocks; power rack-and-pinion steering with vehicle speed-sensing assist; front disc/rear drum brakes with 4 wheel anti-lock braking system; 20 gal capacity fuel tank; 3 doors with sliding right rear passenger door, liftback rear cargo door; front and rear body-colored bumpers with black rub strip, rear step bumper; black bodyside molding; monotone paint; aero-composite halogen fully automatic headlamps with daytime running lights and delay-off feature; additional exterior lights include center high mounted stop light, underhood light; driver and passenger power remote black folding outside mirrors; front and rear 15" x 6" steel wheels with full wheel covers; P205/70SR15 BSW AS front and rear tires; underbody mounted compact steel spare wheel; air conditioning, air filter; AM/FM stereo with clock, seek-scan, 4 speakers and window grid antenna; power door locks, child safety rear door locks, remote hatch release; 3 power accessory outlets; analog instrumentation display includes oil pressure gauge, water temp gauge, volt gauge, PRNDL in instrument panel, trip odometer; warning indicators include oil pressure, water temp warning, low oil level, low coolant, lights on, key in ignition, low fuel; dual airbags, door mounted side airbags for front passengers; tinted windows, manual 1/4 vent windows; variable intermittent front windshield wipers, fixed interval rear wiper; seating capacity of 7, front bucket seats with tilt adjustable headrests and front armrests, driver seat includes 6-way direction control with easy entry feature, passenger seat includes 4-way direction control; removeable full folding 2nd row bench seat; 3rd row removeable full folding bench seat; front height adjustable seatbelts; cloth seats, cloth door trim insert, full cloth headliner, full carpet floor covering with carpeted floor mats; interior lights include dome light; steering wheel with tilt adjustment; vanity mirrors; day-night rearview mirror; mini

VENTURE CHEVROLET

| CODE | DESCRIPTION | INVOICE | MSRP |

overhead console with storage, locking glove box with light, front and rear cupholders, instrument panel covered bin, dashboard storage, 2 seat back storage pockets, driver and passenger door bins; carpeted cargo floor, plastic cargo lid, cargo tie downs, cargo light; chrome grille, black side window moldings, black front windshield molding, black rear window molding, black door handles.

4-DOOR (in addition to or instead of 3-DOOR equipment): 40-60 folding and reclining split-bench 2nd row seat; 50-50 folding and reclining split-bench 3rd row seat; deluxe sound insulation; cargo net.

3-DOOR EXTENDED (in addition to or instead of 4-DOOR equipment): 25 gal capacity fuel tank.

4-DOOR EXTENDED (in addition to or instead of 3-DOOR EXTENDED equipment): Deluxe sound insulation; cargo net.

Base Prices

Code	Description	Invoice	MSRP
1UN06	3-door	18325	20249
1UN16	4-door	19393	21429
1UM06	3-door Extended	19610	21669
1UM16	4-door Extended	20144	22259
	Destination Charge:	570	570

Accessories

Code	Description	Invoice	MSRP
AG1	6-Way Power Driver's Seat	232	270
	NOT AVAILABLE with 1SA, 1SB, 1SE, 1SF.		
ABD	7 Passenger Seating with 2nd Row Captains Chairs	228	265
	Includes 3rd row split-bench seat. NOT AVAILABLE with 1SA, 1SB, AN2, AN5, ABB, 1SE, 1SF.		
ABB	7 Passenger Seating with Rear Buckets	99	115
	NOT AVAILABLE with 1SA, 1SB, ABD, 1SE, 1SF.		
ABA	7 Passenger Seating with Split-Back Rear (Regular Length)	288	335
	Includes split folding rear seat. NOT AVAILABLE with (1SA) Preferred Equipment Group 1SA, (1SC) Preferred Equipment Group 1SC.		
ABA	7 Passenger Seating with Split-Back Rear (Regular Length)	NC	NC
	Includes split folding rear seat. NOT AVAILABLE with (1SA) Preferred Equipment Group 1SA, (1SB) Preferred Equipment Group 1SB.		
YF5	California Emissions	146	170
	Automatically added to vehicles shipped to and/or sold to retailers in California. Out-of-state retailers must order on vehicles to be registered or leased in California. NOT AVAILABLE with (NG1) MA/NY/CT Emissions.		
AJ1	Deep Tinted Glass	236	275
	Includes B-pillar blackout treatment with dark granite (32U) or dark sapphire (28U) paint. REQUIRES (C49) electric rear window defogger. NOT AVAILABLE with (R9W) rear window defogger not desired.		
AN5	Dual Integrated Child Safety Seats	194	225
	NOT AVAILABLE with (ABD) 7 passenger seating with 2nd row captains chairs, (AN2) integrated child safety seat.		

CHEVROLET VENTURE

CODE	DESCRIPTION	INVOICE	MSRP
C49	Electric Rear Window Defogger	146	170

NOT AVAILABLE with (R9W) rear window defogger not desired.

K05	Engine Block Heater	17	20
C34	Front & Rear Air Conditioning (Extended Length)	387	450

REQUIRES (AJ1) deep tinted glass and (C49) electric rear window defogger. NOT AVAILABLE with (R9W) rear window defogger not desired.

AN2	Integrated Child Safety Seat	108	125

NOT AVAILABLE with (ABD) 7 passenger seating with 2nd row captains chairs, (AN5) dual integrated child safety seats.

V54	Luggage Carrier	150	175

NOT AVAILABLE with (1SA) Preferred Equipment Group 1SA.

NG1	MA/NY/CT Emissions	146	170

Automatically added to vehicles shipped to and/or sold to retailers in Massachusetts/New York/Connecticut. Out-of-state retailers must order on vehicles to be registered or leased in Massachusetts/New York/Connecticut. NOT AVAILABLE with (YF5) California Emissions.

E58	Power Sliding Door	374	435

Passenger side. Includes rear vent power window. REQUIRES 1SF. NOT AVAILABLE with 1SA, 1SC, 1SE, 1SG, 1SH.

E58	Power Sliding Door	331	385

Passenger side. NOT AVAILABLE with 1SA, 1SB, 1SE, 1SF.

1SA	Preferred Equipment Group 1SA (Regular Length)	NC	NC

Includes vehicle with standard equipment. REQUIRES C49 or R9W. NOT AVAILABLE with DK6, E58, V54, ABA, R7D, AG1, ABB, ABD, FE3, XPU, P42, NW9, V92.

1SB	Preferred Equipment Group 1SB (Regular Length)	559	650

Includes power windows with driver's side express down, remote keyless entry with panic alarm, speed control with resume speed. REQUIRES C49 or R9W. NOT AVAILABLE with DK6, E58, R7D, AG1, ABB, ABD, FE3, ABA, NW9, V92.

1SC	Preferred Equipment Group 1SC (3-door)	1324	1540

Includes power windows with driver's side express down, remote keyless entry with panic alarm, speed control with resume speed, LS Decor: cargo net, custom interior panel trim, adjustable headrests, driver's and passenger's lumbar support, custom cloth seat trim, rear vent power window, AM/FM stereo with cassette and seek-scan, 7 passenger seating with split-back rear bench seats. REQUIRES C49 or R9W. NOT AVAILABLE with UM6, ABA, E58.

1SC	Preferred Equipment Group 1SC (4-door)	1036	1205

Includes power windows with driver's side express down, remote keyless entry with panic alarm, speed control with resume speed, LS Decor: cargo net, custom interior panel trim, adjustable headrests, driver's and passenger's lumbar support, custom cloth seat trim, rear vent power window, AM/FM stereo with cassette and seek-scan. REQUIRES C49 or R9W. NOT AVAILABLE with E58, UM6.

1SE	Preferred Equipment Group 1SE (Extended Length)	NC	NC

Includes vehicle with standard equipment. REQUIRES C49 or R9W. NOT AVAILABLE with DK6, E58, R7D, AG1, ABB, ABD, FE3, XPU, P42, NW9, V92.

VENTURE — CHEVROLET

CODE	DESCRIPTION	INVOICE	MSRP
1SF	**Preferred Equipment Group 1SF (Extended Length)**	559	650
	Includes speed control with resume speed, power windows with driver's side express down, remote keyless entry with panic alarm. REQUIRES C49 or R9W. NOT AVAILABLE with DK6, E58, R7D, AG1, ABB, ABD, FE3, NW9, V92.		
1SG	**Preferred Equipment Group 1SG (Extended Length)**	1036	1205
	Includes speed control with resume speed, power windows with driver's side express down, remote keyless entry with panic alarm, LS Decor: cargo net, custom interior panel trim, adjustable headrests, driver's and passenger's lumbar support, custom cloth seat trim, rear vent power window, AM/FM stereo with cassette and seek-scan. REQUIRES C49 or R9W. NOT AVAILABLE with E58, UM6, FE3.		
1SH	**Preferred Equipment Group 1SH (Extended)**	2065	2401
	Includes speed control with resume speed, power windows with driver's side express down, remote keyless entry with panic alarm, LS Decor: cargo net, custom interior panel trim, adjustable headrests, driver's and passenger's lumbar, custom cloth seat trim, rear vent power window, AM/FM stereo with cassette and seek-scan, 6-way power driver's seat, deep tinted glass, electric rear window defogger, P215/70R15 touring SBR tires, luggage carrier, roof console with driver's information center, dual illuminated visor vanity mirrors, NOT AVAILABLE with E58, UM6, R9W, XPU, FE3.		
UL0	**Radio: AM/FM Stereo with Cassette**	232	270
	Includes digital clock, automatic tone control, theft lock and premium front and rear coaxial speakers. NOT AVAILABLE with UM6, UN0, UN7, 1SC, 1SG, or 1SH.		
UM6	**Radio: AM/FM Stereo with Cassette**	142	165
	Includes digital clock. NOT AVAILABLE with UL0, UN0, UN7, UK6, 1SC, 1SG, 1SH.		
UN7	**Radio: AM/FM Stereo with Cassette & CD**	404	470
	Includes seek-scan, cassette player with auto reverse, CD player, auto-tone control, digital clock, theft lock, premium front and rear coaxial speakers and speed compensated volume. REQUIRES 1SA or 1SB or 1SE or 1SF. NOT AVAILABLE with UL0, UM6, UN0.		
UN7	**Radio: AM/FM Stereo with Cassette & CD**	172	200
	Includes seek-scan, cassette player with auto reverse, CD player, auto-tone control, digital clock, theft lock, premium front and rear coaxial speakers and speed compensated volume. REQUIRES 1SC or 1SG or 1SH. NOT AVAILABLE with UL0, UM6, UN0.		
UN0	**Radio: AM/FM Stereo with CD**	318	370
	Includes auto-tone control, digital clock, theft lock, premium front and rear coaxial speakers and speed compensated volume. REQUIRES 1SA or 1SB or 1SE or 1SF. NOT AVAILABLE with UL0, UM6, UN7.		
UN0	**Radio: AM/FM Stereo with CD**	86	100
	Includes auto-tone control, digital clock, theft lock, premium front and rear coaxial speakers and speed compensated volume. REQUIRES 1SC or 1SG or 1SH. NOT AVAILABLE with UL0, UM6, UN7.		
UK6	**Rear Seat Audio Controls with Jacks**	103	120
	REQUIRES UL0 or UN0 or UN7. NOT AVAILABLE with UM6.		
R9W	**Rear Window Defogger Not Desired**	NC	NC
	NOT AVAILABLE with AJ1, C49, 1SH, C34.		

CHEVROLET VENTURE

CODE	DESCRIPTION	INVOICE	MSRP
DK6	Roof Console	233	271
	Includes driver's information center, dual illuminated visor vanity mirrors. NOT AVAILABLE with 1SA, 1SB, 1SE, 1SF.		
R7D	Safety & Security System (Extended Length)	211	245
	Includes theft deterrent system, P215/70R15 touring SBR self-sealing tires. NOT AVAILABLE with (1SE) Preferred Equipment Group 1SE, (1SF) Preferred Equipment Group 1SF.		
R7D	Safety & Security System (Regular Length)	245	285
	Includes theft deterrent system, P215/70R15 touring SBR self-sealing tires. NOT AVAILABLE with (1SA) Preferred Equipment Group 1SA, (1SB) Preferred Equipment Group 1SB.		
R7D	Safety & Security System with FE3	181	210
	Includes theft deterrent system, P215/70R15 touring SBR self-sealing tires. REQUIRES FE3. NOT AVAILABLE with 1SA, 1SB, 1SE, 1SF.		
P42	Self-Sealing Tires (Extended Length)	159	185
	Includes P215/70R15 touring SBR tires. NOT AVAILABLE with (1SE) Preferred Equipment Group 1SE.		
P42	Self-Sealing Tires (Regular Length)	194	225
	Includes P215/70R15 touring SBR tires. NOT AVAILABLE with (1SA) Preferred Equipment Group 1SA, (1SB) Preferred Equipment Group 1SB.		
XPU	Tires: P215/70R15 Touring SBR (Extended Length)	NC	NC
	NOT AVAILABLE with (1SE) Preferred Equipment Group 1SE, (1SF) Preferred Equipment Group 1SF, (1SG) Preferred Equipment Group 1SG.		
XPU	Tires: P215/70R15 Touring SBR (Extended Length)	30	35
	NOT AVAILABLE with (1SE) Preferred Equipment Group 1SE, (1SH) Preferred Equipment Group 1SH.		
XPU	Tires: P215/70R15 Touring SBR (Regular Length)	64	75
	NOT AVAILABLE with (1SA) Preferred Equipment Group 1SA.		
FE3	Touring Suspension Group with 1SC (Regular Length)	245	285
	Includes load leveling suspension with auxiliary air inflator, P215/70R15 touring SBR tires. NOT AVAILABLE with (1SA) Preferred Equipment Group 1SA, (1SB) Preferred Equipment Group 1SB.		
FE3	Touring Suspension Group with 1SG (Extended Length)	211	245
	Includes load leveling suspension with auxiliary air inflator, P215/70R15 touring SBR tires. NOT AVAILABLE with (1SE) Preferred Equipment Group 1SE, (1SF) Preferred Equipment Group 1SF, (1SH) Preferred Equipment Group 1SH.		
FE3	Touring Suspension Group with 1SH (Extended Length)	181	210
	Includes load leveling suspension with auxiliary air inflator, P215/70R15 touring SBR tires. NOT AVAILABLE with (1SE) Preferred Equipment Group 1SE, (1SF) Preferred Equipment Group 1SF, (1SG) Preferred Equipment Group 1SG.		
NW9	Traction Control	168	195
	NOT AVAILABLE with 1SA, 1SB, 1SE, 1SF.		
V92	Trailer Towing Package	129	150
	Includes HD transmission oil cooler, HD engine oil cooler. REQUIRES FE3. NOT AVAILABLE with 1SA, 1SB, 1SE, 1SF.		
PH3	Wheels: 15" Cast Aluminum	254	295

TOWN & COUNTRY   CHRYSLER

1998 TOWN & COUNTRY

1998 Chrysler Town & Country LXi

What's New?

Chrysler's luxury minivans get a few improvements this year, with the addition of a new Chrysler-signature grille, more powerful 3.8-liter V-6, high-performance headlights, and three fancy new colors.

Review

Elegance and expressiveness. Grace and grandeur. These are the words that describe Chrysler's posh rendition of the Dodge/Plymouth minivan.

Oh sure, you get the same fresh shape and interior space in a lower-priced Caravan or Voyager, the same car-like ride/handling qualities, the same practical virtues as a people and cargo hauler. What Chrysler adds to that mix is luxury: plenty of it—and that's enough to attract a fair share of extra customers to the Chrysler end of the minivan spectrum.

Town & Country customers have three distinct models to choose from: the LX model, an "ultimate" LXi that promises features ordinarily found only on luxury cars; the short-wheelbase (113.3-inch) SX version. The SX is Chrysler's sporty minivan. It offers cast aluminum wheels, touring tires, and a very inexpensive touring and handling package. Properly outfitted, the SX transforms into a quick, little sport van capable of embarrassing most sedan owners.

AWD is optional on the LX and LXi models of the T & C. Since these minivans only have 5" of ground clearance, they aren't meant for serious off-road adventure. They do, however, give drivers the security of knowing that their traction is improved when driving on slippery surfaces. They also make piloting the extended length minivans a little more fun, by evening out the weight distribution and providing some rear-wheel motive power. Chrysler's AWD minivans also replace the standard rear drum brakes with discs.

All three minivans feature seven-passenger seating, with an "Easy-Out" rollaway back seat. A newly revised 3.8-liter V-6 now offers 180 horsepower and 240 lbs.-ft. torque. This engine is standard in the LXi, and optional in its mates, which otherwise come with a 3.3-liter engine. Both engines drive a four-speed automatic transmission, which delivers neat and smooth gearchanges. Minivanners who do lots of highway cruising and Interstate hopping might be happier with the bigger engine, which lets the T & C pass and merge into traffic with greater confidence and briskness.

CHRYSLER TOWN & COUNTRY

Extras in the LXi edition include dual zone control heat/air conditioning, eight-way leather trimmed driver and passenger seats, plus a memory for both the seats and outside mirrors. A roof rack is standard on the LXi, and optional on the others. If you want luxury and spaciousness, but you just can't abide the thought of a boxy Volvo wagon or lethargic Audi A6, drop by your local Chrysler store and try the Town & Country on for size.

Safety Data

Driver Airbag: *Standard*
Side Airbag: *Not Available*
Traction Control: *Opt. (LX/SX); Std. (LXi)*
Driver Crash Test Grade: *Good (SX); Average (LX/LXi)*

Passenger Airbag: *Standard*
4-Wheel ABS: *Standard*
Integrated Child Seat(s): *Optional*
Passenger Crash Test Grade: *Good*

Standard Equipment

TOWN & COUNTRY SX: 3.3L V-6 OHV SMPI 12-valve engine; 4-speed electronic overdrive automatic transmission with lock-up; 500-amp battery; 120-amp HD alternator; front wheel drive, traction control, 3.61 axle ratio; stainless steel exhaust; firm ride suspension, front independent strut suspension with anti-roll bar, front coil springs, front shocks, rear non-independent suspension with rear leaf springs, rear shocks; power rack-and-pinion steering; front disc/rear drum brakes with 4 wheel anti-lock braking system; 20 gal capacity fuel tank; rear lip spoiler; 4 doors with sliding left rear passenger door, sliding right rear passenger door, liftback rear cargo door; front and rear body-colored bumpers with chrome bumper insert, rear step bumper; body-colored bodyside molding with chrome bodyside insert; monotone paint; aero-composite halogen headlamps with delay-off feature; additional exterior lights include front fog/driving lights, underhood light; driver and passenger power remote black folding outside mirrors; front and rear 16" x 6.5" silver alloy wheels; P215/65TR16 BSW AS front and rear tires; underbody mounted compact steel spare wheel; dual zone front air conditioning; AM/FM stereo with clock, seek-scan, cassette, 4 speakers and fixed antenna; cruise control with steering wheel controls; power door locks with remote keyless entry, child safety rear door locks; 2 power accessory outlets, driver foot rest; analog instrumentation display includes tachometer gauge, water temp gauge, compass, exterior temp, PRNDL in instrument panel, trip computer, trip odometer; warning indicators include oil pressure, water temp warning, battery, lights on, key in ignition, low fuel, low washer fluid, door ajar, trunk ajar; dual airbags; panic alarm; tinted windows, power front windows with driver 1-touch down, fixed rear windows, power 1/4 vent windows; variable intermittent front windshield wipers, variable intermittent rear wiper, rear window defroster; seating capacity of 7, front bucket seats with tilt adjustable headrests, driver and passenger armrests, driver seat includes 4-way direction control with lumbar support, passenger seat includes 4-way direction control with lumbar support; removeable reclining bucket 2nd row seats with adjustable rear headrests, 3rd row removeable full folding and reclining bench seat with adjustable headrests; front and rear height adjustable seatbelts; premium cloth seats, cloth door trim insert, full cloth headliner, full carpet floor covering with carpeted floor mats, wood trim; interior lights include dome light with fade, front reading lights, 2 door curb lights, illuminated entry; leather-wrapped steering wheel with tilt adjustment; dual illuminated vanity mirrors, dual auxiliary visors; day-night rearview mirror; full overhead console with storage, glove box with light, front and rear cupholders, instrument panel covered bin, 1 seat back storage pocket, driver and passenger door bins, front underseat tray; carpeted cargo floor, vinyl trunk lid, cargo light; chrome grille, black side window moldings, black front windshield molding, black rear window molding, body-colored door handles.

LX (in addition to or instead of SX equipment): Deluxe sound insulation.

AWD LX (in addition to or instead of LX equipment): 3.8L engine; 600-amp battery; full-time 4 wheel drive, 3.45 axle ratio; auto-levelling suspension.

TOWN & COUNTRY — CHRYSLER

LXi (in addition to or instead of LX equipment): 3.8L engine; traction control, 3.61 axle ratio; roof rack; body-colored bodyside cladding; fully automatic headlamps; full-size temporary spare wheel; rear air conditioning with separate controls, rear heater; premium stereo with single CD player, graphic equalizer; garage door opener; security system; deep tinted windows; heated wipers; driver seat includes 6-way power seat with lumbar support, passenger seat includes 6-way power seat with lumbar support; leather seats, leatherette door trim insert; memory on driver seat with 2 memory setting(s) including rearview mirror and exterior mirrors; ; auto-dimming rearview mirror.

LXi AWD (in addition to or instead of LXi equipment): 600-amp battery; full-time 4 wheel drive, 3.45 axle ratio; auto-levelling suspension.

Base Prices

Code	Description	Invoice	MSRP
NSYP52	SX	24218	26680
NSYP53	LX	24619	27135
NSCP53	LX AWD	27259	30135
NSYS53	LXi	28654	31720
NSCS53	LXi AWD	30744	34095
Destination Charge:		580	580

Accessories

Code	Description	Invoice	MSRP
DGB	4-Speed Automatic Transmission	NC	NC
CYR	7 Passenger Deluxe Seating with 2 Child Seats (All except SX)	NC	NC
	NOT AVAILABLE with (FL) seats, (25P) Quick Order Package 25P, (28P) Quick Order Package 28P.		
YCF	Border State (California) Emissions	145	170
	NOT AVAILABLE with (NAE) CA/CT/MA/NY Emissions.		
NAE	CA/CT/MA/NY Emissions	145	170
	Automatically coded. NOT AVAILABLE with 25F, 25H, YCF, 25P, 25R.		
PH2	Candy Apple Red Metallic Clear Coat	170	200
AAB	Climate Group III (LX FWD/LX AWD)	344	405
	Includes rear heater and air conditioning. NOT AVAILABLE with (4XN) rear air conditioning bypass, (25P) Quick Order Package 25P, (28P) Quick Order Package 28P.		
AA2	Convenience Group VI (SX/LX FWD/LX AWD)	204	240
	Includes security alarm, universal garage door opener. NOT AVAILABLE with 25F, 28F, 25P, 28P.		
NHK	Engine Block Heater	30	35
EGA	Engine: 3.3L MPI V6 (SX/LX FWD)	NC	NC
	NOT AVAILABLE with (29H) Quick Order Package 29H.		
EGM	Engine: 3.3L V6 FFV (SX/LX FWD)	NC	NC
	NOT AVAILABLE with (28F) Quick Order Package 28F, (28H) Quick Order Package 28H, (29H) Quick Order Package 29H.		
EGH	Engine: 3.8L MPI V6 (LX AWD/LXi AWD/LXi FWD)	NC	NC
EGH	Engine: 3.8L MPI V6 (SX/LX FWD)	285	335
	NOT AVAILABLE with (28F) Quick Order Package 28F, (28H) Quick Order Package 28H.		

CHRYSLER TOWN & COUNTRY

CODE	DESCRIPTION	INVOICE	MSRP
PWP	Golden White Pearl Tri-Coat	170	200
AAT	Handling Group II (LX FWD)	400	470
	Includes 16" x 6.5" aluminum wheels, HD suspension, front and rear stabilizer bars. NOT AVAILABLE with 25P, 28P, AAR.		
AAT	Handling Group II (LX FWD)	370	435
	Includes 16" x 6.5" aluminum wheels, front and rear stabilizer bars. REQUIRES AAR. NOT AVAILABLE with 25P, 28P.		
CMA	Heated Front Seats (LXi FWD/LXi AWD)	213	250
FL	Leather Seat Trim (SX/LX FWD/LX AWD)	757	890
	NOT AVAILABLE with 25F, 28F, CYR, 25P, 28P.		
SER	Load Leveling & Height Control (LX FWD)	247	290
	NOT AVAILABLE with (25P) Quick Order Package 25P, (28P) Quick Order Package 28P.		
AAP	Loading & Towing Group II (LX FWD)	123	145
	Includes P215/65R15 AS BSW touring tires, 15" wheel covers. REQUIRES AAT. NOT AVAILABLE with 25P, 28P, AAR, 25R, 28R, 29R.		
AAR	Loading & Towing Group III (LX FWD/LX AWD)	323	380
	Includes 120-amp alternator, Loading and Towing Group II: HD suspension, P215/65R15 AS BSW touring tires, 15" wheel covers; 685-amp maintenance free battery, heavy duty front disc/rear drum brakes. NOT AVAILABLE with 25P, 28P, AAP.		
25F	Quick Order Package 25F (SX)	NC	NC
	Includes vehicle with standard equipment. REQUIRES EGM and DGB. NOT AVAILABLE with AA2, RAZ, FL, NAE.		
25H	Quick Order Package 25H (SX)	1288	1515
	Manufacturer Discount	(1080)	(1270)
	Net Price	208	245
	Includes sunscreen glass, AM/FM stereo with cassette, roof rack, 8-way power driver's seat, 10/200w Infinity speakers. REQUIRES EGM and DGB. NOT AVAILABLE with AAP, NAE.		
25P	Quick Order Package 25P (LX FWD)	NC	NC
	Includes vehicle with standard equipment. REQUIRES EGM and DGB. NOT AVAILABLE with RAZ, AAB, SER, AAR, WNB, AAT, FL, AAP, AA2, NAE, CYR, 4XN.		
25R	Quick Order Package 25R (LX FWD)	1046	1230
	Manufacturer Discount	(973)	(1145)
	Net Price	73	85
	Includes sunscreen glass, AM/FM stereo with cassette, 8-way power driver's seat, 10/200w Infinity speakers. REQUIRES EGM and DGB and (AAB or 4XN). NOT AVAILABLE with AAP, NAE.		
28F	Quick Order Package 28F (SX)	NC	NC
	Includes vehicle with standard equipment. REQUIRES EGA and DGB and NAE. NOT AVAILABLE with EGH, EGM, AA2, RAZ, FL.		

TOWN & COUNTRY — CHRYSLER

CODE	DESCRIPTION	INVOICE	MSRP
28H	Quick Order Package 28H (SX)	1288	1515
	Manufacturer Discount	(1080)	(1270)
	Net Price	208	245

Includes sunscreen glass, AM/FM stereo with cassette, roof rack, 8-way power driver's seat, 10/200w Infinity speakers. REQUIRES EGA and DGB and NAE. NOT AVAILABLE with EGH, EGM, AAP.

28P	Quick Order Package 28P (LX FWD)	NC	NC

Includes vehicle with standard equipment. REQUIRES EGA and DGB and NAE. NOT AVAILABLE with RAZ, AAB, SER, AAR, WNB, AAT, FL, AAP, AA2, CYR, 4XN.

28R	Quick Order Package 28R (LX FWD)	1046	1230
	Manufacturer Discount	(973)	(1145)
	Net Price	73	85

Includes sunscreen glass, AM/FM stereo with cassette, 8-way power driver's seat, 10/200w Infinity speakers. REQUIRES EGA and DGB and NAE and (AAB or 4XN). NOT AVAILABLE with AAP.

29H	Quick Order Package 29H (SX)	1288	1515
	Manufacturer Discount	(1080)	(1270)
	Net Price	208	245

Includes sunscreen glass, AM/FM stereo with cassette, roof rack, 8-way power driver's seat, 10/200w Infinity speakers. REQUIRES EGH and DGB. NOT AVAILABLE with EGA, EGM, AAP.

29R	Quick Order Package 29R (LX AWD)	1046	1230
	Manufacturer Discount	(973)	(1145)
	Net Price	73	85

Includes sunscreen glass, AM/FM stereo with cassette, 8-way power driver's seat, 10/200w Infinity speakers. REQUIRES EGH and DGB and (4XN or AAB).

29R	Quick Order Package 29R (LX FWD)	1046	1230
	Manufacturer Discount	(973)	(1145)
	Net Price	73	85

Includes sunscreen glass, AM/FM stereo with cassette, 8-way power driver's seat, 10/200w Infinity speakers. REQUIRES EGH and DGB and (AAB or 4XN). NOT AVAILABLE with AAP.

29Y	Quick Order Package 29Y (LXi AWD)	NC	NC

Includes vehicle with standard equipment. REQUIRES (EGH) engine and (DGB) transmission.

29Y	Quick Order Package 29Y (LXi FWD)	NC	NC

Includes vehicle with standard equipment. REQUIRES (EGH) engine and (DGB) transmission.

RAZ	Radio: AM/FM Stereo with CD & Cassette (SX/LX FWD/LX AWD)	264	310

NOT AVAILABLE with 25F, 28F, 25P, 28P.

4XN	Rear Air Conditioning Bypass (LX FWD/LX AWD)	NC	NC

NOT AVAILABLE with (AAB) Climate Group III, (25P) Quick Order Package 25P, (28P) Quick Order Package 28P.

MWG	Roof Rack (LX FWD/LX AWD)	149	175

NOT AVAILABLE with (25P) Quick Order Package 25P, (28P) Quick Order Package 28P.

CHRYSLER TOWN & COUNTRY

CODE	DESCRIPTION	INVOICE	MSRP
AWS	Smoker's Group	17	20
	Includes cigar lighter.		
AHT	Trailer Tow Group (LXi FWD/LXi AWD)	230	270
	Includes 685-amp maintenance free battery, heavy duty front disc/rear drum brakes, HD suspension.		
WNB	Wheels: 16" X 6.5" Aluminum (LX FWD/LX AWD)	349	410
	NOT AVAILABLE with (25P) Quick Order Package 25P, (28P) Quick Order Package 28P.		

Take Advantage of Warranty Gold!

Savings up to 50% off Dealer's Extended Warranty Prices. Protect and enhance YOUR investment with the best extended warranty available.

Call Toll Free   1-800-580-9889

One 15-minute call could save you 15% or more on car insurance.

America's 6th Largest Automobile Insurance Company

1-800-555-2758

CARAVAN   DODGE

1998 CARAVAN

1998 Dodge Caravan

What's New?

Available this year is a 3.8-liter V-6 that puts out 180 horsepower and 240 lbs.-ft of torque. And for convenience, the Caravans come with rear-seat mounted grocery bag hooks, and driver's-side easy-entry Quad seat. All Chrysler products are equipped with "Next Generation" depowered airbags.

Review

If there is a perfect family vehicle in existence, it is the Dodge Caravan. What's the data say? The average American has two kids and spends a little more than $20,000 on a new car or truck. The Dodge Caravan fits into this scenario better than Velveeta in a grilled cheese sandwich.

We like the Caravan SE because it is the most flexible trim level and upgrades seating positions from five to seven. You can go with the bare-bones $20,000 edition, or add luxury items like remote keyless entry, CD player with premium sound, and a security alarm. A third way to spec an SE model is with a Sport Option Package, which includes a firmer suspension, alloy wheels, fog lights, and monochromatic trim. Oddly, the 3.8-liter V-6 engine cannot be purchased on an SE model, which means the most sport your Sport can attain uses the 158 horsepower churned out by the 3.3-liter V-6 that comes with the package. Still, a Caravan Sport is the raciest minivan you can buy, short of popping an extra four grand for the LE model and its 3.8-liter V-6.

Step up to LE trim level, and you buy your ticket to a stronger engine, traction control, trip computer, snazzy trim, and leather seating. Just for fun, let's see what a loaded LE runs...Whoa! $30,000 for a packed Caravan LE! Not much value here, folks. Stick with the SE.

Caravan offers several thoughtful details, but the most important are the easy-out rolling seats and the innovative driver-side sliding door—a feature that makes so much sense, it's amazing that no one tried this before. Easy-out seats are a snap to release and remove, though lifting the seat from the rear of the van may still require two sets of biceps. Optional on base and SE, and standard on LE, the driver's side sliding door offers the convenience of loading kids and cargo from either side of the Caravan. Also intriguing is the windshield-wiper de-icer, which also comes standard on the LE.

DODGE CARAVAN

Cupholders not only are numerous, they "ratchet down" to a smaller size. Except for an overabundance of climate controls, and an oddly-shaped column gearshift, the attractively curved dashboard is a pleasure to consult. Seats are soft but reasonably supportive, with moderate side bolstering.

Light steering response gives the Caravan an undeniably car-like feel, with an exceptionally smooth ride. Highly maneuverable and easy to control, the minivan delivers just a hint that you could exceed its capabilities, as when rounding a sharp curve. A 150-horsepower 16-valve dual-cam four serves as the base engine, with a 3.0-, 3.3-, or 3.8-liter V-6 optional. The Sport package features specially tuned shocks and springs.

New for 1998 is a high-output 3.8-liter V-6 engine that's optional on the LE. Other new stuff includes fresh paint colors, rear-seat grocery bag hooks, and easy-entry for the second driver's side door.

Chrysler notes that the Caravan is 3.6 inches shorter than a Mercury Villager and nearly 15 inches shorter than a Ford Windstar, but offers more cargo space than either rival. The Caravan doesn't feel nearly so massive from the driver's seat, which is one of its many charms. Definitely investigate the Dodge Caravan if a smaller minivan meets your needs.

Safety Data

Driver Airbag: *Standard*
Side Airbag: *Not Available*
Traction Control: *Optional*
Driver Crash Test Grade: *Good*

Passenger Airbag: *Standard*
4-Wheel ABS: *Optional*
Integrated Child Seat(s): *Optional*
Passenger Crash Test Grade: *Good*

Standard Equipment

BASE: 2.4L I-4 DOHC SMPI 16-valve engine; 3-speed automatic transmission; 600-amp battery; 90-amp alternator; front wheel drive, 3.19 axle ratio; stainless steel exhaust; comfort ride suspension, front independent strut suspension with anti-roll bar, front coil springs, front shocks, rear non-independent suspension with rear leaf springs, rear shocks; power rack-and-pinion steering; front disc/rear drum brakes; 20 gal capacity fuel tank; front mud flaps, rear lip spoiler; 3 doors with sliding right rear passenger door, liftback rear cargo door; front and rear colored bumpers; colored bodyside molding; monotone paint; aero-composite halogen headlamps; additional exterior lights include center high mounted stop light; driver and passenger manual black folding outside mirrors; front and rear 14" x 6" steel wheels, full wheel covers; P205/75SR14 BSW AS front and rear tires; underbody mounted compact steel spare wheel; AM/FM stereo with clock, seek-scan, 4 speakers and fixed antenna; child safety rear door locks; 2 power accessory outlets, driver foot rest; analog instrumentation display includes water temp gauge, PRNDL in instrument panel, trip odometer; warning indicators include oil pressure, water temp warning, battery, lights on, key in ignition, low fuel, low washer fluid, door ajar, trunk ajar; dual airbags; tinted windows, fixed rear windows, manual 1/4 vent windows; variable intermittent front windshield wipers, variable intermittent wiper; seating capacity of 5, front bucket seats with fixed adjustable headrests, driver and passenger armrests, driver seat includes 4-way direction control, passenger seat includes 4-way direction control; removeable rear bench seat; front and rear height adjustable seatbelts; cloth seats, vinyl door trim insert, full cloth headliner, full carpet floor covering; interior lights include dome light, front reading lights; vanity mirrors; day-night rear-view mirror; glove box, front and rear cupholders, instrument panel bin, interior concealed storage; carpeted cargo floor, vinyl trunk lid, cargo light; body-colored grille, black door handles.

SE (in addition to or instead of BASE): 3L V-6 SOHC SMPI 12-valve engine; 4-speed electronic overdrive automatic transmission with lock-up; 500-amp battery; 3.61 axle ratio; firm ride suspension; front disc/rear drum brakes with 4 wheel anti-lock braking system; 4 doors with

CARAVAN — DODGE

sliding left rear passenger door, sliding right rear passenger door, liftback rear cargo door; driver and passenger power remote black folding outside mirrors; front and rear 15" x 6.5" P215/65SR15 BSW AS tires; rear heat ducts; AM/FM stereo with seek-scan, cassette; cruise control with steering wheel controls; includes tachometer gauge, water temp gauge; seating capacity of 7; removable full folding bench rear bench seat with mounted outboard only; 3rd row seat removable full folding bench; steering wheel with tilt adjustment; instrument panel bin, interior concealed storage, front underseat tray; cargo net, cargo light.

LE (in addition to or instead of SE): 3.3L V-6 OHV SMPI 12-valve engine, requires flexible fuel; colored bodyside molding, colored bodyside cladding; monotone paint with bodyside accent stripe; aero-composite halogen headlamps with delay off feature; additional exterior lights include center high mounted stop light, underhood light; driver and passenger power remote black heated folding outside mirrors; air conditioning, rear heat ducts; clock; remote keyless entry controls trunk, power remote hatch/trunk release; includes tachometer gauge, oil pressure gauge, water temp gauge, volt gauge, compass, exterior temp, PRNDL in instrument panel, trip computer, trip odometer; panic alarm; deep tinted windows, power front windows with driver 1-touch down, fixed rear windows, power 1/4 vent windows; variable intermittent front windshield wipers with heated wipers, variable intermittent wiper rear window defroster; with adjustable headrests, driver seat includes 4-way direction control with lumbar support; adjustable rear headrest; adjustable 3rd row headrest; premium cloth seats, full carpet floor covering with carpeted floor mats, deluxe sound insulation; interior lights include front reading lights, 2 door curb lights, illuminated entry; dual illuminated vanity mirrors dual auxiliary visors; full overhead console with storage, glove box with light, instrument panel covered bin, interior concealed storage, 1 seatback storage pocket, front underseat tray; body-colored grille, body-colored door handles.

Base Prices

Code	Description	Invoice	MSRP
NSKL52	Base	15845	17415
NSKH52	SE	19255	21290
NSKP52	LE	22546	25030
	Destination Charge:	580	580

Accessories

Code	Description	Invoice	MSRP
DGB	4-Speed Automatic Transmission with OD (Base)	213	250
BGF	4-Wheel Antilock Brakes (Base)	480	565
CYS	7-Passenger Deluxe Quad Seating (SE/LE)	553	650
	Includes front reclining buckets with armrest, middle reclining and folding buckets with armrest and rear 3 passenger reclining and folding bench with adjustable headrests, adjustable track and easy out roller system. NOT AVAILABLE with 28A, 26A, 26B, 25B, 28B, 25C, 28C, CYR, 25J, 28J.		
CYR	7-Passenger Deluxe Seating with 2 Child Seats (SE/LE)	191	225
	Includes front reclining buckets with armrest, middle 2 passenger reclining and folding bench with 2 integrated child seats, adjustable headrests, armrest and easy out roller system and rear 3 passenger reclining and folding bench with adjustable headrests, adjustable track and easy out roller system. NOT AVAILABLE with 28A, 26A, 25J, 28J, FL, CYS.		
CYE	7-Passenger Seating (Base)	298	350
	Recommended: (TYH) LT245/75R16E A/T BSW tires. NOT AVAILABLE with (CYK) 7-passenger seating with integrated child seat.		

DODGE CARAVAN

CODE	DESCRIPTION	INVOICE	MSRP
CYK	7-Passenger Seating with Integrated Child Seat (Base)	242	285
	Includes passenger assist grab handle (Rt roof header), standard lighter receptacle and ignition key light with time delay. NOT AVAILABLE with (22S) quick order package 22S, (CYE) 7-passenger seating.		
HAA	Air Conditioning (Base/SE)	731	860
	NOT AVAILABLE with (4XA) air conditioning bypass.		
4XA	Air Conditioning Bypass (Base/SE)	NC	NC
	NOT AVAILABLE with 22T, 24T, 28T, 25D, 25B, 26B, 26D, 28B, 28D, HAA, 25C, 25E, 28E, 28C.		
RAS	AM/FM Stereo with Cassette (Base)	153	180
	NOT AVAILABLE with (22S) quick order package 22S, (RBR) radio.		
RBR	AM/FM Stereo with CD (Base)	276	325
	NOT AVAILABLE with (22S) quick order package 22S, (RAS) radio.		
RAZ	AM/FM Stereo with CD, Cassette, EQ (LE)	264	310
	Includes graphic equalizer and 4 speakers. NOT AVAILABLE with (25J) quick order package 25J, (28J) quick order package 28J.		
RAZ	AM/FM Stereo with CD, Cassette, EQ (SE)	276	325
	Includes graphic equalizer and 4 speakers. NOT AVAILABLE with (28A) quick order package 28A, (26A) quick order package 26A.		
YCF	Border State (Non-Federal) Emissions	145	170
	NOT AVAILABLE with 28A, 28B, 28D, 28T, NAE.		
NAE	CA/CT/MA/NY Emissions	145	170
	Automatically coded. NOT AVAILABLE with 24T, 26A, 25B, 26B, 25C, 25E, 25D, 26D, 25J, 25K, YCF, EFA.		
PH2	Candy Apple Red Metallic Clear Coat (SE/LE)	170	200
	NOT AVAILABLE with 26A, 28A, 26B, 28B, 25B, 26D, 25D, 28D.		
AAA	Climate Group II (Base/SE)	383	450
	Includes air conditioning, sunscreen/solar glass. NOT AVAILABLE with 22S, 28A, 26A, AAA, 25C, 25E, 28E, 28C.		
AAC	Convenience Group I (Base)	370	435
	Includes power fold-away mirrors, speed control, tilt steering. NOT AVAILABLE with 22S, AAE, AAC, 22T, 24T, 28T.		
AAE	Convenience Group II	268	315
	Includes power door locks. NOT AVAILABLE with 26A, 28A, AAE, 25B, 26B, 26D, 28B, 28D, 25D, 25C, 25E, 28C, 28E.		
AAE	Convenience Group II (Base)	638	750
	Includes power door locks. NOT AVAILABLE with (22S) quick order package 22S, (AAC) convenience group I.		
AAF	Convenience Group III	582	685
	Includes convenience group II: power door locks, power windows. NOT AVAILABLE with 28A, 26A, AAF, 25B, 26B, 25D, 26D, 28B, 28D, 25C, 25E, 28C, 28E.		
AAG	Convenience Group IV (SE)	200	235
	Includes headlight off time delay, illuminated entry, remote keyless entry, convenience group II: power door locks, power windows. NOT AVAILABLE with 28A, 25B, 26A, 26B, 28B, 25C, 28C, AAH.		

CARAVAN — DODGE

CODE	DESCRIPTION	INVOICE	MSRP
AAH	Convenience Group V (LE)	128	150
	Includes security alarm. NOT AVAILABLE with (28J) quick order package 28J, (25J) quick order package 25J.		
AAH	Convenience Group V (SE)	327	385
	Includes security alarm. NOT AVAILABLE with 28A, 25B, 26A, 26B, 28B, 25C, 28C, AAG.		
TBB	Conventional Spare Tire	94	110
	NOT AVAILABLE with 22S, 28A, 26A, 25J, 28J, TBB, 22T, 24T, 28T, 25B, 26B, 25D, 26D, 28B, 28D, 25K, 28K, 29K, 25C, 25E, 28C, 28E.		
NHK	Engine Block Heater	30	35
EFA	Engine: 3.0L MPI V6 (Base)	655	770
	NOT AVAILABLE with (NAE) CA/CT/MA/NY Emissions.		
EFA	Engine: 3.0L MPI V6 (SE)	NC	NC
	NOT AVAILABLE with (NAE) CA/CT/MA/NY Emissions.		
EGA	Engine: 3.3L MPI V6 (Base)	825	970
EGA	Engine: 3.3L MPI V6 (SE)	170	200
EGM	Engine: 3.3L V6 Ethanol Flexible Fuel (LE)	NC	NC
EGM	Engine: 3.3L V6 Ethanol Flexible Fuel (SE)	170	200
EGH	Engine: 3.8L MPI V6 (LE)	285	335
RCE	Infinity Speaker System (SE/LE)	336	395
	NOT AVAILABLE with 26A, 28A, 26B, 25B, 28B, 25C, 28C, 28J, 25J.		
SER	Load Leveling & Height Control (LE)	247	290
	NOT AVAILABLE with (25J) quick order package 25J, (28J) quick order package 28J.		
AAP	Loading & Towing Group II (LE)	123	145
	Includes P215/65R15 BSW A/S tires and 15" disc/drum brakes, heavy duty rear suspension, conventional spare tire. NOT AVAILABLE with 25J, 28J, AAR, AAP.		
AAP	Loading & Towing Group II (SE)	153	180
	Includes P215/65R15 BSW A/S tires and 15" disc/drum brakes, heavy duty rear suspension, conventional spare tire. NOT AVAILABLE with 28A, 26A, AAP, 25C, 25E, 28E, 28C, 25B, 26B, 25D, 26D, 28B, 28D, 25J, 28J, AAR, 28K, 29K, 25K.		
AAR	Loading & Towing Group III (LE)	378	445
	Includes 120-amp alternator, 685-CCA battery, heavy duty rear suspension, conventional spare tire. NOT AVAILABLE with (AAP) loading and towing group II, (25J) quick order package 25J, (28J) quick order package 28J.		
22S	Quick Order Package 22S (Base)	NC	NC
	Includes vehicle with standard equipment. REQUIRES (HAA or 4XA) and EDZ and DGA. NOT AVAILABLE with AAA, AAC, AAE, RAS, RBR, MWG, CYK, TBB.		
22T	Quick Order Package 22T (Base)	1050	1235
	Manufacturer Discount	(1050)	(1235)
	Net Price	NC	NC
	Includes air conditioning, under seat lockable drawer, 7-passenger seating. REQUIRES EDZ and DGA. NOT AVAILABLE with 4XA, AAA, AAC, TBB.		

EDMUND'S 1998 NEW TRUCKS

DODGE CARAVAN

CODE	DESCRIPTION	INVOICE	MSRP
24T	Quick Order Package 24T (Base)	1050	1235
	Manufacturer Discount	(731)	(860)
	Net Price	319	375

Includes air conditioning, under seat lockable drawer, 7-passenger seating. REQUIRES EFA and DGA. NOT AVAILABLE with 4XA, NAE, AAA, AAC, TBB.

25B	Quick Order Package 25B (SE)	1024	1205
	Manufacturer Discount	(859)	(1010)
	Net Price	165	195

Includes air conditioning, rear window defroster, windshield wiper de-icer, heated mirrors, 7-passenger deluxe seating. REQUIRES EGM and DGB. NOT AVAILABLE with CYS, 4XA, NAE, AAG, AAH, AAA, AAE, AAF, TBB, AAP, RCE, WNG, PH2, GFA.

25C	Quick Order Package 25C (SE)	2108	2480
	Manufacturer Discount	(1092)	(1285)
	Net Price	1016	1195

Includes air conditioning, rear window defroster, windshield wiper de-icer, heated mirrors, Dodge Sport Group: roof rack, Caravan badging, body side molding, Wheels/Handling Group II; Sport Handling Group: heavy duty rear suspension, front and rear stabilizer bars, 16" wheels, fog lights, sunscreen/solar glass, 7-passenger deluxe seating, leather-wrapped steering wheel, P215/65R16 touring AS tires, power windows. REQUIRES EGM and DGB. NOT AVAILABLE with NAE, CYS, AAG, AAH, RCE, 4XA, AAA, AAP, AAE, AAF, TBB, PTK, PCN, PC5, PTE, PMT, GFA.

25D	Quick Order Package 25D (SE)	1904	2240
	Manufacturer Discount	(1114)	(1310)
	Net Price	790	930

Includes air conditioning, rear window defroster, windshield wiper de-icer, heated mirrors, front and rear carpeted floor mats, Light Group: illuminated glove box, Convenience Group: power door locks, power windows, dual illuminated visor vanity mirrors, 7-passenger deluxe seating. REQUIRES EGM and DGB. NOT AVAILABLE with NAE, 4XA, AAA, AAE, AAF, TBB, AAP, WNG, PH2, GFA.

25E	Quick Order Package 25E (SE)	2988	3515
	Manufacturer Discount	(1347)	(1585)
	Net Price	1641	1930

Includes air conditioning, rear window defroster, windshield wiper de-icer, heated mirrors, Dodge Sport Group: roof rack, Caravan badging, body side molding, Wheels/Handling Group II; Sport Handling Group: heavy duty rear suspension, front and rear stabilizer bars, 16" wheels, front and rear carpeted floor mats, fog lights, sunscreen/solar glass, Light Group: illuminated glove box, Convenience Group: power door locks, power windows, dual illuminated visor vanity mirrors, 7-passenger deluxe seating, leather-wrapped steering wheel, P215/65R16 touring AS tires. REQUIRES EGM and DGB. NOT AVAILABLE with NAE, 4XA, AAA, AAP, AAE, AAF, TBB, PCN, PTK, PC5, PTE, PMT, GFA.

25J	Quick Order Package 25J (LE)	NC	NC

Includes vehicle with standard equipment. REQUIRES EGM and DGB. NOT AVAILABLE with NAE, AAH, SER, AAP, AAR, RAZ, MWG, CYR, CYS, TBB, WNG, FL, RCE.

CARAVAN DODGE

CODE	DESCRIPTION	INVOICE	MSRP
25K	Quick Order Package 25K (LE)	1084	1275
	Manufacturer Discount	(1012)	(1190)
	Net Price	72	85

Includes air conditioning with dual temp control, sunscreen/solar glass, AM/FM stereo with cassette, 8-way power driver's seat, Infinity speaker system. REQUIRES EGM and DGB. NOT AVAILABLE with NAE, AAP, TBB.

26A	Quick Order Package 26A (SE)	NC	NC

Includes vehicle with standard equipment. REQUIRES (HAA or 4XA) and EFA and DGB. NOT AVAILABLE with CYR, CYS, NAE, AAA, AAE, AAF, AAG, AAH, TBB, AAP, RAZ, MWG, RCE, WNG, PH2.

26B	Quick Order Package 26B (SE)	1024	1205
	Manufacturer Discount	(859)	(1010)
	Net Price	165	195

Includes air conditioning, rear window defroster, windshield wiper de-icer, heated mirrors, 7-passenger deluxe seating. REQUIRES EFA and DGB. NOT AVAILABLE with CYS, 4XA, NAE, AAG, AAH, AAA, AAE, AAF, TBB, AAP, RCE, WNG, PH2, GFA.

26D	Quick Order Package 26D (SE)	1904	2240
	Manufacturer Discount	(1114)	(1310)
	Net Price	790	930

Includes air conditioning, rear window defroster, windshield wiper de-icer, heated mirrors, front and rear carpeted floor mats, Light Group: illuminated glove box, Convenience Group: power door locks, power windows, dual illuminated visor vanity mirrors, 7-passenger deluxe seating. REQUIRES EFA and DGB. NOT AVAILABLE with 4XA, NAE, AAA, AAE, AAF, TBB, AAP, WNG, PH2, GFA.

28A	Quick Order Package 28A (SE)	NC	NC

Includes vehicle with standard equipment. REQUIRES (HAA or 4XA) and EGA and DGB and NAE. NOT AVAILABLE with CYR, CYS, AAA, AAE, AAF, AAG, AAH, TBB, AAP, RAZ, MWG, RCE, YCF, WNG, PH2.

28B	Quick Order Package 28B (SE)	1024	1205
	Manufacturer Discount	(859)	(1010)
	Net Price	165	195

Includes air conditioning, rear window defroster, windshield wiper de-icer, heated mirrors, 7-passenger deluxe seating. REQUIRES EGA and DGB and NAE. NOT AVAILABLE with CYS, 4XA, AAG, AAH, AAA, AAE, AAF, TBB, AAP, YCF, RCE, WNG, PH2, GFA.

28C	Quick Order Package 28C (SE)	2108	2480
	Manufacturer Discount	(1092)	(1285)
	Net Price	1016	1195

Includes air conditioning, rear window defroster, windshield wiper de-icer, heated mirrors, Dodge Sport Group: roof rack, Caravan badging, body side molding, Wheels/Handling Group II: Sport Handling Group: heavy duty rear suspension, front and rear stabilizer bars, 16" wheels, fog lights, sunscreen/solar glass, 7-passenger deluxe seating, leather-wrapped steering wheel, P215/65R16 touring AS tires, power windows. REQUIRES EGA and DGB and NAE. NOT AVAILABLE with CYS, AAG, AAH, RCE, 4XA, AAA, AAP, AAE, AAF, TBB, PC5, PTK, PTE, PMT, PCN, GFA.

DODGE CARAVAN

CODE	DESCRIPTION	INVOICE	MSRP
28D	Quick Order Package 28D (SE)	1904	2240
	Manufacturer Discount	(1114)	(1310)
	Net Price	790	930

Includes air conditioning, rear window defroster, windshield wiper de-icer, heated mirrors, front and rear carpeted floor mats, Light Group: illuminated glove box, Convenience Group: power door locks, power windows, dual illuminated visor vanity mirrors, 7-passenger deluxe seating. REQUIRES EGA and DGB and NAE. NOT AVAILABLE with 4XA, AAA, AAE, AAF, TBB, AAP, YCF, WNG, PH2, GFA.

28E	Quick Order Package 28E (SE)	2988	3515
	Manufacturer Discount	(1347)	(1585)
	Net Price	1641	1930

Includes air conditioning, rear window defroster, windshield wiper de-icer, heated mirrors, Dodge Sport Group: roof rack, Caravan badging, body side molding, Wheels/Handling Group II: Sport Handling Group: heavy duty rear suspension, front and rear stabilizer bars, 16" wheels, front and rear carpeted floor mats, fog lights, sunscreen/solar glass, Light Group: illuminated glove box, Convenience Group: power door locks, power windows, dual illuminated visor vanity mirrors, 7-passenger deluxe seating, leather-wrapped steering wheel, P215/65R16 touring AS tires. REQUIRES EGA and DGB and NAE. NOT AVAILABLE with 4XA, AAA, AAP, AAE, AAF, TBB, PCN, PTK, PC5, PTE, PMT, GFA.

28J	Quick Order Package 28J (LE)	NC	NC

Includes vehicle with standard equipment. REQUIRES EGA and DGB and NAE. NOT AVAILABLE with CYR, CYS, AAH, TBB, AAP, AAR, RAZ, MWG, SER, WNG, FL, RCE.

28K	Quick Order Package 28K (LE)	1084	1275
	Manufacturer Discount	(1012)	(1190)
	Net Price	72	85

Includes air conditioning with dual temp control, sunscreen/solar glass, AM/FM stereo with cassette, 8-way power driver's seat, Infinity speaker system. REQUIRES EGA and DGB and NAE. NOT AVAILABLE with TBB, AAP.

28T	Quick Order Package 28T (Base)	1050	1235
	Manufacturer Discount	(731)	(860)
	Net Price	319	375

Includes air conditioning, under seat lockable drawer, 7-passenger seating. REQUIRES NAE and EGA and DGB. NOT AVAILABLE with 4XA, AAA, AAC, TBB, YCF.

29K	Quick Order Package 29K (LE)	1084	1275
	Manufacturer Discount	(1012)	(1190)
	Net Price	72	85

Includes air conditioning with dual temp control, sunscreen/solar glass, AM/FM stereo with cassette, 8-way power driver's seat, Infinity speaker system. REQUIRES EGH and DGB. NOT AVAILABLE with TBB, AAP.

GFA	Rear Window Defroster (Base)	166	195

Includes windshield wiper de-icer, heated mirrors.

GFA	Rear Window Defroster (SE)	196	230

Includes heated mirrors, windshield wiper de-icer. NOT AVAILABLE with 26B, 28B, 25B, 26D, 25D, 28D, 25C, 28C, 25E, 28E.

MWG	Roof Rack	149	175

NOT AVAILABLE with 22S, 26A, 28A, 25J, 28J.

CARAVAN / DAKOTA — DODGE

CODE	DESCRIPTION	INVOICE	MSRP
FL	Seats: Lowback Leather Buckets (LE)	757	890
	REQUIRES CYS. NOT AVAILABLE with 28J, 25J, CYR.		
AWS	Smokers Group	17	20
	Includes cigar lighter and 3 ash receiver inserts.		
BNM	Traction Control (LE)	149	175
AAT	Wheels/Handling Group II (LE)	370	435
	Includes P215/65R16 AST LBL SBR tires, sport handling group: heavy duty rear suspension, front and rear stabilizer bars. REQUIRES (AAR) loading and towing group III. NOT AVAILABLE with (25J) quick order package 25J, (28J) quick order package 25J, (28J) quick order package 28J.		
AAT	Wheels/Handling Group II (LE)	400	470
	Includes P215/65R16 AST LBL SBR tires, sport handling group, heavy duty rear suspension, front and rear stabilizer bars. NOT AVAILABLE with (25J) quick order package 25J, (28J) quick order package 28J.		
WNG	Wheels: 16" Forged Aluminum (Genesis) (LE)	349	410
	REQUIRES 28K or 25K or 29K. NOT AVAILABLE with 28J, 25J.		
WNG	Wheels: 16" Forged Aluminum (Genesis) (SE)	225	265
	REQUIRES 25C or 28C or 28E or 25E. NOT AVAILABLE with 26A, 28A, 26B, 28B, 25B, 26D, 25D, 28D.		

1998 DAKOTA

1998 Dodge Dakota Sport 4X2

What's New?

The Dakota R/T, featuring a 250 horsepower V-8 is available for those seeking a performance pickup. The passenger airbag can now be deactivated in all Dakotas, so a rear-facing child seat is perfectly safe. The Dakota is also available in three new colors.

DODGE DAKOTA

CODE	DESCRIPTION	INVOICE	MSRP

Review

The Dakota was completely redesigned inside and out in 1997, so this year the changes are kept to a minimum. A passenger airbag cutoff switch makes the Dakota available to those with small children, and a new R/T edition makes its way into the lineup in the Spring of '98, which is bound to spark interest from enthusiasts. The R/T gets the 5.9-liter Magnum V-8 with 250 hp and 335 lbs.-ft torque, sport bucket seats, a sport-tuned suspension, new wheels, and various R/T decals. And it will no doubt be a blast to drive.

Inside the Dakota, user-friendly controls and displays pass the same work-glove ease-of-operation test that the bigger Dodge Ram does. Seats are king-of-the-road high, and infinitely more comfortable. Club Cab models will carry up to six people. Dual airbags are standard. The Club Cab offers no third door option. Seems odd from the company that pioneered the fourth sliding door on minivans and has a Quad Cab full-size Ram for 1998. To get this convenience, you've got to buy a Chevy S-10 or GMC Sonoma. Press materials indicate that the new Dakota is equipped with side door guard beams, but makes no mention that these beams pass 1999 side-impact standards for trucks. Why didn't engineers just put the stronger beams in from the get-go, rather than wait a couple of years? Dodge had the chance to build the perfect compact pickup, and we'll have to wait to see if they ever decide to add more doors.

Still, it's a nice piece of work. Base, Sport, SLT and R/T models are available. Regular cab 2WD models feature a 2.5-liter inline four-cylinder engine that provides 120 horsepower. Club Cab and 4WD models get a 3.9-liter V-6 good for 175 horsepower and 225 lbs../ft. of torque. Optional on all models (except R/T) is a 5.2-liter V-8 engine that makes 230 horsepower and 300 lbs../ft. of torque at 3,200 rpm. Crammed into a regular cab shortbed with 2WD, the V-8 transforms the Dakota into a storming sport truck.

Overall, the Dakota is quite a truck. Want the best-looking, best-performing compact pickup on the market? Look no further.

Safety Data

Driver Airbag: *Standard*
Side Airbag: *Not Available*
Traction Control: *Not Available*
Driver Crash Test Grade: *Good*

Passenger Airbag: *Standard*
4-Wheel ABS: *Standard*
Integrated Child Seat(s): *Not Available*
IPassenger Crash Test Grade: *Good*

Standard Equipment

2WD REGULAR CAB SHORTBED: 2.5L I-4 OHV SMPI 8-valve engine; 5-speed overdrive manual transmission; 600-amp battery; 117-amp alternator; rear wheel drive, 3.55 axle ratio; stainless steel exhaust; front independent suspension with anti-roll bar, front coil springs, HD front shocks, rear suspension with rear leaf springs, HD rear shocks; power rack-and-pinion steering; front disc/rear drum brakes with rear wheel anti-lock braking system; 15 gal capacity fuel tank; regular pick-up box; front and rear argent bumpers with black rub strip; monotone paint; aero-composite halogen headlamps; additional exterior lights include center high mounted stop light; front and rear 15" x 6" silver styled steel wheels, hub wheel covers; P215/75SR15 BSW AS tires; underbody mounted full-size conventional steel spare wheel; AM/FM stereo with clock, seek-scan, cassette, 4 speakers and fixed antenna; 1 power accessory outlet; analog instrumentation display includes oil pressure gauge, water temp gauge, volt gauge, trip odometer; warning indicators include battery, lights on, key in ignition, low fuel, low washer fluid; driver side airbag, passenger side cancelable airbag; tinted windows; variable intermittent front windshield wipers; seating capacity of 3, bench front seat with fixed adjustable headrests, driver seat includes 2-way direction control, passenger seat includes 2-way direction control; front height adjustable seatbelts; vinyl seats, full cloth headliner, full vinyl floor covering , cabback insulator; interior dome light; sport steering wheel; day-night rear-view mirror; locking glove box, front cupholder; vinyl cargo floor; black grille, black door handles.

2WD REGULAR CAB LONGBED (same standard equipment as 2WD Regular Cab Shortbed).

DAKOTA — DODGE

CODE	DESCRIPTION	INVOICE	MSRP

4WD REGULAR CAB SHORTBED (in addition to or instead of 2WD Regular Cab Shortbed): 3.9L V-6 OHV SMPI 12-valve engine; part-time 4 wheel drive, with auto locking hub control and manual shift; front torsion springs, front torsion bar; power re-circulating ball steering.

2WD EXTENDED CAB (in addition to or instead of 2WD Regular Cab Shortbed): 3.21 axle ratio; deep tinted windows, vented rear windows; seating capacity of 6, 40-20-40 split-bench front seat center armrest with storage, driver seat includes 4-way direction control with lumbar support, passenger seat includes 4-way direction control; fixed full folding split-bench rear seat; premium cloth seats, full carpet floor covering; carpeted cargo floor.

4WD EXTENDED CAB (in addition to or instead of 2WD Extended Cab): 3.9L V-6 OHV SMPI 12-valve engine; part-time 4 wheel drive, with auto locking hub control and manual shift; front torsion springs, front torsion bar; power re-circulating ball steering.

Base Prices

Code	Description	Invoice	MSRP
AN1L61	Base 2WD Reg. Cab Shortbed	11818	12975
AN1L62	Base 2WD Reg. Cab Longbed	12223	13435
AN1L31	Base 2WD Club Cab-Extended Cab	14665	16170
AN5L61	Base 4WD Reg. Cab Shortbed	15355	16955
AN5L31	Base 4WD Club Cab-Extended Cab	17854	19755
	Destination Charge:	510	510

Accessories

Code	Description	Invoice	MSRP
NFB	22 Gallon Fuel Tank	47	55
DMC	3.21 Axle Ratio (2WD Reg Cab)	NC	NC
	NOT AVAILABLE with DSA, 21W, 24W, 24B, 25B, 24E, 25E, Z1E, 21B, 23B, AGB, 21F, 24F, 25F, Z1D, 23F, 23G, 24G, 25G.		
DMD	3.55 Axle Ratio	34	40
	REQUIRES 23W or 23E and Z1E or 23W or 23E. NOT AVAILABLE with 21B, 21F, 24F.		
DMH	3.90 Axle Ratio	34	40
	REQUIRES 24W or 24E and Z1E. NOT AVAILABLE with 23W.		
DGB	4-Speed Automatic Transmission	808	950
	Includes prndl in instrument panel. NOT AVAILABLE with (EPE) engine.		
BGK	4-Wheel Antilock Brakes	425	500
DDC	5-Speed Manual Transmission (2WD Reg Cab)	NC	NC
	Manufacturer Discount	(170)	(200)
	Net Price	(170)	(200)
	NOT AVAILABLE with (EPE) engine, (EHC) engine.		
DDQ	5-Speed Manual Transmission (Std)	NC	NC
	Manufacturer Discount	(170)	(200)
	Net Price	(170)	(200)
	NOT AVAILABLE with (ELF) engine.		
JPS	6-Way Power Driver's Seat (2WD/4WD X-cab)	272	320
HAA	Air Conditioning	680	800
	NOT AVAILABLE with (4XA) air conditioning bypass.		

DODGE DAKOTA

CODE	DESCRIPTION	INVOICE	MSRP
4XA	Air Conditioning Bypass	NC	NC
	NOT AVAILABLE with (HAA) air conditioning, (25H) quick order package 25H, (26H) quick order package 26H.		
6D1	Black CC with Light Driftwood SG (2WD Reg Cab)	166	195
K17	Bodyside Molding (Reg Cab)	64	75
YCF	Border State (California) Emissions	145	170
	NOT AVAILABLE with (NAE) CA/CT/MA/NY Emissions.		
6DA	Bright Jade with Light Driftwood SG (Reg Cab)	166	195
6D7	Bright White CC with Light Driftwood SG (Reg Cab)	166	195
NAE	CA/CT/MA/NY Emissions	145	170
	Automatically coded. NOT AVAILABLE with (YCF) border state emissions.		
M5	Cloth & Vinyl Bucket Seats (2WD Reg Cab)	170	200
G1	Cloth Bench Seats (Reg Cab)	47	55
6D9	Deep Amethyst PC with Light Driftwood SG (2WD Reg Cab)	166	195
AJK	Deluxe Convenience Group	332	390
	Available as a fleet option on base model. electronic speed control, tilt steering column. NOT AVAILABLE with 21B.		
GT4	Dual Power Black Fold Away Mirrors (2WD Reg Cab)	136	160
	REQUIRES 21F or 23F or 24F or 25F or 26F or 23B or 24B or 25B or 26B. NOT AVAILABLE with GUR.		
GT4	Dual Power Black Fold Away Mirrors (2WD/4WD X-Cab)	17	20
	Fold-away. REQUIRES 23G or 24G or 25G or 26G or 25H or 26H. NOT AVAILABLE with GUR.		
6D8	Emerald Green PC with Light Driftwood SG (Reg Cab)	166	195
NHK	Engine Block Heater	30	35
EHC	Engine: 3.9 L MPI Magnum V-6 (2WD Reg Cab)	425	500
	NOT AVAILABLE with (DDC) transmission, 21B, 21F.		
EHC	Engine: 3.9 L MPI Magnum V-6 (4WD Reg Cab)	NC	NC
	NOT AVAILABLE with (Z5C) payload: 2000 lbs., (DHC) full time transfer case, (DDC) transmission.		
ELF	Engine: 5.2L MPI Magnum V8 (2WD Reg Cab)	927	1090
	NOT AVAILABLE with (DDQ) transmission, 21B, 21F.		
ELF	Engine: 5.2L MPI Magnum V8 (4WD)	502	590
	NOT AVAILABLE with (DDQ) transmission.		
6D5	Flame Red CC with Light Driftwood SG (Reg Cab)	166	195
LNJ	Fog Lamps (2WD Reg Cab)	102	120
6D3	Forest Green PC with Light Driftwood SG (Reg Cab)	166	195
CLA	Front Floor Mats (2WD Reg Cab)	26	30
DHC	Full Time Transfer Case (4WD)	336	395
	NOT AVAILABLE with (EHC) engine.		
ADH	HD Electrical Group	102	120
	Includes HD 136-amp alternator.		
NMC	HD Engine Cooler	51	60
	REQUIRES 21W or 23W or 21B or 23B or 25B or 23E or 25E or 23F or 25F or 23G or 25G or 25H.		

DAKOTA — DODGE

CODE	DESCRIPTION	INVOICE	MSRP
NMC	HD Engine Cooler	102	120

REQUIRES 24W or 24B or 26B or 24E or 26E or 24B or 26B or 24F or 26F or 24G or 26G or 26H.

ADJ	HD Service Group	251	295

Includes 22 gallon fuel tank, HD engine cooler, HD Electrical Group: HD 136-amp alternator. REQUIRES 23W or 24B or 26B. NOT AVAILABLE with 21W, 21B, 24W.

ADJ	HD Service Group (Base)	302	355

Includes tachometer, 22 gallon fuel tank, HD engine cooler, HD Electrical Group: HD 136-amp alternator. REQUIRES 24W. NOT AVAILABLE with 21W or 23W.

ADJ	HD Service Group (Reg Cab)	204	240

Includes HD Electrical Group: HD 136-amp alternator, HD engine cooler. REQUIRES 24E or 26E or 24B or 26B or 24F or 26F or 24G or 26G or 26H.

ADJ	HD Service Group (Reg Cab)	153	180

Includes HD Electrical Group: HD 136-amp alternator, HD engine cooler. REQUIRES 23E or 25E or 23B or 25B or 23F or 25F or 23G or 25G or 25H.

ADJ	HD Service Group (Reg Cab)	200	235

Includes HD Electrical Group: HD 136-amp alternator, 22 gallon fuel tank, HD engine cooler. REQUIRES 23B or 25B. NOT AVAILABLE with 21B.

RCK	Infinity Sound Speakers (2WD Reg Cab)	149	175

NOT AVAILABLE with RA8, RBN, RAZ, RBR.

6D2	Intense Blue PC with Light Driftwood SG (Reg Cab)	166	195
ADA	Light Group	106	125

Includes ash receiver light, courtesy light (under instrument panel), ignition switch with time delay, exterior cargo light, glove box light, underhood light, auxiliary electrical receptacle.

6DB	Magenta (4WD Reg Cab)	166	195
3CF	Manual Transmission Bonus Discount (2WD X-Cab)	NC	NC

NOT AVAILABLE with 23F, 24F, 25F, 26F, 24W.

6D6	Metallic Red CC with Light Driftwood SG (Reg Cab)	166	195
AJL	Overhead SLT PLUS Convenience Group (2WD/4WD X-Cab)	183	215

Includes overhead console, automatic dimming rearview mirror. REQUIRES 23G or 24G or 25G or 26G. NOT AVAILABLE with 23F, 24F, 25F, 26F, AJL.

Z1C	Payload: 1800 lbs (2WD Reg Cab)	497	585

NOT AVAILABLE with 21W, (Z1E) payload: 2600 lbs, (TS1) tires.

Z1C	Payload: 1800 lbs (2WD Reg Cab)	89	105

NOT AVAILABLE with (Z1E) payload: 2600 lbs, (TS1) tires.

Z5B	Payload: 1800 lbs (4WD X-Cab)	34	40
Z1D	Payload: 2000 lbs (2WD X-Cab)	157	185

Includes P235/75R15 AS BSW tires. REQUIRES (23B and (DMD or DMH)) or (24B and DMH) or 25B or 26B or ((23F or 23G) and (DMD or DMH)) or ((24F or 24G) and DMH) or (25F or 26F or 25G or 26G). NOT AVAILABLE with EPE, AGB, DMC.

Z5C	Payload: 2000 lbs. (4WD Reg Cab)	47	55

Includes rear drum brakes. NOT AVAILABLE with (EHC) engine.

Z1E	Payload: 2600 lbs (2WD Reg Cab)	153	180

REQUIRES ((23E or 25E or 26E) and (DMD or DMH)) or (24E and DMH).

DODGE DAKOTA

CODE	DESCRIPTION	INVOICE	MSRP
Z1E	**Payload: 2600 lbs (2WD Reg Cab)**	561	660
	Includes P235/75R15 AS BSW tires. REQUIRES (23W and DMD or DMH) or (24W and DMH).		
AJP	**Power Convenience Group (2WD Reg Cab)**	485	570
	Includes power door locks, power windows with driver's one touch down, remote keyless entry with 2 transmitters.		
AJP	**Power Convenience Group (2WD X-Cab)**	476	560
	Includes power door locks, power windows with driver's one touch down, remote keyless entry with 2 transmitters.		
GUR	**Power Mirrors (2WD Reg Cab)**	119	140
	NOT AVAILABLE with (GT4) dual power black fold away mirrors.		
AJL	**Power Overhead Convenience Group (2WD Reg Cab)**	667	785
	Includes overhead console, automatic dimming rearview mirror, Power Convenience Group: power door locks, power windows with driver's one touch down, remote keyless entry with 2 transmitters. REQUIRES 23F or 24F or 25F or 26F. NOT AVAILABLE with 23G, 24G, 25G, 26G, AJL.		
21B	**Quick Order Package 21B (2WD Reg Cab)**	1390	1635
	Manufacturer Discount	(553)	(650)
	Net Price	837	985
	Includes front seat area carpet, cloth door trim panel with map pocket, 40/20/40 cloth bench seat, Sport Appearance Group: 15" x 7" aluminum 5 spoke design wheels, painted body color grille, front and rear body colored fascia, cloth sun visors, P215/75R15 RWL AS tires, 3.55 axle ratio. REQUIRES (HAA or 4XA) and EPE and DDQ. NOT AVAILABLE with AJK, ADJ, DMC, AHC.		
21B	**Quick Order Package 21B (2WD X-Cab)**	880	1035
	Manufacturer Discount	(880)	(1035)
	Net Price	NC	NC
	Includes cloth door trim panel with map pocket, 22 gallon fuel tank, tachometer, Sport Appearance Group: 15" x 7" aluminum 5 spoke design wheels, painted body color grille, front and rear body colored fascia, cloth sun visors, P215/75R15 AS RWL tires, 3.90 axle ratio. REQUIRES ((HAA or 4XA)) and DDQ. NOT AVAILABLE with EHC, ELF, DMC, DMD.		
21F	**Quick Order Package 21F (2WD X-Cab)**	1653	1945
	Manufacturer Discount	(850)	(1000)
	Net Price	803	945
	Includes air conditioning, cloth door trim panel with map pocket, 22 gallon fuel tank, Light Group: exterior cargo light, glove box light, underhood light, auxiliary electrical receptacle, SLT Decor Group: front and rear body colored fascia, painted body color grille, 15" x 7" aluminum 5 spoke design wheels, cloth sun visors, tachometer, P215/75R15 AS RWL tires, 3.90 axle ratio. REQUIRES DDQ. NOT AVAILABLE with EHC, ELF, DMC, DMD.		
21W	**Quick Order Package 21W (2WD Reg Cab)**	NC	NC
	Includes 3.55 axle ratio. REQUIRES (HAA or 4XA) and EPE and DDQ. NOT AVAILABLE with ADJ, Z1C, Z1E, DMC, AHC.		
21W	**Quick Order Package 21W (2WD X-Cab)**	NC	NC
	Includes vehicle with standard equipment. REQUIRES ((HAA or 4XA)) and EHC and DDQ.		

DAKOTA — DODGE

CODE	DESCRIPTION	INVOICE	MSRP
23B	Quick Order Package 23B (2WD Reg Cab)	1390	1635
	Manufacturer Discount	(553)	(650)
	Net Price	837	985

Includes front seat area carpet, cloth door trim panel with map pocket, 40/20/40 cloth bench seat, Sport Appearance Group: 15" x 7" aluminum 5 spoke design wheels, painted body color grille, front and rear body colored fascia, cloth sun visors, tachometer, P215/75R15 RWL AS tires, 3.21 axle ratio. REQUIRES (HAA or 4XA) and EHC and DDQ.

23B	Quick Order Package 23B (2WD X-Cab)	880	1035
	Manufacturer Discount	(880)	(1035)
	Net Price	NC	NC

Includes cloth door trim panel with map pocket, 22 gallon fuel tank, Sport Appearance Group: 15" x 7" aluminum 5 spoke design wheels, painted body color grille, front and rear body colored fascia, cloth sun visors, tachometer, P215/75R15 AS RWL tires, 3.21 axle ratio. REQUIRES (HAA or 4XA) and EHC and DDQ. NOT AVAILABLE with DMC.

23B	Quick Order Package 23B (4WD Reg Cab Shortbed)	1543	1815
	Manufacturer Discount	(553)	(650)
	Net Price	990	1165

Includes front seat area carpet, cloth door trim panel with map pocket, 40/20/40 cloth bench seat, Sport Appearance Group: 15" x 7" aluminum 5 spoke design wheels, painted body color grille, front and rear body colored fascia, cloth sun visors, tachometer, P235/75R15 AS OWL tires, 3.55 axle ratio. REQUIRES (HAA or 4XA) and EHC and DDQ.

23B	Quick Order Package 23B (4WD X-Cab)	1020	1200
	Manufacturer Discount	(1020)	(1200)
	Net Price	NC	NC

Includes cloth door trim panel with map pocket, 22 gallon fuel tank, Sport Appearance Group: 15" x 7" aluminum 5 spoke design wheels, painted body color grille, front and rear body colored fascia, cloth sun visors, tachometer, P235/75R15 AS OWL tires, 3.55 axle ratio. REQUIRES (HAA or 4XA) and EHC and DDQ.

23E	Quick Order Package 23E (2WD Reg Cab)	2244	2640
	Manufacturer Discount	(553)	(650)
	Net Price	1691	1990

Includes air conditioning, front seat area carpet, cloth door trim panel with map pocket, 22 gallon fuel tank, Light Group: exterior cargo light, glove box light, underhood light, auxiliary electrical receptacle, SLT Decor Group: front and rear body colored fascia, painted body color grille, 15" x 7" aluminum 5 spoke design wheels, cloth sun visors, 40/20/40 cloth bench seat, tachometer, P215/75R15 RWL AS tires, 3.21 axle ratio. REQUIRES (EHC) engine and (DDQ) transmission.

23E	Quick Order Package 23E (4WD Reg Cab Shortbed)	2397	2820
	Manufacturer Discount	(553)	(650)
	Net Price	1844	2170

Includes air conditioning, front seat area carpet, cloth door trim panel with map pocket, 22 gallon fuel tank, Light Group: exterior cargo light, glove box light, underhood light, auxiliary electrical receptacle, SLT Decor Group: front and rear body

DODGE DAKOTA

CODE	DESCRIPTION	INVOICE	MSRP

colored fascia, painted body color grille, 15" x 7" aluminum 5 spoke design wheels, cloth sun visors, 40/20/40 cloth bench seat, tachometer, P235/75R15 AS OWL tires, 3.55 axle ratio. REQUIRES (EHC) engine and (DDQ) transmission.

23F Quick Order Package 23F (2WD X-Cab) 1653 1945
Manufacturer Discount .... (850) (1000)
Net Price 803 945
With 25B (4WD Reg Cab Shortbed) 435 506

Includes air conditioning, cloth door trim panel with map pocket, 22 gallon fuel tank, Light Group: exterior cargo light, glove box light, underhood light, auxiliary electrical receptacle, SLT Decor Group: front and rear body colored fascia, painted body color grille, 15" x 7" aluminum 5 spoke design wheels, cloth sun visors, tachometer, P215/75R15 AS RWL tires, 3.21 axle ratio. REQUIRES EHC and DDQ. NOT AVAILABLE with HAA, DMC, AJL, 3CF.

23F Quick Order Package 23F (4WD X-Cab) 1806 2125
Manufacturer Discount .... (1020) (1200)
Net Price 786 925

Includes air conditioning, cloth door trim panel with map pocket, 22 gallon fuel tank, Light Group: exterior cargo light, glove box light, underhood light, auxiliary electrical receptacle, SLT Decor Group: front and rear body colored fascia, painted body color grille, 15" x 7" aluminum 5 spoke design wheels, cloth sun visors, tachometer, P235/75R15 AS OWL tires, 3.55 axle ratio. REQUIRES (EHC) engine and (DDQ) transmission. NOT AVAILABLE with (AJL) overhead SLT PLUS convenience group.

23G Quick Order Package 23G SLT Plus (2WD X-Cab) 2814 3310
Manufacturer Discount .... (1318) (1550)
Net Price 1496 1760

Includes air conditioning, Deluxe Convenience Group: electronic speed control, tilt steering column, cloth door trim panel with map pocket, 22 gallon fuel tank, Light Group: exterior cargo light, glove box light, underhood light, auxiliary electrical receptacle, power mirrors, Power Convenience Group: power door locks, power windows with driver's one touch down, remote keyless entry with 2 transmitters, SLT Decor Group: front and rear body colored fascia, painted body color grille, 15" x7" aluminum 5 spoke design wheels, cloth sun visors, anti-theft security system, tilt steering column, tachometer, P215/75R15 AS RWL tires, sliding rear window, 3.21 axle ratio. REQUIRES EHC and DDQ. NOT AVAILABLE with HAA, DMC, AJL.

23G Quick Order Package 23G SLT Plus (4WD X-Cab) 2967 3490
Manufacturer Discount .... (1318) (1550)
Net Price 1649 1940

Includes air conditioning, Deluxe Convenience Group: electronic speed control, tilt steering column, cloth door trim panel with map pocket, 22 gallon fuel tank, Light Group: exterior cargo light, glove box light, underhood light, auxiliary electrical receptacle, power mirrors, Power Convenience Group: power door locks, power windows with driver's one touch down, remote keyless entry with 2 transmitters, SLT Decor Group: front and rear body colored fascia, painted body color grille, 15" x7" aluminum 5 spoke design wheels, cloth sun visors, anti-theft security system, tachometer, P235/75R15 AS OWL tires, sliding rear window, 3.55 axle ratio. REQUIRES (EHC) engine and (DDQ) transmission. NOT AVAILABLE with (AJL) overhead SLT PLUS convenience group.

DAKOTA — DODGE

CODE	DESCRIPTION	INVOICE	MSRP
23W	Quick Order Package 23W (2WD Reg Cab)	NC	NC
	Includes 3.21 axle ratio. REQUIRES (HAA or 4XA) and EHC and DDQ. NOT AVAILABLE with DMH.		
23W	Quick Order Package 23W (2WD X-Cab)	NC	NC
	Includes 3.21 axle ratio. REQUIRES (HAA or 4XA) and EHC and DDQ.		
23W	Quick Order Package 23W (4WD Reg Cab Shortbed)	NC	NC
	Includes 3.55 axle ratio. REQUIRES (HAA or 4XA) and EHC and DDQ. NOT AVAILABLE with ADJ.		
23W	Quick Order Package 23W (4WD X-Cab)	NC	NC
	Includes 3.55 axle ratio. REQUIRES (HAA or 4XA) and EHC and DDQ.		
24B	Quick Order Package 24B (2WD Reg Cab)	1390	1635
	Manufacturer Discount	(553)	(650)
	Net Price	837	985
	Includes front seat area carpet, cloth door trim panel with map pocket, 40/20/40 cloth bench seat, Sport Appearance Group: 15" x 7" aluminum 5 spoke design wheels, painted body color grille, front and rear body colored fascia, cloth sun visors, tachometer, P215/75R15 RWL AS tires, 3.55 axle ratio. REQUIRES (HAA or 4XA) and EHC and DGB. NOT AVAILABLE with DMC.		
24B	Quick Order Package 24B (2WD X-Cab)	880	1035
	Manufacturer Discount	(880)	(1035)
	Net Price	NC	NC
	Includes cloth door trim panel with map pocket, 22 gallon fuel tank, Sport Appearance Group: 15" x 7" aluminum 5 spoke design wheels, painted body color grille, front and rear body colored fascia, cloth sun visors, tachometer, P215/75R15 AS RWL tires, 3.55 axle ratio. REQUIRES (HAA or 4XA) and EHC and DGB. NOT AVAILABLE with DMC.		
24B	Quick Order Package 24B (4WD Reg Cab Shortbed)	1543	1815
	Manufacturer Discount	(553)	(650)
	Net Price	990	1165
	Includes front seat area carpet, cloth door trim panel with map pocket, 40/20/40 cloth bench seat, Sport Appearance Group: 15" x 7" aluminum 5 spoke design wheels, painted body color grille, front and rear body colored fascia, cloth sun visors, tachometer, P235/75R15 AS OWL tires, 3.90 axle ratio. REQUIRES (HAA or 4XA) and EHC and DGB.		
24B	Quick Order Package 24B (4WD X-Cab)	1020	1200
	Manufacturer Discount	(1020)	(1200)
	Net Price	NC	NC
	Includes cloth door trim panel with map pocket, 22 gallon fuel tank, Sport Appearance Group: 15" x 7" aluminum 5 spoke design wheels, painted body color grille, front and rear body colored fascia, cloth sun visors, tachometer, P235/75R15 AS OWL tires, 3.90 axle ratio. REQUIRES (HAA or 4XA) and EHC and DGB.		
24E	Quick Order Package 24E (2WD Reg Cab)	2244	2640
	Manufacturer Discount	(553)	(650)
	Net Price	1691	1990
	Includes air conditioning, front seat area carpet, cloth door trim panel with map pocket, 22 gallon fuel tank, Light Group: exterior cargo light, glove box light, underhood light, auxiliary electrical receptacle, SLT Decor Group: front and rear body		

DODGE DAKOTA

CODE	DESCRIPTION	INVOICE	MSRP

colored fascia, painted body color grille, 15" x 7" aluminum 5 spoke design wheels, cloth sun visors, 40/20/40 cloth bench seat, tachometer, P215/75R15 RWL AS tires, 3.55 axle ratio. REQUIRES (EHC) engine and (DGB) transmission. NOT AVAILABLE with (DMC) 3.21 axle ratio.

24E Quick Order Package 24E (4WD Reg Cab Shortbed) 2397   2820
Manufacturer Discount .... (553)   (650)
Net Price 1844   2170

Includes air conditioning, front seat area carpet, cloth door trim panel with map pocket, 22 gallon fuel tank, Light Group: exterior cargo light, glove box light, underhood light, auxiliary electrical receptacle, SLT Decor Group: front and rear body colored fascia, painted body color grille, 15" x 7" aluminum 5 spoke design wheels, cloth sun visors, 40/20/40 cloth bench seat, tachometer, P235/75R15 AS OWL tires, 3.90 axle ratio. REQUIRES (EHC) engine and (DGB) transmission.

24F Quick Order Package 24F (2WD X-Cab) 1653   1945
Manufacturer Discount .... (850)   (1000)
Net Price 803   945

Includes air conditioning, cloth door trim panel with map pocket, 22 gallon fuel tank, Light Group: exterior cargo light, glove box light, underhood light, auxiliary electrical receptacle, SLT Decor Group: front and rear body colored fascia, painted body color grille, 15" x 7" aluminum 5 spoke design wheels, cloth sun visors, tachometer, P215/75R15 AS RWL tires, 3.55 axle ratio. REQUIRES EHC and DGB. NOT AVAILABLE with HAA, DMC, AJL, 3CF, DMD.

24F Quick Order Package 24F (4WD X-Cab) 1806   2125
Manufacturer Discount .... (1020) (1200)
Net Price 786   925

Includes air conditioning, cloth door trim panel with map pocket, 22 gallon fuel tank, Light Group: exterior cargo light, glove box light, underhood light, auxiliary electrical receptacle, SLT Decor Group: front and rear body colored fascia, painted body color grille, 15" x 7" aluminum 5 spoke design wheels, cloth sun visors, tachometer, P235/75R15 AS OWL tires, 3.90 axle ratio. REQUIRES (EHC) engine and (DGB) transmission. NOT AVAILABLE with (AJL) overhead SLT PLUS convenience group.

24G Quick Order Package 24G SLT Plus (2WD X-Cab) 2814   3310
Manufacturer Discount .... (1318) (1550)
Net Price 1496   1760

Includes air conditioning, Deluxe Convenience Group: electronic speed control, tilt steering column, cloth door trim panel with map pocket, 22 gallon fuel tank, Light Group: exterior cargo light, glove box light, underhood light, auxiliary electrical receptacle, power mirrors, Power Convenience Group: power door locks, power windows with driver's one touch down, remote keyless entry with 2 transmitters, SLT Decor Group: front and rear body colored fascia, painted body color grille, 15" x 7" aluminum 5 spoke design wheels, cloth sun visors, anti-theft security system, tilt steering column, tachometer, P215/75R15 AS RWL tires, sliding rear window, 3.55 axle ratio. REQUIRES EHC and DGB. NOT AVAILABLE with HAA, DMC, AJL.

DAKOTA — DODGE

CODE	DESCRIPTION	INVOICE	MSRP
24G	Quick Order Package 24G SLT Plus (4WD X-Cab)	2967	3490
	Manufacturer Discount	(1318)	(1550)
	Net Price	1649	1940

Includes air conditioning, Deluxe Convenience Group: electronic speed control, tilt steering column, cloth door trim panel with map pocket, 22 gallon fuel tank, Light Group: exterior cargo light, glove box light, underhood light, auxiliary electrical receptacle, power mirrors, Power Convenience Group: power door locks, power windows with driver's one touch down, remote keyless entry with 2 transmitters, SLT Decor Group: front and rear body colored fascia, painted body color grille, 15" x 7" aluminum 5 spoke design wheels, cloth sun visors, anti-theft security system, tachometer, P235/75R15 AS OWL tires, sliding rear window, 3.90 axle ratio. REQUIRES (EHC) engine and (DGB) transmission. NOT AVAILABLE with (AJL) overhead SLT PLUS convenience group.

| 24W | Quick Order Package 24W (2WD Reg Cab) | NC | NC |

Includes 3.55 axle ratio. REQUIRES (HAA or 4XA) and EHC and DGB. NOT AVAILABLE with DMC.

| 24W | Quick Order Package 24W (2WD X-Cab) | NC | NC |

Includes 3.55 axle ratio. REQUIRES (HAA or 4XA) and EHC and DGB. NOT AVAILABLE with 3CF, DMC.

| 24W | Quick Order Package 24W (4WD Reg Cab Shortbed) | NC | NC |

Includes 3.90 axle ratio. REQUIRES (HAA or 4XA) and EHC and DGB. NOT AVAILABLE with ADJ.

| 24W | Quick Order Package 24W (4WD X-Cab) | NC | NC |

Includes 3.90 axle ratio. REQUIRES (HAA or 4XA) and EHC and DGB.

25B	Quick Order Package 25B (2WD Reg Cab)	1390	1635
	Manufacturer Discount	(553)	(650)
	Net Price	837	985

Includes front seat area carpet, cloth door trim panel with map pocket, 40/20/40 cloth bench seat, Sport Appearance Group: 15" x 7" aluminum 5 spoke design wheels, painted body color grille, front and rear body colored fascia, cloth sun visors, tachometer, P215/75R15 RWL AS tires, 3.21 axle ratio. REQUIRES (HAA or 4XA) and ELF and DDC. NOT AVAILABLE with DMC.

25B	Quick Order Package 25B (2WD X-Cab)	880	1035
	Manufacturer Discount	(880)	(1035)
	Net Price	NC	NC

Includes cloth door trim panel with map pocket, 22 gallon fuel tank, Sport Appearance Group: 15" x 7" aluminum 5 spoke design wheels, painted body color grille, front and rear body colored fascia, cloth sun visors, tachometer, P215/75R15 AS RWL tires, 3.55 axle ratio. REQUIRES (HAA or 4XA) and ELF and DDC. NOT AVAILABLE with DMC.

25B	Quick Order Package 25B (4WD Reg Cab Shortbed)	1543	1815
	Manufacturer Discount	(553)	(650)
	Net Price	990	1165

Includes front seat area carpet, cloth door trim panel with map pocket, 40/20/40 cloth bench seat, Sport Appearance Group: 15" x 7" aluminum 5 spoke design

DODGE DAKOTA

CODE	DESCRIPTION	INVOICE	MSRP

wheels, painted body color grille, front and rear body colored fascia, cloth sun visors, tachometer, P235/75R15 AS OWL tires, 3.55 axle ratio. REQUIRES (HAA or 4XA) and ELF and DDC.

25B Quick Order Package 25B (4WD X-Cab) 1020 1200
 Manufacturer Discount .... (1020) (1200)
 Net Price .... NC NC

Includes cloth door trim panel with map pocket, 22 gallon fuel tank, Sport Appearance Group: 15" x 7" aluminum 5 spoke design wheels, painted body color grille, front and rear body coloured fascia, cloth sun visors, tachometer, P235/75R15 AS OWL tires, 3.55 axle ratio. REQUIRES (HAA or 4XA) and ELF and DDC.

25E Quick Order Package 25E (2WD Reg Cab Longbed) 2244 2640
 Manufacturer Discount .... (535) (650)
 Net Price 1709 1990

Includes air conditioning, front seat area carpet, cloth door trim panel with map pocket, 22 gallon fuel tank, Light Group: exterior cargo light, glove box light, underhood light, auxiliary electrical receptacle, SLT Decor Group: front and rear body colored fascia, painted body color grille, 15" x 7" aluminum 5 spoke design wheels, cloth sun visors, 40/20/40 cloth bench seat, tachometer, P215/75R15 RWL AS tires, 3.55 axle ratio. REQUIRES (ELF) engine and (DDC) transmission. NOT AVAILABLE with (DMC) 3.21 axle ratio.

25E Quick Order Package 25E (2WD Reg Cab Shortbed) 2244 2640
 Manufacturer Discount .... (553) (650)
 Net Price 1691 1990

Includes air conditioning, front seat area carpet, cloth door trim panel with map pocket, 22 gallon fuel tank, Light Group: exterior cargo light, glove box light, underhood light, auxiliary electrical receptacle, SLT Decor Group: front and rear body colored fascia, painted body color grille, 15" x 7" aluminum 5 spoke design wheels, cloth sun visors, 40/20/40 cloth bench seat, tachometer, P215/75R15 RWL AS tires, 3.21 axle ratio. REQUIRES (ELF) engine and (DDC) transmission. NOT AVAILABLE with (DMC) 3.21 axle ratio.

25E Quick Order Package 25E (4WD Reg Cab Shortbed) 2397 2820
 Manufacturer Discount .... (553) (650)
 Net Price 1844 2170

Includes air conditioning, front seat area carpet, cloth door trim panel with map pocket, 22 gallon fuel tank, Light Group: exterior cargo light, glove box light, underhood light, auxiliary electrical receptacle, SLT Decor Group: front and rear body coloured fascia, front and rear body coloured fascia, painted body color grille, 15" x 7" aluminum 5 spoke design wheels, cloth sun visors, 40/20/40 cloth bench seat, tachometer, P235/75R15 AS OWL tires, 3.55 axle ratio. REQUIRES (ELF) engine and (DDC) transmission.

25F Quick Order Package 25F (2WD X-Cab) 1653 1945
 Manufacturer Discount .... (850) (1000)
 Net Price 803 945

Includes air conditioning, cloth door trim panel with map pocket, 22 gallon fuel tank, Light Group: exterior cargo light, glove box light, underhood light, auxiliary electrical

DAKOTA DODGE

CODE	DESCRIPTION	INVOICE	MSRP

receptacle, SLT Decor Group: front and rear body colored fascia, painted body color grille, 15" x 7" aluminum 5 spoke design wheels, cloth sun visors, tachometer, P215/75R15 AS RWL tires, 3.55 axle ratio. REQUIRES ELF and DDC. NOT AVAILABLE with HAA, DMC, AJL, 3CF.

25F	Quick Order Package 25F (4WD X-Cab)	1806	2125
	Manufacturer Discount	(1020)	(1200)
	Net Price	786	925

Includes air conditioning, cloth door trim panel with map pocket, 22 gallon fuel tank, Light Group: exterior cargo light, glove box light, underhood light, auxiliary electrical receptacle, SLT Decor Group: front and rear body colored fascia, painted body color grille, 15" x 7" aluminum 5 spoke design wheels, cloth sun visors, tachometer, P235/75R15 AS OWL tires, 3.55 axle ratio. REQUIRES (ELF) engine and (DDC) transmission. NOT AVAILABLE with (AJL) overhead SLT PLUS convenience group.

25G	Quick Order Package 25G SLT Plus (2WD X-Cab)	2814	3310
	Manufacturer Discount	(1318)	(1550)
	Net Price	1496	1760

Includes air conditioning, Deluxe Convenience Group: electronic speed control, tilt steering column, cloth door trim panel with map pocket, 22 gallon fuel tank, Light Group: exterior cargo light, glove box light, underhood light, auxiliary electrical receptacle, power mirrors, Power Convenience Group: power door locks, power windows with driver's one touch down, remote keyless entry with 2 transmitters, SLT Decor Group: front and rear body colored fascia, painted body color grille, 15" x7" aluminum 5 spoke design wheels, cloth sun visors, anti-theft security system, tilt steering column, tachometer, P215/75R15 AS RWL tires, sliding rear window, 3.55 axle ratio. REQUIRES ELF and DDC. NOT AVAILABLE with HAA, DMC, AJL.

25G	Quick Order Package 25G SLT Plus (4WD X-Cab)	2967	3490
	Manufacturer Discount	(1318)	(1550)
	Net Price	1649	1940

Includes air conditioning, Deluxe Convenience Group: electronic speed control, tilt steering column, cloth door trim panel with map pocket, 22 gallon fuel tank, Light Group: exterior cargo light, glove box light, underhood light, auxiliary electrical receptacle, power mirrors, Power Convenience Group: power door locks, power windows with driver's one touch down, remote keyless entry with 2 transmitters, SLT Decor Group: front and rear body colored fascia, painted body color grille, 15" x7" aluminum 5 spoke design wheels, cloth sun visors, anti-theft security system, tachometer, P235/75R15 AS OWL tires, sliding rear window, 3.55 axle ratio. REQUIRES (ELF) engine and (DDC) transmission. NOT AVAILABLE with (AJL) overhead SLT PLUS convenience group.

25H	Quick Order Package 25H Sport Plus (4WD X-Cab)	2962	3485
	Manufacturer Discount	(1318)	(1550)
	Net Price	1644	1935

Includes air conditioning, Deluxe Convenience Group: electronic speed control, tilt steering column, cloth door trim panel with map pocket, fog lamps, 22 gallon fuel

DODGE DAKOTA

CODE	DESCRIPTION	INVOICE	MSRP

tank, Light Group: exterior cargo light, glove box light, underhood light, auxiliary electrical receptacle, power mirrors, cloth and vinyl bucket seats, Sport Appearance Group: 15" x 7" aluminum 5 spoke design wheels, painted body color grille, front and rear body colored fascia, cloth sun visors, tachometer, 31 X 10.5R15 AS OWL tires, sliding rear window, 3.55 axle ratio. REQUIRES (ELF) engine and (DDC) transmission. NOT AVAILABLE with (4XA) air conditioning bypass.

26B	Quick Order Package 26B (2WD Reg Cab)	1390	1635
	Manufacturer Discount	(553)	(650)
	Net Price	837	985

Includes front seat area carpet, cloth door trim panel with map pocket, 40/20/40 cloth bench seat, Sport Appearance Group: 15" x 7" aluminum 5 spoke design wheels, painted body color grille, front and rear body colored fascia, cloth sun visors, tachometer, P215/75R15 RWL AS tires, 3.55 axle ratio. REQUIRES (HAA or 4XA) and ELF and DGB.

26B	Quick Order Package 26B (2WD X-Cab)	880	1035
	Manufacturer Discount	(880)	(1035)
	Net Price	NC	NC

Includes cloth door trim panel with map pocket, 22 gallon fuel tank, Sport Appearance Group: 15" x 7" aluminum 5 spoke design wheels, painted body color grille, front and rear body colored fascia, cloth sun visors, tachometer, P215/75R15 AS RWL tires, 3.55 axle ratio. REQUIRES (HAA or 4XA) and ELF and DGB.

26B	Quick Order Package 26B (4WD Reg Cab Shortbed)	1543	1815
	Manufacturer Discount	(553)	(650)
	Net Price	990	1165

Includes front seat area carpet, cloth door trim panel with map pocket, 40/20/40 cloth bench seat, Sport Appearance Group: 15" x 7" aluminum 5 spoke design wheels, painted body color grille, front and rear body colored fascia, cloth sun visors, tachometer, P235/75R15 AS OWL tires, 3.55 axle ratio. REQUIRES (HAA or 4XA) and ELF and DGB.

26B	Quick Order Package 26B (4WD X-Cab)	1020	1200
	Manufacturer Discount	(1020)	(1200)
	Net Price	NC	NC

Includes cloth door trim panel with map pocket, 22 gallon fuel tank, Sport Appearance Group: 15" x 7" aluminum 5 spoke design wheels, painted body color grille, front and rear body colored fascia, cloth sun visors, tachometer, P235/75R15 AS OWL tires, 3.55 axle ratio. REQUIRES (HAA or 4XA) and ELF and DGB.

26E	Quick Order Package 26E (2WD Reg Cab)	2244	2640
	Manufacturer Discount	(553)	(650)
	Net Price	1691	1990

Includes air conditioning, front seat area carpet, cloth door trim panel with map pocket, 22 gallon fuel tank, Light Group: exterior cargo light, glove box light, underhood light, auxiliary electrical receptacle, SLT Decor Group: front and rear body colored fascia, painted body color grille, 15" x 7" aluminum 5 spoke design wheels, cloth sun visors, 40/20/40 cloth bench seat, tachometer, P215/75R15 RWL AS tires, 3.55 axle ratio. REQUIRES (ELF) engine and (DGB) transmission.

DAKOTA DODGE

CODE	DESCRIPTION	INVOICE	MSRP
26E	Quick Order Package 26E (4WD Reg Cab Shortbed)	2397	2820
	Manufacturer Discount	(553)	(650)
	Net Price	1844	2170

Includes air conditioning, front seat area carpet, cloth door trim panel with map pocket, 22 gallon fuel tank, Light Group: exterior cargo light, glove box light, underhood light, auxiliary electrical receptacle, SLT Decor Group: front and rear body colored fascia, painted body color grille, 15" x 7" aluminum 5 spoke design wheels, cloth sun visors, 40/20/40 cloth bench seat, tachometer, P235/75R15 AS OWL tires, 3.55 axle ratio. REQUIRES (ELF) engine and (DGB) transmission.

26F	Quick Order Package 26F (2WD X-Cab)	1653	1945
	Manufacturer Discount	(850)	(1000)
	Net Price	803	945

Includes air conditioning, cloth door trim panel with map pocket, 22 gallon fuel tank, Light Group: exterior cargo light, glove box light, underhood light, auxiliary electrical receptacle, SLT Decor Group: front and rear body colored fascia, painted body color grille, 15" x 7" aluminum 5 spoke design wheels, cloth sun visors, tachometer, P215/75R15 AS RWL tires, 3.55 axle ratio. REQUIRES ELF and DGB. NOT AVAILABLE with HAA, AJL, 3CF.

26F	Quick Order Package 26F (4WD X-Cab)	1806	2125
	Manufacturer Discount	(1020)	(1200)
	Net Price	786	925

Includes air conditioning, cloth door trim panel with map pocket, 22 gallon fuel tank, Light Group: exterior cargo light, glove box light, underhood light, auxiliary electrical receptacle, SLT Decor Group: front and rear body colored fascia, painted body color grille, 15" x 7" aluminum 5 spoke design wheels, cloth sun visors, tachometer, P235/75R15 AS OWL tires, 3.55 axle ratio. REQUIRES (ELF) engine and (DGB) transmission. NOT AVAILABLE with (AJL) overhead SLT PLUS convenience group.

26G	Quick Order Package 26G SLT Plus (2WD X-Cab)	2814	3310
	Manufacturer Discount	(1318)	(1550)
	Net Price	1496	1760

Includes air conditioning, Deluxe Convenience Group: electronic speed control, tilt steering column, cloth door trim panel with map pocket, 22 gallon fuel tank, Light Group: exterior cargo light, glove box light, underhood light, auxiliary electrical receptacle, power mirrors, Power Convenience Group: power door locks, power windows with driver's one touch down, remote keyless entry with 2 transmitters, SLT Decor Group: front and rear body colored fascia, painted body color grille, 15" x7" aluminum 5 spoke design wheels, cloth sun visors, anti-theft security system, tilt steering column, tachometer, P215/75R15 AS RWL tires, sliding rear window, 3.55 axle ratio. REQUIRES ELF and DGB. NOT AVAILABLE with HAA, AJL.

26G	Quick Order Package 26G SLT Plus (4WD X-Cab)	2967	3490
	Manufacturer Discount	(1318)	(1550)
	Net Price	1649	1940

Includes air conditioning, Deluxe Convenience Group: electronic speed control, tilt steering column, cloth door trim panel with map pocket, 22 gallon fuel tank, Light Group: exterior cargo light, glove box light, underhood light, auxiliary electrical receptacle, power mirrors, Power Convenience Group: power door locks, power

DODGE DAKOTA

CODE	DESCRIPTION	INVOICE	MSRP

windows with driver's one touch down, remote keyless entry with 2 transmitters, SLT Decor Group: front and rear body colored fascia, painted body color grille, 15" x 7" aluminum 5 spoke design wheels, cloth sun visors, anti-theft security system, tachometer, P235/75R15 AS OWL tires, sliding rear window, 3.55 axle ratio. REQUIRES (ELF) engine and (DGB) transmission. NOT AVAILABLE with (AJL) overhead SLT PLUS convenience group.

26H	Quick Order Package 26H Sport Plus (4WD X-Cab)	2962	3485
	Manufacturer Discount	(1318)	(1550)
	Net Price	1644	1935

Includes air conditioning, Deluxe Convenience Group: electronic speed control, tilt steering column, cloth door trim panel with map pocket, fog lamps, 22 gallon fuel tank, Light Group: exterior cargo light, glove box light, underhood light, auxiliary electrical receptacle, power mirrors, cloth and vinyl bucket seats, Sport Appearance Group: 15" x 7" aluminum 5 spoke design wheels, painted body color grille, front and rear body colored fascia, cloth sun visors, tachometer, 31 X 10.5R15 AS OWL Tires, sliding rear window, 3.55 axle ratio. REQUIRES (ELF) engine and (DGB) transmission. NOT AVAILABLE with (4XA) air conditioning bypass.

RA8	Radio Delete	(85)	(100)
	NOT AVAILABLE with RAZ, RBN, RBR, RCK.		
RBN	Radio: AM/FM Stereo with Cassette, EQ (2WD Reg Cab)	255	300
	Includes Infinity sound speakers. NOT AVAILABLE with (RAZ) radio, (RBR) radio, (RA8) radio delete.		
RBR	Radio: AM/FM Stereo with CD (2WD Reg Cab)	408	480
	Includes Infinity sound speakers. NOT AVAILABLE with (RBN) radio, (RAZ) radio, (RA8) radio delete.		
RAZ	Radio: AM/FM Stereo with CD, Cassette, EQ (2WD Reg Cab)	561	660
	Includes Infinity sound speakers. NOT AVAILABLE with (RBN) radio, (RBR) radio, (RA8) radio delete.		
MBV	Rear Valance Panel (Reg Cab)	47	55
	NOT AVAILABLE with (AHC) trailer tow group.		
AJB	Security Alarm (2WD Reg Cab)	128	150
	Includes anti-theft security system. REQUIRES (AJP) Power Convenience Group.		
ADL	Skid Plate Group (4WD)	111	130
	Includes fuel tank skid plate shield and front suspension skid plate.		
GFD	Sliding Rear Window	98	115
DSA	Sure Grip Axle	242	285
JAY	Tachometer	51	60
	NOT AVAILABLE with (EPE) engine, 21W.		
SUA	Tilt Steering Column	119	140
AGB	Tire & Handling Package (2WD X-Cab)	196	230
	Includes P235/70R15 AS OWL tires, rear stabilizer bar. REQUIRES (23B and DMD or DMH) or 24B or 25B or 26B or (23F or 23G and DMD or DMH) or 24F or 25F or 26F or 24G or 25G or 26G. NOT AVAILABLE with DMC, Z1D, TS1.		
TUT	Tires: 31 X 10.5R15 AS OWL (4WD)	340	400
TSH	Tires: P235/70R15 AS OWL (2WD Reg Cab)	174	205
	Includes 15" x 7" aluminum 5 spoke design wheels. NOT AVAILABLE with 21B, Z1E, TS1, Z1C.		

DAKOTA / DURANGO — DODGE

CODE	DESCRIPTION	INVOICE	MSRP
TS1	Tires: P235/75R15 AS BSW (2WD Reg Cab)	55	65
	NOT AVAILABLE with (Z1C) payload: 1800 lbs, (Z1E) payload: 2600 lbs, (AGB) tire and handling package.		
TS1	Tires: P235/75R15 AS BSW (Base)	162	190
	NOT AVAILABLE with (EPE) engine, (Z1C) payload: 1800 lbs, (Z1E) payload: 2600 lbs.		
AHC	Trailer Tow Group	208	245
	Includes trailer hitch receiver (Class IV). REQUIRES ADJ. NOT AVAILABLE with EPE, 21W, 21B, MBV.		

1998 DURANGO

1998 Dodge Durango

What's New?

As the most recent addition to the Dodge truck lineup, the Durango makes quite an entry. Offering the most cargo space in its class, along with an optional Magnum V-8 engine, eight-passenger seating, and three-and-a-half tons of towing capacity, the Durango is the most versatile sport-utility on the market.

Review

Remember the Ramcharger? Neither do we, with the help of the Dodge Durango. Based on the Dakota platform, the Durango is Dodge's latest attempt at a sport-utility vehicle. And from the looks of things, the Dodge boys have done their homework.

Competing directly with the sales king Ford Explorer is no easy task. But the Durango can seat three more passengers than the Explorer. With its more powerful engine, it can tow more weight. It has better ground clearance. More cargo capacity. Bigger. Stronger. Faster. Less expensive. Sounds like a winning formula.

The Durango is larger than anything else in its class, which explains the expansive interior. Yet it's smaller than the Chevrolet Tahoe or Ford Expedition, so we can't call it full-sized. But the niche is filled. Need more room than an Explorer, Blazer or Cherokee? Don't want to fork over the price of an Expedition? Take a good look at the Dodge Durango; it's the only option.

DODGE DURANGO

CODE	DESCRIPTION	INVOICE	MSRP

Although currently available only as a four-wheel drive, a 2WD model is in the works for next year, meaning that even more buyers are soon likely to defect from the competition's ranks. With fresh new styling, superior versatility, and an attractive price, the newest Dodge makes a statement all its own. It says, "Buy me."

Safety Data

Driver Airbag: *Standard*
Side Airbag: *Not Available*
Traction Control: *Not Available*
Driver Crash Test Grade: *Not Available*

Passenger Airbag: *Standard*
4-Wheel ABS: *Optional*
Integrated Child Seat(s): *Not Available*
Passenger Crash Test Grade: *Not Available*

Standard Equipment

4WD DURANGO: 3.9L V-6 OHV SMPI 12-valve engine; 4-speed electronic overdrive automatic transmission with lock-up; 600-amp battery; 117-amp alternator; part-time 4-wheel drive, auto locking hub control and manual shift, 3.55 axle ratio; stainless steel exhaust; front independent suspension with anti-roll bar, front torsion springs, front torsion bar, HD front shocks, rear suspension with anti-roll bar, rear leaf springs, HD rear shocks; power re-circulating ball steering with engine speed-sensing assist; front disc/rear drum brakes with rear wheel anti-lock braking system; 25 gal capacity fuel tank; front license plate bracket; liftback rear cargo door; roof rack; front body-colored bumper rear argent bumper with rear step; monotone paint; aero-composite halogen headlamps; additional exterior lights include center high mounted stop light; driver and passenger power remote black folding outside mirrors; front and rear 15" x 7" silver alloy wheels; P235/75SR15 BSW AS front and rear tires; underbody mounted full-size conventional steel spare wheel; air conditioning, rear heat ducts; AM/FM stereo with clock, seek-scan, cassette, 4 speakers and fixed antenna; 1 power accessory outlet; analog instrumentation display includes tachometer gauge, oil pressure gauge, water temp gauge, trip odometer; warning indicators include oil pressure, battery, lights on, key in ignition, low fuel, low washer fluid, trunk ajar; driver side airbag, passenger side cancelable airbag; deep tinted windows, manual rear windows, fixed 1/4 vent windows; variable intermittent front windshield wipers, fixed interval rear wiper, rear window defroster; seating capacity of 5, front bucket seats with fixed adjustable headrests, center armrest with storage, driver seat includes 4-way direction control with lumbar support, passenger seat includes 4-way direction control; 40-20-40 folding rear split-bench seat with fixed rear headrest; front and rear height adjustable seatbelts; cloth seats, vinyl door trim insert, full cloth headliner, full carpet floor covering; interior lights include dome light; sport steering wheel; vanity mirrors; day-night rearview mirror; partial floor console, locking glove box, front cupholder, 2 seatback storage pockets; carpeted cargo floor, carpeted trunk lid, cargo tie downs, cargo light, cargo concealed storage; chrome grille, black side window moldings, black front windshield molding, black rear window molding, black door handles.

Base Prices

DN5L74	Durango SLT	23318	25810
Destination Charge:		525	525

Accessories

DMH	3.92 Axle Ratio	34	40
BGK	4-Wheel Antilock Brakes	480	565
V9	40/20/40 Cloth Bench Seat	NC	NC
	Includes center armrest, console delete. NOT AVAILABLE with (JPS) 6-way power driver's seat, (LJ) seats.		

DURANGO — DODGE

CODE	DESCRIPTION	INVOICE	MSRP
ADL	4WD Protection Group	77	90
	Includes fuel tank, transfer case and front suspension skid plate shield.		
GT4	6 X 9 Power Fold Away Mirrors	21	25
JPS	6-Way Power Driver's Seat	272	320
	NOT AVAILABLE with (V9) seats.		
DSA	Anti-Spin Differential Axle	242	285
	REQUIRES (24D and DMH) or (26D or 26F or 28F).		
K17	Bodyside Molding	68	80
YCF	Border State (California) Emissions	145	170
NAE	CA/CT/MA/NY Emissions	145	170
	Automatically coded.		
—	Door Ajar Indicator Light	NC	NC
NHK	Engine Block Heater	30	35
EHC	Engine: 3.9L MPI V-6 (Std)	NC	NC
	NOT AVAILABLE with (CFP) third rear seat, (TUT) tires.		
ELF	Engine: 5.2L MPI Magnum V8	502	590
EML	Engine: 5.9L SMPI Magnum V8	752	885
LNJ	Fog Lamps	204	240
	REQUIRES (HBA) rear air conditioning.		
LNJ	Fog Lamps	102	120
CLE	Front & Rear Floor Mats	43	50
DHC	Full Time Transfer Case	336	395
ADJ	HD Service Group	204	240
	Includes HD electrical group: HD 136-amp alternator, 750-amp maintenance free battery, maximum engine cooler.		
RCK	Infinity Speaker System	281	330
LJ	Leather High-Back Bucket Seats	570	670
	NOT AVAILABLE with (V9) seats, 24D, 26D.		
AFH	Overhead Convenience Group	349	410
	Includes Overhead Console: instrumentation, map/reading lights, automatic dimming rearview mirror, dual sunvisors. NOT AVAILABLE with 26F SLT Plus, 28F SLT Plus.		
24D	Quick Order Package 24D	1530	1800
	Manufacturer Discount	(595)	(700)
	Net Price	935	1100
	Includes payload, Deluxe Convenience Group: electronic speed control, tilt steering column, Power Convenience Group: door ajar indicator light, illuminated entry, remote keyless entry system, panic alarm, power door locks, power windows, SLT Decor Group: badging, floor console, door trim, Light Group: illuminated glove box, map/reading lights, auxiliary electrical receptacle, underhood light, heavy duty sound insulation, body color fascias, cloth/vinyl highback bucket seats, tires: P235/75R15 AS WOL SBR. REQUIRES (EHC) engine and (DGB) transmission. NOT AVAILABLE with (LJ) seats.		

DODGE DURANGO

CODE	DESCRIPTION	INVOICE	MSRP
26D	Quick Order Package 26D	1530	1800
	Manufacturer Discount	(595)	(700)
	Net Price	935	1100

Includes payload, Deluxe Convenience Group: electronic speed control, tilt steering column, Power Convenience Group: door ajar indicator light, illuminated entry, remote keyless entry system, panic alarm, power door locks, power windows, SLT Decor Group: badging, floor console, door trim, Light Group: illuminated glove box, map/reading lights, auxiliary electrical receptacle, underhood light, heavy duty sound insulation, body color fascias, cloth/vinyl highback bucket seats, tires: P235/75R15 AS WOL SBR. REQUIRES (ELF) engine and (DGB) transmission. NOT AVAILABLE with (LJ) seats.

26F	Quick Order Package 26F SLT Plus	2763	3250
	Manufacturer Discount	(850)	(1000)
	Net Price	1913	2250

Includes payload, Deluxe Convenience Group: electronic speed control, tilt steering column, front and rear floor mats, fog lamps, bodyside molding, Power Convenience Group: door ajar indicator light, illuminated entry, remote keyless entry system, panic alarm, power door locks, power windows, AM/FM stereo with CD, Cassette, EQ radio, Infinity speaker system, SLT Decor Group: badging, floor console, door trim, Light Group: illuminated glove box, map/reading lights, auxiliary electrical receptacle, underhood light, heavy duty sound insulation, body color fascias, 6-way power driver's seat, cloth/vinyl highback bucket seats, Security Group: security system, tires: P235/75R15 AS WOL SBR. REQUIRES (ELF) engine and (DGB) transmission.

28F	Quick Order Package 28F SLT Plus	2763	3250
	Manufacturer Discount	(850)	(1000)
	Net Price	1913	2250

Includes payload, Deluxe Convenience Group: electronic speed control, tilt steering column, front and rear floor mats, fog lamps, bodyside molding, Power Convenience Group: door ajar indicator light, illuminated entry, remote keyless entry system, panic alarm, power door locks, power windows, AM/FM Stereo with CD, Cassette, EQ Radio: Infinity speaker system, SLT Decor Group: badging, floor console, door trim, Light Group: illuminated glove box, map/reading lights, auxiliary electrical receptacle, underhood light, heavy duty sound insulation, body color fascias, 6-way power driver's seat, cloth/vinyl highback bucket seats, Security Group: security system, tires: P235/75R15 AS WOL SBR. REQUIRES (EML) engine and (DGB) transmission.

RAZ	Radio: AM/FM Stereo with CD, Cassette, EQ	255	300

Includes Infinity speaker system.

HBA	Rear Air Conditioning	366	430

Does not include heater. NOT AVAILABLE with (4XN) rear air conditioning bypass.

4XN	Rear Air Conditioning Bypass	NC	NC

NOT AVAILABLE with (HBA) rear air conditioning.

AJB	Security Group	128	150

Includes security system.

CFP	Third Rear Seat	468	550

When leather seats are ordered, the third row bench seat is vinyl. REQUIRES (ELF) engine or (EML) engine. NOT AVAILABLE with (EHC) engine.

DURANGO / GRAND CARAVAN — DODGE

CODE	DESCRIPTION	INVOICE	MSRP
TUT	Tires: 31 X 10.5R15 AS OWL	429	505
	REQUIRES (ELF) engine or (EML) engine. NOT AVAILABLE with (EHC) engine.		
AHC	Trailer Tow Group	208	245
	7 lead wiring harness (mounted on hitch) and 7/4 pin adaptor wiring pigtail, trailer hitch receiver (class IV). REQUIRES (ADJ) HD service group.		
DGB	Transmission: 4-Speed Automatic	NC	NC

1998 GRAND CARAVAN

1998 Dodge Grand Caravan ES

What's New?

The best-selling minivan gets a higher output (180 horsepower) 3.8-liter V-6 this year, along with four new exterior colors, and "next generation" depowered airbags.

Review

Who's the minivan champ? Why, Chrysler Corporation is, of course. They pioneered the concept of a 7-passenger box-on-wheels way back in 1984 and have dominated this market since. Last year, the Chrysler minivans received a complete makeover that instantly relegated newcomers Ford Windstar and Honda Odyssey to runner-up status. Dodge's interpretation of the minivan concept doesn't look much different from Plymouth's. That's because it differs little in design and engineering, but Dodge offers a broader selection of models: base, SE, and top-of-the-line LE. LE models can be ordered with an ES trim package that includes traction control, automatic light-sensitive headlights, driver's-side lumbar adjustable seat, alloy wheels, special exterior trim, and a firmer suspension. SE models get a standard 3.0-liter engine.

A 2.4-liter 4-cylinder engine is standard on base models, but these sizeable vans benefit from little extra oomph. Acceleration with the 3.3-liter engine (standard in the LE) is pretty strong from startup, but sometimes unimpressive when merging into an expressway. Many buyers are likely to elect the more potent 3.8-liter V-6 instead. Automatic-transmission shifts are neat and smooth. Engine and tire sounds are virtually absent.

Though tautly suspended, the ride is seldom harsh or jarring, unless you get onto truly rough surfaces. Even then, the seven-passenger minivan behaves itself well. Light steering-wheel

DODGE GRAND CARAVAN

response makes handling even more car-like than in the past. Visibility is great, courtesy of more glass and a reduced-height cOWL. Dodge claims that 85 percent of controls can be reached "without leaning."

An innovative left-side sliding door has attracted plenty of notice, and with good cause—it's an idea whose time clearly has come. Better yet, its sliding track is hidden at the base of the glass. Also tempting is the available electric windshield-wiper de-icer. A rollaway rear seat is handy, but it still weighs 95 pounds, so removal can be a chore. Outboard seatbelts are height adjustable, in both the front and middle positions. Front-seat occupants enjoy loads of leg, head, and elbow room.

So, how do engineers improve a nearly perfect package for 1998? More power for the 3.8-liter V6! The SE model comes standard with a 3.0-liter 4EATX engine, and the ES gets automatic headlights and an Automatic Night Vision Safety driver's side mirror. And a new five-point belt system makes it easier to buckle Junior into the child safety seat.

This minivan exhibits not a hint of looseness, squeaks, or rattles, feeling tight all over. Ford's Windstar is the strongest challenger, but we think that the Grand Caravan is the superior minivan.

Safety Data

Driver Airbag: *Standard*
Side Airbag: *Not Available*
Traction Control: *N/A (Base/SE); Opt. (LE/ES)*
Driver Crash Test Grade: *Average*

Passenger Airbag: *Standard*
4-Wheel ABS: *Opt. (Base); Std. (SE/LE/ES)*
Integrated Child Seat(s): *Optional*
Passenger Crash Test Grade: *Good*

Standard Equipment

GRAND CARAVAN BASE: 3.0L V-6 engine; 3-speed automatic transmission; 600-amp battery; 90-amp alternator; front wheel drive, 3.19 axle ratio; stainless steel exhaust; comfort ride suspension, front independent strut suspension with anti-roll bar, front coil springs, front shocks, rear non-independent suspension with rear leaf springs, rear shocks; power rack-and-pinion steering; front disc/rear drum brakes; 20 gal capacity fuel tank; rear lip spoiler; 4 doors with sliding left rear passenger door, sliding right rear passenger door, liftback rear cargo door; front and rear colored bumpers, rear step bumper; colored bodyside molding; monotone paint; aero-composite halogen headlamps; additional exterior lights include center high mounted stop light; driver and passenger manual black folding outside mirrors; front and rear 14" x 6" steel wheels with full wheel covers; P205/75SR14 BSW AS front and rear tires; underbody mounted compact steel spare wheel; AM/FM stereo with clock, seek-scan, 4 speakers and fixed antenna; child safety rear door locks; 2 power accessory outlets, driver foot rest; analog instrumentation display includes water temp gauge, PRNDL in instrument panel, trip odometer; warning indicators include oil pressure, water temp warning, battery, lights on, key in ignition, low fuel, low washer fluid, door ajar, trunk ajar; dual airbags; tinted windows, fixed rear windows, manual 1/4 vent windows; variable intermittent front windshield wipers, variable intermittent rear wiper; seating capacity of 7, front bucket seats with fixed adjustable headrests and driver and passenger armrests, driver seat includes 4-way direction control, passenger seat includes 4-way direction control; removable 2nd row bench seat; removable 3rd row full folding bench seat; front and rear height adjustable seatbelts; cloth seats, vinyl door trim insert, full cloth headliner, full carpet floor covering; interior lights include dome light, front reading lights; vanity mirrors; day-night rearview mirror; glove box, front and rear cupholders, instrument panel bin; carpeted cargo floor, cargo light; body-colored grille, black side window moldings, black front windshield molding, black rear window molding, black door handles.

SE (in addition to or instead of BASE equipment): 4-speed electronic overdrive transmission with lock-up; firm ride suspension; 4 wheel anti-lock braking system; 15" x 6.5" wheels; rear heat ducts; cassette player; cruise control with steering wheel controls; tachometer gauge; service interval warning indicator; full folding 2nd row bench seat; cloth door trim insert; cargo net.

GRAND CARAVAN — DODGE

SE AWD (in addition to or instead of SE equipment): 3.8L OHV engine; 600-amp battery; full-time 4 wheel drive; auto-levelling suspension, rear semi-independent suspension; warning indicators include water temp warning, trunk ajar.

LE (in addition to or instead of SE equipment): 3.3L V-6 engine; delay-off headlight feature; additional exterior lights include underhood light; air conditioning; remote keyless entry, power remote hatch release; oil pressure gauge, volt gauge, compass, exterior temp, trip computer; panic alarm; deep tinted windows, power front windows with driver 1-touch down, power 1/4 vent windows; heated wipers, rear window defroster; tilt adjustable front headrests, driver seat includes lumbar support; premium cloth seats, carpeted floor mats, deluxe sound insulation; interior lights include 2 door curb lights, illuminated entry; illuminated dual auxiliary visors; full overhead console with storage with light, covered instrument panel bin, 1 seat back storage pocket; body-colored door handles.

LE AWD (in addition to or instead of LE equipment): 3.8L V-6 engine; 600-amp battery; full-time 4 wheel drive; auto-levelling suspension, rear semi-independent suspension; warning indicators include water temp warning, trunk ajar; 2nd row reclining seat with adjustable rear headrest; 3rd row reclining seat with adjustable 3rd row headrest.

ES/ES AWD (in addition to or instead of LE/LE AWD equipment): Front and rear body-colored bumpers; body-colored wide bodyside molding, body-colored sill moldings, gold trim, tape stripe, side window outline.

Base Prices

Code	Description	Invoice	MSRP
NSKL53	Base	18270	20125
NSKH53	SE	20171	22285
NSKP53	LE	23462	26025
NSKP53	ES	23972	26605
NSDH53	SE AWD	23132	25650
NSDP53	LE AWD	26256	29200
NSDP53	ES AWD	26714	29720
Destination Charge:		580	580

Accessories

Code	Description	Invoice	MSRP
DGA	3-Speed Automatic Transmission (Base)	NC	NC
DGB	4-Speed Automatic Transmission (All except Base)	NC	NC
DGB	4-Speed Automatic Transmission (Base)	213	250
BGF	4-Wheel Antilock Brakes (Base)	480	565
CYR	7 Passenger Deluxe Seating with 2 Child Seats (All except Base)	191	225
	Includes front reclining buckets with armrests, middle 2 passenger reclining and folding bench with 2 integrated child seats and adjustable headrests, and rear 3 passenger reclining and folding bench with adjustable headrests and adjustable track. NOT AVAILABLE with 26A, 28A, CYS, 25J, 28J, FL.		
CYK	7 Passenger Seating with 2 Child Seats (Base)	242	285
	Includes front reclining buckets with armrests, middle 2 passenger reclining and folding bench with 2 integrated child seats and adjustable headrests, and rear 3 passenger folding bench with adjustable track. NOT AVAILABLE with 24S or 28S.		

DODGE GRAND CARAVAN

CODE	DESCRIPTION	INVOICE	MSRP
CYS	7 Passenger Seating with Quad Buckets (All except Base)	553	650
	Includes front reclining buckets with armrests, middle reclining and folding buckets with armrests, and rear 3 passenger reclining and folding bench with adjustable headrests, adjustable track and easy out roller system. NOT AVAILABLE with 26A, 28A, 26B, 25B, 28B, CYR, 25C, 28C, 25J, 28J.		
HAA	Air Conditioning (Base/SE FWD)	731	860
	NOT AVAILABLE with 4XA, 24T, 28T, 26B, 25B, 28B, 26D, 25D, 28D, 25C, 28C, 25E, 28E.		
4XA	Air Conditioning Bypass (Base/SE FWD/SE AWD)	NC	NC
	NOT AVAILABLE with 24T, 28T, 26B, 25B, 28B, 26D, 25D, 28D, 25C, 28C, 25E, 28E.		
YCF	Border State (California) Emissions	145	170
NAE	CA/CT/MA/NY Emissions	145	170
	Automatically coded. NOT AVAILABLE with 24S, 25B, 25C, 25D, 25E, 25K, 25M, 26A, 26B, 26D, YCF, 25J, 24T.		
PH2	Candy Apple Red Metallic (LE FWD/LE AWD/ES FWD/ES AWD)	170	200
AAA	Climate Group II (Base/SE FWD/SE AWD)	383	450
	Includes sunscreen glass. NOT AVAILABLE with 24S, 28S, AAA, 26A, 28A, 25C, 28C, 25E, 28E.		
AAB	Climate Group III (ES FWD/ES AWD)	344	405
	REQUIRES 25M or 28M or 29M. NOT AVAILABLE with 25J, 28J.		
AAB	Climate Group III (LE FWD/LE AWD)	400	470
	REQUIRES 25K or 28K or 29K. NOT AVAILABLE with 25J, 28J.		
AAB	Climate Group III (SE FWD)	961	1130
	Includes overhead console, rear heater, air conditioning with dual temp control. REQUIRES 26B or 25B or 28B. NOT AVAILABLE with 26A, 28A, 25C, 28C, 25E, 28E.		
AAB	Climate Group III (SE FWD/SE AWD)	867	1020
	Includes air conditioning with dual temp control. REQUIRES 26D or 25D or 28D or 29D. NOT AVAILABLE with 26A, 28A, 25C, 28C, 25E, 28E.		
AAB	Climate Group III with Sport Pkg. (SE FWD)	429	505
	Includes overhead console, rear heater, air conditioning with dual temp control. REQUIRES 25E or 28E. NOT AVAILABLE with 25C or 28C.		
AAB	Climate Group III with Sport Pkg. (SE FWD)	523	615
	Includes overhead console, rear heater, air conditioning with dual temp control. REQUIRES 25C or 28C. NOT AVAILABLE with 25E or 28E.		
AAC	Convenience Group I (Base)	370	435
	Includes speed control, tilt steering, power mirrors. NOT AVAILABLE with 24S, 28S, AAC.		
AAE	Convenience Group II (Base)	638	750
	Includes Convenience Group I: speed control, tilt steering, power mirrors; power door locks. NOT AVAILABLE with 24S or 28S.		
AAE	Convenience Group II (SE FWD)	268	315
	Includes Convenience Group I: speed control, tilt steering, power mirrors; power door locks. Some items may be standard on SE models. NOT AVAILABLE with 26A, 28A, AAH, 26D, 25D, 28D, AAF, 25E, 28E.		

GRAND CARAVAN — DODGE

CODE	DESCRIPTION	INVOICE	MSRP
AAF	Convenience Group III (SE FWD)	582	685

Includes Convenience Group II: speed control, tilt steering, power mirrors, power door locks; power windows, power quarter vent windows. Some items may be standard on SE models. NOT AVAILABLE with 26A, 28A, AAE, 26D, 25D, 28D, 25E, 28E.

AAG	Convenience Group IV (SE FWD/SE AWD)	200	235

Includes Convenience Group III: speed control, tilt steering, power mirrors, power door locks, power windows, power quarter vent windows; illuminated entry, remote keyless entry, headlamp-off time delay. Some items may be standard on SE models. NOT AVAILABLE with 26A, 28A, 26B, 25B, 28B, AAE, 25C, 28C.

AAH	Convenience Group V (LE FWD/LE AWD/ES FWD/ES AWD)	128	150

Includes Convenience Group IV: speed control, tilt steering, power mirrors, power door locks, power windows, power quarter vent windows, illuminated entry, remote keyless entry, headlamp-off time delay; security alarm. Some items may be standard on LE and ES models. NOT AVAILABLE with 25J or 28J.

AAH	Convenience Group V (SE FWD/SE AWD)	327	385

Includes Convenience Group IV: speed control, tilt steering, power mirrors, power door locks, power windows, power quarter vent windows, illuminated entry, remote keyless entry, headlamp-off time delay; security alarm. Some items may be standard on SE models. NOT AVAILABLE with 26A, 28A, 26B, 25B, 28B, AAE, 25C, 28C.

CODE	DESCRIPTION	INVOICE	MSRP
NHK	Engine Block Heater	30	35
EFA	Engine: 3.0L V6 MPI (Base/SE FWD)	NC	NC
EGA	Engine: 3.3L MPI V6 (Base/SE FWD)	170	200
EGA	Engine: 3.3L MPI V6 (LE FWD/ES FWD)	NC	NC
EGM	Engine: 3.3L V6 FFV (LE FWD/ES FWD)	NC	NC
EGM	Engine: 3.3L V6 FFV (SE FWD)	170	200
EGH	Engine: 3.8L MPI V-6 (AWD)	NC	NC
EGH	Engine: 3.8L MPI V6 (LE FWD/ES FWD)	285	335
PWP	Golden White Pearl Tri-Coat (ES FWD/ES AWD)	170	200
RCE	Infinity Sound System (SE FWD/SE AWD)	336	395

Includes 10 speakers. REQUIRES RAZ. NOT AVAILABLE with 26A, 28A, 26B, 25B, 28B, 25C, 28C.

FL	Leather Low Back Bucket Seats (LE FWD/LE AWD/ES FWD/ES AWD)	757	890

REQUIRES CYS. NOT AVAILABLE with 25J, 28J, CYR.

SER	Load Leveling & Height Control (SE FWD/LE FWD/ES FWD)	247	290

NOT AVAILABLE with 26A, 28A, 26B, 25B, 28B, 28C, 25C, 25J, 28J.

AAP	Loading & Towing Group II (SE FWD/LE FWD)	153	180

Includes full size spare tire, HD suspension. NOT AVAILABLE with 26A, 28A, 25C, 28C, 25E, 28E, TBB, 25J, 28J, AAP, AAT.

AAP	Loading & Towing Group II with AAT (LE FWD/ES FWD)	123	145

Includes full size spare tire, HD suspension. REQUIRES AAT. NOT AVAILABLE with 25J, 28J, AAP.

AAR	Loading & Towing Group III (ES FWD/ES AWD)	293	345

Includes 685-amp battery, HD radiator, HD brakes, 120-amp alternator, HD transmission oil cooler. REQUIRES 25M or 28M or 29M.

DODGE GRAND CARAVAN

CODE	DESCRIPTION	INVOICE	MSRP
AAR	Loading & Towing Group III (SE FWD/SE AWD/LE FWD/LE AWD)	378	445
	Includes 685-amp battery, HD radiator, HD brakes, 120-amp alternator, HD transmission oil cooler. REQUIRES 26D or 25D or 28D or 25E or 28E or 25K or 28K or 29K or 29D. NOT AVAILABLE with 26A, 28A, 26B, 25B, 28B, 25C, 28C, AAB, 25J, 28J.		
AAR	Loading & Towing Group III (SE FWD/SE AWD/LE FWD/LE AWD)	323	380
	Includes 685-amp battery, HD radiator, HD brakes, 120-amp alternator, HD transmission oil cooler. REQUIRES AAB and (26D or 25D or 28D or 25E or 28E or 25K or 28K or 29K or 29D). NOT AVAILABLE with 26A, 28A, 26B, 25B, 28B, 25C, 28C, 25J, 28J.		
24S	Quick Order Package 24S (Base)	NC	NC
	Includes vehicle with standard equipment. REQUIRES 4XA and (EFA and DGA). NOT AVAILABLE with CYK, AAA, AAC, AAE, TBB, RAS, MWG, NAE, RBR.		
24T	Quick Order Package 24T (Base)	752	885
	Manufacturer Discount	(731)	(860)
	Net Price	21	25
	Includes air conditioning, under seat lockable drawer, rear floor silencer pad. REQUIRES EFA and DGA. NOT AVAILABLE with 4XA, AAA, AAC, NAE, TBB.		
25B	Quick Order Package 25B (SE FWD)	1024	1205
	Manufacturer Discount	(859)	(1010)
	Net Price	165	195
	Includes 7 passenger seating, windshield wiper de-icer. REQUIRES EGM and DGB. NOT AVAILABLE with WNG, CYS, 4XA, AAH, AAR, YCF, NAE, SER, AAA, AAE, AAF, TBB, AAP, RCE, AAB.		
25C	Quick Order Package 25C (SE FWD)	2108	2480
	Manufacturer Discount	(1092)	(1285)
	Net Price	1016	1195
	Includes Sport Package: fog lights, sunscreen glass, body colored bodyside moldings, body colored roof rack, 7 passenger seating, front and rear stabilizer bars, leather wrapped steering wheel, HD suspension, P215/65R16 AS SBR tires. REQUIRES EGM and DGB. NOT AVAILABLE with AAA, AAE, AAF, NAE, AAP, PC5, PMT, PTE, PTK, SER, RCE, MWG, CYS, PCN, AAH, AAR, AAB.		
25D	Quick Order Package 25D (SE FWD)	1904	2240
	Manufacturer Discount	(1114)	(1310)
	Net Price	790	930
	Includes deluxe sound insulation, Light Group with illuminated glove box, Convenience Group III: cruise control, tilt steering wheel, power door locks, power windows, power quarter vent windows; dual illuminated visor vanity mirrors, 7 passenger seating. REQUIRES EGM and DGB. NOT AVAILABLE with WNG, 4XA, AAA, AAE, AAF, YCF, NAE, TBB, AAP, AAR, AAB.		
25E	Quick Order Package 25E (SE FWD)	2988	3515
	Manufacturer Discount	(1347)	(1585)
	Net Price	1641	1930
	Includes Sport Package: fog lights, sunscreen glass, deluxe sound insulation, Light Group with illuminated glove box, Convenience Group III: cruise control, tilt steering		

GRAND CARAVAN — DODGE

CODE	DESCRIPTION	INVOICE	MSRP

wheel, power door locks, power windows, power quarter vent windows; dual illuminated visor vanity mirrors, body colored bodyside moldings, body colored roof rack, 7 passenger seating, front and rear stabilizer bars, leather wrapped steering wheel, HD suspension, P215/65R16 AS SBR tires. REQUIRES EGM AND DGB. NOT AVAILABLE with AAA, AAE, AAF, NAE, AAP, PC5, PMT, PTE, PTK, MWG, PCN, AAB, AAR.

25J   Quick Order Package 25J (LE FWD) .... NC   NC
Includes vehicle with standard equipment. REQUIRES EGM and DGB. NOT AVAILABLE with WNG, NAE, CYR, CYS, AAB, AAH, TBB, AAP, AAR, RAZ, MWG, SER, FL, 4XN, PWP, AAT.

25K   Quick Order Package 25K (LE FWD) 1084   1275
Manufacturer Discount .... (1012)   (1190)
Net Price 72   85
Includes air conditioning with dual temp control, sunscreen glass, AM/FM stereo with cassette, 8-way power driver's seat, 10 speaker Infinity sound system. REQUIRES EGM and DGB. NOT AVAILABLE with NAE, TBB, AAP, PWP.

25M   Quick Order Package 25M (ES FWD) 1500   1765
Manufacturer Discount .... (1012)   (1190)
Net Price 488   575
Includes air conditioning with dual temp control, passenger's assist handle, sunscreen glass, fog lights, automatic headlamps, electrochromic driver's mirror, automatic dimming rearview mirror, AM/FM stereo with cassette, 8-way power driver's seat, 10 speaker Infinity sound system, front and rear stabilizer bars, leather wrapped steering wheel, HD suspension, P215/65R16 AS touring tires, traction control, 16" aluminum wheels with gold accents, windshield wiper de-icer. REQUIRES EGM and DGB. NOT AVAILABLE with NAE, AAT, PC5, PMT, PPJ, PTK, PW7, TBB, WNG, PTE, AAP.

26A   Quick Order Package 26A (SE FWD) .... NC   NC
Includes vehicle with standard equipment. REQUIRES 4XA and (EFA and DGB). NOT AVAILABLE with WNG, 4XN, NAE, CYR, CYS, AAA, AAB, AAF, AAE, AAH, TBB, AAP, AAR, RAZ, MWG, SER, RCE.

26B   Quick Order Package 26B (SE FWD) 1024   1205
Manufacturer Discount .... (859)   (1010)
Net Price 165   195
Includes 7 passenger seating, windshield wiper de-icer. REQUIRES EFA and DGB. NOT AVAILABLE with WNG, NAE, 4XA, SER, AAA, AAE, AAF, TBB, AAP, RCE, CYS, AAH, AAR, AAB.

26D   Quick Order Package 26D (SE FWD) 1904   2240
Manufacturer Discount .... (1114)   (1310)
Net Price 790   930
Includes deluxe sound insulation, Light Group with illuminated glove box, Convenience Group III: cruise control, tilt steering wheel, power door locks, power windows, power quarter vent windows; dual illuminated visor vanity mirrors, 7 passenger seating. REQUIRES EFA and DGB. NOT AVAILABLE with WNG, NAE, 4XA, AAE, AAF, TBB, AAP, AAA, AAR, AAB.

DODGE GRAND CARAVAN

CODE	DESCRIPTION	INVOICE	MSRP
28A	Quick Order Package 28A (SE FWD)	NC	NC

Includes vehicle with standard equipment. NOT AVAILABLE with 4XA, EGA, DGB, NAE, WNG, 4XN, YCF, CYR, CYS, AAA, AAB, AAF, AAE, AAH, TBB, AAP, AAR, MWG, SER, RAZ, RCE.

28B	Quick Order Package 28B (SE FWD)	1024	1205
	Manufacturer Discount	(859)	(1010)
	Net Price	165	195

Includes 7 passenger seating, windshield wiper de-icer. REQUIRES EGA and DGB and NAE. NOT AVAILABLE with WNG, YCF, CYS, AAH, AAR, SER, AAA, AAE, AAF, TBB, AAP, RCE, 4XA, AAB.

28C	Quick Order Package 28C (SE FWD)	2108	2480
	Manufacturer Discount	(1092)	(1285)
	Net Price	1016	1195

Includes Sport Package: fog lights, sunscreen glass, body colored bodyside moldings, body colored roof rack, 7 passenger seating, front and rear stabilizer bars, leather wrapped steering wheel, HD suspension, P215/65R16 AS SBR tires. REQUIRES EGA and DGB and NAE. NOT AVAILABLE with YCF, CYS, AAH, AAP, SER, PC5, PMT, PTE, PTK, AAE, AAF, RCE, MWG, PCN, AAA, AAR, AAB.

28D	Quick Order Package 28D (SE FWD)	1904	2240
	Manufacturer Discount	(1114)	(1310)
	Net Price	790	930

Includes deluxe sound insulation, Light Group with illuminated glove box, Convenience Group III: cruise control, tilt steering wheel, power door locks, power windows, power quarter vent windows; dual illuminated visor vanity mirrors, 7 passenger seating. REQUIRES EGA and DGB and NAE. NOT AVAILABLE with WNG, YCF, 4XA, AAA, AAE, AAF, TBB, AAP, AAR, AAB.

28E	Quick Order Package 28E (SE FWD)	2988	3515
	Manufacturer Discount	(1347)	(1585)
	Net Price	1641	1930

Includes Sport Package: fog lights, sunscreen glass, body colored bodyside moldings, body colored roof rack, 7 passenger seating, front and rear stabilizer bars, leather wrapped steering wheel, HD suspension, P215/65R16 AS SBR tires, deluxe sound insulation, Light Group with illuminated glove box, Convenience Group III: cruise control, tilt steering wheel, power door locks, power windows, power quarter vent windows; dual illuminated visor vanity mirrors. REQUIRES EGA and DGB and NAE. NOT AVAILABLE with YCF, AAP, PC5, PTK, PCN, AAE, AAF, PMT, PTE, MWG, AAA, AAB, AAR.

28J	Quick Order Package 28J (LE FWD)	NC	NC

Includes vehicle with standard equipment. REQUIRES EGA and DGB and NAE. NOT AVAILABLE with WNG, YCF, CYR, CYS, AAB, AAH, TBB, AAP, AAR, RAZ, SER, FL, 4XN, PWP, MWG, AAT.

28M	Quick Order Package 28M (ES FWD)	1500	1765
	Manufacturer Discount	(1012)	(1190)
	Net Price	488	575

Includes air conditioning with dual temp control, passenger's assist handle, sunscreen glass, fog lights, automatic headlamps, electrochromic driver's mirror, automatic dimming rearview mirror, AM/FM stereo with cassette, 8-way power driver's seat,

GRAND CARAVAN — DODGE

CODE	DESCRIPTION	INVOICE	MSRP
	10 speaker Infinity sound system, front and rear stabilizer bars, leather wrapped steering wheel, HD suspension, P215/65R16 AS touring tires, traction control, 16" aluminum wheels with gold accents, windshield wiper de-icer. REQUIRES EGA and DGB and NAE. NOT AVAILABLE with YCF, AAT, PC5, PMT, PPJ, PTK, PW7, TBB, WNG, PTE, AAP.		
28S	Quick Order Package 28S (Base)	NC	NC
	Includes vehicle with standard equipment. REQUIRES EGA and DGB and NAE and 4XA. NOT AVAILABLE with YCF, AAA, AAC, AAE, CYK, MWG, RAS, RBR, TBB.		
28T	Quick Order Package 28T (Base)	752	885
	Manufacturer Discount	(731)	(860)
	Net Price	21	25
	Includes air conditioning, under seat lockable drawer, rear floor silencer pad. REQUIRES NAE and EGA and DGB. NOT AVAILABLE with 4XA, AAA, AAC, TBB, YCF.		
29M	Quick Order Package 29D (ES AWD)	1352	1590
	Manufacturer Discount	(935)	(1100)
	Net Price	417	490
	Includes air conditioning with dual temp control, interior assist handle, fog lights, sunscreen glass, automatic headlamps, automatic dimming rearview mirror, electrochromic driver's mirror, AM/FM stereo with cassette, 8-way power driver's seat, 10 speaker Infinity sound system, leather wrapped steering wheel, P215/70R15 AS BSW tires, 16" aluminum wheels with gold accents. REQUIRES EGH and DGB. NOT AVAILABLE with AAR, PC5, PMT, PPJ, PTE, PTK, PW7.		
29D	Quick Order Package 29D (SE AWD)	1904	2240
	Manufacturer Discount	(1114)	(1310)
	Net Price	790	930
	Includes air conditioning, rear window defroster, front and rear floor mats, deluxe sound insulation, Light Group with illuminated glove box, dual illuminated visor vanity mirrors, power quarter vent windows, power windows with driver's one touch down, windshield wiper de-icer. REQUIRES (EGH) engine and (DGB) transmission.		
29K	Quick Order Package 29K (LE AWD)	1084	1275
	Manufacturer Discount	(1012)	(1190)
	Net Price	72	85
	Includes air conditioning with dual temp control, sunscreen glass, AM/FM stereo with cassette, 8-way power driver's seat, 10 speaker Infinity sound system. REQUIRES EGH and DGB. NOT AVAILABLE with AAR, PWP.		
29K	Quick Order Package 29K (LE FWD)	1084	1275
	Manufacturer Discount	(1012)	(1190)
	Net Price	72	85
	Includes air conditioning with dual temp control, sunscreen glass, AM/FM stereo with cassette, 8-way power driver's seat, 10 speaker Infinity sound system. REQUIRES EGH and DGB. NOT AVAILABLE with TBB, AAP, PWP.		
29M	Quick Order Package 29M (ES FWD)	1500	1765
	Manufacturer Discount	(1012)	(1190)
	Net Price	488	575
	Includes air conditioning with dual temp control, passenger's assist handle, sunscreen glass, fog lights, automatic headlamps, electrochromic driver's mirror, automatic		

DODGE GRAND CARAVAN

CODE	DESCRIPTION	INVOICE	MSRP
	dimming rearview mirror, AM/FM stereo with cassette, 8-way power driver's seat, 10 speaker Infinity sound system, front and rear stabilizer bars, leather wrapped steering wheel, HD suspension, P215/65R16 AS touring tires, traction control, 16" aluminum wheels with gold accents, windshield wiper de-icer. REQUIRES EGH and DGB. NOT AVAILABLE with AAT, PC5, PMT, PPJ, PTK, PW7, TBB, WNG, PTE, AAP.		
RAS	Radio: AM/FM Stereo with Cassette (Base) .... NOT AVAILABLE with 24S, 28S.	153	180
RBR	Radio: AM/FM Stereo with CD (Base) .... NOT AVAILABLE with 24S, 28S.	276	325
RAZ	Radio: AM/FM Stereo with CD & Cassette (LE FWD/LE AWD/ES FWD/ES AWD) NOT AVAILABLE with 25J, 28J.	264	310
RAZ	Radio: AM/FM Stereo with CD & Cassette (SE FWD/SE AWD) .... NOT AVAILABLE with 26A, 28A.	276	325
4XN	Rear Air Conditioning Bypass (All except Base) .... With AAB (SE FWD) NOT AVAILABLE with 26A, 28A, 25J, 28J.	NC 241	NC 280
GFA	Rear Window Defroster (Base) .... With AAF (SE FWD) Includes exterior mirror heating element, windshield wiper de-icer.	166 NC	195 NC
GFA	Rear Window Defroster (Base/SE FWD) .... Includes exterior mirror heating element, windshield wiper de-icer. REQUIRES AAA or AAB or AAC. NOT AVAILABLE with 26B, 25B, 28B, 26D, 25D, 28D, 25C, 28C, 25E, 28E.	196	230
MWG	Roof Rack .... NOT AVAILABLE with 24S, 28S, 26A, 28A, 25C, 28C, 25E, 28E, 25J, 28J.	149	175
AWS	Smokers Group .... Includes cigar lighter and ash trays.	17	20
TBB	Tires: Full Size Spare .... NOT AVAILABLE with AAP, 24S, 28S, 26A, 28A, 25C, 28C, 25E, 28E, 25J, 28J.	94	110
BNM	Traction Control (LE FWD)	149	175
AAT	Wheels & Handling Group II (LE FWD) .... Includes HD suspension, 16" aluminum wheels, front and rear stabilizer bars. NOT AVAILABLE with 25J, 28J, AAP.	400	470
AAT	Wheels & Handling Group II with AAR (LE FWD) .... Includes HD suspension, 16" aluminum wheels, front and rear stabilizer bars. REQUIRES AAR. NOT AVAILABLE with 25J, 28J, AAP.	370	435
WNG	Wheels: 16" Aluminum (LE FWD/LE AWD) .... NOT AVAILABLE with 25J, 28J.	349	410
WNG	Wheels: 16" Aluminum (SE FWD) .... NOT AVAILABLE with 26A, 28A, 26B, 25B, 28B, 26D, 25D, 28D.	225	265

RAM 1500   DODGE

| CODE | DESCRIPTION | INVOICE | MSRP |

1998 RAM 1500

1998 Dodge Ram SST

What's New?

Available as a sedan! The Ram Quad Cab, as in four doors, becomes the first pickup on the market with two rear access doors. And for convenience, the front seat belts are now integrated into the front seats, making for obstruction-free rear access. All Rams get a totally redesigned interior, standard passenger-side airbag with cutoff switch, and all airbags are "depowered" for safety.

Review

The Dodge boys had to know they had a winner when their bold Ram pickup debuted for 1994. Few trucks have turned as many heads, or prompted so much comment. Whether decked out in Sport trim or wearing conventional chrome on its chest-thumping grille, this is macho mentality sculpted in steel.

Under the hood, the goods range from modest to mammoth. For the practical-minded, there's a mild-mannered 3.9-liter V-6; or, a Cummins diesel whose throbbing note and power make a guy want to grab his Stetson and haul on out.

Those who'd like a little more muscle have a pair of V-8s to choose from. Whoa! You're still not satisfied? Like TV's Tim the Tool Man, you want "more power?" Say no more. Just check the option list and you can barrel homeward with an 8.0-liter V-10, blasting out 300 horses, and a locomotive-like 450 pounds-feet of torque. The Magnum V-10 is available only in heavy-duty 2500 and 3500 series pickups.

One first-season criticism centered on space. Only the regular cab was available, seating three on a bench. Dodge claimed its cab was the most spacious in the industry, but that was little consolation to potential buyers who needed to carry extra people. Two years ago, Dodge introduced a Club Cab that seated six adults, even if access to the rear wasn't so easy. Last year, Club Cab models received standard rear-quarter window glass. For 1998, the rules have changed again. Dodge now offers a Ram Quad Cab, which means rear-access doors on either side of the cab. This is truly the most convenient truck you can buy.

Inside, the Ram is finally redesigned, creating ergonomics to match the utility of the rest of the truck. A new passenger-side airbag comes standard, and with a cutoff switch, it's safe to strap in a child seat up front. With any engine, tromping the gas produces a reassuring roar—

DODGE RAM 1500

a reverberation of vitality. Otherwise, it's fairly quiet. Ride and handling are so competent that you almost forget you're in a full-size pickup, though occupants will notice plenty of bumps. Visibility is great, and controls are excellent. Automatic-transmission shifts are firm, but not harsh, and the column-mounted gearshift operates easily. For such a large and bulky vehicle, the Ram is surprisingly agile and reasonably sure-footed, but think twice before making any quick maneuvers.

More than 1,000,000 Rams went to customers during the first three years of production. Demand is still strong, and Chrysler recently opened a new plant to keep the supply lines full. Curiosity has tapered off, but when pickup owners try to sleep on the idea of buying a new truck, they count Rams.

Safety Data

Driver Airbag: *Standard*
Side Airbag: *Not Available*
Traction Control: *Not Available*
Driver Crash Test Grade: *Good*

Passenger Airbag: *Standard*
4-Wheel ABS: *Optional*
Integrated Child Seat(s): *Not Available*
Passenger Crash Test Grade: *Not Available*

Standard Equipment

2WD REGULAR CAB SB: 3.9L V-6 OHV SMPI 12-valve engine; 5-speed overdrive manual transmission; 600-amp battery; 117-amp alternator; rear wheel drive, 3.21 axle ratio; stainless steel exhaust; front independent suspension with anti-roll bar, front coil springs, HD front shocks, rear suspension with rear leaf springs, HD rear shocks; power re-circulating ball steering with vehicle speed-sensing assist; front disc/rear drum brakes with rear wheel anti-lock braking system; 26 gal capacity fuel tank; regular pick-up box; front and rear chrome bumpers with black rub strip; monotone paint; aero-composite halogen headlamps; additional exterior lights include center high mounted stop light, pickup cargo box light; driver and passenger manual black folding outside mirrors; front and rear 16" x 7"; front and rear silver styled steel wheels, hub wheel covers with trim rings; P225/75SR16 BSW AS front and rear tires; underbody mounted full-size conventional steel spare wheel; AM/FM stereo with clock, seek-scan, cassette, 4 speakers and fixed antenna; 2 power accessory outlets; analog instrumentation display includes oil pressure gauge, water temp gauge, volt gauge, trip odometer; warning indicators include low oil level, lights on, key in ignition; driver side airbag, passenger side cancelable airbag; tinted windows; variable intermittent front windshield wipers; seating capacity of 3, 40-20-40 bench front seat with adjustable headrests, center armrest with storage, driver seat includes 4-way direction control, passenger seat includes 4-way direction control; front height adjustable seatbelts; vinyl seats, full cloth headliner, full vinyl floor covering , CABback insulator; interior lights include dome light; day-night rear-view mirror; glove box, front cupholder, instrument panel bin; cargo concealed storage; chrome grille, black door handles.

2WD REGULAR CAB WS LB (in addition to or instead of 2WD REGULAR CAB SB): 35 gal capacity fuel tank.

4WD REGULAR CAB SB (in addition to or instead of 2WD REGULAR CAB SB): 5.2L V-8 OHV SMPI 16-valve engine; part-time 4 wheel drive, with auto locking hub control and manual shift, 3.55 axle ratio; front non-independent suspension with anti-roll bar.

4WD REGULAR CAB LB (in addition to or instead of 4WD REGULAR CAB SB): 35 gal capacity fuel tank.

2WD EXTENDED CAB SB (in addition to or instead of 2WD REGULAR CAB SB): 5.2L V-8 OHV SMPI 16-valve engine; deep tinted windows, vented rear windows; seating capacity of 6, 40-20-40 split-bench front seat driver seat includes 4-way direction control, easy entry, passenger seat includes 4-way direction control, easy entry; fixed full folding rear bench seat.

RAM 1500 DODGE

CODE	DESCRIPTION	INVOICE	MSRP

2WD EXTENDED CAB LB (in addition to or instead of 2WD EXTENDED CAB SB): 35 gal capacity fuel tank.

4WD EXTENDED CAB SB (in addition to or instead of 2WD EXTENDED CAB SB): Part-time 4 wheel drive with auto locking hub control and manual shift, 3.55 axle ratio; front non-independent suspension with anti-roll bar; additional exterior lights include center high mounted stop light; P245/75SR16 BSW AS front and rear tires; sport steering wheel; front and rear cupholders.

4WD EXTENDED CAB LB (in addition to or instead of 4WD EXTENDED CAB SB): 35 gal capacity fuel tank; front and rear silver styled steel wheels, hub wheel covers; LT225/75SR16 BSW AS front and rear tires.

2WD QUAD CAB SB (in addition to or instead of 2WD REGULAR CAB SB): 5.2L V-8 OHV SMPI 16-valve engine; deep tinted windows, vented rear windows; seating capacity of 6, 40-20-40 split-bench front seat driver seat includes 4-way direction control, easy entry, passenger seat includes 4-way direction control, easy entry; fixed full folding rear bench seat.

2WD QUAD CAB LB (in addition to or instead of 2WD QUAD CAB SB): 35 gal capacity fuel tank.

4WD QUAD CAB SB (in addition to or instead of 2WD QUAD CAB SB): Part-time 4 wheel drive, with auto locking hub control and manual shift, 3.55 axle ratio; front non-independent suspension with anti-roll bar; P245/75SR16 BSW AS front and rear tires; sport steering wheel; front and rear cupholders.

4WD QUAD CAB LB (in addition to or instead of 4WD QUAD CAB SB): 35 gal capacity fuel tank; LT225/75SR16 BSW AS front and rear tires.

Base Prices

Code	Description	Invoice	MSRP
BR1L61	WS Regular Cab 2WD SB	13232	14485
BR1L62	WS Regular Cab 2WD LB	13469	14755
BR1L61	Regular Cab 2WD SB	14306	16260
BR1L62	Regular Cab 2WD LB	14548	16545
BR6L61	Regular Cab 4WD SB	17373	19815
BR6L62	Regular Cab 4WD LB	17662	20155
BE1L31	Extended Cab 2WD SB	16649	18975
BE1L32	Extended Cab 2WD LB	16887	19255
BE6L31	Extended Cab 4WD SB	19434	22205
BE6L32	Extended Cab 4WD LB	19715	22535
BE1L33	Quad Cab 2WD SB	17296	19725
BE1L34	Quad Cab 2WD LB	17534	20005
BE6L33	Quad Cab 4WD SB	20072	22955
BE6L34	Quad Cab 4WD LB	20352	23285
Destination Charge:		640	640

DODGE RAM 1500

CODE	DESCRIPTION	INVOICE	MSRP

Accessories

CODE	DESCRIPTION	INVOICE	MSRP
DMD	3.55 Axle Ratio	43	50
DMH	3.92 Axle Ratio	43	50
	REQUIRES (DSA) sure grip axle. NOT AVAILABLE with 22A.		
DGB	4-Speed Automatic Transmission	808	950
	NOT AVAILABLE with (23A), (23G), (ADJ) HD service group.		
BGK	4-Wheel Antilock Brakes	425	500
DDC	5-Speed Manual Transmission (Std)	NC	NC
	NOT AVAILABLE with 24A, 26A, 24G, 26G, EML.		
JPS	6-Way Power Driver's Seat	272	320
	NOT AVAILABLE with (AGG) Sport Appearance Group, (SX) seats, (D3) seats.		
GPC	7"x10" Dual Bright Mirrors	(81)	(95)
	For camper and towing applications. NOT AVAILABLE with (AGL) Super Sport Truck Performance (SS/T).		
GPC	7"x10" Dual Bright Mirrors	43	50
	For camper and towing applications.		
JPV	8-Way Power Driver's Seat	306	360
	NOT AVAILABLE with (SX) seats.		
HAA	Air Conditioning	680	800
	NOT AVAILABLE with (4XA) air conditioning bypass.		
AMR	Behind Seat Storage (WS)	81	95
	Modular system. Includes storage tray and cab back stowage.		
K17	Black Bodyside Molding with Bright Insert	89	105
6C8	Black CC with Flame Red CC	183	215
	NOT AVAILABLE with (AGG) Sport Appearance Group, (AGL) Super Sport Truck Performance (SS/T).		
6D1	Black CC with Light Driftwood SG	166	195
	NOT AVAILABLE with (AGG) Sport Appearance Group, (AGL) Super Sport Truck Performance (SS/T).		
6C1	Black CC with Light Driftwood SG	183	215
	NOT AVAILABLE with (AGG) Sport Appearance Group, (AGL) Super Sport Truck Performance (SS/T).		
YCF	Border State (California) Emissions	145	170
	NOT AVAILABLE with (NAE) CA/CT/MA/NY Emissions.		
6D7	Bright White CC with Light Driftwood SG	166	195
	NOT AVAILABLE with (AGG) Sport Appearance Group, (AGL) Super Sport Truck Performance (SS/T).		
6C9	Bright White CC with Light Driftwood SG	183	215
	NOT AVAILABLE with (AGG) Sport Appearance Group, (AGL) Super Sport Truck Performance (SS/T).		
NAE	CA/CT/MA/NY Emissions	145	170
	Automatically coded. NOT AVAILABLE with (YCF) border state emissions.		
LNC	Cab Clearance Lights	68	80
	NOT AVAILABLE with (AGL) Super Sport Truck Performance (SS/T).		
LPE	Cargo Light (WS)	34	40

RAM 1500 — DODGE

CODE	DESCRIPTION	INVOICE	MSRP
S9	Cloth 40/20/40 Split Bench Seat	94	110
	REQUIRES (AGG) Sport Appearance Group. NOT AVAILABLE with (D3) seats, (TY) seats.		
D3	Cloth/Vinyl Bench Seat (WS)	94	110
6C4	Dark Chestnut PC with Light Driftwood SG	183	215
	NOT AVAILABLE with (AGG) Sport Appearance Group, (AGL) Super Sport Truck Performance (SS/T).		
6D4	Dark Chestnut PC with Light Driftwood SG	166	195
	NOT AVAILABLE with (AGG) Sport Appearance Group, (AGL) Super Sport Truck Performance (SS/T).		
6CD	Deep Amethyst PC with Light Driftwood SG	183	215
	NOT AVAILABLE with (AGG) Sport Appearance Group, (AGL) Super Sport Truck Performance (SS/T).		
6DD	Deep Amethyst PC with Light Driftwood SG	166	195
	NOT AVAILABLE with (AGG) Sport Appearance Group, (AGL) Super Sport Truck Performance (SS/T).		
AJK	Deluxe Convenience Group	332	390
	Includes electronic speed control.		
GTS	Dual Power Black Heated Mirrors	123	145
	NOT AVAILABLE with (GPC) 7"x10" dual bright mirrors.		
6C7	Emerald Green PC with Light Driftwood SG	183	215
	NOT AVAILABLE with (AGG) Sport Appearance Group, (AGL) Super Sport Truck Performance (SS/T).		
6D8	Emerald Green PC with Light Driftwood SG	166	195
	NOT AVAILABLE with (AGG) Sport Appearance Group, (AGL) Super Sport Truck Performance (SS/T).		
NHK	Engine Block Heater	34	40
EHC	Engine: 3.9L MPI V-6 (Std)	NC	NC
ELF	Engine: 5.2L MPI V-8 Magnum	502	590
ELF	Engine: 5.2L MPI V-8 Magnum (Std)	NC	NC
	NOT AVAILABLE with 26A, 26G.		
EML	Engine: 5.9L MPI V-8 Magnum	752	885
EML	Engine: 5.9L MPI V-8 Magnum	251	295
	NOT AVAILABLE with 23A, 24A, 23G, 24G, DDC.		
6D5	Flame Red CC with Light Driftwood SG	166	195
	NOT AVAILABLE with (AGG) Sport Appearance Group, (AGL) Super Sport Truck Performance (SS/T).		
LNJ	Fog Lamps	102	120
6D3	Forest Green PC with Light Driftwood SG	166	195
	NOT AVAILABLE with (AGG) Sport Appearance Group, (AGL) Super Sport Truck Performance (SS/T).		
6C3	Forest Green PC with Light Driftwood SG	183	215
	NOT AVAILABLE with (AGG) Sport Appearance Group, (AGL) Super Sport Truck Performance (SS/T).		
CKE	Front Seat Area Carpet	94	110
NHB	HD Aux. Auto Transmission Oil Cooler	51	60
	REQUIRES DGB or NMC. NOT AVAILABLE with 21A, 22A, 23A, 23G.		

DODGE RAM 1500

CODE	DESCRIPTION	INVOICE	MSRP
ADJ	**HD Service Group**	183	215
	Includes 136-amp alternator. NOT AVAILABLE with 24A, 26A, 24G, 26G, ADJ.		
ADJ	**HD Service Group with Auto Trans**	293	345
	Includes 136-amp alternator, maximum engine cooler, HD aux. auto transmission oil cooler. NOT AVAILABLE with 21A, 22A, 23A, 23G, ADJ.		
ADJ	**HD Service Group with Auto Trans (4WD)**	332	390
	Includes maximum engine cooler, 136-amp alternator, HD aux. auto transmission oil cooler. REQUIRES DGB. NOT AVAILABLE with 23A, 23G, ADJ.		
ADJ	**HD Service Group with Manual Trans (4WD)**	221	260
	Includes 136-amp alternator. NOT AVAILABLE with 24A, 26A, 24G, 26G, ADJ, DGB.		
TY	**HD Vinyl Bench Seat (Quad Cab)**	NC	NC
	NOT AVAILABLE with (S9) seats.		
6D2	**Intense Blue PC with Light Driftwood SG**	166	195
	NOT AVAILABLE with (AGG) Sport Appearance Group, (AGL) Super Sport Truck Performance (SS/T).		
6C2	**Intense Blue PC with Light Driftwood SG**	183	215
	NOT AVAILABLE with (AGG) Sport Appearance Group, (AGL) Super Sport Truck Performance (SS/T).		
AJD	**Leather Interior Group**	1309	1540
	Includes woodgrain instrument panel bezel, Travel Convenience Group, leather 40/20/40 double split bench seat, 8-way power driver's seat. NOT AVAILABLE with (SX) seats, (S9) seats.		
AJD	**Leather Interior Group**	1190	1400
	Includes woodgrain instrument panel bezel, Travel Convenience Group, 6-way power driver's seat, leather 40/20/40 double split bench seat. NOT AVAILABLE with (SX) seats, (D3) seats.		
ADA	**Light Group**	102	120
	Includes passenger assist grab handle (right roof header), full deluxe cloth headliner and ignition key light with time delay, underhood compartment light.		
NMC	**Maximum Engine Cooler**	111	130
	REQUIRES (DGB) transmission. NOT AVAILABLE with 23A, 23G.		
6C5	**Metallic Red CC with Light Driftwood SG**	183	215
	NOT AVAILABLE with (AGG) Sport Appearance Group, (AGL) Super Sport Truck Performance (SS/T).		
6D6	**Metallic Red CC with Light Driftwood SG**	166	195
	NOT AVAILABLE with (AGG) Sport Appearance Group, (AGL) Super Sport Truck Performance (SS/T).		
4XM	**No Rear Bumper (WS)**	NC	NC
	NOT AVAILABLE with (MBD) rear argent bumper.		
21A	**Quick Order Package 21A (2WD Regular Cab)**	NC	NC
	Includes 3.21 axle ratio. REQUIRES (HAA or 4XA) and EHC and DDC. NOT AVAILABLE with AHC, ADJ, NHB.		
21W	**Quick Order Package 21W (2WD Regular Cab WS)**	NC	NC
	Includes radio delete, 3.21 axle ratio. REQUIRES (HAA or 4XA) and EHC and DDC.		
22A	**Quick Order Package 22A (2WD Regular Cab)**	NC	NC
	Includes 3.55 axle ratio. REQUIRES (HAA or 4XA) and EHC and DGB. NOT AVAILABLE with DMH, AHC, ADJ, NHB.		

RAM 1500 — DODGE

CODE	DESCRIPTION	INVOICE	MSRP
22W	Quick Order Package 22W (2WD Regular Cab WS)	NC	NC
	Includes radio delete, 3.55 axle ratio. REQUIRES (HAA or 4XA) and EHC and DGB.		
23A	Quick Order Package 23A (2WD)	NC	NC
	Includes 3.21 axle ratio. REQUIRES (HAA or 4XA) and ELF and DDC. NOT AVAILABLE with ADJ, NHB, NMC.		
23A	Quick Order Package 23A (4WD)	NC	NC
	Includes 3.55 axle ratio. REQUIRES (4XA or HAA) and ELF and DDC. NOT AVAILABLE with ADJ, EML, DGB, NMC, NHB.		
23G	Quick Order Package 23G (2WD)	2639	3105
	Manufacturer Discount	(595)	(700)
	Net Price	2044	2405
	Includes air conditioning, front seat area carpet, Deluxe Convenience Group: electronic speed control, dual electric horn, underhood compartment light, Light Group, dual power black heated mirrors, black bodyside molding with bright insert, SLT Decor Group: cloth sun visors, cloth with lower carpet door trim, driver's/passenger's door storage bins, deluxe sound insulation, Power Convenience Group, premium cloth 40/20/40 split bench seat, front bumper sight shields, tachometer, P245/75R16 BSW AS tires, 16" x 7" cast aluminum wheels, non-matching spare wheel, 3.21 axle ratio. REQUIRES ELF and DDC.		
23G	Quick Order Package 23G (4WD)	2639	3105
	Manufacturer Discount	(595)	(700)
	Net Price	2044	2405
	Includes air conditioning, front seat area carpet, Deluxe Convenience Group: electronic speed control, dual electric horn, underhood compartment light, Light Group, dual power black heated mirrors, black bodyside molding with bright insert, Power Convenience Group, SLT Decor Group: cloth sun visors, cloth with lower carpet door trim, driver's/passenger's door storage bins, deluxe sound insulation, premium cloth 40/20/40 split bench seat, front bumper sight shields, tachometer, P245/75R16 BSW AS tires, cast aluminum wheels, non-matching spare wheel, 3.55 axle ratio. REQUIRES ELF and DDC. NOT AVAILABLE with ADJ, AGL, NHB, NMC.		
23G	Quick Order Package 23G (4WD Laramie)	2529	2975
	Manufacturer Discount	(595)	(700)
	Net Price	1934	2275
	Includes air conditioning, front seat area carpet, Deluxe Convenience Group: electronic speed control, dual electric horn, Light Group, dual power black heated mirrors, black bodyside molding with bright insert, Power Convenience Group, SLT Decor Group: cloth sun visors, cloth with lower carpet door trim, driver's/passenger's door storage bins, deluxe sound insulation, premium cloth 40/20/40 split bench seat, front bumper sight shields, tachometer, cast aluminum wheels, non-matching spare wheel, 3.55 axle ratio. REQUIRES ELF and DDC. NOT AVAILABLE with ADJ, EML, DGB, NMC, NHB.		
24A	Quick Order Package 24A (2WD)	NC	NC
	Includes 3.55 axle ratio. REQUIRES (HAA or 4XA) and ELF and DGB. NOT AVAILABLE with ADJ.		

DODGE   RAM 1500

CODE	DESCRIPTION	INVOICE	MSRP
24A	Quick Order Package 24A (4WD)	NC	NC

Includes 3.55 axle ratio. REQUIRES (4XA or HAA) and ELF and DGB. NOT AVAILABLE with ADJ, EML, DDC.

24G	Quick Order Package 24G (4WD)	2529	2975
	Manufacturer Discount	(595)	(700)
	Net Price	1934	2275

Includes air conditioning, front seat area carpet, Deluxe Convenience Group: electronic speed control, dual electric horn, underhood compartment light, Light Group, dual power black heated mirrors, black bodyside molding with bright insert, Power Convenience Group, SLT Decor Group: cloth sun visors, cloth with lower carpet door trim, driver's/passenger's door storage bins, deluxe sound insulation, premium cloth 40/20/40 split bench seat, front bumper sight shields, tachometer, cast aluminum wheels, non-matching spare wheel, 3.55 axle ratio. REQUIRES ELF and DGB. NOT AVAILABLE with ADJ, EML, DDC.

24G	Quick Order Package 24G (2WD)	2639	3105
	Manufacturer Discount	(595)	(700)
	Net Price	2044	2405

Includes air conditioning, front seat area carpet, Deluxe Convenience Group: electronic speed control, dual electric horn, underhood compartment light, Light Group, dual power black heated mirrors, black bodyside molding with bright insert, Power Convenience Group, SLT Decor Group: cloth sun visors, cloth with lower carpet door trim, driver's/passenger's door storage bins, deluxe sound insulation, premium cloth 40/20/40 split bench seat, front bumper sight shields, tachometer, P245/75R16 BSW AS tires, 16" x 7" cast aluminum wheels, non-matching spare wheel, 3.55 axle ratio. REQUIRES ELF and DGB.

26A	Quick Order Package 26A	NC	NC

Includes 3.55 axle ratio. REQUIRES (HAA or 4XA) and EML and DGB. NOT AVAILABLE with ADJ, DDC, ELF.

26G	Quick Order Package 26G (2WD)	2639	3105
	Manufacturer Discount	(595)	(700)
	Net Price	2044	2405

Includes air conditioning, front seat area carpet, Deluxe Convenience Group: electronic speed control, dual electric horn, underhood compartment light, Light Group, dual power black heated mirrors, black bodyside molding with bright insert, Power Convenience Group, SLT Decor Group: cloth sun visors, cloth with lower carpet door trim, driver's/passenger's door storage bins, deluxe sound insulation, premium cloth 40/20/40 split bench seat, front bumper sight shields, tachometer, P245/75R16 BSW AS tires, 16" x 7" cast aluminum wheels, non-matching spare wheel, 3.55 axle ratio. REQUIRES (EML) engine and (DGB) transmission. NOT AVAILABLE with (ADJ) HD Service Group.

26G	Quick Order Package 26G (4WD)	2529	2975
	Manufacturer Discount	(595)	(700)
	Net Price	1934	2275

Includes air conditioning, front seat area carpet, Deluxe Convenience Group: electronic speed control, dual electric horn, Light Group, dual power black heated mirrors, black bodyside molding with bright insert, Power Convenience Group, SLT Decor Group: cloth sun visors, cloth with lower carpet door trim, driver's/passenger's door storage

RAM 1500 — DODGE

CODE	DESCRIPTION	INVOICE	MSRP
	bins, deluxe sound insulation, premium cloth 40/20/40 split bench seat, front bumper sight shields, tachometer, cast aluminum wheels, non-matching spare wheel, 3.55 axle ratio. REQUIRES EML and DGB. NOT AVAILABLE with ADJ, ELF, DDC.		
26G	Quick Order Package 26G (4WD Regular Cab)	2639	3105
	Manufacturer Discount	(595)	(700)
	Net Price	2044	2405
	Includes air conditioning, front seat area carpet, Deluxe Convenience Group: electronic speed control, dual electric horn, underhood compartment light, Light Group, dual power black heated mirrors, black bodyside molding with bright insert, Power Convenience Group, SLT Decor Group: cloth sun visors, cloth with lower carpet door trim, driver's/passenger's door storage bins, deluxe sound insulation, premium cloth 40/20/40 split bench seat, front bumper sight shields, tachometer, P245/75R16 BSW AS tires, cast aluminum wheels, non-matching spare wheel, 3.55 axle ratio. REQUIRES EML and DGB. NOT AVAILABLE with (ADJ) HD Service Group.		
RAS	Radio: AM/FM Stereo with Cassette (WS)	340	400
RBN	Radio: AM/FM Stereo with Cassette, EQ	285	335
	NOT AVAILABLE with (RAZ) radio, (RBR) radio.		
RAZ	Radio: AM/FM Stereo with CD, Cassette, EQ	587	690
	NOT AVAILABLE with (RBN) radio, (RBR) radio.		
RBR	Radio: AM/FM Stereo with CD	434	510
	NOT AVAILABLE with (RBN) radio, (RAZ) radio.		
MBD	Rear Argent Bumper (WS)	115	135
	NOT AVAILABLE with (4XM) no rear bumper.		
CF8	Rear Seat Delete (Quad Cab)	NC	NC
MBQ	Rear Step Body Color Bumper	43	50
	REQUIRES AGG or AGL.		
GXM	Remote Keyless Entry System	162	190
	Includes 2 transmitters.		
LSA	Security Alarm	128	150
	REQUIRES (GXM) remote keyless entry system.		
GFD	Sliding Rear Window	119	140
AGG	Sport Appearance Group (2WD)	327	385
	Includes dual electric horns, 'Sport' decal, front bumper sight shields, tachometer (in analog cluster), cast aluminum wheels, color keyed grille, fog lamps, front color keyed bumper, bodyside with insert molding delete, P245/75R16 OWL AS tires. NOT AVAILABLE with AGL, JPS, SX.		
AGG	Sport Appearance Group (4WD)	570	670
	Deletes tailgate applique from SLT Decor Group and SLT badges. front color keyed bumper, color keyed grille, 'Sport' decal on rear quarter box, fog lamps, P265/75R16 OWL AT tires, color-keyed rear valance panel. NOT AVAILABLE with TYZ, TYV.		
AGL	Super Sport Truck Performance (SS/T) (2WD)	1156	1360
	Includes sight shields, tachometer, 'Dodge' and '1500 Magnum V-8 Engine' decals and dual electric horns, front color keyed bumper, color keyed grille, fog lamps, sport tuned exhaust with chrome tip, P275/60R17 goodyear tires, dual wide center stripe, 17" x 9" cast aluminum wheels. NOT AVAILABLE with 23G, 24G, LNC, GPC, AGG, WDB.		

DODGE RAM 1500 / 2500

CODE	DESCRIPTION	INVOICE	MSRP
DSA	Sure Grip Axle	242	285
	REQUIRES (DMD) 3.55 axle ratio or (DMH) 3.92 axle ratio.		
JAY	Tachometer	68	80
	INCLUDED in 23G, 24G, 26G.		
TYU	Tires: P245/75R16 BSW AS	111	130
	NOT AVAILABLE with (TYX) tires.		
TYX	Tires: P245/75R16 BSW AT (4WD)	128	150
TYX	Tires: P245/75R16 BSW AT (4WD Regular Cab)	238	280
	NOT AVAILABLE with (TYU) tires.		
TYV	Tires: P245/75R16 OWL AS (4WD Quad Cab)	128	150
	NOT AVAILABLE with (TYZ) tires, (TXW) tires, (AGG) Sport Appearance Group.		
TYZ	Tires: P245/75R16 OWL AT (4WD)	234	275
	NOT AVAILABLE with (TYV) tires, (TXW) tires, (AGG) Sport Appearance Group.		
TYV	Tires: P245/75R16C AS OWL	111	130
	NOT AVAILABLE with (TYZ) tires, (TXW) tires, (AGG) Sport Appearance Group.		
TXW	Tires: P265/75R16 OWL AT (4WD)	353	415
	NOT AVAILABLE with (TYV) tires, (TYZ) tires.		
AHC	Trailer Tow Group	208	245
	Includes HD flasher. REQUIRES (ADJ) HD service group. NOT AVAILABLE with 21A, 22A.		
AWK	Travel Convenience Group	251	295
SX	Vinyl 40/20/40 Split Bench Seat	NC	NC
	NOT AVAILABLE with D3, AJD, AGG, JPS, JPV.		
WDB	Wheels: Chrome Steel	NC	NC
	NOT AVAILABLE with (AGL) Super Sport Truck Performance (SS/T).		
WDB	Wheels: Chrome Steel	293	345

1998 RAM 2500

Safety Data

Driver Airbag: *Standard*
Side Airbag: *Not Available*
Traction Control: *Not Available*
Driver Crash Test Grade: *Good*

Passenger Airbag: *Standard*
4-Wheel ABS: *Optional*
Integrated Child Seat(s): *Not Available*
Passenger Crash Test Grade: *Not Available*

Standard Equipment

2WD REGULAR CAB: 5.9L V-8 OHV SMPI 16-valve engine; 5-speed overdrive manual transmission; 600-amp battery; 117-amp alternator; rear wheel drive, 3.54 axle ratio; stainless steel exhaust; front independent suspension with anti-roll bar, front coil springs, HD front shocks, rear suspension with rear leaf springs, HD rear shocks; power re-circulating ball steering with vehicle speed-sensing assist; front disc/rear drum brakes with rear wheel anti-lock braking system; 35 gal capacity fuel tank; front and rear chrome bumpers with black rub strip, rear step; monotone paint; aero-composite halogen headlamps; additional exterior lights include center high mounted stop light, pickup cargo box light; driver and passenger manual black folding outside mirrors; front and rear 16" x 6.5" silver styled steel wheels with hub wheel covers with trim rings; LT245/75SR16 BSW AS front and rear tires; underbody mounted full-size conventional steel spare wheel; AM/FM stereo, clock, with seek-scan, cassette, 4 speakers

RAM 2500 DODGE

CODE	DESCRIPTION	INVOICE	MSRP

and fixed antenna; 2 power accessory outlets; analog instrumentation display includes oil pressure gauge, water temp gauge, volt gauge, trip odometer; warning indicators include low oil level, lights on, key in ignition; driver side airbag, passenger side cancelable airbag; tinted windows; variable intermittent front windshield wipers; seating capacity of 3, 40-20-40 split-bench front seat with fixed adjustable headrests, with center armrest with storage, driver seat includes 4-way direction control, passenger seat includes 4-way direction control; front height adjustable seatbelts; vinyl seats, full cloth headliner, full vinyl floor covering, cabback insulator; interior lights include dome light; day-night rearview mirror; glove box, front cupholder, instrument panel bin; cargo concealed storage; chrome grille, black side window moldings, black front windshield molding, black rear window molding, black door handles.

2WD EXTENDED CAB & QUAD CAB (in addition to or instead of 2WD REGULAR CAB): 34 gal capacity fuel tank; deep tinted windows, vented rear windows; seating capacity of 6, driver seat includes easy entry, passenger seat includes easy entry; full folding rear bench seat.

4WD REGULAR CAB (in addition to or instead of 2WD EXTENDED CAB & QUAD CAB): Part-time 4 wheel drive, auto locking hub control and manual shift; front non-independent suspension; black bodyside molding with chrome bodyside insert; additional exterior lights include underhood light; driver power remote outside mirror, passenger manual remote outside mirror; full-size temporary spare wheel; air conditioning; cruise control with steering wheel controls; includes tachometer gauge; warning indicators include battery, low fuel, low washer fluid; tinted windows, power front windows with driver 1-touch down; seating capacity of 3; premium cloth seats, cloth door trim insert, carpet floor covering with carpeted floor mats, deluxe sound insulation; interior lights include; leather-wrapped sport steering wheel; passenger side vanity mirror; mini overhead console with storage, with light, driver and passenger door bins; cargo net, cargo concealed storage.

4WD EXTENDED CAB & QUAD CAB (in addition to or instead of 4WD REGULAR CAB): 34 gal capacity fuel tank; full-size conventional spare wheel; deep tinted windows, vented rear windows; seating capacity of 6, driver seat includes easy entry, passenger seat includes easy entry; full folding rear bench seat; vinyl seats, vinyl floor covering.

Base Prices

Code	Description	Invoice	MSRP
BR2L62	Regular Cab 2WD	17069	19510
BE2L31	Extended Cab 2WD SB	18617	21290
BE2L32	Extended Cab 2WD LB	18778	21480
BE2L33	Quad Cab 2WD SB	19264	22040
BE2L34	Quad Cab 2WD LB	19426	22230
BR7L62	Regular Cab 4WD	20016	22925
BE7L31	Extended Cab 4WD SB	21415	24535
BE7L32	Extended Cab 4WD LB	21576	24725
BE7L33	Quad Cab 4WD SB	22052	25285
BE7L34	Quad Cab 4WD LB	22214	25475
Destination Charge:		640	640

Accessories

Code	Description	Invoice	MSRP
DGB	4-Speed Automatic Transmission	808	950
	Includes PRNDL in instrument panel. NOT AVAILABLE with EWA, ETB, 25A, 27A, 29A, 25G, 27G, 29G, NMC.		

DODGE RAM 2500

CODE	DESCRIPTION	INVOICE	MSRP
BGK	4-Wheel Antilock Brakes	425	500
DMF	4.09 Axle Ratio	43	50
	NOT AVAILABLE with (DMF) 4.09 axle ratio.		
DDX	5-Speed Manual Transmission	NC	NC
	NOT AVAILABLE with EWA, 25A, 26A, 28A, 2YA, 25G, 26G, 28G, 2YG, ETB, AGG, EML, NMC.		
DDP	5-Speed Manual Transmission (Std)	NC	NC
	NOT AVAILABLE with AGG, EWA, ETB, 26A, 27A, 28A, 29A, 2YA, 26G, 27G, 28G, 29G, 2YG, NMC.		
GPC	7"x10" Dual Bright Mirrors	(81)	(95)
	For camper and towing applications.		
GPC	7"x10" Dual Bright Mirrors	(80)	(95)
	For camper and towing applications.		
GPC	7"x10" Dual Bright Mirrors (ST)	43	50
	For camper and towing applications. NOT AVAILABLE with (GTS) dual power heated folding mirrors.		
JPS	8-Way Power Driver's Seat (Reg Cab)	272	320
	NOT AVAILABLE with (SX) seats.		
HAA	Air Conditioning (ST)	680	800
	NOT AVAILABLE with (4XA) air conditioning bypass.		
4XA	Air Conditioning Bypass (ST)	NC	NC
	NOT AVAILABLE with (HAA) air conditioning.		
K17	Black Bodyside Molding With Bright Insert (ST)	89	105
	NOT AVAILABLE with (AGG) Sport Appearance Group.		
6C8	Black CC with Flame Red CC	183	215
	NOT AVAILABLE with (AGG) Sport Appearance Group.		
6D1	Black CC with Lt. Driftwood SG	166	195
	NOT AVAILABLE with (AGG) Sport Appearance Group.		
6C1	Black CC with Lt. Driftwood SG	183	215
	NOT AVAILABLE with (AGG) Sport Appearance Group.		
CKJ	Black Rubber Floor Covering	NC	NC
YCF	Border State (California) Emissions	145	170
	NOT AVAILABLE with (NAE) CA/CT/MA/NY emissions.		
6C9	Bright White CC with Lt. Driftwood SG	183	215
	NOT AVAILABLE with (AGG) Sport Appearance Group.		
6D7	Bright White CC with Lt. Driftwood SG	166	195
	NOT AVAILABLE with (AGG) Sport Appearance Group.		
NAE	CA/CT/MA/NY Emissions	145	170
	Automatically coded. NOT AVAILABLE with (YCF) border state emissions.		
LNC	Cab Clearance Lights	68	80
AHJ	Camper Special Package	81	95
	Includes auxiliary springs. REQUIRES NMC or 29A or 2YA or 29G or 2YG.		
S9	Cloth 40/20/40 Split Bench Seat (ST)	94	110
	NOT AVAILABLE with (TY) seats, (CF8) rear seat delete (fleet only).		
6D4	Dark Chestnut PC with Lt. Driftwood SG	166	195
	NOT AVAILABLE with (AGG) Sport Appearance Group.		

RAM 2500 — DODGE

CODE	DESCRIPTION	INVOICE	MSRP
6C4	Dark Chestnut PC with Lt. Driftwood SG	183	215
	NOT AVAILABLE with (AGG) Sport Appearance Group.		
6DD	Deep Amethyst PC with Lt. Driftwood SG	166	195
	NOT AVAILABLE with (AGG) Sport Appearance Group.		
6CD	Deep Amethyst PC with Lt. Driftwood SG	183	215
	NOT AVAILABLE with (AGG) Sport Appearance Group.		
AJK	Deluxe Convenience Group (ST)	332	390
	Includes speed control, tilt steering.		
GTS	Dual Power Heated Folding Mirrors (ST)	123	145
	NOT AVAILABLE with (GPC) 7"x10" dual bright mirrors.		
6D8	Emerald Green PC with Lt. Driftwood SG	166	195
	NOT AVAILABLE with (AGG) Sport Appearance Group.		
6C7	Emerald Green PC with Lt. Driftwood SG	183	215
	NOT AVAILABLE with (AGG) Sport Appearance Group.		
NHK	Engine Block Heater	34	40
ETB	Engine: 5.9L Cummins Turbo Diesel	3778	4445
	Includes 'Cummins Turbo Diesel' nameplate on exterior right and left doors. engine block heater, HD Service Group with manual transmission/Diesel: 136-amp alternator, HD engine cooler, dual batteries. NOT AVAILABLE with 25A, 26A, 27A, 28A, 29A, DDP, AGG, 25G, 26G, 27G, 2YG, 28G, 29G.		
EML	Engine: 5.9L MPI V-8 (Std)	NC	NC
	REQUIRES DDP or DGB. NOT AVAILABLE with DDX, 27A, 28A, 29A, 2YA, 27G, 28G, 29G, 2YG, AGG.		
EWA	Engine: 8.0L MPI V-10	829	975
	Includes HD Service Group with Manual Trans/V10: 136-amp alternator, HD engine cooler. NOT AVAILABLE with DDP, 25A, 26A, 29A, 2YA, 28A, 27A, AGG, 25G, 26G, 28G, 29G, 2YG, 27G.		
6D5	Flame Red CC with Lt. Driftwood SG	166	195
	NOT AVAILABLE with (AGG) Sport Appearance Group.		
LNJ	Fog Lights	102	120
	NOT AVAILABLE with (2YG).		
6C3	Forest Green PC with Lt. Driftwood SG	183	215
	NOT AVAILABLE with (AGG) Sport Appearance Group.		
6D3	Forest Green PC with Lt. Driftwood SG	166	195
	NOT AVAILABLE with (AGG) Sport Appearance Group.		
MXB	Front Air Dam	21	25
CKE	Front Seat Area Carpet (ST)	94	110
NMC	HD Engine Cooler	60	70
	REQUIRES DDP or DDX or 25A or 27A or 25G or 27G. NOT AVAILABLE with DGB.		
NMC	HD Engine Cooler	111	130
	REQUIRES DGB or 26A or 28A or 26G or 28G. NOT AVAILABLE with DDP, DDX.		
ADJ	HD Service Group with Auto Trans (4WD)	332	390
	Includes 136-amp alternator. REQUIRES 26A or 28A or 26G or 28G. NOT AVAILABLE with AHD.		
ADJ	HD Service Group with Auto Trans/V8 (2WD)	293	345
	Includes 136-amp alternator, HD engine cooler. REQUIRES 26A or 26G. NOT AVAILABLE with 25A, 27A, 28A, 29A, 2YA, 25G, 27G, 28G, 29G, 2YG.		

DODGE   RAM 2500

CODE	DESCRIPTION	INVOICE	MSRP
ADJ	HD Service Group with Manual Trans (4WD)	281	330
	Includes 136-amp alternator, HD engine cooler. REQUIRES 25A or 27A or 25G or 27G. NOT AVAILABLE with AHD.		
ADJ	HD Service Group with Manual Trans/V8 (2WD)	242	285
	Includes 136-amp alternator, HD engine cooler. REQUIRES 25A or 25G. NOT AVAILABLE with 26A, 27A, 28A, 29A, 2YA, 26G, 27G, 28G, 29G, 2YG.		
AHD	HD Snow Plow Prep Group with Manual	157	185
	Manufacturer Discount	(72)	(85)
	Net Price	85	100
	Recommended: (TY1) LT245/75R16E A/T BSW tires, (LNC) front clearance and I.D. lights (5). Height adjustable front coil springs, shift-on-the-fly transfer case. REQUIRES 25A or 27A or 26A or 28A or 25G or 27G or 26G or 28G. NOT AVAILABLE with AHD.		
TY	HD Vinyl Bench Seat (Quad Cab)	NC	NC
	REQUIRES (CF8) rear seat delete (fleet only). NOT AVAILABLE with (S9) seats.		
6C2	Intense Blue PC with Lt. Driftwood SG	183	215
	NOT AVAILABLE with (AGG) Sport Appearance Group.		
6D2	Intense Blue PC with Lt. Driftwood SG	166	195
	NOT AVAILABLE with (AGG) Sport Appearance Group.		
AJD	Leather Interior Group	1309	1540
	Includes woodgrain I/P bezel. Travel Convenience Group: automatic dimming rearview mirror, compass/temperature display, dual illuminated visor vanity mirrors, leather 40/20/40 split bench seat, 8-way power driver's seat. NOT AVAILABLE with (SX) seats.		
AJD	Leather Interior Group (Reg Cab)	1190	1400
	Includes woodgrain I/P bezel. Travel Convenience Group: automatic dimming rearview mirror, compass/temperature display, dual illuminated visor vanity mirrors, 8-way power driver's seat, leather 40/20/40 split bench seat. NOT AVAILABLE with (SX) seats.		
ADA	Light Group (ST)	102	120
	Includes passenger assist grab handle (RT roof header), cloth full deluxe headliner and ignition key light with time delay, overhead console with storage, glove box light, reading/map lights.		
6D6	Metallic Red CC with Lt. Driftwood SG	166	195
	NOT AVAILABLE with (AGG) Sport Appearance Group.		
6C5	Metallic Red CC with Lt. Driftwood SG	183	215
	NOT AVAILABLE with (AGG) Sport Appearance Group.		
25A	Quick Order Package 25A	NC	NC
	Includes vehicles with standard equipment. REQUIRES (HAA or 4XA) and EML and DDP. NOT AVAILABLE with AHC, DMF, DGB, DDX, EWA, ETB.		
25G	Quick Order Package 25G	2512	2955
	Manufacturer Discount	(595)	(700)
	Net Price	1917	2255
	Includes air conditioning, front seat area carpet, Deluxe Convenience Group: speed control, tilt steering; Light Group: overhead console with storage, glove box light, reading/map lights, dual power heated folding mirrors, black bodyside molding with		

RAM 2500 — DODGE

CODE	DESCRIPTION	INVOICE	MSRP

bright insert, Power Convenience Group: power door locks, power windows with driver's one touch down, SLT Decor Group: black sport leather wrap steering wheel, dual cloth visors, front floor mats, premium cloth 40/20/40 split bench seat, front bumper sight shield, tachometer, 16" x 6.5" chrome wheels. REQUIRES EML and DDP. NOT AVAILABLE with DMF, AGG, AHC, AHD, EWA, ETB, DDX, DGB.

26A Quick Order Package 26A .... NC NC
Includes vehicle with standard equipment. REQUIRES (HAA or 4XA) and EML and DGB. NOT AVAILABLE with AHC, AHD, DMF, EWA, ETB, DDP, DDX.

26G Quick Order Package 26G 2512 2955
Manufacturer Discount .... (595) (700)
Net Price 1917 2255
Includes air conditioning, front seat area carpet, Deluxe Convenience Group: speed control, tilt steering, Light Group: overhead console with storage, glove box light, reading/map lights, dual power heated folding mirrors, black bodyside molding with bright insert, Power Convenience Group: power door locks, power windows with driver's one touch down, SLT Decor Group: black sport leather wrap steering wheel, dual cloth visors, front floor mats, premium cloth 40/20/40 split bench seat, front bumper sight shield, tachometer, 16" x 6.5" chrome wheels. REQUIRES EML and DGB. NOT AVAILABLE with DMF, AGG, AHC, AHD, EWA, ETB, DDP, DDX.

27A Quick Order Package 27A .... NC NC
Includes vehicle with standard equipment. REQUIRES (HAA or 4XA) and DDX. NOT AVAILABLE with DMF, EML, ETB, DDP, DGB.

27G Quick Order Package 27G (2WD) 2512 2955
Manufacturer Discount .... (595) (700)
Net Price 1917 2255
Includes air conditioning, front seat area carpet, Deluxe Convenience Group: speed control, tilt steering, Light Group: overhead console with storage, glove box light, reading/map lights, dual power heated folding mirrors, black bodyside molding with bright insert, Power Convenience Group: power door locks, power windows with driver's one touch down, SLT Decor Group: black sport leather wrap steering wheel, dual cloth visors, front floor mats, premium cloth 40/20/40 split bench seat, front bumper sight shield, tachometer, 16" x 6.5" chrome wheels. REQUIRES DDX. NOT AVAILABLE with DMF, AGG, EML, ETB, DDP, DGB.

27G Quick Order Package 27G (4WD) 2512 2955
Manufacturer Discount .... (595) (700)
Net Price 1917 2255
Includes air conditioning, Deluxe Convenience Group: speed control, tilt steering, front seat area carpet, Light Group: overhead console with storage, glove box light, reading/map lights, dual power heated folding mirrors, black bodyside molding with bright insert, Power Convenience Group: power door locks, power windows with driver's one touch down, SLT Decor Group: black sport leather wrap steering wheel, dual cloth visors, front floor mats, premium cloth 40/20/40 split bench seat, front bumper sight shield, tachometer, 16" x 6.5" chrome wheels. REQUIRES (EWA) engine and (DDX) transmission.

DODGE RAM 2500

CODE	DESCRIPTION	INVOICE	MSRP
28A	Quick Order Package 28A	NC	NC

Includes vehicle with standard equipment. REQUIRES (HAA or 4XA) and DGB. NOT AVAILABLE with DMF, EML, ETB, DDP, DDX.

28G	Quick Order Package 28G (2WD)	2512	2955
	Manufacturer Discount	(680)	(800)
	Net Price	1832	2155

Includes air conditioning, front seat area carpet, Deluxe Convenience Group: speed control, tilt steering, Light Group: overhead console with storage, glove box light, reading/map lights, dual power heated folding mirrors, black bodyside molding with bright insert, Power Convenience Group: power door locks, power windows with driver's one touch down, SLT Decor Group: black sport leather wrap steering wheel, dual cloth visors, front floor mats, premium cloth 40/20/40 split bench seat, front bumper sight shield, tachometer, 16" x 6.5" chrome wheels. REQUIRES DGB. NOT AVAILABLE with DMF, AGG, EML, ETB, DDP, DDX.

28G	Quick Order Package 28G (4WD)	2512	2955
	Manufacturer Discount	(595)	(700)
	Net Price	1917	2255

Includes air conditioning, Deluxe Convenience Group: speed control, tilt steering, front seat area carpet, Light Group: overhead console with storage, glove box light, reading/map lights, dual power heated folding mirrors, black bodyside molding with bright insert, Power Convenience Group: power door locks, power windows with driver's one touch down, SLT Decor Group: black sport leather wrap steering wheel, dual cloth visors, front floor mats, premium cloth 40/20/40 split bench seat, front bumper sight shield, tachometer, 16" x 6.5" chrome wheels. REQUIRES (EWA) engine and (DGB) transmission.

29A	Quick Order Package 29A (2WD)	NC	NC

Includes vehicle with standard equipment. REQUIRES (HAA or 4XA) and DDX. NOT AVAILABLE with DMF, EML, EWA, DDP, DGB.

29A	Quick Order Package 29A (4WD)	NC	NC

Includes vehicle with standard equipment. REQUIRES (HAA or 4XA) and (ETB and DDX).

29G	Quick Order Package 29G (2WD)	2512	2955
	Manufacturer Discount	(595)	(700)
	Net Price	1917	2255

Includes air conditioning, front seat area carpet, Deluxe Convenience Group: speed control, tilt steering, Light Group: overhead console with storage, glove box light, reading/map lights, dual power heated folding mirrors, black bodyside molding with bright insert, Power Convenience Group: power door locks, power windows with driver's one touch down, SLT Decor Group: black sport leather wrap steering wheel, dual cloth visors, front floor mats, driver's and passenger's door bin, cloth door trim panels, premium cloth 40/20/40 split bench seat, front bumper sight shield, tachometer, 16" x 6.5" chrome wheels. REQUIRES DDX. NOT AVAILABLE with DMF, AGG, EML, EWA, DDP, DGB.

RAM 2500 — DODGE

CODE	DESCRIPTION	INVOICE	MSRP
29G	Quick Order Package 29G (4WD)	2512	2955
	Manufacturer Discount	(595)	(700)
	Net Price	1917	2255

Includes air conditioning, Deluxe Convenience Group: speed control, tilt steering, front seat area carpet, Light Group: overhead console with storage, glove box light, reading/map lights, dual power heated folding mirrors, black bodyside molding with bright insert, Power Convenience Group: power door locks, power windows with driver's one touch down, SLT Decor Group: black sport leather wrap steering wheel, dual cloth visors, front floor mats, premium cloth 40/20/40 split bench seat, tachometer, 16" x 6.5" chrome wheels. REQUIRES (ETB) engine and (DDX) transmission.

| 2YA | Quick Order Package 2YA (2WD) | NC | NC |

Includes vehicle with standard equipment. REQUIRES (HAA or 4XA) and DGB. NOT AVAILABLE with DMF, EML, EWA, DDP, DDX.

| 2YA | Quick Order Package 2YA (4WD) | NC | NC |

Includes vehicle with standard equipment. REQUIRES (HAA or 4XA) and (ETB and DGB).

2YG	Quick Order Package 2YG (2WD)	2512	2955
	Manufacturer Discount	(595)	(700)
	Net Price	1917	2255

Includes air conditioning, front seat area carpet, Deluxe Convenience Group: speed control, tilt steering, Light Group: overhead console with storage, glove box light, reading/map lights, dual power heated folding mirrors, black bodyside molding with bright insert, Power Convenience Group: power door locks, power windows with driver's one touch down, SLT Decor Group: black sport leather wrap steering wheel, dual cloth visors, front floor mats, driver's and passenger's door bin, cloth door trim panels, premium cloth 40/20/40 split bench seat, front bumper sight shield, tachometer, 16" x 6.5" chrome wheels. REQUIRES DGB. NOT AVAILABLE with DMF, AGG, EML, EWA, DDP, DDX.

2YG	Quick Order Package 2YG (4WD)	2512	2955
	Manufacturer Discount	(595)	(700)
	Net Price	1917	2255

Includes air conditioning, Deluxe Convenience Group: speed control, tilt steering, front seat area carpet, Light Group: overhead console with storage, glove box light, reading/map lights, dual power heated folding mirrors, black bodyside molding with bright insert, Power Convenience Group: power door locks, power windows with driver's one touch down, SLT Decor Group: black sport leather wrap steering wheel, dual cloth visors, front floor mats, premium cloth 40/20/40 split bench seat, tachometer, 16" x 6.5" chrome wheels. REQUIRES (ETB) engine and (DGB) transmission.

| RBN | Radio: AM/FM Stereo with Cassette, EQ | 285 | 335 |

Includes CD changer control. NOT AVAILABLE with (RAZ) radio, (RBR) radio.

| RBR | Radio: AM/FM Stereo with CD | 434 | 510 |

NOT AVAILABLE with (RBN) radio, (RAZ) radio.

| RAZ | Radio: AM/FM Stereo with CD, Cassette, EQ | 587 | 690 |

NOT AVAILABLE with (RBN) radio, (RBR) radio.

DODGE RAM 2500

CODE	DESCRIPTION	INVOICE	MSRP
GXM	Remote Keyless Entry System	162	190
	Includes 2 transmitters.		
LSA	Security Alarm	128	150
	REQUIRES (GXM) remote keyless entry system.		
DHG	Shift-On-The-Fly Transfer Case	85	100
GFD	Sliding Rear Window	119	140
AGG	Sport Appearance Group (2WD)	366	430
	Includes dual electric horns, front bumper sight shields, tachometer located in analog cluster and 16"x5" aluminum wheels, Deletes tailgate applique. front color keyed bumper, fog lights, tires: LT245/75R16EAS OWL, sport decal, color keyed grille. NOT AVAILABLE with 6F6, 6F4, 6F5, 6F9, 6FC, 6D1, 6D7, 6D4, 6DD, 6D8, 6D5, 6D2, 6D6, 6C8, 6C1, 6C9, 6C4, 6CD, 6C7, 6C3, 6C2, 6C5, 6D3, AGG, 2YG, ETB, TY1.		
AGG	Sport Appearance Group (4WD)	383	450
	Includes dual electric horns, front bumper sight shields and tachometer (in analog cluster), color keyed front and rear bumpers, color keyed grille, tires: LT245/75R16E OWL all terrain, bodyside moldings delete. REQUIRES 2YG. NOT AVAILABLE with TYN, 6F6, 6F4, 6F5, 6F9, 6D4, 6D1, 6D2, 6D3, 6D8, 6D5, 6D6, 6D7, 6C4, 6C1, 6C8, 6C2, 6C3, 6C7, 6C5, 6C9.		
AGG	Sport Appearance Group (4WD)	485	570
	Includes dual electric horns, front bumper sight shields and tachometer (in analog cluster), color keyed front and rear bumpers, color keyed grille, fog lights, tires: LT245/75R16E OWL all terrain, bodyside moldings delete. REQUIRES 25G OR 26G OR 27G OR 28G OR 29G. NOT AVAILABLE with TYN.		
AGG	Sport Appearance Group With Diesel-Auto (2WD)	264	310
	Includes dual electric horns, front bumper sight shields, tachometer located in analog cluster and 16"x5" aluminum wheels, Deletes tailgate applique. front color keyed bumper, tires: LT245/75R16E AS OWL, sport decal, color keyed grille. NOT AVAILABLE with DGB, 6F6, 6F4, 6F5, 6F9, 6FC, 6D1, 6D7, 6D4, 6DD, 6D8, 6D5, 6D2, 6D6, 6C8, 6C1, 6C9, 6C4, 6CD, 6C7, 6C3, 6C2, 6C5, 6D3, AGG, 25G, 27G, EWA, DDP, 26G, 28G, 29G, EML.		
DSA	Sure Grip Axle	242	285
	REQUIRES DMF or (25A or 27A or 28A or 29A or 2YA) or (25G or 27G or 28G or 29G or 2YG).		
JAY	Tachometer (ST)	68	80
TYN	Tires: LT245/75R16E AS OWL	106	125
	NOT AVAILABLE with (TY1) tires, (AGG) Sport Appearance Group.		
TY1	Tires: LT245/75R16E AT BSW	119	140
	NOT AVAILABLE with (AGG) Sport Appearance Group, (TYN) tires.		
TY2	Tires: LT245/75R16E OWL All Terrain	225	265
	NOT AVAILABLE with (AGG) Sport Appearance Group, (TYN) tires, (TY1) tires.		
AHC	Trailer Tow Group	208	245
	Includes adaptor plug and HD flasher, trailer hitch receiver (class IV). REQUIRES 25A or 26A or 27A or 28A or 29A or 2YA or 25G or 26G or 27G or 28G or 29G or 2YG. NOT AVAILABLE with AHD.		

RAM 2500 / 3500 — DODGE

CODE	DESCRIPTION	INVOICE	MSRP
AWK	Travel Convenience Group	251	295
	Includes reading lamps, automatic dimming rearview mirror, compass/temperature display, dual illuminated visor vanity mirrors.		
SX	Vinyl 40/20/40 Split Bench Seat	NC	NC
	NOT AVAILABLE with (AJD) Leather Interior Group, (JPS) 8-way power driver's seat, (JPV) 8-way power driver's seat.		
WDT	Wheels: 16" X 6.5 Aluminum 8-Stud	NC	NC
WDC	Wheels: 16" X 6.5" Chrome	276	325

1997 RAM 3500

Safety Data

Driver Airbag: *Standard*
Side Airbag: *Not Available*
Traction Control: *Not Available*
Driver Crash Test Grade: *Good*

Passenger Airbag: *Not Available*
4-Wheel ABS: *Optional*
Integrated Child Seat(s): *Not Available*
Passenger Crash Test Grade: *Not Available*

Standard Equipment

RAM 3500 REGULAR CAB: Driver's airbag, power front disc/rear drum brakes with rear ABS, argent front bumper, headlights-on warning buzzer, digital clock, cigarette lighter, auxiliary power outlet, 5.9-liter V-8 engine, black rubber floor covering, voltmeter, oil pressure gauge, engine temperature gauge, trip odometer, tinted glass, chrome grille, heavy-duty service group (750-amp HD battery, 136-amp HD alternator, HD engine cooling, skid plates (4WD), auxiliary transmission oil cooler (w/automatic transmission), 10 front/side/rear clearance and identification lights, fender flares, day/night rearview mirror, dual chrome power exterior mirrors, power steering, AM/FM stereo with cassette player and 4 speakers, vinyl bench seat with head restraints, heavy-duty front and rear shocks, LT215/85R16D blackwall all-season tires, underbody spare tire carrier, 5-speed manual transmission, 16"x 6" steel wheels, 2-speed intermittent windshield wipers, heavy-duty 2-speed transfer case with shift-on-the-fly auto-locking front hubs (4WD).

3500 CLUB CAB (in addition to or instead of REGULAR CAB equipment): Deluxe cloth 40/20/40 split bench seat, deluxe cloth rear bench seat, front stabilizer bar.

Base Prices

BR3L62	2WD Regular Cab Duallie	17702	20255
BR3L32	2WD Club Cab Duallie	19730	22600
BR8L62	4WD Regular Cab Duallie	19875	22770
BR8L32	4WD Club Cab Duallie	21912	25120
	Destination Charge:	640	640

Accessories

25G	Laramie SLT Option Package 25G (Club Cab)	1832	2155
	Manufacturer Discount	(340)	(400)
	Net Price	1492	1755
	Includes Laramie SLT Decor (black bodyside moldings, full floor carpeting, 40/20/40 split bench seat, tailgate applique, front floor mats, chrome front bumper, under		

DODGE RAM 3500

CODE	DESCRIPTION	INVOICE	MSRP

hood sound insulation, dual horns, premium cloth upholstery, passenger visor vanity mirror), power convenience group (power windows, power door locks), deluxe convenience group (tilt steering wheel, cruise control), light group (cloth headliner, passenger assist grip, glovebox light, exterior cargo light, overhead console with storage and reading lights, under hood light), air conditioning, tachometer, chrome front and rear bumpers

25G   Laramie SLT Option Package 25G (Reg Cab) 2729   3210
       Manufacturer Discount .... (680)   (800)
       Net Price 2049   2410

Includes Laramie SLT Decor (black bodyside moldings, full floor carpeting, 40/20/40 split bench seat, tailgate applique, front floor mats, chrome front bumper, under hood sound insulation, dual horns, premium cloth upholstery, passenger visor vanity mirror), power convenience group (power windows, power door locks), deluxe convenience group (tilt steering wheel, cruise control), light group (cloth headliner, passenger assist grip, glovebox light, exterior cargo light, overhead console with storage and reading lights, under hood light), behind seat storage, air conditioning, tachometer, wheel dress-up package (chrome wheel skins), chrome front and rear bumpers

26G   Laramie SLT Option Package 26G (Club Cab) 2640   3105
       Manufacturer Discount .... (340)   (400)
       Net Price 2300   2705

Includes Laramie SLT Decor (black bodyside moldings, full floor carpeting, 40/20/40 split bench seat, tailgate applique, front floor mats, chrome front bumper, under hood sound insulation, dual horns, premium cloth upholstery, passenger visor vanity mirror), power convenience group (power windows, power door locks), deluxe convenience group (tilt steering wheel, cruise control), light group (cloth headliner, passenger assist grip, glovebox light, exterior cargo light, overhead console with storage and reading lights, under hood light), air conditioning, tachometer, chrome front and rear bumpers, 4-speed automatic transmission

26G   Laramie SLT Option Package 26G (Reg Cab) 3537   4160
       Manufacturer Discount .... (680)   (800)
       Net Price 2857   3360

Includes Laramie SLT Decor (black bodyside moldings, full floor carpeting, 40/20/40 split bench seat, tailgate applique, front floor mats, chrome front bumper, under hood sound insulation, dual horns, premium cloth upholstery, passenger visor vanity mirror), power convenience group (power windows, power door locks), deluxe convenience group (tilt steering wheel, cruise control), light group (cloth headliner, passenger assist grip, glovebox light, exterior cargo light, overhead console with storage and reading lights, under hood light), behind seat storage, air conditioning, tachometer, wheel dress-up package (chrome wheel skins), chrome front and rear bumpers, 4-speed automatic transmission

27G   Laramie SLT Option Package 27G (Club Cab) 2661   3130
       Manufacturer Discount .... (340)   (400)
       Net Price 2321   2730

Includes Laramie SLT Decor (black bodyside moldings, full floor carpeting, 40/20/40 split bench seat, tailgate applique, front floor mats, chrome front bumper, under hood sound insulation, dual horns, premium cloth upholstery, passenger visor vanity

RAM 3500

CODE	DESCRIPTION	INVOICE	MSRP

mirror), power convenience group (power windows, power door locks), deluxe convenience group (tilt steering wheel, cruise control), light group (cloth headliner, passenger assist grip, glovebox light, exterior cargo light, overhead console with storage and reading lights, under hood light), air conditioning, tachometer, chrome front and rear bumpers, 8.0-liter V-10 engine

27G	Laramie SLT Option Package 27G (Reg Cab)	3558	4185
	Manufacturer Discount	(680)	(800)
	Net Price	2878	3385

Includes Laramie SLT Decor (black bodyside moldings, full floor carpeting, 40/20/40 split bench seat, tailgate applique, front floor mats, chrome front bumper, under hood sound insulation, dual horns, premium cloth upholstery, passenger visor vanity mirror), power convenience group (power windows, power door locks), deluxe convenience group (tilt steering wheel, cruise control), light group (cloth headliner, passenger assist grip, glovebox light, exterior cargo light, overhead console with storage and reading lights, under hood light), behind seat storage, air conditioning, tachometer, wheel dress-up package (chrome wheel skins), chrome front and rear bumpers, 8.0-liter V-10 engine.

28G	Laramie SLT Option Package 28G (Club Cab)	3469	4080
	Manufacturer Discount	(340)	(400)
	Net Price	3129	3680

Includes Laramie SLT Decor (black bodyside moldings, full floor carpeting, 40/20/40 split bench seat, tailgate applique, front floor mats, chrome front bumper, under hood sound insulation, dual horns, premium cloth upholstery, passenger visor vanity mirror), power convenience group (power windows, power door locks), deluxe convenience group (tilt steering wheel, cruise control), light group (cloth headliner, passenger assist grip, glovebox light, exterior cargo light, overhead console with storage and reading lights, under hood light), air conditioning, tachometer, chrome front and rear bumpers, 8.0-liter V-10 engine, 4-speed automatic transmission

28G	Laramie SLT Option Package 28G (Reg Cab)	4366	5135
	Manufacturer Discount	(680)	(800)
	Net Price	3686	4335

Includes Laramie SLT Decor (black bodyside moldings, full floor carpeting, 40/20/40 split bench seat, tailgate applique, front floor mats, chrome front bumper, under hood sound insulation, dual horns, premium cloth upholstery, passenger visor vanity mirror), power convenience group (power windows, power door locks), deluxe convenience group (tilt steering wheel, cruise control), light group (cloth headliner, passenger assist grip, glovebox light, exterior cargo light, overhead console with storage and reading lights, under hood light), behind seat storage, air conditioning, tachometer, wheel dress-up package (chrome wheel skins), chrome front and rear bumpers, 8.0-liter V-10, 4-speed automatic transmission

29G	Laramie SLT Option Package 29G (Club Cab)	5542	6520
	Manufacturer Discount	(340)	(400)
	Net Price	5202	6120

Includes Laramie SLT Decor (black bodyside moldings, full floor carpeting, 40/20/40 split bench seat, tailgate applique, front floor mats, chrome front bumper, under hood sound insulation, dual horns, premium cloth upholstery, passenger visor vanity mirror), power convenience group (power windows, power door locks), deluxe

DODGE RAM 3500

CODE	DESCRIPTION	INVOICE	MSRP

convenience group (tilt steering wheel, cruise control), light group (cloth headliner, passenger assist grip, glovebox light, exterior cargo light, overhead console with storage and reading lights, under hood light), air conditioning, tachometer, chrome front and rear bumpers, 5.9-liter Cummins Turbodiesel engine, two 750-amp batteries, diesel sound insulation, engine block heater, message center with warning lights.

29G   **Laramie SLT Option Package 29G (Reg Cab)** 6443   7580
     Manufacturer Discount .... (680)   (800)
     Net Price 5763   6780

Includes Laramie SLT Decor (black bodyside moldings, full floor carpeting, 40/20/40 split bench seat, tailgate applique, front floor mats, chrome front bumper, under hood sound insulation, dual horns, premium cloth upholstery, passenger visor vanity mirror), power convenience group (power windows, power door locks), deluxe convenience group (tilt steering wheel, cruise control), light group (cloth headliner, passenger assist grip, glovebox light, exterior cargo light, overhead console with storage and reading lights, under hood light), behind seat storage, air conditioning, tachometer, wheel dress-up package (chrome wheel skins), chrome front and rear bumpers, 5.9-liter Cummins Turbodiesel engine, two 750-amp batteries, diesel sound insulation, engine block heater, message center with warning lights.

2YG   **Laramie SLT Option Package 2YG (Club Cab)** 6350   7470
     Manufacturer Discount .... (340)   (400)
     Net Price 6010   7070

Includes Laramie SLT Decor (black bodyside moldings, full floor carpeting, 40/20/40 split bench seat, tailgate applique, front floor mats, chrome front bumper, under hood sound insulation, dual horns, premium cloth upholstery, passenger visor vanity mirror), power convenience group (power windows, power door locks), deluxe convenience group (tilt steering wheel, cruise control), light group (cloth headliner, passenger assist grip, glovebox light, exterior cargo light, overhead console with storage and reading lights, under hood light), air conditioning, tachometer, chrome front and rear bumpers, 5.9-liter Cummins Turbodiesel engine, 4-speed automatic transmission, two 750-amp batteries, diesel sound insulation, engine block heater, message center with warning lights.

2YG   **Laramie SLT Option Package 2YG (Reg Cab)** 7251   8530
     Manufacturer Discount .... (680)   (800)
     Net Price 6571   7730

Includes Laramie SLT Decor (black bodyside moldings, full floor carpeting, 40/20/40 split bench seat, tailgate applique, front floor mats, chrome front bumper, under hood sound insulation, dual horns, premium cloth upholstery, passenger visor vanity mirror), power convenience group (power windows, power door locks), deluxe convenience group (tilt steering wheel, cruise control), light group (cloth headliner, passenger assist grip, glovebox light, exterior cargo light, overhead console with storage and reading lights, under hood light), behind seat storage, air conditioning, tachometer, wheel dress-up package (chrome wheel skins), chrome front and rear bumpers, 5.9-liter Cummins Turbodiesel engine, 4-speed automatic transmission, two 750-amp batteries, diesel sound insulation, engine block heater, message center with warning lights.

RAM 3500 — DODGE

CODE	DESCRIPTION	INVOICE	MSRP
26A	LT Option Package 26A (Reg Cab)	808	950
	Includes 4-speed automatic transmission		
27A	LT Option Package 27A (Reg Cab)	829	975
	Includes 8.0-liter V-10 engine		
28A	LT Option Package 28A (Reg Cab)	1637	1925
	Includes 8.0-liter V-10 engine and 4-speed automatic transmission		
29A	LT Option Package 29A (Reg Cab)	3778	4445
	Includes 5.9-liter Cummins Turbodiesel engine, two 750-amp batteries, diesel sound insulation, engine block heater, message center with warning lights, tachometer		
2YA	LT Option Package 2YA (Reg Cab)	4586	5395
	Includes 5.9-liter Cummins Turbodiesel engine, 4-speed automatic transmission, two 750-amp batteries, diesel sound insulation, engine block heater, message center with warning lights, tachometer		
26C	ST Option Package 26C (Club Cab)	808	950
	Includes 4-speed automatic transmission		
27C	ST Option Package 27C (Club Cab)	829	975
	Includes 8.0-liter V-10 engine		
28C	ST Option Package 28C (Club Cab)	1637	1925
	Includes 8.0-liter V-10 engine and 4-speed automatic transmission		
29C	ST Option Package 29C (Club Cab)	3778	4445
	Includes 5.9-liter Cummins Turbodiesel engine, two 750-amp batteries, diesel sound insulation, engine block heater, message center with warning lights, tachometer		
2YC	ST Option Package 2YC (Club Cab)	4586	5395
	Includes 5.9-liter Cummins Turbodiesel engine, 4-speed automatic transmission, two 750-amp batteries, diesel sound insulation, engine block heater, message center with warning lights, tachometer		
HAA	Air Conditioning	680	800
	INCLUDED in Laramie SLT Option Packages		
BGK	Anti-lock Brakes	425	500
AMR	Behind Seat Storage (Reg Cab)	81	95
	INCLUDED in ST Decor Package and in Laramie SLT Packages		
K17	Bodyside Moldings	89	105
YCF	Border States Emissions	145	170
NAE	Calif./Mass./New York Emissions	145	170
AHJ	Camper Special Package	78	92
	Includes stabilizer bars and auxiliary springs		
AJK	Deluxe Convenience Group	332	390
	Includes tilt steering column and cruise control		
GNC	Dual Illuminated Visor Vanity Mirrors	81	95
	REQUIRES purchase of a Laramie SLT Option Package		
NHK	Engine Block Heater	34	40
GPC	Exterior Mirrors — Chrome Manual	(43)	(50)
	Sized 7"x 10"		
LNJ	Fog Lights	102	120
	REQUIRES purchase of a Laramie SLT Option Package		
MXB	Front Air Dam	21	25

DODGE RAM 3500

CODE	DESCRIPTION	INVOICE	MSRP
AJD	Leather Interior Group (Club Cab)	1292	1520
	Includes leather upholstery, power driver's seat with 6-way adjustment, woodgrain interior trim, travel convenience group (overhead console with compass, reading lights, and outside temperature readout; automatic dimming rearview mirror), dual illuminated visor vanity mirrors; REQUIRES purchase of a Laramie SLT Option Package		
AJD	Leather Interior Group (Reg Cab)	1207	1420
	Includes leather upholstery, power driver's seat with 6-way adjustment, woodgrain interior trim, travel convenience group (overhead console with compass, reading lights, and outside temperature readout; automatic dimming rearview mirror), dual illuminated visor vanity mirrors; REQUIRES purchase of a Laramie SLT Option Package		
ADA	Light Group (Club Cab)	102	120
	Includes cloth headliner, passenger assist grip, glove box light, exterior cargo light, overhead console with storage and reading lights, under hood light		
ADA	Light Group (Reg Cab)	136	160
	Includes cloth headliner, passenger assist grip, glove box light, exterior cargo light, overhead console with storage and reading lights, under hood light		
6B	Paint — Two-tone	213	250
	With 25G (Club Cab)	162	190
	With 25G (Reg Cab)	162	190
	With 26G (Club Cab)	162	190
	With 26G (Reg Cab)	162	190
	With 27G (Reg Cab)	162	190
	With 27G (Club Cab)	162	190
	With 28G (Club Cab)	162	190
	With 28G (Reg Cab)	162	190
	With 29G (Reg Cab)	162	190
	With 29G (Club Cab)	162	190
	With 2YG (Reg Cab)	162	190
	With 2YG (Club Cab)	162	190
JPS	Power Driver's Seat	272	320
	REQUIRES purchase of a Laramie SLT Option Package		
DM	Rear Axle — Optional Ratio	43	50
MBD	Rear Step Bumper — Painted (Reg Cab)	115	135
GXM	Remote Keyless Entry	162	190
	REQUIRES purchase of a Laramie SLT Option Package		
CKJ	Rubber Floor Covering	NC	NC
	REQUIRES purchase of ST Decor Group on Regular Cab models; NOT AVAILABLE with Laramie SLT Option Packages on Regular Cab models		
B3	Seats — Deluxe Cloth & Vinyl Bench (Reg Cab)	85	100
T9	Seats — Deluxe Cloth 40/20/40 Split Bench (Reg Cab)	225	265
TX	Seats — Heavy-duty Vinyl 40/20/40 Split Bench (Club Cab)	NC	NC
TX	Seats — Heavy-duty Vinyl 40/20/40 Split Bench (Reg Cab)	225	265
	With 25G (Reg Cab)	NC	NC
	With 26G (Reg Cab)	NC	NC
	With 27G (Reg Cab)	NC	NC

RAM 3500 — DODGE

CODE	DESCRIPTION	INVOICE	MSRP
	With 28G (Reg Cab)	NC	NC
	With 29G (Reg Cab)	NC	NC
	With 2YG (Reg Cab)	NC	NC
	With AMP (Reg Cab)	NC	NC
GFD	Sliding Rear Window	119	140
AHD	Snow Plow Prep Group (4WD)	72	85
	Manufacturer Discount	(72)	(85)
	Net Price	NC	NC
	Includes extra-duty front suspension and warning light for automatic transmission oil overheat; REQUIRES trailer tow group and rear bumper		
AGG	Sport Appearance Group	425	500
	With 25G (Reg Cab)	255	300
	With 25G (Club Cab)	255	300
	With 26G (Reg Cab)	255	300
	With 26G (Club Cab)	255	300
	With 27G (Reg Cab)	255	300
	With 27G (Club Cab)	255	300
	With 28G (Reg Cab)	255	300
	With 28G (Club Cab)	255	300
	With 29G (Club Cab)	255	300
	With 29G (Reg Cab)	255	300
	With 2YG (Club Cab)	255	300
	With 2YG (Reg Cab)	255	300
	Includes color-keyed bumpers, dual horns, tachometer, chrome wheel skins, Sport decal, color-keyed grille, fog lights; REQUIRES ST Decor Group on Regular Cab trucks		
AMP	ST Decor Group (Reg Cab)	876	1030
	Manufacturer Discount	(340)	(400)
	Net Price	536	630
	Includes deluxe cloth 40/20/40 split bench seat, floor carpeting, chrome bumpers, chrome wheel skins, behind seat storage tray, cab back panel storage; NOT AVAILABLE with Laramie SLT Option Packages		
RA8	Stereo — Delete Credit	(85)	(100)
	NOT AVAILABLE with Laramie SLT Option Packages		
RBN	Stereo — Uplevel w/cassette	285	335
	AM/FM stereo with cassette player, graphic equalizer, and clock		
RAZ	Stereo — Uplevel w/cassette & CD players	587	690
	AM/FM stereo with cassette and CD players, graphic equailzer, and clock; REQUIRES purchase of a Laramie SLT Option Package		
RBR	Stereo — w/CD player	434	510
	AM/FM stereo with CD changer; REQUIRES purchase of a Laramie SLT Option Package		
DSA	Sure Grip Axle	242	285
JAY	Tachometer	68	80
TVW	Tires — LT215/85R16D (2WD)	170	200
	Blackwall all-terrain tires		

DODGE RAM 3500 / RAM VAN / RAM WAGON

CODE	DESCRIPTION	INVOICE	MSRP
TV2	Tires — LT215/85R16E (4WD)	170	200
	Blackwall all-terrain tires		
AHC	Trailer Tow Group	208	245
	Includes heavy-duty flashers, class IV trailer hitch receiver, and adaptor plug; REQUIRES a rear bumper		
AWK	Travel Convenience Group	179	210
	Includes overhead console with compass, reading lights, and outside temperature display; automatic dimming rearview mirror; REQUIRES purchase of a Laramie SLT Option Package		
WMG	Wheel Dress-up Package (Reg Cab)	259	305
	Includes chrome wheel skins		

1997 RAM VAN / WAGON

1997 Dodge Ram Wagon

What's New?

New this year are wider cargo doors, upgraded stereo systems, and an improved ignition switch with anti-theft protection. Front quarter vent windows disappear for 1997, and underhood service points feature colored identification.

Review

Dodge's full-size vans and wagons haven't changed all that much through nearly three decades of existence. Squint your eyes and focus away from the front end (which was redesigned in 1994), and the latest big Rams could almost be mistaken for 1971 models. Does that matter to their fans? Not in the least. Dodge's brawny haulers have earned an enviable reputation over the years, proving their worth against rivals from Ford and General Motors. Like those makes, Dodge offers a bewildering selection of models, in three capacities with payloads as great as 4,264 pounds—not to mention the dazzlingly long list of options to be considered. Wagons can be equipped to carry as many as 15 passengers.

RAM VAN / WAGON — DODGE

| CODE | DESCRIPTION | INVOICE | MSRP |

A driver's airbag is standard, and all Rams have rear-wheel anti-lock braking (four-wheel on the Wagons). Base engine in the 1500 and 2500 series is a 3.9-liter V-6, but most buyers would be better off with a V-8 (standard in the 3500 series). With 295 pound-feet of torque on tap, the 5.2-liter V-8 yields a rewarding combination of strength and economy, but no Ram vehicle ranks miserly at the gas pump.

For demanding applications, whether in cargo-carrying or passenger-seating, the 5.9-liter V-8, packing 330 pound-feet of twisting force, might be a better bet. To compensate for thirsty engine choices, Dodge includes a 35-gallon gas tank on all Ram Vans and Wagons.

New this year are wider cargo doors, upgraded stereo systems, and an improved ignition switch with anti-theft protection (Like theft is a problem here. Ooooh! Can't wait to get my thieving hands on that antique Dodge Van in mint condition...hey! Wait a minute! That's an airbag. This van is new!). Front quarter vent windows disappear for 1997, and underhood service points feature colored identification.

Plenty of RV converters turn out fancied-up variants of the Dodge Ram, but even the stock models can be fitted with a few comforts and conveniences to make driving pleasant, if not exactly posh. Wagons can have a power driver's seat, for instance, and you can even get a CD player with a graphic equalizer and Infinity speakers. An upscale SLT Wagon Package includes cupholders, seat map pockets, and cloth trim panels. Standard gear includes dual side doors, tinted windows, power steering, and a front stabilizer bar.

We find the Ram Van and Wagon to be packed full of value and think that they are a reasonable alternative to the full-size offerings from Ford and Chevy for those on a strict budget. When searching in this market segment, price is often the only thing separating somewhat unequal competitors.

Safety Data

Driver Airbag: *Standard*
Side Airbag: *Not Available*
Traction Control: *Not Available*
Driver Crash Test Grade: *Average*

Passenger Airbag: *Not Available*
4-Wheel ABS: *Optional*
Integrated Child Seat(s): *Not Available*
Passenger Crash Test Grade: *Good*

RAM VAN

Standard Equipment

RAM VAN 1500/2500: 3.9-liter V-6 engine, 3-speed automatic transmission, power recirculating ball steering, power front disc/rear drum brakes, rear anti-lock brake system, 15"x 6.5" wheels, hub caps, P235/75R15XL tires, driver airbag, dual hinged right side cargo doors, painted front and rear bumpers, painted dark silver metallic grille, tinted front door glass and windshield, lockable glovebox, black rubber floor covering, hardboard front headliner, woodgrain applique on instrument panel, door sill scuff pads, front sunvisors, dual exterior mirrors, AM/FM stereo with clock and 2 speakers, heavy-duty vinyl bucket seats, conventional spare tire, rear door windows, 2-speed intermittent wipers

3500 (in addition to 1500/2500 equipment): 5.2-liter V-8 engine, 4-speed automatic transmission, larger front and rear brakes, 16"x 6" wheels, LT225/75R16 tires

Base Prices

AB1L11	1500 SWB	15289	16845
AB1L12	1500 LWB	15344	17505
AB2L11	2500 SWB	15480	17665

DODGE RAM VAN / WAGON

CODE	DESCRIPTION	INVOICE	MSRP
AB2L12	2500 LWB	15519	17710
AB2L13	2500 Maxivan	16921	19360
AB3L12	3500 LWB	17720	20300
AB3L13	3500 Maxivan	18209	20875
	Destination Charge:	615	615

Accessories

CODE	DESCRIPTION	INVOICE	MSRP
HAA	Air Conditioning	825	970
BAZ	Alternator — 136 amp	132	155
	INCLUDED in Trailer Tow Prep Group		
BGK	Anti-lock Brakes	425	500
NHB	Auxiliary Transmission Oil Cooler (1500/2500)	55	65
	REQUIRES Maximum Engine Cooling; INCLUDED in Trailer Tow Prep Group		
GMF	Cargo Door — Single Rear	NC	NC
	NOT AVAILABLE with No Glass Group		
GKF	Cargo Door — Sliding Right Side	NC	NC
MBF	Chrome Bumpers	255	300
24C	Commercial Package 24C (1500/2500)	502	590
	Includes 5.2-liter V-8 engine		
28C	Commercial Package 28C (2500 LWB)	986	1160
	Includes 5.9-liter V-8 engine and 4-speed automatic transmission		
28C	Commercial Package 28C (3500)	230	270
	Includes 5.9-liter V-8 engine		
26C	Commericial Package 26C (1500/2500)	757	890
	Includes 5.2-liter V-8 engine and 4-speed automatic transmission		
AJK	Convenience Group — Deluxe	332	390
	Includes tilt steering wheel and cruise control		
AJP	Convenience Package	591	695
	Includes power windows and door locks		
GAE	Deep Tinted Glass	349	410
	With GHB	102	120
	With GHD	208	245
	REQUIRES purchase of a Window Group		
YCF	Emissions — Border States	145	170
	On 1500 SWB models, this emissions system REQUIRES the 3.55 Rear Axle Ratio on vans not equipped with Commercial Package 24C or 26C		
NAE	Emissions — Calif./Mass./New York	145	170
	On 1500 SWB models, this emissions system REQUIRES the 3.55 Rear Axle Ratio on vans not equipped with Commercial Package 24C or 26C		
NHK	Engine Block Heater	43	50
CUB	Engine Cover Console	132	155
AEA	Exterior Appearance Group	319	375
	Includes chrome bumpers and grille		
Z3B	GVWR — 8,510 lb. (3500 LWB)	344	405
Z3D	GVWR — 9,000 lb. (3500 Maxivan)	221	260
	REQUIRES Commercial Package 28C		

RAM VAN / WAGON — DODGE

CODE	DESCRIPTION	INVOICE	MSRP
BCQ	Heavy-duty Battery — 750 CCA	51	60
	INCLUDED in Trailer Tow Prep Group		
GXE	Lock Group	9	10
	Includes separate keys for ignition, front doors, and rear doors		
DSA	Locking Differential	242	285
	NOT AVAILABLE with 3.90 Rear Axle Ratio or 9000 lb. GVWR		
TBW	Matching Spare Wheel (1500/2500)	85	100
	With WJA (1500/2500)	55	65
	With WJM (1500/2500)	85	100
	REQUIRES purchase of Styled Steel Wheels or Chrome Styled Steel Wheels		
NMC	Maximum Engine Cooling (1500/2500)	55	65
	REQUIRES Auxiliary Transmission Oil Cooler; INCLUDED in Trailer Tow Prep Group		
GHA	No Glass Group	(51)	(60)
	Removes rear door glass		
CYA	Passenger Seat Delete	(153)	(180)
GPS	Power Exterior Mirrors — 6 x 9 Painted Black	136	160
DMD	Rear Axle Ratio — 3.55 (1500)	34	40
	NOT AVAILABLE with Commercial Package 26C		
DMD	Rear Axle Ratio — 3.55 (2500)	34	40
	REQUIRES Commercial Package 24C		
DMH	Rear Axle Ratio — 3.90 (1500)	34	40
	REQUIRES Commercial Package 26C		
DMH	Rear Axle Ratio — 3.90 (2500)	34	40
	REQUIRES Commercial Package 26C or 28C		
DMF	Rear Axle Ratio — 4.10 (3500)	34	40
	REQUIRES Locking Differential		
K5	Seats — Cloth & Vinyl Highback Buckets	132	155
	NOT AVAILABLE with Passenger Seat Delete		
N5	Seats — Reclining Cloth & Vinyl Buckets	179	210
	With CYA	89	105
	NOT AVAILABLE with Tradesman Package		
N6	Seats — Vinyl Highback Buckets	60	70
	With CYA	30	35
RAS	Stereo — w/cassette	187	220
RA8	Stereo Delete	(85)	(100)
WJM	Styled Steel Wheels — Chrome (1500/2500)	340	400
WJA	Styled Steel Wheels — Painted (1500/2500)	213	250
SUA	Tilt Steering Wheel	115	135
	INCLUDED in Deluxe Convenience Group		
TWT	Tires — LT225/75R16E (3500 LWB)	145	170
TSD	Tires — P235/75R15 Whitewalls (2500 Maxivan)	81	95
TSF	Tires — P235/75R15XL OWL (1500/2500)	106	125
	Outline white-lettered all-season tires		

DODGE RAM VAN / WAGON

CODE	DESCRIPTION	INVOICE	MSRP
ASF	Tradesman Package (2500 LWB)	1156	1360
	Manufacturer Discount	(310)	(365)
	Net Price	846	995
	Includes ladder rack, cargo area floor mat, and metal partition behind front seats		
AHC	Trailer Tow Prep Group (2500)	327	385
	Includes 136-amp alternator, heavy-duty battery, maximum engine cooling, auxiliary transmission oil cooler, and heavy-duty flashers; REQUIRES Commercial Package 24C, 26C, or 28C		
AHC	Trailer Tow Prep Group (3500)	217	255
	Includes 136-amp alternator, heavy-duty battery, and heavy-duty flashers		
GAH	Vented Windows	187	220
	With GHB	51	60
	With GHD	119	140
	With GHJ	119	140
	REQUIRES purchase of a Window Group		
WMC	Wheel Trim Rings (3500)	111	130
GHD	Window Group — Fixed Rear and Side Door Glass	38	45
GHB	Window Group — Fixed Rear Door Glass	NC	NC
GHG	Window Group — Vision Van All Around Glass	128	150
	Includes windows all around, and a larger day/night rearview mirror		
GHJ	Window Group — Vision Van Curb Side Glass	64	75
	Includes windows in rear doors and along right side of van		

RAM WAGON

Standard Equipment

RAM WAGON 1500: 3.9-liter V-6 engine, 3-speed automatic transmission, power recirculating ball steering, power front disc/rear drum brakes with rear anti-lock system, 15"x 6.5" styled steel wheels, P235/75R15XL tires, driver airbag, convenience group (glovebox light, cigarette lighter, underhood light), single rear door with vent window, dual hinged side doors with vent windows, chrome bumpers, tinted windows, lockable glove compartment, front air conditioning, front and rear carpeting, spare tire cover, cloth headliner, woodgrain applique on instrument panel, door sill scuff pads, dual front sunvisors, dual exterior mirrors, AM/FM stereo with cassette player, clock, and 4 speakers; 8-passenger seating, premium vinyl front bucket seats, conventional spare tire, vented glass windows, 2-speed intermittent windshield wipers

2500 (in addition to or instead of 1500 equipment): 5.2-liter V-8 engine, 4-speed automatic transmission

3500 (in addition to or instead of 2500 equipment): Larger front and rear brakes, 16"x 6" steel wheels, LY225/75R16 tires, hub caps and trim rings, deluxe floor mat, 15-passenger seating (Maxiwagon)

RAM VAN / WAGON — DODGE

CODE	DESCRIPTION	INVOICE	MSRP

Base Prices

CODE	DESCRIPTION	INVOICE	MSRP
AB1L51	1500 SWB	17886	19740
AB2L52	2500 LWB	19164	21940
AB3L52	3500 LWB	20184	23140
AB3L53	3500 Maxiwagon	21723	24950
	Destination Charge:	615	615

Accessories

CODE	DESCRIPTION	INVOICE	MSRP
HBB	Air Conditioning — Rear (2500/3500)	650	765
	With AHC (2500/3500 LWB)	604	710
	With AHC (3500 Maxiwagon)	604	710
	Includes rear heater, heavy-duty battery, and heavy-duty alternator; INCLUDED in SLT Option Packages on 3500 models		
WJC	Aluminum Wheels (1500/2500)	NC	NC
	REQUIRES purchase of an SLT Option Package		
BGK	Anti-lock Brakes	425	500
NHB	Auxiliary Transmission Oil Cooler (All except 3500 Maxivan)	55	65
	Requires Maximum Engine Cooling; INCLUDED in Trailer Tow Prep Group		
CKZ	Carpet Delete	NC	NC
	Replaces carpet on 1500, 2500 and 3500 models (w/SLT Option Package) with black rubber floor covering		
MBF	Chrome Rear Step Bumper	81	95
AJK	Convenience Group — Deluxe	332	390
	Includes cruise control and tilt steering wheel; INCLUDED in SLT Option Packages		
GAE	Deep Tinted Glass	349	410
	INCLUDED in SLT Option Packages		
YCF	Emissions — Border States	145	170
	On 1500 models without an Option Package, this emissions system REQUIRES the 3.55 Rear Axle Ratio		
NAE	Emissions — Calif./Mass./New York	145	170
	On 1500 models without an Option Package, this emissions system REQUIRES the 3.55 Rear Axle Ratio		
NHK	Engine Block Heater	43	50
CUB	Engine Cover Console Storage	132	155
	INCLUDED in SLT Option Packages		
CKE/CKN	Floor Carpeting (3500)	136	160
Z3B	GVWR — 8,510 lb. (3500 LWB)	344	405
Z3D	GVWR — 9,000 lb. (3500 Maxiwagon)	221	260
	REQUIRES purchase of Value Package 28B or SLT Option Package 28E		
BCQ	Heavy-duty Battery	51	60
	INCLUDED with Rear Air Conditioning and Trailer Tow Prep Group		
RCE	Infinity Sound System	149	175
	Included in SLT Option Packages		
DSA	Locking Differential	242	285
	NOT AVAILABLE with 3.90 Rear Axle Ratio		

DODGE RAM VAN / WAGON

CODE	DESCRIPTION	INVOICE	MSRP
TBW	Matching Spare Wheel (1500/2500)	55	65
	With WJC (1500/2500)	85	100
	With WJM (1500/2500)	85	100
	REQUIRES purchase of an SLT Option Package with Aluminum Wheels		
NMC	Maximum Engine Cooling (All except 3500 Maxivan)	55	65
	Requires Auxiliary Transmission Oil Cooler; INCLUDED in Trailer Tow Prep Group		
6P	Paint — Two-tone Center Band	336	395
	With 26E (1500)	251	295
	With 26E (2500 LWB)	251	295
	With 26E (3500)	251	295
	With 28E (2500 LWB)	251	295
	With 28E (3500)	251	295
6L	Paint — Two-tone Lower Break	298	350
	With 26E (1500)	196	230
	With 26E (2500 LWB)	196	230
	With 26E (3500)	196	230
	With 28E (2500 LWB)	196	230
	With 28E (3500)	196	230
CSR	Passenger Assist Handle	31	37
	INCLUDED in SLT Option Packages		
AJP	Power Convenience Group	591	695
	Includes power windows and door locks; INCLUDED in SLT Option Packages		
JPS	Power Driver's Seat	255	300
	REQUIRES purchase of an SLT Option Package		
DMD	Rear Axle Ratio — 3.55 (1500)	34	40
	INCLUDED in Option Packages		
DMH	Rear Axle Ratio — 3.90 (1500)	34	40
	REQUIRES purchase of an Option Package; NOT AVAILABLE with Locking Differential		
DMH	Rear Axle Ratio — 3.90 (2500)	34	40
	NOT AVAILABLE with Locking Differential		
DMF	Rear Axle Ratio — 4.10 (3500)	34	40
	REQUIRES Locking Differential		
GLC	Rear Door — Dual w/Vented Glass	NC	NC
GMC	Rear Door — Single w/Vented Glass	NC	NC
HDA	Rear Heater	179	211
	INCLUDED with Rear Air Conditioning		
GFA	Rear Window Defroster	153	180
	REQUIRED in New York State; REQUIRES Single Rear Door		
K5	Seat Trim — Cloth & Vinyl	72	85
	INCLUDED in SLT Option Packages		
CYH	Seating Downgrade — 12-passenger (3500 Maxiwagon)	(242)	(285)
26E	SLT Option Package 26E (1500)	3103	3650
	Manufacturer Discount	(128)	(150)
	Net Price	2975	3500
	Includes 5.2-liter V-8 engine, 4-speed automatic transmission, SLT Decor (reclining cloth and vinyl front bucket seats, front door armrests, full floor carpeting, engine cover console, extra sound insulation, passenger's illuminated visor vanity mirror,		

RAM VAN / WAGON — DODGE

CODE	DESCRIPTION	INVOICE	MSRP

bodyside moldings, dual horns), deluxe convenience group (cruise control tilt steering wheel), deep tinted glass, power exterior mirrors, Infinity sound system, passenger assist handles, power convenience group (power windows and door locks), chrome wheels

26E   SLT Option Package 26E (2500 LWB) 2427   2855
       Manufacturer Discount .... (170)   (200)
       Net Price 2257   2655

Includes SLT Decor (reclining cloth and vinyl front bucket seats, front door armrests, full floor carpeting, engine cover console, extra sound insulation, passenger's illuminated visor vanity mirror, bodyside moldings, dual horns), deluxe convenience group (cruise control tilt steering wheel), deep tinted glass, power exterior mirrors, Infinity sound system, power convenience group (power windows and door locks), chrome wheels, whitewall tires

26E   SLT Option Package 26E (3500) 3005   3535
       Manufacturer Discount .... (255)   (300)
       Net Price 2750   3235

Includes SLT Decor (reclining cloth and vinyl front bucket seats, front door armrests, full floor carpeting, engine cover console, extra sound insulation, passenger's illuminated visor vanity mirror, bodyside moldings, dual horns), rear heater and air conditioning, deluxe convenience group (cruise control tilt steering wheel), deep tinted glass, power exterior mirrors, Infinity sound system, power convenience group (power windows and door locks)

28E   SLT Option Package 28E (2500 LWB) 2657   3125
       Manufacturer Discount .... (170)   (200)
       Net Price 2487   2925

Includes 5.9-liter V-8 engine, SLT Decor (reclining cloth and vinyl front bucket seats, front door armrests, full floor carpeting, engine cover console, extra sound insulation, passenger's illuminated visor vanity mirror, bodyside moldings, dual horns), deluxe convenience group (cruise control tilt steering wheel), deep tinted glass, power exterior mirrors, Infinity sound system, power convenience group (power windows and door locks), chrome wheels, whitewall tires

28E   SLT Option Package 28E (3500) 3235   3805
       Manufacturer Discount .... (255)   (300)
       Net Price 2980   3505

Includes 5.9-liter V-8 engine, SLT Decor (reclining cloth and vinyl front bucket seats, front door armrests, full floor carpeting, engine cover console, extra sound insulation, passenger's illuminated visor vanity mirror, bodyside moldings, dual horns), rear heater and air conditioning, deluxe convenience group (cruise control tilt steering wheel), deep tinted glass, power exterior mirrors, Infinity sound system, power convenience group (power windows and door locks)

RBN   Stereo — Uplevel w/cassette 132   155
       Includes graphic equalizer; REQUIRES purchase of an SLT Option Package

RBR   Stereo — Uplevel w/CD player 264   310
       Includes graphic equalizer; REQUIRES purchase of an SLT Option Package

WJM   Styled Steel Chrome Wheels (1500/2500) 128   150
       INCLUDED in SLT Option Packages

DODGE RAM VAN / WAGON

CODE	DESCRIPTION	INVOICE	MSRP
SUA	Tilt Steering Wheel	115	135
	INCLUDED in Deluxe Convenience Group and in SLT Option Packages		
TSC	Tire Downgrade — P235/75R15 Blackwalls (2500)	NC	NC
	REQUIRES purchase of an SLT Option Package		
TSF	Tires — P235/75R15 OWL (1500)	106	125
	Outline white-lettered all-season tires; REQUIRES purchase of an SLT Option Package		
TSF	Tires — P235/75R15 OWL (2500)	26	31
	Outline white-lettered all-season tires; REQUIRES purchase of an SLT Option Package		
TSD	Tires — P235/75R15 Whitewalls (1500)	81	95
	REQUIRES purchase of an SLT Option Package		
AHC	Trailer Tow Prep Group (2500/3500 LWB)	196	230
	Includes 136-amp alternator, heavy-duty battery, maximum engine cooling, auxiliary engine oil cooler, and heavy-duty flashers		
AHC	Trailer Tow Prep Group (3500 Maxiwagon)	85	100
	Includes 136-amp alternator, heavy-duty battery, and heavy-duty flashers		
26C	Value Option Package 26C (1500)	757	890
	Includes 5.2-liter V-8 engine and 4-speed automatic transmission		
28B	Value Option Package 28B (3500)	230	270
	Includes 5.9-liter V-8 engine		

Take Advantage of Warranty Gold!

Savings up to 50% off Dealer's Extended Warranty Prices. Protect and enhance YOUR investment with the best extended warranty available.

Call Toll Free 1-800-580-9889

For a guaranteed low price on a new vehicle in your area, call

1-800-CAR-CLUB

CLUB WAGON   FORD

| CODE | DESCRIPTION | INVOICE | MSRP |

1998 CLUB WAGON

1998 Ford Club Wagon Chateau

What's New?

New interior and exterior packages appear on the Club Wagon and Econoline vans.

Review

Tough and roomy, rugged and reliable, Ford's full-size vans and wagons have a favorable, well-earned reputation that reaches way back to the Sixties. Ford calls the Econoline/Club Wagon group the U.S. industry's only family of body-on-frame vans and passenger wagons, adding that the Econoline leads in sales to aftermarket conversions—the folks who turn no-frills vans into alluring recreational vehicles.

All Econoline and Club Wagon vans ride on a 138-inch wheelbase. All of Ford's full-size vans have four-wheel anti-lock brakes and dual air bags. These features, and their large size result in better than average crash test scores, make the Ford vans some of the safest vehicles on the road.

Driving a Club Wagon, despite its passenger seating, differs little from piloting a delivery vehicle, so it's not a logical choice for everyday motoring—though quite a few families happily employ their Wagons exactly that way. The virtues of sitting tall with a panoramic view of the road ahead can outweigh many a minor inconvenience—such as the difficulty of squeezing these biggies into urban parking spots and compact garages. Handling is light, seats are acceptably comfortable, and Club Wagons don't ride badly at all, considering the old-fashioned suspension configurations they employ.

As with most full-size vans, the Club Wagon and Econoline feature a wide choice of powerplants. Exclusive to Ford, however, is the industry's first SOHC engines found in a van. The three SOHC engines include a 4.6-liter V-8 producing 215 horsepower, a 5.4-liter V-8 producing 235 horsepower, and 6.8-liter V-10 that produces 265 horsepower and a massive 411 lbs./ft. of torque. Ford claims that a natural gas version of the 5.4-liter will be available later this year.

Full-size vans fell out of favor with families when the minivan was introduced. Few find their way into suburban driveways anymore. The Ford Club Wagon and Econoline are some of the best, and can be had at prices that rival Ford's own Windstar. For your money, wouldn't you rather have more space and utility?

FORD CLUB WAGON

| CODE | DESCRIPTION | INVOICE | MSRP |

Safety Data

Driver Airbag: *Standard*
Side Airbag: *Not Available*
Traction Control: *Not Available*
Driver Crash Test Grade: *Good*

Passenger Airbag: *Standard*
4-Wheel ABS: *Standard*
Integrated Child Seat(s): *Not Available*
Passenger Crash Test Grade: *Average*

Standard Equipment

XL: 4.2L V-6 OHV SMPI 12-valve engine; 4-speed overdrive automatic transmission with lock-up; 72-amp battery; 95-amp alternator; rear-wheel drive, 3.31 axle ratio; stainless steel exhaust; front independent suspension, front coil springs, front shocks, rear suspension with rear leaf springs, rear shocks; power re-circulating ball steering; front disc/rear drum brakes with 4 wheel anti-lock braking system; 35 gal capacity fuel tank; 3 doors with split swing-out right rear passenger door, split swing-out rear cargo door; front and rear colored bumpers; monotone paint; sealed beam halogen headlamps; additional exterior lights include center high-mounted stop light; driver and passenger manual black folding outside mirrors; front and rear 15" x 6" steel wheels, hub wheel covers; P235/75SR15 BSW AS front and rear tires; underbody mounted full-size conventional steel spare wheel; air conditioning; AM/FM stereo with clock, seek-scan, 4 speakers and fixed antenna; 1 power accessory outlet; analog instrumentation display, PRNDL in instrument panel; dual airbags; tinted windows, vented rear windows, fixed 1/4 vent windows; variable intermittent front windshield wipers; seating capacity of 8, front bucket seats with adjustable headrests, driver seat includes 2-way direction control, passenger seat includes 2-way direction control; fixed bench 2nd row seat; 3rd row fixed bench seatt; front height adjustable seatbelts with pretensioners; vinyl seats, full cloth headliner, full vinyl floor covering; interior lights include dome light; passenger side vanity mirror; day-night rear-view mirror; engine cover console with storage, front cupholder, dashboard storage; vinyl cargo floor, cargo light; colored grille, black side windows, black front windshield trim, black rear window trim, and black door handles.

XL HD (in addition to or instead of XL equipment): 5.4L V-8 SOHC SMPI 16-valve engine; 4-speed electronic overdrive automatic transmission with lock-up; 3.55 axle ratio; front independent suspension with anti-roll bar, HD front shocks, HD rear shocks; Class 1 trailer harness; front and rear 16" x 7" wheels; LT225/75SR16 BSW AS front and rear tires; and seating capacity of 12.

XLT (in addition to or instead of XL equipment): 5.4L V-8 SOHC SMPI 16-valve engine; 4-speed electronic overdrive automatic transmission with lock-up; front independent suspension with anti-roll bar, HD front shocks, HD rear shocks; Class 1 trailer harness, front and rear chrome bumpers; aero-composite halogen headlamps; front and rear steel wheels, full wheel covers; 6 speakers; warning indicators include lights on; power front windows; front captain seats with driver and passenger armrests, driver seat includes 4-way direction control, passenger seat includes 4-way direction control; cloth seats, door trim with carpet lower, full carpet floor covering , deluxe sound insulation; interior lights include front reading lights, illuminated entry; dashboard storage, driver and passenger door bins; and carpeted cargo floor.

XLT HD (in addition to or instead of XL HD): Front and rear chrome bumpers; aero-composite halogen headlamps; front and rear steel wheels, full wheel wheel covers; LT235/75SR16 BSW AS rear tires; 6 speakers; warning indicators include lights on; power front windows; front captain seats, driver and passenger armrests, driver seat includes 4-way direction control, passenger seat includes 4-way direction control; cloth seats, door trim with carpet lower, full carpet floor covering, deluxe sound insulation; interior lights include front reading lights, illuminated entry; dashboard storage, driver and passenger door bins; carpeted cargo floor; and chrome grille.

CLUB WAGON — FORD

CODE	DESCRIPTION	INVOICE	MSRP

Base Prices

Code	Description	Invoice	MSRP
E11	XL	19002	21755
E31	XL HD	21454	24640
E11	XLT	20655	23700
E31	XLT HD	23043	26510
	Destination Charge:	615	615

Accessories

Code	Description	Invoice	MSRP
X19	3.55 Axle Ratio (XL HD/XLT HD)	38	45
X32	4.10 Axle Ratio (XL HD/XLT HD)	38	45
	NOT AVAILABLE with (XC4) 3.73 limited slip differential or (XC9) 3.55 limited slip differential.		
961	Auxiliary Idle Control (XL HD/XLT HD)	170	200
	REQUIRES (99F) engine. NOT AVAILABLE with (99S) engine.		
548	Bright Swing-Out Recreational Mirrors	51	60
	DELETES power mirrors when equipped.		
422	California Emissions	145	170
	Required on all units for California/Massachusetts/New York/Connecticut (if specified) registration. NOT AVAILABLE with (428) High Altitude Principal Use.		
77C	Chateau Appearance Package (XLT)	876	1030
	Includes rear door badge, lower accent two-tone paint, leather-wrapped steering wheel, 7-passenger seating with 4 captain chairs and 1 bench seat, privacy glass, and bright cast aluminum wheels.		
77C	Chateau Appearance Package (XLT HD)	702	825
	Includes rear door badge, lower accent two-tone paint, leather-wrapped steering wheel, and 7-passenger seating with 4 captain chairs and 1 bench seat.		
768	Chrome Rear Step Bumper	102	120
	NOT AVAILABLE with (769) painted rear step bumper.		
C2	Cloth Trim (XL)	NC	NC
415	Deluxe Engine Cover Console (XL)	128	150
	Includes 2 cupholders, storage area, and rack for cassettes.		
419	Dual Illuminated Visor Mirrors (XLT/XLT HD)	43	50
41H	Engine Block Heater	30	35
996	Engine: 4.6L EFI V8 (XL/XLT)	613	720
	Includes HD alternator. NOT AVAILABLE with (44E) transmission or (574) high capacity dual zone air conditioning.		
99L	Engine: 5.4L EFI V8 (XL/XLT)	1105	1300
	Includes 3.55 axle ratio. REQUIRES (44E) transmission.		
99S	Engine: 6.8L EFI V-10 (XL HD/XLT HD)	472	555
	Includes 3.73 axle ratio. NOT AVAILABLE with (XC9) 3.55 limited slip differential or (961) auxiliary idle control.		
99F	Engine: 7.3L V8 Turbo Diesel (XL HD/XLT HD)	4085	4805
	Includes HD alternator. NOT AVAILABLE with (XC4) limited slip differential and 3.73 axle ratio or (634) HD auxiliary battery.		

FORD CLUB WAGON

CODE	DESCRIPTION	INVOICE	MSRP
18A	Exterior Upgrade Package (XL)	285	335

Includes aero-composite halogen headlamps and chrome grille. NOT AVAILABLE with (769) rear step painted bumper.

639	Extra HD Alternator (XLT HD)	493	580

REQUIRES (99F) engine.

—	Front Air Conditioning Delete (XL)	(723)	(915)
633	HD Alternator (XL)	68	80
634	HD Auxiliary Battery (XLT/XLT HD)	123	145

Includes 78-amp battery and deep-cycle non-starting. NOT AVAILABLE with (99F) engine.

428	High Altitude Principal Use	NC	NC
574	High Capacity Dual Zone Air Conditioning (XL)	702	825

Includes overhead ducts. NOT AVAILABLE with (996) engine.

18G	Interior Upgrade Package (XL)	522	615

Includes illuminated entry, headlights-on audible alert/chime, full length carpeting, and cloth trim.

XH9	Limited Slip Differential (XL/XLT)	221	260

REQUIRES (X19) 3.55 axle ratio.

XC9	Limited Slip Differential with 3.55 (XL HD/XLT HD)	221	260

NOT AVAILABLE with 99S, XC4, XC2, X32.

XC4	Limited Slip Differential with 3.73 (XL HD/XLT HD)	221	260

REQUIRES 99S. NOT AVAILABLE with 99F, XC2, XC9, X32.

XC2	Limited Slip Differential with 4.10 (XL HD/XLT HD)	221	260

REQUIRES (X32) 4.10 axle ratio. NOT AVAILABLE with (XC4) 3.73 limited slip axle ratio or (XC9) 3.55 limited slip axle

903	Power Convenience Group (XL)	421	495

Includes XLT door trim panels and memory lock module with sliding cargo door, power windows, power door locks, door bin storage, and carpet door trim.

90P	Power Driver's Seat (XLT/XLT HD)	332	390
700A	Preferred Equipment Package 700A (XL)	NC	NC

Includes front air conditioning and 8 passenger seating with vinyl trim (A2).

705A	Preferred Equipment Package 705A (XLT)	1428	1680
	Manufacturer Discount	(408)	(480)
	Net Price	1020	1200

Includes high capacity dual zone air conditioning, Power Convenience Group: power windows, power door locks, door bin storage, carpet door trim, HD alternator, and deluxe engine cover console; Tilt and Cruise Convenience Group: tilt steering and speed control; AM/FM stereo with cassette, clock radio, and power sail mount mirrors.

710A	Preferred Equipment Package 710A (XL HD)	NC	NC

Includes 5.4L V-8 engine, 4-spd elecronic transmission, front air conditioning, full wheel covers, 12-passenger vinyl seating.

713A	Preferred Equipment Package 713A (XLT HD)	1428	1680
	Manufacturer Discount	(408)	(480)
	Net Price	1020	1200

Includes 5.4L V-8 engine, electronic 4-speed automatic transmission, full wheel

CLUB WAGON   FORD

CODE	DESCRIPTION	INVOICE	MSRP
	covers, high capacity dual zone air conditioning, HD alternator, deluxe engine cover console, AM/FM stereo with cassette, clock radio, power sail mount mirrors, Tilt and Cruise Convenience Group: tilt steering and speed control; Power Convenience Group: power windows, power door locks, door bin storage, and carpet door trim.		
924	Privacy Glass (XLT/XLT HD)	357	420
589	Radio: AM/FM Stereo with Cassette and Clock (XL)	132	155
	Includes 4 speakers.		
588	Radio: Premium AM/FM Stereo with Cassette (XLT/XLT HD)	64	75
	Includes clock and 6 speakers.		
769	Rear Step Painted Bumper (XL)	102	120
	Includes light charcoal paint. NOT AVAILABLE with (768) chrome rear step bumper or (18A) Exterior Upgrade Package.		
948	Remote Keyless Entry with Panic Alarm	170	200
	Includes remote entry transmitters (2). REQUIRES (18G) Interior Upgrade Package and (903) Power Convenience Group.		
60S	Sliding Side Cargo Door	NC	NC
52N	Tilt and Cruise Convenience Group (XL)	328	385
	Includes tilt steering and speed control.		
T38	Tires: LT245/75R16E AS BSW (XL HD/XLT HD)	119	140
535	Trailer Towing Package (Class II/III/IV) (XL/XLT HD)	162	190
	Includes electric brake controller tap-in capability and relay system for backup, running lights.		
535	Trailer Towing Package (Class II/III/IV) (XLT)	93	110
	Includes electric brake controller tap-in capability and relay system for backup, running lights.		
44E	Transmission: Electronic 4-Spd Automatic	NC	NC
	NOT AVAILABLE with (996) engine.		
645	Wheels: Bright Cast Aluminum (XLT)	263	310
	Includes 15" steel spare.		

Save hundreds, even thousands,
off the sticker price
of the new car you want.

Call Autovantage®
your FREE auto-buying service

1-800-201-7703

No purchase required. No fees.

FORD ECONOLINE

1998 ECONOLINE

1998 Ford Econoline Van XL

What's New?

New interior and exterior packages appear on the Club Wagon and Econoline vans.

Review

Tough and roomy, rugged and reliable, Ford's full-size vans and wagons have a favorable, well-earned reputation that reaches way back to the Sixties. Ford calls the Econoline/Club Wagon group the U.S. industry's only family of body-on-frame vans and passenger wagons, adding that the Econoline leads in sales to aftermarket conversions—the folks who turn no-frills vans into alluring recreational vehicles.

All Econoline and Club Wagon vans ride on a 138-inch wheelbase. All of Ford's full-size vans have four-wheel anti-lock brakes and dual air bags. These features, and their large size better than average crash test scores, make the Ford vans some of the safest vehicles on the road.

Driving a Club Wagon, despite its passenger seating, differs little from piloting a delivery vehicle, so it's not a logical choice for everyday motoring—though quite a few families happily employ their Wagons exactly that way. The virtues of sitting tall with a panoramic view of the road ahead can outweigh many a minor inconvenience—such as the difficulty of squeezing these biggies into urban parking spots and compact garages. Handling is light, seats are acceptably comfortable, and Club Wagons don't ride badly at all, considering the old-fashioned suspension configurations they employ.

As with most full-size vans, the Club Wagon and Econoline feature a wide choice of powerplants. Exclusive to Ford, however, is the industry's first SOHC engines found in a van. The three SOHC engines include a 4.6-liter V-8 producing 215 horsepower, a 5.4-liter V-8 producing 235 horsepower, and 6.8-liter V-10 that produces 265 horsepower and a massive 411 ft./lbs. of torque. Ford claims that a natural gas version of the 5.4-liter will be available later this year.

Full-size vans fell out of favor with families when the minivan was introduced. Few find their

ECONOLINE   FORD

| CODE | DESCRIPTION | INVOICE | MSRP |

way into suburban driveways anymore. The Ford Club Wagon and Econoline are some of the best, and can be had at prices that rival Ford's own Windstar. For your money, wouldn't you rather have more space and utility?

Safety Data

Driver Airbag: *Standard*
Side Airbag: *Not Available*
Traction Control: *Not Available*
Driver Crash Test Grade: *Good*

Passenger Airbag: *Standard*
4-Wheel ABS: *Standard*
Integrated Child Seat(s): *Not Available*
Passenger Crash Test Grade: *Average*

Standard Equipment

ECONOLINE: 4.2-liter V-6 engine (E150/E250), 5.4-liter V-8 engine (E350), 4-speed automatic transmission, power steering, power front disc/rear drum brakes, gas shock absorbers, handling package (E350), P225/75R15L tires (E150), LT225/75R16D (E250) tires, LT245/75R16E tires (E250 H/D/E350), 15" wheels (E150), 16" wheels (E250/E350), hub caps, charcoal colored grille and bumpers, halogen headlamps, hinged side cargo door, solar tinted glass, black outside mirrors, interval windshield wipers, driver's side airbag, passenger's side airbag (E150/E250), front dome light, gray interior, rear cargo light, courtesy lights, AM radio, clock, black vinyl floor mats, and vinyl sun visors.

Base Prices

		INVOICE	MSRP
E14	E150 Cargo	16813	19180
E24	E250 Cargo	17077	19490
S24	E250 Super	17672	20190
E34	E350	19287	22090
S34	E350 Super	20119	23070
Destination Charge:		615	615

Accessories

		INVOICE	MSRP
996	4.6-liter V-8 Engine (E150)	613	720
	REQUIRES *optional payload package.*		
99L	5.4-liter V-8 Engine (E150/E250)	1105	1300
	REQUIRES *(44E) transmission.*		
99S	6.8-liter V-10 Engine (E350)	472	555
99F	7.3-liter Power Stroke Diesel (E350)	3889	4575
572	Air Conditioning	827	973
574	Air Conditioning/Auxiliary Heater	1530	1800
	Includes *auxiliary heater, front air conditioning, HD alternator, and Light and Convenience Group.*		
17W	All-Around Windows	298	350
44E	Automatic Transmission	NC	NC
	REQUIRES *(99L) engine.*		
57J	Auxiliary Heater Connector Package	21	24
X—	Axle Ratio	NC	NC
422	California Emission System	145	170
21W	Captain's Chairs Delete	NC	NC

EDMUND'S 1998 NEW TRUCKS

FORD ECONOLINE

CODE	DESCRIPTION	INVOICE	MSRP
768	Chrome Rear Step Bumper	136	164
	Includes front chrome bumper.		
B	Cloth Seats	17	20
551	Deluxe Insulation Package	149	175
41H	Engine Block Heater	68	80
415	Engine Cover Console	128	150
173	Fixed Rear Cargo Door Glass	50	59
178	Fixed Side/Rear Cargo Door Glass	111	130
671	Front GAWR-One Up (E150)	26	30
684	Handling Package (150/250)	67	79
	Includes front stabilizer bar and HD front and rear shocks. NOT AVAILABLE with (534).		
633	Heavy Duty Alternator	56	66
634	Heavy Duty Auxiliary Battery	123	145
53C	Heavy Duty Service Package (150/250)	153	180
53C	Heavy Duty Service Package (350)	73	85
683	Heavy Duty Suspension (150)	75	88
683	Heavy Duty Suspension (250)	275	323
428	High Altitude Principal Use Emissions	NC	NC
153	License Plate Bracket	NC	NC
593	Light and Convenience Group	128	150
	Includes headlights on audible alert and illuminated entry.		
X—	Limited Slip Axle Ratio	221	260
	Includes standard axle ratio.		
X—	Limited Slip Axle Ratio	259	305
	Includes alternate axle.		
769	Painted Rear Step Bumper	104	122
202	Payload Package 202 (150)	85	100
205	Payload Package 205 (250 Super)	NC	NC
207	Payload Package 207 (E250 Reg)	NC	NC
90P	Power Driver's Seat	330	388
	Includes power lumbar support.		
740A	Preferred Equipment Package 740A (150)	NC	NC
	Includes vehicle with standard equipment.		
750A	Preferred Equipment Package 750A (250)	NC	NC
	Includes vehicle with standard equipment.		
760A	Preferred Equipment Package 760A (350)	NC	NC
	Includes vehicle with standard equipment.		
588	Premium Stereo with Cassette	63	74
924	Privacy Glass	251	295
58Y	Radio Credit Option	(52)	(61)
58R	Radio Prep Package	(132)	(155)
60S	Sliding Side Cargo Door	NC	NC
516	Spare Tire and Wheel Delete	(129)	(151)
52N	Speed Control/Tilt Steering Wheel	328	385
589	Stereo with Cassette	132	155

ECONOLINE / EXPEDITION — FORD

CODE	DESCRIPTION	INVOICE	MSRP
548	Swing-out Recreational Mirrors	50	59
179	Swing-out Side/Rear Cargo Door Glass	158	185
T76	Tires — P225/75R15SL BSW (150)	NC	NC
T32	Tires — LT225/75R16D BSW (250)	NC	NC
T37	Tires — LT225/75R16E BSW (250)	73	85
T38	Tires — LT245/75R16E BSW (350)	NC	NC
T77	Tires — P235/75R15XL BSW (150)	72	84
T7Q	Tires — P235/75R15XL OWL (150)	177	209
T78	Tires — P235/75R15XL WSW (150)	158	185
535	Trailer Towing Package (150/250) Class II/III/IV.	349	410
534	Trailer Towing Package (Class I)	196	230
535	Trailer Towing Pkg (Class II/III/IV) (350)	162	190
64B	Wheel Covers	84	99
644	Wheels Covers, Sport	73	85
645	Wheels: Bright Cast Aluminum	265	312
64F	Wheels: Forged Aluminum	265	312

1998 EXPEDITION

1998 Ford Expedition Eddie Bauer

What's New?

After an insanely successful first year, the Ford Expedition pounds its way into 1998 without changes. Next year expect to see a minor facelift to keep the truck current with the F-150.

FORD EXPEDITION

| CODE | DESCRIPTION | INVOICE | MSRP |

Review

After allowing GM to dominate the full-size SUV arena for years, Ford introduced a vehicle in 1997 that had its sights squarely aimed at the Chevy Tahoe and GMC Yukon. Ford boasts that its Expedition is superior to the GM full-size sport-utes in every way. We had the chance to drive many of these brute/utes this year, and here is what we found out.

Larger than the Tahoe and Yukon, the Expedition can seat nine people with its optional third-row bench seat; the Tahoe and Yukon can only seat six. Unlike the Suburban, which may have difficulty fitting into a standard garage, the Expedition can be handled with ease in most parking maneuvers. The Expedition also has the best payload and towing capacity in its class: 2,000-lbs. and 8000-lbs. respectively.

On the road the Expedition is well mannered. It's obvious that this is not a car, but compared to the vehicle it replaces the Expedition rides like a limousine. Interior ergonomics are first rate and will be familiar to anyone who has spent time in the new F-150. From the front seat forward the Expedition is nearly identical to the new pickup. That's a good thing; we love the cab of the 1997 F-150 with its easy-to-use climate and stereo controls, steering wheel mounted cruise control, plenty of cupholders and great storage space.

Ford has put a lot of time and money into making this truck the next sales leader in their already dominant light-truck lineup. We came away impressed and think you will too. The Expedition comes standard with dual airbags, a first in this segment, anti-lock brakes, and fold-flat second row seats; features that we feel are important in this increasingly competitive segment. Our few gripes stem from the powertrain. After driving a few Vortec powered Suburbans this year, we've become spoiled by the GM engine's gobs of torque and horsepower. The Expedition's power output won't be confused with a Chevy Tracker, but it did leave us wondering if we could squeeze one of GM's 5.7-liter powerhouses into the engine bay. One option that we think everyone should investigate is the lighted running boards. The Expedition towers above the ground, and entering and exiting this truck will take its toll on most passengers after a few days.

We've seen a lot of these monsters turning up in our neighborhood and after driving the Expedition ourselves we know why. If you're thinking of buying a full-size SUV in the near future, you owe it to yourself to take a look at this truck.

Safety Data

Driver Airbag: *Standard*
Side Airbag: Not Available
Traction Control: Not Available
Driver Crash Test Grade: Not Available

Passenger Airbag: *Standard*
4-Wheel ABS: *Standard*
Integrated Child Seat(s): Not Available
Passenger Crash Test Grade: Not Available

Standard Equipment

XLT 2WD: 4.6L V-8 SOHC SMPI 16-valve engine; 4-speed overdrive automatic transmission with lock-up; 650 amp battery with run down protection; 130-amp alternator; rear wheel drive, 3.31 axle ratio; stainless steel exhaust; front independent suspension with anti-roll bar, front coil springs, front shocks, rear multi-link suspension with anti-roll bar, rear coil springs, rear shocks; power re-circulating ball steering with vehicle speed-sensing assist; 4-wheel disc brakes with 4-wheel anti-lock braking system; 26 gal capacity fuel tank; liftback rear cargo door; class II trailer harness; front and rear chrome bumpers front with body-colored rub strip, body-colored bodyside molding, chrome bodyside insert; monotone paint; aero-composite halogen headlamps; additional exterior lights include center high mounted stop light, underhood light; driver and passenger power remote chrome folding outside mirrors; front and rear 16" x 7" silver styled steel wheels, hub wheel covers; P255/70SR16 BSW AS front and rear tires; underbody mounted full-size temporary steel spare wheel; air conditioning, rear heat ducts; premium AM/FM stereo with clock, seek-scan, cassette, 4 speakers and fixed antenna; power door locks,

EXPEDITION   FORD

CODE	DESCRIPTION	INVOICE	MSRP

remote keyless entry, child safety rear door locks, power remote hatch/trunk release; 2 power accessory outlet, driver foot rest, retained accessory power; analog instrumentation display includes tachometer gauge, oil pressure gauge, water temp gauge, volt gauge, PRNDL in instrument panel, trip odometer; warning indicators include oil pressure, water temp warning, battery, low oil level, lights-on, key-in-ignition, low fuel, low washer fluid, door ajar; dual airbags; ignition disable, panic alarm; tinted windows, power front windows with driver 1-touch down, power rear windows, fixed 1/4 vent windows; variable intermittent front windshield wipers, flip-up rear window, fixed interval rear wiper, rear window defroster; seating capacity of 6, 40-60 split-bench front seat with fixed adjustable headrests, center armrest with storage, driver seat includes 4-way direction control with lumbar support, passenger seat includes 4-way direction control; 60-40 folding split-bench second row seat with reclining and adjustable headrest, center armrest with storage; front and rear height adjustable seatbelts; cloth seats, door trim with carpet lower, full cloth headliner, full carpet floor covering with carpeted floor mats; interior lights include dome light, front reading lights, 2 door curb lights, illuminated entry; steering wheel with tilt adjustment; dual auxiliary visors, passenger side vanity mirror, day-night rearview mirror; glove box with light, front and rear cupholders, instrument panel bin, dashboard storage, driver and passenger door bins, rear door bins; carpeted cargo floor, cargo tie downs, cargo light, cargo concealed storage; chrome grille, black side windows, and body-colored door handles.

EDDIE BAUER 2WD (in addition to or instead of XLT 2WD equipment): Roof rack; front and rear chrome bumpers with colored rub strip; body-colored bodyside molding, rocker panel extensions, wheel well extentions; monotone paint with bodyside accent stripe; aero-composite halogen fully automatic headlamps with delay-off feature; additional exterior lights include front fog/driving lights; driver and passenger power remote body-colored folding outside mirrors; front and rear silver alloy wheels, hub wheel covers; P255/70SR16 OWL AT front and rear tires; clock, rear controls; cruise control with steering wheel controls; 3 power accessory outlet, driver foot rest, retained accessory power; compass, trip computer, trip odometer; deep tinted power windows with driver 1-touch down, power 1/4 vent windows; seating capacity of 5, front captain seats with driver and passenger armrests, driver seat includes 8-way direction control with lumbar support, passenger seat includes 4-way direction control with lumbar support; leather seats; leather-wrapped steering wheel with with tilt adjustment; dual illuminated vanity mirrors, dual auxiliary visors; body-colored grille and body-colored door handles.

XLT 4WD (in addition to or instead of XLT 2WD equipment): Part-time 4-wheel drive, auto locking hub control and electronic shift, 3.55 axle ratio; front independent torsion suspension with anti-roll bar, front torsion springs; 30 gal capacity fuel tank; front chrome bumper with body-colored rub strip, and tow hook(s).

EDDIE BAUER 4WD (in addition to or instead of XLT 4WD equipment): Part-time 4-wheel drive, auto locking hub control and electronic shift, 3.55 axle ratio; front independent torsion suspension with anti-roll bar, front torsion springs; 30 gal capacity fuel tank; front chrome bumper with body-colored rub strip, and tow hook(s).

Base Prices

U17	XLT 2WD	24533	27985
U18	XLT 4WD	26743	30585
U17	Eddie Bauer 2WD	27908	31955
U18	Eddie Bauer 4WD	30148	34590
Destination Charge:		640	640

FORD EXPEDITION

CODE	DESCRIPTION	INVOICE	MSRP

Accessories

Code	Description	Invoice	MSRP
91P	6-Disc CD Changer	404	475
	NOT AVAILABLE with (684A) Preferred Equipment Package 684A, or (FD) seats.		
422	California Emissions	144	170
	Required on all units for California, Massachusetts or New York registration. NOT AVAILABLE (41H) engine block heater, or (428) high altitude principal use.		
FD	Delete Cloth Captain Seats with Console (XLT)	(285)	(335)
	REQUIRES (685A) Preferred Equipment Package 685A. NOT AVAILABLE with (684A) Preferred Equipment Package 684A or (91P) 6-Disc CD Changer.		
41H	Engine Block Heater	30	35
	NOT AVAILABLE with (685A) Preferred Equipment Package 685A, (686A) Preferred Equipment Package 686A, or (422) California emissions.		
99L	Engine: 5.4L EFI V8	565	665
	Includes super engine cooling. REQUIRES (44E) transmission. NOT AVAILABLE with XH7, 535, 428, XH9, 647.		
63W	Extreme Weather Group (Eddie Bauer 2WD/Eddie Bauer 4WD)	68	80
	Includes heated mirrors and engine block heater. NOT AVAILABLE with (687A) Preferred Equipment Package 687A.		
63W	Extreme Weather Group (XLT)	162	190
	Includes heated mirrors, front fog lamps, and engine block heater. NOT AVAILABLE with (684A) Preferred Equipment Package 684A.		
916	Ford MACH Cassette Audio System (Eddie Bauer 2WD/Eddie Bauer 4WD)	302	355
	Includes 7 premium speakers.		
68P	Four Corner Load Leveling Suspension (XLT 4WD/Eddie Bauer 4WD)	692	815
	NOT AVAILABLE with (684A) Preferred Equipment Package 684A.		
428	High Altitude Principal Use	NC	NC
186	Illuminated Running Boards	370	435
1	Leather Captain's Seats with Console (XLT)	1105	1300
	Includes 6-way power driver seat and driver/passenger manual lumbar adjustments, floor console, seatback storage pockets, power point, and rear radio controls. NOT AVAILABLE with (684A) Preferred Equipment Package 684A, or (FD) seats.		
XH7	Limited Slip Differential with 3.31 (XLT 2WD/Eddie Bauer 2WD)	217	255
	NOT AVAILABLE with (687A) Preferred Equipment Package 687A, (99L) engine, or (44E) transmission.		
XH9	Limited Slip Differential with 3.55 (XLT 4WD/Eddie Bauer 2WD)	217	255
	NOT AVAILABLE with (687A) Preferred Equipment Package 687A, (99L) engine, or (44E) transmission.		
XH6	Limited Slip Differential with 3.73 (Eddie Bauer 4WD)	NC	NC
	Includes engine oil cooler. REQUIRES (687A) Preferred Equipment Package 687A, (99L) engine and (44E) transmission.		
XH6	Limited Slip Differential with 3.73 (XLT 4WD)	267	315
	Includes engine oil cooler. REQUIRES (99L) engine and (44E) transmission. NOT AVAILABLE with (687A) Preferred Equipment Package 687A.		

EXPEDITION — FORD

CODE	DESCRIPTION	INVOICE	MSRP
43M	**Power Moonroof with Sunshade (Eddie Bauer 2WD/Eddie Bauer 4WD)**	680	800
	Includes power flip-our rear quarter window switches, trip computer with electronic display, and mini overhead console. NOT AVAILABLE with (574) rear auxiliary air conditioning and heater.		
684A	**Preferred Equipment Package 684A (XLT 2WD)**	NC	NC
	Includes styled steel wheels and cloth 40/60 split bench. NOT AVAILABLE with T65, 645, 63W, 68L, 91P, FD.		
684A	**Preferred Equipment Package 684A (XLT 2WD)**	NC	NC
	Includes styled steel wheels and cloth 40/60 split bench. NOT AVAILABLE with T5N, T65, 645, 647, 63W, 91P, FD, 68P.		
685A	**Preferred Equipment Package 685A (XLT 2WD)**	1505	1770
	Manufacturer Discount	(612)	(720)
	Net Price	893	1050
	Includes cast aluminum wheels, cloth captain seat with console, seatback storage pockets, power point, rear radio controls, speed control, Popular Equipment Group: 6-way power driver's seat, privacy glass, dual illuminated visor vanity mirrors, and luggage rack. NOT AVAILABLE with (41H) engine block heater, (875) seats.		
685A	**Preferred Equipment Package 685A (XLT 4WD)**	1505	1770
	Manufacturer Discount	(612)	(720)
	Net Price	893	1050
	Includes cast aluminum wheels, cloth captain seat with console, seatback storage pockets, power point, rear radio controls, speed control, Popular Equipment Group: 6-way power driver's seat, privacy glass, dual illuminated visor vanity mirrors, and luggage rack. NOT AVAILABLE with (41H) engine block heater, (875) seats.		
686A	**Preferred Equipment Package 686A (Eddie Bauer 2WD)**	NC	NC
	Includes P255/70R16 AS BSW tires, cast aluminum wheels, leather captain's seats with console, speed control, Popular Equipment Group: 6-way power driver's seat, privacy glass, dual illuminated visor vanity mirrors, and luggage rack. NOT AVAILABLE with (41H) engine block heater.		
686A	**Preferred Equipment Package 686A (Eddie Bauer 4WD)**	NC	NC
	Includes P255/70R16 AS BSW tires, cast aluminum wheels, leather captain's seats with console, speed control, tow hooks, Popular Equipment Group: 6-way power driver's seat, privacy glass, dual illuminated visor vanity mirrors, and luggage rack. NOT AVAILABLE with (41H) engine block heater.		
687A	**Preferred Equipment Package 687A (Eddie Bauer 2WD)**	1279	1505
	Manufacturer Discount	(488)	(575)
	Net Price	791	930
	Includes 5.4L EFI V-8 Engine, super engine cooling, transmission: electronic 4 speed auto, P255/70R16 AS BSW tires, cast aluminum wheels, leather captain's seats with console, power signal mirrors, illuminated running boards, speed control, Ford Mach cassette audio system, Popular Equipment Group: 6-way power driver's seat, privacy glass, dual illuminated visor vanity mirrors, and luggage rack. NOT AVAILABLE with (XH7) limited slip differential with 3.31, (63W) Extreme Weather Group, (535) Trailer Towing Package (Class III).		

FORD EXPEDITION

CODE	DESCRIPTION	INVOICE	MSRP
687A	Preferred Equipment Package 687A (Eddie Bauer 4WD)	1832	2155
	Manufacturer Discount	(638)	(750)
	Net Price	1194	1405

Includes 5.4L EFI V-8 Engine, super engine cooling, transmission: electronic 4 speed auto P265/70R17 AT OWL tires, 17" cast aluminum wheels, leather captain's seats with console, power signal mirror, illuminated running boards, speed control, tow hooks, Ford Mach cassette audio system, Popular Equipment Group: 6-way power driver's seat, privacy glass, dual illuminated visor vanity mirrors, and luggage rack. NOT AVAILABLE with XH6, XH9, 63W, 535.

574	Rear Air Conditioning and Heater (Eddie Bauer 2WD/Eddie Bauer 4WD)	599	705

Includes mini overhead console. NOT AVAILABLE with (43M) power moonroof with sunshade.

574	Rear Air Conditioning and Heater (XLT)	642	755

Includes mini overhead console.

68L	Rear Load Leveling (XLT 2WD/Eddie Bauer 2WD)	417	490

Includes 30 gallon fuel tank. NOT AVAILABLE with (684) Preferred Equipment Package 684A.

413	Skid Plate Package (XLT 4WD/Eddie Bauer 4WD)	89	105

Includes front differential/suspension plates and skid plates for fuel tank and transfer case.

525	Speed Control (XLT)	200	235
875	Third Row Seat	727	855

Includes cupholders in the quarter trim panel.

875	Third Row Seat	510	600

Available in front seat material. NOT AVAILABLE with (685A) Preferred Equipment Package 685A.

T65	Tires: P255/70R16SL AS BSW (XLT)	196	230

NOT AVAILABLE with (684A) Preferred Equipment Package 684A or (647) Wheels.

T5N	Tires: P265/70R17 OWL (Eddie Bauer 4WD)	128	150

REQUIRES (647) wheels and (99L) engine.

T5N	Tires: P265/70R17 AT OWL (XLT 4WD)	323	380

REQUIRES (647) wheels. NOT AVAILABLE with 684A.

53T	Tow Hooks (XLT 4WD)	34	40
535	Trailer Towing Package (Class III) (XLT 2WD/Eddie Bauer 2WD)	748	880

Includes frame mounted trailer hitch (class III), engine oil cooler, HD battery, rear load leveling: 30 gallon fuel tank, and super engine cooling. NOT AVAILABLE with 99L, 44E, 687A.

535	Trailer Towing Package (Class III) (XLT 4WD/Eddie Bauer 4WD)	383	450

Includes frame mounted trailer hitch (class III), engine oil cooler, HD battery, and engine oil cooler. REQUIRES (99L) engine and (44E) transmission.

535	Trailer Towing Package (Class III) (XLT 4WD/Eddie Bauer 4WD)	332	390

Includes frame mounted trailer hitch (class III), engine oil cooler, HD battery, and super engine cooling. NOT AVAILABLE with 99L, 44E, 687A.

535	Trailer Towing Package (Class III) with 99L (XLT 2WD/Eddie Bauer 2WD)	799	940

Includes frame mounted trailer hitch (class III), engine oil cooler, HD battery, rear load leveling: 30 gallon fuel tank, and engine oil cooler. REQUIRES (99L) engine and (44E) transmission.

EXPEDITION / EXPLORER FORD

CODE	DESCRIPTION	INVOICE	MSRP
44E	Transmission: Electronic 4-Speed Auto OD .... NOT AVAILABLE with XH7, 428, 535, XH9, 647.	NC	NC
645	Wheels: 16" Chrome Steel .... NOT AVAILABLE with (684A) Preferred Equipment Package 684A or (647) wheels.	NC	NC
647	Wheels: 17" Cast Aluminum .... NOT AVAILABLE with (684A) Preferred Equipment Package 684A, (T65) tires, or (645) wheels.	158	185

1998 EXPLORER

1998 Ford Explorer Sport

What's New?

The Ford Explorer gets a restyled tailgate for 1998. Ford is obviously unwilling to mess too much with the third-best selling vehicle in America.

Review

Since its introduction in 1991, the Ford Explorer has resided at the top of the sport-utility sales heap. With good reason; the Explorer combined style, comfort and room is one go-anywhere package. The modern day Country Squire, some have called it, after the segment leading station wagon of the 1950s.

We think that there's a good reason for this. Simply stated, the Explorer is a more refined vehicle than the competition at Jeep and General Motors. The interior instills a feeling of quality that is missing from the Grand Cherokee and the Blazer. An organically sweeping dashboard houses radio controls that can actually be operated without a magnifying glass. Materials look and feel rich. Rear seat comfort surpasses Chevy, and entry/exit is easier than Jeep. Explorers offer more cargo capacity than most rivals, and five passengers can ride with ease. Exterior styling is a subjective matter, but we think that the Explorer is one of the most attractive SUVs on the road.

The Explorer's standard 4.0-liter V-6 is the puniest engine found in a domestic sport-ute. Acceleration is fine from a standstill, but step on the gas at 50 mph and not much happens. That's not good news when there's a need to pass or merge. Fortunately, Ford introduced an

FORD EXPLORER

optional SOHC V-6 in 1997 that offers nearly as much power as the V-8, for a lot less money. We recommend this engine over the other two engine choices due to its great power and affordable price.

Changes for 1998 are limited to revising the truck's tailgate. Nothing to write home about, especially when compared to the sweeping changes of last year, which saw the first-ever application of 5-speed transmission technology in a truck. This 5-speed is, in fact, the first ever developed for an American passenger vehicle. Ford claims that the additional gear, which occurs between the former 1st and 2nd gears, allows for more precise shifting, allowing the truck to move uphill and off-road more authoritatively. When combined with the optional V-6, this should make the Explorer much more fun to drive.

Unlike the reworked Chevy Blazer, Explorers retain a distinctly truck-like character, which could be a bonus or a demerit. They're tough and solid, and easy to maneuver, though steering is a little slow and ponderous, and the body leans through tight corners. Braking is excellent, and the suspension has a compliant attitude, but Ford's Explorer can bounce around, making occupants regret the Denver omelet they had for breakfast.

Ford has a philosophy of building vehicles that everyone can be happy with. Sure, the Jeep Grand Cherokee feels sportier, and the GMC Jimmy looks cooler, but the Explorer has just the right amount of class and ruggedness to make it America's best-selling off-roader. If you are thinking about buying an SUV, chances are you've already checked out the Explorer. If you haven't, do yourself a favor and find out why there are so many of these trucks on the road.

Safety Data

Driver Airbag: *Standard*
Side Airbag: *Not Available*
Traction Control: *None*
Driver Crash Test Grade: *Good*

Passenger Airbag: *Standard*
4-Wheel ABS: *Standard*
Integrated Child Seat(s): *Optional (4dr)*
Passenger Crash Test Grade: *Good*

Standard Equipment

SPORT 2WD: 4L V-6 OHV SMPI 12-valve engine; 5-speed overdrive manual transmission; 650-amp battery with run down protection; HD radiator; 95-amp alternator; rear wheel drive, 3.27 axle ratio; steel exhaust; front independent suspension with anti-roll bar, front torsion springs, front torsion bar, HD front shocks, rear suspension with anti-roll bar, rear leaf springs, HD rear shocks; power rack-and-pinion steering; 4-wheel disc brakes with 4-wheel anti-lock braking system; 17.5 gal capacity fuel tank; liftback rear cargo door; front and rear black bumpers with black rub strip; body-colored bodyside molding, rocker panel extensions, black fender flares; monotone paint; aero-composite halogen headlamps; additional exterior lights include center high mounted stop light; driver and passenger power remote black folding outside mirrors; front and rear 15" x 7"; front and rear silver alloy wheels, hub wheel covers; P225/70SR15 BSW AS front and rear tires; underbody mounted full-size temporary steel spare wheel; air conditioning, rear heat ducts; AM/FM stereo with clock, seek-scan, cassette, 4 speakers and fixed antenna; cruise control with steering wheel controls; power door locks with 2 stage unlock, power remote hatch/trunk release; 2 power accessory outlet, retained accessory power; analog instrumentation display includes tachometer gauge, oil pressure gauge, water temp gauge, volt gauge, trip odometer; warning indicators include oil pressure, battery, lights-on, key-in-ignition, door ajar; dual airbags; deep tinted windows, power front windows with driver 1-touch down, vented rear windows, fixed 1/4 vent windows; variable intermittent front windshield wipers, flip-up rear window, fixed interval wipers, rear window defroster; seating capacity of 5, front bucket seats with fixed adjustable headrests, driver seat includes 4-way direction control, passenger seat includes 4-way direction control; fixed 50-50 folding bench rear seat 2nd row seat with tilt rear headrest; front height adjustable seatbelts; vinyl seats, vinyl door trim insert with carpet lower, full cloth headliner, full carpet floor covering , deluxe sound insulation; interior lights include dome light with fade, front reading lights, illuminated entry;

EXPLORER

| CODE | DESCRIPTION | INVOICE | MSRP |

steering wheel with tilt adjustment; dual illuminated vanity mirrors dual auxiliary visors; day-night rear-view mirror; glove box with light, driver and passenger door bins; carpeted cargo floor, vinyl trunk lid, cargo cover, cargo tie downs, cargo light; body-colored grille, and body-colored door handles.

SPORT 4WD (in addition to or instead of SPORT 2WD equipment): Part-time 4-wheel drive, with auto locking hub control and electronic shift; and skid plates.

XL 2WD 4-DOOR (in addition to or instead of SPORT 2WD equipment): Front coil springs; 21 gal capacity fuel tank; liftback rear cargo door; front and rear chrome bumpers with black rub strip; rocker panel extensions; driver and passenger manual black folding outside mirrors; front and rear steel wheels, hub wheel covers; underbody mounted full-size conventional spare wheel; child safety rear door locks; 2 power accessory outlet; warning indicators include oil pressure, battery, lights on, key in ignition; tinted windows, manual rear windows, fixed 1/4 vent windows; flip-up rear window; fixed 60-40 folding bench rear seat; passenger side vanity mirror; cargo tie downs, cargo light; chrome grille, and body-colored door handles.

XLT 2WD (in addition to or instead of XL equipment): Body-colored bodyside molding, chrome bodyside insert, rocker panel extensions; monotone paint with bodyside accent stripe; driver and passenger power remote black folding outside mirrors; front and rear silver alloy wheels, hub wheel covers; underbody mounted full-size temporary spare wheel; cruise control with steering wheel controls; power remote hatch/trunk release; retained accessory power; deep tinted windows, power front windows with driver 1-touch down, power rear windows, fixed 1/4 vent windows; fixed interval wiper, rear window defroster; front captain seats center armrest; premium cloth seats, vinyl door trim insert with carpet lower, deluxe sound insulation; leather-wrapped steering wheel with tilt adjustment; dual illuminated vanity mirrors dual auxiliary visors; partial floor console, front cupholders, and driver and passenger door bins.

EDDIE BAUER 2WD (in addition to or instead of XLT 2WD equipment): 4L V-6 SOHC SMPI 12-valve engine; 5-speed electronic overdrive automatic transmission; 4.1 axle ratio; roof rack; front and rear chrome bumpers with body-colored rub strip; colored fender flares; two-tone paint with bodyside accent stripe; front and rear 16" x 7"; front and rear chrome alloy wheels, hub wheel covers; P255/70SR16 OWL AT front and rear tires; premium AM/FM stereo with seek-scan, single in-dash CD, 4 performance speakers, amplifier; PRNDL in instrument panel, trip odometer; front sports seats driver seat includes 4-way power seat, 8-way direction control with power lumbar support, passenger seat includes 4-way direction control with power lumbar support; full carpet floor covering with carpeted floor mats; instrument panel bin, driver and passenger door bins; cargo cover, cargo tie downs, cargo light.

LIMITED EDITION 2WD (in addition to or instead of EDDIE BAUER 2WD equipment): 3.55 axle ratio; running boards; front and rear body-colored bumpers with body-colored rub strip; monotone paint with bodyside accent stripe; aero-composite halogen fully automatic headlamps with delay off feature; additional exterior lights include front fog/driving lights, underhood light; driver and passenger power remote black heated folding outside mirrors; front and rear 15" x 7"; front and rear silver alloy wheels, hub wheel covers; P235/75SR15 OWL AT front and rear tires; air conditioning with climate control, rear air conditioning with with separate controls, rear heat ducts; JBL AM/FM stereo with clock, seek-scan, cassette, single in-dash CD, 4 brand speakers, amplifier, and power retractable antenna, remote keyless entry, power remote hatch/trunk release; compass, exterior temp, systems monitor, panel, trip computer, trip odometer; warning indicators include oil pressure, battery, lights-on, key-in-ignition, low fuel, low washer fluid, door ajar, trunk ajar, service interval; panic alarm, security system; front premium bucket seats with tilt adjustable headrests, center armrest with storage, passenger seat includes 8-way direction control with power lumbar support; leather seats, leather door trim insert, memory on driver seat with 3 memory setting(s); interior lights include front and rear reading lights, illuminated

FORD EXPLORER

entry; auto-dimming day-night rear-view mirror; full floor console, full overhead console with storage, front and rear cupholders, driver and passenger door bins; body-colored grille, and body-colored door handles.

XL 4WD (in addition to or instead of XL 2WD equipment): Part-time 4 wheel drive, with auto locking hub control and electronic shift, 3.55 axle ratio; and 21 gal capacity fuel tank.

XLT 4WD (in addition to or instead of XLT 2WD equipment): Part-time 4 wheel drive, with auto locking hub control and electronic shift, 3.55 axle ratio; and 21 gal capacity fuel tank.

EDDIE BAUER 4WD (in addition to or instead of EDDIE BAUER 2WD equipment): Part-time 4 wheel drive, with auto locking hub control and electronic shift, 3.55 axle ratio; 21 gal capacity fuel tank, and P255/70SR16 OWL AT front and rear tires.

LIMITED 4WD (in addition to or instead of LIMITED 4WD equipment): Part-time 4 wheel drive, with auto locking hub control and electronic shift, 3.55 axle ratio; 21 gal capacity fuel tank, 72-amp battery with run down protection; automatic ride control; P235/75SR15 OWL AT front and rear tires; auto-leveling and skid plates.

XLT AWD (in addition to or instead of XLT 4WD equipment): Full-time 4-wheel drive, 3.55 axle ratio, and skid plates.

EDDIE BAUER AWD (in addition to or instead of EDDIE BAUER 4WD equipment): Full-time 4-wheel drive, 4.1 axle ratio, and roof rack.

LIMITED AWD (in addition to or instead of LIMITED 4WD equipment): Full-time 4-wheel drive.

Base Prices

Code	Description	Invoice	MSRP
U22	Sport 2WD	18119	19880
U24	Sport 4WD	20558	22650
U32	XL 2WD	19532	21485
U34	XL 4WD	21221	23405
U32	XLT 2WD	22286	24615
U34	XLT 4WD	24051	26620
U35	XLT AWD	24051	26620
U32	Eddie Bauer 2WD	25956	28785
U34	Eddie Bauer 4WD	27721	30790
U35	Eddie Bauer AWD	27324	30340
U32	Limited 2WD	28425	31590
U34	Limited 4WD	30189	33595
U35	Limited AWD	29792	33145
Destination Charge:		525	525

Accessories

Code	Description	Invoice	MSRP
X45	3.55 Axle Ratio (2WD)	NC	NC
	REQUIRES 99E and 44D. NOT AVAILABLE with XD2 or 99P.		
X46	3.73 Axle Ratio (Sport/XL/XLT)	NC	NC
44U	4-Speed Automatic Transmission with OD	803	945
	NOT AVAILABLE with (99E) engine.		

EXPLORER — FORD

CODE	DESCRIPTION	INVOICE	MSRP
44D	**5-Speed Automatic Transmission (Sport/XL/XLT)**	905	1065
	REQUIRES ((941A) Preferred Equipment Package 941A) or (945A) Preferred Equipment Package 945A.		
Z	**6-Way Power Cloth Bucket Seats (XLT)**	553	650
	Includes power lumbar support and floor console. NOT AVAILABLE with (M) seats.		
M	**60/40 Cloth Split-Bench Seat (XLT)**	8	10
	Includes stowage bin and floor consolette. REQUIRES 44U or 44D. NOT AVAILABLE with 945A or Z.		
68P	**Automatic Ride Control (Eddie Bauer 4WD/Limited 4WD)**	553	650
	NOT AVAILABLE with (942A) Preferred Equipment Package 942A.		
422	**California Emissions**	144	170
	Required on units for California/Massachusetts/New York/Connecticut (if specified) registration. NOT AVAILABLE with (428) high altitude principal use.		
J	**Cloth Captain's Chairs (XL)**	238	280
	Includes floor console.		
Z	**Cloth Sport Bucket Seats (Sport)**	867	1020
	Includes driver power 6-way and power lumbar support.		
52N	**Convenience Group (Sport/XL)**	565	665
	Includes leather-wrapped tilt steering wheel, speed control, and intermittent rear wiper with washer.		
59B	**Electrochromic Mirror (Sport/XLT/Eddie Bauer/Limited)**	158	185
	Includes automatic headlamps. NOT AVAILABLE with (931A) Preferred Equipment Package 931A, (941A) Preferred Equipment Package 941A, or (942A) Preferred Equipment Package 942A.		
151	**Electronics Group (Eddie Bauer 2WD/Eddie Bauer 4WD)**	352	415
	Keypad is color-keyed. Includes puddle lamps on outside mirrors, keyless remote transmitters (2).		
41H	**Engine Block Heater**	30	35
	400 watt single element.		
99E	**Engine: 4.0L SOHC V6 (Sport/XL/XLT)**	459	540
	REQUIRES 44D, (941A AND 44D) or 945A. NOT AVAILABLE with X46 or 44U.		
99P	**Engine: 5.0L EFI V8 (Eddie Bauer 2WD and AWD /Limited 2WD and AWD)**	366	430
	Includes limited slip performance axle: trailer towing package. REQUIRES (44U) transmission. NOT AVAILABLE with (XD2) limited slip performance axle.		
99P	**Engine: 5.0L EFI V8 (XLT 2WD and AWD)**	956	1125
	Includes limited slip performance axle and trailer towing package. REQUIRES 941A and 44U. NOT AVAILABLE with X46, 44D, or X45.		
99P	**Engine: 5.0L EFI V8 (XLT 2WD and AWD)**	854	1005
	Includes limited slip performance axle, and trailer towing package. REQUIRES (945A) Preferred Equipment Package 945A and (44U) transmission. NOT AVAILABLE with (X45) 3.55 Axle Ratio.		
167	**Floor Mats (Sport)**	73	85
86D	**Floor Mats/Cargo Cover Group (XLT)**	140	165
	Includes floor mats and cargo cover.		
916	**Ford MACH Audio System (Sport)**	680	800
	Includes cassette, CD, clock, sub-woofer, amp, digital signal processor and power antenna. REQUIRES 44D. NOT AVAILABLE with 931A, 582, 58K, or 47P.		

FORD EXPLORER

CODE	DESCRIPTION	INVOICE	MSRP
916	Ford MACH Audio System (XLT/Eddie Bauer/Limited)	553	650
	Includes cassette, CD, clock, sub-woofer, amp, digital signal processor and power antenna. REQUIRES 44D and 47P or 418. NOT AVAILABLE with 931A, 58K, or 941A.		
428	High Altitude Principal Use	NC	NC
418	High Series Floor Console (Eddie Bauer 2WD/Eddie Bauer 4WD)	323	380
	Includes rear heat and A/C controls and rear radio controls. REQUIRES (151) Electronics Group.		
87C	Integrated Rear Child Seat (XL/XLT/Eddie Bauer/Limited)	170	200
	Includes rear seat recliner.		
XD4	Limited Slip Performance Axle	302	355
	Includes trailer towing package. REQUIRES X46. NOT AVAILABLE with 934A, 47P, XD2, or X45.		
XD2	Limited Slip Performance Axle	263	310
	Includes trailer towing package. REQUIRES 931A AND 47P or 934A AND 47P. NOT AVAILABLE with X45, 99P, or 44U.		
XD4	Limited Slip Performance Axle	263	310
	Includes trailer towing package. REQUIRES 44D and X46. NOT AVAILABLE with 47P, XD2, or X45.		
615	Luggage Rack (XL)	119	140
	100 lbs. max. capacity.		
91P	Multi-Disc CD Changer (Sport/XLT/Eddie Bauer/Limited)	314	370
	REQUIRES 44D and 58K, or 418 and 58K. NOT AVAILABLE with 931A or 941A.		
439	Power Moonroof (Sport 2WD/XLT 2WD/Eddie Bauer 2WD/Limited 2WD)	680	800
	Includes front overhead console. NOT AVAILABLE with (931A) Preferred Equipment Package 931A, (941A) Preferred Equipment Package 941A or (942A) Preferred Equipment Package 942A.		
931A	Preferred Equipment Package 931A (Sport 2WD)	553	650
	Manufacturer Discount	(489)	(575)
	Net Price	64	75
	Includes P235/75R15 AT OWL tires, luggage rack, cloth captain's chairs, and 3.73 axle ratio. REQUIRES (BONUS) Special Bonus Discount. NOT AVAILABLE with (439) power moonroof with shade or (91P) multi-disc CD changer.		
931A	Preferred Equipment Package 931A (Sport 4WD)	553	650
	Manufacturer Discount	(489)	(575)
	Net Price	64	75
	Includes P235/75R15 AT OWL tires, luggage rack, cloth captain's chairs, and 3.73 axle ratio. REQUIRES (BONUS) Special Bonus Discount. NOT AVAILABLE with (439) power moonroof with shade or (91P) multi-disc CD changer.		
934A	Preferred Equipment Package 934A (Sport 2WD)	3086	3630
	Manufacturer Discount	(1139)	(1340)
	Net Price	1947	2290
	Includes P235/75R15 AT OWLI tires, luggage rack, 5-speed automatic transmission, 6-way power cloth bucket seats, Luxury Group: high series floor console: rear heat and A/C controls, rear radio controls, front overhead console, Electronics Group: keyless remote transmitters (2), anti-theft, and keypad; fog lamps, floor mats, and 3.73 axle ratio. NOT AVAILABLE with (BONUS) Special Bonus Discount.		

EXPLORER — FORD

CODE	DESCRIPTION	INVOICE	MSRP
934A	Preferred Equipment Package 934A (Sport 4WD)	3086	3630
	Manufacturer Discount	(1139)	(1340)
	Net Price	1947	2290

Includes P235/75R15 AT OWL tires, luggage rack, 5-speed automatic transmission, 6-way power cloth overhead console, Electronics Group: keyless remote transmitters (2), anti-theft, and keypad; fog lamps, floor mats, and 3.73 axle ratio. NOT AVAILABLE with (BONUS) Special Bonus Discount.

940A	Preferred Equipment Package 940A (XL 2WD)	NC	NC

Includes 15" chrome steel wheels, knitted vinyl bucket seats, and 3.27 axle ratio.

940A	Preferred Equipment Package 940A (XL 4WD)	NC	NC

Includes 15" chrome steel wheels, knitted vinyl bucket seats, and 3.27 axle ratio.

941A	Preferred Equipment Package 941A (XLT 2WD)	247	290
	Manufacturer Discount	(247)	(290)
	Net Price	NC	NC

Includes AM/FM stereo with CD, clock radio, luggage rack, cloth captain's chairs, Convenience Group: leather-wrapped tilt steering wheel, speed control, intermittent rear wiper with washer, and 3.27 axle ratio. NOT AVAILABLE with (439) power moonroof with shade, (91P) multi-disc CD changer, or (954) paint.

941A	Preferred Equipment Package 941A (XLT 4WD)	247	290
	Manufacturer Discount	(247)	(290)
	Net Price	NC	NC

Includes AM/FM stereo with CD, clock radio, luggage rack, cloth, captain's chairs, Convenience Group: leather-wrapped tilt steering wheel, speed control, intermittent rear wiper with washer, and 3.27 axle ratio. NOT AVAILABLE with (439) power moonroof with shade, (91P) multi-disc CD changer, or (954) paint.

941A	Preferred Equipment Package 941A (XLT AWD)	247	290
	Manufacturer Discount	(247)	(290)
	Net Price	NC	NC

Includes AM/FM stereo with CD, clock radio, luggage rack, cloth captain's chairs, Convenience Group: leather-wrapped tilt steering wheel, speed control, intermittent rear wiper with washer, and 3.27 axle ratio. NOT AVAILABLE with (439) power moonroof with shade, (91P) multi-disc CD changer, or (954) paint.

942A	Preferred Equipment Package 942A (Eddie Bauer 2WD)	893	1050
	Manufacturer Discount	(893)	(1050)
	Net Price	NC	NC

Includes AM/FM stereo with CD, clock radio, luggage rack, leather sport bucket seats, running boards, Convenience Group: leather-wrapped tilt steering wheel, speed control, intermittent rear wiper with washer, Floor Mats/Cargo Cover Group: floor mats, cargo cover, and 4.10 axle ratio. NOT AVAILABLE with (516) voice activated cellular telephone or (439) power moonroof with shade.

942A	Preferred Equipment Package 942A (Eddie Bauer 4WD)	893	1050
	Manufacturer Discount	(893)	(1050)
	Net Price	NC	NC

Includes AM/FM stereo with CD, clock radio, luggage rack, leather sport bucket seats, running boards, Convenience Group: leather-wrapped tilt steering wheel, speed control, intermittent rear wiper with washer, Floor Mats/Cargo Cover Group: floor

FORD EXPLORER

CODE	DESCRIPTION	INVOICE	MSRP

mats, cargo cover, and 4.10 axle ratio. NOT AVAILABLE with (516) voice activated cellular telephone, (439) power moonroof with shade, or (68P) automatic ride control.

942A Preferred Equipment Package 942A (Eddie Bauer AWD) 893 1050
Manufacturer Discount .... (893) (1050)
Net Price .... NC NC
Includes AM/FM stereo with CD, clock radio, luggage rack, leather sport bucket seats, running boards, Convenience Group: leather-wrapped tilt steering wheel, speed control, intermittent rear wiper with washer, Floor Mats/Cargo Cover Group: floor mats, cargo cover, and 4.10 axle ratio. NOT AVAILABLE with (516) voice activated cellular telephone, (439) power moonroof with shade, or (8P) automatic ride control.

943A Preferred Equipment Package 943A (Limited 2WD) .... NC NC
Includes vehicle with standard equipment.

943A Preferred Equipment Package 943A (Limited 4WD) .... NC NC
Includes vehicle with standard equipment.

943A Preferred Equipment Package 943A (Limited AWD) .... NC NC
Includes vehicle with standard equipment.

945A Preferred Equipment Package 945A (XLT 2WD) 2767 3255
Manufacturer Discount .... (1152) (1355)
Net Price 1615 1900
Includes AM/FM stereo with CD, clock radio, luggage rack, 6-way power cloth bucket seats, Luxury Group: high series floor console: rear heat and A/C controls, rear radio controls, front overhead console, Electronics Group: keyless remote transmitters (2), fog lamps, 5-speed automatic transmission, Floor Mats/Cargo Cover Group: floor mats, cargo cover, Convenience Group: leather-wrapped tilt steering wheel, speed control, intermittent rear wiper with washer, and 3.73 axle ratio. NOT AVAILABLE with (M) Seats.

945A Preferred Equipment Package 945A (XLT 4WD) 2767 3255
Manufacturer Discount .... (1152) (1355)
Net Price 1615 1900
Includes AM/FM stereo with CD, clock radio, luggage rack, 6-way power cloth bucket seats, Luxury Group: high series floor console: rear heat and A/C controls, rear radio controls, front overhead console, Electronics Group: keyless remote transmitters (2), anti-theft, and keypad; fog lamps, 5-speed automatic transmission, Floor Mats/Cargo Cover Group: floor mats, cargo cover, Convenience Group: leather-wrapped tilt steering wheel, speed control, intermittent rear wiper with washer, and 3.73 axle ratio. NOT AVAILABLE with (M) Seats.

945A Preferred Equipment Package 945A (XLT AWD) 2767 3255
Manufacturer Discount .... (1152) (1355)
Net Price 1615 1900
Includes AM/FM stereo with CD, clock radio, luggage rack, 6-way power cloth bucket seats, Luxury Group: high series floor console: rear heat and A/C controls, rear radio controls, front overhead console, Electronics Group: keyless remote transmitters (2), anti-theft, and keypad; fog lamps, 5-speed automatic transmission, Floor Mats/

EXPLORER — FORD

Code	Description	Invoice	MSRP
	Cargo Cover Group: floor mats, cargo cover, Convenience Group: leather-wrapped tilt steering wheel, speed control, intermittent rear wiper with washer, and 3.73 axle ratio. NOT AVAILABLE with (M) Seats.		
946A	**Preferred Equipment Package 946A (Eddie Bauer 2WD)**	2869	3375
	Manufacturer Discount	(1334)	(1570)
	Net Price	1535	1805
	Includes luggage rack, Luxury Group: high series floor console: rear heat and A/C controls, rear radio controls, front overhead console, Electronics Group: keyless remote transmitters (2), anti-theft, and keypad; fog lamps, Floor Mats/Cargo Cover Group: floor mats, cargo cover, leather sport bucket seats, Premium Group: message center, Ford Mach audio system, running boards, and 4.10 axle ratio. NOT AVAILABLE with (58K) Radio.		
946A	**Preferred Equipment Package 946A (Eddie Bauer 4WD)**	2869	3375
	Manufacturer Discount	(1334)	(1570)
	Net Price	1535	1805
	Includes luggage rack, Luxury Group: high series floor console: rear heat and A/C controls, rear radio controls, front overhead console, Electronics Group: keyless remote transmitters (2), anti-theft, and keypad; fog lamps, Floor Mats/Cargo Cover Group: floor mats, cargo cover, leather sport bucket seats, Premium Group: message center, Ford Mach audio system, running boards, and 4.10 axle ratio. NOT AVAILABLE with (58K) Radio.		
946A	**Preferred Equipment Package 946A (Eddie Bauer AWD)**	2869	3375
	Manufacturer Discount	(1334)	(1570)
	Net Price	1535	1805
	Includes luggage rack, Luxury Group: high series floor console: rear heat and A/C controls, rear radio controls, front overhead console, Electronics Group: keyless remote transmitters (2), anti-theft, and keypad; fog lamps, Floor Mats/Cargo Cover Group: floor mats, cargo cover, leather sport bucket seats, Premium Group: message center, Ford Mach audio system, running boards, and 4.10 axle ratio. NOT AVAILABLE with (58K) Radio.		
47P	**Premium Sport Package (Sport)**	1700	2000
	Manufacturer Discount	(850)	(1000)
	Net Price	850	1000
	Includes wheellip moulding system, front and rear bumpers, side step bar, 15" chrome steel wheels, tow hooks (rear), AM/FM stereo with CD and clock radio. NOT AVAILABLE with (58K) radio.		
58K	**Radio: AM/FM CD with Cassette (Sport)**	277	325
	NOT AVAILABLE with (582) radio, (58K) radio, or (47P) Premium Sport Package.		
58K	**Radio: AM/FM CD with Cassette (XLT/Eddie Bauer/Limited)**	149	175
	Includes CD and cassette player. REQUIRES (47P) Premium Sport Package. NOT AVAILABLE with (58K) radio, (946A) Preferred Equipment Package 946A.		
582	**Radio: AM/FM Stereo with CD and Clock (Sport/XL)**	128	150
	Includes premium sound. REQUIRES (52N) Convenience Group. NOT AVAILABLE with (58K) radio.		
186	**Running Boards (XLT)**	336	395
	Deletes rocker moldings.		

FORD EXPLORER / F-150 PICKUP

CODE	DESCRIPTION	INVOICE	MSRP
182	Side Step Bar (Sport)	251	295
	In medium graphite.		
BONUS	Special Bonus Discount (Sport)	(413)	(485)
	NOT AVAILABLE with (934A) Preferred Equipment Package 934A.		
F	Sport Buckets with Leather Surface (Sport/XLT)	557	655
	Includes driver power 6-way and power lumbar support. NOT AVAILABLE with (931A) Preferred Equipment Package 931A, (941A) Preferred Equipment Package 941A, or (M) seats.		
T7R	Tires: P235/75R15SL AT OWL (XLT)	196	230
	Includes full-size spare.		
954	Two-Tone Rocker Paint (XLT)	102	120
	NOT AVAILABLE with (941A) Preferred Equipment Package 941A.		
516	Voice Activated Cellular Telephone (Eddie Bauer/Limited)	587	690
	NOT AVAILABLE with (942A) Preferred Equipment Package 942A.		

1998 F-150

1998 Ford F-150 XLT SuperCab 4WD

What's New?

The brutish F-350 and heavy-duty F-250 models will finally join the rest of the F-Series family in their redesign early in the 1998 calendar year.

Review

When Ford introduced the new family of F-Series trucks in 1996, as a 1997 model, there was an uproar among old-school Blue Oval fans. Gone were their beloved Twin-I-Beam suspensions, pushrod engines, and traditional styling. The new model appeared with a short- and long-arm front suspension, overhead cam engines, and more swoops than a Dairy Queen sundae.

Now that the vehicle has been out for two years, naysayers have put their fears to rest. The SLA suspension provides excellent on- and off-road articulation giving the most demanding drivers the best ride available in any truck. Overhead cam engines provide capable acceleration

F-150 PICKUP   FORD

and enough power to tow Rhode Island to the West Coast. The swoopy exterior means that parking an F-Series truck in a crowded parking lot may be a bit of a challenge, but the outstanding visibility it gives when off-roading more than makes up for its somewhat sissified shape.

The Ford F-Series' interior is also a breakthrough. Stepping out of one of the competitive vehicles, like a Chevy or Dodge, and into the F-Series is like going from a Yugo to a Lincoln. All of the Ford's hard edges have been softened, and the interior materials are not something that one would expect to see in a vehicle meant for a hard day's work. When put to the test, however, the Ford's interior can stand up to the rigors thrown at it by the meanest of foreman and orneriest of ranch hands. Until this vehicle came onto the scene, ergonomic and truck were not words that we were likely to use in the same sentence. The positioning of the F-Series' controls, however, make this vehicle easier to drive than many mid-size sedans.

Our main gripe about the new F-Series is its overly twitchy steering and the tall step-in on the four-wheel drive model. Not too much to complain about, if you ask us.

After driving several F-150s, it appears that Ford has taken a path designed to bring more personal use buyers into the Ford fold without alienating truck buyers who work their pickups hard. Styling, always a subjective point, might turn potential buyers off with its free-flowing forms and smooth contours. We, however, like its clean lines and lack of clutter, particularly around the grille. If you are in the market for a full-size pickup, you need to see why the F-150 has been the best selling truck on the market for the last decade. Ford redefined excellence when it introduced its latest full-size truck, the others are still trying to catch up. Chevrolet will be coming out with a new model for the 1999 model year, we don't think that there will be any serious competition for Ford's F-Series trucks until then.

Safety Data

Driver Airbag: *Standard*
Side Airbag: *Not Available*

Passenger Airbag: *Standard*
4-Wheel ABS: *Standard (Lariat); Opional (Standard/XL/XLT)*

Traction Control: *Not Available*
Driver Crash Test Grade: *Good*

Integrated Child Seat(s): *Not Available*
Passenger Crash Test Grade: *Excellent*

Standard Equipment

STANDARD STANDARD CAB 2WD: 4.2L V-6 OHV SMPI 12-valve engine; 5-speed overdrive manual transmission; 540-amp battery with run down protection; 95-amp alternator; rear wheel drive, 3.08 axle ratio; stainless steel exhaust; front independent suspension with anti-roll bar, front coil springs, front shocks, rear suspension with rear leaf springs, rear shocks; power re-circulating ball steering; front disc/rear drum brakes with rear-wheel anti-lock braking system; 25 gal capacity fuel tank; trailer harness; argent bumper; monotone paint; aero-composite halogen headlamps; additional exterior lights include center high mounted stop light; driver and passenger manual black folding outside mirrors; front and rear 16" x 7" silver steel wheels with hub wheel covers; P235/70SR16 BSW AS front and rear tires; underbody mounted full-size conventional steel spare wheel; AM/FM stereo and clock with seek-scan, 4 speakers and fixed antenna; 2 power accessory outlets, driver foot rest; analog instrumentation display includes oil pressure gauge, water temp gauge, volt gauge, trip odometer; warning indicators include oil pressure, water temp warning, battery, key-in-ignition, low fuel, door ajar; driver side airbag, passenger side cancellable airbag; tinted windows; variable intermittent front windshield wipers; seating capacity of 3, bench front seat with fixed adjustable headrests, driver seat includes 2-way direction control, passenger seat includes 2-way direction control; front height adjustable seatbelts; vinyl seats, vinyl door trim insert, front cloth headliner, full vinyl floor covering, interior lights include dome light; day-night rearview mirror; glove box, front cupholder, instrument panel bin; vinyl cargo floor; colored grille, black side window moldings, black front windshield molding, black rear window molding, and black door handles.

FORD F-150 PICKUP

STANDARD SUPERCAB 2WD (in addition to or instead of STANDARD STANDARD CAB 2WD equipment): 25.1 gal capacity fuel tank; fixed rear windows; seating capacity of 6; 60-40 folding rear bench seat; vinyl seats, and full headliner.

STANDARD STANDARD CAB 4WD (in addition to or instead STANDARD STANDARD CAB 2WD equipment): Part-time 4 wheel drive, auto locking hub control and manual shift; front torsion suspension front torsion springs, front torsion bar; 24.5 gal capacity fuel tank; and colored wheel well molding.

STANDARD SUPERCAB 4WD (in addition to or instead of STANDARD STANDARD CAB 4WD equipment): 4.6L V-8 SOHC engine and 130-amp alternator.

XL STANDARD CAB 2WD (in addition to or instead of STANDARD STANDARD CAB 2WD equipment): Chrome bumper with black rub strip; additional exterior lights include underhood light; cloth seats; interior lights include; passenger side vanity mirror; and chrome grille.

XL SUPERCAB 2WD (in addition to or instead of XL STANDARD CAB 2WD equipment): Front suspension front coil springs; 25.1 gal capacity fuel tank; fixed rear windows; seating capacity of 6; and 60-40 folding rear bench seat.

XL STANDARD CAB 4WD (in addition to or instead of XL STANDARD CAB 2WD equipment): Part-time 4 wheel drive, auto locking hub control and manual shift; front torsion suspension, front torsion springs, front torsion bar; 24.5 gal capacity fuel tank; and colored wheel well molding.

XLT STANDARD CAB 2WD (in addition to or instead of XL STANDARD CAB 2WD equipment): Front suspension with front coil springs; 25 gal capacity fuel tank; front and rear chrome bumpers with black rub strip, rear step bumper; body-colored bodyside molding with chrome bodyside insert; additional exterior lights include pickup cargo box light, retained accessory power; tachometer gauge; power front windows with driver 1-touch down; 60-40 split-bench front seat with center armrest with storage, driver seat includes 4-way direction control with lumbar support, passenger seat includes 4-way direction control; premium cloth seats, carpet floor covering; interior lights include 2 door curb lights; driver side auxiliary visor; driver and passenger door bins; carpeted cargo floor, cargo concealed storage; and body-colored door handles.

XLT SUPERCAB 2WD (in addition to or instead of XLT STANDARD CAB 2WD equipment): 25.1 gal capacity fuel tank; deep tinted windows, vented rear windows, seating capacity of 6; and 60-40 folding rear bench seat.

XLT STANDARD CAB 4WD (in addition to or instead of XLT STANDARD CAB 2WD equipment): Part-time 4-wheel drive, auto locking hub control and manual shift; front torsion suspension, front torsion springs, front torsion bar; 24.5 gal capacity fuel tank; and tow hooks.

XLT SUPERCAB 4WD (in addition to or instead of XLT STANDARD CAB 4WD equipment): Rear wheel anti-lock braking system; 25.1 gal capacity fuel tank; deep tinted windows, vented rear windows; seating capacity of 6; and 60-40 folding rear bench seat.

LARIAT STANDARD CAB 2WD (in addition to or instead XLT STANDARD CAB 2WD equipment): 3.55 axle ratio; 4 wheel anti-lock braking system; body-colored wheel well molding; leather seats, door trim front headliner, carpet floor covering with carpeted floor mats; and leather-wrapped steering wheel.

LARIAT SUPERCAB 2WD (in addition to or instead of LARIAT STANDARD CAB 2WD equipment): 25.1 gal capacity fuel tank; deep tinted windows, vented rear windows seating capacity of 6; and 60-40 folding rear bench seat.

F-150 PICKUP — FORD

| CODE | DESCRIPTION | INVOICE | MSRP |

LARIAT STANDARD CAB 4WD (in addition to or instead of LARIAT SUPERCAB 2WD equipment): Part-time 4 wheel drive, auto locking hub control and manual shift; front torsion suspension front torsion springs, front torsion bar; 24.5 gal capacity fuel tank; and tow hooks.

LARIAT SUPERCAB 4WD (in addition to or instead of LARIAT STANDARD CAB 4WD equipment): 25.1 gal capacity fuel tank; deep tinted windows, vented rear windows seating capacity of 6; and 60-40 folding rear bench seat.

Base Prices

Code	Description	Invoice	MSRP
X18	XLT SuperCab 4WD Styleside SB	21531	24730
F17	Standard Std. Cab 2WD Styleside SB	13477	14735
F17-8	Standard Std. Cab 2WD Styleside LB	13732	15025
X17	Standard Std. Cab 2WD Styleside SB	15550	17090
X17-8	Standard SuperCab 2WD Styleside LB	15804	17380
F18	Standard Std. Cab 4WD Styleside SB	16354	18005
F18-8	Standard Std. Cab 4WD Styleside LB	16610	18295
X18	Standard SuperCab 4WD Styleside SB	18735	20710
X18-8	Standard SuperCab 4WD Styleside LB	18990	21000
F17	XL Std. Cab 2WD Styleside SB	13910	15765
F17-8	XL Std. Cab 2WD Styleside SB	14165	16065
F07	XL Std. Cab 2WD Flareside	14769	16775
F18	XL Std. Cab 4WD Styleside SB	16792	19155
X17	XL SuperCab 2WD Styleside SB	15984	18205
F18-8	XL Std. Cab 4WD Styleside LB	17047	19455
X17-8	XL Supercab 2WD Styleside LB	16239	18505
X07	XL SuperCab 2WD Flareside	16737	19090
F08	XL Std. Cab 4WD Flareside	17442	19920
X18	XL SuperCab 4WD Styleside SB	19172	21955
X18-8	XL SuperCab 4WD Styleside LB	19427	22255
X08	XL SuperCab 4WD Flareside	19822	22720
F17	XLT Std. Cab 2WD Styleside SB	16162	18415
F17-8	XLT Std. Cab 2WD LB	16417	18715
F07	XLT Std. Cab 2WD Flareside	17022	19425
X17-8	XLT SuperCab 2WD Styleside LB	18696	21395
X07	XLT SuperCab 2WD Flareside	19091	21860
F18	XLT Std. Cab 4WD Styleside SB	18755	21465
F18-8	XLT Std. Cab 4WD Styleside LB	19010	21765
F08	XLT Std. Cab 4WD Styleside SB	19406	22230
X17	XLT SuperCab 4WD Styleside SB	18441	21095
X18-8	XLT SuperCab WD Styleside LB	21786	25030
X08	XLT SuperCab 4WD Flareside	22181	25495
F17	Lariat Std. Cab 2WD Stylside SB	18233	20850
F17-8	Lariat Std. Cab 2WD Styleside LB	18488	21150

FORD F-150 PICKUP

CODE	DESCRIPTION	INVOICE	MSRP
F07	Lariat Std. Cab 2WD Flareside	19091	21860
X07	Lariat SuperCab 2WD Flareside	21161	24295
X17	Lariat SuperCab 2WD Styleside SB	20511	23530
X17-8	Lariat SuperCab 2WD Styleside LB	20766	23830
F18	Lariat Std. Cab 4WD Styleside SB	20825	23900
F18-8	Lariat Std. Cab 4WD Styleside LB	21080	24200
F08	Lariat Std. Cab 4WD Flareside	21475	24665
X18	Lariat SuperCab 4WD Styleside SB	23061	26530
X18-8	Lariat SuperCab 4WD Styleside LB	23316	26830
X08	Lariat SuperCab 4WD Flareside	23711	27295
Destination Charge:		640	640

Accessories

CODE	DESCRIPTION	INVOICE	MSRP
X19	3.55 Axle Ratio (Standard 2WD/XL 2WD/XLT 2WD)	43	50
67B	4-Wheel Antilock Brakes (Standard/XL/XLT)	425	500
M	40/60 Split Bench with Driver's Lumbar (XL)	128	150
	NOT AVAILABLE with (A) seats.		
543	Aero Power Chrome Exterior Mirrors (XLT 2WD)	85	100
54M	Aero Power Color-Keyed Mirrors (XLT 4WD/Lariat 4WD)	85	100
572	Air Conditioning (Standard/XL/XLT)	684	805
769	Argent Rear Step Bumper (Standard)	85	100
18E	Black Cab Steps (Std. Cab)	272	320
	Black platform type.		
18E	Black Cab Steps (SuperCab)	314	370
	Black platform type.		
422	California Emissions	144	170
	Required on units for California/Massachusetts/New York/Connecticut (if specified) registration.		
16G	Carpet Delete (Lariat)	(85)	(100)
	Replace with black vinyl mat and deletes floor mats.		
16G	Carpet Delete (XLT)	(43)	(50)
	Replace with black vinyl mat. NOT AVAILABLE with (167) carpeted color-keyed floor mats.		
167	Carpeted Color-Keyed Floor Mats (XLT Std. Cab)	26	30
	NOT AVAILABLE with (16G) carpet delete.		
167	Carpeted Color-Keyed Floor Mats (XLT SuperCab)	43	50
	Includes front and rear mats. NOT AVAILABLE with (16G) carpet delete.		
F	Cloth Captain's Seats (XLT)	417	490
	Includes driver lumbar, center console.		
168	Color-Keyed Carpeting (XL)	85	100
653	Dual Fuel Tank (LB)	115	135
	REQUIRES 99Z and (66N or 66P). NOT AVAILABLE with 99L, 44U, 535, or 63H.		
215	Electric Shift-On-The-Fly 4WD (XLT 4WD/Lariat 4WD)	128	150
	REQUIRES (996) engine or (99L) engine.		

F-150 PICKUP — FORD

CODE	DESCRIPTION	INVOICE	MSRP
41H	**Engine Block Heater**	77	90
	NOT AVAILABLE with (535) Trailer Towing Group with automatic, (63H) HD Electrical/Cooling Package with automatic, or (53C) Snow Plow Prep Pkg. with manual.		
996	**Engine: 4.6L EFI V8 (Standard/XL/XLT)**	540	635
	Includes 130-amp alternator. NOT AVAILABLE with 44E, 94B, 535, 63H, T55, T34, 53C, or 202.		
99Z	**Engine: 5.4L Bi-Fuel Prep Engine (Lariat)**	692	815
	Includes single fuel tank. REQUIRES 44E AND (66N or 66P). NOT AVAILABLE with 44U, 535, or 63H.		
99Z	**Engine: 5.4L Bi-Fuel Prep Engine (Standard/XL/XLT)**	1233	1450
	Includes single fuel tank. REQUIRES 44E and (66N or 66P). NOT AVAILABLE with 44U, 535, or 63H.		
99L	**Engine: 5.4L EFI V8 (XL/XLT)**	1105	1300
	Includes 3.55 axle ratio, optional payload package #1, 130-amp alternator, and super engine cooling. REQUIRES 44E. NOT AVAILABLE with 202, 44U, XH9, 63H, T55, T34, 94B, or 53C.		
99L	**Engine: 5.4L EFI V8 (XL/XLT/Lariat)**	565	665
	Includes optional payload package #1 and super engine cooling. REQUIRES 44E. NOT AVAILABLE with 202, 44U, 63H, XH9, 535, or 53C.		
595	**Fog Lamps (Standard 4WD/XL 4WD/XLT 4WD)**	119	140
63H	**HD Electrical/Cooling Package with Automatic**	178	210
	Includes auxiliary transmission oil cooler.		
H	**Leather Captain's Seats (Lariat)**	417	490
	Includes driver lumbar support and center console.		
XH9	**Limited Slip Differential (2WD)**	221	260
	REQUIRES X19. NOT AVAILABLE with 535.		
954D	**Lower Two-Tone Paint Delete (XL)**	(81)	(95)
	REQUIRES (62N) XL Special Appearance Package.		
66N	**Natural Gas Fuel System (Standard 2WD)**	6217	7315
	REQUIRES 99Z. NOT AVAILABLE with 99L, 44U, 535, or 63H.		
55R	**Off-Road Package (Lariat 4WD)**	633	745
	Includes skid plates, frame front crossmember, P265/70R17SL AT OL tires, 17" cast aluminum wheels, fog lamps, tachometer, HD shocks, transfer case, and fuel tank skid plates.		
55R	**Off-Road Package (XLT 4WD)**	973	1145
	Includes off-road decal, skid plates, frame front crossmember. tP265/70R17SL AT OWL tires, 17" cast aluminum wheels, fog lamps, tachometer, transfer case, fuel tank skid plates, HD shocks, and 3.55 axle ratio. REQUIRES (996) engine or (99L) engine. NOT AVAILABLE with (53C) Snow Plow Prep Package with manual.		
202	**Payload Package #2**	43	50
	Includes max. payload of 2030 lbs and GVWR of 6000 lbs. HD shocks and springs. REQUIRES X19. NOT AVAILABLE with 99L, 996, or 44U.		
203	**Payload Package #3 (Standard 2WD)**	357	420
	Includes HD shocks and springs, maximum payload: 2435 lbs., GVWR: 6550 lbs., styled steel wheels, LT245/75R16D AS BSW tires: 3.55 axle ratio. REQUIRES (996) engine and (44U) transmission and (X19) 3.55 axle ratio.		

FORD F-150 PICKUP

CODE	DESCRIPTION	INVOICE	MSRP
203	Payload Package #3 (XL 2WD)	187	220
	Includes HD shocks and springs, maximum payload: 2435 lbs., P255/70R16SL AS BSW tires, GVWR 6550 lbs., and styled steel wheels. REQUIRES (996, 44U, and X19) or (99L and 44E).		
203	Payload Package #3 (XLT 2WD)	17	20
	Includes HD shocks and springs, maximum payload: 2435 lbs., P255/70R16SL AS BSW tires, GVWR 6550 lbs., and styled steel wheels. REQUIRES (996, 44U, and X19) or (99L and 44E).		
61T	Pickup Box Security Group (Standard/XL)	38	45
	Includes integral cargo light and tailgate lock.		
C	Poly Knit Bench Seat (Standard)	85	100
90P	Power Driver's Seat (XLT)	306	360
	Includes autolamp. REQUIRES (44U or 44E) or 507A.		
500A	Preferred Equipment Package 500A (Standard)	NC	NC
	Includes vehicles with standard equipment.		
502A	Preferred Equipment Package 502A (XL)	298	350
	Manufacturer Discount	(298)	(350)
	Net Price	NC	NC
	Includes styled steel wheels and chrome rear step bumper.		
507A	Preferred Equipment Package 507A (XLT)	1293	1520
	Manufacturer Discount	(1293)	(1520)
	Net Price	NC	NC
	Includes aluminum wheels, air conditioning, pickup box security group, speed control: tilt steering, AM/FM stereo with cassette, clock, Power Convenience Group: power windows, power door locks, speed dependent interval wipers, door curb lights, delayed accessory power, and SuperCab rear seat.		
508A	Preferred Equipment Package 508A (Lariat)	1428	1680
	Manufacturer Discount	(1428)	(1680)
	Net Price	NC	NC
	Includes air conditioning, carpeted color-keyed floor mats, aero power chrome exterior mirrors, pickup box security group, power driver's seat: autolamp, speed control, tilt steering, AM/FM stereo with cassette, clock, Power Convenience Group: power windows, power door locks, speed dependent interval wipers, door curb lights, delayed accessory power, and power signal mirror.		
66P	Propane Fuel System (Standard 2WD)	4208	4950
	REQUIRES 99Z. NOT AVAILABLE with 99L, 44U, 535, or 63H.		
924	Quarter/Rear Window Privacy Glass (XL SuperCab)	85	100
589	Radio: AM/FM Stereo with Cassette (Standard/XL)	111	130
	Includes 4 speakers.		
91P	Radio: AM/FM Stereo with CD and Cassette (XLT/Lariat)	340	400
	Includes 6 disc changer.		
436	Rear Quarter Flip Window (Standard SuperCab)	38	45
87D	Rear Seat Deletion (Standard SuperCab)	(352)	(415)
61S	Rear Storage Bin (Standard)	77	90
904	Remote Keyless Entry (XLT)	225	265
	Includes 2 key fobs, perimeter anti-theft system, and illuminated entry.		

F-150 PICKUP — FORD

CODE	DESCRIPTION	INVOICE	MSRP
433	Sliding Rear Window	107	125
53C	Snow Plow Prep Package with Manual (4WD)	429	505
	Manufacturer Discount	(59)	(70)
	Net Price	370	435
	REQUIRES 769. NOT AVAILABLE with 53C, T3P, 55R, or 44E.		
—	Special Disc. w/ Manual Transmission & Air Conditioning (Standard/XL/XLT)	(425)	(500)
	NOT AVAILABLE with 99L, 44U, 44E, or 63H.		
52N	Speed Control (Standard/XL)	328	385
	Includes tilt steering.		
94B	STX Package (XLT)	506	595
	Includes 4x4 grille insert, 17" cast aluminum wheels, P275/60R17 AS BSW tires, body colored painted bumpers, color-keyed grille, body colored mirrors, 3.55 axle ratio, unique STX decal, NOT AVAILABLE with (996) engine, (99L) engine.		
T34	Tires: LT245/75R16D AS BSW (Lariat 2WD)	77	90
	REQUIRES (99L) engine. NOT AVAILABLE with (T34) tires.		
T34	Tires: LT245/75R16D AS BSW (Standard 2WD)	328	385
	Includes 3.55 axle ratio. NOT AVAILABLE with 996, 62N, T34, or T55.		
T34	Tires: LT245/75R16D AS BSW (XL 2WD)	221	260
	Includes 3.55 axle ratio. REQUIRES 62N and 99L. NOT AVAILABLE with T34 or 996.		
T3P	Tires: LT245/75R16D AT OWL (Lariat 4WD)	293	345
T3P	Tires: LT245/75R16D AT OWL (Standard 4WD)	607	715
	Includes 3.55 axle ratio and styled steel wheels. NOT AVAILABLE with (53C) Snow Plow Prep Package with manual.		
T3P	Tires: LT245/75R16D AT OWL (XL 4WD)	437	515
	Includes 3.55 axle ratio. NOT AVAILABLE with (53C) Snow Plow Prep Package with manual.		
T53	Tires: P235/70R16SL AS OWL (XLT 2WD)	107	125
	Includes 6-spoke cast aluminum wheels. NOT AVAILABLE with (T55) or (T34) tires.		
T65	Tires: P255/70R16SL AT OWL (Lariat 4WD)	111	130
T65	Tires: P255/70R16SL AT OWL (Standard 4WD)	340	400
	Includes 3.55 axle ratio.		
53T	Tow Hooks (Standard 4WD/XL 4WD)	34	40
535	Trailer Towing Group with Auto (2WD)	340	400
	Includes 7-pin trailer wiring harness, HD Electrical/Cooling Package with auxiliary transmission oil cooler, HD shocks. NOT AVAILABLE with ((XH9) limited slip differential or (53C) Snow Plow Prep Package with manual.		
413	Transfer Case and Fuel Tank Skid Plates (Std. Cab 4WD)	68	80
44U	Transmission: 4-Speed Automatic	824	970
	Includes PRNDL in instrument panel. NOT AVAILABLE with 99L, 63H, 535, 53C, or 202.		
44E	Transmission: Electronic 4 Speed Automatic	824	970
	Includes PRNDL display in instrument panel. NOT AVAILABLE with 996, 63H, 535, or 53C.		
954	Two-Tone Lower Paint (XLT/Lariat)	162	190
	NOT AVAILABLE with (94B) STX Package.		

FORD F-150 PICKUP / F-250 PICKUP

CODE	DESCRIPTION	INVOICE	MSRP
A	Vinyl Bench Seat (XL)	(85)	(100)
	NOT AVAILABLE with (M) seats.		
645	Wheels: 16" Chrome Steel (XL)	170	200
62N	XL Special Appearance Package (XL)	437	515
	Manufacturer Discount	(213)	(250)
	Net Price	224	265
	Includes two-tone lower paint, 16" styled steel wheels, and P235/70R16SL AS OWL tires. NOT AVAILABLE with (T34) tires.		

1998 F-250

Safety Data

Driver Airbag: *Standard*
Side Airbag: *Not Available*

Passenger Airbag: *Standard*
4-Wheel ABS: *Standard (Lariat); Opional (Standard/XL/XLT)*

Traction Control: *Not Available*
Driver Crash Test Grade: *Good*

Integrated Child Seat(s): *Not Available*
Passenger Crash Test Grade: *Excellent*

Standard Equipment

STANDARD REGULAR CAB 2WD: 4.6L V-8 SOHC SMPI 16-valve engine; 5-speed overdrive manual transmission; 540-amp battery with run down protection; 130-amp HD alternator; rear wheel drive, 3.31 axle ratio; stainless steel exhaust; firm ride suspension, front independent double-wishbone suspension with anti-roll bar, front coil springs, front shocks, rear suspension with rear leaf springs, rear shocks; power re-circulating ball steering; front disc/rear drum brakes with rear wheel anti-lock braking system; 30 gal capacity fuel tank; trailer harness; front argent bumper; monotone paint; aero-composite halogen headlamps; additional exterior lights include center high mounted stop light; driver and passenger manual black folding outside mirrors; front and rear 16" x 7" silver styled steel wheels, hub wheel covers; P255/70SR16 BSW AS front and rear tires; underbody mounted full-size conventional steel spare wheel; AM/FM stereo with clock, seek-scan, 4-speakers and fixed antenna; 2 power accessory outlet; analog instrumentation display includes oil pressure gauge, water temp gauge, volt gauge, trip odometer; warning indicators include oil pressure, water temp warning, battery, key-in-ignition, low fuel, door ajar; driver side airbag, passenger side cancellable airbag; tinted windows; variable intermittent front windshield wipers; seating capacity of 3, bench front seat with adjustable headrests, driver seat includes 2-way direction control, passenger seat includes 2-way direction control; front height adjustable seatbelts; vinyl seats, vinyl door trim insert, full cloth headliner, full vinyl floor covering , interior lights include dome light; day-night rear-view mirror; glove box, front cupholder, instrument panel bin, dashboard storage; vinyl cargo floor, cargo tie downs; colored grille, and black door handles.

XL 2WD (in addition to or instead of STANDARD 2WD equipment): Front chrome bumper with black rub strip; underhood light; cloth seats; interior lights include front reading lights; passenger side vanity mirror; instrument panel bin, dashboard storage, driver door bin; and chrome grille.

XLT 2WD (in addition to or instead of XL 2WD equipment): Rear chrome bumper; body-colored bodyside molding; pickup cargo box light, driver and passenger manual chrome folding

F-250 PICKUP — FORD

outside mirrors; 2 power accessory outlet, retained accessory power; tachometer gauge, power front windows with driver 1-touch down); 40-60 split-bench front seat center armrest with storage, driver seat includes 4-way direction control with lumbar support, passenger seat includes 4-way direction control; vinyl door trim insert with carpet lower, full carpet floor covering ; interior lights include front reading lights, 2 door curb lights; driver side auxiliary visor; carpeted cargo floor, cargo tie downs, cargo concealed storage; chrome grille and body-colored door handles.

LARIAT 2WD (in addition to or instead of XLT 2WD equipment): 4-wheel disc brakes with 4-wheel anti-lock braking system; body-colored bodyside molding, driver and passenger power remote body-colored folding outside mirrors; front and rear chrome styled steel wheels, hub wheel covers; P255/70SR16 OWL AS front and rear tires; underbody mounted full-size temporary spare wheel; leather seats, full carpet floor covering with carpeted floor mats; leather-wrapped steering wheel; body-colored grille, and body-colored door handles.

STANDARD 4WD (in addition to or instead of STANDARD 2WD equipment): Part-time 4-wheel drive with auto locking hub control and manual shift; front torsion springs, front torsion bar; and LT245/75SR16 BSW AS front and rear tires.

XL 4WD (in addition to or instead of XL 2WD equipment): Part-time 4-wheel drive with auto locking hub control and manual shift; front torsion springs, front torsion bar; and LT245/75SR16 BSW AS front and rear tires.

XLT 4WD (in addition to or instead of XL T 2WD equipment): Front and rear chrome bumpers front with black rub strip, tow hook(s) rear; part-time 4-wheel drive with auto locking hub control and manual shift; front torsion springs, front torsion bar; and LT245/75SR16 BSW AS front and rear tires.

LARIAT 4WD (in addition to or instead of LARIAT 2WD equipment): Part-time 4-wheel drive with auto locking hub control and manual shift; front torsion springs, front torsion bar; and LT245/75SR16 BSW AS front and rear tires.

SUPERCAB CAB (in addition to or instead of REGULAR CAB): Third door access; fixed rear windows; seating capacity of 6; and 60-40 folding bench rear seat.

Base Prices

Code	Description	Invoice	MSRP
F27	Standard Std Cab 2WD LB	15215	16710
X27	Standard SuperCab 2WD SB	16975	18710
F28	Standard Std Cab 4WD LB	17903	19765
X28	Standard SuperCab 4WD SB	19633	21765
F27	XL Std Cab 2WD LB	15648	17810
X27	XL SuperCab 2WD SB	17413	19885
F28	XL Std Cab 4WD SB	18339	20975
X28	XL SuperCab 4WD SB	20103	23050
F27	XLT Std Cab 2WD LB	17829	20375
X27	XLT SuperCab 2WD SB	19902	22815
F28	XLT Std Cab 4WD LB	20422	23425
X28	XLT SuperCab 4WDSB	22495	25865
F27	Lariat Std Cab 2WD LB	19359	22175

FORD F-250 PICKUP

CODE	DESCRIPTION	INVOICE	MSRP
X28	XLT SuperCab 4WDSB	22495	25865
F27	Lariat Std Cab 2WD LB	19359	22175
X27	Lariat SuperCab 2WD SB	21432	24615
F28	Lariat Std Cab 4WD LB	21952	25225
X28	Lariat SuperCab 4WD SB	24025	27665
	Destination Charge:	640	640

Accessories

CODE	DESCRIPTION	INVOICE	MSRP
X26	3.73 Axle Ratio	43	50
	Includes engine oil cooler with 5.4L engine (99L).		
67B	4-Wheel Antilock Brakes (Standard/XL/XLT)	476	560
215	4x4 Electric Shift-On-The-Fly (XLT 4WD/Lariat 4WD)	128	150
	REQUIRES (44E) transmission or (44U) transmission.		
543	Aero Power Chrome Exterior Mirrors (XLT)	85	100
54M	Aero Power Color-Keyed Mirrors (XLT 4WD/Lariat 4WD)	85	100
572	Air Conditioning (Standard/XL/XLT)	684	805
18E	Black Cab Steps	272	320
422	California Emissions	144	170
	Required on all units for California registration.		
16G	Carpet Delete (Lariat)	(85)	(100)
	Also deletes floor mats.		
16G	Carpet Delete (XLT)	(43)	(50)
	NOT AVAILABLE with (167) Carpeted Color-Keyed Floor Mats.		
167	Carpeted Color-Keyed Floor Mats (XLT Std Cab)	26	30
	NOT AVAILABLE with (16G) Carpet Delete.		
167	Carpeted Color-Keyed Floor Mats (XLT SuperCab 2WD)	43	50
	Includes front and rear mats. NOT AVAILABLE with (16G) Carpet Delete.		
M	Cloth 40/60 Split Bench (XL)	128	150
	Includes driver's lumbar. No storage in center console.		
F	Cloth Captain's Seats (XLT)	417	490
	Includes driver's lumbar and floor console. REQUIRES (44E OR 44U) OR (517A).		
52N	Convenience Group (Standard/XL)	328	385
	Includes tilt steering and speed control.		
653	Dual In-Bed Fuel Tank	115	135
	NOT AVAILABLE with 99L, 99M, 44U, 535, or 53C.		
41H	Engine Block Heater	77	90
	Includes 600-watt element. Recommended when minimum temperature is -10 degrees F or below. HD 78ah battery. NOT AVAILABLE with (535) Trailer Towing Group (Class III), (63H) HD Electrical/Cooling Package, (53C) Snow Plow Prep Package.		
99Z	Engine: 5.4L Bi-Fuel Prep Engine	692	815
	Includes natural gas auxiliary fuel tank and 3.73 axle ratio. NOT AVAILABLE with (44U) transmission, (535) Trailer Towing Group (Class III), or (53C) Snow Plow Prep Package.		
99L	Engine: 5.4L EFI V8	565	665
	Includes 130-amp HD alternator and engine oil cooler. NOT AVAILABLE with 44U, 653, 66N, 66P, or 535.		

F-250 PICKUP — FORD

CODE	DESCRIPTION	INVOICE	MSRP
99M	Engine: 5.4L Natural Gas (Standard/XL)	4692	5520
	Includes natural gas auxiliary fuel tank, 3.73 axle ratio, and engine oil cooler. REQUIRES 44E. NOT AVAILABLE with 44U, 535, 66N, 66P, 63H, 209, or 653.		
595	Fog Lamps (Standard 4WD/XL 4WD/XLT 4WD)	119	140
63H	HD Electrical/Cooling Package	128	150
	This package or (535) class III trailer group required to tow over 4,000 lbs. super engine cooling. REQUIRES 44E. NOT AVAILABLE with 99Z, 66N, 66P, or 653.		
H	Leather Captain's Seats (Lariat)	417	490
	Includes driver's lumbar and floor console.		
XB6	Limited Slip Rear Axle	221	260
	REQUIRES (X26) 3.73 axle ratio.		
68P	Load Leveling Suspension (XL/XLT/Lariat)	417	490
	Includes HD rear shocks. REQUIRES 67B and 63H or (67B or 518A).		
66N	Natural Gas Fuel System	6217	7315
	NOT AVAILABLE with 99L, 99M, 44U, 66P, 535, or 53C.		
207	Optional Payload Package #2 (2WD)	41	50
	Includes 7500 lbs GVWR and 3085 lbs payload. spring upgrades. REQUIRES T34 and (X26 or XB6 or 44E or 44U). NOT AVAILABLE with T55.		
209	Optional Payload Package #2 (2WD)	41	50
	Includes 7700 lbs GVWR and 3350 lbs payload and spring upgrades. REQUIRES T34 and (X26 or XB6 or 44E) or 99L or 99Z. NOT AVAILABLE with 99M or T55.		
61T	Pickup Box Security Group (Standard/XL)	38	45
	Includes tailgate lock and cargo light.		
C	Poly Knit Bench Seat (Standard)	85	100
90P	Power Driver's Seat (XLT/Lariat)	306	360
	Includes autolamp. REQUIRES (517A) or (44E or 44U).		
510A	Preferred Equipment Package 510A (Standard Std Cab 4WD)	NC	NC
	Includes LT245/75R16 AS BSW tires and vinyl bench seat.		
510A	Preferred Equipment Package 510A (Standard Std. Cab)	NC	NC
	Includes vinyl bench seat and Supercab rear seat.		
510A	Preferred Equipment Package 510A (Standard Std. Cab 2WD)	NC	NC
	Includes vinyl bench seat.		
510A	Preferred Equipment Package 510A (Standard SuperCab 4WD)	NC	NC
	Includes LT245/75R16d AS BSW tires, vinyl bench seat, and Supercab rear seat.		
512A	Preferred Equipment Package 512A (XL Std Cab 2WD)	128	150
	Manufacturer Discount	(128)	(150)
	Net Price	NC	NC
	Includes poly knit bench seat and chrome rear step bumper.		
512A	Preferred Equipment Package 512A (XL Std Cab 4WD)	128	150
	Manufacturer Discount	(128)	(150)
	Net Price	NC	NC
	Includes LT245/75R16 AS BSW tires, poly knit bench seat, and chrome rear step bumper.		
512A	Preferred Equipment Package 512A (XL SuperCab 2WD)	128	150
	Manufacturer Discount	(128)	(150)
	Net Price	NC	NC
	Includes poly knit bench seat, chrome rear step bumper, and SuperCab rear seat.		

FORD F-250 PICKUP

CODE	DESCRIPTION	INVOICE	MSRP
512A	Preferred Equipment Package 512A (XL SuperCab 4WD)	128	150
	Manufacturer Discount	(128)	(150)
	Net Price	NC	NC
	Includes LT245/75R16 AS BSW tires, poly knit bench seat, chrome rear step bumper, and SuperCab rear seat.		
517A	Preferred Equipment Package 517A (XLT Std Cab 2WD)	1293	1520
	Manufacturer Discount	(1293)	(1520)
	Net Price	NC	NC
	Includes chrome styled steel wheels, cloth 40/60 split bench, air conditioning, chrome rear step bumper, Convenience Group: tilt steering, speed control, AM/FM stereo with cassette, clock radio, Power Convenience Group: power door locks, door curb lights, XLT door trim panels, speed dependent interval wipers, power windows with driver's 1 touch down: delayed accessory power, Pickup Box Security Group: tailgate lock, and cargo light.		
517A	Preferred Equipment Package 517A (XLT Std Cab 4WD)	1293	1520
	Manufacturer Discount	(1293)	(1520)
	Net Price	NC	NC
	Includes chrome styled steel wheels, cloth 40/60 split bench, air conditioning, chrome rear step bumper, Convenience Group: tilt steering, speed control, AM/FM stereo with cassette, clock radio, Power Convenience Group: power door locks, door curb lights, XLT door trim panels, speed dependent interval wipers, power windows with driver's 1 touch down: delayed accessory power, Pickup Box Security Group: tailgate lock, cargo light, tow hooks, and LT245/75R16 AS BSW tires.		
517A	Preferred Equipment Package 517A (XLT SuperCab 2WD)	1293	1520
	Manufacturer Discount	(1293)	(1520)
	Net Price	NC	NC
	Includes chrome styled steel wheels, cloth 40/60 split bench, air conditioning, chrome rear step bumper, Convenience Group: tilt steering, speed control, AM/FM stereo with cassette, clock radio, Power Convenience Group: power door locks, door curb lights, XLT door trim panels, speed dependent interval wipers, power windows with driver's 1 touch down: delayed accessory power, Pickup Box Security Group: tailgate lock, cargo light, and SuperCab rear seat.		
517A	Preferred Equipment Package 517A (XLT SuperCab 4WD)	1293	1520
	Manufacturer Discount	(1293)	(1520)
	Net Price	NC	NC
	Includes chrome styled steel wheels, cloth 40/60 split bench, air conditioning, chrome rear step bumper, Convenience Group: tilt steering, speed control, AM/FM stereo with cassette, clock radio, Power Convenience Group: power door locks, door curb lights, XLT door trim panels, speed dependent interval wipers, power windows with driver's 1 touch down: delayed accessory power, Pickup Box Security Group: tailgate lock, cargo light, tow hooks, LT245/75R16 AS BSW tires, and SuperCab		
518A	Preferred Equipment Package 518A (Lariat Std Cab 2WD)	1428	1680
	Manufacturer Discount	(1428)	(1680)
	Net Price	NC	NC
	Includes P255/70R16SL AS OWL tires, leather 60/40 bench seat, 4-wheel antilock brakes, air conditioning, chrome rear step bumper, power driver's seat: autolamp, Convenience Group: tilt steering, speed control, AM/FM stereo with		

F-250 PICKUP — FORD

CODE	DESCRIPTION	INVOICE	MSRP

cassette and clock, Power Convenience Group: power door locks, door curb lights, XLT door trim panels, speed dependent interval wipers, power windows with driver's 1-touch down: delayed accessory power, chrome styled steel wheels, carpeted color-keyed floor mats, Pickup Box Security Group: tailgate lock, cargo light, power signal mirror, and power signal mirror.

518A	Preferred Equipment Package 518A (Lariat Std Cab 4WD)	1428	1680
	Manufacturer Discount	(1428)	(1680)
	Net Price	NC	NC

Includes P255/70R16SL AS OWL tires, leather 60/40 bench seat, 4-wheel antilock brakes, air conditioning, chrome rear step bumper, power driver's seat: autolamp, Convenience Group: tilt steering, speed control, AM/FM stereo with cassette and clock, Power Convenience Group: power door locks, door curb lights, XLT door trim panels, speed dependent interval wipers, power windows with driver's 1-touch down: delayed accessory power, chrome styled steel wheels, carpeted color-keyed floor mats, Pickup Box Security Group: tailgate lock, cargo light, power signal mirror, power signal mirror, tow hooks, LT245/75R16 AS BSW tires, fog lamps, and SuperCab rear seat.

518A	Preferred Equipment Package 518A (Lariat SuperCab 2WD)	1428	1680
	Manufacturer Discount	(1428)	(1680)
	Net Price	NC	NC

Includes P255/70R16SL AS OWL tires, leather 60/40 bench seat, 4-wheel antilock brakes, air conditioning, chrome rear step bumper, power driver's seat: autolamp, Convenience Group: tilt steering, speed control, AM/FM stereo with cassette and clock, Power Convenience Group: power door locks, door curb lights, XLT door trim panels, speed dependent interval wipers, power windows with driver's 1-touch down: delayed accessory power, chrome styled steel wheels, carpeted color-keyed floor mats, Pickup Box Security Group: tailgate lock, cargo light, power signal mirror, and supercab rear seat.

518A	Preferred Equipment Package 518A (Lariat SuperCab 4WD)	1428	1680
	Manufacturer Discount	(1428)	(1680)
	Net Price	NC	NC

Includes P255/70R16SL AS OWL tires, leather 60/40 bench seat, 4-wheel antilock brakes, air conditioning, chrome rear step bumper, power driver's seat: autolamp, Convenience Group: tilt steering, speed control, AM/FM stereo with cassette and clock, Power Convenience Group: power door locks, door curb lights, XLT door trim panels, speed dependent interval wipers, power windows with driver's 1-touch down: delayed accessory power, chrome styled steel wheels, carpeted color-keyed floor mats, Pickup Box Security Group: tailgate lock, cargo light, power signal mirror, tow hooks, LT245/75R16 AS BSW tires, fog lamps, and SuperCab rear seat.

66P	Propane Fuel System	4208	4950
	NOT AVAILABLE with 99L, 99M, 44U, 66N, 535, or 53C.		
589	Radio: AM/FM Stereo with Cassette and Clock (Standard/XL)	111	130
	Includes 4 speakers.		
91P	Radio: AM/FM Stereo with CD and Cassette (XLT/Lariat)	340	400
	Includes 6-disc CD changer and storage tray delete.		

FORD F-250 PICKUP / F-350 PICKUP

CODE	DESCRIPTION	INVOICE	MSRP
436	Rear Quarter Flip Window (SuperCab)	38	45
924	Rear Qtr. Window Privacy Glass (XL SuperCab/XLT SuperCab/Lariat SuperCab)	85	100
769	Rear Step Painted Bumper (Standard)	85	100
61S	Rear Storage Bin (Standard Std Cab/XL Std Cab)	77	90
904	Remote Keyless Entry (XLT/Lariat)	225	265
	Includes anti-theft and 2 key fobs, panic alarm, and illuminated entry.		
413	Skid Plates (4WD)	136	160
	Includes transfer case and fuel tank skid plates.		
433	Sliding Rear Window	107	125
53C	Snow Plow Prep Package (4WD)	387	455
	Includes P245/75R16D AT OWL tires and full size temporary tires. REQUIRES 769. NOT AVAILABLE with 99Z, 66N, 66P, 653, or 44E.		
T34	Tires: LT245/75R16D AS BSW (Lariat)	77	90
T34	Tires: LT245/75R16D AS BSW (Standard 2WD/XL 2WD)	182	215
	NOT AVAILABLE with (T55) tires.		
T3P	Tires: P245/75R16D AT OWL (Standard 4WD/XL 4WD)	217	255
	Includes spare full size temporary tires.		
T55	Tires: P255/70R16SL AS OWL (XLT 2WD)	107	125
	Includes BSW all-season spare. NOT AVAILABLE with (T34) tires, (209) Optional Payload Package #2, or (207) Optional Payload Package #2.		
53T	Tow Hooks (Standard 4WD/XL 4WD)	34	40
	Includes 2 cast iron front tow hooks.		
535	Trailer Towing Group (Class III)	383	450
	NOTE: This package or (63H) HD electrical/cooling package required to tow over 4,000 lbs. Trailer hitch and harness, HD Electrical/Cooling Package: super engine cooling, general and trailering weights. REQUIRES 769. NOT AVAILABLE with 53C, 66N, 66P, or 653.		
44U	Transmission: Electronic 4 Speed Auto OD	824	970
	NOT AVAILABLE with 99L, 99M, 653, 99Z, 66N, 66P, 63H, or 535.		
44E	Transmission: Electronic 4-Speed Automatic	824	970
	NOT AVAILABLE with (535) Trailer Towing Group (Class III) or (53C) Snow Plow Prep Package.		
954	Two-Tone Lower Paint (XLT/Lariat)	162	190
A	Vinyl Bench Seat (XL)	(85)	(100)
643	Wheels: Chrome Styled Steel (XL)	170	200
	Includes chrome hub.		

1997 F-350 PICKUP

What's New?

Until an all-new truck goes into production for release in the spring, we're stuck with the same old truck that's been on the road since 1980.

F-350 PICKUP FORD

CODE	DESCRIPTION	INVOICE	MSRP

Safety Data

Driver Airbag: *Not Available*
Side Airbag: *Not Available*
Traction Control: *Not Available*
Driver Crash Test Grade: *Not Available*

Passenger Airbag: *Not Available*
4-Wheel ABS: *Not Available*
Integrated Child Seat(s): *Not Available*
Passenger Crash Test Grade: *Not Available*

Base Prices

Code	Description	Invoice	MSRP
F35	Reg. Cab 2WD	16119	18340
F36	Reg. Cab 4WD	18787	21445
F35	Reg. Cab 2WD DRW	16787	19125
X35	SuperCab 2WD DRW	18754	21440
W35	Crew Cab 2WD	19048	21785
W35	Crew Cab 2WD DRW	19544	22370
W36	Crew Cab 4WD	21717	24925
	Destination Charge:	640	640

Accessories

Code	Description	Invoice	MSRP
209	161" WB Optional Payload Package #2 (DRW 2WD)	27	32
99Y	4.9-liter I-6 Engine (2WD Regular Cab)	(933)	(1098)
85D	4x4 Off-road Decal Delete	NC	NC
99H	5.8-liter EFI V-8 Engine	NC	NC
	STANDARD on all models except Chassis Cab 4WD and Super Cab 2WD		
99F	7.3-liter Powerstroke Diesel V-8 Engine	3518	4139
99F	7.3-liter Powerstroke Diesel V-8 Engine (Chassis 4WD, Super 4WD)	3192	3755
99G	7.5-liter EFI V-8 Engine	327	384
99G	7.5-liter EFI V-8 Engine (Chassis 4WD, Super 2WD)	NC	NC
572	Air Conditioning	685	806
44G	Automatic Transmission	631	743
44E	Automatic Transmission	825	971
	electronic 4-speed		
435	Auxiliary Fuel Tap	26	30
545	Bright Low-mount Swing-away Mirrors	38	45
	with 618A (Super Cab DRW 2WD)	7	9
	with 642A (Reg Cab SRW 4WD)	7	9
	with 651A (Reg Cab SRW 2WD)	7	9
	with 661A (Crew Cab SRW)	7	9
	with 671A (Crew Cab DRW 2WD)	7	9
	with 183	7	9
	w/o 183 Chrome Appearance Package		
543	Bright Power Mirrors	84	99

FORD F-350 PICKUP

CODE	DESCRIPTION	INVOICE	MSRP
548	Bright Swing-out Recreational Mirrors	46	54
	with 618A (Super Cab DRW 2WD)	7	9
	with 642A (Reg Cab SRW 4WD)	7	9
	with 651A (Reg Cab SRW 2WD)	7	9
	with 661A (Crew Cab SRW)	7	9
	with 671A (Crew Cab DRW 2WD)	7	9
	w/o 183 Chrome Appearance Package		
422	California Emissions System	85	100
532	Camper/Trailer Towing Package	253	297
	with 55R (4WD)	(102)	(120)
	CREDIT w/55R Off-Road Package		
167	Carpeted Floor Mats	43	50
183	Chrome Appearance Package	153	180
768	Chrome Rear Step Bumper	128	150
7	Cloth & Vinyl Bench Seat (Reg Cab)	85	100
7	Cloth and Vinyl Bench Seat (Super Cab)	85	100
7	Cloth Bench Seat (Crew Cab)	85	100
	with 661A (Crew Cab SRW)	NC	NC
	with 671A (Crew Cab DRW 2WD)	NC	NC
8	Cloth Bench Seats (Super Cab)	NC	NC
	Includes cloth rear bench seat		
4	Cloth Captain's Chairs (Super Cab)	664	782
	with 618A (Super Cab DRW 2WD)	528	621
	Includes floor console, power lumbar, cloth rear bench seat		
5	Cloth Flight Bench Seat (Crew Cab)	NC	NC
	w/661A or 671A Package		
5	Cloth Flight Bench Seat (Reg Cab)	NC	NC
	w/651A or 642A Package		
186	Color-keyed Cab Steps	340	400
952	Deluxe Two-tone Paint (DRW)	141	166
	with 651A (Reg Cab SRW 2WD)	234	276
	with 642A (Reg Cab SRW 4WD)	234	276
	with 661A (Crew Cab SRW)	234	276
41H	Engine Block Heater	28	33
	with 99G	56	66
	with 99G (Super 2WD)	56	66
	w/4.9- or 5.8-liter engine		
166	Floor Mat	NC	NC
	REPLACES carpet		
649	Forged Aluminum Wheels	708	833
	with 671A (Crew Cab DRW 2WD)	454	534
	with 651A (Reg Cab SRW 2WD)	454	534
	with 618A (Super Cab DRW 2WD)	454	534
684	Handling Package	102	120
	Includes front/rear stabilizer bars		
44C	HD 5-Speed Manual Transmission	NC	NC
	REQUIRES 99F 7.3-liter Powerstroke Diesel V-8		

F-350 PICKUP — FORD

CODE	DESCRIPTION	INVOICE	MSRP
44W	HD 5-speed Manual Transmission	NC	NC
674	HD Front Suspension Package	23	27
428	High Altitude Principal Use Emissions	NC	NC
593	Interior Enhancement/Light Group	66	78
	Includes under hood light, dual beam dome/map light, headlights on audible alert, map pocket, RH visor vanity mirror, mini-console (Regular Cab only), headliner and insulation package (Regular Cab only)		
6	Knitted Vinyl Bench Seat (Super Cab)	NC	NC
B	Knitted Vinyl Bench Seats (Super Cab)	NC	NC
	w/618A Package		
153	License Plate Bracket	NC	NC
—	Limited Slip Rear Axle	215	252
—	Limited Slip Rear Axle	252	296
	Includes optional axle ratio upgrade		
954	Lower Accent Two-tone Paint	155	183
21M	Manual Locking Hubs	NC	NC
55R	Off-road Package (4WD)	220	259
	with 99F	145	171
	with 99F (Super 4WD)	145	171
	Includes skid plate, front/rear stabilizer bars, and 4x4 off-road decal		
—	Optional Axle Ratio (upgrade)	37	44
66D	Pickup Box Delete	(532)	(626)
90P	Power Driver's Seat (Super Cab)	247	290
	40/20/40 Bench Seat; w/618A Package		
617A	Preferred Equipment Package 617A (Super Cab DRW 2WD)	NC	NC
	Includes vehicles w/standard equipment		
618A	Preferred Equipment Package 618A (Super Cab DRW 2WD)	1759	2070
	Includes black rub strip w/front bumper, bright manual mirrors, argent headlamp/parking bezels, bright windshield molding, color-keyed lower bodyside protection, headlight-on alert signal, vinyl door trim w/large perforated vinyl/upper insert, other accents and moldings, color-keyed speaker grilles, black mat floor covering, color-keyed cloth, dual note horn, color-keyed instrument panel w/storage bin, air conditioning, power door locks/windows, interior enhancement/light group, speed control/tilt steering wheel, electronic AM/FM stereo/clock/cassette/4 speakers		
640A	Preferred Equipment Package 640A (Reg Cab SRW 4WD)	NC	NC
	Includes vehicle w/standard equipment		
642A	Preferred Equipment Package 642A (Reg Cab SRW 4WD)	2133	2510
	Includes black rub strip w/front bumper, bright manual mirrors, argent headlamp/parking bezels, bright windshield moldings, color-keyed lower bodyside protection, headlight-on alert signal, vinyl door trim w/large perforated vinyl/upper insert, other accents and moldings, color-keyed speaker grilles, black mat floor covering, color-keyed cloth, dual note horn, color-keyed instrument panel w/storage bin, air conditioning, power door locks/windows, interior enhancement/light group, speed control/tilt steering wheel, forged aluminum deep dish wheels, electronic AM/FM stereo/clock/cassette/4 speakers		

FORD F-350 PICKUP

CODE	DESCRIPTION	INVOICE	MSRP
650A	Preferred Equipment Package 650A (Reg Cab SRW 2WD)	NC	NC
	Includes vehicle w/standard equipment		
651A	Preferred Equipment Package 651A (Reg Cab SRW 2WD)	1811	2130
	Includes black rub strip w/front bumper, bright manual mirrors, argent headlamp/parking bezels, bright windshield moldings, color-keyed lower bodyside protection, headlight-on alert signal, vinyl door trim w/large perforated vinyl/upper insert, other accents and moldings, color-keyed speaker grilles, black mat floor covering, color-keyed cloth, air conditioning, power door locks/windows, interior enhancement/light group, speed control/tilt steering wheel, electronic AM/FM stereo/clock/cassette/4 speakers		
660A	Preferred Equipment Package 660A (Crew Cab SRW)	NC	NC
	Includes vehicle w/standard equipment		
661A	Preferred Equipment Package 661A (Crew Cab SRW)	2252	2650
	Includes black rub strip w/front bumper, bright manual mirrors, argent headlamp/parking bezels, bright windshield moldings, color-keyed lower bodyside protection, headlight-on alert signal, n\vinyl door trim w/large perforated vinyl/upper insert, other accents and moldings, color-keyed speaker grilles, black mat floor covering, color-keyed cloth, dual note horn, color-keyed instrument panel w/storage bin, air conditioning, power door locks/windows, interior enhancement/light group, speed control/tilt steering wheel, forged aluminum deep dish wheels, electronic AM/FM stereo/clock/cassette/4 speakers		
670A	Preferred Equipment Package 670A (Crew Cab DRW 2WD)	NC	NC
	Includes vehicle w/standard equipment		
671A	Preferred Equipment Package 671A (Crew Cab DRW 2WD)	2184	2570
	Includes black rub strip w/front bumper, bright manual mirrors, argent headlamp/parking bezels, bright windshield moldings, color-keyed lower bodyside protection, headlight-on alert signal, vinyl door trim w/large perforated vinyl/upper insert, other accents and moldings, color-keyed speaker grilles, black mat floor covering, color-keyed cloth, dual note horn, color-keyed instrument panel w/storage bin, air conditioning, power door locks/windows, interior enhancement/light group, speed control/tilt steering wheel, electronic AM/FM stereo/clock/cassette/4 speakers		
R	Premium Cloth 40/20/40 Bench (Crew Cab)	528	621
	w/661A or 671A Package		
R	Premium Cloth 40/20/40 Bench Seat (Reg Cab)	445	523
	w/651A or 642A Package		
J	Premium Cloth 40/20/40 Bench Seats (Super Cab)	528	621
	with 642A (Reg Cab SRW 4WD)	445	523
	with 651A (Reg Cab SRW 2WD)	445	523
	w/618A Package		
582	Premium Stereo w/CD Player	573	556
	with 642A (Reg Cab SRW 4WD)	NC	NC
	with 661A (Crew Cab SRW)	254	299
	with 671A (Crew Cab DRW 2WD)	254	299
	with 651A (Reg Cab SRW 2WD)	254	299
	with 618A (Super Cab DRW 2WD)	254	299
	Includes clock		
58Y	Radio Credit Option	(52)	(61)

F-350 PICKUP — FORD

CODE	DESCRIPTION	INVOICE	MSRP
924	Rear Privacy Glass	84	99
76C	Rear Step Bumpers	85	100
	argent colored		
66H	Receiving Trailer Hitch	126	149
948	Remote Keyless Entry	145	171
592	Roof Clearance Lights	45	52
651	Single Fuel Tank	(98)	(116)
433	Sliding Rear Window	96	113
513	Spare Rear Wheel	114	134
515	Spare Tire & Wheel — LT235/85R16E (4WD) BSW	251	295
512	Spare Tire & Wheel — LT215/85R16D BSW	210	248
—	Spare Tire and Wheel LT235/85R16E BSW	227	267
52N	Speed Control/Tilt Steering Wheel	325	383
644	Sport Wheel Covers	86	101
589	Stereo w/cassette	219	257
	with 587	93	110
	Includes clock		
587	Stereo w/clock	125	148
624	Super Engine Cooling	86	101
152	Tachometer	50	59
T63	Tires — LT215/85R16D BSW (DRW 2WD)	NC	NC
T6C	Tires — LT215/85R16D BSW All-Terrain (DRW 2WD)	95	112
T35	Tires — LT235/85R16E BSW (SRW 2WD)	NC	NC
T3N	Tires — LT235/85R16E BSW (SRW 2WD)	95	112
	rear tires		
T35	Tires — LT235/85R16E BSW (SRW 4WD)	NC	NC
TEE	Tires — LT235/85R16E BSW All-Terrain (DRW)	143	168
TE5	Tires — LT235/85R16E BSW All-Terrain (DRW 4WD)	NC	NC
6	Vinyl Bench Seat (Crew Cab)	NC	NC
6	Vinyl Bench Seat (Reg Cab)	NC	NC

Take Advantage of Warranty Gold!

Savings up to 50% off Dealer's Extended Warranty Prices. Protect and enhance YOUR investment with the best extended warranty available.

Call Toll Free 1-800-580-9889

FORD RANGER

| CODE | DESCRIPTION | INVOICE | MSRP |

1998 RANGER

1998 Ford Ranger Splash SuperCab 2WD

What's New?

The Ford Ranger gets new sheetmetal on the flanks and hood, as well as a new grille and headlamps. The wheelbase on regular and SuperCab models has been stretched and the engines' displacement have been increased. A short- and long-arm (SLA) suspension replaces the Twin-I-Beam suspension found on last year's models. Look for a radical 4-door Ranger to join the lineup early this spring. An electric model debuts as well, the first electric vehicle sold by Ford.

Review

Whether it's image or utility that attracts you to a compact truck, Ford stands ready to seduce you into its strong-selling Ranger. Trim levels range from the practical XL through the well-trimmed XLT, all the way to the beguiling little Ranger Splash with its fiberglass Flareside bed, chrome wheels, and lowered suspension.

With the optional 4.0-liter V-6 engine, in particular, acceleration is impressively brisk, whether from a standstill or when merging and passing. The base four cylinder engine can overtax the Ranger when carrying a heavy load, although its increase in displacement for 1998 should help a little bit. Automatic-transmission upshifts are crisp and barely noticed, with just a slight jolt under hard throttle, and downshifts deliver only slightly more harshness. Push-button four-wheel-drive, if installed, is a snap to use.

Well-controlled overall, with good steering feedback, Rangers handle easily, corner capably, maneuver neatly, and stay reasonably stable on curves. Occupants aren't likely to complain about the ride, either, though it can grow bouncy around town. Gas mileage isn't the greatest with the big engine and automatic, as expected.

Ranger sports a worldwide industry first for safety protection. An optional passenger side airbag is available, and it can be disabled with the flick of a switch in the event that a car seat is installed in the truck. The Ranger is also the only small truck to be available with a 5-speed automatic transmission. Ford claims that the 5-speed automatic allows better acceleration, trailering, and hill climbing by their capable Ranger.

Ford lost its deathgrip on the small truck segment when Dodge introduced the outstanding new-for-97 Dakota. In a retaliatory effort, Ford gives the 1998 Ranger an unneeded facelift that

RANGER   FORD

we think renders the truck less attractive than before. With that facelift comes an increase in wheelbase, a larger base engine, a new suspension, rack-and-pinion steering and a 4-door model (set to appear after the first of the year). Also new for 1998 is the presence of an electric model. Marketed primarily to fleets, the electric Ranger boasts a top speed of 75 mph and a 700-lb. payload.

Ford has had the best-selling small trucks in the country for years. We think it's because Rangers are all truck, with few pretensions toward any other identity, but can be loaded with gadgets like a luxury auto. Fun to drive, sharp looking, and well built, they deliver a solid compact-pickup experience. Even though we're not crazy about the new styling, we're certain that they will continue to be a big hit.

Safety Data

Driver Airbag: *Standard*
Side Airbag: *Not Available*
Traction Control: *Not Available*
Driver Crash Test Grade: *Good*

Passenger Airbag: *Standard*
4-Wheel ABS: *Optional*
Integrated Child Seat(s): *Not Available*
Passenger Crash Test Grade: *Good*

Standard Equipment

XL 2WD: 2.3L I-4-SOHC SMPI 8-valve engine; 5-speed overdrive manual transmission; 540-amp battery with run down protection; 95-amp alternator; rear-wheel drive, 3.45 axle ratio; partial stainless steel exhaust; front independent suspension with anti-roll bar, front coil springs, front shocks, rear suspension with rear leaf springs, rear shocks; power rack-and-pinion steering; front disc/rear drum brakes with rear-wheel anti-lock braking system; 17 gal capacity fuel tank; front and rear mud flaps; front and rear colored bumpers with rear step; monotone paint; aero-composite halogen headlamps; additional exterior lights include center high mounted stop light; driver and passenger manual black folding outside mirrors; front and rear 14" x 5.5" silver styled steel wheels with hub wheel covers; P205/75SR14-BSW AS front and rear tires; underbody mounted full-size conventional steel spare wheel; 2 power accessory outlets; analog instrumentation display includes oil pressure gauge, water temp gauge, volt gauge, trip odometer; warning indicators include battery, lights on, key in ignition, door ajar; driver side airbag, passenger side cancellable airbag; tinted windows; variable intermittent front windshield wipers; seating capacity of 3, 60-40 split-bench front seat with adjustable headrests, driver seat includes 2-way direction control, passenger seat includes 2-way direction control; front height adjustable seatbelts; vinyl seats, full cloth headliner, full vinyl floor covering; interior lights include dome light, illuminated entry; day-night rearview mirror; glove box, front cupholders; vinyl cargo floor; colored grille, and black door handles.

XL SUPERCAB 2WD (in addition to or instead of XL 2WD equipment): 3.73 axle ratio; fixed rear windows; seating capacity of 5; and 50-50 folding rear jump side facing seat.

XL 4WD (in addition to or instead of XL 2WD equipment): 3L V-6 OHV engine; part-time 4-wheel drive, auto locking hub control and electronic shift; HD front shocks, rear anti-roll bar, HD rear shocks; skid plates; front and rear colored bumpers, rear tow hooks; and colored fender flares.

XL SUPERCAB 4WD (in addition to or instead of XL 4WD equipment): Seating capacity of 5; 50-50 folding rear jump facing side seat.

XLT 2WD (in addition to or instead of XL 2WD equipment): 17 gal capacity fuel tank; trailer harness; front and rear chrome bumpers with black rub strip; bodyside accent stripe; additional exterior lights include pickup cargo box light; AM/FM stereo, clock, with seek-scan, 2 speakers and fixed antenna; center armrest with storage; cloth seats, cloth door trim insert, carpet floor

FORD RANGER

covering; passenger side vanity mirror; partial floor console, driver and passenger door bins; carpeted cargo floor, cargo concealed storage; chrome grille, and body-colored door handles.

XLT SUPERCAB 2WD (in addition to or instead of XLT 2WD equipment): 20 gal capacity fuel tank; fixed rear windows; seating capacity of 5; 50-50 folding rear jump facing side seat; cargo cover, cargo net; chrome grille.

XLT 4WD (in addition to or instead of XLT 2WD equipment): 3L V-6 OHV engine, part-time 4-wheel drive, auto-locking hub control and electronic shift; HD front shocks, HD rear shocks; skid plates; and colored fender flares.

XLT SUPERCAB 4WD (in addition to or instead of XLT 4WD equipment): 4 speakers; fixed rear windows; seating capacity of 5; 50-50 folding rear side facing jump seat; cargo cover, cargo net; and chrome grille.

SPLASH 2WD (in addition to or instead of XLT 2WD equipment): Rear anti-roll bar; trailer harness; flare side pick-up box; front and rear body-colored bumpers; and Splash badging.

SPLASH SUPERCAB 2WD (in addition to or instead of SPLASH 2WD equipment): 50-50 folding rear side facing jump seats and cargo net.

SPLASH 4WD (in addition to or instead of SPLASH 2WD equipment): 3L V-6 OHV engine, part-time 4-wheel drive, auto-locking hub control and electronic shift; HD front shocks, HD rear shocks; skid plates; and colored fender flares.

SPLASH SUPERCAB 4WD (in addition to or instead of SPLASH 4WD equipment): 4 speakers; fixed rear windows; seating capacity of 5; 50-50 folding rear side facing jump seat; and cargo net.

Base Prices

Code	Description	Invoice	MSRP
R10	XL Std Cab 2WD SB	10835	11385
R10-7	XL Std Cab 2WD LB	11267	11855
R11	XL Std Cab 4WD SB	14864	15765
R11-7	XL Std Cab 4WD LB	15296	16235
R14	XL SuperCab 2WD	13419	14840
R15	XL SuperCab 4WD	15646	17370
R10	XLT Std Cab 2WD SB	11981	13205
R10-7	XLT Std Cab 2WD LB	12465	13755
R11	XLT Std Cab 4WD SB	15580	17295
R11-7	XLT Std Cab 4WD LB	16099	17885
R14	XLT SuperCab 2WD	13863	15345
R15	XLT SuperCab 4WD	16886	18780
R10	Splash Std Cab 2WD	13511	14945
R11	Splash Std Cab 4WD	16873	18765
R14	Splash SuperCab 2WD	14946	16575
R15	Splash SuperCab 4WD	17604	19595
Destination Charge:		510	510

RANGER — FORD

CODE	DESCRIPTION	INVOICE	MSRP
	Accessories		
X92	3.08 Axle Ratio (XLT/Splash)	NC	NC
	REQUIRES 99X. NOT AVAILABLE with 99U, XF6, or XR5.		
X95	3.55 Axle Ratio (XLT/Splash)	NC	NC
X86	3.73 Axle Ratio	NC	NC
	REQUIRES T80, 202, 864A or 867A. NOT AVAILABLE with XF6, 99X, or XR5.		
X96	3.73 Axle Ratio (XLT 4WD/Splash 4WD)	NC	NC
	REQUIRES 99X and 428. NOT AVAILABLE with 44T, XF6, XF7, or XR6.		
44T	4-Speed Automatic Transmission With OD	909	1070
	NOT AVAILABLE with 99X, XF6, X96, or XR6.		
67B	4-Wheel Antilock Brakes	425	510
X87	4.10 Axle Ratio	NC	NC
	REQUIRES 44T. NOT AVAILABLE with XF6, XF7, 99X, 44D, or XR6.		
—	4X4 Value Discount (4WD)	(298)	(350)
44D	5-Speed Automatic Transmission (XLT/Splash)	939	1105
	REQUIRES 99X engine. NOT AVAILABLE with 99U, X87, XF6, or XF7.		
E	60/40 Split Cloth Bench Seat (XL Std Cab)	247	290
572	Air Conditioning	684	805
965	Bodyside Protection Mouldings (XLT)	102	120
	NOT AVAILABLE with (173) flareside box.		
—	Bonus Discount With 2.5L Engine (99C)	(425)	(500)
	NOT AVAILABLE with (99U) engine, (99X) engine.		
422	California Emissions	144	170
	Required on units for California/Massachusetts/New York/Connecticut registration. NOT AVAILABLE with (428) High Altitude Principal Use.		
G	Cloth Sport Bucket Seats (XLT/Splash)	306	360
	Includes floor console. NOT AVAILABLE with (864A) Preferred Equipment Package 864A.		
—	Delete 649 Aluminum Wheels Credit (XLT)	(213)	(250)
954	Deluxe Two-Tone Paint (XLT)	200	235
99U	Engine: 3.0L V-6 (XL/XLT/Splash)	383	450
	REQUIRES 587. NOT AVAILABLE with X92, XR5, or 44D.		
99X	Engine: 4.0L V-6 (XLT 2WD/Splash 2WD)	765	900
	Includes 3.55 axle ratio. NOT AVAILABLE with (X86) 3.73 axle ratio, (XF6) limited slip differential with 3.73, and (44T) transmission.		
99X	Engine: 4.0L V-6 (XLT 4WD/Splash 4WD)	383	450
	NOT AVAILABLE with XF6, XF7, X87, or 44T.		
173	Flareside Box (XL/XLT)	387	455
	NOT AVAILABLE with (646) wheels.		
47F	Flareside Plus Package (XLT 2WD)	599	705
	Manufacturer Discount	(263)	(310)
	Net Price	336	395
	Includes flareside box, full face chrome wheels, P225/70R15 AS OWL tires, AM/FM stereo with CD, clock, and tachometer.		

EDMUND'S 1998 NEW TRUCKS — www.edmunds.com

FORD RANGER

CODE	DESCRIPTION	INVOICE	MSRP
47F	Flareside Plus Package (XLT 4WD)	625	735
	Manufacturer Discount	(289)	(340)
	Net Price	336	395
	Includes flareside box, AM/FM stereo with CD and clock, and fog lamps.		
595	Fog Lamps (XLT)	158	185
	REQUIRES (99U) engine or (99X) engine.		
428	High Altitude Principal Use	NC	NC
529	Leather Wrapped Steering Wheel (XLT)	43	50
XR5	Limited Slip Differential with 3.55 (2WD)	229	270
	REQUIRES 99X and 202. NOT AVAILABLE with 99U, X86, X92, or XF6.		
XF6	Limited Slip Differential with 3.73	229	270
	REQUIRES 99U and 202 or 20W. NOT AVAILABLE with X86, 99X, X92, XR5, 44T, X87, 44D, or X96.		
XR6	Limited Slip Differential with 3.73 (4WD)	229	270
	REQUIRES 99X. NOT AVAILABLE with 44T, X87, or X96.		
XF7	Limited Slip Differential with 4.10 (4WD)	229	270
	REQUIRES 20W and 44T. NOT AVAILABLE with X87, 99X, 44D, or X96.		
91R	Off-Road Package (XLT)	336	395
	Manufacturer Discount	(170)	(200)
	Net Price	166	195
	Includes off-road shocks, painted front and rear bumpers, fog lamps, painted grille, 4x4 off-road decal, P235/70R16SL AT OWL tires, and argent wheels.		
20F	Optional Payload Package #2 (Splash 2WD)	51	60
	Includes 5140 lbs GVWR and 1440 lbs maximum payload.		
20P	Optional Payload Package #2 (Splash 4WD)	51	60
	Maximum payload 1500 lbs with GVWR 5060 lbs.		
20B	Optional Payload Package #2 (XL 2WD/XLT 2WD)	51	60
	Includes 4880 lbs GVWR and 1550 lbs maximum payload. REQUIRES (T80) tires. NOT AVAILABLE with (646) wheels.		
202	Optional Payload Package #2 (XL 2WD/XLT 2WD)	51	60
	Maximum payload 1660 lbs with GVWR 4740 lbs. REQUIRES T80 tires. NOT AVAILABLE with (646) wheels.		
20T	Optional Payload Package #2 (XL 4WD/XLT 4WD)	51	60
	Includes 5120 lbs GVWR and 1500 lbs maximum payload.		
20W	Optional Payload Package #2 (XL 4WD/XLT 4WD)	51	60
	Maximum payload 1500 lbs with GVWR 4980 lbs.		
903	Power Equipment Group (Splash)	336	395
	Includes color-keyed power mirrors, power windows with driver's one-touch down, and power door locks.		
903	Power Equipment Group (XLT)	455	535
	Includes power windows with driver's one-touch down and power door locks.		
543	Power Mirrors (XLT)	119	140
	REQUIRES (903) Power Equipment Group.		

RANGER — FORD

CODE	DESCRIPTION	INVOICE	MSRP
47P	Power Security Group (Splash)	569	670
	Manufacturer Discount	(233)	(275)
	Net Price	336	395
	Includes Power Equipment Group: power windows with driver's one-touch down, power door locks, and remote keyless entry.		
47P	Power Security Group (XLT)	688	810
	Manufacturer Discount	(233)	(275)
	Net Price	455	535
	Includes Power Equipment Group: power windows with driver's one-touch down, power door locks, and remote keyless entry.		
861A	Preferred Equipment Package 861A (XL Std Cab 4WD SB)	NC	NC
	Includes 3.0L V-6 engine, argent wheels, vinyl bench seat, 3.73 axle ratio, radio credit option.		
861A	Preferred Equipment Package 861A (XL Std Cab 2WD LB)	NC	NC
	Includes P205/75R14SL AS BSW SBR tires, argent wheels, vinyl bench seat, and radio credit option. REQUIRES (99U) engine.		
861A	Preferred Equipment Package 861A (XL Std Cab 2WD SB)	NC	NC
	Includes P205/75R14SL AS BSW SBR tires, argent wheels, vinyl bench seat, and radio credit option. REQUIRES (99U) engine.		
861A	Preferred Equipment Package 861A (XL Std Cab 4WD LB)	NC	NC
	Includes 3.0L V-6 engine, argent wheels, vinyl bench seat, 3.73 axle ratio, and radio credit option.		
861A	Preferred Equipment Package 861A (XL SuperCab 4WD)	NC	NC
	Includes 3.0L V-6 engine, argent wheels, vinyl bench seat, 3.73 axle ratio, and radio credit option.		
861A	Preferred Equipment Package 861A (XL SuperCab 4WD)	NC	NC
	Includes P205/75R14SL AS BSW SBR tires, argent wheels, vinyl bench seat, radio credit option, and 3.73 axle ratio. REQUIRES (99U) engine.		
864A	Preferred Equipment Package 864A (XLT Std Cab 2WD LB)	688	810
	Manufacturer Discount	(688)	(810)
	Net Price	NC	NC
	Includes XLT Group: sliding rear tinted window, tape stripe, AM/FM stereo with cassette and clock, 60/40 split cloth bench seat, floor consolette, P225/70R14SL AS OWL SBR tires, deep dish cast aluminum wheels. REQUIRES 99U or 99X. NOT AVAILABLE with G, 58K.		
864A	Preferred Equipment Package 864A (XLT Std Cab 2WD SB)	544	640
	Manufacturer Discount	(544)	(640)
	Net Price	NC	NC
	Includes 3.0L V-6 engine, P235/75R15SLAT OWL tires, cast aluminum wheels, 60/40 split cloth bench seat, floor consolette, sliding rear tinted window, AM/FM stereo with cassette and clock, tape stripe, 3.73 axle ratio. NOT AVAILABLE with (G) seats.		

FORD RANGER

CODE	DESCRIPTION	INVOICE	MSRP
864A	Preferred Equipment Package 864A (XLT Std Cab 2WD SB)	688	810
	Manufacturer Discount	(688)	(810)
	Net Price	NC	NC

Includes XLT Group: sliding rear tinted window, tape stripe, AM/FM stereo with cassette and clock, 60/40 split cloth bench seat, floor consolette, P225/70R14SL AS OWL SBR tires, and deep dish cast aluminum wheels. REQUIRES 99U or 99X. NOT AVAILABLE with G or 58K.

864A	Preferred Equipment Package 864A (XLT Std Cab 4WD LB)	544	640
	Manufacturer Discount	(544)	(640)
	Net Price	NC	NC

Includes 3.0L V-6 engine, P235/75R15SL AT OWL tires, cast aluminum wheels, 60/40 split cloth bench seat, floor consolette, sliding rear tinted window, AM/FM stereo with cassette and clock, XLT Group: tape stripe and 3.73 axle ratio. NOT AVAILABLE with (G) Seats.

864A	Preferred Equipment Package 864A (XLT SuperCab 2WD)	688	810
	Manufacturer Discount	(688)	(810)
	Net Price	NC	NC

Includes XLT Group: sliding rear tinted window, tape stripe, AM/FM stereo with cassette and clock, 60/40 split cloth bench seat; floor consolette, P225/70R14SL AS OWL SBR tires, deep dish cast aluminum wheels, 3.73 axle ratio. REQUIRES 99U or 99X. NOT AVAILABLE with G or 58K.

864A	Preferred Equipment Package 864A (XLT SuperCab 4WD)	544	640
	Manufacturer Discount	(544)	(640)
	Net Price	NC	NC

Includes 3.0L V-6 engine, P235/75R15SL AT OWL tires, cast aluminum wheels, 60/40 split cloth bench seat, floor consolette, sliding rear tinted window, AM/FM stereo with cassette and clock, XLT Group: tape stripe and 3.73 axle ratio. NOT AVAILABLE with (G) Seats.

866A	Preferred Equipment Package 866A (Splash Std Cab 2WD)	407	480
	Manufacturer Discount	(203)	(240)
	Net Price	204	240

Includes 60/40 split cloth bench seat, floor consolette, Splash Group: sliding rear tinted window, bodyside protection moldings, AM/FM stereo with CD and clock, full face chrome wheels, power mirrors, and 3.73 axle ratio. REQUIRES (99U) engine OR (99X) Engine.

866A	Preferred Equipment Package 866A (Splash Std Cab 4WD)	407	480
	Manufacturer Discount	(203)	(240)
	Net Price	204	240

Includes 3.0L V-6 engine, P235/75R15SL AT OWL tires, cast aluminum wheels, 60/40 split cloth bench seat, floor consolette, flareside box, bodyside protection moldings, power mirrors, sliding rear tinted window, 3.73 axle ratio, and AM/FM stereo with CD and clock.

RANGER — FORD

CODE	DESCRIPTION	INVOICE	MSRP
866A	Preferred Equipment Package 866A (Splash SuperCab 2WD)	407	480
	Manufacturer Discount	(203)	(240)
	Net Price	204	240

Includes AM/FM stereo with cassette and clock, 60/40 split cloth bench seat, floor consolette, Splash Group: sliding rear tinted window, bodyside protection moldings, AM/FM stereo with CD and clock, full face chrome wheels, power mirrors, 3.0L V-6 engine, and 3.73 axle ratio.

866A	Preferred Equipment Package 866A (Splash SuperCab 4WD)	407	480
	Manufacturer Discount	(203)	(240)
	Net Price	204	240

Includes 3.0L V-6 engine, P235/75R15SL AL OWL tires, cast aluminum wheels, 60/40 split cloth bench seat, floor consolette, flareside box, bodyside protection moldings, power mirrors, sliding rear tinted window, 3.73 axle ratio, and AM/FM stereo with CD and clock.

867A	Preferred Equipment Package 867A (XLT Std Cab 2WD LB)	2529	2975
	Manufacturer Discount	(1012)	(1190)
	Net Price	1517	1785

Includes XLT Group: sliding rear tinted window, tape stripe, 60/40 split cloth bench seat, floor consolette, Luxury Group: air conditioning, speed control, tilt steering wheel, remote keyless entry, Power Equipment Group: power windows with driver's one-touch down, power door locks, AM/FM stereo with CD and clock. REQUIRES (99U) engine or (99X) engine.

867A	Preferred Equipment Package 867A (XLT Std Cab 2WD SB)	2529	2975
	Manufacturer Discount	(1012)	(1190)
	Net Price	1517	1785

Includes XLT Group sliding rear tinted window tape stripe, 60/40 split cloth bench seat, floor consolette, Luxury Group: air conditioning, speed control: tilt steering wheel, remote keyless entry, Power Equipment Group: power windows with driver's one-touch down, power door locks, AM/FM stereo with CD and clock. REQUIRES (99U) engine or (99X) engine.

867A	Preferred Equipment Package 867A (XLT Std Cab 4WD LB)	2333	2745
	Manufacturer Discount	(931)	(1095)
	Net Price	1402	1650

Includes 3.0L V-6 engine, P235/75R15SL AT OWL tires, cast aluminum wheels, 60/40 split cloth bench seat, floor consolette, air conditioning, Luxury Group: remote keyless entry, Power Equipment Group: power windows with driver's one-touch down, power door locks, AM/FM stereo with CD and clock, XLT Group: sliding rear tinted window, tape stripe, 3.73 axle ratio, speed control, and tilt steering wheel. NOT AVAILABLE with (58Z) radio.

867A	Preferred Equipment Package 867A (XLT Std Cab 4WD SB)	2333	2745
	Manufacturer Discount	(931)	(1095)
	Net Price	1402	1650

Includes 3.0L V-6 engine, P235/75R15SL AT OWL tires, cast aluminum wheels, 60/40 split cloth bench seat, floor consolette, air conditioning, Luxury Group: remote keyless entry, Power Equipment Group: power windows with driver's one-touch down,

FORD RANGER

CODE	DESCRIPTION	INVOICE	MSRP

power door locks, AM/FM stereo with CD and clock, XLT Group: sliding rear tinted window, tape stripe, 3.73 axle ratio, speed control, and tilt steering wheel. NOT AVAILABLE with (58Z) radio.

Code	Description	Invoice	MSRP
867A	**Preferred Equipment Package 867A (XLT SuperCab 2WD)**	2529	2975
	Manufacturer Discount	(1012)	(1190)
	Net Price	1517	1785

Includes XLT Group: sliding rear tinted window, tape stripe, 60/40 split cloth bench seat, floor consolette, Luxury Group: air conditioning, speed control, tilt steering wheel, remote keyless entry, Power Equipment Group: power windows with driver's one-touch down, power door locks, AM/FM stereo with CD and clock, and 3.73 axle ratio. REQUIRES (99U) engine or (99X) engine. NOT AVAILABLE with (58Z) radio.

Code	Description	Invoice	MSRP
867A	**Preferred Equipment Package 867A (XLT SuperCab 4WD)**	2333	2745
	Manufacturer Discount	(931)	(1095)
	Net Price	1402	1650

Includes 3.0L V-6 engine, P235/75R15SL AT OWL tires, cast aluminum wheels, 60/40 split cloth bench seat, floor consolette, air conditioning, Luxury Group: air conditioning, speed control, tilt steering wheel, remote keyless entry, Power Equipment Group: power windows with driver's one-touch down, power door locks, AM/FM stereo with CD and clock, XLT Group: sliding rear tinted window, tape stripe, and 3.73 axle ratio. NOT AVAILABLE with (58Z) radio.

Code	Description	Invoice	MSRP
589	**Radio: AM/FM Stereo with Cassette and Clock (XL)**	273	320
	Includes 4 speakers. NOT AVAILABLE with (587) radio.		
58Z	**Radio: AM/FM Stereo with CD and Clock (Splash)**	192	225
	Includes 4 speakers. NOT AVAILABLE with (587) radio.		
58Z	**Radio: AM/FM Stereo with CD and Clock (XLT)**	81	95
	Includes 4 speakers. NOT AVAILABLE with (867A) Preferred Equipment Package 867A and (587) radio.		
587	**Radio: AM/FM Stereo with Clock (XL)**	153	180
	Includes 2 speakers.		
58K	**Radio: Premium AM/FM Dual Media (XLT/Splash)**	115	135
	Includes CD and cassette player with 80-watt rating. NOT AVAILABLE with (864A) Preferred Equipment Package 864A.		
904	**Remote Keyless Entry (XLT/Splash)**	233	275
	Includes anti-theft and 2 remote transmitters. REQUIRES 903 and 152.		
52N	**Speed Control (Splash)**	336	395
	Includes tilt steering wheel.		
52N	**Speed Control (XLT)**	336	395
	Includes tilt steering wheel.		
152	**Tachometer (XLT 2WD/Splash 2WD)**	51	60
T80	**Tires: P225/70R14SL AS OWL SBR (XL)**	204	240
	Includes P205 temporary spare. REQUIRES (642) wheels.		
T7K	**Tires: P225/70R15 AS OWL (XLT 2WD)**	47	55
	Includes full size spare tire.		
T7R	**Tires: P235/75R15SL AT OWL (XL 4WD/XLT 4WD)**	59	70
	Includes full-size spare. REQUIRES (642) wheels or (20W) Optional Payload Package #2.		

RANGER / WINDSTAR — FORD

CODE	DESCRIPTION	INVOICE	MSRP
T7S	Tires: P265/75R15SL AT OWL (XLT 4WD)	93	110
	Includes P235 temporary spare.		
646	Wheels: Full Face Chrome (XLT)	34	40
	NOT AVAILABLE with (202) Optional Payload Package #2 or (173) flareside box.		
642	Wheels: Full Face Steel (XL 2WD)	85	100
64G	Wheels: Full Face Steel (XL 4WD)	85	100
43H	Windows: Pivoting Quarter (XLT SuperCab 2WD/Splash SuperCab 2WD)	51	60
	Includes privacy glass.		
472	XLT Appearance Package (XLT 2WD)	362	425
	Manufacturer Discount	(170)	(200)
	Net Price	192	225
	Includes deluxe two-tone paint, full face chrome wheels, P225/70R15 AS OWL tires, AM/FM stereo with CD and clock.		
472	XLT Appearance Package (XLT 4WD)	438	515
	Manufacturer Discount	(213)	(250)
	Net Price	225	265
	Includes deluxe two-tone paint, AM/FM stereo with CD and clock, and fog lamps.		

1998 WINDSTAR

1998 Ford Windstar LX

What's New?

Ford widens the driver's door as a stop-gap measure until the 1999 Windstar arrives with a fourth door. Subtle styling revisions and a new Limited model round out the changes for 1998.

FORD WINDSTAR

Review

Until mid-1994, nobody had seriously challenged Chrysler's domination of minivan sales. All previous attempts by domestic and imported manufacturers couldn't match the Chrysler standard for user-friendliness. They were either underpowered, too high off the ground, or the wrong size. When Windstars rolled into Ford showrooms, Chrysler finally had been bested at its own game.

For a while, at least. The Windstar's superiority proved to be short-lived. The totally redesigned Chrysler minivans are best-in-class in terms of style and convenience features; the main reasons people buy minivans in the first place. Then, General Motors arrived on the scene with totally redesigned minivans. Gone were the underpowered "dustbusters", the new models are sleek, functional, and attractively priced The Windstar is still a good minivan, but the stiff competition in this segment is forcing Ford to offer sweet lease deals and big incentives.

Not everyone favors the Windstar's styling, but the interior is an ergonomic delight. With room for seven, dual airbags, and a commodious cargo area, the Windstar keeps passengers comfortable. Controls and displays are housed in an attractively swept dashboard, lending a well-crafted tone. The radio is crammed with buttons and tiny lettering; it's time for the new family of Ford radios, complete with big buttons and a volume knob, to debut in this van. Climate controls are mounted low, but are easy to modulate without glancing from the road. An optional center console adds generous amounts of much-needed storage, but cuts access to the rear seats. There's little to complain about, and quite a lot to like. Construction quality is fine and the interior is spacious and attractive. A single body size and style is offered, in cargo van, Base, GL or luxury LX guise, with four-wheel anti-lock brakes.

The Windstar receives interesting changes for 1998. New models show stop-gap features designed to appease potential buyers who can't live without a left-side passenger door. The most notable are the oversize king-door and tip forward driver's seat that are intended to allow passenger access from the left side. To people who feel that it's important to have a left side passenger entry, this is a poor substitute. Fortunately for Ford, the Windstar has other features, which make up for this missing portal. Namely its awesome horsepower available with the optional 3.8-liter engine. Cranking out 200 horsepower, the 3.8-liter equipped Windstar is the fastest minivan on the market.

If you're searching for a minivan with good towing ability, fast acceleration, gobs of interior space and comfortable seating for seven, the Windstar is definitely worth a look. Especially because your local Ford dealer should be offering deep discounts to keep them competitive with the Caravan and new Chevy Venture.

Safety Data

Driver Airbag: *Standard*
Side Airbag: *Not Available*
4-Wheel ABS: *Standard*
Driver Crash Test Grade: *Excellent*
Passenger Crash Test Grade: *Excellent*

Passenger Airbag: *Standard*
Meets 1997 Car Side Impact Standards: *Yes*
Traction Control: *N/A (3.0L); Opt. (GL/LX/Limited)*
Insurance Cost: *Not Available*
Integrated Child Seat(s): *Optional*

Standard Equipment

WINDSTAR 3.0L: 3.0-liter V-6 engine, 4-speed automatic transmission with overdrive, P205/70R15 tires, power rack and pinion steering, gas pressurized shock absorbers, 20-gallon fuel tank, power front disc/rear drum 4-wheel anti-lock brakes, stainless steel antenna, body-color 5-mph bumpers, limo-style front Family Entry System (essentially a fancy name for a big driver's door), tethered fuel cap, solar-tinted glass, body-color grille, dual black foldaway exterior mirrors, full plastic sport wheelcovers, intermittent rear window wiper/washer, interval windshield wipers, dual front airbags, low oil level warning chime, headlights-on warning chime, turn signal on warning chime, second row auxiliary power point, AM/FM stereo with clock and 4 speakers,

WINDSTAR — FORD

CODE	DESCRIPTION	INVOICE	MSRP

liftgate courtesy light switch, 5 cupholders, front door window demisters, dual note horn, front and rear dome lights with automatic dim delay, child-proof sliding side door locks, day/night rearview mirror, 7-passenger seating, highback cloth front bucket seats with integral headrests, dual covered vanity mirrors, rear quarter flip-out glass.

GL (in addition to or instead of 3.0L equipment): Reclining front seats, reclining 2nd row seat, fore-aft adjustment for 3rd row seat.

LX (in addition to or instead of GL equipment): 3.8-liter V-6 engine, P215/70R15 tires, 25-gallon fuel tank, power exterior mirrors, color-keyed bodyside molding, reflective applique for tailgate, 15-inch cast aluminum wheels, power front windows with one-touch down feature and retained accessory power, air conditioning, tachometer, front map lights, glovebox light, footwell lighting, power door locks with backlighting, cargo area lock switch, AM/FM stereo with cassette player, digital clock, and 4 speakers; low-back cloth bucket seats with adjustable headrests, power driver's seat, power lumbar support for driver, seatback map pockets, tip/slide driver's seat, cruise control, tilt leather-wrapped steering wheel, center storage bin, cargo area storage bin, illuminated vanity mirrors, driver's auxiliary sunshade, power rear quarter flip-out glass.

LIMITED (in addition to or instead of LX equipment): P225/60R16 tires, front fog lights, chrome grille surround, color-keyed exterior mirrors, remote keyless entry, polished aluminum wheels, high capacity air conditioning, auxiliary heater, overhead console (includes rear seat audio controls, compass, external temperature display, conversation mirror, coin holder sunglasses holder, and garage door opener), rear window defroster, automatic on/off headlights, electrochromic rearview mirror, premium sound system, quad lowback leather bucket seats, power lumbar support for front passenger.

Base Prices

Code	Description	Invoice	MSRP
A51	3.0L	17977	19380
A51	GL	18980	20960
A51	LX	23316	26205
A51	Limited	26499	29505
	Destination Charge:	580	580

Accessories

Code	Description	Invoice	MSRP
994	3.8-liter Engine (GL)	583	685
	INCLUDED in Option Packages.		
572	Air Conditioning (3.0L/GL)	727	855
	INCLUDED in Option Packages.		
574	Air Conditioning — High Capacity (GL/LX)	404	475
	Includes auxiliary heater; REQUIRES Light Group and Power Convenience Group; INCLUDED in GL Option Package 473A and LX Option Package 477A.		
965	Bodyside Moldings (GL)	68	80
	INCLUDED in Option Packages.		
422	California Emissions	85	100
64D	Cast Aluminum Wheels (GL/LX)	352	415
	INCLUDED in LX Option Package		
51A	Conventional Spare Tire	93	110
	INCLUDED in Trailer Towing Package		

FORD WINDSTAR

CODE	DESCRIPTION	INVOICE	MSRP
52N	Cruise Control and Tilt Steering Wheel (3.0L/GL)	319	375
	INCLUDED in GL Option Packages.		
41H	Engine Block Heater	30	35
414	Floor Console (GL/LX/Limited)	132	155
	Includes cupholder, auxiliary power point, covered storage bin; REQUIRES high-capacity air conditioning and Power Convenience Group.		
167	Floor Mats	77	90
	INCLUDED in LX and Limited Option Packages		
652	Fuel Tank — 25 gallon (GL)	26	30
428	High Altitude Emissions	NC	NC
87C	Integrated Child Seats (3.0L)	242	285
87C	Integrated Child Seats (GL/LX)	191	225
	With 477A (LX)	(433)	(510)
94H	Interior Convenience Group (GL)	43	50
	Includes covered rear storage bin, covered center dashboard bin, and cargo net.		
916	JBL Sound System (Limited)	433	510
916	JBL Sound System (LX)	565	665
	REQUIRES a Premium Stereo		
2	Leather Seat Trim (LX)	735	865
	REQUIRES quad bucket seats		
593	Light Group (3.0L/GL)	63	75
	Includes front map light, glovebox light, footwell lighting; INCLUDED in GL Option Package 473A		
60F	Light Group — Premium (LX)	251	295
	Includes front fog lights, automatic on/off headlights, and electrochromic rearview mirror.		
68S	Load Leveling Air Suspension (LX/Limited)	247	290
615	Luggage Rack (GL/LX/Limited)	149	175
	INCLUDED in GL Option Package 473A, LX Option Package 477A, and Limited Option Package 479A.		
470A	Option Package 470A (3.0L)	1305	1535
	Manufacturer Discount	(446)	(525)
	Net Price	859	1010
	Includes air conditioning and power convenience group (power front windows with one-touch down feature and retained accessory power, power rear quarter flip-out glass)		
472A	Option Package 472A (GL)	2108	2480
	Manufacturer Discount	(578)	(680)
	Net Price	1530	1800
	Includes tip/slide driver's seat, AM/FM stereo with cassette player, 4 speakers, and digital clock; air conditioning, rear window defroster, power convenience group (power windows with one-touch down feature and retained accessory power, power door locks, power exterior mirrors, power rear quarter vent windows), bodyside moldings, cruise control, and tilt steering.		

WINDSTAR — FORD

CODE	DESCRIPTION	INVOICE	MSRP
473A	Option Package 473A (GL)	3745	4405
	Manufacturer Discount	(1131)	(1330)
	Net Price	2614	3075

Includes tip/slide driver's seat, AM/FM stereo with cassette player, 4 speakers, and digital clock; high capacity air conditioning, auxiliary heater, rear window defroster, power convenience group (power windows with one-touch down feature and retained accessory power, power door locks, power exterior mirrors, power rear quarter vent windows), bodyside moldings, cruise control, tilt steering wheel, 3.8-liter V-6 engine, overhead console (includes rear audio controls, conversation mirror, coin holder, sunglasses holder, garage door opener), privacy glass, light group (includes front map lights, glovebox light, footwell lights), and black luggage rack.

CODE	DESCRIPTION	INVOICE	MSRP
477A	Option Package 477A (LX)	2161	2545
	Manufacturer Discount	(821)	(965)
	Net Price	1340	1580

Includes quad low-back bucket seats, power lumbar support for front passenger, rear window defroster, high capacity air conditioning, auxiliary heater, overhead console (includes rear audio controls, conversation mirror, coin holder, sunglasses holder, garage door opener, compass, external temperature display), privacy glass, black luggage rack, floor mats, two-tone paint, and remote keyless entry.

CODE	DESCRIPTION	INVOICE	MSRP
479A	Option Package 479A (Limited)	578	680
	Manufacturer Discount	(578)	(680)
	Net Price	NC	NC

Includes privacy glass, black luggage rack, and floor mats.

CODE	DESCRIPTION	INVOICE	MSRP
41N	Overhead Console (GL)	85	100

Includes garage door opener, conversation mirror, sunglasses storage, coin holder, rear audio controls and headphone jacks. REQUIRES Light Group

CODE	DESCRIPTION	INVOICE	MSRP
41N	Overhead Console (LX)	153	180

Includes garage door opener, conversation mirror, sunglasses storage, coin holder, compass, external temperature display, rear audio controls and headphone jacks. REQUIRES Light Group

CODE	DESCRIPTION	INVOICE	MSRP
903	Power Convenience Group (3.0L/GL)	578	680

Includes power windows with one-touch down feature and retained accessory power, power door locks, power exterior mirrors, and power quarter vent windows; INCLUDED in Option Packages

CODE	DESCRIPTION	INVOICE	MSRP
924	Privacy Glass (GL/LX/Limited)	325	415

INCLUDED in GL Option Package 473A, LX Option Package 477A, and Limited Option Package 479A.

CODE	DESCRIPTION	INVOICE	MSRP
21Q	Quad Bucket Seats (GL)	607	715

REQUIRES Option Package 473A.

CODE	DESCRIPTION	INVOICE	MSRP
21K	Quad Bucket Seats (LX)	532	625

INCLUDED in Option Package.

CODE	DESCRIPTION	INVOICE	MSRP
588	Radio: Premium AM/FM Stereo with cassette (LX)	132	155

AM/FM stereo with cassette player, digital clock, and 4 premium speakers

FORD WINDSTAR

CODE	DESCRIPTION	INVOICE	MSRP
582	Radio: Premium AM/FM Stereo with CD player (GL/LX)	420	495
	With 472A (GL)	276	325
	With 473A (GL)	276	325
	With 477A (LX)	276	325
	AM/FM stereo with CD player, digital clock, and 4 premium speakers; REQUIRES Light Group, cruise control, and tilt steering wheel.		
589	Radio: AM/FM Stereo with cassette (3.0L/GL)	144	170
	AM/FM stereo with cassette player, 4 speakers, and digital clock; INCLUDED in GL Option Packages		
57Q	Rear Window Defroster (3.0L/GL/LX)	144	170
	INCLUDED in GL and LX Option Packages		
948	Remote Keyless Entry (GL/LX)	149	175
	REQUIRES Power Convenience Group; INCLUDED in LX Option Package.		
21D	Seat Bed (GL)	522	615
151	Security Group (LX/Limited)	171	200
	Includes trainable transmitter capable of handling up to 3 different programs, perimeter anti-theft system; REQUIRES remote keyless entry on LX models		
582	Stereo — Premium with CD player (Limited)	144	170
	AM/FM stereo with CD player, digital clock, and 4 premium speakers		
87S	Tip/slide Driver's Seat (3.0L/GL)	128	150
	INCLUDED in GL Option Packages		
T75	Tires — Self-sealing (GL/LX)	208	245
	P215/70R15 all-season tires. REQUIRES 64D cast aluminum wheels.		
67A	Traction Control (GL/LX/Limited)	336	395
	All-speed system; REQUIRES 3.8-liter Engine, Cruise Control, and Tilt Steerig Column on GL models		
539	Trailer Towing Package (GL/LX)	370	435
	With 473A (GL)	347	410
	With 477A (LX)	347	410
	Includes heavy-duty battery, engine oil cooler, power steering cooler, class II wiring harness, conventional spare tire, auxiliary transmission oil cooler. REQUIRES 3.8-liter engine on GL models		
539	Trailer Towing Package (Limited)	347	410
	Includes heavy-duty battery, engine oil cooler, power steering cooler, class II wiring harness, conventional spare tire, and auxiliary transmission oil cooler.		
95M	Two-tone Paint (LX)	200	235
	INCLUDED in Option Package.		
95M	Two-tone Paint Delete (LX)	(115)	(135)
	REQUIRES Option Package.		

JIMMY — GMC

| CODE | DESCRIPTION | INVOICE | MSRP |

1998 JIMMY

1998 GMC Jimmy SLT 4-Door

What's New?

A revised interior contains dual second-generation airbags, improved climate controls, and available premium sound systems. Outside, the front bumper, grille, and headlights are new. Side cladding is restyled, and SLT models have new alloy wheels. Fresh colors inside and out sum up the changes.

Review

GMC has the unenviable job of marketing the Jimmy as a luxury SUV now that the Pontiac-GMC merger is complete and crazed brand managers think GMC products need to be perceived as upscale from Chevrolet. Essentially identical to the Blazer and Oldsmobile Bravada, with no distinguishing characteristics to set it apart from either of these models, Jimmy marketers have their work cut out for them. Tightly sandwiched between the Blazer and Bravada, there is only one way to convince buyers that the Jimmy is the one to buy - slick advertising.

Despite a minor redesign for 1998, four-door styling is on the staid side, but two-doors are fastback-profiled with a distinctive side-window treatment. A Jimmy is comfortable, easy to handle, and fun to drive. Upgraded versions can be luxuriously equipped, but each rugged rendition looks and feels tough - a little more truck-like than the similar Blazer. An under-the-floor spare tire on four-doors increases cargo space. Headroom is immense, elbow space excellent. There's room for two in back; maybe three if you enjoy hearing comfort complaints while you drive, but the short seat feels hard and there's no room under front seats for feet. Basically, the back seat should be reserved for kiddies.

Though exceptionally sure-footed most of the time, a Jimmy can feel momentarily unstable and top-heavy in a sharp maneuver - but only if you forget what you're driving. On snowy pavement, you almost have to try to make a four-wheel-drive Jimmy skid. Whether maintaining traction while accelerating, or trying to recapture grip through a turn, 4WD delivers a strong feeling of confidence

All-wheel drive, formerly an option, is no longer available on the Jimmy. Four-wheel anti-lock braking helps haul the sport-ute to a prompt halt, and all models gain four-wheel discs for 1998. Drivers and passengers face second generation de-powered airbags. Acceleration is strong

GMC JIMMY

| CODE | DESCRIPTION | INVOICE | MSRP |

from the standard 4300 Vortec V6 engine, and the smooth four-speed automatic suffers little lag when downshifting. A five-speed manual transmission is available on two-door models.

Other news for the new year includes a revised interior with a softer appearance and better ergonomics. Body side cladding has been restyled, and the top-of-the-line SLT 4WD is equipped with some God-awful alloy wheels. The back bumper gets a center step cutout to improve access to the cargo area and roof rack. New audio systems debut, and buyers of the SLT 4WD can opt for heated front seats. Something called a Truck Body Computer controls the PassLock theft deterrent system, automatic headlights, battery rundown protection, retained accessory power, and lockout prevention features. Exterior mirrors can be ordered with a defrost mode for snowy days and nights.

The hardest duty in Jimmy-shopping is deciding what to include. Suspension choices stretch from smooth to off-road. Expect some bounce and roll from the Luxury Ride suspension, but it's compliant and responds quickly. Sport (SLS), comfort (SLE) and touring (SLT) decor packages are available. Then there's the huge option list to contend with. Overdo it, and the toll can zip skyward in a hurry, though this GMC represents slightly better value than Oldsmobile's all-wheel drive Bravada.

Safety Data

Driver Airbag: *Standard*
Side Airbag: *Not Available*
Traction Control: *Not Available*
Driver Crash Test Grade: *Not Available*

Passenger Airbag: *Standard*
4-Wheel ABS: *Standard*
Integrated Child Seat(s): *Not Available*
Passenger Crash Test Grade: *Not Available*

Standard Equipment

2WD 2-DOOR: 4.3L V-6 OHV SMPI 12-valve engine; 4-speed electronic overdrive automatic transmission with lock-up; 525-amp battery; engine oil cooler; 100-amp alternator; transmission oil cooler; rear wheel drive, 3.08 axle ratio; stainless steel exhaust; front independent suspension with anti-roll bar, front coil springs, front shocks, rear suspension with anti-roll bar, rear leaf springs, rear shocks; power re-circulating ball steering; 4-wheel disc brakes with 4-wheel anti-lock braking system; 19 gal capacity fuel tank; front license plate bracket; tailgate rear cargo door; trailer harness; front and rear body-colored bumpers, rear step bumper; monotone paint; aero-composite halogen headlamps with daytime running lights; additional exterior lights include center high mounted stop light, underhood light; driver and passenger manual black folding outside mirrors; front and rear 15" x 7" painted steel wheels with hub wheel covers and trim rings; P205/75SR15 BSW AS front and rear tires; inside mounted compact steel spare wheel; air conditioning with climate control, rear heat ducts; AM/FM stereo with clock, seek-scan, 4 speakers and fixed antenna; 1 power accessory outlet; analog instrumentation display includes tachometer gauge, oil pressure gauge, water temp gauge, volt gauge, trip odometer; warning indicators include battery, lights on, key in ignition; dual airbags; ignition disable; deep tinted windows, vented rear windows, fixed 1/4 vent windows; variable intermittent front windshield wipers, flip-up rear window; front bucket seats with tilt adjustable headrests, center armrest with storage, driver seat includes 4-way direction control with lumbar support, passenger seat includes 4-way direction control with lumbar support and easy entry feature; cloth seats, full cloth headliner, full carpet floor covering with carpeted floor mats; interior lights include dome light; passenger side vanity mirror; day-night rearview mirror; full floor console, glove box with light, front and rear cupholders, instrument panel bin, dashboard storage, driver and passenger door bins; carpeted cargo floor, cargo tie downs, cargo light; black grille, black side window moldings, black front windshield molding, black rear window molding, black door handles.

4WD 2-DOOR: (in addition to or instead of 2WD 2-DOOR equipment): Part-time 4 wheel drive, auto locking hub control with electronic shift; front torsion suspension with front torsion bar; tow hooks.

JIMMY

| CODE | DESCRIPTION | INVOICE | MSRP |

2WD 4-DOOR (in addition to or instead of 2WD 2-DOOR equipment): 18 gal capacity fuel tank; underbody mounted spare wheel; child safety rear door locks; manual rear windows; 60-40 split-bench front seat; rear height adjustable seatbelts; 2 seat back storage pockets.

4WD 4-DOOR (in addition to or instead of 2WD 4-DOOR equipment): Part-time 4 wheel drive, auto locking hub control with electronic shift; front torsion suspension with front torsion bar; tow hooks.

Base Prices

Code	Description	Invoice	MSRP
TS10516-R9S	2WD 2-door	19716	21786
TS10506-R9S	2WD 4-door	21600	23867
TT10516-R9S	4WD 2-door	21515	23774
TT10506-R9S	4WD 4-door	23399	25855
	Destination Charge:	515	515

Accessories

Code	Description	Invoice	MSRP
GU6	3.42 Axle Ratio	NC	NC
GT4	3.73 Axle Ratio (4WD)	NC	NC
	REQUIRES G80 and Z85 or ZM6. NOT AVAILABLE with M50, Z83.		
M50	5-Speed Manual Transmission (2-door)	(765)	(890)
	REQUIRES GU6 and G80 and Z85. NOT AVAILABLE with GT4.		
AG1	6-Way Power Driver's Seat	335	390
	Includes remote keyless entry. REQUIRES 1SB or 1SD.		
ANL	Air Deflector & Fog Lamps (2WD)	99	115
	REQUIRES 1SB or 1SD or 1SE.		
YF5	California Emissions	146	170
	Automatically added to vehicles shipped to and/or sold to retailers in California. Out-of-state retailers must order on vehicles to be registered or leased in California. NOT AVAILABLE with (NG1) MA/NY/CT Emissions.		
RYJ	Cargo Cover (4WD 2-door)	59	69
	REQUIRES (P16) spare tire carrier. NOT AVAILABLE with (1SA) Marketing Option Package 1SA.		
AN3	Cloth Front Bucket Seats (4-door)	(516)	(600)
	REQUIRES (1SF) Marketing Option Package 1SF. Replaces leather with cloth.		
V10	Cold Climate Package	77	89
	Includes HD battery.		
ZQ3	Convenience Group	340	395
	Includes tilt steering, speed control. REQUIRES 1SA or 1SC.		
ZY2	Conventional Two-Tone Paint (4-door)	148	172
	NOT AVAILABLE with (1SC) Marketing Option Package 1SC.		
ZQ6	Driver's Convenience (2-door)	460	535
	Includes power windows, power door locks, power mirrors. REQUIRES 1SA.		
ZQ6	Driver's Convenience (4-door)	611	710
	Includes power windows, power door locks, power mirrors. REQUIRES 1SC.		
DK2	Electric Defogging Outside Mirror	99	115
	Includes light sensitive rearview mirror. REQUIRES 1SB or 1SD.		

GMC JIMMY

CODE	DESCRIPTION	INVOICE	MSRP
CF5	**Electric Glass Sunroof**	598	695
	Includes express open feature and wind deflector. REQUIRES (DK6) overhead console.		
Z85	**Euro Ride Suspension Package**	169	197
	Includes urethane jounce bumpers front and rear, Bilstein shock absorbers, HD springs. REQUIRES 1SA or 1SC.		
UA1	**HD Battery**	48	56
KA1	**Heated Seats (4-door)**	194	225
	REQUIRES (1SF) Marketing Option Package 1SF.		
UG1	**Homelink Transmitter**	112	130
	3-channel capability with trip computer. REQUIRES (DK6) overhead console.		
G80	**Locking Differential**	217	252
	REQUIRES GU6 or GT4.		
V54	**Luggage Carrier**	108	126
	Roof mounted and painted black. REQUIRES 1SA or 1SC.		
ZW7	**Luxury Ride Suspension Package (4-door)**	169	197
	Includes urethane jounce bumpers, Bilstein shock absorbers. REQUIRES 1SC.		
NG1	**MA/NY/CT Emissions**	146	170
	Automatically added to vehicles shipped to and/or sold to retailers in Massachusetts/New York/Connecticut. Out-of-state retailers must order on vehicles to be registered or leased in Massachusetts/New York/Connecticut. NOT AVAILABLE with (YF5) California Emissions.		
1SA	**Marketing Option Package 1SA (2-door)**	NC	NC
	Includes SL decor package.		
1SB	**Marketing Option Package 1SB (2-door)**	2387	2776
	Manufacturer Discount	(1204)	(1400)
	Net Price	1183	1376
	Includes SLS Sport decor: cargo net, cloth covered door panels, dual front reading lamps, 2-dash-mounted power outlets, leather-wrapped steering wheel, illuminated visor vanity mirrors, visor extensions, rear window defogger, rear window wiper/washer, body-color grille, lower body stripe, aluminum wheels, deep-tinted glass; euro-ride suspension package, P235/70R15 AS BSW tires, AM/FM stereo with cassette, power windows, power door locks, power exterior mirrors, tilt steering wheel, cruise control, luggage rack.		
1SC	**Marketing Option Package 1SC (4-door)**	NC	NC
	Includes SL decor package.		
1SD	**Marketing Option Package 1SD (4-door)**	2275	2645
	Manufacturer Discount	(1204)	(1400)
	Net Price	1071	1245
	Includes SLS Sport decor: floor shift console, cargo compartment shade, cargo net, cloth covered door panels, dual front reading lamps, 2-dash-mounted power outlets, leather-wrapped steering wheel, illuminated visor vanity mirrors, visor extensions, rear window defogger, rear window wiper/washer, body-color grille, lower body stripe, aluminum wheels, deep tinted glass; rear liftgate, luxury ride suspension package, P235/70R15 AS BSW tires, AM/FM stereo with cassette, power windows, power door locks, power exterior mirrors, tilt steering wheel, cruise control, luggage rack.		

JIMMY — GMC

CODE	DESCRIPTION	INVOICE	MSRP
1SE	Marketing Option Package 1SE (4-door)	3164	3679
	Manufacturer Discount	(1204)	(1400)
	Net Price	1960	2279

Includes SLE Comfort decor floor shift console, cargo compartment shade, cargo net, cloth covered door panels, 2-dash-mounted power outlets, leather-wrapped steering wheel, illuminated visor vanity mirrors, visor extensions, rear window defogger, rear window wiper/washer, body-color grille with chrome trim, body-color bodyside moldings, lower body stripe, aluminum wheels, deep tinted glass, remote keyless entry, rear liftgate, luxury ride suspension package, P235/70R15 AS BSW tires, power windows, power door locks, power defogging exterior mirrors, tilt steering wheel, cruise control, luggage rack; AM/FM stereo with cassette, automatic tone control, speed sensitive volume control, and 6 speakers; overhead console: reading lamps, outside temperature gauge, compass, storage for sunglasses and garage door opener; 6-way power driver's seat.

1SF	Marketing Option Package 1SF (4-door)	4194	4877
	Manufacturer Discount	(1204)	(1400)
	Net Price	2990	3477

Includes SLT Touring decor floor shift console, cargo compartment shade, cargo net, simulated leather covered door panels, 2-dash-mounted power outlets, leather-wrapped steering wheel, illuminated visor vanity mirrors, visor extensions, rear window defogger, rear window wiper/washer, body-color grille with chrome trim, body-color bodyside moldings, lower body stripe, aluminum wheels, deep tinted glass, remote keyless entry, rear liftgate, luxury ride suspension package, P235/70R15 AS BSW tires, power windows, power door locks, power exterior defogging mirrors, tilt steering wheel, cruise control, electrochromic rearview mirror, leather bucket seats with 2-way power lumbar supports, 4-way adjustable front headrests, power driver's recliner, luggage rack; AM/FM stereo with cassette, automatic tone control, speed sensitive volume control, and 6 speakers; overhead console: reading lamps, outside temperature gauge, compass, storage for sunglasses and garage door opener; 6-way power driver's seat; fog lamps on 2WD models.

ZM6	Off-Road Suspension Package (4WD 2-door)	210	244

Includes urethane jounce bumpers front and rear, larger body mounts, upsized torsion bars, front and rear stabilizer bars, Bilstein shock absorbers. NOT AVAILABLE with Z83.

DK6	Overhead Console	126	147

Includes storage for eye glasses and garage door opener, reading lamps, compass/temperature display, electric defogging outside mirror. REQUIRES 1SB or 1SD.

UL5	Radio Delete (2-door)	(194)	(226)

NOT AVAILABLE with UM6, UL0, UP0, UN0, 1SB.

UM6	Radio: AM/FM Stereo with Cassette	105	122

Includes digital clock. NOT AVAILABLE with (UL5) radio, 1SB, 1SD.

UL0	Radio: AM/FM Stereo with Cassette	69	80

Includes digital clock, theft lock and speed compensated volume. REQUIRES 1SB or 1SD.

UN0	Radio: AM/FM Stereo with CD	155	180

Includes automatic tone control, digital clock, theft lock and 6 speakers. REQUIRES 1SB or 1SD.

GMC JIMMY

CODE	DESCRIPTION	INVOICE	MSRP
UN0	Radio: AM/FM Stereo with CD (4-door)	86	100
	Includes automatic tone control, digital clock, theft lock and 6 speakers. REQUIRES 1SE or 1SF.		
UP0	Radio: AM/FM Stereo with CD & Cassette (2-door)	241	280
	NOT AVAILABLE with 1SA, UL5, UL0, UN0.		
ZM8	Rear Window Convenience Package	277	322
	Includes electric gate release, rear window defogger and wiper/washer. REQUIRES 1SA or 1SB or 1SC.		
ZM5	Shield Package (4WD)	108	126
	Includes transfer case shield, front differential skid plates, steering linkage and fuel tank shields.		
Z83	Smooth Ride Suspension Package (2-door)	NC	NC
	Includes front and rear twin tube gas shocks and urethane jounce bumpers, front and rear stabilizer bars, rear springs. REQUIRES (1SA) Marketing Option Package 1SA. NOT AVAILABLE with (GT4) 3.73 axle ratio.		
Z83	Smooth Ride Suspension Package (2-door)	(71)	(83)
	Includes front and rear twin tube gas shocks and urethane jounce bumpers, front and rear stabilizer bars, rear springs. NOT AVAILABLE with (1SA) Marketing Option Package 1SA, (GT4) 3.73 axle ratio.		
ZQ1	Smooth Ride Suspension Package (4-door)	NC	NC
	Includes urethane jounce bumpers and twin tube gas shocks. REQUIRES (1SC) Marketing Option Package 1SC.		
ZQ1	Smooth Ride Suspension Package (4-door)	(71)	(83)
	Includes urethane jounce bumpers and twin tube gas shocks. REQUIRES 1SD or 1SE or 1SF.		
P16	Spare Tire & Wheel Carrier (4WD 2-door)	137	159
	Includes gray cover with GMC lettering. Tailgate mounted.		
—	Spare Tire: Full-size	64	75
QCE	Tires: P205/75R15 AS BSW	NC	NC
	REQUIRES 1SA or 1SC.		
QCA	Tires: P205/75R15 AS WOL (2WD)	104	121
	REQUIRES 1SA or 1SC.		
QBF	Tires: P235/70R15 AS BSW	165	192
	REQUIRES 1SA or 1SC.		
QBG	Tires: P235/70R15 AS WOL SBR	280	325
	REQUIRES 1SA or 1SC.		
QBG	Tires: P235/70R15 AS WOL SBR	114	133
	NOT AVAILABLE with 1SA, 1SC.		
QEB	Tires: P235/75R15 AT WOL (4WD)	288	335
	REQUIRES 1SA and P16 on 2-door models; 1SC on 4-door models.		
QEB	Tires: P235/75R15 AT WOL	123	143
	REQUIRES P16 on 2-door models. NOT AVAILABLE with 1SA, 1SC.		
Z82	Trailering Equipment	181	210
	Includes 8-wire harness (7-wire with CHMSL wire), trailering hitch platform and heavy duty flasher.		
N60	Wheels: Aluminum (2WD)	241	280
	REQUIRES 1SA or 1SC.		

JIMMY / SAFARI — GMC

CODE	DESCRIPTION	INVOICE	MSRP
N90	Wheels: Aluminum (4WD)	241	280
	REQUIRES 1SA or 1SC.		
PF2	Wheels: Aluminum (4WD 4-door)	NC	NC
	REQUIRES (1SF) Marketing Option Package 1SF.		

1998 SAFARI

1998 GMC Safari

What's New?

New colors, a theft deterrent system, and automatic transmission refinements are all the changes to the Safari. This van is one of the few GM models that retains full-power airbags for 1998.

Review

Choosing between a Chevrolet Astro and a GMC Safari is more a matter of image than necessity. Do you want to see Chevrolet's badge every time you approach? Or would it be viscerally satisfying to face those bold "GMC" block letters, with their implication, as brand managers hope, of upscale luxury?

Tangible differences between the two are modest—a fact that's true of most Chevrolet and GMC cousins. Once you've decided that a rear-drive (or all-wheel-drive) General Motors mid-size van is the rational choice, you'll likely be satisfied with either one.

Because of their traditional-type full-frame construction and rear-drive layout, Safaris are most adept at heavy hauling and burly trailer towing. Not everyone will relish the truck-like ride over harsh surfaces, but it's not bad at all when the highway smoothes out. Don't expect top-notch fuel mileage, though.

Dual airbags are housed in an artfully styled dashboard, and anti-lock brakes are standard. For added safety and visibility, daytime running lights blaze the trail. Integrated child safety seats are available for the center bench seat, and the sliding door has a child safety lock. Rear seat heat ducts direct warm air to freezing rear passengers. For 1998, a PassLock theft deterrent system has been added to the Safari.

GMC SAFARI

One slick feature sure to be appreciated by the parents of teenagers is the middle radio option. The driver and front passenger can listen to Casey Kasem up front, or nothing at all, while Junior blasts the local alternative music station into his eardrums via a set of headphone jacks that plugs into a separate radio unit in the center row. This option alone is worth the savings in family therapy, don't you think?

GM's 4300 Vortec V6 is standard, sending 190 horsepower to an electronically controlled four-speed automatic transmission. Long-life engine coolant and 100,000 mile spark plugs help keep maintenance costs to a minimum. This year brings transmission refinements that result in improved fuel economy, better shift quality, and increased reliability.

Safaris come in three trim levels. The FE2 touring suspension option has stiffer shocks, a rear stabilizer bar, and grabby Goodyear rubber for a firmer, controlled ride. Eight-passenger seating is standard in Safaris with SLE or SLT trim, and available in the base SLX rendition. Several new colors are available for 1997.

Whether rear-drive or running full-time all-wheel drive, Safaris serve the muscular tasks that a front-drive minivan just cannot handle—yet convey a family in a fashion that won't produce pangs of pain.

Safety Data

Driver Airbag: *Standard*
Side Airbag: *Not Available*
Traction Control: *Not Available*

Driver Crash Test Grade: *Average*

Passenger Airbag: *Standard*
4-Wheel ABS: *Standard*
Integrated Child Seat(s): *Opt. (Pass. Van); N/A (Cargo Van)*

Passenger Crash Test Grade: *Average*

Standard Equipment

SAFARI CARGO VAN: 4.3-liter Vortec V-6 engine, 4-speed automatic transmission, speed-sensitive power steering, hydraulic power front disc/rear drum anti-lock brakes, 15" x 6" styled steel wheels, P215/75R15 tires, dual front airbags, front air conditioning, side-impact door beams (do not meet 1999 truck standards), trip odometer, Scotchgard fabric protectant, vinyl reclining bucket seats, AM/FM stereo with seek/scan and digital clock, vinyl sunvisors with map bands, headlights-on warning buzzer, intermittent variable wipers, daytime running lights, dual black exterior foldaway mirrors, adjustable 3-point front seatbelts, brake/transmission shift interlock system, tachometer, PassLock theft deterrent system.

PASSENGER VAN (in addition to or instead of CARGO VAN equipment): Cloth and carpet door panel trim, cloth headliner, delayed entry interior lighting, vinyl 3-passenger center bench seat, left rear quarter storage compartment, cloth sunvisors with extensions, swing out windows, black center caps for wheel, rear door child safety locks.

Base Prices

CODE	DESCRIPTION	INVOICE	MSRP
TM11005	Cargo Van SL	17561	19404
TL11005	Cargo Van SL AWD	19733	21804
TM11006	Passenger Van	18225	20138
TL11006	Passenger Van AWD	20306	22438
	Destination Charge:	585	585

SAFARI — GMC

CODE	DESCRIPTION	INVOICE	MSRP

Accessories

CODE	DESCRIPTION	INVOICE	MSRP
YG6	Air Conditioning Not Desired (Cargo)	(727)	(845)
B74	Bodyside Moldings	104	121
	NOT AVAILABLE with 1SB on Passenger Van.		
YF5	California Emissions	146	170
V10	Cold Climate Package	40	46
	Includes engine block heater and extra coolant protection.		
ZQ3	Convenience Group (Cargo)	329	383
	Includes cruise control, tilt steering wheel.		
ZQ2	Convenience Group (Cargo)	408	474
	Includes power door locks, power windows.		
NG1	CT/MA/NY Emissions	146	170
AJ1	Deep Tinted Glass (Cargo)	225	262
	REQUIRES ZW6.		
AJ1	Deep Tinted Glass (Cargo)	46	54
	REQUIRES ZW2.		
AJ1	Deep Tinted Glass (Cargo)	92	107
	REQUIRES ZW3.		
AJ1	Deep Tinted Glass (Passenger)	249	290
	REQUIRES 1SA.		
E54	Dutch Doors	313	364
	REQUIRES 1SA. REQUIRES 1SA or 1SB on Passenger Van.		
E54	Dutch Doors (Passenger)	262	305
	REQUIRES 1SC or 1SD or 1SE.		
B37	Floor Mats (Passenger)	40	47
	REQUIRES 1SA or 1SB and ZP5.		
B37	Floor Mats (Passenger)	59	69
	REQUIRES 1SA or 1SB and ZP7 or ZP8.		
C69	Front & Rear Air Conditioning (Passenger)	450	523
A18	Glass: Swing-Out Rear & Side Cargo Door Windows (Cargo)	117	136
A19	Glass: Swing-Out Side Cargo Door Window (Cargo)	66	77
B94	Gold Appearance package (Passenger)	NC	NC
Z82	HD Trailering Equipment	266	309
	Includes trailer hitch platform and 8-wire harness.		
UG1	Homelink Transmitter (Passenger)	99	115
AN5	Integrated Child Safety Seats (Passenger)	206	240
522/922	Leather Upholstery (Passenger)	817	950
NP5	Leather-Wrapped Steering Wheel (Passenger)	46	54
	NOT AVAILABLE with 1SE.		
G80	Locking Differential	217	252
V54	Luggage Rack (Passenger)	108	126
	REQUIRES 1SA or 1SB or 1SC.		
1SA	Marketing Option Package 1SA	NC	NC
	Includes vehicle with standard equipment.		

GMC SAFARI

CODE	DESCRIPTION	INVOICE	MSRP
1SB	Marketing Option Package 1SB (Passenger)	1837	2136
	Manufacturer Discount	(516)	(600)
	Net Price	1321	1536

Includes vehicle with standard equipment plus Convenience Group 1: tilt steering wheel, cruise control, convenience net, power door locks, power windows, deep tinted windows, courtesy lights, dual reading lights; Seat Package: inboard/outboard armrests on front seats, map pocket, manually adjustable lumbar support; uplevel grille with chrome accents, composite headlights, bodyside moldings with chrome insert.

CODE	DESCRIPTION	INVOICE	MSRP
AU3	Power Door Locks	192	223
	NOT AVAILABLE with ZQ2, 1SB, 1SC, 1SD, 1SE.		
AG1	Power Driver's Seat (Passenger)	206	240
	REQUIRES 1SA or 1SB or 1SD.		
D48	Power Exterior Mirrors (Passenger)	84	98
	REQUIRES 1SA or 1SB.		
AG2	Power Passenger's Seat (Passenger)	206	240
UM6	Radio: AM/FM Stereo with Cassette	126	147
	Includes seek-scan and digital clock. REQUIRES 1SA on Cargo Van. REQUIRES 1SA or 1SB on Passenger Van.		
UL0	Radio: AM/FM Stereo with Cassette	264	307
	Includes automatic tone control, speed compensated volume, seek-scan, digital clock, and theft lock. REQUIRES 1SA on Cargo Van. REQUIRES 1SA or 1SB on Passenger Van.		
UP0	Radio: AM/FM Stereo with Cassette & CD (Passenger)	436	507
	Includes automatic tone control, speed compensated volume, seek-scan, digital clock, and theft lock.		
UN0	Radio: AM/FM Stereo with CD (Passenger)	350	407
	Includes automatic tone control, speed compensated volume, seek-scan, digital clock, and theft lock. NOT AVAILABLE with 1SE.		
UL5	Radio: Delete (Cargo)	(164)	(191)
UK6	Radio: Rear Seat Controls (Passenger)	108	125
C95	Reading & Dome Lamps (Cargo)	28	33
C36	Rear Heater	176	205
C49	Rear window defogger	132	154
	REQUIRES E54.		
AU0	Remote Keyless Entry	129	150
	NOT AVAILABLE with 1SD, 1SE.		
FE2	Ride & Handling Package (2WD Passenger)	263	306
	Includes front and rear gas shocks, rear stabilizer bar, P235/65R15 WOL tires.		
ZP5	Seats: 5-Passenger Seating (Passenger)	NC	NC
ZP7	Seats: 7-Passenger Seating (Passenger)	273	318
	Includes front and middle row captain's chairs. REQUIRES 1SC or 1SD.		
ZP8	Seats: 8-Passenger Seating (Passenger)	340	395
	REQUIRES 1SA or 1SB.		
AN6	Seats: Lumbar Supports (Passenger)	86	100
	On middle row captain's chairs. REQUIRES ZP7.		

SAFARI GMC

CODE	DESCRIPTION	INVOICE	MSRP
AN0	Seats: Seat Package	144	168

Includes armrests, map pocket, manually adjustable lumbar supports. REQUIRES 1SA.

1SC	SLE Marketing Option Package 1SC (Passenger)	2920	3395
	Manufacturer Discount	(602)	(700)
	Net Price	2318	2695

Includes SLE decor cargo net, color-keyed rubber floor mats, two sets of adjustable reading lights, rear dome light, stepwell lighting, ashtray light, glovebox light, power door locks, 8-passenger seating: front reclining buckets with armrests, map pockets, manual lumbar supports, adjustable headrests, center and rear removeable bench seats, special cloth trim; tilt steering wheel, cruise control, lower bodyside cladding, uplevel grille with chrome trim, composite halogen headlights, 15"x 6.5" painted silver styled steel wheels, swing-out glass for rear windows and side door window; remote keyless entry, AM/FM stereo with seek-scan, cassette player, and clock.

1SD	SLE Marketing Option Package 1SD (Passenger)	3598	4184
	Manufacturer Discount	(602)	(700)
	Net Price	2996	3484

Includes SLE decor cargo net, color-keyed rubber floor mats, two sets of adjustable reading lights, rear dome light, stepwell lighting, ashtray light, glovebox light, power door locks, 8-passenger seating: front reclining buckets with armrests, map pockets, manual lumbar supports, adjustable headrests, center and rear removeable bench seats, special cloth trim; tilt steering wheel, cruise control, lower bodyside cladding, uplevel grille with chrome trim, composite halogen headlights, 15"x 6.5" brushed aluminum wheels, swing-out glass for rear windows and side door window; remote keyless entry, AM/FM stereo with seek-scan, cassette player, and clock; luggage rack, power driver's seat, Convenience Group 3: deep tinted windows, power exterior mirrors, overhead console, underseat storage on passenger's side, illuminated visor vanity mirrors.

1SE	SLT Marketing Option Package 1SE (Passenger)	4987	5799
	Manufacturer Discount	(688)	(800)
	Net Price	4299	4999

Includes SLT decor cargo net, color-keyed rubber floor mats, two sets of adjustable reading lights, rear dome light, stepwell lighting, ashtray light, glovebox light, power door locks, 8-passenger seating: front reclining buckets with armrests, map pockets, manual lumbar supports, adjustable headrests, center and rear removeable bench seats, fold-down rear center console with convenience tray and dual cupholders, special cloth trim; tilt steering wheel, cruise control, lower bodyside cladding, uplevel grille with chrome trim, composite halogen headlights, 15"x 6.5" brushed aluminum wheels, swing-out glass for rear windows and side door window, additional cupholders, overhead console with storage, lighting, compass, and exterior temperature readout; power windows, remote keyless entry, leather-wrapped steering wheel, illuminated visor vanity mirrors, power exterior mirrors, deep tinted glass, luggage rack, AM/FM stereo with seek-scan, CD player, and and clock; Convenience Group 4: power driver's seat, underseat storage on passenger's side.

| QCM | Tires: P215/75R15 AS White Lettered (Passenger) | 76 | 88 |

GMC SAFARI / SAVANA

CODE	DESCRIPTION	INVOICE	MSRP
TL1	**Uplevel Grille & Headlights**	129	150
	Includes uplevel grille with chrome accents and composite headlights. REQUIRES 1SA.		
PF3	**Wheels: Brushed Aluminum (Passenger)**	314	365
	REQUIRES 1SA.		
PF3	**Wheels: Brushed Aluminum (Passenger)**	235	273
	REQUIRES 1SB or 1SC.		
PC2	**Wheels: Chrome**	292	340
	REQUIRES 1SA.		
PC2	**Wheels: Chrome (Passenger)**	(22)	(25)
	REQUIRES 1SE.		
PC2	**Wheels: Chrome (Passenger)**	213	248
	REQUIRES 1SB or 1SC or 1SD.		
PA6	**Wheels: Silver Painted Styled Steel**	79	92
	REQUIRES 1SA. NOT AVAILABLE with FE2, 1SE on Passenger Van.		
ZW6	**Windows: Complete Body (Cargo)**	316	368
ZW2	**Windows: Rear Panel Door (Cargo)**	75	87
ZW3	**Windows: Sliding Door and Rear Panel Door (Cargo)**	133	155

1998 SAVANA

1998 GMC Savana Passenger Van

What's New?

New colors, transmission enhancements, more power for the diesel engine, revised uplevel stereos, and the addition of a PassLock theft deterrent system mark the changes for 1998. A mini-module driver's airbag is new, but it and the passenger airbag still deploy at full-force levels.

SAVANA — GMC

| CODE | DESCRIPTION | INVOICE | MSRP |

Review

Believe it or not, it had been 25 years since GM redesigned its full-size van lineup when the Savana arrived in small numbers for 1996. The GMC Rally Van and Vandura were introduced in 1971, and sold steadily until the end. Competition and safety regulations forced GM to redo the big vans — heck, since 1971 Ford had re-engineered the Club Wagon and Econoline twice! To distinguish the new design, GMC rebadged the van Savana.

Savana features flush glass and door handles, hidden door hinges, standard anti-lock brakes and dual airbags. Doors contain side impact guard beams, though they do not meet 1999 safety standards yet. Front foot and leg room is adequate, and front seats offer a wide range of fore and aft travel. Rear heat ducts are standard, but for better warming (and cooling) an optional rear heating and air conditioning unit is available. Front air conditioning is standard. The center console contains two cupholders, an auxiliary power outlet, and storage for items like CDs and cassettes. Five sound systems are offered, and uplevel units have been improved for 1998. Savana is available in base SL or luxury SLE trim levels.

New for 1998 is a steering wheel with a mini-module airbag. Rear seats receive seat belt comfort guides, while a new PassLock theft deterrent system is designed to keep thieves from absconding with the Savana. Automatic transmission refinements result in lower levels of vibration and noise.

Buyers may select either a 135-inch or a 155-inch wheelbase. There is a choice of side-entry doors as well: a sliding door or a pair of 60/40 hinged doors. Inside the short-wheelbase Savana you'll find 267 cubic feet of cargo area, while the longer wheelbase model provides a whopping 317 cubic feet of volume. Up to 15 passengers can be seated within the longer van, on as many as five bench seats. Hinged rear doors open 180 degrees for easy loading, and do not conceal high-mounted taillights when opened up. Gross vehicle weight ratings of up to 9,500 pounds are available on either wheelbase.

The base engine is a Vortec 4300 V6 making 200 horsepower. Optional motors include the new GM family of V8's, ranging from the popular Vortec 5000 to the monster Vortec 7400. Also available is a newly robust turbo-diesel V8 good for 195 horsepower and 430 stump-pulling lbs.-ft. of torque.

Like most product in showrooms these days, the Savana's styling is rounded and bulbous, with a front end that mimics the corporate look carried by most of GM's truck family. This design should wear well into the next century.

Safety Data

Driver Airbag: *Standard*
Side Airbag: *Not Available*
Traction Control: *Not Available*
Driver Crash Test Grade: *Not Available*

Passenger Airbag: *Standard*
4-Wheel ABS: *Standard*
Integrated Child Seat(s): *Not Available*
Passenger Crash Test Grade: *Not Available*

Standard Equipment

G1500 CARGO VAN: 4.3L V-6 OHV SMPI 12-valve engine; 4-speed electronic overdrive automatic transmission with lock-up; 600-amp HD battery; 100-amp alternator; rear wheel drive, 3.42 axle ratio; stainless steel exhaust; front independent suspension with anti-roll bar, front coil springs, front shocks, suspension with rear leaf springs, rear shocks; power steering with vehicle speed-sensing assist; front disc/rear drum brakes with 4 wheel anti-lock braking system; 31 gal capacity fuel tank; 3 doors with split swing-out right rear passenger door, split swing-out rear cargo door; front and rear argent bumpers with rear step; sealed beam halogen headlamps with daytime running lights; additional exterior lights include center high mounted stop light, underhood light; folding passenger convex outside mirror; front and rear 15" x 6" silver styled steel wheels with hub wheel covers; P215/75SR15 BSW AS front and rear tires; underbody mounted full-size conventional steel spare wheel; AM/FM stereo with clock, seek-scan, 4

GMC SAVANA

speakers and fixed antenna; child safety rear door locks; 2 power accessory outlets; analog instrumentation display includes oil pressure gauge, water temp gauge, volt gauge, trip odometer; warning indicators include lights on; dual airbags; tinted windows; variable intermittent front windshield wipers; seating capacity of 2, front bucket seats with fixed adjustable headrests, driver seat includes 4-way direction control, passenger seat includes 4-way direction control; vinyl seats, front vinyl headliner, full vinyl floor covering; day-night rearview mirror; engine cover console with storage; vinyl cargo floor, plastic trunk lid, cargo light; colored grille.

G2500 CARGO VAN (in addition to or instead of G1500 CARGO VAN equipment): Front and rear 16" x 6.5" wheels.

G3500 CARGO VAN (in addition to or instead of G2500 CARGO VAN equipment): 5.7L V-8 engine; 3.73 axle ratio.

G1500 PASSENGER VAN (in addition to or instead of G1500 CARGO VAN equipment): Front suspension with HD front springs, rear suspension with HD rear springs; re-circulating ball steering with engine speed-sensing assist; trailer harness; monotone paint; air conditioning; PRNDL in instrument panel; warning indicators include battery, key in ignition; ignition disable; vented rear windows, fixed 1/4 vent windows; vented rear window; seating capacity of 8; 2nd row bench seat with adjustable rear headrests; 3rd row removeable bench seat with adjustable 3rd row headrests; cloth door trim insert, full cloth headliner; interior lights include dome light; glove box, instrument panel covered bin, 2 seat back storage pockets, driver and passenger door bins; black grille, black side window moldings, black front windshield molding, black rear window molding, black door handles.

G2500/G3500 PASSENGER VAN (in addition to or instead of G1500 PASSENGER VAN equipment): 5.7L V-8 engine; 124-amp alternator; 3.73 axle ratio, seating capacity of 12.

Base Prices

Code	Description	Invoice	MSRP
TG11405-R9S	G1500 Cargo Van Regular Length	17129	19576
TG21405-R9S	G2500 Cargo Van Regular Length	17501	20001
TG21705-R9S	G2500 Cargo Van Extended Length	18288	20901
TG31405-R9S	G3500 Cargo Van Regular Length	18840	21535
TG31705-R9S	G3500 Cargo Van Extended Length	19627	22435
TG11406-R9S	G1500 Passenger Van Regular Length	19972	22825
TG21406-R9S	G2500 Passenger Van Regular Length	22159	25325
TG21706-R9S	G2500 Passenger Van Extended Length	22947	26225
TG31406-R9S	G3500 Passenger Van Regular Length	22409	25614
TG31706-R9S	G3500 Passenger Van Extended Length	23196	26514
Destination Charge:		615	615

Accessories

Code	Description	Invoice	MSRP
KW2	124-Amp Alternator (G1500 Passenger/G1500 & G2500 Cargo) NOT AVAILABLE with C69.	52	60
ZP3	15 Passenger Seating (G3500 Passenger) Includes 2 front buckets, three 3 passenger bench seats, and one 4 passenger bench seat.	319	371
GU6	3.42 Axle Ratio REQUIRES L29. NOT AVAILABLE with L65, G80, YF2, KL5.	NC	NC

SAVANA — GMC

CODE	DESCRIPTION	INVOICE	MSRP
GT4	3.73 Axle Ratio	NC	NC
	REQUIRES C5Y or C6P. NOT AVAILABLE with L30, GT5.		
MT1	4-Speed HD Automatic Transmission (All except G1500 Cargo)	NC	NC
	REQUIRES (GT4 or GT5) and C6P. NOT AVAILABLE with L30.		
GT5	4.10 Axle Ratio (G2500/G3500)	NC	NC
	REQUIRES (C6P) GVWR: 8600 lbs. NOT AVAILABLE with (L30) engine, (GT4) 3.73 axle ratio.		
AG1	6-Way Power Driver's Seat	206	240
AG2	6-Way Power Passenger's Seat (Passenger)	206	240
	REQUIRES (AG1) 6-way power driver's seat.		
ZP8	8 Passenger Seating (G2500/G3500 Passenger)	(319)	(371)
C60	Air Conditioning (Cargo)	838	975
	REQUIRES 1SA. NOT AVAILABLE with (R6G) air conditioning not desired.		
R6G	Air Conditioning Not Desired (Cargo)	NC	NC
	NOT AVAILABLE with 1SB, C60, C69, DE5, YF2.		
KL5	Alternative Fuel Conversion	108	125
	REQUIRES L31. NOT AVAILABLE with L30, L65, L29, YF2, GU6.		
ZR7	Appearance Package (Cargo)	272	316
	Includes chrome bumpers, chrome grille, composite headlamps.		
TR9	Auxiliary Lighting	138	160
	Includes dome lamp, override switch, stepwell lamps, underhood retractable lamp, front reading lamps. NOT AVAILABLE with 1SB (on cargo van), 1SC, 1SD.		
C36	Auxiliary Rear Heater	206	240
	NOT AVAILABLE with C69.		
B31	Black Vinyl Floor Covering (Cargo)	NC	NC
	Includes front full width vinyl floor covering and rear cargo mat delete.		
YF5	California Emissions	146	170
	REQUIRES (1SA or 1SB) or (L30 or L31 or L65).		
B30	Carpet Floor Covering (Passenger)	126	147
	Includes front and rear mats, cargo space carpet. NOT AVAILABLE with 1SC, 1SD.		
V10	Cold Climate Package	41	48
	Includes engine block heater. NOT AVAILABLE with (L65) engine, (C6P) GVWR: 8600 lbs.		
ZQ3	Convenience Group	331	385
	Includes tilt steering, speed control. REQUIRES 1SA.		
—	Custom Cloth Seat Trim	NC	NC
AJ1	Deep Tinted Glass (Cargo)	120	140
AJ1	Deep Tinted Glass (Passenger)	335	390
	NOT AVAILABLE with 1SD.		
ZX1	Driver's Side Reclining Bucket Seat Only (Cargo)	(350)	(407)
	Includes driver's side reclining bucket seat only with passenger's airbag delete.		
DE5	Dual Exterior Power Remote Mirrors	97	113
	Includes electric defoggers and right side convex mirror. REQUIRES (C60 or C69) and ZQ2. NOT AVAILABLE with R6G, 1SD.		
DH6	Dual Illuminated Visor Vanity Mirrors (Passenger)	64	75
	NOT AVAILABLE with (1SD) Marketing Option Package 1SD.		

GMC SAVANA

CODE	DESCRIPTION	INVOICE	MSRP
L65	**Engine: 6.5L V8 Turbo Diesel (G2500/G3500 Passenger)**	3290	3825
	Also includes glow plugs, integral 2-stage fuel filter, fuel and water separator with instrument panel warning light, fuel filter change signal, dual batteries, engine oil cooler, HD radiator, extra sound insulation, engine block heater. REQUIRES MT1 and (GT4 or GT5). NOT AVAILABLE with KL5, V10.		
L65	**Engine: 6.5L V8 Turbo Diesel (G3500 Cargo)**	2460	2860
	Includes glow plugs, integral 2-stage fuel filter, fuel and water separator with instrument panel warning light, fuel filter change signal, dual batteries, engine oil cooler, HD radiator, extra sound insulation, engine block heater. NOT AVAILABLE with (KL5) alternative fuel conversion, (V10) cold climate package, (GU6) 3.42 axle ratio.		
L30	**Engine: Vortec 5000 V8 SFI (G1500/G2500 Cargo & G1500 Passenger)**	426	495
	NOT AVAILABLE with GT4, MT1, GT5, C6P, XHF, YHF, ZHF, KL5.		
L31	**Engine: Vortec 5700 V8 SFI (G1500/G2500 Cargo & G1500 Passenger)**	830	965
	NOT AVAILABLE with GT4.		
L29	**Engine: Vortec 7400 V8 SFI (G3500)**	516	600
	NOT AVAILABLE with (KL5) alternative fuel conversion.		
ZP5	**Five Passenger Seating (G1500 Passenger)**	(319)	(371)
	Includes two front bucket seats and one rear 3-passenger bench seat.		
ZW3	**Fixed Glass Package (Cargo)**	86	100
	Includes fixed rear cargo door glass, side cargo door with fixed glass. NOT AVAILABLE with ZW2, ZW6, A18.		
ZW2	**Fixed Rear Door Glass (Cargo)**	52	60
	NOT AVAILABLE with ZW3, ZW6, A19, YF2.		
ZW6	**Full Body Glass (Cargo)**	267	311
	Includes right and left hand rear quarter fixed glass, fixed rear cargo door glass, side cargo door with fixed windows. NOT AVAILABLE with ZW2, ZW3, A18, YF2.		
C5Y	**GVWR: 7100 Lbs. (G1500 Cargo)**	267	310
	REQUIRES (XHA) tires or (XHB) tires or (XHM) tires.		
C6P	**GVWR: 8600 lbs. (G2500/G3500 Cargo)**	357	415
	REQUIRES XHF and KW2. NOT AVAILABLE with L30, C6P, KL5, V10.		
Z82	**HD Trailering Equipment**	267	310
	Includes trailering hitch platform and 8 wire harness.		
NP5	**Leather-Wrapped Steering Wheel**	52	60
G80	**Locking Differential**	217	252
	NOT AVAILABLE with (GU6) 3.42 axle ratio.		
1SA	**Marketing Option Package 1SA**	NC	NC
	Includes standard decor package.		
1SB	**Marketing Option Package 1SB (Cargo)**	1307	1520
	Includes standard decor package, air conditioning, auxiliary lighting with front reading lamps, Convenience Group: tilt steering, speed control. NOT AVAILABLE with (R6G) air conditioning not desired.		
1SB	**Marketing Option Package 1SB (Passenger)**	739	859
	Includes standard decor package, Power Convenience Group: power door locks, power windows; Convenience Group: tilt steering, speed control.		

SAVANA — GMC

CODE	DESCRIPTION	INVOICE	MSRP
AJ3	Passenger's Airbag Delete (Cargo)	(189)	(220)
	REQUIRES (C6P) GVWR: 8600 lbs. NOT AVAILABLE with (ZX1) driver's side reclining bucket seat only.		
U75	Power Antenna	73	85
	NOT AVAILABLE with UL5, UN0, UL0, UP0.		
ZQ2	Power Convenience Group	408	474
	Includes power door locks, power windows. NOT AVAILABLE with 1SB (on Passenger models), 1SC, 1SD.		
UL5	Radio Delete (Cargo)	(264)	(307)
	NOT AVAILABLE with (UM6) radio, (U75) power antenna.		
UM6	Radio: AM/FM Stereo with Cassette	126	147
	Includes seek-scan and digital clock. REQUIRES 1SA or 1SB.		
UL0	Radio: AM/FM Stereo with Cassette (Passenger)	380	442
	Includes auto reverse cassette player with music search, automatic tone control, digital clock, 8 speakers, power antenna. REQUIRES ZQ2. NOT AVAILABLE with UM6, UN0, UP0.		
UP0	Radio: AM/FM Stereo with Cassette & CD (Passenger)	552	642
	Includes automatic tone control, digital clock, 8 speakers, power antenna. REQUIRES ZQ2. NOT AVAILABLE with UM6, UL0, UN0.		
UN0	Radio: AM/FM Stereo with CD Player (Passenger)	466	542
	Includes automatic tone control, digital clock, 8 speakers, power antenna. REQUIRES ZQ2. NOT AVAILABLE with UM6, UL0, UP0.		
P06	Rally Wheel Trim	52	60
	Includes chrome trim rings and bright center caps. REQUIRES 1SA or 1SB.		
C69	Rear Air Conditioning (G1500 Passenger)	740	860
	Includes auxiliary rear heater, 124-amp alternator.		
C69	Rear Air Conditioning (G1500/G2500 Cargo)	1578	1835
	Includes front and rear air conditioning, auxiliary rear heater, 124-amp alternator. NOT AVAILABLE with (R6G) air conditioning not desired.		
C69	Rear Air Conditioning (G2500/G3500 Passenger)	691	804
	Includes auxiliary rear heater.		
C69	Rear Air Conditioning (G3500 Cargo)	1530	1779
	Includes air conditioning, auxiliary rear heater. NOT AVAILABLE with (R6G) air conditioning not desired.		
AU0	Remote Keyless Entry (Passenger)	129	150
	Includes 2 transmitters and illuminated entry. REQUIRES 1SC.		
1SC	SLE Marketing Option Package 1SC (Passenger)	1423	1655
	Includes Power Convenience Group: power door locks, power windows; Convenience Group: tilt steering, speed control, SLE Decor Package: illuminated visor vanity mirrors, carpet floor covering with cargo space carpet, auxiliary lighting with front reading lamps, custom cloth seat trim, chrome bumpers, chrome grille, composite halogen headlamps, lower bodyside moldings, wheel trim rings and bright center hub caps.		
1SD	SLE Marketing Option Package 1SD (G1500 Passenger)	2789	3243
	Includes Power Convenience Group: power door locks, power windows; Convenience Group: tilt steering, speed control, SLE Decor Package: illuminated visor vanity mirrors, carpet floor covering with cargo space carpet, auxiliary lighting with front		

GMC SAVANA

CODE	DESCRIPTION	INVOICE	MSRP

reading lamps, custom cloth seat trim, chrome bumpers, chrome grille, composite halogen headlamps, lower bodyside moldings, wheel trim rings and bright center hub caps; front and rear air conditioning with auxiliary rear heater, deep tinted glass, remote keyless entry, illuminated entry, dual exterior power remote mirrors, dual illuminated visor vanity mirrors.

Code	Description	Invoice	MSRP
1SD	**SLE Marketing Option Package 1SD (G2500/G3500 Passenger)**	2741	3187
	Includes Power Convenience Group: power door locks, power windows; Convenience Group: tilt steering, speed control, SLE Decor Package: illuminated visor vanity mirrors, carpet floor covering with cargo space carpet, auxiliary lighting with front reading lamps, custom cloth seat trim, chrome bumpers, chrome grille, composite halogen headlamps, lower bodyside moldings, wheel trim rings and bright center hub caps; front and rear air conditioning with auxiliary rear heater, deep tinted glass, remote keyless entry, illuminated entry, dual exterior power remote mirrors, dual illuminated visor vanity mirrors.		
YA2	**Sliding Rear Door**	NC	NC
ZX9	**Spare Tire: Delete (G1500)**	(95)	(110)
	Deletes spare tire, wheel, hoist, jack and tools.		
ZX9	**Spare Tire: Delete (G2500)**	(217)	(252)
	Deletes spare tire, wheel, hoist, jack and tools.		
ZX9	**Spare Tire: Delete (G3500)**	(256)	(298)
	Deletes spare tire, wheel, hoist, jack and tools.		
A18	**Swing-Out Rear Door Glass (Cargo)**	69	80
	REQUIRES ZW2. NOT AVAILABLE with ZW3, ZW6, YF2.		
A19	**Swing-Out Side Cargo Door Glass (Cargo)**	135	157
	REQUIRES ZW3 or ZW6. NOT AVAILABLE with ZW2.		
ZHA	Tire: P235/75R15 BSW AS Spare (G1500)	NC	NC
ZHM	Tire: P235/75R15 OWL AS Spare (G1500 Cargo)	49	57
ZHM	Tire: P235/75R15 OWL AS Spare (G1500 Passenger)	22	25
ZHB	Tire: P235/75R15 WSW AS Spare (G1500 Cargo)	45	52
ZHB	Tire: P235/75R15 WSW AS Spare (G1500 Passenger)	17	20
ZHF	Tire: Spare LT225/75R16E AS BSW (G2500)	NC	NC
	NOT AVAILABLE with (L30) engine.		
XHF	Tires: Front LT225/75R16E AS BSW (G2500 except Passenger Extended)	NC	NC
	REQUIRES YHF and ZHF. NOT AVAILABLE with (L30) engine.		
XHA	Tires: Front P235/75R15 AS BSW (G1500)	NC	NC
	REQUIRES YHA and ZHA.		
XHM	**Tires: Front P235/75R15 AS WOL (G1500 Cargo)**	98	114
	REQUIRES YHM and ZHM.		
XHM	**Tires: Front P235/75R15 AS WOL (G1500 Passenger)**	43	50
	REQUIRES YHM and ZHM.		
XHB	**Tires: Front P235/75R15 AS WSW (G1500 Cargo)**	89	104
	REQUIRES YHB and ZHB.		
XHB	**Tires: Front P235/75R15 AS WSW (G1500 Passenger)**	34	40
	REQUIRES YHB and ZHB.		
YHA	Tires: P235/75R15 BSW AS Rear (G1500)	NC	NC
	REQUIRES ZHA.		

SAVANA / SIERRA 1500 — GMC

CODE	DESCRIPTION	INVOICE	MSRP
YHM	Tires: P235/75R15 OWL AS Rear (G1500 Cargo) .... *REQUIRES ZHM.*	98	114
YHM	Tires: P235/75R15 OWL AS Rear (G1500 Passenger) .... *REQUIRES ZHM.*	43	50
YHB	Tires: P235/75R15 WSW AS Rear (G1500 Cargo) .... *REQUIRES ZHB.*	89	104
YHB	Tires: P235/75R15 WSW AS Rear (G1500 Passenger) .... *REQUIRES ZHB.*	34	40
YHF	Tires: Rear LT225/75R16E AS BSW (G2500) .... *REQUIRES ZHF. NOT AVAILABLE with (L30) engine.*	NC	NC
N90	Wheels: Aluminum (G1500 Passenger) .... *REQUIRES 1SA or 1SB.*	267	310
N90	Wheels: Aluminum (G1500 Passenger) .... *REQUIRES 1SC or 1SD.*	215	250
N83	Wheels: Chrome (G1500 Passenger) .... *REQUIRES 1SA or 1SB.*	267	310
N83	Wheels: Chrome (G1500 Passenger) .... *REQUIRES 1SC or 1SD.*	215	250

1998 SIERRA 1500

1998 GMC Sierra K1500 Extended Cab

What's New?

With an all-new Sierra just one year away, changes are minimal. Diesel engines make more power and torque, extended cab models get rear heater ducts, a PassLock theft deterrent system is standard, 1500-series trucks get reduced rolling resistance tires, and three new colors debut. Second generation airbags are standard.

GMC SIERRA 1500

Review

GM has figured out a way to steal some thunder from the Dodge Ram and the new Ford F-Series. Their entire line of truck engines is infused with notable horsepower and torque output figures, which goes a long way toward selling the consumer on these aging pickups.

Every Sierra gasoline engine, from the base V6 to the king-of-the-hill V8, benefits from Vortec technology which provides healthy power and torque ratings. For example, the standard 4300 V6 makes an ample 200 horsepower, and the optional 5700 V8 is a much more satisfying powerplant than Ford's new overhead cam designs. Also available are regular- and heavy-duty turbodiesels sporting 6.5 liters of displacement. For 1998, turbodiesels are infused with additional power and torque. All Sierras have four-wheel anti-lock braking.

The optional side access panel makes the extended cab model a true family vehicle. Loading cargo into the rear of the cab is much easier too. To qualify for the side access panel, you must order a 1500-series extended cab equipped with SLE or SLT trim and a Vortec 5000 or Vortec 5700 engine mated to an automatic transmission. In contrast, Ford provides a third door standard on all extended cab models, making life much easier. And, for 1998, Dodge offers optional rear doors on both sides of the truck.

Creature comforts aren't forgotten in the Sierra. Automakers are constantly trying to make their trucks more car-like, so GM has made rear seat heating ducts standard on the Sierra extended cab. Shoulder belts are height adjustable to fit a variety of physiques, and upholstery choices include leather. Heck, you'd hardly know this was a truck, especially with the passenger car tires that give some versions of the Sierra a nicer ride and quieter interior.

Improvements for 1998 include second-generation airbags for front seat passengers, a standard PassLock theft deterrent system, reduced rolling resistance tires on 1500-series models, and three new exterior colors. An all-new Sierra is due in mid-1998 as a 1999 model, so revisions this year are understandably minimal.

Although Chevrolet's own C/K Series garners the greatest amount of publicity, GMC's equivalents are pretty strong sellers themselves. Sierras, in fact, account for close to half of GMC output. Americans continue to clamor for burly pickups, whether for their macho image or for real down and dirty work. Whether you choose a light-duty two-wheel-drive (C1500) or the massive four-wheel-drive K3500 Club Coupe on a 155.5-inch wheelbase, GMC gives both Chevrolet and its Ford/Dodge rivals a run for their money.

Safety Data

Driver Airbag: *Standard*
Side Airbag: *Not Available*
Traction Control: *Not Available*
Driver Crash Test Grade: *Excellent*

Passenger Airbag: *Standard*
4-Wheel ABS: *Standard*
Integrated Child Seat(s): *Not Available*
Passenger Crash Test Grade: *Good*

Standard Equipment

C1500 REGULAR CAB: 4.3L V-6 OHV SMPI 12-valve engine; 5-speed overdrive manual transmission; 600-amp battery; 100-amp alternator; rear wheel drive, 3.08 axle ratio; stainless steel exhaust; front independent suspension with anti-roll bar, front coil springs, front shocks, rear suspension with anti-roll bar, rear leaf springs, rear shocks; power re-circulating ball steering with engine speed-sensing assist; front disc/rear drum brakes with 4 wheel anti-lock braking system; 30 gal capacity fuel tank (40.8 gal on Longbed models); trailer harness; front chrome bumper, rear black bumper with rear step; monotone paint; sealed beam halogen headlamps with daytime running lights; additional exterior lights include center high mounted stop light, pickup cargo box light, underhood light; driver and passenger manual black folding outside mirrors; front and rear 15" x 7" painted styled steel wheels with hub wheel covers; P235/75SR15 BSW AS front and rear tires; underbody mounted full-size conventional steel spare

SIERRA 1500 — GMC

wheel; AM/FM stereo with clock, seek-scan, 4 speakers and fixed antenna; 3 power accessory outlets; analog instrumentation display includes tachometer gauge, oil pressure gauge, water temp gauge, volt gauge, trip odometer; warning indicators include battery, lights on, key in ignition, door ajar; driver side airbag, passenger side cancellable airbag; ignition disable; tinted windows; variable intermittent front windshield wipers; seating capacity of 3, front bench seat with tilt adjustable headrests, driver seat includes 2-way direction control, passenger seat includes 2-way direction control; front height adjustable seatbelts; vinyl seats, full vinyl headliner, full vinyl floor covering, cab-back insulator; interior lights include dome light, front reading lights; sport steering wheel; passenger side vanity mirror; day-night rearview mirror; glove box with light, front cupholder, driver and passenger door bins; colored grille, black side window moldings, black front windshield molding, black rear window molding; black door handles.

C1500 EXTENDED CAB SHORTBED (in addition to or instead of C1500 REGULAR CAB equipment): 3.42 axle ratio; 30 gal capacity fuel tank; vented rear windows; seating capacity of 6, 60-40 split-bench front seat with center armrest with storage, driver seat includes 4-way direction control with easy entry feature, passenger seat includes 4-way direction control with easy entry feature; full folding rear bench seat with adjustable rear headrests.

C1500 EXTENDED CAB LONGBED (in addition to or instead of C1500 EXTENDED CAB SHORTBED equipment): 5.0L V-8 engine; 3.08 axle ratio; 40.8 gal capacity fuel tank, rear window molding, black door handles.

K1500 (in addition to or instead of C1500 equipment): HD battery; engine oil cooler; part-time 4 wheel drive, auto locking hub control with manual shift, 3.73 axle ratio; front torsion suspension, front torsion springs, front torsion bar; tow hooks; front and rear 16"x 6.5" wheels.

Base Prices

Code	Description	Invoice	MSRP
TC10703	C1500 X81 Special Regular Cab SB	13575	15000
TC10903	C1500 X81 Special Regular Cab LB	13865	15320
TC10703	C1500 Wideside Regular Cab SB	14372	16425
TC10903	C1500 Wideside Regular Cab LB	14634	16725
TC10703	C1500 Sportside Regular Cab SB	14875	17000
TC10753	C1500 Wideside Extended Cab SB	16122	18425
TC10953	C1500 Wideside Extended Cab LB	16818	19220
TC10703	C1500 Sportside Extended Cab SB	20273	23169
TK10703	K1500 X81 Special Regular Cab SB	16924	18700
TK10903	K1500 X81 Special Regular Cab LB	17213	19020
TK10703	K1500 Wideside Regular Cab SB	16997	19425
TK10903	K1500 Wideside Regular Cab LB	17259	19725
TK10703	K1500 Sportside Regular Cab SB	17500	20000
TK10753	K1500 Wideside Extended Cab SB	18747	21425
TK10953	K1500 Wideside Extended Cab LB	19442	22220
TK10753	K1500 Sportside Extended Cab SB	22898	26169
Destination Charge:		625	625

GMC SIERRA 1500

Accessories

Code	Description	Invoice	MSRP
GU4	3.08 Axle Ratio (C1500) .... *NOT AVAILABLE with G80.*	NC	NC
GU6	3.42 Axle Ratio .... *NOT AVAILABLE with 1SJ, 1SW.*	NC	NC
GT4	3.73 Axle Ratio .... *REQUIRES L30 or L31 or L56 on C1500 models.*	116	135
C60	Air Conditioning (All except X-cab Sportside) .... *REQUIRES 1SA or 1SL.*	692	805
YG6	Air Conditioning Not Desired (All except X-cab Sportside) .... *REQUIRES 1SA or 1SL.*	NC	NC
BZY	Bedliner (All except Sportside)	194	225
FG5	Bilstein 46mm Gas Shock Absorbers (C1500)	194	225
B85	Bodyside Moldings (Reg Cab Sportside) .... *REQUIRES 1SA or 1SB.*	65	76
R9Q	Bright Appearance Group (Wideside except X81) .... *Includes chrome front and rear bumpers, color-keyed grille with chrome accent, chrome wheel trim rings with bright center caps, composite halogen headlights, bodyside moldings with chrome insert. REQUIRES 1SA or 1SB.*	415	483
R9R	Bright Appearance Group Discount (All except X81) .... *REQUIRES R9Q.*	(172)	(200)
R9Q	Bright Appearance Package (Reg Cab Sportside) .... *Includes chrome front and rear bumpers, color-keyed grille with chrome accent, chrome wheel trim rings with bright center caps, composite halogen headlights, bodyside moldings with chrome insert. REQUIRES 1SA or 1SB.*	389	452
B85	Bright Exterior Moldings (Wideside except X81) .... *Includes bright wheel opening moldings. REQUIRES 1SA or 1SB.*	92	107
YF5	California Emissions	146	170
DF2	Camper Style Mirrors (All except X-cab Sportside & X81) .... *Stainless steel 7.5"x 10.5." REQUIRES 1SA or 1SB.*	46	53
DF2	Camper Style Mirrors (All except X81) .... *Stainless steel 7.5"x 10.5." REQUIRES 1SC or 1SD or 1SG.*	(39)	(45)
VG3	Chrome Front Bumper (All except X-cab Sportside & X81) .... *NOT AVAILABLE with 1SC, 1SD, 1SG, R9Q.*	22	26
VB3	Chrome Rear Bumper (All except X-cab Sportside & X81) .... *REQUIRES VG3. NOT AVAILABLE with 1SC, 1SD, 1SG, R9Q.*	85	99
V10	Cold Climate Package (All except X-cab Sportside) .... *Includes engine block heater. NOT AVAILABLE with L56, 1SC, 1SD, 1SG.*	28	33
ZQ3	Convenience Package (All except X-cab Sportside) .... *Includes tilt steering wheel and cruise control. REQUIRES 1SA or 1SL or 1SW.*	331	385
AJ1	Deep Tinted Glass (Reg Cab) .... *REQUIRES A28.*	30	35
AJ1	Deep Tinted Glass (X-cab) .... *NOT AVAILABLE with C49.*	92	107
AJ1	Deep Tinted Glass (X-cab) .... *REQUIRES C49.*	62	72

SIERRA 1500 — GMC

CODE	DESCRIPTION	INVOICE	MSRP
V22	Deluxe Front Appearance Package (All except X-cab Sportside & X81)	164	191
	Includes color-keyed grille with chrome accent, composite halogen headlights. REQUIRES 1SA or 1SB.		
C49	Electric Rear window defogger (X-cab)	132	154
	REQUIRES 1SC or 1SD or 1SG.		
DD7	Electrochromic Rearview Mirror with Compass (All except X81)	125	145
	REQUIRES 1SC or 1SD or 1SG.		
NP1	Electronic Shift Transfer Case (K1500)	129	150
	REQUIRES M30 or MT1 and ZQ3.		
KC4	Engine Oil Cooler	116	135
	REQUIRES GU6 or GU4. NOT AVAILABLE with L56.		
L56	Engine: 6.5L Turbo Diesel V-8 (X-cab except LB)	3487	4055
L56	Engine: 6.5L Turbo Diesel V-8 (X-cab LB)	3062	3560
L30	Engine: Vortec 5.0L V-8 (All except X-cab & X81)	426	495
L31	Engine: Vortec 5.7L V-8 (Reg Cab except X81)	1028	1195
L31	Engine: Vortec 5.7L V-8 (X-cab)	602	700
	NOT AVAILABLE with 1SG.		
BG9	Floor Covering: Color-Keyed Rubber (Reg Cab except X81)	(30)	(35)
	REQUIRES 1SC or 1SD or 1SG.		
BG9	Floor Covering: Color-Keyed Rubber (X-cab)	(44)	(51)
	REQUIRES 1SC or 1SD or 1SG.		
B30	Floor Covering: Full Carpet (Reg Cab except X81)	47	55
	REQUIRES 1SA or 1SB.		
B30	Floor Covering: Full Carpet (X-cab except Sportside & X81)	75	87
	REQUIRES 1SA or 1SB.		
V76	Front Tow Hooks (C1500)	33	38
1SW	Handy Max Commercial Package 1SW (X81)	1526	1775
	Includes 6,100 lb. GVWR, air conditioning, 4-speed automatic transmission, P235/75R15 AS BSW tires, 3.42 axle ratio, front bench seat.		
TP2	HD Battery (All except X81)	115	134
	Includes 600 cold cranking amps. REQUIRES L30 or L31.		
F44	HD Chassis Equipment (K1500)	198	230
	NOT AVAILABLE with L56.		
F60	HD Front Springs (K1500)	54	63
	NOT AVAILABLE with VYU, Z71, L56.		
F51	HD Shock Absorbers	34	40
	NOT AVAILABLE with Z82, VYU, Z71.		
Z82	HD Trailering Equipment	175	204
	Includes trailer hitch platform and HD shocks. NOT AVAILABLE with 1SL, VYU, Z71, FG5.		
Z82	HD Trailering Equipment (All except X81)	141	164
	Includes trailer hitch platform. REQUIRES Z71 or VYU or FG5. NOT AVAILABLE with 1SL.		
KNP	HD Transmission Cooling System (All except X81)	83	96
	NOT AVAILABLE with MG5, M50, MT1, GU4. REQUIRES L31 or L56.		
K47	High Capacity Air Cleaner	22	25
	NOT AVAILABLE with L56.		

GMC SIERRA 1500

CODE	DESCRIPTION	INVOICE	MSRP
1SG	**Image Max SLE Marketing Option Package 1SG (X-cab Sportside)**	894	1040

Includes 5.7-liter V-8 engine, 4-speed automatic transmission, SLE decor front air conditioning, AM/FM stereo with seek-scan, cassette player, digital clock, and 4 speakers; tilt steering wheel, cruise control, full floor color-keyed carpeting, floor mats, power door locks, power windows, leather-wrapped steering wheel, behind seat storage tray, chrome front bumper with black rub strip and chrome insert, chrome rear bumper with step pad, color-keyed grille with chrome accent, composite halogen headlamps, power exterior mirrors, black bodyside molding with chrome accent, chrome wheel opening trim, rally wheel trim: chrome trim rings and bright center caps. NOT AVAILABLE with 1SC, 1SD.

1SG	**Image Max SLE Marketing Option Package 1SG (X-cab Wideside)**	4765	5541
	Manufacturer Discount	(645)	(750)
	Net Price	4120	4791

Includes 5.7-liter V-8 engine, 4-speed automatic transmission, SLE decor front air conditioning, AM/FM stereo with seek-scan, cassette player, digital clock, and 4 speakers; tilt steering wheel, cruise control, full floor color-keyed carpeting, floor mats, power door locks, power windows, leather-wrapped steering wheel, behind seat storage tray, chrome front bumper with black rub strip and chrome insert, chrome rear bumper with step pad, color-keyed grille with chrome accent, composite halogen headlamps, power exterior mirrors, black bodyside molding with chrome accent, chrome wheel opening trim, rally wheel trim: chrome trim rings and bright center caps. NOT AVAILABLE with 1SA, 1SB, 1SC, 1SD.

1SG	**Image Max SLT Marketing Option Package 1SG (X-cab Sportside)**	2167	2520

Includes 5.7-liter V-8 engine, 4-speed automatic transmission, SLT decor front air conditioning, AM/FM stereo with seek-scan, auto-reverse and music search cassette player, digital clock, speed compensated volume, theft lock, automatic tone control, and enhanced performance 6 speaker sound system; tilt steering wheel, cruise control, full floor color-keyed carpeting, floor mats, power door locks, power windows, leather-wrapped steering wheel, behind seat storage tray, chrome front bumper with black rub strip and chrome insert, chrome rear bumper with step pad, color-keyed grille with chrome accent, composite halogen headlamps, power exterior mirrors, black bodyside molding with chrome accent, chrome wheel opening trim, rally wheel trim: chrome trim rings and bright center caps, leather 60/40 split bench seat with power lumbar supports, center fold down armrest with storage and writing board, behind seat storage pockets, aluminum wheels, remote keyless entry, powerdriver's seat. NOT AVAILABLE with 1SC, 1SD.

1SG	**Image Max SLT Marketing Option Package 1SG (X-cab Wideside)**	6038	7021
	Manufacturer Discount	(645)	(750)
	Net Price	5393	6271

Includes 5.7-liter V-8 engine, 4-speed automatic transmission, SLT decor front air conditioning, AM/FM stereo with seek-scan, auto-reverse and music search cassette player, digital clock, speed compensated volume, theft lock, automatic tone control, and enhanced performance 6 speaker sound system; tilt steering wheel, cruise control, full floor color-keyed carpeting, floor mats, power door locks, power windows, leather-wrapped steering wheel, behind seat storage tray, chrome front bumper with black rub strip and chrome insert, chrome rear bumper with step pad, color-keyed grille with chrome accent, composite halogen headlamps, power exterior mirrors, black bodyside

SIERRA 1500 — GMC

CODE	DESCRIPTION	INVOICE	MSRP
	molding with chrome accent, chrome wheel opening trim, rally wheel trim: chrome trim rings and bright center caps, leather 60/40 split bench seat with power lumbar supports, center fold down armrest with storage and writing board, behind seat storage pockets, aluminum wheels, remote keyless entry, power driver's seat. NOT AVAILABLE with 1SC, 1SD.		
G80	Locking Rear Differential .... *NOT AVAILABLE with GU4.*	217	252
1SA	Marketing Option Package 1SA (All except X-cab Sportside & X81) .... *Includes vehicle with standard SL decor passenger side assist handle, coat hooks, color-keyed vinyl floor covering, cloth headliner, rear heat ducts (extended cab models), vinyl 60/40 front bench seat with easy entry feature (extended cab models), swing-out rear quarter glass (extended cab models).*	NC	NC
1SA	Mktg. Option Pkg. 1SA with MG5 or M50 (All except X-cab Sportside & X81) Manufacturer Discount .... Net Price .... *Includes vehicle with standard SL decor passenger side assist handle, coat hooks, color-keyed vinyl floor covering, cloth headliner, rear heat ducts (extended cab models), vinyl 60/40 front bench seat with easy entry feature (extended cab models), swing-out rear quarter glass (extended cab models). REQUIRES MG5 or M50.*	NC (430) (430)	NC (500) (500)
1SB	Marketing Option Package 1SB (All except X-cab Sportside & X81) .... Manufacturer Discount .... Net Price .... *Includes standard SL decor passenger side assist handle, coat hooks, color-keyed vinyl floor covering, cloth headliner, rear heat ducts (extended cab models), vinyl 60/40 front bench seat with easy entry feature (extended cab models), swing-out rear quarter glass (extended cab models) plus air conditioning, AM/FM stereo with seek-scan, cassette player, digital clock, and 4 speakers; tilt steering wheel, cruise control.*	1150 (430) 720	1337 (500) 837
1SB	Mktg. Option Pkg. 1SB with MG5 or M50 (All except X-cab Sportside & X81) Manufacturer Discount .... Net Price .... *Includes standard SL decor passenger side assist handle, coat hooks, color-keyed vinyl floor covering, cloth headliner, rear heat ducts (extended cab models), vinyl 60/40 front bench seat with easy entry feature (extended cab models), swing-out rear quarter glass (extended cab models) plus air conditioning, AM/FM stereo with seek-scan, cassette player, digital clock, and 4 speakers; tilt steering wheel, cruise control. REQUIRES MG5 or M50.*	1150 (860) 290	1337 (1000) 337
Z71	Off-Road Chassis Equipment Package (K1500 except X81) .... *Includes skid plates and Bilstein shocks. NOT AVAILABLE with 1SA, 1SB, 1SJ, XGA, XGB, L30, M30, GU6, Z82.*	232	270
ZY2	Paint: Conventional Two-Tone (All except X81) .... *REQUIRES 1SC or 1SD or 1SG.*	163	190
AU3	Power Door Locks (All except X-cab Sportside)	134	156
UL5	Radio Delete (All except X-cab Sportside) .... *REQUIRES 1SA or 1SL.*	(247)	(287)

EDMUND'S 1998 NEW TRUCKS   www.edmunds.com

GMC SIERRA 1500

CODE	DESCRIPTION	INVOICE	MSRP
UM7	**Radio: AM/FM Stereo (All except X-cab Sportside)**	NC	NC
	Includes AM/FM stereo with seek-scan, digital clock, and 4 speakers. REQUIRES 1SA or 1SL or 1SW.		
UM6	**Radio: AM/FM Stereo with Cassette (All except X-cab Sportside)**	126	147
	Includes AM/FM stereo with seek-scan, cassette player, digital clock, and 4 speakers. REQUIRES 1SA or 1SL or 1SW.		
UL0	**Radio: AM/FM Stereo with Cassette (All except X81)**	77	90
	Includes AM/FM stereo with seek-scan, auto-reverse and music search cassette player, speed sensitive volume control, automatic tone control, theft lock, digital clock, and enhanced 6 speaker sound system. REQUIRES 1SC or 1SG (SLE).		
UN0	**Radio: AM/FM Stereo with CD (All except X81)**	163	190
	Includes AM/FM stereo with seek-scan, CD player, speed sensitive volume control, automatic tone control, theft lock, digital clock, and enhanced 6 speaker sound system. REQUIRES 1SC or 1SD or 1SG.		
UP0	**Radio: AM/FM Stereo with CD and Cassette (All except X81)**	249	290
	Includes AM/FM stereo with seek-scan, auto-reverse and music search cassette player, CD player, speed sensitive volume control, automatic tone control, theft lock, digital clock, and enhanced 6 speaker sound system. REQUIRES 1SC or 1SD or 1SG. NOT AVAILABLE with MG5 or M50.		
EF1	**Rear Bumper Delete (All except X-cab Sportside & X81)**	(112)	(130)
	NOT AVAILABLE with Z82, 1SC, 1SB, 1SG.		
EF1	**Rear Bumper Delete (All except X81)**	(172)	(200)
	REQUIRES 1SC or 1SD or 1SG. NOT AVAILABLE with Z82.		
AU0	**Remote Keyless Entry (All except X81)**	129	150
	REQUIRES 1SC or 1SG (SLE).		
AE7	**Seats: Front 60/40 Split Reclining Bench (Reg Cab except X81)**	150	174
	REQUIRES 1SC or 1SG (SLE).		
A95	**Seats: Front Reclining Bucket Seats (Reg Cab except X81)**	332	386
	NOT AVAILABLE with 1SD or 1SG (SLT).		
A95	**Seats: Front Reclining Bucket Seats (X-cab)**	232	270
	REQUIRES 1SC or 1SG (SLE).		
AG9	**Seats: Power Driver's Seat (X-cab)**	206	240
	REQUIRES 1SC or 1SG (SLE) and AE7 or A95.		
NZZ	**Skid Plates (K1500)**	82	95
	Includes shields for differential and transfer case. NOT AVAILABLE with Z71.		
1SC	**SLE Marketing Option Package 1SC (All except X-cab Sportside & X81)**	2611	3036
	Manufacturer Discount	(645)	(750)
	Net Price	1966	2286
	Includes SLE decor front air conditioning, AM/FM stereo with seek-scan, cassette player, digital clock, and 4 speakers; tilt steering wheel, cruise control, full floor color-keyed carpeting, floor mats, power door locks, power windows, leather-wrapped steering wheel, behind seat storage tray, chrome front bumper with black rub strip and chrome insert, chrome rear bumper with step pad, color-keyed grille with chrome accent, composite halogen headlamps, power exterior mirrors, black bodyside molding with chrome accent, chrome wheel opening trim, rally wheel trim: chrome trim rings and bright center caps.		

SIERRA 1500 — GMC

CODE	DESCRIPTION	INVOICE	MSRP
1SC	**SLE Marketing Option Package 1SC (X-cab Sportside)**	NC	NC

Includes SLE decor front air conditioning, AM/FM stereo with seek-scan, cassette player, digital clock, and 4 speakers; tilt steering wheel, cruise control, full floor color-keyed carpeting, floor mats, power door locks, power windows, leather-wrapped steering wheel, behind seat storage tray, chrome front bumper with black rub strip and chrome insert, chrome rear bumper with step pad, color-keyed grille with chrome accent, composite halogen headlamps, power exterior mirrors, black bodyside molding with chrome accent, chrome wheel opening trim, rally wheel trim: chrome trim rings and bright center caps.

1SC	**SLE Mktg. Option Pkg. 1SC w/ MG5 or M50 (All except X-cab Sportside & X81)**	2611	3036
	Manufacturer Discount	(1075)	(1250)
	Net Price	1536	1786

Includes SLE decor front air conditioning, AM/FM stereo with seek-scan, cassette player, digital clock, and 4 speakers; tilt steering wheel, cruise control, full floor color-keyed carpeting, floor mats, power door locks, power windows, leather-wrapped steering wheel, behind seat storage tray, chrome front bumper with black rub strip and chrome insert, chrome rear bumper with step pad, color-keyed grille with chrome accent, composite halogen headlamps, power exterior mirrors, black bodyside molding with chrome accent, chrome wheel opening trim, rally wheel trim: chrome trim rings and bright center caps.

1SC	**SLE Marketing Option Package 1SC with MG5 or M50 (X-cab Sportside)**	NC	NC
	Manufacturer Discount	(1075)	(1250)
	Net Price	(1075)	(1250)

Includes SLE decor front air conditioning, AM/FM stereo with seek-scan, cassette player, digital clock, and 4 speakers; tilt steering wheel, cruise control, full floor color-keyed carpeting, floor mats, power door locks, power windows, leather-wrapped steering wheel, behind seat storage tray, chrome front bumper with black rub strip and chrome insert, chrome rear bumper with step pad, color-keyed grille with chrome accent, composite halogen headlamps, power exterior mirrors, black bodyside molding with chrome accent, chrome wheel opening trim, rally wheel trim: chrome trim rings and bright center caps.

A28	**Sliding Rear Window**	99	115

NOT AVAILABLE with C49.

1SD	**SLT Marketing Option Package 1SD (Reg Cab except X81)**	4119	4790
	Manufacturer Discount	(645)	(750)
	Net Price	3474	4040

Includes SLT decor front air conditioning, AM/FM stereo with seek-scan, auto-reverse and music search cassette player, digital clock, speed compensated volume, theft lock, automatic tone control, and enhanced performance 6 speaker sound system; tilt steering wheel, cruise control, full floor color-keyed carpeting, floor mats, power door locks, power windows, leather-wrapped steering wheel, behind seat storage tray, chrome front bumper with black rub strip and chrome insert, chrome rear bumper with step pad, color-keyed grille with chrome accent, composite halogen headlamps, power exterior mirrors, black bodyside molding with chrome accent, chrome wheel opening trim, rally wheel trim: chrome trim rings and bright center caps, leather 60/

GMC SIERRA 1500

CODE	DESCRIPTION	INVOICE	MSRP
	40 split bench seat with power lumbar supports, center fold down armrest with storage and writing board, behind seat storage pockets, aluminum wheels, remote keyless entry, power driver's seat.		
1SD	**SLT Marketing Option Package 1SD (X-cab Sportside)**	1565	1820
	Includes SLT decor front air conditioning, AM/FM stereo with seek-scan, auto-reverse and music search cassette player, digital clock, speed compensated volume, theft lock, automatic tone control, and enhanced performance 6 speaker sound system; tilt steering wheel, cruise control, full floor color-keyed carpeting, floor mats, power door locks, power windows, leather-wrapped steering wheel, behind seat storage tray, chrome front bumper with black rub strip and chrome insert, chrome rear bumper with step pad, color-keyed grille with chrome accent, composite halogen headlamps, power exterior mirrors, black bodyside molding with chrome accent, chrome wheel opening trim, rally wheel trim: chrome trim rings and bright center caps, leather 60/40 split bench seat with power lumbar supports, center fold down armrest with storage and writing board, behind seat storage pockets, aluminum wheels, remote keyless entry, power driver's seat.		
1SD	**SLT Marketing Option Package 1SD (X-cab Wideside)**	4176	4856
	Manufacturer Discount	(645)	(750)
	Net Price	3531	4106
	Includes SLT decor front air conditioning, AM/FM stereo with seek-scan, auto-reverse and music search cassette player, digital clock, speed compensated volume, theft lock, automatic tone control, and enhanced performance 6 speaker sound system; tilt steering wheel, cruise control, full floor color-keyed carpeting, floor mats, power door locks, power windows, leather-wrapped steering wheel, behind seat storage tray, chrome front bumper with black rub strip and chrome insert, chrome rear bumper with step pad, color-keyed grille with chrome accent, composite halogen headlamps, power exterior mirrors, black bodyside molding with chrome accent, chrome wheel opening trim, rally wheel trim: chrome trim rings and bright center caps, leather 60/40 split bench seat with power lumbar supports, center fold down armrest with storage and writing board, behind seat storage pockets, aluminum wheels, remote keyless entry, power driver's seat.		
VYU	**Snow Plow Prep Package (K1500 Reg Cab)**	136	158
	Includes HD front torsion bars, HD shocks, HD power steering cooler. REQUIRES KC4 and GU6. NOT AVAILABLE with Z71, L56.		
VYU	**Snow Plow Prep Package (K1500 Reg Cab except X81)**	47	55
	Includes HD power steering cooler. REQUIRES Z71 and KC4 and GU6. NOT AVAILABLE with L56.		
1SL	**Special Package 1SL (X81)**	NC	NC
	Manufacturer Discount	(430)	(500)
	Net Price	(430)	(500)
E24	**Third Door (X-cab except Sportside)**	361	420
	REQUIRES M30 and L30 or L31 and 1SC or 1SD or 1SG. NOT AVAILABLE with BG9.		
E24	**Third Door (X-cab Sportside)**	NC	NC
	REQUIRES M30 and L30 or L31 and 1SC or 1SD or 1SG. NOT AVAILABLE with BG9.		
XBN	**Tires: Front LT245/75R16 On-Off BSW (K1500 except X81)**	19	22

SIERRA 1500 — GMC

CODE	DESCRIPTION	INVOICE	MSRP
XBX	Tires: Front LT245/75R16 On-Off Road WOL (K1500 except X81)	62	72
XFN	Tires: Front P235/75R15 AS White Lettered (C1500)	43	50
XGB	Tires: Front P245/75R16 All Terrain WOL (K1500)	43	50
	NOT AVAILABLE with Z71.		
XGC	Tires: P265/75R16 All Terrain BSW (K1500 except X81)	46	54
	REQUIRES PF4. REQUIRES GT4 except with L31.		
ZGC	Tires: P265/75R16 All Terrain BSW (K1500 except X81)	23	27
	REQUIRES PF4. REQUIRES GT4 except with L31.		
XGD	Tires: P265/75R16 All Terrain WOL (K1500 except X81)	89	104
	REQUIRES PF4. REQUIRES GT4 except with L31.		
YBN	Tires: Rear LT245/75R16 On-Off Road BSW (K1500 except X81)	19	22
YBX	Tires: Rear LT245/75R16 On-Off Road WOL (K1500 except X81)	62	72
YFN	Tires: Rear P235/75R15 AS White Lettered (C1500 except X81)	43	50
YGB	Tires: Rear P245/75R16 All Terrain WOL (K1500)	43	50
	NOT AVAILABLE with Z71.		
YGC	Tires: Rear P265/75R16 All Terrain BSW (K1500 except X81)	46	54
	REQUIRES PF4. REQUIRES GT4 except with L31.		
YGD	Tires: Rear P265/75R16 All Terrain WOL (K1500 except X81)	89	104
	REQUIRES PF4. REQUIRES GT4 except with L31.		
ZBN	Tires: Spare LT245/75R16 On-Off Road BSW (K1500 except X81)	9	11
ZBX	Tires: Spare LT245/75R16 On-Off Road WOL (K1500 except X81)	31	36
ZFN	Tires: Spare P235/75R15 AS White Lettered (C1500 except X81)	22	25
ZGB	Tires: Spare P245/75R16 All Terrain WOL (K1500)	22	25
	NOT AVAILABLE with Z71.		
ZGD	Tires: Spare P265/75R16 All Terrain WOL (K1500 except X81)	45	52
	REQUIRES PF4. REQUIRES GT4 except with L31.		
M30	Transmission: 4-Speed Automatic (All except X-cab Sportside)	834	970
	NOT AVAILABLE with 1SG, 1SW.		
M50	Transmission: 5-Speed Manual	NC	NC
	NOT AVAILABLE with 1SD, 1SG.		
MG5	Transmission: 5-Speed Manual	NC	NC
	NOT AVAILABLE with 1SD, 1SG.		
MT1	Transmission: HD 4-Speed Automatic	834	970
	Includes transmission oil cooler. NOT AVAILABLE with KNP.		
1SJ	Value Max Option Package (Reg Cab Wideside except X81)	1612	1875
	Manufacturer Discount	(602)	(700)
	Net Price	1010	1175
	Includes 3.42 axle ratio, air conditioning, tilt steering wheel, cruise control, full floor color-keyed carpeting, AM/FM stereo with seek-scan, cassette player, digital clock; Bright Appearance Group: chrome front and rear bumpers, bodyside moldings with chrome accent, chrome trim rings, bright center caps, color-keyed grille with chrome accent, composite halogen headlamps. REQUIRES MG5 or M50.		
1SJ	Value Max Option Package 1SJ (Reg Cab Sportside)	1586	1844
	Manufacturer Discount	(602)	(700)
	Net Price	984	1144
	Includes 3.42 axle ratio, air conditioning, tilt steering wheel, cruise control, full floor color-keyed carpeting, AM/FM stereo with seek-scan, cassette player, digital clock;		

GMC SIERRA 1500 / 2500

CODE	DESCRIPTION	INVOICE	MSRP
	Bright Appearance Group: chrome front and rear bumpers, bodyside moldings with chrome accent, chrome trim rings, bright center caps, color-keyed grille with chrome accent, composite halogen headlamps. REQUIRES MG5 or M50.		
1SJ	Value Max Option Package 1SJ with MG5 or M50 (Reg Cab Sportside)	1586	1844
	Manufacturer Discount	(1032)	(1200)
	Net Price	554	644
	Includes 3.42 axle ratio, air conditioning, tilt steering wheel, cruise control, full floor color-keyed carpeting, AM/FM stereo with seek-scan, cassette player, digital clock; Bright Appearance Group: chrome front and rear bumpers, bodyside moldings with chrome accent, chrome trim rings, bright center caps, color-keyed grille with chrome accent, composite halogen headlamps. REQUIRES MG5 or M50.		
1SJ	Value Max Option Pkg. 1SJ w/ MG5 or M50 (Reg Cab Wideside except X81)	1612	1875
	Manufacturer Discount	(1032)	(1200)
	Net Price	580	675
	Includes 3.42 axle ratio, air conditioning, tilt steering wheel, cruise control, full floor color-keyed carpeting, AM/FM stereo with seek-scan, cassette player, digital clock; Bright Appearance Group: chrome front and rear bumpers, bodyside moldings with chrome accent, chrome trim rings, bright center caps, color-keyed grille with chrome accent, composite halogen headlamps.		
N90	Wheels: 15"x 7" Aluminum (C1500 except X-cab Sportside & X81)	344	400
	NOT AVAILABLE with 1SC, 1SD, 1SG, R9L, R9Q.		
N90	Wheels: 15"x 7" Aluminum (C1500 except X81)	215	250
	REQUIRES 1SC or 1SG (SLE) or R9L or R9Q.		
N83	Wheels: 15"x 7" Chrome (C1500 except X-cab Sportside & X81)	267	310
	NOT AVAILABLE with 1SC, 1SD, 1SG, R9L, R9Q.		
N83	Wheels: 15"x 7" Chrome (C1500 except X81)	215	250
	REQUIRES 1SC or or 1SG (SLE) or R9L or R9Q.		
PF4	Wheels: 16"x 7" Aluminum (K1500 except X-cab Sportside & X81)	344	400
	NOT AVAILABLE with 1SC, 1SD, 1SG, R9L, R9Q.		
PF4	Wheels: 16"x 7" Aluminum (K1500 except X81)	292	340
	REQUIRES 1SC or 1SG (SLE) or R9L or R9Q.		
P06	Wheels: Rally Wheel Trim (All except X-cab Sportside)	52	60
	NOT AVAILABLE with 1SC, 1SD, 1SG, 1SJ, R9Q.		

1998 SIERRA 2500

Safety Data

Driver Airbag: *Std. only on C1500 X-cab SB/C1500 Reg Cab LD*
Side Airbag: *Not Available*
Traction Control: *Not Available*
Driver Crash Test Grade: *Excellent (LD); Not Available (HD)*

Passenger Airbag: *Std. only on C1500 X-cab SB/ C1500 Reg Cab LD*
4-Wheel ABS: *Standard*
Integrated Child Seat(s): *Not Available*
Passenger Crash Test Grade: *Good (LD); Not Available (HD)*

SIERRA 2500 — GMC

CODE	DESCRIPTION	INVOICE	MSRP

Standard Equipment

C2500 REGULAR CAB: 5.0L V-8 OHV SMPI 16-valve engine; 5-speed overdrive manual transmission; 600-amp battery; 100-amp alternator; rear wheel drive, 3.42 axle ratio; stainless steel exhaust; front independent suspension with anti-roll bar, front coil springs, front shocks, rear suspension with rear leaf springs, rear shocks; power re-circulating ball steering with engine speed-sensing assist; front disc/rear drum brakes with 4 wheel anti-lock braking system; 34 gal capacity fuel tank; trailer harness; regular pick-up box; front chrome bumper; monotone paint; sealed beam halogen headlamps with daytime running lights; additional exterior lights include center high mounted stop light, pickup cargo box light, underhood light; driver and passenger manual black folding outside mirrors; front and rear 16" x 6.5" painted styled steel wheels with hub wheel covers; LT225/75SR16 BSW AS front and rear tires; underbody mounted full-size conventional steel spare wheel; AM/FM stereo with clock, seek-scan, 4 speakers and fixed antenna; 3 power accessory outlets; analog instrumentation display includes tachometer gauge, oil pressure gauge, water temp gauge, volt gauge, trip odometer; warning indicators include battery, lights on, key in ignition, door ajar; driver side airbag, passenger side cancellable airbag; tinted windows; variable intermittent front windshield wipers; seating capacity of 3, bench front seat with tilt adjustable headrests, driver seat includes 2-way direction control, passenger seat includes 2-way direction control; front height adjustable seatbelts; vinyl seats, full cloth headliner, full vinyl floor covering, cab-back insulator; interior lights include dome light, front reading lights; sport steering wheel; day-night rearview mirror; glove box with light, front cupholder, driver and passenger door bins; vinyl cargo floor; colored grille, black side window moldings, black front windshield molding, black rear window molding, black door handles.

C2500 HD REGULAR CAB (in addition to or instead of C2500 REGULAR CAB equipment): 5.7L engine tinted windows; full vinyl floor covering; interior lights include front reading lights; vinyl cargo floor; colored grille, black side windows moldings, black front windshield molding, black rear window molding, black door handles.

C2500 EXTENDED CAB SHORTBED (in addition to or instead of C2500 REGULAR CAB equipment): 25 gal capacity fuel tank; vented rear windows; seating capacity of 6, 60-40 split-bench front seat, driver seat includes 4-way direction control with easy entry feature, passenger seat includes 4-way direction control with easy entry feature; full folding rear bench seat with adjustable rear headrest.

C2500 EXTENDED CAB LONGBED (in addition to or instead of C2500 EXTENDED CAB SHORTBED equipment): 5.7L engine; 3.73 axle ratio; 34 gal capacity fuel tank; interior lights include illuminated entry; dashboard storage.

K2500 HD REGULAR CAB (in addition to or instead of C2500 HD REGULAR CAB equipment): Engine oil cooler; part-time 4 wheel drive, auto locking hub control with manual shift, power take-off, 3.73 axle ratio; front torsion suspension, front torsion springs, front torsion bar; 34 gal capacity fuel tank; tow hooks; colored fender flares; dashboard storage.

K2500 HD EXTENDED CAB (in addition to or instead of K2500 REGULAR CAB HD LONGBED equipment): 25 gal capacity fuel tank; vented rear windows; seating capacity of 6, 60-40 split-bench front seat, driver seat includes 4-way direction control with easy entry feature, passenger seat includes 4-way direction control with easy entry feature; full folding rear bench seat with adjustable rear headrests; cab-back insulator; cargo concealed storage.

Base Prices

Code	Description	Invoice	MSRP
TC20903	C2500 LD Regular Cab Longbed	15664	17902
TC20903	C2500 HD Regular Cab Longbed	16578	18950
TC20753	C2500 LD Extended Cab Shortbed	17953	20518

GMC SIERRA 2500

CODE	DESCRIPTION	INVOICE	MSRP
TC20953	C2500 LD Extended Cab Longbed	17981	20554
TK20903	K2500 HD Regular Cab Longbed	18988	21705
TK20753	K2500 HD Extended Cab Shortbed	20699	23660
TK20953	K2500 HD Extended Cab Longbed	20810	23787
Destination Charge:		625	625

Accessories

GT4	3.73 Axle Ratio (C2500 LD)	116	135
	Includes water to oil cooler.		
MT1	4-Speed Automatic Transmission	834	970
	Includes HD transmission oil cooler. REQUIRES 1SA or 1SB or 1SC or 1SD.		
M30	4-Speed Automatic Transmission (C2500 LD)	834	970
	NOT AVAILABLE with L56, KL5, L29, L65, GT5.		
GT5	4.10 Axle Ratio	NC	NC
	REQUIRES MW3 or MT1. NOT AVAILABLE with M30, KL6.		
MW3	5-Speed Manual Transmission (All except C2500 X-cab)	NC	NC
	Includes deep low. NOT AVAILABLE with KL5, KNP, UPO, 1SD, 1SH.		
M50	5-Speed Manual Transmission (C2500 LD)	NC	NC
	NOT AVAILABLE with L29, L56, L65, Z82, KL5, KNP, UPO, 1SD, 1SH.		
AG9	6-Way Power Driver's Seat	206	240
	REQUIRES 1SC and AE7 or A95.		
AE7	60/40 Split-Bench Seat (Reg Cab)	150	174
	REQUIRES 1SC.		
C60	Air Conditioning	692	805
	REQUIRES 1SA. NOT AVAILABLE with (YG6) air conditioning not desired.		
YG6	Air Conditioning Not Desired	NC	NC
	NOT AVAILABLE with 1SB, 1SC, 1SD, 1SH, 1SR, C60.		
KL5	Alternative Fuel Conversion (All except C2500 X-cab)	108	125
	Conversion ready engine. Internal modifications for operation of natural or propane gas. REQUIRES MT1 and GT4 or GT5. NOT AVAILABLE with L56, M50, M30, L29, L65, MW3.		
V22	Appearance Package	164	191
	Includes dual horns, composite halogen headlamps, color keyed grille with chrome accents. REQUIRES 1SA or 1SB.		
B85	Bodyside Black Moldings with Chrome Insert (C2500)	92	107
	REQUIRES 1SA or 1SB.		
B85	Bodyside Black Moldings with Chrome Insert (K2500)	65	76
	REQUIRES 1SA or 1SB.		
R9R	Bright Appearance Group Discount	(172)	(200)
	REQUIRES R9Q. NOT AVAILABLE with 1SC, 1SD, 1SR, 1SH.		
R9Q	Bright Appearance Package (C2500)	415	483
	Includes Appearence Package: composite halogen headlamps, color keyed grille with chrome accents, chrome front bumper with rub strip, rear chrome step bumper with rub strip, bodyside black moldings with chrome insert, chrome trim rings and bright center hub caps. REQUIRES 1SA or 1SB.		

SIERRA 2500 — GMC

CODE	DESCRIPTION	INVOICE	MSRP
R9Q	**Bright Appearance Package (K2500)**	389	452
	Includes Appearance Package: composite halogen headlamps, color keyed grille with chrome accent, chrome front bumper with rub strip, rear chrome step bumper with rub strip, bodyside black moldings with chrome insert, chrome trim rings and bright center hub caps. REQUIRES 1SA or 1SB.		
YF5	**California Emissions**	146	170
	Automatically added to vehicles shipped to and/or sold to retailers in California. Out-of-state retailers must order on vehicles to be registered or leased in California. NOT AVAILABLE with (L56) engine, (U01) roof marker lamps.		
Z81	**Camper Equipment Package with Diesel Engine**	NC	NC
	Includes wiring harness, camper type mirrors. REQUIRES L56 or L65 and 1SC or 1SD, or 1SH.		
Z81	**Camper Equipment Package with Diesel Engine**	85	99
	Includes wiring harness, camper type mirrors. REQUIRES L56 or L65. NOT AVAILABLE with 1SC, 1SD, L29, KL6, 1SH.		
Z81	**Camper Equipment Package with Gasoline Engine**	116	135
	Includes wiring harness, HD auxiliary battery, camper type mirrors. NOT AVAILABLE with L56, 1SA, 1SB, L65, KL6, 1SR.		
Z81	**Camper Equipment Package with Gasoline Engine**	200	233
	Includes wiring harness, HD auxiliary battery, camper type mirrors. NOT AVAILABLE with L56, 1SC, 1SD, L65, KL6, 1SH.		
DF2	**Camper Type Mirrors**	46	53
	7.5" x 10.5" stainless steel. Adjustable arm feature to provide field of vision for vehicles to 96" wide. Shipped loose for dealer installation. NOT AVAILABLE with 1SC, 1SD, 1SH.		
DF2	**Camper Type Mirrors**	(39)	(45)
	7.5" x 10.5" stainless steel. Adjustable arm feature to provide field of vision for vehicles to 96" wide. Shipped loose for dealer installation. REQUIRES 1SC, 1SD, or 1SH.		
B30	**Carpet Floor Covering (Reg Cab)**	47	55
B30	**Carpet Floor Covering (X-cab)**	61	71
	REQUIRES (YG4) seats.		
B30	**Carpet Floor Covering (X-cab)**	75	87
VG3	**Chrome Front Bumper with Rub Strip**	22	26
	Includes black bumper guards with diesel engines. REQUIRES 1SA or 1SB.		
—	**Cloth Seat Trim**	NC	NC
	NOT AVAILABLE with 1SC, 1SD, 1SH.		
V10	**Cold Climate Package**	28	33
	Includes special insulation, engine block heater. NOT AVAILABLE with (L56) engine, (L65) engine.		
BG9	**Color-Keyed Rubber Flooring (Reg Cab)**	(30)	(35)
	Replaces carpet and floor mats.		
BG9	**Color-Keyed Rubber Flooring (X-cab)**	(44)	(51)
	Replaces carpet and floor mats.		
ZQ3	**Convenience Group**	331	385
	Includes tilt steering, cruise control. REQUIRES 1SA.		

GMC SIERRA 2500

CODE	DESCRIPTION	INVOICE	MSRP
ZY2	Conventional Two-Tone Paint	163	190
	NOT AVAILABLE with 1SA, 1SB.		
—	Custom Cloth Seat Trim	NC	NC
	Includes seatback storage pockets. NOT AVAILABLE with 1SA, 1SB, 1SR, 1SD.		
AJ1	Deep Tinted Glass (Reg Cab)	30	35
	REQUIRES (A28) sliding rear window.		
AJ1	Deep Tinted Glass (X-cab)	62	72
	Includes light tinted rear window. REQUIRES (C49) electric rear window defogger.		
AJ1	Deep Tinted Glass (X-cab)	92	107
	NOT AVAILABLE with (C49) electric rear window defogger.		
C49	Electric Rear window defogger	132	154
	NOT AVAILABLE with A28, 1SA, 1SB, 1SR.		
DD7	Electrochromic Rearview Mirror	125	145
	Includes 8 point compass. REQUIRES 1SC or 1SD or 1SH.		
NP1	Electronic Shift Transfer Case (K2500)	129	150
	REQUIRES (MT1) Transmission and (ZQ3) Convenience Group.		
KC4	Engine Oil Cooler (C2500)	116	135
	NOT AVAILABLE with (L29) engine, (L56) engine, (L65) engine.		
L65	Engine: 6.5L V8 Turbo Diesel (All except C2500 LD)	2460	2860
	Includes hydraulic brakes, extra sound insulation, glow plugs, integral two stage fuel filter, fuel and water separator with instrument panel warning light and fuel filter change signal, dual batteries, HD radiator. NOT AVAILABLE with M50, M30, KL5, KC4, TP2, Z81, KL6, V10.		
L56	Engine: 6.5L V8 Turbo Diesel (C2500 LD)	3062	3560
	Includes hydraulic brakes, extra sound insulation, glow plugs, integral two stage fuel filter, fuel and water separator with instrument panel warning light and fuel filter change signal, dual batteries, HD radiator. REQUIRES MT1. NOT AVAILABLE with M50, M30, YF5, KL5, K47, KC4, TP2, V10, Z81.		
L31	Engine: Vortec 5700 V8 (C2500 LD)	602	700
L29	Engine: Vortec 7400 V8 (All except 2500 LD)	516	600
	NOT AVAILABLE with M50, M30, KL5, KC4, Z81, KL6, 1SH.		
TP2	HD Auxiliary Battery	115	134
	600 cold cranking amps. NOT AVAILABLE with (L56) engine, (L65) engine.		
F60	HD Front Springs (K2500)	54	63
Z82	HD Trailering Equipment	141	164
	Includes trailer hitch platform. REQUIRES KC4 on C2500 LD models. NOT AVAILABLE with L29, L56, L65, GT4, GT5 on C2500 LD models. NOT AVAILABLE with MG5 or M50.		
KNP	HD Transmission Oil Cooler	83	96
	REQUIRES L56 and M30. NOT AVAILABLE with M50, MT1, MW3.		
A95	High Back Reclining Bucket Seats (Reg Cab)	332	386
	Includes inboard armrests, floor console, dual adjustable headrests, power lumbar supports, storage pockets behind seats and custom cloth trim. REQUIRES 1SC.		
A95	High Back Reclining Bucket Seats (X-cab)	232	270
	Includes inboard armrests, floor console, dual adjustable headrests, power lumbar supports, storage pockets behind seats and custom cloth trim. REQUIRES 1SC.		

SIERRA 2500 — GMC

CODE	DESCRIPTION	INVOICE	MSRP
K47	**High Capacity Air Cleaner**	22	25
	NOT AVAILABLE with (L56) engine.		
G80	**Locking Differential**	217	252
	REQUIRES (GT4) 3.73 axle ratio.		
1SA	**Marketing Option Package 1SA**	NC	NC
	Includes standard SL decor package.		
1SB	**Marketing Option Package 1SB**	1150	1337
	Manufacturer Discount	(430)	(500)
	Net Price	720	837
	Includes standard SL decor package, air conditioning, AM/FM stereo with cassette and seek-scan, Convenience Group with tilt steering and cruise control.		
KL6	**Natural Gas Provisions (C2500 HD Reg Cab)**	4988	5800
	REQUIRES MT1 and GT4 and XHH. NOT AVAILABLE with Z81, BZY, L29, L65, GT5.		
1SR	**Performax Marketing Option Package 1SR (C2500 HD Reg Cab)**	2399	2790
	Manufacturer Discount	(602)	(700)
	Net Price	1797	2090
	Includes 5.7L V8 engine, 4-speed automatic transmission with HD transmission oil cooler, air conditioning, Convenience Group with tilt steering and cruise control, AM/FM stereo with cassette and seek-scan, front bench seat, Bright Appearance Group with chrome front and rear bumpers, black bodyside moldings with chrome insert, body-color grille with chrome accent, composite halogen headlights, chrome wheel trim rings with chrome center hub caps. REQUIRES 1SA.		
1SR	**Performax Marketing Option Package 1SR (K2500 Reg Cab)**	2373	2759
	Manufacturer Discount	(602)	(700)
	Net Price	1771	2059
	Includes 5.7L V8 engine, 4-speed automatic transmission with HD transmission oil cooler, air conditioning, Convenience Group with tilt steering and cruise control, AM/FM stereo with cassette and seek-scan, front bench seat, Bright Appearance Group with chrome front and rear bumpers, black bodyside moldings with chrome insert, body-color grille with chrome accent, composite halogen headlights, chrome wheel trim rings with chrome center hub caps. REQUIRES 1SA.		
AU3	**Power Door Locks**	134	156
	REQUIRES 1SA.		
1SH	**Powermax Marketing Option Package 1SH**	1350	1570
	Manufacturer Discount	(645)	(750)
	Net Price	705	820
	Includes 7.4L V8 engine, 4-speed automatic transmission with HD transmission oil cooler, GVWR: 8600 lbs. REQUIRES 1SC.		
1SH	**Powermax Marketing Option Package 1SH (Reg Cab)**	1407	1636
	Manufacturer Discount	(645)	(750)
	Net Price	762	886
	Includes 7.4L V8 engine, 4-speed automatic transmission with HD transmission oil cooler, GVWR: 8600 lbs. REQUIRES 1SD.		

GMC SIERRA 2500

CODE	DESCRIPTION	INVOICE	MSRP
1SH	**Powermax Marketing Option Package 1SH (X-cab)**	1350	1570
	Manufacturer Discount	(645)	(750)
	Net Price	705	820
	Includes 7.4L V8 engine, 4-speed automatic transmission with HD transmission oil cooler, GVWR: 8600 lbs. REQUIRES 1SD.		
UL5	**Radio Delete**	(247)	(287)
	Includes front fender antenna hole plug, instrument panel storage bin. NOT AVAILABLE with 1SB, 1SC, 1SD, 1SR, UM6, ULO, UPO, UNO, 1SH.		
UM6	**Radio: AM/FM Stereo with Cassette**	126	147
	Includes digital clock and 4 speakers. NOT AVAILABLE with (UL5) radio delete, 1SD, 1SH.		
UL0	**Radio: AM/FM Stereo with Cassette**	77	90
	Includes auto-tone controls, digital clock, theft lock, auto reverse cassette with music search and an enhanced performance 6 speaker sound system. NOT AVAILABLE with UL5, 1SA, 1SB, 1SR, UNO, UPO.		
UNO	**Radio: AM/FM Stereo with CD**	163	190
	Includes auto-tone controls, digital clock, theft lock and an enhanced performance 6 speaker sound system. Also includes digital clock. NOT AVAILABLE with UL5, 1SA, 1SB, 1SR, ULO, UPO.		
UPO	**Radio: AM/FM with Cassette & CD**	249	290
	Includes auto-tone controls, digital clock, theft lock, seek and scan, auto reverse cassette with music search, CD player, and an enhanced performance 6 speaker sound system. NOT AVAILABLE with UL5, 1SA, 1SB, 1SR, M50, UNO, ULO, MW3.		
EF1	**Rear Bumper Delete**	(112)	(130)
	REQUIRES 1SA or 1SB or 1SR. NOT AVAILABLE with Z82.		
EF1	**Rear Bumper Delete**	(172)	(200)
	REQUIRES 1SC or 1SD or 1SH. NOT AVAILABLE with Z82.		
VB3	**Rear Chrome Step Bumper with Rub Strip**	85	99
	REQUIRES VG3 and 1SA or 1SB.		
YG4	**Rear Seat Delete (X-cab)**	(374)	(435)
	NOT AVAILABLE with 1SC, 1SD, 1SH.		
AU0	**Remote Keyless Entry**	129	150
	REQUIRES 1SC.		
U01	**Roof Marker Lamps**	47	55
	NOT AVAILABLE with (YF5) California Emissions.		
NZZ	**Skid Plates (K2500)**	82	95
	Includes differential and transfer case shields.		
1SC	**SLE Marketing Option Package 1SC**	2611	3036
	Manufacturer Discount	(645)	(750)
	Net Price	1966	2286
	Includes air conditioning, AM/FM stereo with cassette and seek-scan, Convenience Group with tilt steering and cruise control, SLE Decor Package: full color-keyed floor carpeting, rubber floor mats, power door locks, power windows, leather-wrapped steering wheel, black front rub strip with chrome insert, color-keyed grille with chrome accent, composite halogen headlights, power exterior mirrors, black bodyside molding with chrome insert, chrome wheel well trim, chrome wheel trim rings and center hub caps.		

SIERRA 2500 — GMC

CODE	DESCRIPTION	INVOICE	MSRP
A28	Sliding Rear Window	99	115
	NOT AVAILABLE with (C49) electric rear window defogger.		
1SD	SLT Marketing Option Package 1SD (Reg Cab)	3827	4450
	Manufacturer Discount	(645)	(750)
	Net Price	3182	3700
	Includes air conditioning, Convenience Group with tilt steering and cruise control, SLT Decor Package: full color-keyed floor carpeting, rubber floor mats, power door locks, power windows, leather-wrapped steering wheel, black front rub strip with chrome insert, color-keyed grille with chrome accent, composite halogen headlights, rear chrome step bumper with rub strip, power exterior mirrors, black bodyside molding with chrome insert, chrome wheel well trim, chrome wheel trim rings and center hub caps, AM/FM stereo with auto reverse and music search cassette, seek-scan, speed sensitive volume control, theft lock, automatic tone control, and enhanced 6 speaker sound system; leather seating with fold-down front center console with writing console, power lumbar supports; remote keyless entry.		
1SD	SLT Marketing Option Package 1SD (X-cab)	3884	4516
	Manufacturer Discount	(645)	(750)
	Net Price	3239	3766
	Includes air conditioning, Convenience Group with tilt steering and cruise control, SLT Decor Package: full color-keyed floor carpeting, rubber floor mats, power door locks, power windows, leather-wrapped steering wheel, black front rub strip with chrome insert, color-keyed grille with chrome accent, composite halogen headlights, rear chrome step bumper with rub strip, power exterior mirrors, black bodyside molding with chrome insert, chrome wheel well trim, chrome wheel trim rings and center hub caps, AM/FM stereo with auto reverse and music search cassette, seek-scan, speed sensitive volume control, theft lock, automatic tone control, and enhanced 6 speaker sound system; leather seating with fold-down front center console with writing console, power lumbar supports, seatback map pockets; remote keyless entry, 6-way power seat adjuster.		
VYU	Snow Plow Prep Package (K2500 Reg Cab)	101	118
	Includes HD front springs, HD power steering cooler.		
ZHR	Spare Tire: LT225/75R16-D BSW (C2500 LD)	9	11
	NOT AVAILABLE with XHH, YHH, YGK, ZHH, ZGK.		
ZHH	Spare Tire: LT245/75R16-E AS BSW (All except C2500 LD)	NC	NC
	NOT AVAILABLE with YHR, ZHR, YGK, ZGK.		
ZHH	Spare Tire: LT245/75R16-E AS BSW (C2500 LD)	39	46
	NOT AVAILABLE with YHR, YHH, ZHR, ZHH.		
ZGK	Spare Tire: LT245/75R16-E AT BSW (All except C2500 LD)	9	11
	NOT AVAILABLE with YHR, YHH, ZHR, ZHH.		
ZGK	Spare Tire: LT245/75R16-E AT BSW (C2500 LD)	48	57
	NOT AVAILABLE with YHR, YHH, ZHR, ZHH.		
YHR	Tires Rear: LT225/75R16-D BSW AT (C2500 LD)	19	22
	REQUIRES ZHR. NOT AVAILABLE with XHH, YHH, YGK, ZHH, ZGK.		
YHH	Tires Rear: LT245/75R16-E BSW AS (All except C2500 LD)	NC	NC
	NOT AVAILABLE with YHR, ZHR, YGK, ZGK.		
YHH	Tires Rear: LT245/75R16-E BSW AS (C2500 LD)	77	92
	NOT AVAILABLE with YHR, ZHR, YGK, ZGK.		

GMC SIERRA 2500 / 3500

CODE	DESCRIPTION	INVOICE	MSRP
YGK	Tires Rear: LT245/75R16-E BSW AT (All except C2500 LD)	19	22
	NOT AVAILABLE with YHR, YHH, ZHR, ZHH.		
YGK	Tires Rear: LT245/75R16-E BSW AT (C2500 LD)	96	114
	NOT AVAILABLE with YHR, YHH, ZHR, ZHH.		
XHH	Tires: Front LT245/75R16E AS BSW (All except C2500 LD)	NC	NC
	REQUIRES (YHH and ZHH) or (YGK and ZGK). NOT AVAILABLE with YHR, ZHR.		
XHH	Tires: Front LT245/75R16E AS BSW (C2500 LD)	77	92
	REQUIRES (YHH and ZHH) or (YGK and ZGK). NOT AVAILABLE with YHR, ZHR.		
XGK	Tires: Front LT245/75R16E AT BSW (K2500)	19	22
	Includes front tires only. REQUIRES YGK and ZGK.		
V76	Tow Hooks (front) (C2500)	33	38
P06	Trim Rings & Bright Center Hub Caps	52	60
	REQUIRES 1SA or 1SB.		
BZY	Under Rail Bedliner	194	225
	NOT AVAILABLE with (KL6) natural gas provisions.		

1997 SIERRA 3500

Safety Data

Driver Airbag: *Not Available*
Side Airbag: *Not Available*
Traction Control: *Not Available*
Driver Crash Test Grade: *Not Available*

Passenger Airbag: *Not Available*
4-Wheel ABS: *Standard*
Integrated Child Seat(s): *Not Available*
Passenger Crash Test Grade: *Not Available*

Standard Equipment

SIERRA 3500 REGULAR CAB: Vortec 5700 V-8 engine, 5-speed manual transmission, speed-sensitive power steering, power front disc/rear drum 4-wheel anti-lock brakes, light argent grille with dark argent air intakes, chrome front bumper, intermittent windshield wipers, tinted glass, dual exterior mirrors, vinyl floor covering, cloth headliner, AM/FM stereo with seek/scan, clock, and 4 speakers; trip odometer, tachometer, daytime running lights, headlights-on warning buzzer, dual in-dash auxiliary power outlets, passenger's visor vanity mirror, vinyl bench seat, simulated leather-wrapped steering wheel, 8-wire trailering harness, silver painted styled steel wheels with black center caps, LT245/75R16E all-season tires, front tow hooks (4WD)

3500 EXTENDED CAB (in addition to or instead of REGULAR CAB equipment): Roof marker lights, 60/40 split bench seat with easy entry passenger seat, folding rear bench seat, LT225/75R16 all-season tires

3500 CREW CAB (in addition to or instead of REGULAR CAB equipment): Black bumper rub strip, black bodyside moldings with bright insert, front seat headrests, fixed rear bench seat with folding back, steel wheels that haven't been styled, wheel flares (4WD)

SIERRA 3500 — GMC

CODE	DESCRIPTION	INVOICE	MSRP

Base Prices

Code	Description	Invoice	MSRP
C30903	C3500 Regular Cab	16168	18477
C30953	C3500 Club Coupe Duallie	19166	21903
C30943	C3500 Crew Cab	21684	24781
K30903	K3500 Regular Cab	18793	21477
K30953	K3500 Club Coupe Duallie	21625	24714
K30943	K3500 Crew Cab	21684	24781
	Destination Charge:	625	625

Accessories

Code	Description	Invoice	MSRP
1SB	SL Option Package 1SB (Crew Cab)	692	805
	Includes air conditioning		
1SB	SL Option Package 1SB (Reg Cab/X-cab)	1148	1335
	Manufacturer Discount	(430)	(500)
	Net Price	718	835
	Includes air conditioning, AM/FM stereo with cassette player, seek/scan, clock, and 4 speakers; convenience package (tilt steering wheel and cruise control)		
1SC	SL Option Package 1SC (Crew Cab)	1148	1335
	Includes air conditioning, AM/FM stereo with cassette player, seek/scan, clock, and 4 speakers; convenience package (tilt steering wheel and cruise control)		
1SC	SLE Option Package 1SC (Crew Cab)	3266	3798
	Includes air conditioning, AM/FM stereo with cassette player, seek/scan, clock, and 4 speakers; convenience package (tilt steering wheel and cruise control), SLE Decor (appearance package including color-keyed grille, composite headlights, and dual horn; rally wheel trim, chrome bumpers, floor carpeting, power windows, power door locks, power exterior mirrors, leather-wrapped steering wheel, behind seat storage)		
1SC	SLE Option Package 1SC (Reg Cab/X-cab)	2721	3164
	Manufacturer Discount	(645)	(750)
	Net Price	2076	2414
	Includes air conditioning, AM/FM stereo with cassette player, seek/scan, clock, and 4 speakers; convenience package (tilt steering wheel and cruise control), SLE Decor (appearance package including color-keyed grille, composite headlights, and dual horn; rally wheel trim, chrome bumpers, floor carpeting, power windows, power door locks, power exterior mirrors, leather-wrapped steering wheel, behind seat storage)		
1SD	SLT Option Package 1SD (Crew Cab)	4702	5468
	Includes air conditioning, convenience package (tilt steering wheel and cruise control), SLE Decor (appearance package including color-keyed grille, composite headlights, and dual horn; rally wheel trim, chrome bumpers, floor carpeting, power windows, power door locks, power exterior mirrors, leather-wrapped steering wheel, behind seat storage), and SLT Decor (leather 60/40 split bench seat with headrests, center storage console, power lumbar support, behind seat storage pockets, AM/FM stereo with auto-reverse cassette, seek/scan, clock, theft lock, automatic tone control, music search feature, and enhanced performance 6 speaker sound system, remote keyless entry, power driver's seat)		

GMC SIERRA 3500

CODE	DESCRIPTION	INVOICE	MSRP
1SD	SLT Option Package 1SD (Reg Cab)	3928	4568
	Manufacturer Discount	(645)	(750)
	Net Price	3283	3818

Includes air conditioning, convenience package (tilt steering wheel and cruise control), SLE Decor (appearance package including color-keyed grille, composite headlights, and dual horn; rally wheel trim, chrome bumpers, floor carpeting, power windows, power door locks, power exterior mirrors, leather-wrapped steering wheel, behind seat storage), and SLT Decor (leather 60/40 split bench seat with headrests, center storage console, power lumbar support, behind seat storage pockets, AM/FM stereo with auto-reverse cassette, seek/scan, clock, theft lock, automatic tone control, music search feature, and enhanced performance 6 speaker sound system, remote keyless entry)

CODE	DESCRIPTION	INVOICE	MSRP
1SD	SLT Option Package 1SD (X-cab)	3985	4634
	Manufacturer Discount	(645)	(750)
	Net Price	3340	3884

Includes air conditioning, convenience package (tilt steering wheel and cruise control), SLE Decor (appearance package including color-keyed grille, composite headlights, and dual horn; rally wheel trim, chrome bumpers, floor carpeting, power windows, power door locks, power exterior mirrors, leather-wrapped steering wheel, behind seat storage), and SLT Decor (leather 60/40 split bench seat with headrests, center storage console, power lumbar support, behind seat storage pockets, AM/FM stereo with auto-reverse cassette, seek/scan, clock, theft lock, automatic tone control, music search feature, and enhanced performance 6 speaker sound system, remote keyless entry, leather rear bench seat, power driver's seat)

CODE	DESCRIPTION	INVOICE	MSRP
C60	Air Conditioning	692	805
	INCLUDED in Option Packages		
R9Q	Appearance Package R9Q (2WD Reg Cab)	527	613

Includes appearance package V22 (color-keyed grille, composite headlights, dual horns), chrome bumpers, bodyside moldings with bright insert (except Duallie), rally wheels trim (chrome trim rings and bright center caps); INCLUDED in SLE and SLT Option Packages

CODE	DESCRIPTION	INVOICE	MSRP
R9Q	Appearance Package R9Q (4WD Reg Cab)	500	582
	Manufacturer Discount	(172)	(200)
	Net Price	328	382

Includes appearance package V22 (color-keyed grille, composite headlights, dual horns), chrome bumpers, bodyside moldings with bright insert (except Duallie), rally wheels trim (chrome trim rings and bright center caps); INCLUDED in SLE and SLT Option Packages

CODE	DESCRIPTION	INVOICE	MSRP
V22	Appearance Package V22	164	191
	Includes color-keyed grille, composite headlights, and dual horn		
MT1	Automatic Transmission	834	970
BZY	Bedliner	194	225
B85	Bodyside Moldings (2WD Reg Cab)	92	107
	INCLUDED in SLE and SLT Option Packages, and in Appearance Package R9Q; NOT AVAILABLE with Dual Rear Wheels		

SIERRA 3500 — GMC

CODE	DESCRIPTION	INVOICE	MSRP
B85	**Bodyside Moldings (4WD Reg Cab)**	65	76
	INCLUDED in SLE and SLT Option Packages, and in Appearance Package R9Q; NOT AVAILABLE with Dual Rear Wheels		
VB3	**Bumper — Chrome Rear Step with Rub Strip**	197	229
	REQUIRES front bumper rub strip; INCLUDED in SLE and SLT Option Package, and in Appearance Package R9Q		
VG3	**Bumper — Front Rub Strip (Reg Cab/X-cab)**	22	26
	Includes front bumper guards when ordered with 6.5-liter Turbodiesel V-8 Engine; INCLUDED in SLE and SLT Option Package, and in Appearance Package R9Q		
V43	**Bumper — Painted Rear Step**	112	130
	NOT AVAILABLE with SLE or SLT Option Packages, or with Appearance Package R9Q		
EF1	**Bumper — Rear Delete Credit**	(172)	(200)
	NOT AVAILABLE with SLE or SLT Option Packages, or with Trailering Equipment		
YF5	**California Emissions**	145	170
Z81	**Camper Equipment**	116	135
	With L65	NC	NC
	Includes special wiring harness, stainless-steel exterior mirrors, and heavy-duty battery; REQUIRES 9,600 lb. GVWR on Crew Cab; REQUIRES purchase of an SLE or SLT Option Package		
Z81	**Camper Equipment**	200	233
	With L65	85	99
	Includes special wiring harness, stainless-steel exterior mirrors, and heavy-duty battery; REQUIRES 9,600 lb. GVWR on Crew Cab; NOT AVAILABLE with SLE or SLT Option Packages		
DF2	**Camper Type Exterior Mirrors**	46	53
	With 1SC (Reg Cab/X-cab)	(39)	(45)
	With 1SC (Crew Cab)	(39)	(45)
	With 1SD (Crew Cab)	(39)	(45)
	With 1SD (X-cab)	(39)	(45)
	With 1SD (Reg Cab)	(39)	(45)
	Stainless-steel; INCLUDED with Camper Equipment		
B30	**Carpeted Floor Covering (Reg Cab)**	47	55
	Includes rubber floor mats; INCLUDED in SLE and SLT Option Packages		
B30	**Carpeted Floor Covering (X-cab)**	75	87
	Includes rubber floor mats; INCLUDED in SLE and SLT Option Packages		
V10	**Cold Climate Package**	28	33
	Includes engine block heater; INCLUDED with 6.5-liter Turbodiesel V-8 Engine		
ZQ3	**Convenience Package ZQ3**	329	383
	Includes tilt steering wheel and cruise control; NOT AVAILABLE with option packages except SL Option Package 1SB on Crew Cab		
AJ1	**Deep Tinted Glass (Crew Cab)**	183	215
	With C49 (X-cab/Crew Cab)	155	180
AJ1	**Deep Tinted Glass (Reg Cab)**	30	35
	REQUIRES Sliding Rear Window		
AJ1	**Deep Tinted Glass (X-cab)**	92	107
	With C49 (X-cab/Crew Cab)	62	72

GMC SIERRA 3500

CODE	DESCRIPTION	INVOICE	MSRP
R05	Dual Rear Wheels (Crew Cab)	737	857
	Includes roof marker lights; REQUIRES 10,000 lb. GVWR		
R05	Dual Rear Wheels (Reg Cab)	821	955
	Includes roof marker lights; REQUIRES 10,000 lb. GVWR		
DD7	Electrochromic Rearview Mirror (Reg Cab/X-cab)	125	145
	Includes 8-point compass; REQUIRES purchase of an SLE Option Package		
L65	Engine — 6.5-liter Turbodiesel	2460	2860
	Includes dual batteries, hydraulic brakes, heavy-duty radiator, engine oil cooler, additional sound insulation, engine block heater, instrument panel warning lights; REQUIRES purchase of an SLE Option Package and Bucket Seats when ordered on 2WD Club Coupe		
L29	Engine — Vortec 7400 V-8	516	600
VK3	Front License Plate Bracket	NC	NC
V76	Front Tow Hooks (2WD)	33	38
C7A	GVWR — 10,000 lb. (Reg Cab/Crew Cab)	NC	NC
	REQUIRES Dual Rear Wheels; NOT AVAILABLE with Camper Equipment		
C6Y	GVWR — 9,600 lb. (2WD Crew Cab)	NC	NC
	REQUIRES Camper Equipment; NOT AVAILABLE with Dual Rear Wheels		
TP2	Heavy-duty Battery	115	134
	INCLUDED with 6.5-liter Turbodiesel V-8 Engine and Camper Equipment		
F60	Heavy-duty Front Springs (4WD)	54	63
	INCLUDED in Snow Plow Prep Package		
K47	High Capacity Air Cleaner	22	25
	NOT AVAILABLE with 6.5-liter Turbodiesel V-8 Engine		
G80	Locking Differential	217	252
NG1	Massachusetts/New York Emissions	NC	NC
AU3	Operating Convenience Package (Crew Cab)	192	223
	Includes power door locks		
AU3	Operating Convenience Package (Reg Cab/X-cab)	134	156
	Includes power door locks		
ZY2	Paint — Conventional Two-tone (Reg Cab/X-cab)	155	180
ZY4	Paint — Deluxe Two-tone (Reg Cab/X-cab)	237	275
	REQUIRES purchase of an SLE Option Package		
AG9	Power Driver's Seat (X-cab/Crew Cab)	206	240
	REQUIRES purchase of an SLE Option Package		
P06	Rally Wheel Trim (Reg Cab/X-cab)	52	60
	Includes chrome trim rings and bright center caps; INCLUDED with SLE and SLT Option Packages, and in Appearance Package R9Q		
GT5	Rear Axle Ratio — 4.10	NC	NC
HC4	Rear Axle Ratio — 4.56	NC	NC
	REQUIRES Locking Differential		
C49	Rear window defogger (X-cab/Crew Cab)	132	154
	REQUIRES purchase of an SLE or SLT Option Package; NOT AVAILABLE with Sliding Rear Window		
AU0	Remote Keyless Entry	120	140
	REQUIRES purchase of an SLE Option Package and Operating Convenience Package		

SIERRA 3500 — GMC

CODE	DESCRIPTION	INVOICE	MSRP
U01	Roof Marker Lights (Reg Cab/Crew Cab)	45	52
	INCLUDED with Dual Rear Wheels; NOT AVAILABLE with California Emissions		
BG9	Rubber Floor Covering (Reg Cab)	(30)	(35)
BG9	Rubber Floor Covering (X-cab)	(44)	(51)
AE7	Seats — 60/40 Split Reclining Bench (Crew Cab)	86	100
	REQUIRES purchase of an SLE Option Package		
AE7	Seats — 60/40 Split Reclining Bench (Reg Cab)	150	174
	REQUIRES purchase of an SLE Option Package		
A95	Seats — Bucket Seats (High-back Reclining) (Crew Cab)	335	390
	Includes power lumbar support, floor storage console, and inboard armrests; REQUIRES purchase of an SLE or SLT Option Package		
A95	Seats — Bucket Seats (High-back Reclining) (Reg Cab)	332	386
	Includes power lumbar support, floor storage console, and inboard armrests; REQUIRES purchase of an SLE Option Package		
A95	Seats — Bucket Seats (High-back Reclining) (X-cab)	230	270
	Includes power lumbar support, floor storage console, and inboard armrests; REQUIRES purchase of an SLE or SLT Option Package; NOTE: This is a required option on Club Coupes ordered with the 6.5-liter Turbodiesel V-8 Engine		
YG4	Seats — Rear Seat Delete Credit (X-cab)	(374)	(435)
	NOT AVAILABLE with SLE or SLT Option Packages		
NZZ	Skid Plate Package (4WD)	82	95
	Includes skid plates for transfer case and differential		
A28	Sliding Rear Window	97	113
	NOT AVAILABLE with Rear window defogger		
VYU	Snow Plow Prep Package (4WD Reg Cab)	101	118
	Includes heavy-duty front springs and power steering cooler		
UL5	Stereo — Delete Credit	(247)	(287)
	NOT AVAILABLE with Option Packages except SL Option Package 1SB on Crew Cab		
UP0	Stereo — Premium w/cassette & CD players	249	290
	AM/FM stereo with CD player and auto-reverse cassette player, seek/scan, clock, theft lock, automatic tone control, music search feature, and enhanced performance 6 speaker sound system; REQUIRES purchase of an SLE or SLT Option Package and Automatic Transmission		
UL0	Stereo — Uplevel w/cassette	77	90
	AM/FM stereo with auto-reverse cassette player, seek/scan, clock, theft lock, automatic tone control, music search feature, and enhanced performance 6 speaker sound system; REQUIRES purchase of an SLE Option Package		
UN0	Stereo — Uplevel w/CD player	163	190
	AM/FM stereo with CD player, seek/scan, clock, theft lock, automatic tone control, and enhanced performance 6 speaker sound system; REQUIRES purchase of an SLE or SLT Option Package		
UM6	Stereo — w/cassette (Reg Cab/X-cab)	126	147
	AM/FM stereo with cassette player, seek/scan, clock, and 4 speakers; NOT AVAILABLE with Option packages except SL Option Package 1SB for Crew Cab		
XYK/YYK/ZYK	Tires — LT215/85R16D (2WD X-cab)	456	531
	Blackwall highway tires; REQUIRES Dual Rear Wheels		

GMC SIERRA 3500

CODE	DESCRIPTION	INVOICE	MSRP
XYL/YYL/ZYL	Tires — LT215/85R16D (4WD Reg Cab)	874	1016
	On/off road blackwall tires; REQUIRES Dual Rear Wheels and Heavy-duty Front Springs		
XYL/YYL/ZYL	Tires — LT215/85R16D (4WD X-cab)	596	693
	On/off road blackwall tires; REQUIRES Dual Rear Wheels and Heavy-duty Front Springs		
XYK/YYK/ZYK	Tires — LT215/85R16D (4WD X-cab)	427	497
	Blackwall highway tires; REQUIRES Dual Rear Wheels		
XYK/YYK/ZYK	Tires — LT215/85R16D (Crew Cab)	707	820
	Blackwall highway tires; REQUIRES Dual Rear Wheels		
XYL/YYL/ZYL	Tires — LT215/85R16D (Crew Cab)	876	1016
	On/off road blackwall tires; REQUIRES Dual Rear Wheels and Heavy-duty Front Springs		
XYK/YYK/ZYK	Tires — LT215/85R16D (Reg Cab)	705	820
	Blackwall highway tires; REQUIRES Dual Rear Wheels		
XHP/YHP/ZHP	Tires — LT225/75R16D (2WD X-cab)	29	34
	All-season blackwall; REQUIRES Dual Rear Wheels		
XHR/YHR/ZHR	Tires — LT225/75R16D (4WD Crew Cab)	344	400
	On/off road blackwall tires; REQUIRES Dual Rear Wheels		
XHP/YHP/ZHP	Tires — LT225/75R16D (Crew Cab)	278	323
	All-season blackwall tires; REQUIRES Dual Rear Wheels		
XHR/YHR/ZHR	Tires — LT225/75R16D (Reg Cab)	344	400
	On/off road blackwall tires; REQUIRES Dual Rear Wheels		
XHP/YHP/ZHP	Tires — LT225/75R16D (Reg Cab)	278	323
	All-season blackwall tires; REQUIRES Dual Rear Wheels		
XHR/YHR/ZHR	Tires — LT225/75R16D (X-cab)	66	77
	On/off road blackwall tires; REQUIRES Dual Rear Wheels		
XGK/YGK/ZGK	Tires — LT245/75R16E (4WD Reg Cab)	48	55
	On/off road blackwall tires; NOT AVAILABLE with Dual Rear Wheels		
Z82	Trailering Equipment	141	164
	Includes trailer hitch and heavy-duty flashers; REQUIRES rear step bumper		

Don't forget to swing by the Townhall when you visit Edmund's website at http://www.edmunds.com. Talk to our editors and compare notes on your favorite cars and trucks. Join others to scope out smart shopping stategies, get answers to your questions, or share your expertise. To get to the Townhall, just click on the link on the homepage or go directly to http://www.edmund.com/edweb/townhall/welcomeconflist.html.

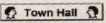

SONOMA — GMC

CODE DESCRIPTION INVOICE MSRP

1997 SONOMA

1997 GMC Sonoma Sportside

What's New?

What's New for GMC Sonoma in 1997 — Nothing much. Changes are limited to availability of the Sport Suspension on extended cab models, engine and transmission improvements, lighter-weight plug-in half shafts for 4WD Sonomas, and console-mounted shifter for trucks equipped with a center console and bucket seats. New colors arrive, and the remote keyless entry key fob is redesigned.

Review

Compact trucks are hot sellers, and GMC's entry into that market delivers hard-to-beat value—even if it doesn't stand at the top of its class in every way. A driver airbag with knee bolster and daytime running lights are standard. All Sonomas are equipped with 4-wheel anti-lock braking, and a handy side access panel is optional on the extended cab.

Sonomas can be fitted to suit just about any requirement, from strict utility to sporty style and performance. Choose from three wheelbases, two cab types, a regular-size or long cargo bed in Fleetside or Sportside configuration, and two- or four-wheel drive. Whew! You still have to consider three trim levels, five suspension systems, three engines (a four or two V-6 choices), and manual or automatic shift.

GMC changes little for 1997. Extended cab models can be equipped with the Sport Suspension for the first time, and powertrains have been improved for better efficiency. Order bucket seats and a center console, and you'll get a floor-mounted shifter rather than one sticking out of the steering column. Remote keyless entry key fobs are redesigned, and Fairway Green and Smoky Caramel replace Radar Purple and Bright Teal on the color chart. Plug-in half-shafts on 4WD models are lighter-weight and easier to service.

With the high-output, 180-horsepower Vortec 4300 V-6 on tap, and the Sport Suspension package, the Sonoma performs as energetically as high-priced sports cars did a decade or so ago. By any definition, that's progress. The Sportside box and sharp 5-spoke alloys nicely complement the top powertrain and suspension, turning the Sonoma into a true factory sport truck. For off-roading duties, GMC offers the Highrider, riding three-ply all-terrain tires and

GMC SONOMA

sporting a reinforced frame (four inches wider, two inches taller) and toughened suspension. Either Sonoma outperforms the Ranger on or off the pavement, but when it comes to interior fittings, only the Nissan Truck is more archaic.

Inside, Sonomas and Chevrolet S-Series pickups are virtually identical, with a roomy cab marred by an aesthetic disaster of a dashboard, which looks and feels as though it were lifted from some defunct Buick project, and uncomfortable bucket seats. A passenger airbag is unavailable. On extended cab trucks, an optional left side access panel makes loading passengers or cargo into the rear of the cab much easier, but takes the place of one of the fold-out jump seats in the rear.

Ford's Ranger, Dodge's Dakota, and Toyota's Tacoma come across as more refined, and their sticker prices reflect this impression. In compact-truck value per dollar, though, GMC just might deliver all the goods you're seeking.

Safety Data

Driver Airbag: *Standard*
Side Airbag: *Not Available*
Traction Control: *Not Available*
Driver Crash Test Grade: *Average*

Passenger Airbag: *Not Available*
4-Wheel ABS: *Standard*
Integrated Child Seat(s): *Not Available*
Passenger Crash Test Grade: *Poor*

Standard Equipment

SONOMA SL 2WD: 2.2-liter inline 4-cylinder engine, 5-speed manual transmission, power front disc/rear drum 4-wheel anti-lock brakes, variable power recirculating ball steering, front stabilizer bar, 15"x 7" steel wheels, P205/75R15 tires all-season tires, brake/transmission shift interlock system, daytime running lights, driver airbag, AM/FM stereo with seek/scan and clock, trip odometer, intermittent windshield wipers, tinted glass, vinyl bench seat, side-door guard beams (do not meet 1999 truck side-impact standards), 5-wire trailer harness

SL 4WD (in addition to or instead of SL 2WD equipment): 4.3-liter V-6 engine, front tow hooks, P235/70R15 all-season tires

SLS 2WD/4WD (in addition to or instead of SL 2WD/4WD equipment): Body-color grille, body-color bumpers, body stripe, wheel trim rings and center cap, composite headlights, dual illuminated visor vanity mirrors, sunvisor extensions, elastic visor straps, illuminated entry, map lights, auxiliary dash-mounted power outlets, 60/40 cloth reclining split bench seat, center storage armrest, rear jump seats (extended cab), cloth and carpet door trim, floor carpeting, black vinyl floor mats

Base Prices

Code	Description	Invoice	MSRP
S10603	2WD SL Reg. Cab Shortbed	10979	11617
S10803	2WD SL Reg. Cab Longbed	11262	11917
S10603	2WD SLS Reg. Cab Shortbed	11506	12714
S10803	2WD SLS Reg. Cab Longbed	11778	13014
S10653	2WD SLS Club Coupe	13317	14714
T10603	4WD SL Reg. Cab Shortbed	15467	16367
T10803	4WD SL Reg. Cab Longbed	15781	16699
T10603	4WD SLS Reg. Cab Shortbed	15850	17514
T10803	4WD SLS Reg. Cab Longbed	16237	17941
T10653	4WD SLS Club Coupe	17570	19414
Destination Charge:		510	510

SONOMA — GMC

CODE	DESCRIPTION	INVOICE	MSRP

Accessories

Code	Description	Invoice	MSRP
C60	Air Conditioning	692	805
	INCLUDED in Option Packages 1SD, 1SP, 1SQ, 1SR, 1ST, 1SU, 1SW, 1SX, and 1SY		
ANL	Air Dam with Fog Lights (SLS 2WD)	99	115
	INCLUDED in Option Packages 1SS, 1ST, 1SX, and 1SY		
N60	Aluminum Wheels (SL 2WD)	292	340
	15"x 7" size		
N90	Aluminum Wheels (SL 4WD)	292	340
	15"x 7" size		
N60	Aluminum Wheels (SLS 2WD)	213	248
	15"x 7" size; INCLUDED in SLE Comfort Decor and Option Packages 1SM, 1SN, 1SP, 1SQ, and 1SU; NOT AVAILABLE with Sport Suspension Package		
N90	Aluminum Wheels (SLS 4WD)	241	280
	15"x 7" size; INCLUDED in SLE Comfort Decor and Option Packages 1SR and 1SW		
YF5	California Emissions	146	170
V10	Cold Climate Package	77	89
	Includes heavy-duty battery and engine block heater		
ZQ3	Convenience Package ZQ3	340	395
	Includes tilt steering wheel and cruise control		
AJ1	Deep Tinted Glass (Reg Cab)	61	71
	With A28	31	36
AJ1	Deep Tinted Glass (X-cab)	92	107
	With A28	62	72
NP1	Electronic Shift Transfer Case (SLS 4WD)	106	123
LF6	Engine — Vortec 4300 V-6 (2WD)	851	990
	Includes transmission oil cooler with automatic; REQUIRES M50 or M30 Transmission; INCLUDED in Option Packages 1SS and 1SX		
L35	Engine — Vortec 4300 V-6 (High Output) (4WD)	223	259
	Includes transmission oil cooler with automatic		
L35	Engine — Vortec 4300 V-6 (High-Output) (2WD)	1074	1249
	Includes transmission oil cooler with automatic; REQUIRES M50 or M30 Transmission		
B30	Floor Carpeting (SL)	34	40
C5T	GVWR — 4,200 lb. (2WD Reg Cab SB)	NC	NC
	REQUIRES Smooth Ride Suspension Package or Sport Suspension Package		
C3A	GVWR — 4,400 lb. (2WD X-cab)	NC	NC
	REQUIRES Convenience Package ZQ3 or Sport Suspension Package and a V-6 engine		
C5D	GVWR — 4,600 lb. (2WD)	NC	NC
	REQUIRES Heavy-duty Suspension Package; NOT AVAILABLE on Longbed models with V-6 engine		
C5X	GVWR — 4,650 lb. (4WD Reg Cab SB)	NC	NC
	REQUIRES Convenience Package ZQ3 or Highrider Suspension Package		
C5X	GVWR — 4,650 lb. (4WD X-cab)	NC	NC
	REQUIRES Convenience Package ZQ3 or Highrider Suspension Package		
C5A	GVWR — 4,900 lb. (2WD Reg Cab LB)	NC	NC
	REQUIRES Heavy-duty Suspension Package and a V-6 engine		

GMC SONOMA

CODE	DESCRIPTION	INVOICE	MSRP
C5A	GVWR — 4,900 lb. (4WD X-cab)	NC	NC
	REQUIRES Highrider Suspension Package		
C6F	GVWR — 5,150 lb. (4WD)	NC	NC
	REQUIRES Heavy-duty Suspension Package or Off-road Suspension Package		
UA1	Heavy-duty Battery	48	56
	INCLUDED in Cold Climate Package		
NP5	Leather Wrapped Steering Wheel (SLS)	46	54
G80	Locking Rear Differential	217	252
NG1	Massachusetts/New York Emissions	146	170
ZQ6	Operating Convenience Package	460	535
	Includes power door locks, power windows, power exterior mirrors		
1SB	Option Package 1SB (SL Reg Cab)	(242)	(281)
	This package deletes the stereo and rear bumper from the base truck		
1SD	Option Package 1SD (Regional) (SLS)	692	805
	Manufacturer Discount	(129)	(150)
	Net Price	563	655
	Includes air conditioning; NOT AVAILABLE with Automatic Transmission; NOTE: This package is only available in AL, AK, CA, DC, FL, GA, HA, LA, MD, MS, NC, OK, SC, TN, TX, VA, WV and parts of DE, IN, KS, KY, MO, NM, and Ohio.		
1SM	Option Package 1SM (SLS 2WD Reg Cab)	213	248
	Manufacturer Discount	(213)	(248)
	Net Price	NC	NC
	Includes aluminum wheels and powertrain bonus discount; NOT AVAILABLE with V-6 Engine		
1SN	Option Package 1SN (X-cab)	318	370
	Manufacturer Discount	(318)	(370)
	Net Price	NC	NC
	Includes aluminum wheels, AM/FM stereo with cassette, seek/scan, 4 speakers, and clock		
1SP	Option Package 1SP (Regional) (SLS 2WD Reg Cab)	906	1053
	Manufacturer Discount	(342)	(398)
	Net Price	564	655
	Includes air conditioning, aluminum wheels, and powertrain bonus discount; NOT AVAILABLE with V-6 Engine; NOTE: This package is only available in AL, AK, CA, DC, FL, GA, HA, LA, MD, MS, NC, OK, SC, TN, TX, VA, WV and parts of DE, IN, KS, KY, MO, NM, and Ohio.		
1SQ	Option Package 1SQ (2WD X-cab)	3122	3630
	Manufacturer Discount	(553)	(643)
	Net Price	2569	2987
	Includes aluminum wheels, AM/FM stereo with cassette, seek/scan, 4 speakers, and clock; LF6 Vortec 4300 V-6 Engine, automatic transmission, air conditioning, and convenience package (tilt steering wheel and cruise control)		

SONOMA — GMC

CODE	DESCRIPTION	INVOICE	MSRP
1SR	Option Package 1SR (4WD X-cab)	1585	1843
	Manufacturer Discount	(523)	(643)
	Net Price	1062	1200

Includes aluminum wheels, AM/FM stereo with cassette, seek/scan, 4 speakers, and clock; automatic transmission, air conditioning, cloth bucket seats with driver's lumbar support, and convenience package (tilt steering wheel and cruise control)

1SS	Option Package 1SS (SLS 2WD Reg Cab SB)	1867	2171
	Manufacturer Discount	(306)	(356)
	Net Price	1561	1815

Includes LF6 Vortec 4300 V-6 Engine, Sport Suspension Package (shortened coil springs, heavy-duty stabilizer bars, bilstein front and rear shocks, urethane jounce bumpers, 16"x 8" aluminum wheels, P235/55R16 all-season tires), AM/FM stereo with cassette, seek/scan, 4 speakers, and clock; cloth bucket seats with driver's lumbar support, and air dam with fog lights

1ST	Option Package 1ST (2WD X-cab)	2899	3371
	Manufacturer Discount	(646)	(751)
	Net Price	2253	2620

Includes AM/FM stereo with cassette, seek/scan, 4 speakers, and clock; LF6 4300 Vortec V-6 Engine, air conditioning, cloth bucket seats with driver's lumbar support, convenience package (tilt steering wheel and cruise control), Sport Suspension Package (shortened coil springs, heavy-duty stabilizer bars, Bilstein front and rear shocks, urethane jounce bumpers, 16"x 8" aluminum wheels, P235/55R16 all-season tires) and air dam with fog lights; NOT AVAILABLE with SLE Comfort Decor

1SU	Option Package 1SU (Regional) (2WD X-cab)	1011	1175
	Manufacturer Discount	(447)	(520)
	Net Price	564	655

Includes air conditioning, AM/FM stereo with cassette, seek/scan, 4 speakers, and clock; and aluminum wheels; NOTE: This package is only available in AL, AK, CA, DC, FL, GA, HA, LA, MD, MS, NC, OK, SC, TN, TX, VA, WV and parts of DE, IN, KS, KY, MO, NM, and Ohio.

1SW	Option Package 1SW (Regional) (4WD X-cab)	1585	1843
	Manufacturer Discount	(682)	(793)
	Net Price	903	1050

Includes air conditioning, AM/FM stereo with cassette, seek/scan, 4 speakers, and clock; aluminum wheels, convenience package (tilt steering wheel and cruise control), and cloth bucket seats with driver's manual lumbar adjustment; NOTE: This package is only available in AL, AK, CA, DC, FL, GA, HA, LA, MD, MS, NC, OK, SC, TN, TX, VA, WV and parts of DE, IN, KS, KY, MO, NM, and Ohio.

1SX	Option Package 1SX (Regional) (SLS 2WD Reg Cab SB)	2559	2976
	Manufacturer Discount	(435)	(506)
	Net Price	2124	2470

Includes air conditioning, LF6 Vortec 4300 V-6 Engine, Sport Suspension Package (shortened coil springs, heavy-duty stabilizer bars, bilstein front and rear shocks, urethane jounce bumpers, 16"x 8" aluminum wheels, P235/55R16 all-season tires), AM/FM stereo with cassette, seek/scan, 4 speakers, and clock; cloth bucket

GMC SONOMA

Code	Description	Invoice	MSRP
	seats with driver's lumbar support, and air dam with fog lights; NOTE: This package is only available in AL, AK, CA, DC, FL, GA, HA, LA, MD, MS, NC, OK, SC, TN, TX, VA, WV and parts of DE, IN, KS, KY, MO, NM, and Ohio.		
1SY	Option Package 1SY (Regional) (2WD X-cab)	2899	3371
	Manufacturer Discount	(775)	(901)
	Net Price	2124	2470
	Includes air conditioning, AM/FM stereo with cassette, seek/scan, 4 speakers, and clock; convenience package (tilt steering wheel and cruise control), cloth bucket seats with driver's manual lumbar adjustment, LF6 Vortec 4300 V-6 Engine, Sport Suspension Package (shortened coil springs, heavy-duty stabilizer bars, bilstein front and rear shocks, urethane jounce bumpers, 16"x 8" aluminum wheels, P235/55R16 all-season tires) and air dam with fog lights; NOT AVAILABLE with SLE Comfort Decor; NOTE: This package is only available in AL, AK, CA, DC, FL, GA, HA, LA, MD, MS, NC, OK, SC, TN, TX, VA, WV and parts of DE, IN, KS, KY, MO, NM, and Ohio.		
ZY3	Paint — Special Two-tone (SLS)	255	297
	NOT AVAILABLE with Sportside Cargo Box		
LN2	Powertrain Bonus Discount (2WD Reg Cab)	(215)	(250)
	Credit issued to buyers of 2WD Regular Cab Sonomas equipped with the standard 2.2-liter 4-cylinder engine; INCLUDED in Option Packages 1SM and 1SP		
GU4	Rear Axle Ratio — 3.08	NC	NC
	REQUIRES Locking Rear Differential when ordered on 2WD trucks or when ordered with L35 Vortec 4300 V-6 High Output Engine and a manual transmission; REQUIRES Smooth Ride Suspension Package when ordered on 4WD trucks with an Automatic Transmission; NOT AVAILABLE on trucks equipped with the Locking Rear Differential and an Automatic Transmission. Got all that?		
GU6	Rear Axle Ratio — 3.42	NC	NC
	REQUIRES Automatic Transmission on 2WD trucks; REQUIRES Locking Rear Differential on 4WD trucks equipped with the SLE Comfort Decor, Vortec 4300 V-6 High Output Engine, and a manual transmission		
GT4	Rear Axle Ratio — 3.73	NC	NC
	REQUIRES Locking Rear Differential on 2WD trucks, and 4WD trucks equipped with 5,150 lb. GVWR		
GT5	Rear Axle Ratio — 4.10 (2WD)	NC	NC
	NOT AVAILABLE with Locking Rear Differential		
VF7	Rear Bumper Delete (SL)	NC	NC
	Includes rear valance panel; INCLUDED in Option Package 1SB		
A28	Rear Sliding Window	97	113
AU0	Remote Keyless Entry (SLS)	120	140
	REQUIRES Operating Convenience Package		
AV5	Seats — Cloth Buckets (SLS 2WD)	83	96
	With M30	207	241
	With M50 (2WD)	207	241
	Reclining seats with manual driver's lumbar support; Includes floor console when ordered with M50 Manual Transmission or M30 Automatic Transmission; INCLUDED in Option Packages 1SR, 1SS, 1ST, 1SW, 1SX, and 1SY		
AV5	Seats — Cloth Buckets (SLS 4WD)	207	241
	Reclining seats with manual driver's lumbar support and floor console		

SONOMA — GMC

CODE	DESCRIPTION	INVOICE	MSRP
ZM5	Skid Plate Package (4WD)	108	126

Includes skid plates for transfer case, front differential, fuel tank, and steering linkage; INCLUDED in Highrider Suspension Package

YC5	SLE Comfort Decor (SLS 2WD)	707	822

Includes gray painted bumpers with gray rub strips and bright inserts, gray grille with bright trim, gray bodyside moldings, conventional two-tone paint, and aluminum wheels; REQUIRES purchase of an Option Package; NOT AVAILABLE with Option Packages 1SX, 1ST, or 1SY

—	Spare Tire — Full-size	65	75
E62	Sportside Cargo Box (SLS Reg Cab SB)	407	450
E62	Sportside Cargo Box (X-cab)	407	450
UL5	Stereo — Delete Credit (SL)	(194)	(226)

INCLUDED in Option Package 1SB

UX1	Stereo — Uplevel w/cassette	243	282

AM/FM stereo with cassette player, seek/scan, 4 speakers, and clock

UM6	Stereo — w/cassette	105	122

AM/FM stereo with cassette player, seek/scan, 4 speakers, and clock; INCLUDED in Option Packages 1SN, 1SQ, 1SR, 1SS, 1ST, 1SU, 1SW, 1SX and 1SY

U1C	Stereo — w/CD player (SLS)	349	406

AM/FM stereo with CD player, seek/scan, 4 speakers, and clock

Z85	Suspension Package — Heavy-duty (2WD Reg Cab SB)	55	64

Includes heavy-duty shocks and springs; REQUIRES 4,600 lb. GVWR

Z85	Suspension Package — Heavy-duty (2WD X-cab)	NC	NC

Includes heavy-duty shocks and springs; REQUIRES 4,600 lb. GVWR

Z85	Suspension Package — Heavy-duty (4WD except Reg Cab LB)	220	256

Includes heavy-duty shocks and springs; REQUIRES 5,150 lb. GVWR and P235/75R15 tires or P235/70R15 tires (QEB or QBF)

Z85	Suspension Package — Heavy-duty (Reg Cab LB)	NC	NC

Includes heavy duty shocks and springs; REQUIRES 5,150 lb. GVWR and P235/75R15 tires or P235/70R15 tires (QEB or QBF) on 4WD models; REQUIRES 4,900 lb. GVWR with 2WD 4-cylinder models

ZR2	Suspension Package — Highrider (4WD X-cab)	1501	1745

Includes wheel flares, 46mm Bilstein shocks, Skid Plate Package (transfer case, front differential, fuel tank, steering linkage), enhanced chassis, heavy-duty springs, 31x10.5R15 on-off road tires (QJJ); REQUIRES 4,900 lb. GVWR, Cloth Bucket Seats, and 3.73 Rear Axle Ratio; NOT AVAILABLE with Sportside Cargo Box

ZR2	Suspension Package — Highrider (SLS 4WD Reg Cab SB)	1501	1745

Includes wheel flares, 46mm Bilstein shocks, Skid Plate Package (transfer case, front differential, fuel tank, steering linkage), enhanced chassis, heavy-duty springs, 31x10.5R15 on-off road tires (QJJ); REQUIRES 4,650 lb. GVWR, Cloth Bucket Seats, and 3.73 Rear Axle Ratio; NOT AVAILABLE with Sportside Cargo Box

ZM6	Suspension Package — Off-road (4WD Reg Cab SB)	560	651

Includes Bilstein gas shocks, larger torsion bar, jounce bumpers, stabilizer bar, heavy-duty springs, and P235/75R15 on-off road outline white-lettered tires (QEB); REQUIRES 5,150 lb. GVWR

GMC SONOMA

CODE	DESCRIPTION	INVOICE	MSRP
ZM6	Suspension Package — Off-road (4WD X-cab)	560	651
	Includes Bilstein gas shocks, larger torsion bar, jounce bumpers, stabilizer bar, heavy-duty springs, and P235/75R15 on-off road outline white-lettered tires (QEB); REQUIRES 5,150 lb. GVWR		
Z83	Suspension Package — Smooth Ride (2WD X-cab)	(55)	(64)
	Includes heavy-duty shocks and P205/75R15 tires (QCE)		
Z83	Suspension Package — Smooth Ride (4WD X-cab)	NC	NC
	Includes heavy-duty shocks and P205/75R15 tires (QCE)		
Z83	Suspension Package — Smooth Ride (Reg Cab SB)	NC	NC
	Includes heavy-duty shocks and P205/75R15 tires (QCE); REQUIRES 4,200 lb. GVWR on 2WD models; REQUIRES 4,650 lb. GVWR on 4WD models		
ZQ8	Suspension Package — Sport (2WD X-cab)	605	703
	Includes shortened coil springs, heavy-duty front and rear stabilizer bars, Bilstein front and rear shocks, urethane jounce bumpers, 16"x 8" aluminum wheels, and P235/55R16 all-season tires (QCB); INCLUDED in Option Packages 1ST and 1SY		
ZQ8	Suspension Package — Sport (SLS 2WD Reg Cab SB)	605	703
	Includes shortened coil springs, heavy-duty front and rear stabilizer bars, Bilstein front and rear shocks, urethane jounce bumpers, 16"x 8" aluminum wheels, and P235/55R16 all-season tires (QCB); INCLUDED in Option Packages 1SS and 1SX		
U16	Tachometer	51	59
	INCLUDED with V-6 engine		
E24	Third Door (X-cab)	323	375
QCE	Tires — P205/75R15 (All except 4WD Reg Cab LB)	NC	NC
	All-season blackwall tires		
QCA	Tires — P205/75R15 (All except 4WD Reg Cab LB)	104	121
	All-season outline white-lettered tires		
QBF	Tires — P235/70R15 (4WD)	NC	NC
	All-season blackwall tires; REQUIRES Heavy-duty Suspension Package		
QEB	Tires — P235/75R15 (4WD)	187	218
	On/off road outline white-lettered tires including full-size spare tire; REQUIRES Heavy-duty Suspension Package; INCLUDED in Off-road Suspension Package		
M30	Transmission — Automatic 4-speed	920	1070
	Includes brake/transmission shift interlock		
M50	Transmission — Manual 5-speed (2WD)	NC	NC

SUBURBAN — GMC

| CODE | DESCRIPTION | INVOICE | MSRP |

1998 SUBURBAN 1500

1998 GMC Suburban

What's New?

De-powered second-generation airbags protect front seat occupants for 1998. A new innovation called carpeted floor mats finally appears inside the big 'Burban. Standard equipment now includes PassLock theft deterrent system, power driver's seat, electrochromic rearview mirror, and automatic four-wheel drive on K-series models.

Review

Gaze down the side of a Suburban and all you see is steel and more steel, stretching rearward. Hike yourself aboard and you can't help but feel you're in a truck, ready for the long haul—which is exactly what pleases many owners of these biggies. Compact-SUV fans have a hard time grasping the appeal, but full-size "truck wagons" have been luring more and more upscale motorists.

GMC claims this mammoth combines the comfort of a luxury sedan with the "tenacity and utility of a packhorse." Except for the nearly-identical Chevrolet model, also named Suburban and priced just slightly lower, there was nothing else quite like it on the market, until Ford crashed the party last year with the new Expedition.

For 1998, GMC has added some standard equipment to make its version of the Suburban more upscale. A power driver's seat, PassLock theft deterrent system, and electrochromic rearview mirror are all part of the base price this year. A new Luxury Convenience Package adds a 3-channel HomeLink transmitter, 46mm Bilstein shocks, heated front seats, heated electrochromic rearview mirrors, and a power front passenger seat to the top-level SLT. Suburbans with 4WD get a new Autotrac transfer case. Autotrac is a fully automatic 4WD system that will transfer power to the front axle when rear wheel slippage is detected. If rear wheel slippage is excessive, the system switches to "4-Hi" mode with no driver input. Basically, you set it and forget it. Three new colors add some zip to the exterior.

Inside, the modern instrument panel holds a selection of white-on-black analog gauges with zone markings and red-orange needles. Climate controls are easy to grasp and use, within easy reach of each occupant. Dual cupholders ease out of a compartment at the center of the

GMC SUBURBAN

dashboard, but are poorly located so that beverages sit in front of the air vents. Three assist handles help entry/exit. Passenger car tires make less rough-and-tumble Suburbans ride smoothly and quietly. For 1998, carpeted floor mats and a cargo area mat are standard.

Despite its pickup truck heritage, the Suburban produces a stable and reasonably comfortable, if not exactly cushiony, ride—at least until you stray away from smooth pavement. We do wish the driver's seat backrest didn't feel reclined when in its most upright position. Gasoline engines tend to guzzle as expected, and if you're planning to carry heavy loads much of the time (or haul a trailer) give the big-block Vortec 7400 V8 a whirl before deciding to accept the base engine.

The Suburban is one of our favorites. It's a no-holds barred, no apologies kind of truck that can carry or tow just about anything you'd want to move without professional assistance. With a strong lineup of engines and more room inside than the Ford Expedition or 1998 Lincoln Navigator, we'd take the Suburban so long as we could live with it occupying the driveway rather than the garage.

Safety Data

Driver Airbag: *Standard*
Side Airbag: *Not Available*
Traction Control: *Not Available*
Driver Crash Test Grade: *Good*

Passenger Airbag: *Standard*
4-Wheel ABS: *Standard*
Integrated Child Seat(s): *Not Available*
Passenger Crash Test Grade: *Good*

Standard Equipment

C1500: 5.7L V-8 OHV SMPI 16-valve engine; 4-speed electronic overdrive automatic transmission with lock-up; 600-amp HD battery; 100-amp alternator; rear wheel drive, 3.42 axle ratio; stainless steel exhaust; front independent suspension with HD anti-roll bar, front coil springs, HD front shocks, rear suspension with anti-roll bar, rear leaf springs, HD rear shocks; power re-circulating ball steering with engine speed-sensing assist; front disc/rear drum brakes with 4 wheel anti-lock braking system; 42 gal capacity fuel tank; split swing-out rear cargo door; trailer harness; front and rear chrome bumpers with black rub strip, front rub strip with chrome bumper insert, rear step bumper; black bodyside molding with chrome bodyside insert, chrome wheel well molding; monotone paint; sealed beam halogen headlamps with daytime running lights; additional exterior lights include center high mounted stop light, underhood light; driver and passenger manual black folding outside mirrors; front and rear 15" x 7" painted styled steel wheels with hub wheel covers; P235/75SR15 BSW AS front and rear tires; inside mounted full-size conventional steel spare wheel; rear heat ducts; AM/FM stereo with clock, seek-scan, 4 speakers and fixed antenna; power door locks, child safety rear door locks, power remote tailgate release; 3 power accessory outlets; analog instrumentation display includes tachometer gauge, oil pressure gauge, water temp gauge, volt gauge, PRNDL in instrument panel, trip odometer; warning indicators include battery, lights on, key in ignition, door ajar; dual airbags; ignition disable; tinted windows, manual rear windows, fixed 1/4 vent windows; variable intermittent front windshield wipers; seating capacity of 3, front bench seat with tilt adjustable headrests, driver seat includes 2-way direction control, passenger seat includes 2-way direction control; front height adjustable seatbelts; vinyl seats, full cloth headliner, full vinyl floor covering; interior lights include dome light with fade, front reading lights, illuminated entry; sport steering wheel; passenger side vanity mirror; day-night rearview mirror; glove box with light, front cupholder, instrument panel bin, driver and passenger door bins, rear door bins; vinyl cargo floor, cargo tie downs, cargo light; colored grille, black side window moldings, black front windshield molding, black rear window molding, black door handles.

K1500 (in addition to or instead of C1500 equipment): Part-time 4 wheel drive, auto locking hub control with electronic shift; front torsion springs, front torsion bar; tow hooks; front and rear 16" x 6.5" wheels.

SUBURBAN — GMC

CODE	DESCRIPTION	INVOICE	MSRP

Base Prices

TC10906-R9S	C1500	21988	25129
TK10906-R9S	K1500	24613	28129
	Destination Charge:	675	675

Accessories

CODE	DESCRIPTION	INVOICE	MSRP
GT4	**3.73 Axle Ratio** — Includes water to oil cooler. NOT AVAILABLE with L65, MT1, KC4, K47, C3F, QIZ, Z82, C5I.	116	135
MT1	**4-Speed HD Automatic Transmission** — Includes HD auxiliary transmission oil cooler. NOT AVAILABLE with GT4, QHM, N90, K47, YF5, KC4, V10, PF4, QBN, QBX, QGB.	NC	NC
AG9	**6-Way Power Driver's Seat** — REQUIRES 1SA and AE7.	206	240
YG6	**Air Conditioning Not Desired** — NOT AVAILABLE with C60, C69, 1SB, 1SC.	NC	NC
C36	**Auxiliary Rear Heater** — REQUIRES 1SA.	176	205
YF5	**California Emissions** — Automatically added to vehicles shipped to and/or sold to retailers in California. Out-of-state retailers must order on vehicles to be registered or leased in California. NOT AVAILABLE with L65, MT1, U01, C3F.	146	170
DF2	**Camper Type Exterior Mirrors** — 7.5" x 10.5" stainless steel. Includes adjustable arm feature to provide field of vision for vehicles to 96" wide. Shipped loose for dealer installation. REQUIRES 1SB or 1SC.	(39)	(45)
DF2	**Camper Type Exterior Mirrors** — 7.5" x 10.5" stainless steel. Includes adjustable arm feature to provide field of vision for vehicles to 96" wide. Shipped loose for dealer installation. REQUIRES (1SA) Marketing Option Package 1SA.	46	53
AS3	**Center & Rear Bench Seating** — REQUIRES 1SA. NOT AVAILABLE with (AT5) center folding bench seat, (YG4) rear seat not desired.	1017	1182
AT5	**Center Folding Bench Seat** — Includes easy entry feature on passenger side for access to rear seat/cargo area. REQUIRES 1SA. NOT AVAILABLE with (AS3) center and rear bench seating, (YG4) rear seat not desired.	544	632
V10	**Cold Climate Package** — Includes engine block heater. NOT AVAILABLE with L65, MT1, C3F, C5I.	28	33
ZQ3	**Convenience Package: Tilt/Speed Control** — REQUIRES 1SA.	329	383
ZY2	**Conventional Two-Tone Paint** — REQUIRES 1SB or 1SC. NOT AVAILABLE with (1SA) Marketing Option Package 1SA.	172	200
AJ1	**Deep Tinted Glass** — REQUIRES 1SA.	262	305

GMC SUBURBAN

CODE	DESCRIPTION	INVOICE	MSRP
C49	Electric Rear window defogger	NC	NC
	REQUIRES 1SB or 1SC or ZP6.		
C49	Electric Rear window defogger	132	154
	REQUIRES 1SA.		
NP8	Electronic Active Transfer Case (K1500)	NC	NC
	REQUIRES ZQ3 or 1SB or 1SC.		
KC4	Engine Oil Cooler	116	135
	NOT AVAILABLE with GT4, MT1, C3F, L65, C5I.		
L65	Engine: 6.5L V8 Turbo Diesel	2460	2860
	Includes hydraulic brakes, glow plugs, integral two-stage fuel filter, fuel and water separator w/instrument panel warning light, fuel filter change signal, black front bumper guards, dual 600 CCA batteries, HD radiator, extra sound insulation, engine block heater, engine oil cooler. REQUIRES MT1 and C3F and QIZ. NOT AVAILABLE with GT4, K47, YF5, V10, QHM, Z82, N90, KC4, PF4, QBN, QBX, QGB.		
U01	Exterior Roof Marker Lamps (5)	47	55
	NOT AVAILABLE with (YF5) California Emissions.		
C69	Front & Rear Air Conditioning	1200	1395
	Includes dual controls and rear overhead vents. REQUIRES 1SA. NOT AVAILABLE with (YG6) air conditioning not desired.		
C60	Front Air Conditioning	727	845
	REQUIRES 1SA. NOT AVAILABLE with (YG6) air conditioning not desired.		
C3F	GVWR: 7700 Lbs. (C1500)	NC	NC
	REQUIRES MT1. NOT AVAILABLE with 1SB, 1SC, GT4, QHM, N90, YF5, KC4, V10, K47.		
C5I	GVWR: 8050 Lbs. (K1500)	NC	NC
	REQUIRES MT1. NOT AVAILABLE with GT4, QGB, QBN, QBX, KC4, V10, PF4, F60, Z82.		
KNP	HD Auxiliary Transmission Oil Cooler	83	96
F60	HD Front Springs (K1500)	54	63
	NOT AVAILABLE with C5I.		
Z82	HD Trailering Equipment	184	214
	Includes platform hitch and HD hazard flasher. REQUIRES KC4. NOT AVAILABLE with NZZ, QBN, QIW, QBX, A52, AE7, L65.		
A95	High Back Reclining Bucket Seats	335	390
	Includes recliners, dual adjustable headrests, storage pockets behind seats, roof console, floor console, dual power lumbars, inboard armrests. REQUIRES 1SB. NOT AVAILABLE with 1SA, 1SC, YG4.		
K47	High Capacity Air Cleaner	22	25
	NOT AVAILABLE with L65, C3F, MT1, GT4.		
G80	Locking Rear Differential	217	252
ZM9	Luxury Convenience Package	856	995
	Includes heated bucket seats, power driver's and passenger's seats, Homelink security system, electrochromic heated outside rear view mirror, premium ride suspension package. REQUIRES 1SC.		
1SA	Marketing Option Package 1SA	NC	NC
	Includes SL Decor Package. REQUIRES C60 or C69 or YG6. NOT AVAILABLE with Z82, ZY2, UNO, UPO, A95, AG9.		

SUBURBAN — GMC

CODE	DESCRIPTION	INVOICE	MSRP
NZZ	**Off Road Skid Plates (K1500)**	194	225

Includes differential and transfer case shields. NOT AVAILABLE with (Z82) HD trailering equipment, (BVE) Running Boards.

UM6	**Radio: AM/FM Stereo & Cassette**	126	147

Includes digital clock. REQUIRES 1SA. NOT AVAILABLE with 1SB, 1SC, UP0.

UN0	**Radio: AM/FM Stereo & CD**	86	100

Includes theft lock, digital clock and enhanced performance 8 speaker system. NOT AVAILABLE with (UP0) radio, (1SA) Marketing Option Package 1SA, (1SC) Marketing Option Package 1SC.

UP0	**Radio: AM/FM Stereo with CD & Cassette**	172	200

Includes theft lock, auto reverse/music search cassette player, CD player, automatic tone control, digital clock and enhanced performance 8 speaker system. NOT AVAILABLE with UN0, UM6, 1SA, 1SC.

YG4	**Rear Seat Not Desired**	NC	NC

Deletes third seat. REQUIRES 1SA. NOT AVAILABLE with 1SB, 1SC, YG4, AS3, AT5, A95.

YG4	**Rear Seat Not Desired with 1SB**	(531)	(618)

Deletes third seat. REQUIRES 1SB. NOT AVAILABLE with 1SA, 1SC, YG4.

YG4	**Rear Seat Not Desired with 1SC**	(875)	(1018)

Deletes third seat. REQUIRES 1SC. NOT AVAILABLE with 1SA, 1SB, YG4, A95.

ZP6	**Rear Window Equipment**	NC	NC

Includes electric rear window defogger, intermittent rear window wiper/washer. REQUIRES 1SB or 1SC.

ZP6	**Rear Window Equipment**	240	279

Includes electric rear window defogger, intermittent rear window wiper/washer. REQUIRES 1SA.

AE7	**Reclining 60/40 Split-Bench Seat**	86	100

Includes coin holder, map net, writing board, storage pockets behind seat, center fold down storage armrest, dual power lumbars. REQUIRES (1SA) Marketing Option Package 1SA. NOT AVAILABLE with (A95) seats, (Z82) HD trailering equipment.

AU0	**Remote Keyless Entry System**	129	150

REQUIRES 1SA.

BVE	**Running Boards**	236	275

Shipped loose for dealer installation. NOT AVAILABLE with (NZZ) Skid Plate Package.

1SB	**SLE Marketing Option Package 1SB**	6513	7573

Includes SLE Decor front and rear air conditioning, AM/FM stereo with cassette, automatic tone control, and enhanced performance 8 speaker sound system; cargo net, tilt steering wheel, cruise control, color-keyed full floor carpeting, carpeted and color-keyed floor mats, electrochromic rearview mirror with 8-point compass and outside temperature indicator, power windows with driver's express-down, cloth 3-passenger front bench seat with fold-down storage armrest, 6-way power adjustable driver's seat, storage pockets, adjustable headrests, folding center bench seat with headrests, folding rear bench seat with headrests, leather-wrapped steering wheel, visor extensions, illuminated visor vanity mirrors, color-keyed grille with chrome

GMC SUBURBAN

CODE	DESCRIPTION	INVOICE	MSRP

accents, composite halogen headlights, black luggage carrier, power exterior mirrors, chrome trim rings and hub wheel covers, deep tinted glass, push-button four-wheel drive (on 4WD models); remote keyless entry, carpeted load floor mats, auxiliary rear heater. NOT AVAILABLE with L65, QIZ, MT1, YG6, R9S, Z82, UM6, YG4.

1SB — **SLE Marketing Option Package 1SB with L65** 6298 7323
Includes SLE Decor front and rear air conditioning, AM/FM stereo with cassette, automatic tone control, and enhanced performance 8 speaker sound system; cargo net, tilt steering wheel, cruise control, color-keyed full floor carpeting, carpeted and color-keyed floor mats, electrochromic rearview mirror with 8-point compass and outside temperature indicator, power windows with driver's express-down, cloth 3-passenger front bench seat with fold-down storage armrest, 6-way power adjustable driver's seat, storage pockets, adjustable headrests, folding center bench seat with headrests, folding rear bench seat with headrests, leather-wrapped steering wheel, visor extensions, illuminated visor vanity mirrors, color-keyed grille with chrome accents, composite halogen headlights, black luggage carrier, power exterior mirrors, chrome trim rings and hub wheel covers, deep tinted glass, push-button four-wheel drive (on 4WD models); remote keyless entry, carpeted load floor mats, auxiliary rear heater. REQUIRES L65. NOT AVAILABLE with YG6, R9S, Z82, UM6, YG4.

1SC — **SLT Marketing Option Package 1SC** 8267 9613
Includes SLT Decor front and rear air conditioning, AM/FM stereo with cassette, CD player, automatic tone control, and enhanced performance 8 speaker sound system; cargo net, tilt steering wheel, cruise control, color-keyed full floor carpeting, carpeted and color-keyed floor mats, electrochromic rearview mirror with 8-point compass and outside temperature indicator, power windows with driver's express-down, leather front bucket seats inboard armrests and center storage console, 6-way power adjustable driver's seat, storage pockets, adjustable headrests, roof console, power lumbar supports, folding center bench seat with headrests, folding rear bench seat with headrests, leather-wrapped steering wheel, visor extensions, illuminated visor vanity mirrors, color-keyed grille with chrome accents, composite halogen headlights, black luggage carrier, power exterior mirrors, chrome trim rings and hub wheel covers, deep tinted glass, push-button four-wheel drive (on 4WD models), extra cupholders for rear passengers; remote keyless entry, carpeted load floor mats, auxiliary rear heater.

1SC — **SLT Marketing Option Package 1SC with L65** 8052 9363
Includes SLT Decor front and rear air conditioning, AM/FM stereo with cassette, CD player, automatic tone control, and enhanced performance 8 speaker sound system; cargo net, tilt steering wheel, cruise control, color-keyed full floor carpeting, carpeted and color-keyed floor mats, electrochromic rearview mirror with 8-point compass and outside temperature indicator, power windows with driver's express-down, leather front bucket seats inboard armrests and center storage console, 6-way power adjustable driver's seat, storage pockets, adjustable headrests, roof console, power lumbar supports, folding center bench seat with headrests, folding rear bench seat with headrests, leather-wrapped steering wheel, visor extensions, illuminated visor vanity mirrors, color-keyed grille with chrome accents, composite halogen headlights, black luggage carrier, power exterior mirrors, chrome trim rings and hub wheel covers,

SUBURBAN GMC

CODE	DESCRIPTION	INVOICE	MSRP
	deep tinted glass, push-button four-wheel drive (on 4WD models), extra cupholders for rear passengers; remote keyless entry, carpeted load floor mats, auxiliary rear heater.		
QBN	Tires: LT245/75R16C AT BSW (K1500)	47	55
	NOT AVAILABLE with L65, MT1, C5I, QGB, QBX, QIZ, QIW, Z82.		
QBX	Tires: LT245/75R16C AT WOL (K1500)	155	180
	NOT AVAILABLE with L65, MT1, C5I, QGB, QBN, QIZ, QIW, Z82.		
QIZ	Tires: LT245/75R16E AS BSW (C1500)	391	459
	NOT AVAILABLE with N90, GT4, QHM, 1SB, 1SC.		
QIZ	Tires: LT245/75R16E AS BSW (K1500)	146	174
	NOT AVAILABLE with GT4, PF4, QBX, QBN, QGB, QIW, 1SB, 1SC.		
QIW	Tires: LT245/75R16E AT BSW (K1500)	194	229
	NOT AVAILABLE with QGB, QBN, QBX, QIZ, PF4, Z82.		
QHM	Tires: P235/75R15 AS WOL (C1500)	155	180
	NOT AVAILABLE with L65, MT1, C3F, QIZ.		
QGB	Tires: P245/75R16 AT WOL (K1500)	120	140
	NOT AVAILABLE with L65, MT1, C5I, QBN, QBX, QIZ, QIW.		
V76	Tow Hooks (front) (C1500)	33	38
V96	Trailer Hitch Ball & Mount Provisions	26	30
	REQUIRES (Z82) HD trailering equipment.		
P06	Trim Rings & Bright Center Hub Caps	52	60
	REQUIRES 1SA.		
P06	Trim Rings & Bright Center Hub Caps	NC	NC
	REQUIRES 1SB or 1SC.		
B71	Wheel Flare Moldings (K1500)	155	180
PF4	Wheels: Aluminum (K1500)	NC	NC
	Includes steel spare wheel. REQUIRES 1SB or 1SC. NOT AVAILABLE with L65, QIZ, QIW, MT1, C5I.		
PF4	Wheels: Aluminum (K1500)	267	310
	Includes steel spare wheel. REQUIRES 1SA. NOT AVAILABLE with L65, QIZ, QIW, MT1, C5I.		
N90	Wheels: Cast Aluminum (C1500)	NC	NC
	Includes steel spare wheel. REQUIRES 1SB or 1SC. NOT AVAILABLE with L65, MT1, C3F, QIZ, 1SA.		
N90	Wheels: Cast Aluminum (C1500)	267	310
	Includes steel spare wheel. REQUIRES 1SA. NOT AVAILABLE with 1SB, 1SC, L65, MT1, C3F, QIZ.		

1998 SUBURBAN 2500

Standard Equipment

C2500: 5.7L V-8 OHV SMPI 16-valve engine; 4-speed electronic overdrive automatic transmission with lock-up; 600-amp HD battery; 100-amp alternator; HD transmission oil cooler; rear wheel drive, 3.73 axle ratio; stainless steel exhaust; front independent suspension with HD anti-roll bar, front coil springs, HD front shocks, rear suspension with anti-roll bar, rear leaf springs, HD

GMC SUBURBAN

rear shocks; power re-circulating ball steering with engine speed-sensing assist; front disc/rear drum brakes with 4 wheel anti-lock braking system; 42 gal capacity fuel tank; split swing-out rear cargo door; trailer harness; front and rear chrome bumpers with black rub strip, front rub strip with chrome bumper insert, rear step bumper; black bodyside molding with chrome bodyside insert, chrome wheel well molding; monotone paint; sealed beam halogen headlamps with daytime running lights; additional exterior lights include center high mounted stop light, underhood light; driver and passenger manual black folding outside mirrors; front and rear 16" x 6.5" painted styled steel wheels with hub wheel covers; LT245/75SR16 BSW AS front and rear tires; inside mounted full-size conventional steel spare wheel; rear heat ducts; AM/FM stereo with clock, seek-scan, 4 speakers and fixed antenna; power door locks, child safety rear door locks; 3 power accessory outlets; analog instrumentation display includes tachometer gauge, oil pressure gauge, water temp gauge, volt gauge, PRNDL in instrument panel, trip odometer; warning indicators include battery, lights on, key in ignition, door ajar; dual airbags; ignition disable; tinted windows, manual rear windows, fixed 1/4 vent windows; variable intermittent front windshield wipers; front bench seat with tilt adjustable headrests, driver seat includes 2-way direction control, passenger seat includes 2-way direction control, front height adjustable seatbelts; vinyl seats, full cloth headliner, full vinyl floor covering; interior lights include dome light with fade, front reading lights; passenger side vanity mirror; day-night rearview mirror; glove box with light, front cupholder, instrument panel bin, driver and passenger door bins, rear door bins; vinyl cargo floor, cargo tie downs, cargo light; colored grille, black side window moldings, black front windshield molding, black rear window molding, black door handles.

K2500 (in addition to or instead of C2500 equipment): Part-time 4 wheel drive, auto locking hub control with electronic shift, 4.1 axle ratio; front torsion suspension, front torsion springs, front torsion bar; tow hooks; colored fender flares; front and rear height adjustable seatbelts.

Base Prices

TC20906-R9S	C2500	23370	26713
TK20906-R9S	K2500	25995	29713
Destination Charge:		675	675

Accessories

Code	Description	Invoice	MSRP
GU6	3.42 Axle Ratio	NC	NC
MT1	4-Speed HD Automatic Transmission	NC	NC
	Includes HD auxiliary transmission oil cooler.		
GT5	4.10 Axle Ratio	NC	NC
	REQUIRES (L29) engine OR (L65) engine.		
AE7	60/40 Reclining Split Bench Seat	86	100
	Includes center fold down storage armrest with coin holder, map net, writing board and power lumbar. seatback storage pockets. REQUIRES 1SA. NOT AVAILABLE with A95.		
Y6G	Air Conditioning Not Desired	NC	NC
	NOT AVAILABLE with (C60) front air conditioning, (C69) front and rear air conditioning.		
C36	Auxiliary Rear Passenger Heater	176	205
	REQUIRES 1SA.		
YF5	California Emissions	146	170
	Automatically added to vehicles shipped to and/or sold to retailers in California. Out-of-state retailers must order on vehicles to be registered or leased in California. NOT AVAILABLE with (U01) exterior roof marker lamps (5).		

SUBURBAN — GMC

CODE	DESCRIPTION	INVOICE	MSRP
AS3	**Center and Rear Bench Seats**	1017	1182
	Includes headrests, center and rear folding bench seats, adjustable front and rear seatbelts, rear cupholders.		
AT5	**Center Folding Bench Seat**	544	632
	Includes headrests, center fold-down armrests, easy entry feature on passenger side for access to rear seat/cargo area, adjustable front and rear seatbelts, rear cupholders. REQUIRES 1SA.		
V10	**Cold Climate Package**	28	33
	Includes engine block heater. NOT AVAILABLE with (L65) engine.		
ZQ3	**Convenience Package**	329	383
	Includes tilt wheel, speed control. REQUIRES 1SA.		
AJ1	**Deep Tinted Glass**	262	305
	REQUIRES 1SA.		
C49	**Electric Rear window defogger**	132	154
	REQUIRES 1SA.		
L65	**Engine: 6.5L V8 Turbo Diesel**	2460	2860
	Includes hydraulic brakes, glow plugs, integral two-stage fuel filter, fuel and water separator with instrument panel warning light, fuel filter change signal, black front bumper guards, HD radiator, engine oil cooler, extra sound insulation, engine block heater, dual batteries. NOT AVAILABLE with (K47) high capacity air cleaner, (V10) Cold Climate Package.		
L29	**Engine: 7.4L V8**	516	600
U01	**Exterior Roof Marker Lamps (5)**	47	55
	NOT AVAILABLE with (YF5) California Emissions.		
C69	**Front & Rear Air Conditioning**	1200	1395
	Includes dual controls and rear overhead vents. REQUIRES 1SA. NOT AVAILABLE with (Y6G) air conditioning not desired.		
C60	**Front Air Conditioning**	727	845
	REQUIRES 1SA. NOT AVAILABLE with (Y6G) air conditioning not desired.		
V76	**Front Tow Hooks**	33	38
KNP	**HD Auxiliary Transmission Oil Cooler**	83	96
F60	**HD Front Springs (K2500)**	54	63
Z82	**HD Trailering Equipment**	184	214
	Includes platform hitch and HD hazard flasher.		
K47	**High Capacity Air Cleaner**	22	25
	NOT AVAILABLE with (L65) engine.		
G80	**Locking Differential**	217	252
ZM9	**Luxury Convenience Package**	856	995
	Includes heated front seats, 6-way power adjustable driver's seat, electrochromic rearview mirror, Homelink transmitter, 46mm Bilstein shocks. REQUIRES 1SC and A95.		
1SA	**Marketing Option Package 1SA**	NC	NC
	Includes SL Decor Package. REQUIRES Y6G or C60 or C69. NOT AVAILABLE with YG4, AE7, A95, ULO, AUO, ZY2.		
NZZ	**Off-Road Skid Plates (K2500)**	194	225
ZY2	**Paint: Conventional Two-Tone**	172	200
	NOT AVAILABLE with (1SA) Marketing Option Package 1SA.		

GMC SUBURBAN / 2500

CODE	DESCRIPTION	INVOICE	MSRP
UL0	**Radio: AM/FM Stereo with Cassette**	NC	NC
	Includes theft lock, automatic tone control, auto reverse cassette player with music search, digital clock and enhanced 8 speaker system. NOT AVAILABLE with 1SA, 1SC, UM6, UN0, UP0.		
UM6	**Radio: AM/FM Stereo with Cassette**	126	147
	Includes digital clock and 4 speakers. REQUIRES 1SA. NOT AVAILABLE with (UL0) radio, (UN0) radio, (UP0) radio.		
UN0	**Radio: AM/FM Stereo With CD**	86	100
	Includes automatic tone control, theft lock, digital clock and enhanced 8 speaker system. REQUIRES 1SB. NOT AVAILABLE with UM6, UL0, UP0.		
UP0	**Radio: AM/FM Stereo with CD & Cassette**	172	200
	Includes automatic tone control, theft lock, auto reverse and music search cassette player, CD player, digital clock and enhanced 8 speaker system. REQUIRES 1SB. NOT AVAILABLE with (UM6) radio, (UN0) radio, (UL0) radio.		
ZP6	**Rear Window Wiper/Washer with Defogger**	240	279
	REQUIRES 1SA.		
A95	**Reclining Bucket Seats**	335	390
	Includes inboard armrests, dual adjustable headrests, power lumbar supports, floor console, overhead console, seatback storage pockets. NOT AVAILABLE with (1SA) Marketing Option Package 1SA, (AE7) seats.		
AU0	**Remote Keyless Entry**	129	150
	REQUIRES 1SA.		
BVE	**Running Boards**	236	275
	Shipped loose for dealer installation. NOT AVAILABLE with (NZZ) Skid Plate Package.		
1SB	**SLE Marketing Option Package 1SB**	6298	7323
	Includes SLE Decor front and rear air conditioning, AM/FM stereo with cassette, automatic tone control, and enhanced performance 8 speaker sound system; cargo net, tilt steering wheel, cruise control, color-keyed full floor carpeting, carpeted and color-keyed floor mats, electrochromic rearview mirror with 8-point compass and outside temperature indicator, power windows with driver's express-down, cloth 3-passenger front bench seat with fold-down storage armrest, 6-way power adjustable driver's seat, storage pockets, adjustable headrests, folding center bench seat with headrests, folding rear bench seat with headrests, leather-wrapped steering wheel, visor extensions, illuminated visor vanity mirrors, color-keyed grille with chrome accents, composite halogen headlights, black luggage carrier, power exterior mirrors, chrome trim rings and hub wheel covers, deep tinted glass, push-button four-wheel drive (on 4WD models); remote keyless entry, carpeted load floor mats, auxiliary rear heater.		
1SC	**SLT Marketing Option Package 1SC**	8052	9363
	Includes SLT Decor front and rear air conditioning, AM/FM stereo with cassette, CD player, automatic tone control, and enhanced performance 8 speaker sound system; cargo net, tilt steering wheel, cruise control, color-keyed full floor carpeting, carpeted and color-keyed floor mats, electrochromic rearview mirror with 8-point compass and outside temperature indicator, power windows with driver's express-down, leather front bucket seats inboard armrests and center storage console, 6-way power		

SUBURBAN / 2500 — GMC

CODE	DESCRIPTION	INVOICE	MSRP

adjustable driver's seat, storage pockets, adjustable headrests, roof console, power lumbar supports, folding center bench seat with headrests, folding rear bench seat with headrests, leather-wrapped steering wheel, visor extensions, illuminated visor vanity mirrors, color-keyed grille with chrome accents, composite halogen headlights, black luggage carrier, power exterior mirrors, chrome trim rings and hub wheel covers, deep tinted glass, push-button four-wheel drive (on 4WD models), extra cupholders for rear passengers; remote keyless entry, carpeted load floor mats, auxiliary rear heater.

Code	Description	Invoice	MSRP
DF2	Stainless Steel Camper Mirrors	46	53
	7.5" x 10.5" stainless steel. Adjustable arm feature to provide field of vision for vehicles to 96" wide. Shipped loose for dealer installation. REQUIRES (1SA) Marketing Option Package 1SA.		
DF2	Stainless Steel Camper Type Mirrors	(39)	(45)
	7.5" x 10.5" stainless steel. Adjustable arm feature to provide field of vision for vehicles to 96" wide. Shipped loose for dealer installation. REQUIRES 1SB or 1SC.		
QIW	Tires: LT245/75R16E AT BSW (K2500)	47	55
V96	Trailering Hitch Ball & Mount	26	30
	REQUIRES (Z82) HD trailering equipment.		
P06	Trim Rings & Bright Center Hub Caps	52	60
	REQUIRES 1SA.		
N90	Wheels: Cast Aluminum (K2500)	267	310
	NOT AVAILABLE with PF4, 1SB, 1SC.		
PF4	Wheels: Cast Aluminum (K2500)	267	310
	REQUIRES 1SA. NOT AVAILABLE with (N90) wheels.		

For expert advice in selecting/buying/leasing a new car, call

1-900-AUTOPRO

($2.00 per minute)

GMC YUKON

1998 YUKON

1998 GMC Yukon 4-Door

What's New?

The two-door model gets the ax this year. Rear seat passengers are cooled by a newly optional rear air conditioning system. A host of new standard features has been added, including carpeted floor mats. Three new colors spruce up the outside a bit, and second-generation airbags are standard inside.

Review

Until this year, General Motors had a lock on the mid-size sport/utility market, but couldn't build enough to meet demand because of a serious lack of production capacity. The result? Inflated prices as dealers struggled to keep the Yukon and its Chevrolet Tahoe twin in stock. Then, GM refurbished a plant in Arlington, Texas, (which used to produce full-size Buick, Chevrolet, and Cadillac sedans) and Yukon/Tahoe production was effectively doubled.

Unfortunately for GM, the additional plant capacity may have come a bit too late. Ford released the mid-sized Expedition last year, and this F-150 pickup-based SUV is more refined but less powerful than the GM twins. This year, Dodge releases the Durango, based on the fresh Dakota platform and sure to be slightly smaller and easier to maneuver than the GM and Ford behemoths. And Lincoln is assaulting our eyesight with the overdone Navigator, which is currently selling faster than condoms at a drive-in theater. Since four-door SUVs sell much better than two-door models, the smaller Yukon has been retired from the lineup this year.

In the size race, the remaining Yukon four-door fits squarely between the Jimmy compact and the big-bruiser Suburban wagons. Squint your eyes, in fact, and the difference between a Yukon and Suburban begins to evaporate, despite the latter's extra 20 inches of steel. Ford's Expedition is a bit larger than the Yukon, while the Dodge Durango is slightly smaller. Both of these competitors offer 8-passenger seating, which is not available on the Yukon.

Yukon's interior has been borrowed from the full-size Sierra pickup. This year, the airbags are of the reduced force second generation variety. Carpeted floor mats and a carpeted reversible cargo mat are standard equipment. Also standard for 1998 is a power driver's seat, a theft-deterrent system, an electrochromic rearview mirror, and a new automatic 4WD system on K-

YUKON

| CODE | DESCRIPTION | INVOICE | MSRP |

series models. Rear air conditioning is newly optional, as is a Luxury Convenience Package that includes heated seats, heated exterior mirrors, a power passenger seat, and a HomeLink transmitter.

How does the Yukon stack up against the Expedition? The Ford is more refined and comfortable, but we prefer Yukon's dated exterior styling and more maneuverable size. Smooth overhead-cam engines power the Ford, but we prefer the torque and roar of GMC's Vortec 5700 V8. Neither is easy to climb into, particularly without running boards, but the Yukon's lower ride height makes access much easier. The Ford boasts optional 8-passenger seating. As drivers, however, we prefer the Yukon's powerful engine over the Expedition's refinement. Naturally, though, you can still expect truck-style ride and handling, but reasonable comfort on the road.

With new competitors arriving annually and increased production capacity, GMC dealers have little reason to gouge customers on Yukon pricing. Just threaten to go down the street and pick up a new Ford Expedition, Lincoln Navigator, or Dodge Durango; the dealer should be eager to play ball.

Safety Data

Driver Airbag: *Standard*
Side Airbag: *Not Available*
Traction Control: *Not Available*
Driver Crash Test Grade: *Good*

Passenger Airbag: *Standard*
4-Wheel ABS: *Standard*
Integrated Child Seat(s): *Not Available*
Passenger Crash Test Grade: *Good*

Standard Equipment

YUKON 2WD: 5.7L V-8 OHV SMPI 16-valve engine; 4-speed electronic overdrive automatic transmission with lock-up; 600-amp battery; 100-amp alternator; rear wheel drive, 3.42 axle ratio; stainless steel exhaust; front independent suspension with anti-roll bar, front coil springs, front shocks, rear suspension with rear leaf springs, rear shocks; power re-circulating ball steering with engine speed-sensing assist; front disc/rear drum brakes with 4 wheel anti-lock braking system; 30 gal capacity fuel tank; split swing-out rear cargo door; trailer harness; roof rack; front and rear chrome bumpers with black rub strip, front rub strip with chrome bumper insert, rear step bumper; black bodyside molding with chrome bodyside insert, chrome wheel well molding; monotone paint; aero-composite halogen headlamps with daytime running lights; additional exterior lights include center high mounted stop light, underhood light; driver and passenger power remote black folding outside mirrors; front and rear 15" x 7" silver alloy wheels; P235/75SR15 BSW AS front and rear tires; underbody mounted full-size temporary steel spare wheel; air conditioning, rear heat ducts; AM/FM stereo with clock, seek-scan, cassette, 8 performance speakers, automatic equalizer, theft deterrent, and fixed antenna; cruise control; power door locks with remote keyless entry, child safety rear door locks, power remote tailgate release; 3 power accessory outlets; analog instrumentation display includes tachometer gauge, oil pressure gauge, water temp gauge, volt gauge, compass, exterior temp, trip odometer; warning indicators include battery, lights on, key in ignition, door ajar; dual airbags; ignition disable; deep tinted windows, power front windows with driver 1-touch down, power rear windows, fixed 1/4 vent windows; variable intermittent front windshield wipers, rear window defroster; seating capacity of 6, 60-40 split-bench front seat with tilt adjustable headrests, center armrest with storage, driver seat includes 4-way power seat with 8-way direction control and power lumbar support, passenger seat includes 4-way direction control with power lumbar support; 60-40 folding split-bench rear seat with adjustable rear headrest, center armrest with storage; front and rear height adjustable seatbelts; premium cloth seats, cloth door trim insert, full cloth headliner, full carpet floor covering with carpeted floor mats; interior lights include dome light, front and rear reading lights, 4 door curb lights, illuminated entry; leather-wrapped sport steering wheel with tilt adjustment; dual illuminated vanity mirrors, dual auxiliary visors; auto-

GMC YUKON

dimming day-night rearview mirror; glove box with light, front and rear cupholders, instrument panel bin, 2 seat back storage pockets, driver and passenger door bins; carpeted cargo floor, cargo cover, cargo net, cargo concealed storage; chrome grille, black side window moldings, black front windshield molding, black rear window molding, black door handles. 4WD (in addition to or instead of 2WD equipment): Part-time 4 wheel drive, auto locking hub control with electronic shift; front torsion suspension, front torsion springs, front torsion bar; tow hooks; front and rear 16"x 6.5" wheels; rubber floor mats.

Base Prices

Code	Description	Invoice	MSRP
C10706	2WD	25904	29604
K10706	4WD	28528	32604
	Destination Charge:	640	640

Accessories

Code	Description	Invoice	MSRP
GT4	3.73 Axle Ratio	116	135
	Includes water to oil cooler. NOT AVAILABLE with (KC4) engine oil cooler.		
AE7	60/40 Reclining Split Bench Seat	NC	NC
	NOT AVAILABLE with (1SD) Marketing Option Package 1SD.		
YF5	California Emissions	146	170
	Required for all vehicles to be registered in the State of California.		
V10	Cold Climate Package	28	33
	Includes engine block heater.		
ZY2	Conventional Two-Tone Paint	172	200
KC4	Engine Oil Cooler	116	135
	NOT AVAILABLE with (GT4) 3.73 axle ratio.		
C69	Front & Rear Air Conditioning	473	550
	REQUIRES 1SD.		
A95	Front High Back Reclining Bucket Seats	204	237
	Includes inboard armrests, dual adjustable headrests, power lumbars, storage pockets behind seats, center storage console, overhead console. REQUIRES 1SD.		
KNP	HD Auxiliary Transmission Cooler	83	96
Z82	HD Trailering Equipment	184	214
	Includes trailering hitch platform and heavy duty hazard flasher. REQUIRES (KC4) engine oil cooler or (GT4) 3.73 axle		
K47	High Capacity Air Cleaner	22	25
G80	Locking Differential	217	252
ZM9	Luxury Convenience Package	856	955
	Includes heated front seats, 6-way power driver's seat, electrochromic rearview mirror with 8-point compass and external temperature readout, Homelink transmitter, 46mm Bilstein shocks. REQUIRES 1SE and A95.		
UN0	Radio: AM/FM Stereo with CD	86	100
	Includes clock, theft lock, automatic tone control, speed sensitive volume and enhanced performance speaker system. NOT AVAILABLE with (UP0) radio, (1SE) SLT Marketing Option Package 1SE.		

YUKON　　　　　　　　　　　　　　　　　　GMC

CODE	DESCRIPTION	INVOICE	MSRP
UP0	Radio: AM/FM Stereo with CD & Cassette	172	200
	Includes clock, theft lock, automatic tone control, speed sensitive volume, auto reverse music search cassette and enhanced performance speaker system. REQUIRES 1SD. NOT AVAILABLE with (UN0) radio.		
BVE	Running Boards	236	275
	Shipped loose for dealer installation. NOT AVAILABLE with (NZZ) Skid Plate Package.		
NZZ	Skid Plate Package (4WD)	82	95
	Includes differential and transfer case shields.		
1SD	SLE Marketing Option Package 1SD	NC	NC
	Includes 6-way power driver's seat, front and rear carpeted floor mats, carpeted cargo area mat, rearview auto-dimming mirror, remote keyless entry. NOT AVAILABLE with (AE7) seats.		
1SE	SLT Marketing Option Package 1SE	1838	2137
	Includes 6-way power driver's seat, front and rear carpeted floor mats, carpeted cargo area mat, rearview auto-dimming mirror, remote keyless entry plus SLT decor package: front and rear air conditioning, AM/FM stereo wiuth CD player, cassette player, seek-scan, clock, automatic tone control, and enhanced 8 speaker sound system; 2 additional rear cupholders, leather highback bucket seats with inboard armrests, adjustable headrests, power lumbar supports, storage pockets, center storage console, overhead console, rear center armrest with tissue holder, visor extensions, illuminated visor vanity mirrors, map storage straps on visors.		
QFN	Tires: P235/75R15 AS RWL SBR (2WD)	120	140
QGB	Tires: P245/75R16 AT WOL (4WD)	120	140
V76	Tow Hooks (front) (2WD)	33	38

**One 15-minute call
could save you 15% or more
on car insurance.**

GEICO DIRECT

America's 6th Largest Automobile Insurance Company

1-800-555-2758

HONDA   CR-V

1997 CR-V

1997 Honda CR-V

What's New?

The first-ever Honda-designed sport-ute has hit the market and is on sale at a dealership near you. Priced competitively with mini-utes, the CR-V offers cargo capacity that is in line with what compact sport-utility buyers are accustomed to. The CR-V comes in one trim level and is available with anti-lock brakes.

Review

For years, Honda has been selling a sport utility vehicle that many consider a fraud. Forget that the Honda Passport is based on the very rugged and capable Isuzu Rodeo, to Honda aficionados it is not a real Honda. (Think of how the Porsche 914 fares in the eyes of diehard Porsche fanatics.) Thus, to many people, the CR-V is the first Honda sport-utility vehicle.

Built on the Civic platform, the CR-V successfully integrates familiar Honda components into an all-new design. Honda's famous four-wheel double wishbone suspension makes an appearance on the CR-V, the first ever application of four-wheel double-wishbone technology on a sport-ute, as does the very familiar four-speed automatic transmission. The 2.0-liter DOHC inline four-cylinder engine makes 126-horsepower and 133 lbs./ft. of torque. The CR-V's real time four-wheel drive system is a derivative of the unit that Honda initially offered on their Civic wagon. The result of using all of these car components is that the CR-V looks and feels rather like, um, a car.

The CR-V's interior is instantly recognizable to anyone who has spent any time in Honda's passenger cars. Functionality takes precedence over style in the CR-V's cabin, and the result is easy-to-read gauges, well-placed controls, and high-quality, if somewhat boring, interior materials. Fit and finish is equal to the highly-acclaimed Accord. The CR-V offers comfortable chairs for its occupants, each of which has excellent visibility and the ability to recline when the trip grows long. The CR-V's cargo capacity is an outstanding 67.2 cubic feet when the rear seats are folded.

CR-V

HONDA

| CODE | DESCRIPTION | INVOICE | MSRP |

Available in only one trim-level, the CR-V is surprisingly well-equipped. Air conditioning with a micron filtration system is standard, as are power windows, power door locks, rear window wiper and defogger, AM/FM stereo, and a folding picnic table that doubles as a cargo area cover. Options include anti-lock brakes and alloy wheels.

The CR-V is not meant to replace hard-core recreational vehicles like the Jeep Wrangler or Toyota 4Runner. Instead, it is meant for the person who wants the functionality of a sport utility without having to pay an exorbitant sticker price and huge gas bills. The CR-V will get people to work and back in all but the worst weather, and to their favorite picnic area, assuming it's not on the Rubicon Trail. Best of all, it's a sport utility vehicle that Honda-lovers can finally call their own.

Safety Data

Driver Airbag: *Standard*
Side Airbag: *Not Available*
Traction Control: *Not Available*
Driver Crash Test Grade: *Not Available*

Passenger Airbag: *Standard*
4-Wheel ABS: *Optional*
Integrated Child Seat(s): *Not Available*
Passenger Crash Test Grade: *Not Available*

Standard Equipment

CR-V: 2.0-liter DOHC 4-cylinder engine, 4-speed automatic transmission, dual front air bags, power front disc/rear drum brakes, speed-sensitive power steering, power windows with driver's side express down, cruise control, air conditioning, tachometer, rear mud guards, digital clock, front and rear stabilizer bars, air filtration system, electric rear window defroster, tilt steering column, map pockets, power door locks, styled steel wheels, 205/70R15 steel belted radial tires, power outside mirrors, visor vanity mirrors, cargo tie-down hooks, AM/FM stereo, front and rear intermittent windshield wipers, cargo area lights, map lights, center armrest, removeable picnic table, outside-mounted spare tire carrier and cover, and remote hatch release.

Base Prices

	Invoice	MSRP
RD184V/RD185V CR-V	17513	19300
Destination Charge:	395	395

Accessories

		Invoice	MSRP
—	Anti-Lock Brakes / Alloy Wheels	907	1000
	NOTE: *Honda refers to vehicles equipped with ABS as a separate model.*		
—	California Emissions	85	100

Don't forget to swing by the Townhall when you visit Edmund's website at http://www.edmunds.com. Talk to our editors and compare notes on your favorite cars and trucks. Join others to scope out smart shopping stategies, get answers to your questions, or share your expertise. To get to the Townhall, just click on the link on the homepage or go directly to http://www.edmund.com/edweb/townhall/welcomeconflist.html.

 Town Hall

HONDA ODYSSEY

1997 ODYSSEY

1997 Honda Odyssey LX

What's New?

No changes for the 1997 Honda Odyssey.

Review

With its doors open and beckoning, Honda's stylish and competent family hauler resembles a tall station wagon more than a minivan. Why? Because instead of the expected sliding side door—a staple of minivan design from the start—you find that all four side doors swing open, like those in a sedan. They contain roll-down windows, too. Naturally, Honda hopes that this unique attribute will help steal sales away from the competition, but a single special feature isn't enough to ensure success in the ferocious minivan market.

Fortunately for Honda, Odysseys possess other virtues. For starters, you get plenty of room for four or five, with a spacious center section that's exceptionally easy to enter. Either bucket seats or a three-place bench can go there. Not enough? Well, a handy two-passenger bench seat pops out of the cargo floor to expand passenger capacity to seven. That back bench folds flat very easily when cargo is the priority, and an inside-mounted, compact spare tire takes up very little space.

The driver occupies a comfortable position, ahead of a low cowl and steering wheel, and a severely sloped windshield, its base stretched far forward. Small front quarter windows do little for visibility in that direction, but mirrors are very good. An unusual slanted dashboard holds a distinctive speedometer. In addition to a large glovebox and ample console storage box, the Odyssey offers a smaller supplementary glovebox. On the safety front, airbags are installed for both the driver and front passenger. So is all-disc anti-lock braking.

Power comes from a VTEC 140-horsepower, 2.2-liter 16-valve four-cylinder engine, borrowed from the Accord. Adequately brisk performance is accompanied, unfortunately, by an excess of buzziness. If noise is a drawback for you, a V-6 choice is likely to arrive soon. Engines in both the LX and EX editions drive an electronically-controlled four-speed automatic transmission, complete with a Grade Logic Control System and controlled by a column-mounted gearshift lever. Both Japanese-built models are well-equipped, priced competitively, and carry on Honda's reputation for solid construction.

CODE	DESCRIPTION		INVOICE	MSRP

Safety Data

Driver Airbag: *Standard*
Side Airbag: *Not Available*
Traction Control: *Not Available*
Driver Crash Test Grade: *Good*

Passenger Airbag: *Standard*
4-Wheel ABS: *Standard*
Integrated Child Seat(s): *Not Available*
Passenger Crash Test Grade: *Good*

Standard Equipment

LX: 2.2-liter 16-valve 4-cylinder SOHC engine, 4-speed automatic transmission, 4-wheel anti-lock disc brakes, independent double-wishbone front and rear suspension, power assisted rack-and-pinion steering, power outside mirrors, 2-speed variable windshield wipers, rear window wiper washer, 15" wheel covers, P205/65R15 tires, dual air bags, tilt steering column, power windows with driver's express down, power locks, cruise control, front and rear air conditioning, illuminated vanity mirrors, AM/FM stereo with cassette, rear seat heater ducts, rear window defroster, digital quartz clock, cloth front bucket seats, 2nd row bench seat (7-passenger seating), 2nd row bucket seats (6-passenger seating), and 3rd row folding rear bench seat.

EX (in addition to or instead of EX): Body-color molding, body-color outside mirrors, power sunroof, 15" alloy wheels, power driver's seat, AM/FM stereo with cassette and 6 speakers, map lights, and remote keyless entry.

Base Prices

RA186V	LX (7-Passenger)		20818	23560
RA184V	LX (6-Passenger)		21180	23970
RA187V	EX		22577	25550
Destination Charge:			395	395

Accessories

—	California Emissions		NC	NC

One 15-minute call could save you 15% or more on car insurance.

GEICO DIRECT

America's 6th Largest Automobile Insurance Company

1-800-555-2758

HONDA PASSPORT

| CODE | DESCRIPTION | INVOICE | MSRP |

1997 PASSPORT

1997 Honda Passport 4WD LX

What's New?

Honda drops the slow-selling DX 4-cylinder Passport.

Review

Honda issued a notable upgrade in 1996, adding airbags for the driver and front passenger. Also new were roof-mounted speakers that expanded available cargo space in the revised interior, plus an improved stereo system. The new dashboard, did away with the old angular look, replacing it with an organically swept affair complete with more legible gauges and improved ergonomics. Nothing has changed since then,

Passports are spacious for five inside, and V-6 models have a swing-out spare tire that creates even greater elbow room. The rear seat folds flat, resulting in a long cargo floor, but the clamshell tailgate design makes it difficult to access the back of the cargo area easily. They are however, better for watching softball games. Fortunately, the rear glass will open independently making it easier to load small items.

Road noise might be a drawback, though the 3.2-liter V-6 engine is quiet-running and strong with either five-speed manual shift or the available four-speed automatic transmission. The 2.6-liter four-cylinder engine, formerly available on the DX model has been discontinued; partially due to poor sales, and to keep the DX from competing with Honda's new mini sport/ute: the CR-V. Passports equipped with automatic transmissions have Power and Winter modes, the latter starting off in third gear to reduce wheel-spin on slippery pavements. Towing capacity is 4,500 pounds with the V-6 engine.

Anyone seeking a capable blend of comfortable highway ride and tempting off-road talents could do well to look for a Honda dealer. However, Isuzu markets a version of the Passport and calls it the Rodeo The Rodeo tends to be a bit less expensive, and comes with a more comprehensive warranty. For those reasons, we suggest you stick with a Rodeo.

PASSPORT / HONDA

| CODE | DESCRIPTION | INVOICE | MSRP |

Safety Data

Driver Airbag: *Std.*
Side Airbag: *N/A*
Traction Control: *N/A*
Driver Crash Test Grade: *Good*

Passenger Airbag: *Std.*
4-Wheel ABS: *Opt.*
Integrated Child Seat(s): *N/A*
Passenger Crash Test Grade: *Avg.*

Standard Equipment

LX (in addition to or instead of DX equipment): Tilt steering wheel, cruise control, air conditioning (4WD), tachometer, power windows, 3.2 liter MFI 24-valve V6 engine, power door locks, power 4-wheel disc brakes w/rear anti-lock braking, AM/FM stereo radio with cassette and 6 speakers, radiator skid plate transfer case (4WD), digital clock, dual visor vanity mirrors, 60/40 split fold-down rear seat, remote control tailgate window release, map pockets, automatic locking hubs (4WD), aluminum alloy wheels (4WD).

LX w/Wheel Pkg (in addition to or instead of LX equipment): 16" alloy wheels, limited slip differential, mud guards, flared wheel opening moldings, P245/70R16 mud and snow SBR tires.

EX (in addition to or instead of LX w/Wheel Pkg equipment): Limited slip differential (4WD), rear privacy glass, removable tilt-up moonroof, air conditioning, leather-wrapped steering wheel, chrome front and rear bumpers, dual map lights, intermittent windshield wipers, rear window wiper/washer, cargo net, dual color-keyed heated power mirrors, front air dam.

Base Prices

Code	Description	Invoice	MSRP
9B214V	LX 2WD 5-Speed	19043	21470
9B224V	LX 2WD Auto	19904	22440
9B314V	LX 4WD 5-Speed	21598	24350
9B324V	LX 4WD Auto	22619	25500
9B315V	LX 4WD w/16" Tires 5-Speed	22042	24850
9B325V	LX 4WD w/16" Tires Auto	23062	26000
9B227V	EX 2WD 5-Speed	23222	26180
9B317V	EX 4WD 5-Speed	24730	27880
9B327V	EX 4WD Auto	25750	29030
Destination Charge:		395	395

Accessories

Code	Description	Invoice	MSRP
—	California Emissions (All)	138	150

CARFINANCE.COM™ Instant Lease & Loan Quotes for New & Used Vehicles!
www.CarFinance.com/edmunds

INFINITI   QX4

| CODE | DESCRIPTION | INVOICE | MSRP |

1997 QX4

1997 Infiniti QX4

What's New?

A version of Nissan's wonderful four-wheeler is introduced by Infiniti, aiming to compete with the Mercury Mountaineer, Acura SLX, and Land Rover Discovery. Differences between the QX4 and the Pathfinder include the Q's full-time four-wheel drive system, a more luxurious interior, and substantially different sheetmetal.

Review

It was only a matter of time. Acura jumped on the luxury SUV bandwagon in early 1996, closely followed by Lexus. Land Rover sales have been shooting up steadily, and even Mercedes-Benz is now producing its version of an off-road luxury vehicle. It's no surprise, then, that Nissan has decided to release a super-luxury version of its capable Pathfinder as an Infiniti.

Nissan took this same course when they decided to introduce a new entry-level sedan to the Infiniti lineup. Like the I30, which is mechanically identical to the Nissan Maxima, the QX4 has little under the skin to distinguish it from its down-market brethren. The QX4 is powered by the same 3.3-liter V-6 found in the lowly Pathfinder XE, but in the Q it is teamed to a 4-speed electronically controlled automatic transmission. Although we haven't yet driven the QX4, we are happy with how this powertrain has performed in the Pathfinder. The QX4 does have one item that stands out, however, and that is the Q's all-mode four-wheel drive which functions continuously without any input from the driver; a must for those who can't be bothered with locking hubs or shifting gears.

Most drivers won't care that the QX4 is so similar to the Pathfinder. For one thing, the Pathfinder rides on one of the best SUV chassis and suspension systems that we've ever experienced. Although most QX4 drivers won't venture far from civilization, it is nice to know that if they do they will be treated to a stable, sure-footed off-road experience. In addition, we must point out that the QX4's steering and on-road manners are unmatched by any other SUV on the market, even the vaunted Toyota 4Runner.

The other reason that drivers won't care about the QX4's mechanical similarities to the Pathfinder is because the QX4 doesn't look at all similar to the truck that it's based on. Dramatically different front and rear end styling render this SUV unique among a segment

QX4

| CODE | DESCRIPTION | INVOICE | MSRP |

famous for look-alike products. Our staff has had mixed reviews about the QX4's styling, but none of us would call it conventional. This may be good or bad, depending on the amount of attention that you like to draw to yourself, but at least you can rest assured that you won't see the freeways cluttered with them on your daily commute.

The QX4's interior is quite comfortable, with supportive seats, excellent ergonomics (for a truck), good visibility, and an easy step in. As befits a $36,000 vehicle, the materials are first-rate and the fit and finish is excellent. Additionally, Infiniti has made optioning the vehicle easy; there are only three non-standard equipment items to choose from the order sheet.

We haven't driven the QX4 yet, but we anticipate getting our hands on one soon. Stay tuned and keep your fingers crossed; hopefully we can have a full road test before camping season is upon us.

Safety Data

Driver Airbag: *Standard*
Side Airbag: *Not Available*
Traction Control: *Not Available*
Driver Crash Test Grade: *Average*

Passenger Airbag: *Standard*
4-Wheel ABS: *Standard*
Integrated Child Seat(s): *Not Available*
Passenger Crash Test Grade: *Average*

Standard Equipment

QX4: 3.3-liter V-6 engine, 4-speed electronically controlled automatic transmission, all-wheel drive, power rack-and-pinion steering, power front disc/rear drum brakes, independent front suspension, multilink rear supsension, front and rear stabilizer bars, 16" aluminum wheels, P245/70R16 tires, full size spare tire, 21 gallon fuel tank, fog lights, roof rack, heated outside mirrors, privacy glass, skid plate, body color running boards, color-keyed grille and bumpers, dual airbags, variable intermittent wipers, liftgate with independent- opening glass, dual illuminated vanity mirrors, overhead console with temperature display, compass, and storage; map lights, leather-wrapped steering wheel, hand brake, and shift knob; tilt steering, cruise control, power windows, power door locks, remote keyless entry, rear window defroster, carpeted floor mats, automatic temperature control, power front bucket seats, amazingly comfortable rear seats, Homelink transmitter, Bose stereo with CD player, cassette, and 6 speakers; power antenna, leather upholstery, wood trim, center console, front and rear cup holders, child-proof rear door locks, cargo area cover, cargo net, and remote fuel filler door release.

Base Prices

| 71017 | QX4 | 31666 | 35550 |
| Destination Charge: | | 495 | 495 |

Accessories

X03	Heated Seats	355	400
J01	Power Sunroof	845	950
S02	Premium Sport Package	1467	1650
	Includes sunroof, limited slip differential, and heated seats.		

EDMUND'S 1998 NEW TRUCKS

ISUZU HOMBRE

1997 HOMBRE

1997 Isuzu Hombre XS

What's New?

A Spacecab model debuts, with seating for 5 passengers and your choice of four-cylinder or V-6 power. Other news includes two fresh paint colors and revised graphics.

Review

Sporting sheetmetal stamped by General Motors do Brasil, and basic mechanical and structural components of the Chevrolet S-10/GMC Sonoma twins, the Hombre is Isuzu's entry into the compact pickup market. Sporting two-wheel drive, a regular cab, and a weak 2.2-liter four cylinder engine upon debut in 1996, the Hombre was not exactly the stuff truck buyers craved.

For 1997, Isuzu introduces a Spacecab model that can be equipped with a 4.3-liter V-6 engine teamed to a four-speed automatic transmission. While this new model may jump-start Hombre sales (this editor has seen two Hombres on the road, both of which were equipped with a large refrigerated box in place of a bed), the two new colors and revised graphics that are new this year likely will not.

At least the Hombre is somewhat of an improvement over the aging Japanese-built pickup the company marketed in 1995. Four-wheel anti-lock brakes and a driver airbag are standard on both models. However, crash test scores, based on the performance of the structurally identical Chevy S-10, are worse than they were for the old Isuzu truck, particularly for the front passenger. Horsepower and torque with the the GM 2.2-liter four-cylinder engine is better than the old truck boasted, and fuel economy has improved. However, front leg room has diminished slightly, payload is down a couple hundred pounds, and the turning circle has widened. This is progress?

Hombre regular cab is available in S and XS trim levels, and options are few. S models are the workhorse Hombres, with vinyl floor covering and options limited to air conditioning, a stereo, and a rear step bumper. XS models are better-equipped, offering custom cloth upholstery, carpeted floors, and a tachometer. All Spacecab models have XS trim.

Isuzu hasn't been selling many pickups in the past several years. As personal use pickup

HOMBRE ISUZU

sales skyrocketed, the company stuck with marketing basic trucks more suited for work than play. First impressions indicate that the Hombre will do little to change Isuzu's fortunes in this segment.

Safety Data

Driver Airbag: *Standard*
Side Airbag: *Not Available*
Traction Control: *Not Available*
Driver Crash Test Grade: *Average*

Passenger Airbag: *Not Available*
4-Wheel ABS: *Standard*
Integrated Child Seat(s): *Not Available*
Passenger Crash Test Grade: *Poor*

Standard Equipment

HOMBRE S: Variable-assist power steering, power front disc/rear drum anti-lock brakes, independent front suspension with stabilizer bar, on-board diagnostic system, maintenance-free battery, driver airbag, side-guard door beams, collapsible steering column, daytime running lights, halogen headlights, dual manual outside mirrors, inside hood release, double-wall cargo bed with two-tier loading, tie-down loops in cargo bed, tinted glass, 15-inch steel wheels with bolt-on wheelcovers, P205/75R15 all-season radial tires, under-bed spare tire carrier with full size spare tire, detachable tailgate, two-sided galvanized steel body sheet metal (except roof and cargo box front panel), tweed cloth bench seat, Scotchgard protective treatment on seating surfaces, dual padded sun visors, intermittent windshield wipers, 2.2-liter I4 OHV SFI engine, 5-speed manual transmission with overdrive, dual cupholders, door pockets, dashboard utility tray and glove compartment, dome light, analog speedometer, trip odometer, gauges for coolant temperature, voltage and fuel level

XS REGULAR CAB (in addition to or instead of HOMBRE S equipment): Rear step bumper, custom cloth 60/40 split bench seat with folding center armrest, cut-pile carpeting, AM/FM stereo with 4 speakers and digital clock

XS SPACECAB (in addition to or instead of XS REGULAR CAB): Dark gray rear bumper, rear quarter swing-out glass, soft cloth upper door trim, front map light, sunvisor extensions, dual illuminated visor vanity mirrors, dual auxiliary power outlets, rear cupholders, vinyl rear jump seats

XS SPACECAB V-6 (in addition to or instead of XS SPACECAB equipment): 4.3-liter V-6 engine, 4-speed automatic transmission, center console with dual cupholders, storage armrest

Base Prices

Code	Description	Invoice	MSRP
P15	S Regular Cab	10370	11272
P25	XS Regular Cab	10646	11699
P55	XS Spacecab	12674	14289
P64	XS Spacecab V-6	14413	16413
	Destination Charge:	485	485

Accessories

Code	Description	Invoice	MSRP
A1	Air Conditioning	710	835
—	Automatic Transmission (All except Spacecab V6)	897	975
B2	California Emissions	145	170
C0	Convenience Package (XS Spacecab V6)	387	425
	Includes tilt steering wheel and cruise control		

EDMUND'S 1998 NEW TRUCKS

ISUZU — HOMBRE

CODE	DESCRIPTION	INVOICE	MSRP
C2	Massachusetts/New York Emissions	145	170
P2	Performance Package (4-cyl. models)	55	65
	Includes heavy-duty suspension and 4.10 rear axle		
P2	Performance Package (XS Spacecab V6)	55	65
	Includes heavy-duty suspension and 3.42 rear axle ratio		
P5	Power Package (XS Spacecab V6)	482	530
	Includes power windows, power door locks, and power exterior mirrors		
P1	Preferred Equipment Package (Reg Cab)	1029	1131
	Includes air conditioning, sliding rear window, AM/FM stereo with cassette player, 4 speakers, and digital clock; tachometer, floor mats		
P6	Preferred Equipment Package (XS Spacecab)	1047	1151
	Includes air conditioning, sliding rear window, AM/FM stereo with CD player, 4 premium speakers, and digital clock; tachometer, floor mats		
P9	Preferred Equipment Package (XS Spacecab)	815	896
	Includes air conditioning, sliding rear window, AM/FM stereo with cassette player, 4 speakers, and digital clock; tachometer, floor mats		
I2	Rear Step Bumper (S)	51	60
F2	Stereo (S)	200	235
	AM/FM stereo with 4 speakers and digital clock		
F3	Stereo — w/cassette (XS Reg Cab)	323	380
	AM/FM stereo with cassette player, 4 speakers, and digital clock		
F5	Stereo — w/cassette (XS Spacecab)	123	145
	AM/FM stereo with cassette player, 4 speakers, and digital clock		

One 15-minute call could save you 15% or more on car insurance.

GEICO DIRECT

America's 6th Largest Automobile Insurance Company

1-800-555-2758

OASIS
ISUZU

CODE   DESCRIPTION   INVOICE   MSRP

1997 OASIS

1997 Isuzu Oasis

What's New?

Cruise control is added to the S model's standard equipment list, and four new colors are available.

Review

For several years, Honda has been purchasing Rodeo sport utilities from Isuzu, and rebadging them as the Honda Passport. Honda dealers were clamoring for an SUV, and rather than wait for engineers to develop a new model from scratch, the company forged a relationship with Isuzu. Starting last year, Honda also began selling an upscale version of the Isuzu Trooper as the Acura SLX, to capitalize on the booming luxury SUV market.

To reciprocate the favor, Honda allows Isuzu to rebadge a Japanese-market sedan for sale across the Pacific, and has donated the slow-selling Odyssey minivan to fill a niche in Isuzu's U.S. lineup. The Oasis has a different grille, different wheels, and an Isuzu-embossed steering wheel center hub.

The Oasis is actually a better deal than the Odyssey, mainly because Isuzu offers a more comprehensive warranty, and the few options available are priced by the factory, not individual dealers, which reduces the dealer's ability to rip off the consumer. Powered by a strong 2.2-liter four-cylinder engine and featuring four conventional doors, the Oasis scores well in government crash tests, and offers side-impact protection that meets 1998 passenger car standards. Anti-lock brakes are standard equipment.

The Oasis S can accommodate up to seven passengers, but LS models have center row captain's chairs which reduces capacity to six. The third row bench seat folds forward, flips backwards for tailgate parties, or folds away into the floor to create a flat load floor. With seats removed and folded, the LS model can hold up to 102.5 cubic feet of cargo.

Despite the distinct lack of V-6 power, we think the Oasis offers solid value as a family wagon. It's roomy, attractive, and well-equipped. Best of all, prices are in line with the new Ford Taurus and Mercury Sable station wagons, as well as the Volkswagen Passat Wagon. Oasis offers more versatility and cargo capacity than any of these competitors, an excellent warranty, and proven Honda mechanicals. What's not to like?

ISUZU OASIS

CODE DESCRIPTION INVOICE MSRP

Safety Data

Driver Airbag: *Standard*
Side Airbag: *Not Available*
Traction Control: *Not Available*
Driver Crash Test Grade: *Good*

Passenger Airbag: *Standard*
4-Wheel ABS: *Standard*
Integrated Child Seat(s): *Not Available*
Passenger Crash Test Grade: *Good*

Standard Equipment

OASIS S: 2.2-liter SOHC 16-valve engine, electronically-controlled 4-speed automatic transmission, front wheel drive, 4-wheel independent double-wishbone suspension, variable-assist power rack-and-pinion steering, power-assisted 4-wheel disc brakes, on-board diagnostic system, maintenance-free battery, 4-wheel anti-lock brake system, driver and front passenger air bags, brake/transmission shift interlock head restraints for all outboard seating positions, power door and tailgate locks, child-safe rear side door locks, 5-mph impact absorbing bumpers, side-guard door beams, halogen headlights, 2-speed intermittent windshield wipers and washers, rear window wiper and washer, front side window defrosters, electric rear window defroster with timer, dual power outside mirrors, liftgate-open warning light, one-piece tailgate with integral air deflector, tinted glass, 15-inch styled steel wheels with bolt-on wheelcovers, P205/65R15 all-season radial tires, body-colored bumpers, bodyside moldings, front and rear splash guards, 7-passenger seating (front bucket seats with inboard armrests, 2nd row 50/50 split folding bench seat, retractable folding 3rd row bench seat), 4-way reclining driver's seat, 4-way reclining front passenger's seat, moquette cloth seat trim, adjustable front shoulder belt anchors, elevated rear "theater-style" seating, dual visor vanity mirrors, full cut-pile carpeting, carpeted floor mats, covered spare tire, passenger assist grips, front and rear air conditioning, AM/FM stereo (with cassette player, anti-theft system, accessory CD controls and 4 speaker sound system), power windows with driver's express-down, adjustable steering column, low fuel warning light, digital clock, courtesy door and cargo area lights, six beverage holders, upper and lower glove compartments, remote hood and fuel-filler door releases, cruise control

OASIS LS (in addition to or instead of OASIS S equipment): Alloy wheels, wheel arch moldings, luggage rack, power sunroof, 6-passenger seating (front bucket seats with inboard armrests, removable 2nd-row bucket seats with inboard armrests, and retractable folding 3rd-row bench seat), AM/FM high-power stereo (cassette player, separate bass and treble, anti-theft system, accessory CD control, and 6-speaker premium sound system), cruise control, remote keyless entry system, map lights.

Base Prices

		Invoice	MSRP
J54	S	21831	23730
J64	LS	23911	25990
Destination Charge:		445	445

Accessories

Code	Description	Invoice	MSRP
CDD	Compact Disc Player (S/LS)	369	470
RST	Rear Seat Tray (LS)	55	70
LRO	Roof Rack (S)	181	230

RODEO ISUZU

1998 RODEO

1998 Isuzu Rodeo LS V6

What's New?

Though it may not look like it, Isuzu has completely revised the Rodeo from top to bottom, giving it more modern styling, a user-friendly interior, more V-6 power, and added room for passengers and cargo.

Review

Choices in the sub-$30,000 sport-utility class are numerous. Figuring out which truck best meets your needs almost always requires a compromise of some sort or another. The closest thing to perfect has been the Ford Explorer, and spectacular sales of this popular SUV prove that buyers find its combination of room, style, and power the best in the segment.

The Explorer is a fine sport-ute, but there's a new face in this neighborhood that deserves consideration. Meet the all-new Isuzu Rodeo, which has been completely re-designed. As you can see, styling is evolutionary, retaining the trademark egg-crate grille and blistered fenders of the old model. The new look is familiar yet contemporary and the 1998 Rodeo is one of the more ruggedly handsome SUVs available today.

Inside, a new interior provides cupholders, excellent ergonomics, the industry's most perfectly designed steering wheel, comfortable seats front and rear, and plastic trim that looks anything but. Clamber aboard and head for the hills; it's easy with push-button 4WD and standard anti-lock brakes to thwart nature's attempts to impede your progress.

Buyers can select either a hatchback that lifts up from top to bottom, or a hatchgate, which employs flip-up glass and tailgate that swings from right to left. The full-size spare tire can be stored under the vehicle or on the hatchgate. S and LS trim levels are available. The basic Rodeo has two-wheel drive and a weak 2.2-liter four-cylinder engine. Step up to the S V-6 and a 205-horsepower 3.2-liter unit whisks you along with verve. LS models are loaded with standard equipment.

Problems with the new design are minimal. The location of the push-button 4WD switch is absurd, located directly next to the cruise control button where it could be activated accidentally. Off-road, the new Isuzu feels somewhat undersprung, but takes bumps and dips easily if speeds are kept down. Finally, there are no rear cupholders for the kiddies.

ISUZU RODEO

The new Rodeo is an excellent blend of old-fashioned truck toughness and modern day car-like convenience. If you're looking for a new $30,000 SUV, this one should be near the top of your shopping list.

Safety Data

Driver Airbag: *Standard*
Side Airbag: *Not Available*
Traction Control: *Not Available*
Driver Crash Test Grade: *Not Available*

Passenger Airbag: *Standard*
4-Wheel ABS: *Standard*
Integrated Child Seat(s): *Not Available*
Passenger Crash Test Grade: *Not Available*

Standard Equipment

S 2WD: 2.2L I-4 DOHC SMPI 16-valve engine; 5-speed overdrive manual transmission; rear wheel drive, 4.55 axle ratio; stainless steel exhaust; front independent double wishbone suspension with anti-roll bar, front torsion springs, front torsion bar, front shocks, rear multi-link suspension with anti-roll bar, rear coil springs, rear shocks; power rack-and-pinion steering with engine speed-sensing assist; front disc/rear drum brakes with 4 wheel anti-lock braking system; 21.1 gal capacity fuel tank; skid plates; conventional rear cargo door; front and rear black bumpers with rear step bumper; monotone paint; aero-composite halogen headlamps; additional exterior lights include center high mounted stop light; driver and passenger manual black folding outside mirrors; front and rear 15" x 6.5" silver styled steel wheels with hub wheel covers; P215/75SR15 BSW M&S front and rear tires; underbody mounted full-size conventional steel spare wheel; AM/FM stereo with seek-scan, cassette, 4 speakers and fixed antenna; child safety rear door locks; 2 power accessory outlets; analog instrumentation display includes tachometer gauge, water temp gauge, in-dash clock, trip odometer; warning indicators include oil pressure, battery, lights on, key in ignition, low fuel, door ajar, trunk ajar; dual airbags; tinted windows, manual rear windows; fixed interval front windshield wipers, flip-up rear window, fixed interval rear wiper, rear window defroster; seating capacity of 5, front bucket seats with tilt adjustable headrests, driver seat includes 4-way direction control, passenger seat includes 4-way direction control; 60-40 folding rear split-bench seat with reclining adjustable rear headrests; front and rear height adjustable seatbelts; cloth seats, full cloth headliner, full carpet floor covering; interior lights include dome light; vanity mirrors; day-night rearview mirror; full floor console, locking glove box, front cupholder, driver and passenger door bins; carpeted cargo floor, plastic trunk lid, cargo tie downs, cargo light; body-colored grille, black side window moldings, black front windshield molding, black rear window molding, black door handles.

S V-6 2WD (in addition to or instead of S 2WD equipment): 3.2L V-6 DOHC SMPI 24-valve engine; 4.3 axle ratio; carpeted floor mats, 4-speed electronic automatic transmission with lock-up (on automatic models); driver selectable program transmission (on automatic models); PRNDL in instrument panel (on automatic models).

S V-6 4WD (in addition to or instead of S V-6 2WD equipment): Part-time 4 wheel drive, auto locking hub control with electronic shift; 4 wheel disc brakes; front and rear mud flaps; trip odometer.

LS V-6 2WD (in addition to or instead of S V-6 2WD equipment): Roof rack; front and rear body-colored bumpers; body-colored bodyside molding; additional exterior lights include front fog/driving lights; heated exterior mirrors; alloy spare wheel; air conditioning; 6 premium performance speakers; cruise control; remote keyless entry, power remote hatchgate release; trip odometer; panic alarm; deep tinted windows, power front windows with driver 1-touch down, power rear windows; variable intermittent front windshield wipers; center armrest with storage; premium cloth seats, cloth door trim insert; interior lights include 4 door curb lights; leather-wrapped steering wheel with tilt adjustment; illuminated visor vanity mirrors; cargo cover, cargo net; body-colored door handles.

RODEO — ISUZU

CODE	DESCRIPTION	INVOICE	MSRP
Base Prices			
P45	S 2WD (5-speed)	16736	17995
R45	S V-6 2WD (5-speed)	18540	20950
R44	S V-6 2WD (automatic)	19426	21950
V45	S V-6 4WD (5-speed)	20451	23240
V44	S V-6 4WD (automatic)	21331	24240
R64	LS V-6 2WD (automatic)	23224	26390
V65	LS V-6 4WD (5-speed)	24421	27910
V64	LS V-6 4WD (automatic)	25296	28910
	Destination Charge:	445	445
Accessories			
AC	Air Conditioning (S)	836	950
CB	Appearance Package (S)	88	100
	Includes color keyed bumpers.		
OM	Bodyside Molding (S)	44	56
B4	California Emissions	167	180
	NOT AVAILABLE with (C4) New York Emissions.		
ENN	Cargo Convenience Net (S)	20	25
UCC	Cargo Cover (S)	70	90
CMC	Cargo Mat	47	60
RCR	Cargo Organizer	68	86
FDC	CD Changer: 6 Disc	506	650
	REQUIRES (P3) Preferred Equipment Package.		
FLY	CD Player	428	550
	REQUIRES (P3) Preferred Equipment Package.		
SCO	Center Armrest Pad (S)	30	39
PHR	Hood Protector	53	68
E2	Leather Seats (LS)	876	995
L1	Limited Slip Differential (LS 4WD)	220	250
H2V	Moonroof Visor	56	71
C4	New York Emissions	167	180
	NOT AVAILABLE with (B4) California Emissions.		
R1	Outside Spare Tire Mount and Cover (S V-6/LS)	NC	NC
H2	Power Moonroof	616	700
P2	Preferred Equipment Package (S)	889	1010
	Includes aero roof rack, air conditioning, cargo cover, cargo convenience net.		
P3	Preferred Equipment Package (S V-6 2WD/S V-6 4WD)	2068	2350
	Includes power windows, power door locks, power tailgate release, cruise control, tilt steering column, AM/FM stereo with cassette, power exterior mirrors, front intermittent wipers, air conditioning, remote keyless entry, panic alarm, aero roof rack, cargo convenience net, cargo cover, courtesy light, center armrest pad.		
RSP	Rear Roof Spoiler	77	98
RBS	Running Boards	280	360
MSG	Splash Guards (S)	31	40

ISUZU RODEO / TROOPER

CODE	DESCRIPTION	INVOICE	MSRP
SP1	Sport Package (S V-6 2WD)	458	520
	Includes aluminum wheels, fog lights, wheel locks.		
SP2	Sport Package (S V-6 4WD)	678	770
	Includes aluminum wheels, fog lights, wheel locks, limited slip differential.		
BST	Sport Side Steps	278	355
TLG	Tail Lamp Trim	66	84
TRO	Trailer Hitch	198	253
M2	Wheels: 16" Aluminum 6-Spoke (S V-6/LS)	176	200
	Includes 245 tires.		

1997 TROOPER

1997 Isuzu Trooper Limited

What's New?

Anti-lock brakes are now standard on all models, and dealers get a wider profit margin to help increase sales. Despite delirious requests by a certain consumer group, Isuzu will not equip the Trooper with training wheels for 1997.

Review

Just more than a decade ago, Isuzu introduced the first Trooper. It was a tough truck, sturdy and boxy in style, with two doors and a sparse interior. Powered by a four-cylinder engine, the original Trooper wasn't prepped to win any drag races, but the truck won fans for its off-road prowess and exceptional reliability. Soon, 4-door models joined the lineup, and a GM-sourced V-6 engine became available. As the sport utility market grew, luxury amenities were added to the Trooper, but by the early nineties, it was apparent that Isuzu needed to redesign the Trooper so that it could remain competitive against steadily improving competitors.

The Rodeo claimed the entry-level slot for Isuzu in 1991, so the Trooper was moved upscale in 1992. Since then, continual refinements have given the Trooper one of the best blends of style, comfort and utility in the class. Dual airbags are standard equipment. For 1997, all

TROOPER ISUZU

CODE	DESCRIPTION	INVOICE	MSRP

Troopers get 4-wheel anti-lock brakes. Fold the rear seats, and a Trooper can carry 90 cubic feet of cargo, ten more than rival Ford Explorer. Ground clearance measures an impressive 8.5 inches with the manual transmission, and rear seat passengers enjoy as much rear leg room as found in a Mercedes S500 sedan.

A 3.2-liter, 24-valve V-6 powers all Troopers, pumping out 190 horsepower. Three trim levels are available: S, LS, and Limited. We think you'd be better off with either the S or the LS. The S model is our favorite, when equipped with alloy wheels and a preferred equipment package (which includes air conditioning, power windows, mirrors and locks, premium sound, cruise, alloy wheels, and a 60/40 split folding rear seat). Add running boards and remote keyless entry, and you've got a comfortable, luxurious $31,000 cruiser that you won't be afraid to take off-roading.

Many of you may have heard a rumor that the Trooper is dangerous, prone to going around corners on two wheels at moderate speeds. Forget it. Government agencies and private test facilities have debunked the myth. The Trooper is no more tippy than any other sport/utility vehicle on the market. However, keep the following in mind: any vehicle with a short wheelbase and a high center of gravity requires care when cornering or traversing rough terrain. The rules of physics necessarily dictate that such a vehicle is more prone to tipping than a longer wheelbase car or truck with a lower center of gravity, as we discovered during an off-road jaunt in a Nissan Pathfinder last summer.

The Trooper has always been one of our favorites, because it has loads of personality and ability. What it doesn't offer is value. As an alternative to the Chevy Tahoe, Ford Explorer XLT and Jeep Grand Cherokee Laredo, the expensive Trooper makes little sense for most suburbanites whose idea of off-road driving is the dirt parking lot at the sweet corn stand. Buyers in this category might want to investigate the Rodeo. As an alternative to more expensive and competent SUV's, like the Toyota Land Cruiser and Land Rover Discovery, the Trooper makes perfect sense.

Safety Data

Driver Airbag: *Standard*
Side Airbag: *Not Available*
Traction Control: *Not Available*
Driver Crash Test Grade: *Average*

Passenger Airbag: *Standard*
4-Wheel ABS: *Standard*
Integrated Child Seat(s): *Not Available*
Passenger Crash Test Grade: *Average*

Standard Equipment

TROOPER S: 3.2-liter V-6 24-valve SOHC engine, 5-speed manual transmission or 4-speed automatic transmission with winter mode, 2-speed part-time transfer case, power 4-wheel disc anti-lock brakes, speed-sensitive power steering, tilt steering column, skid plates, front and rear tow hooks, rocker panel moldings, overfender moldings with integrated mud flaps, tinted glass, cornering lights, outside spare tire carrier with full-size spare tire, P245/70R16 tires, chrome wheel trim, 2-speed intermittent wipers, rear step bumper with step pad, rear ntermittent wiper/washer, rear defogger with timer, dual front airbags, center storage console with dual cupholders, child proof rear door locks, trip odometer, tachometer, day/night rearview mirror, digital clock, rear pasenger heat ducts, front passenger assist grips, rear seat center armrest, rear underseat storage box, front door map pockets, carpeted floor mats, cargo tie-down hooks, cargo net, cargo cover, cargo area light, front and rear door courtesy lights, remote fuel door opener, reclining front bucket seats, pop-up front seat headrests, fabric seat coverings, tilt steering wheel

LS (in addition to or instead of S equipment): Two-tone paint, bronze tinted glass, rear privacy glass, chrome power exterior mirrors with defogger and power folding feature, diversity antenna, aluminum wheels, variable intermittent wipers, power door locks, cargo floor rails, rear passenger foot rests, air conditioning, dual vanity mirrors (passenger side is illuminated), interior illumination time delay feature, front map lights, multi-adjustable front bucket seats with armrests, 60/40 split reclining rear bench seat, velour upholstery, leather-wrapped steering wheel

ISUZU TROOPER

CODE	DESCRIPTION	INVOICE	MSRP

LIMITED (in addition to or instead of LS equipment): Limited slip differential, leather-wrapped parking brake grip, leather-wrapped shift knob, chrome grille, fog lights, power sunroof, headlight wiper/washers, CD changer, compass, altimeter, outside temperature display, outside barometric pressure display, 6-way power driver's seat, 4-way power passenger's seat, front seat heaters, leather upholstery, remote keyless entry system

Base Prices

Code	Description	Invoice	MSRP
L45	S (5-speed)	23099	26550
L44	S (auto)	24186	27800
M64	LS (auto)	27591	32270
M74	Limited (auto)	32481	37990
	Destination Charge:	445	445

Accessories

Code	Description	Invoice	MSRP
B5	California Emissions	162	180
CDT	CD Changer (S/LS)	487	650
CDR	CD Player (S/LS)	412	550
HP	Hood Protector	53	70
E1	Leather Seats (LS)	1912	2250
	Includes 6-way power adjustment for driver and 4-way power adjustment for passenger. Also includes seat heaters.		
L2	Limited Slip Differential (S/LS)	246	290
M9	Multi-information Display (LS)	170	200
	Includes altimeter, compass, outside temperature display, and outside barometric pressure display.		
C5	New York Emissions	162	180
H3	Power Sunroof (LS)	935	1100
P4	Preferred Equipment Package (S)	2714	3190
	Manufacturer Discount	(743)	(1000)
	Net Price	1971	2190
	Includes air conditioning, power windows, power door locks, cruise control, premium AM/FM stereo with cassette player and 6 speakers, 60/40 split folding rear bench seat, dual visor vanity mirrors (passenger side is illuminated), dual power exterior mirrors with defoggers, aluminum wheels, anti-theft system with starter disable feature		
SST	Remote Keyless Entry (S/LS)	188	250
DBV	Running Boards	255	340

Don't forget to swing by the Townhall when you visit Edmund's website at http://www.edmunds.com. Talk to our editors and compare notes on your favorite cars and trucks. Join others to scope out smart shopping stategies, get answers to your questions, or share your expertise. To get to the Townhall, just click on the link on the homepage or go directly to http://www.edmunds.com/edweb/townhall/welcomeconflist.html.

 Town Hall

CHEROKEE — JEEP

1998 CHEROKEE

1998 Jeep Cherokee SE

What's New?

Cherokee Classic and Limited replace the Cherokee Country. A new 2.5-liter four-cylinder engine is now the base engine for the SE, available with an inline three-speed automatic. New colors include Chili Pepper Red, Emerald Green, and Deep Amethyst.

Review

Some things never change much, and the Jeep Cherokee is one of those mainstays. Unlike its posh—and bigger—Grand Cherokee brother, which keeps adding comforts and graceful touches, the ever-practical, affordable Cherokee simply keeps on rolling, looking little different now than when it was first introduced in 1984. This year, however, the Cherokee benefits from some overdue updates, including a new three-speed automatic transmission, optional with the 2.5-liter SE model.

Utilitarian and upright it is, but with a compelling personality that even the Grand Cherokee lacks. The Cherokee Country has been replaced by two new trim levels: Classic and Limited. Four adults fit inside the Cherokee in reasonable comfort, with adequate headroom. Rear legroom is lacking, in a very short seat, and entry to the rear is constricted by a narrow door. Worth noting is the fact that the rear bench folds but doesn't offer a split, meaning you can't haul a toddler and a treadmill simultaneously.

Relatively refined on the road, the compact Cherokee is capable of strutting its stuff when the going gets rough. Acceleration is brisk with the 4.0-liter inline six-cylinder engine, courtesy of 190 horsepower, and we highly recommend this upgrade if you select the SE model. With the 4.0-liter engine, the Cherokee puts the 'sport' into sport utility.

SE and Sport models can have two or four doors, while the step-up Classic and Limited editions are four-door only. All are available with either two- or four-wheel drive. Command-Trac part-time four-wheel drive allows shift-on-the-fly operation. Selec-Trac is Jeep's full-time four-wheel drive system. Standard gear includes power steering, tinted glass, and power front disc brakes. Four-wheel anti-lock braking is optional (six-cylinder only), as are power windows and door locks, keyless entry system, cruise control, air conditioning, and leather seats.

CHEROKEE

Despite its age, the original compact Jeep sport-utility remains a sensible choice in its field, more capable than most of heading into the woods at a moment's notice. What more can anyone ask of a moderately-priced on/off-roader?

Safety Data

Driver Airbag: *Standard*
Side Airbag: *Not Available*
Traction Control: *Not Available*
Driver Crash Test Grade: *Average*

Passenger Airbag: *Standard*
4-Wheel ABS: *Optional*
Integrated Child Seat(s): *Not Available*
Passenger Crash Test Grade: *Average*

Standard Equipment

SE 2DR 2WD: 2.5L I-4 OHV SPI 8-valve engine; 5-speed overdrive manual transmission; 500-amp battery; 117-amp HD alternator; rear wheel drive, 4.1 axle ratio; stainless steel exhaust; front non-independent suspension with anti-roll bar, front coil springs, front shocks, rear suspension with anti-roll bar, rear leaf springs, rear shocks; power rack-and-pinion steering; front disc/rear drum brakes; 20.1 gal capacity fuel tank; liftback rear cargo door; front and rear black bumpers, rear black fender flares; monotone paint; sealed beam halogen headlamps; additional exterior lights include center high mounted stop light; driver and passenger manual black folding outside mirrors; front and rear 15" x 7" silver styled steel wheels, hub wheel covers; P215/75SR15 BSW AS front and rear tires; inside mounted compact steel spare wheel; AM/FM stereo with clock, seek-scan, 2 speakers and fixed antenna; 1 power accessory outlet; analog instrumentation display trip odometer; warning indicators include oil pressure, water temp warning, battery, lights on, key in ignition, trunk ajar; dual airbags; tinted windows, fixed rear windows; variable intermittent front windshield wipers; seating capacity of 5, front bucket seats with fixed adjustable headrests, center armrest with storage, driver seat includes 4-way direction control, passenger seat includes 4-way direction control; removeable full folding bench rear seat; vinyl seats, vinyl door trim insert, full cloth headliner, full carpet floor covering, deluxe sound insulation; interior lights include dome light; day-night rearview mirror; full floor console, locking glove box with light, instrument panel bin; carpeted cargo floor, vinyl trunk lid, cargo tie downs; black grille, black door handles.

SE 2DR 4WD (in addition to or instead of SE 2DR 2WD): Part-time 4-wheel drive, with auto locking hub control and manual shift; rear multi-link suspension with anti-roll bar.

SE 4DR 2WD (in addition to or instead of SE 2DR 2WD): Conventional rear passenger doors; child safety rear door locks; manual rear windows, fixed 1/4 vent windows.

SE 4DR 4WD (in addition to or instead of SE 4DR 2WD): Part-time 4-wheel drive, with auto locking hub control and manual shift; rear multi-link suspension with anti-roll bar.

SPORT 2DR 2WD (in addition to or instead of SE 2DR 2WD): 4L I-6 OHV SMPI 12 valve engine; 3.07 axle ratio; black bodyside molding, black fender flares; monotone paint with badging; P225/75SR15 OWL AT front and rear tires; AM/FM stereo with seek-scan, cassette, 4 speakers; includes tachometer gauge, oil pressure gauge, water temp gauge, volt gauge; warning indicators include oil pressure, water temp warning, battery, lights on, key in ignition, low fuel, trunk ajar; cloth seats.

SPORT 2DR 4WD (in addition to or instead of SPORT 2DR 2WD): Part-time 4-wheel drive, with auto locking hub control and manual shift; rear multi-link suspension with anti-roll bar.

SPORT 4DR 2WD (in addition to or instead of SPORT 2DR 2WD): Conventional rear passenger doors; child safety rear door locks; manual rear windows, fixed 1/4 vent windows.

CHEROKEE — JEEP

CODE	DESCRIPTION	INVOICE	MSRP

SPORT 4DR 4WD (in addition to or instead of SPORT 4DR 2WD): Part-time 4-wheel drive, with auto locking hub control and manual shift; rear multi-link suspension with anti-roll bar.

CLASSIC 4DR 2WD (in addition to or instead of SPORT 4DR 2WD): 4-speed electronic overdrive automatic transmission with lock-up; 3.55 axle ratio; roof rack; front and rear body-colored bumpers, rear body-colored fender flares; monotone paint with bodyside accent stripe; driver and passenger power remote black folding outside mirrors; front and rear silver alloy wheels; P225/70SR15 OWL AT front and rear tires; rear heat ducts; power rear windows, manual 1/4 vent windows; fixed interval wiper; tilt adjustable headrests; premium cloth seats, full carpet floor covering with carpeted floor mats; leather-wrapped steering wheel; front cupholder; body-colored grille.

CLASSIC 4DR 4WD (in addition to or instead of CLASSIC 4DR 2WD): Part-time 4-wheel drive, with auto locking hub control and manual shift; rear multi-link suspension with anti-roll bar.

LIMITED 4DR 2WD (in addition to or instead of CLASSIC 4DR 2WD): Body-colored bodyside insert, body-colored bodyside cladding, body-colored fender flares; sealed beam halogen headlamps with delay off feature; additional exterior lights include center high mounted stop light, underhood light; remote keyless entry; deep tinted windows, power front and rear windows, fixed 1/4 vent windows; leather seats, deluxe sound insulation, wood trim; interior lights include front reading lights; dual illuminated vanity mirrors; full overhead console with storage, instrument panel bin, driver and passenger door bins; cargo cover, cargo tie downs, cargo light.

LIMITED 4DR 4WD (in addition to or instead of LIMITED 4DR 2WD): Part-time 4-wheel drive, with auto locking hub control and manual shift; rear multi-link suspension with anti-roll bar.

Base Prices

Code	Description	Invoice	MSRP
XJTL72	SE 2-Door 2WD	14510	15440
XJJL72	SE 2-Door 4WD	15909	16955
XJTL74	SE 4-Door 2WD	15477	16480
XJJL74	SE 4-Door 4WD	16871	17990
XJTL72	Sport 2-Door 2WD	16348	18055
XJJL72	Sport 2-Door 4WD	17697	19565
XJTL74	Sport 4-Door 2WD	17279	19090
XJJL74	Sport 4-Door 4WD	18628	20600
XJTL74	Classic 4-Door 2WD	18502	20480
XJJL74	Classic 4-Door 4WD	19856	21995
XJTL74	Limited 4-Door 2WD	18502	20480
XJJL74	Limited 4-Door 4WD	19856	21995
Destination Charge:		525	525

Accessories

Code	Description	Invoice	MSRP
DGA	3-Speed Automatic Transmission (SE 2WD)	565	665
DGB	4-Speed Automatic Transmission With OD (SE/Sport)	803	945
	Includes 3.55 axle ratio. NOT AVAILABLE with 23A, 25A, 23B, 25B, 25D, 25J.		
BGK	4-Wheel Antilock Brakes	510	600
	NOT AVAILABLE with 22A, 22B, 23A, 23B.		

JEEP CHEROKEE

CODE	DESCRIPTION	INVOICE	MSRP
RCG	6 Premium Infinity Speakers	298	350
	Includes 8 speakers in 6 locations. REQUIRES (RAZ) radio.		
JPS	6-Way Power Driver's Seat (Sport/Classic)	255	300
	REQUIRES AWH or AWH or 25J or 26J or AWH.		
HAA	Air Conditioning (SE/Sport/Classic)	723	850
	NOT AVAILABLE with (4XA) air conditioning bypass.		
4XA	Air Conditioning Bypass (SE/Sport/Classic)	NC	NC
	NOT AVAILABLE with 25J, 26J, 22B, 23B, 25B, 26B, 26S.		
DSA	Anti-Spin Differential Axle	242	285
	REQUIRES (TBB) conventional spare tire.		
SCG	Black Leather Steering Wheel (SE/Sport/Limited)	43	50
MWG	Black Roof Rack (SE/Sport)	119	140
YCF	Border State Emissions	145	170
	NOT AVAILABLE with (NAE) CA/CT/MA/NY Emissions.		
NAE	CA/CT/MA/NY Emissions	145	170
	Automatically coded. NOT AVAILABLE with (YCF) border state emissions.		
CSC	Cargo Area Cover (SE/Sport)	64	75
M5	Cloth/Vinyl Highback Bucket Seats (SE)	123	145
GTZ	Dual Power Black Folding Mirrors (SE/Sport)	111	130
	REQUIRES (22A or 23A or 25A or 26A) or (22B or 23B or 25B or 26B) or (25D or 26D) or (25J or 26J).		
GTS	Dual Power Heated Folding Mirrors (SE/Sport)	38	45
	REQUIRES GFA and (22B or 23B or 25B or 26B) or GFA and (25J or 26J) or GFA and (25D or 26D) NOT AVAILABLE with GTZ, GTS.		
GTS	Dual Power Heated Folding Mirrors (SE/Sport)	149	175
	REQUIRES GFA and (22A or 23A or 25A or 26A) or GFA and (25D or 26D). NOT AVAILABLE with GTZ, GTS.		
NHK	Engine Block Heater	34	40
ERH	Engine: 4.0L Power-Tech Six (SE)	846	995
	Includes 3.07 axle ratio.		
LNJ	Fog Lamps (Sport/Classic/Limited)	94	110
	REQUIRES GFA and JHB.		
CLE	Front & Rear Floor Mats (SE/Sport)	43	50
MUW	G.S.A. Nomenclature Plate	13	15
ADA	Light Group (SE/Sport/Classic)	136	160
	Includes courtesy light under instrument panel, underhood light, headlights on/time delay, dual illuminated visor vanity mirrors, front map/dome lights. REQUIRES (RAZ) radio.		
CUN	Overhead Console With Storage (Sport/Classic)	200	235
	Includes reading lamps, storage for sunglasses and garage door opener, compass/temperature display. REQUIRES JHB and ADA and AWH.		
AWH	Power Equipment Group (Classic)	574	675
	Includes dual power folding black mirrors, power windows, power door locks, remote keyless entry. REQUIRES (ADA) light group. NOT AVAILABLE with (GTS) dual power heated folding mirrors.		

CHEROKEE — JEEP

CODE	DESCRIPTION	INVOICE	MSRP
AWH	**Power Equipment Group (Sport)**	536	630
	Includes remote keyless entry, power door locks, dual power black folding mirrors, power windows. REQUIRES (ADA) light group and (JHB) rear wiper/washer.		
AWH	**Power Equipment Group (Sport)**	684	805
	Includes power windows, power door locks, remote keyless entry, dual power black folding mirrors. REQUIRES ADA and JHB. NOT AVAILABLE with 25J, 26J, GTS.		
22A	**Quick Order Package 22A (SE 2WD)**	NC	NC
	Includes vehicle with standard equipment. REQUIRES EPE and DGA and (4XA). NOT AVAILABLE with BGK, AHT.		
22A	**Quick Order Package 22A (SE 2WD)**	NC	NC
	Includes vehicle with standard equipment. REQUIRES 4XA and EPE and DGA. NOT AVAILABLE with BGK, AHT, DDQ.		
22B	**Quick Order Package 22B (SE 2WD)**	1084	1275
	Manufacturer Discount	(1084)	(1275)
	Net Price	NC	NC
	Includes air conditioning, dual power black folding mirrors, cloth/vinyl highback bucket seats, rear wiper/washer. REQUIRES EPE and DGA. NOT AVAILABLE with 4XA, BGK, AHT.		
22B	**Quick Order Package 22B (SE 2WD)**	1084	1275
	Manufacturer Discount	(1084)	(1275)
	Net Price	NC	NC
	Includes air conditioning, dual power black folding mirrors, cloth/vinyl highback bucket seats, rear wiper/washer. REQUIRES EPE and DGA. NOT AVAILABLE with 4XA, BGK, AHT, DDQ.		
23A	**Quick Order Package 23A (SE 2WD)**	NC	NC
	Includes vehicle with standard equipment. REQUIRES 4XA and EPE. NOT AVAILABLE with BGK, AHT.		
23A	**Quick Order Package 23A (SE 2WD)**	NC	NC
	Includes vehicle with standard equipment. REQUIRES 4XA and EPE and DDQ. NOT AVAILABLE with BGK, AHT.		
23A	**Quick Order Package 23A (SE 4WD)**	NC	NC
	Includes vehicle with standard equipment. REQUIRES 4XA and EPE. NOT AVAILABLE with AHT, BGK, AWE, DGB.		
23A	**Quick Order Package 23A (SE 4WD)**	NC	NC
	Includes vehicle with standard equipment. REQUIRES 4XA and EPE and DDQ. NOT AVAILABLE with BGK, AWE, AHT.		
23B	**Quick Order Package 23B (SE 2WD)**	1084	1275
	Manufacturer Discount	(1084)	(1275)
	Net Price	NC	NC
	Includes air conditioning, dual power black folding mirrors, cloth/vinyl highback bucket seats, rear wiper/washer. REQUIRES EPE. NOT AVAILABLE with 4XA, BGK, AHT.		

JEEP CHEROKEE

CODE	DESCRIPTION	INVOICE	MSRP
23B	Quick Order Package 23B (SE 2WD)	1084	1275
	Manufacturer Discount	(1084)	(1275)
	Net Price	NC	NC

Includes air conditioning, dual power black folding mirrors, cloth/vinyl highback bucket seats, rear wiper/washer. REQUIRES EPE and DDQ. NOT AVAILABLE with 4XA, BGK, AHT.

23B	Quick Order Package 23B (SE 4WD)	1084	1275
	Manufacturer Discount	(1084)	(1275)
	Net Price	NC	NC

Includes air conditioning, dual power black folding mirrors, cloth/vinyl highback bucket seats, rear wiper/washer. REQUIRES EPE and DDQ. NOT AVAILABLE with 4XA, BGK, AWE, AHT.

23B	Quick Order Package 23B (SE 4WD)	1084	1275
	Manufacturer Discount	(1084)	(1275)
	Net Price	NC	NC

Includes air conditioning, dual power black folding mirrors, cloth/vinyl highback bucket seats, rear wiper/washer. REQUIRES EPE. NOT AVAILABLE with 4XA, BGK, AWE, AHT, DGB.

25A	Quick Order Package 25A (SE 2WD)	NC	NC

Includes vehicle with standard equipment. REQUIRES 4XA and ERH and DDQ. NOT AVAILABLE with AHT.

25A	Quick Order Package 25A (SE 2WD)	NC	NC

Includes vehicle with standard equipment. REQUIRES 4XA air conditioning bypass and (ERH) engine. NOT AVAILABLE with (AHT) trailer tow group.

25A	Quick Order Package 25A (SE 4WD)	NC	NC

Includes vehicle with standard equipment. REQUIRES 4XA and ERH and DDQ. NOT AVAILABLE with AWE, AHT.

25A	Quick Order Package 25A (SE 4WD)	NC	NC

Includes vehicle with standard equipment. REQUIRES 4XA and ERH. NOT AVAILABLE with AWE, AHT, DGB.

25B	Quick Order Package 25B (SE 2WD)	1084	1275
	Manufacturer Discount	(1084)	(1275)
	Net Price	NC	NC

Includes air conditioning, dual power black folding mirrors, cloth/vinyl highback bucket seats, rear wiper/washer. REQUIRES ERH and DDQ. NOT AVAILABLE with 4XA, AHT.

25B	Quick Order Package 25B (SE 2WD)	1084	1275
	Manufacturer Discount	(1084)	(1275)
	Net Price	NC	NC

Includes air conditioning, dual power black folding mirrors, cloth/vinyl highback bucket seats, rear wiper/washer. REQUIRES (ERH) engine. NOT AVAILABLE with (4XA) air conditioning bypass, (AHT) trailer tow group.

CHEROKEE — JEEP

CODE	DESCRIPTION	INVOICE	MSRP
25B	Quick Order Package 25B (SE 4WD)	1084	1275
	Manufacturer Discount	(1084)	(1275)
	Net Price	NC	NC

Includes air conditioning, dual power black folding mirrors, cloth/vinyl highback bucket seats, rear wiper/washer. REQUIRES ERH and DDQ. NOT AVAILABLE with 4XA, AWE, AHT.

25B	Quick Order Package 25B (SE 4WD)	1084	1275
	Manufacturer Discount	(1084)	(1275)
	Net Price	NC	NC

Includes air conditioning, dual power black folding mirrors, cloth/vinyl highback bucket seats, rear wiper/washer. REQUIRES ERH. NOT AVAILABLE with 4XA, AWE, AHT, DGB.

25D	Quick Order Package 25D (Sport 2WD)	NC	NC

Includes vehicle with standard equipment. REQUIRES 4XA and ERH and DDQ. NOT AVAILABLE with AHT.

25D	Quick Order Package 25D (Sport 4WD)	NC	NC

Includes vehicle with standard equipment. REQUIRES 4XA and ERH and DDQ. NOT AVAILABLE with AWE, AHT, DHP, DGB.

25J	Quick Order Package 25J (Sport 2WD 4-door)	1993	2345
	Manufacturer Discount	(1993)	(2345)
	Net Price	NC	NC

Includes air conditioning, front and rear floor mats, Light Group: underhood light, headlights on/time delay, dual illuminated visor vanity mirrors, front map/dome lights, Power Equipment Group: power windows, power door locks, remote keyless entry, dual power black folding mirrors, black roof rack, tilt steering column, black leather steering wheel, rear wiper/washer. REQUIRES ERH and DDQ. NOT AVAILABLE with 4XA, AHT.

25J	Quick Order Package 25J (Sport 2WD 2-door)	1845	2170
	Manufacturer Discount	(1845)	(2170)
	Net Price	NC	NC

Includes air conditioning, front and rear floor mats, Light Group: underhood light, headlights on/time delay, dual illuminated visor vanity mirrors, front map/dome lights, dual power black folding mirrors, Power Equipment Group: power windows, power door locks, remote keyless entry, dual power black folding mirrors, black roof rack, tilt steering column, black leather steering wheel, rear wiper/washer. REQUIRES ERH and DDQ. NOT AVAILABLE with 4XA, AHT.

25J	Quick Order Package 25J (Sport 4WD)	1845	2170
	Manufacturer Discount	(1845)	(2170)
	Net Price	NC	NC

Includes air conditioning, front and rear floor mats, Light Group: underhood light, headlights on/time delay, dual illuminated visor vanity mirrors, front map/dome lights, dual power black folding mirrors, Power Equipment Group: power windows, power door locks, remote keyless entry, dual power black folding mirrors, black roof rack, tilt steering column, black leather steering wheel, rear wiper/washer. REQUIRES ERH and DDQ. NOT AVAILABLE with 4XA, AWE, AHT, DHP, DGB.

EDMUND'S 1998 NEW TRUCKS

JEEP CHEROKEE

CODE	DESCRIPTION	INVOICE	MSRP
25J	Quick Order Package 25J (Sport 4WD)	1993	2345
	Manufacturer Discount	(1993)	(2345)
	Net Price	NC	NC

Includes air conditioning, front and rear floor mats, Light Group: underhood light, headlights on/time delay, dual illuminated visor vanity mirrors, front map/dome lights, dual power black folding mirrors, Power Equipment Group: power windows, power door locks, remote keyless entry, dual power black folding mirrors, black roof rack, tilt steering column, black leather steering wheel, rear wiper/washer. REQUIRES ERH and DDQ. NOT AVAILABLE with 4XA, AWH, AWE, AHT, DHP.

26A	Quick Order Package 26A (SE 2WD)	NC	NC

Includes vehicle with standard equipment. REQUIRES (4XA) air conditioning bypass) and (ERH) engine and (DGB) transmission.

26A	Quick Order Package 26A (SE 4WD)	NC	NC

Includes vehicle with standard equipment. REQUIRES 4XA and ERH and DGB. NOT AVAILABLE with AWE.

26B	Quick Order Package 26B (SE 2WD)	1084	1275
	Manufacturer Discount	(1084)	(1275)
	Net Price	NC	NC

Includes air conditioning, dual power black folding mirrors, cloth/vinyl highback bucket seats, rear wiper/washer. REQUIRES (ERH) engine and (DGB) transmission. NOT AVAILABLE with (4XA) air conditioning bypass.

26B	Quick Order Package 26B (SE 2WD)	1084	1275
	Manufacturer Discount	(1084)	(1275)
	Net Price	NC	NC

Includes air conditioning, dual power black folding mirrors, cloth/vinyl highback bucket seats, rear wiper/washer. REQUIRES ERH and DGB. NOT AVAILABLE with 4XA, DDQ.

26B	Quick Order Package 26B (SE 4WD)	1084	1275
	Manufacturer Discount	(1084)	(1275)
	Net Price	NC	NC

Includes air conditioning, dual power black folding mirrors, cloth/vinyl highback bucket seats, rear wiper/washer. REQUIRES ERH and DGB. NOT AVAILABLE with 4XA, AWE.

26B	Quick Order Package 26B (SE 4WD)	1084	1275
	Manufacturer Discount	(1084)	(1275)
	Net Price	NC	NC

Includes air conditioning, dual power black folding mirrors, cloth/vinyl highback bucket seats, rear wiper/washer. REQUIRES ERH and DGB. NOT AVAILABLE with 4XA, AWE.

26D	Quick Order Package 26D (Sport 2WD)	NC	NC

Includes vehicle with standard equipment. REQUIRES (4XA) air conditioning bypass) and (ERH) engine and (DGB) transmission.

26D	Quick Order Package 26D (Sport 4WD)	NC	NC

Includes vehicle with standard equipment. REQUIRES 4XA and ERH and DGB. NOT AVAILABLE with AWE.

CHEROKEE — JEEP

CODE	DESCRIPTION	INVOICE	MSRP
26H	**Quick Order Package 26H (Limited 2WD)**	3358	3950
	Manufacturer Discount	(1683)	(1980)
	Net Price	1675	1970

Includes air conditioning, speed control, tilt steering column. REQUIRES (ERH) engine and (DGB) transmission.

26H	**Quick Order Package 26H (Limited 4WD)**	3693	4345
	Manufacturer Discount	(1683)	(1980)
	Net Price	2010	2365

Includes air conditioning, speed control, tilt steering column. REQUIRES (ERH) engine and (DGB) transmission.

26J	**Quick Order Package 26J (Sport 2WD)**	1845	2170
	Manufacturer Discount	(1845)	(2170)
	Net Price	NC	NC

Includes air conditioning, front and rear floor mats, Light Group: underhood light, headlights on/time delay, dual illuminated visor vanity mirrors, front map/dome lights, dual power black folding mirrors, Power Equipment Group: power windows, power door locks, remote keyless entry, dual power black folding mirrors, black roof rack, tilt steering column, black leather steering wheel, rear wiper/washer. REQUIRES (ERH) engine and (DGB) transmission. NOT AVAILABLE with (4XA) air conditioning bypass.

26J	**Quick Order Package 26J (Sport 2WD)**	1993	2345
	Manufacturer Discount	(1993)	(2345)
	Net Price	NC	NC

Includes air conditioning, front and rear floor mats, Light Group: underhood light, headlights on/time delay, dual illuminated visor vanity mirrors, front map/dome lights, Power Equipment Group: power windows, power door locks, remote keyless entry, dual power black folding mirrors, black roof rack, tilt steering column, black leather steering wheel, rear wiper/washer. REQUIRES (ERH) engine and (DGB) transmission. NOT AVAILABLE with (4XA) air conditioning bypass.

26J	**Quick Order Package 26J (Sport 4WD)**	1845	2170
	Manufacturer Discount	(1845)	(2170)
	Net Price	NC	NC

Includes air conditioning, front and rear floor mats, Light Group: underhood light, headlights on/time delay, dual illuminated visor vanity mirrors, front map/dome lights, dual power black folding mirrors, Power Equipment Group: power windows, power door locks, remote keyless entry, dual power black folding mirrors, black roof rack, tilt steering column, black leather steering wheel, rear wiper/washer. REQUIRES ERH and DGB. NOT AVAILABLE with 4XA, AWE.

26J	**Quick Order Package 26J (Sport 4WD)**	1993	2345
	Manufacturer Discount	(1993)	(2345)
	Net Price	NC	NC

Includes air conditioning, front and rear floor mats, Light Group: underhood light, headlights on/time delay, dual illuminated visor vanity mirrors, front map/dome lights, dual power black folding mirrors, Power Equipment Group: power windows, power door locks, remote keyless entry, dual power black folding mirrors, black roof rack, tilt steering column, black leather steering wheel, rear wiper/washer. REQUIRES ERH and DGB. NOT AVAILABLE with 4XA, AWH, AWE.

JEEP CHEROKEE

CODE	DESCRIPTION	INVOICE	MSRP
26S	Quick Order Package 26S (Classic)	1551	1825
	Manufacturer Discount	(1551)	(1825)
	Net Price	NC	NC

Includes air conditioning, Light Group: underhood light, headlights on/time delay, dual illuminated visor vanity mirrors, front map/dome lights, Power Equipment Group: power windows, power door locks, remote keyless entry, dual power black folding mirrors, tilt steering column. REQUIRES (ERH) engine and (DGB) transmission. NOT AVAILABLE with (4XA) air conditioning bypass.

CODE	DESCRIPTION	INVOICE	MSRP
26X	Quick Order Package 26X (Classic)	NC	NC

Includes vehicle with standard equipment. REQUIRES (4XA) air conditioning bypass) and (ERH) engine and (DGB) transmission.

CODE	DESCRIPTION	INVOICE	MSRP
26X	Quick Order Package 26X (Classic 4WD)	NC	NC

Includes vehicle with standard equipment. REQUIRES (4XA) air conditioning bypass and (ERH) engine and (DGB) transmission.

CODE	DESCRIPTION	INVOICE	MSRP
RAS	Radio: AM/FM Stereo with Cass. & 4 Speakers (SE)	255	300
	NOT AVAILABLE with (RAZ) radio, (RCG) 6 premium Infinity speakers.		
RAZ	Radio: AM/FM Stereo with CD, Cassette, EQ (SE)	604	710
	Includes 4 speakers.		
RAZ	Radio: AM/FM Stereo with CD, Cassette, EQ (Sport/Classic/Limited)	349	410
	Includes 4 speakers.		
GFA	Rear Window Defroster (SE/Sport)	140	165
	REQUIRES (JHB) rear wiper/washer.		
JHB	Rear Wiper/Washer (SE/Sport)	128	150
DHP	Selec-Trac Transfer Case (Sport 4WD/Classic 4WD)	336	395
	NOT AVAILABLE with 25D or 25J.		
ADL	Skid Plate Group (4WD)	123	145
	Includes skid plates for fuel tank, transfer case, and front suspension.		
CSA	Spare Tire Cover (SE)	43	50
NHM	Speed Control (SE/Sport)	213	250
	REQUIRES (SCG) black leather steering wheel.		
PW1	Stone White Clear Coat	NC	NC
SUA	Tilt Steering Column (SE/Sport)	119	140
TBB	Tire: Conventional Spare (Classic 2WD/Limited 2WD)	238	280
	Includes matching 5th wheel.		
TBB	Tire: Conventional Spare (SE)	102	120
	Includes matching 5th wheel.		
TBB	Tire: Conventional Spare (SE)	64	75
	Includes matching 5th wheel.		
TBB	Tire: Conventional Spare (Sport)	123	145
	Includes matching 5th wheel. NOT AVAILABLE with (WJW) wheels.		
TBB	Tire: Conventional Spare (Sport/Classic)	179	210
	Includes matching 5th wheel. REQUIRES (WJW) wheels.		
TRL	Tires: P225/75R15 Wrangler RT/S AT OWL (SE)	268	315
	NOT AVAILABLE with (TBB) conventional spare tire.		

CHEROKEE — JEEP

CODE	DESCRIPTION	INVOICE	MSRP
AHT	**Trailer Tow Group (4WD)**	208	245
	Includes 7 wire receptacles, 4 wire trailer adaptors, equalizing trailer hitch. REQUIRES (26A or 26B) and TBB or (26D or 26J) and TBB or (26S or 26X) and TBB or 26H and TBB. NOT AVAILABLE with 23A, 25A, 23B, 25B, 25D, 25J, AHT.		
AHT	**Trailer Tow Group (SE/Sport/Limited)**	310	365
	Includes 7 wire receptacles, 4 wire trailer adaptors, and equalizing trailer hitch. REQUIRES TBB and 26A or 26B or 26D or 26J or 26S or 26X or 26H. NOT AVAILABLE with 22A, 23A, 25A, 22B, 23B, 25B, 25D, 25J, AWE, AHT.		
AHT	**Trailer Tow Group (Sport 4WD)**	276	365
	Includes 7 wire receptacles and 4 wire trailer adaptors and equalizing trailer hitch. REQUIRES (26D or 26J) and TBB. NOT AVAILABLE with 25D, 25J, AWE, AHT.		
AWE	**Up Country Suspension Package with Auto Trans (SE 4WD)**	910	1070
	Includes skid plate group, conventional spare tire, delete rear stabilizer bar suspension, up country decals on liftgate, P225/75R15 Wrangler RT/S A/T OWL tires, anti-spin differential axle. REQUIRES 26A or 26B. NOT AVAILABLE with 23A, 25A, 23B, 25B, AHT, AWE.		
AWE	**Up Country Suspension Package with Auto Trans (Sport 4WD)**	663	780
	Includes P225/75 R15 Wrangler RT/S A/T tires, skid plate group, conventional spare tire, delete rear stabilizer bar suspension, up country decals on liftgate, anti-spin differential axle. REQUIRES 26D or 26J. NOT AVAILABLE with 25D, 25J, 25A, 23B, 25B, AHT, AWE.		
AWE	**Up Country Suspension Package with Auto Trans (Sport 4WD/Classic 4WD)** .	718	845
	Includes P225/75 R15 Wrangler RT/S A/T tires, skid plate group, conventional spare tire, delete rear stabilizer bar suspension, up country decals on liftgate, anti-spin differential axle. REQUIRES (26D or 26J) and WJW or 26X or 26S. NOT AVAILABLE with 25D, 25J, AWE, AHT.		
AWE	**Up Country Suspension Package with Manual Trans (SE 4WD)**	876	1030
	Includes skid plate group, conventional spare tire, delete rear stabilizer bar suspension, up country decals on liftgate, P225/75R15 Wrangler RT/S A/T OWL tires, anti-spin differential axle. NOT AVAILABLE with 26A, 26B, AHT, AWE.		
AWE	**Up Country Suspension Package with Manual Trans (Sport 4WD)**	684	805
	Includes P225/75 R15 Wrangler RT/S A/T tires, skid plate group, conventional spare tire, delete rear stabilizer bar suspension, up country decals on liftgate, anti-spin differential axle. REQUIRES (25D or 25J) and WJW. NOT AVAILABLE with 26D, 26J, AHT, AWE.		
AWE	**Up Country Suspension Package with Manual Trans (Sport 4WD)**	629	740
	Includes P225/75 R15 Wrangler RT/S A/T tires, skid plate group, conventional spare tire, delete rear stabilizer bar suspension, up country decals on liftgate, anti-spin differential axle. REQUIRES 25D or 25J. NOT AVAILABLE with 26D, 26J, AHT, AWE, WJW.		
AWE	**Up Country Suspension Package (Limited 4WD)**	646	760
	Includes skid plate group, anti-spin differential axle, conventional spare tire, off-road suspension, delete rear stabilizer bar suspension, up country decals on liftgate, P225/75R15 Wrangler RT/S A/T OWL tires. REQUIRES (26H) Quick Order Package 26H. NOT AVAILABLE with (AHT) trailer tow group.		

JEEP CHEROKEE / GRAND CHEROKEE

CODE	DESCRIPTION	INVOICE	MSRP
WJW	Wheels: 15" X 7" Aluminum (SE)	374	440
WJW	Wheels: 15" X 7" Aluminum (Sport)	208	245

NOT AVAILABLE with (TBB) conventional spare tire, (AWE) up country suspension package with automatic transmission.

1998 GRAND CHEROKEE

1998 Jeep Grand Cherokee 5.9 Limited

What's New?

A 245 horsepower, 345 lbs.-ft torque, 5.9-liter V-8 powers the Grand Cherokee 5.9 Limited, making it the mightiest of the Jeeps. The new Grand Cherokee 5.9 Limited is the only addition to the model lineup this year, replacing the Orvis, and it receives new interior and exterior treatment that also makes it the most expensive of the Jeeps. Two new colors, Wrangler HP VSB tires, and "next generation" airbags round out the changes.

Review

For years, the Ford Explorer has been the best-selling sport utility vehicle in this country, but in 1992 a new challenger called Grand Cherokee arrived to try to wrest the sales crown away from the champ. It was not successful. However, it did outsell every other sport utility on the market, and became the Explorer's biggest threat.

Indeed, this Jeep has the most car-like feel of sport utilities, and is among the most stable on pavement. In fact, with the optional 5.2-liter V8 pumping away under the hood, the Grand Cherokee becomes the Porsche of sport utes. Equipped with a dual airbag system and four-wheel anti-lock disc brakes, Grand Cherokee buyers have a long list of equipment to wade through, including three different drive systems (2WD, part-time 4WD, full-time 4WD), four different trim levels (Laredo, TSI, Limited, 5.9 Limited), and a host of luxury and convenience items.

The exterior is all hard edges and angles, but is instantly recognizable as a Jeep product and looks rugged. A retro touch we could do without is the location of the spare tire. The Grand Cherokee doesn't have tiny tires, and the cargo area is among the smallest in the class to begin with, so why is the tire in the cargo area? It should be under the cargo floor, mounted under the truck or placed on a rack on the liftgate. Otherwise, we have few quibbles with this sport ute.

GRAND CHEROKEE — JEEP

CODE	DESCRIPTION	INVOICE	MSRP

Jeep included several perks to the Grand Cherokee 5.9 Limited for 1998. Mechanical changes are limited to the 5.9-liter V-8 engine and free-lowing exhaust system, reducing back pressure by 25 percent and making the big engine a little easier on gas. The interior sports "premium calf's nap grain" leather seats, a new Infinity 180-watt, 10-speaker audio system, 60/40 folding rear seat with armrest, and leather trim on the doors, armrests, and console. The 5.9 Limited is nothing if not organic. The 5.9 Limited exterior is treated to a body-colored side molding, hood louvers, a front grille with a silvery mesh, and 16" aluminum wheels.

Last year, the TSI model debuted, sporting specific alloy wheels, monotone paint in a choice of three shades, dark blue pinstriping, leather seats, high powered audio system, and more luxurious interior trimmings.

Unfortunately, just as Jeep caught up to and surpassed the Explorer in comfort and safety features last year, Ford went and squeezed a V-8 under the Explorer's hood. This year, Ford is offering a new overhead cam V-6 engine in the Explorer, which puts out 20 more horsepower than the Jeep inline six. The Ford also has more room, a more comfy rear seat, and a lower price tag. Plus, you don't have to load cargo around a big ol' tire in the back. The verdict? For around town family hauling, we prefer the value-packed Explorer XLT. But for speedy fun and off-road prowess, the JGC Laredo V-8 gets our vote.

Safety Data

Driver Airbag: *Standard*
Side Airbag: *Not Available*
Traction Control: *Not Available*
Driver Crash Test Grade: *Average*

Passenger Airbag: *Standard*
4-Wheel ABS: *Standard*
Integrated Child Seat(s): *Not Available*
Passenger Crash Test Grade: *Good*

Standard Equipment

LAREDO 2WD: 4L I-6 OHV SMPI 12-valve engine; 4-speed electronic overdrive automatic transmission with lock-up; 600-amp HD battery; 117-amp HD alternator; rear wheel drive, 3.55 axle ratio; stainless steel exhaust; front non-independent suspension with anti-roll bar, front coil springs, front shocks, rear suspension with anti-roll bar, rear coil springs, rear shocks; power recirculating ball steering; 4-wheel disc brakes with 4-wheel anti-lock braking system; 23 gal capacity fuel tank. conventional rear passenger doors, liftback rear cargo door; roof rack; front and rear black bumpers; black bodyside cladding; monotone paint with bodyside accent stripe; aero-composite halogen headlamps; additional exterior lights include center high mounted stop light, underhood light; driver and passenger power remote black folding outside mirrors; front and rear 15" x 7" silver alloy wheels; P215/75SR15 BSW AS front and rear tires; inside mounted compact steel spare wheel; air conditioning, rear heat ducts; AM/FM stereo with clock, seek-scan, cassette, 4 speakers and fixed antenna; cruise control; power door locks; remote keyless entry that controls trunk, child safety rear door locks, power remote hatch/trunk release; 2 power accessory outlets, driver foot rest; analog instrumentation display includes tachometer gauge, oil pressure gauge, water temp gauge, volt gauge, trip odometer; warning indicators include oil pressure, water temp warning, battery, lights on, key in ignition, low fuel; dual airbags; panic alarm; tinted windows, power front windows with driver 1-touch down, power rear windows, fixed 1/4 vent windows; variable intermittent front windshield wipers, flip-up rear window, fixed interval wiper rear window defroster; seating capacity of 5, front bucket seats with tilt adjustable headrests, center armrest with storage, driver seat includes 4-way direction control, passenger seat includes 4-way direction control; removable 60-40 folding bench rear seat with adjustable rear headrest; front and rear height adjustable seatbelts; cloth seats, full cloth headliner, full carpet floor covering with carpeted floor mats, deluxe sound insulation; interior lights include dome light with fade, front reading lights, illuminated entry; leather-wrapped steering wheel with tilt adjustment; dual illuminated vanity mirrors; day-night rear-view mirror; full floor console, locking glove box with light, front and rear cupholders, driver and passenger door bins; carpeted cargo floor, carpeted trunk lid, cargo cover, cargo net, cargo tie downs, cargo light; chrome grille, black door handles.

JEEP GRAND CHEROKEE

CODE	DESCRIPTION	INVOICE	MSRP

TSI 2WD (in addition to or instead of LAREDO 2WD): Front and rear body-colored bumpers; body-colored bodyside cladding; two-tone paint with badging; front and rear 16" x 7"; P225/70SR16 OWL AS front and rear tires; premium AM/FM stereo with seek-scan, cassette, CD pre-wiring, amplifier, graphic equalizer, radio steering wheel controls; leather seats, deluxe sound insulation, wood trim; interior lights include front reading lights, 2 door curb lights, illuminated entry; full overhead console with storage, 2 seat back storage pockets, driver and passenger door bins; body-colored grill.

LIMITED 2WD (in addition to or instead of TSI 2WD): Monotone paint with badging; additional exterior lights include front fog/driving lights, center high mounted stop light, underhood light; driver and passenger power remote body-colored heated folding outside mirrors; front and rear painted alloy wheels; air conditioning with climate control, rear heat ducts; clock; 2 power accessory outlets, driver foot rest, garage door opener; compass, exterior temp, systems monitor, trip computer, trip odometer; warning indicators include oil pressure, water temp warning, battery, low oil level, low coolant, lights on, key in ignition, low fuel, low washer fluid, bulb failure, door ajar, trunk ajar, service interval; panic alarm, security system; deep tinted windows with driver 1-touch down; driver seat includes 6-way power seat with power lumbar support, passenger seat includes 6-way power seat with power lumbar support; memory on driver seat with 2 memory setting(s) includes settings for door mirrors; interior lights include front and rear reading lights, 2 door curb lights, illuminated entry; dual illuminated vanity mirrors dual auxiliary visors; auto-dimming day-night rearview mirror.

LAREDO 4WD (in addition to or instead of LAREDO 2WD): Part-time 4 wheel drive, with auto locking hub control and manual shift; power rack-and-pinion steering; aero-composite halogen headlamps.

TSI 4WD (in addition to or instead of TSI 2WD): Part-time 4 wheel drive, with auto locking hub control and manual shift; power rack-and-pinion steering; aero-composite halogen headlamps.

LIMITED 4WD (in addition to or instead of LIMITED 2WD): Full-time 4 wheel drive; full overhead console with storage.

LIMITED 5.9 (in addition to or instead of LIMITED 4WD): 5.9L V-8 OHV SMPI 16-valve engine; 150-amp HD alternator; transmission oil cooler; limited slip differential, 3.73 axle ratio; premium front shocks, premium rear shocks; skid plates; front electric sliding and tilting glass with sunshade, regular opening; front and rear body-colored bumpers with tow hook(s); aero-composite halogen fully automatic headlamps; P225/70SR16 BSW AT front and rear tires; inside mounted full-size temporary alloy spare wheel; premium AM/FM stereo with seek-scan, cassette, in-dash CD player, 10 brand speakers; front bucket seats with heated driver and passenger seats; leather door trim insert; mini overhead console.

Base Prices

ZJTL74	Laredo 2WD	23419	25845
ZJJL74	Laredo 4WD	25187	27815
ZJTL74	TSI 2WD	25311	27995
ZJJL74	TSI 4WD	27079	29965
ZJTL74	Limited 2WD	28272	31360
ZJJL74	Limited 4WD	30445	33790
ZJJL74	Limited 5.9 4WD	34304	38175
Destination Charge:		525	525

GRAND CHEROKEE — JEEP

CODE	DESCRIPTION	INVOICE	MSRP
	Accessories		
RAZ	AM/FM, CD, Cassette, Graphic EQ (Laredo)	476	560
	Includes 4 speakers. NOT AVAILABLE with (26Y) quick order package 26Y, (28Y) quick order package 28Y, (ARD) radio.		
DSA	Anti-Spin Differential Axle (Laredo/Limited/TSI)	242	285
PX8	Black Clear Coat (Laredo/TSI/Limited)	NC	NC
YCF	Border State Emissions	145	170
	NOT AVAILABLE with (NAE) CA/CT/MA/NY Emissions.		
NAE	CA/CT/MA/NY Emissions	145	170
	Automatically coded. NOT AVAILABLE with (YCF) border state emissions.		
ARD	Cassette, CD Infinity Speaker Group (Laredo)	799	940
	Includes changer control and 8 Infinity gold speakers in 6 locations. REQUIRES 26E or 26X or 28X. NOT AVAILABLE with 26Y, 28Y, RAZ.		
ARD	Cassette, CD Infinity Speaker Group (Laredo/Limited/TSI)	238	280
	Includes changer control and 8 Infinity gold speakers in 6 locations. REQUIRES 26Y or 28Y. NOT AVAILABLE with RAZ, 26E, 26X, 28X.		
AR3	Cassette, Infinity Speaker Group (Laredo)	561	660
	Includes AM/FM radio, cassette and 8 speakers in 6 locations. NOT AVAILABLE with (RAZ) radio, (ARD) radio.		
TBB	Conventional Full Size Spare Tire (Laredo/TSI/Limited)	136	160
	Includes matching 5th wheel. NOT AVAILABLE with (TRP) tires.		
GEG	Deep Tinted Sunscreen Glass (Laredo)	230	270
NHK	Engine Block Heater	34	40
ELF	Engine: 5.2L V-8 MPI (Laredo 4WD)	1262	1485
	Includes trailer tow prep group: HD radiator, 3.73 axle ratio, conventional full size spare with matching 5th wheel, Quadra-Trac on demand 4WD system. NOT AVAILABLE with DGB, AHT, 26E, 26X, 26Y, ERH, DHR.		
ELF	Engine: 5.2L V-8 MPI (Laredo/Limited/TSI)	748	880
	Includes trailer tow prep group: HD radiator, 3.73 axle ratio. NOT AVAILABLE with AHT, DGB, 26E, 26X, 26Y, 26S, 26G, 26K, ERH.		
LNJ	Fog Lamps (Laredo)	102	120
JPM	Heated Front Seats (Limited)	213	250
EL	Low Back Leather Quad Bucket Seats (Laredo)	493	580
	REQUIRES JPX. NOT AVAILABLE with PS4, PCN, PAW, PFA, 26E, 26X, 28X.		
JPX	Power Heated Seats (Laredo/TSI)	213	250
	NOT AVAILABLE with (26E) quick order package 26E, (26X) quick order package 26X, (28X) quick order package 28X.		
GWA	Power Sunroof (Laredo/TSI/Limited)	646	760
	Includes mini overhead console. REQUIRES 26Y or 28Y. NOT AVAILABLE with 26E, 26X, 28X.		
GWA	Power Sunroof with 26X &28X (Laredo)	718	845
	Includes mini overhead console, electrochromic rearview mirror. REQUIRES 26X or 28X. NOT AVAILABLE with 26E, 26Y, 28Y.		

JEEP GRAND CHEROKEE

CODE	DESCRIPTION	INVOICE	MSRP
DHR	Quadra-Trac On Demand 4WD System (Laredo 4WD)	514	605

Includes conventional full size spare tire with matching 5th wheel. NOT AVAILABLE with (DHR) Quadra-Trac on demand 4WD system, (ELF) engine, (AWE) up country suspension group.

DHR	Quadra-Trac On Demand 4WD System with AWE (Laredo 4WD)	378	445

REQUIRES (AWE) up country suspension group. NOT AVAILABLE with (DHR) Quadra-Trac on demand 4WD system.

26E	Quick Order Package 26E (Laredo 2WD)	NC	NC

Includes vehicle with standard equipment. REQUIRES ERH. NOT AVAILABLE with GWA, AHX, ARD, EL, JPX, ELF, JDH.

26E	Quick Order Package 26E (Laredo 4WD)	NC	NC

Includes vehicle with standard equipment. REQUIRES ERH. NOT AVAILABLE with GWA, AHX, ARD, EL, JPX, ELF.

26G	Quick Order Package 26G (Limited 2WD)	NC	NC

Includes vehicle with standard equipment. REQUIRES (ERH) engine. NOT AVAILABLE with (AHX) trailer tow group IV, (ELF) engine.

26G	Quick Order Package 26G (Limited 4WD)	NC	NC

Includes vehicle with standard equipment. REQUIRES (ERH) engine. NOT AVAILABLE with (AHX) trailer tow group IV, (ELF) engine.

26K	Quick Order Package 26K (Limited)	1097	1290
	Manufacturer Discount	(425)	(500)
	Net Price	672	790

Includes cassette, CD Infinity speaker group radio, heated front seats, power sunroof with mini overhead console. REQUIRES (ERH) engine. NOT AVAILABLE with (AHX) trailer tow group IV, (ELF) engine.

26S	Quick Order Package 26S (TSI 2WD)	2295	2700
	Manufacturer Discount	(1190)	(1400)
	Net Price	1105	1300

Includes overhead console: trip computer, reading/map light (4), TSI Decor Package: door courtesy lamps, carpet and woodgrain door trim, front and rear fascia, color-keyed grille, TSI highland leather/vinyl seat trim, TSI dimensional graphics badge, 16" x 7" - 5 spoke wheels, fog lamps, deep tinted sunscreen glass, Luxury Group: power lumbar adjustment, driver's-side memory-feature seat, power heated exterior mirrors, cassette, Infinity speaker group radio, security alarm. REQUIRES (ERH) engine. NOT AVAILABLE with (AHX) trailer tow group IV, (ELF) engine.

26S	Quick Order Package 26S (TSI 4WD)	2809	3305
	Manufacturer Discount	(1190)	(1400)
	Net Price	1619	1905

Includes overhead console: trip computer, reading/map light (4), TSI Decor Package: door courtesy lamps, carpet and woodgrain door trim, front and rear fascia, color-keyed grille, TSI highland leather/vinyl seat trim, TSI dimensional graphics badge, 16" x 7" - 5 spoke wheels, fog lamps, deep tinted sunscreen glass, Luxury Group: power lumbar adjustment, driver's-side memory-feature seat, power heated exterior mirrors, cassette, Infinity speaker group radio, security alarm. REQUIRES (ERH) engine. NOT AVAILABLE with (AHX) trailer tow group IV, (ELF) engine.

GRAND CHEROKEE — JEEP

CODE	DESCRIPTION	INVOICE	MSRP
26X	Quick Order Package 26X (Laredo)	642	755
	Manufacturer Discount	(595)	(700)
	Net Price	47	55

Includes overhead console: trip computer, reading/map light (4), deep tinted sunscreen glass, P225/75R15 OWL tires. REQUIRES ERH. NOT AVAILABLE with AHX, ARD, GWA, EL, JPX, ELF.

26Y	Quick Order Package 26Y (Laredo)	2248	2645
	Manufacturer Discount	(978)	(1150)
	Net Price	1270	1495

Includes overhead console: trip computer, reading/map light (4), deep tinted sunscreen glass, P225/75R15 OWL tires, Luxury Group: power lumbar adjustment, driver's-side memory-feature seat, cassette, Infinity speaker group radio, power heated exterior mirrors, security alarm, fog lamps. REQUIRES ERH. NOT AVAILABLE with RAZ, ARD, AHX, GWA, PS4, PCN, PAW, PFA, ELF.

28G	Quick Order Package 28G (Limited 2WD)	NC	NC

Includes vehicle with standard equipment. REQUIRES (ELF) engine. NOT AVAILABLE with (ERH) engine.

28G	Quick Order Package 28G (Limited 4WD)	NC	NC

Includes vehicle with standard equipment. REQUIRES (ELF) engine. NOT AVAILABLE with (AHT) trailer tow group III, (ERH) engine.

28K	Quick Order Package 28K (Limited 2WD)	1097	1290
	Manufacturer Discount	(425)	(500)
	Net Price	672	790

Includes cassette, CD Infinity speaker group radio, heated front seats, power sunroof with mini overhead console. REQUIRES (ELF) engine. NOT AVAILABLE with (ERH) engine.

28K	Quick Order Package 28K (Limited 4WD)	1097	1290
	Manufacturer Discount	(425)	(500)
	Net Price	672	790

Includes cassette, CD Infinity speaker group radio, heated front seats, power sunroof with mini overhead console. REQUIRES (ELF) engine. NOT AVAILABLE with (AHT) trailer tow group III, (ERH) engine.

28S	Quick Order Package 28S (TSI 2WD)	2295	2700
	Manufacturer Discount	(1190)	(1400)
	Net Price	1105	1300

Includes overhead console with trip computer, reading/map light (4), TSI decor package: door courtesy lamps, carpet and woodgrain door trim, front and rear fascia, color-keyed grille, TSI highland leather/vinyl seat trim, TSI dimensional graphics badge, 16" x 7" - 5 spoke wheels, fog lamps, deep tinted sunscreen glass, luxury group: power lumbar adjustment, driver's-side memory-feature seat, power heated exterior mirrors, cassette, Infinity speaker group radio, security alarm. REQUIRES (ELF) engine. NOT AVAILABLE with (ERH) engine, (AHT) trailer tow group III.

JEEP GRAND CHEROKEE

CODE	DESCRIPTION	INVOICE	MSRP
28S	Quick Order Package 28S (TSI 4WD)	2809	3305
	Manufacturer Discount	(1190)	(1400)
	Net Price	1619	1905

Includes overhead console with trip computer, reading/map light (4), TSI decor package: door courtesy lamps, carpet and woodgrain door trim, front and rear fascia, color-keyed grille, TSI highland leather/vinyl seat trim, TSI dimensional graphics badge, 16" x 7" - 5 spoke wheels, fog lamps, deep tinted sunscreen glass, luxury group: power lumbar adjustment, driver's-side memory-feature seat, power heated exterior mirrors, Quadra-Trac on demand 4WD system; conventional full size spare with matching 5th wheel, cassette, Infinity speaker group radio, security alarm. REQUIRES (ELF) engine. NOT AVAILABLE with (AHT) trailer tow group III, (ERH) engine.

28X	Quick Order Package 28X (Laredo)	642	755
	Manufacturer Discount	(595)	(700)
	Net Price	47	55

Includes overhead console with trip computer, reading/map light (4), deep tinted sunscreen glass, P225/75R15 OWL tires. REQUIRES ELF. NOT AVAILABLE with EL, ARD, GWA, JPX, AHT, ERH, JDH.

28Y	Quick Order Package 28Y (Laredo 2WD)	2248	2645
	Manufacturer Discount	(978)	(1150)
	Net Price	1270	1495

Includes overhead console wth trip computer, reading/map light (4), fog lamps, deep tinted sunscreen glass, luxury group: power lumbar adjustment, driver's-side memory-feature seat, power heated exterior mirrors, cassette, Infinity speaker group radio, security alarm, P225/75R15 OWL tires. REQUIRES ELF. NOT AVAILABLE with RAZ, AHT, PS4, PCN, ARD, GWA, PAW, PFA, ERH.

28Y	Quick Order Package 28Y (Laredo 4WD)	2248	2645
	Manufacturer Discount	(978)	(1150)
	Net Price	1270	1495

Includes overhead console with trip computer, reading/map light (4), deep tinted sunscreen glass, P225/75R15 OWL tires, luxury group: power lumbar adjustment, driver's-side memory-feature seat, cassette, Infinity speaker group radio, power heated exterior mirrors, security alarm, fog lamps. REQUIRES ELF. NOT AVAILABLE with RAZ, ARD, AHT, GWA, PS4, PCN, PAW, PFA, ERH.

29U	Quick Order Package 29U (Limited 5.9)	NC	NC

Includes 5.9 Limited decor group: bodyside cladding, vinyl and leather door trim (5.9 Limited), front and rear fascia, color-keyed grille, gold bodyside and tailgate striping, overhead console with trip computer, reading/map light (4), gold limited dimensional graphics, carpet and woodgrain door trim, luxury group: power lumbar adjustment, driver's-side memory-feature seat, exterior electric remote painted mirrors, reclining bucket seats, security system, black leather-wrapped steering wheel, universal garage door opener, limited slip differential, roof rack, TSi highland leather/vinyl seat trim, heated front seats, AM/FM audio system with CD and cassette, power sunroof, P225/70R16 BSW/VSB Wrangler HP tires, 16" x 7" ultra star alloy wheels.

GRAND CHEROKEE — JEEP

CODE	DESCRIPTION	INVOICE	MSRP
LSA	Security Alarm (Laredo)	128	150
DHP	Selec-Trac Transfer Case 4WD System (TSI 4WD/Limited 4WD)	NC	NC
	NOT AVAILABLE with (TRP) tires.		
AWN	Skid Plate/Tow Hook Group (Laredo 4WD/TSI 4WD/Ltd. 4WD/Ltd. 5.9)	170	200
	Includes skid plate package, tow hooks.		
GW8	Sunroof Delete (Limited 5.9)	(255)	(300)
	Includes mini overhead console.		
TRT	Tires: P225/75R15 OWL (Laredo)	213	250
	Includes 4 tires. NOT AVAILABLE with (TRL) tires, (AWE) up country suspension group.		
TRL	Tires: P225/75R15 Wrangler RT/S AT (Laredo)	268	315
	Includes 4 tires. REQUIRES (26E) quick order package 26E. NOT AVAILABLE with (TRT) tires, (AWE) up country suspension group.		
TRL	Tires: P225/75R15 Wrangler RT/S AT (Laredo)	55	65
	Includes 4 tires. REQUIRES 26X or 28X or 26Y or 28Y. NOT AVAILABLE with TRT, AWE.		
TRP	Tires: P225/75R16 BSW Wrangler HP (TSI/Limited)	NC	NC
	Includes 5 tires. NOT AVAILABLE with (DHP) Selec-Trac transfer case 4WD system.		
AHT	Trailer Tow Group III (Laredo/Limited/TSI)	306	360
	Includes 25 ft. maximum travel trailer length, 750 lbs maximum tongue weight, frame mounted equalizer hitch receptacle, and 7-pin Bargman outlet with 7 to 4-pin con. Maximum trailering weight (6700 lb), trailer tow prep group: HD radiator, 3.73 axle ratio. REQUIRES ERH. NOT AVAILABLE with 28X, 28Y, 28S, AHX, ELF, 28G, 28K.		
AHX	Trailer Tow Group IV	208	245
	Includes 30 ft. maximum travel trailer length, 750 lb maximum tongue weight, frame mounted equalizer hitch receptacle, and 7-pin Bragman outlet with 7 to 4-pin con. Maximum trailering weight (6700 lb). REQUIRES ELF. NOT AVAILABLE with 26E, 26X, 26Y, 26S, AHT, 26G, 26K.		
AHC	Trailer Tow Prep Group (Laredo/TSI)	89	105
	Includes Spicer 35C rear axle modified with ERH. HD radiator, 3.73 axle ratio.		
AWE	Up Country Suspension Group (Laredo 4WD)	353	415
	Includes shock absorbers front and rear, skid plate package, tow hooks, conventional full size spare tire with matching 5th wheel, P225/70R16 Wrangler HP OWL tires. REQUIRES ELF and 28X or 28Y. NOT AVAILABLE with TRL, DHR, TRT.		
AWE	Up Country Suspension Group (Laredo 4WD)	489	575
	Includes shock absorbers front and rear, skid plate package, tow hooks, conventional full size spare tire with matching 5th wheel, P225/70R16 Wrangler HP OWL tires. REQUIRES 26X or 26Y. NOT AVAILABLE with TRL, DHR, TRT.		
AWE	Up Country Suspension Group (Laredo 4WD)	701	825
	Includes shock absorbers front and rear, skid plate package, tow hooks, conventional full size spare tire with matching 5th wheel, P225/70R16 Wrangler HP OWL tires. REQUIRES 26E. NOT AVAILABLE with TRL, DHR, TRT.		
AWM	Up Country Suspension Package (TSI 4WD/Limited 4WD)	196	230
	Includes shock absorbers front and rear, skid plate package, tow hooks, conventional full size spare tire with matching 5th wheel.		

JEEP WRANGLER

| CODE | DESCRIPTION | INVOICE | MSRP |

1998 WRANGLER

1998 Jeep Wrangler Sport

What's New?

Jeep has improved off-road capability by improving the Wrangler's gear ratio, increasing the axle ratio offered with the 4.0-liter engine, and revising the torsion bar for better steering. Optional this year are a tilting driver's seat, automatic speed control, a combination CD/cassette stereo, a new Smart Key Immobilizer theft deterrent system, and two new colors.

Review

We were a little concerned last year when we heard that Jeep was giving its bad-boy mud-machine an overhaul. Luckily, the Wrangler hasn't received the leather interior, cellular phone makeover that has recently emasculated so much of the sport-utility segment. No, the Wrangler remains the drive-me-hard-through-the-slop beast of yesterday; with a few appreciated improvements.

Jeep Wranglers have long been the standard for those valiant explorers who truly wish to go where no one has gone before. The go-anywhere ability of the Wrangler has been improved by the Quadra-coil suspension which allows an additional seven inches of articulation over the old leaf spring set-up; thus resulting in increased approach and departure angles. Jeep boasts that the Quadra-coil suspension, as well as improved shocks and tires, also greatly improves the Wrangler's on-road manners.

The Wrangler receives minor adjustments to the suspension by combining the Dana 44 rear axle with a 3.73 axle ratio, replacing the 3.55 axle ratio on the 4.0-liter engine. And Jeep claims that a revised torsion bar has improved steering response. Nobody, however, will mistake this vehicle for a smooth-running family sedan; the Wrangler is very much a truck. A five-speed manual transmission remains standard and a three-speed automatic is available for those who don't plan on any serious off-roading.

For 1998, most people will not notice any changes to the Wrangler other than the new Chili Pepper Red and Deep Amethyst exterior colors. Front bumper guards have been added, and a new underhood lamp will aid in finding the wiper fluid reservoir in the dark. A TLEV (Transitional Low Emission Vehicle) 4.0-liter in-line six cylinder engine is available for states adopting California emission regulations, so Jeep owners can feel even closer to nature: they make less smog.

WRANGLER — JEEP

| CODE | DESCRIPTION | INVOICE | MSRP |

Over the past two years, Jeep has done a great job improving the Wrangler. Gone are some of the nagging complaints we had about safety, wind noise and engine roar; what remains is a solid truck with hard-core capabilities and rugged good looks. This is obviously not the truck for everybody, but those willing to put up with a cloth interior and a little road noise will be rewarded with an amazingly fun vehicle. Hey, they even brought back those snazzy round headlights...what's not to like?

Safety Data

Driver Airbag: *Standard*
Side Airbag: *Not Available*
Traction Control: *Not Available*
Driver Crash Test Grade: *Good*

Passenger Airbag: *Standard*
4-Wheel ABS: *Optional*
Integrated Child Seat(s): *Not Available*
Passenger Crash Test Grade: *Excellent*

Standard Equipment

SE: 2.5L I-4 OHV SPI 8-valve engine; 5-speed overdrive manual transmission; 500-amp battery; 81-amp alternator; part-time 4-wheel drive, with auto locking hub control and manual shift, 4.11 axle ratio; stainless steel exhaust; front non-independent suspension with anti-roll bar, front coil springs, front shocks, rear non-independent suspension with anti-roll bar, rear coil springs, rear shocks; power rack-and-pinion steering; front disc/rear drum brakes; 15 gal capacity fuel tank; skid plates; rear tailgate; manual convertible roof with roll-over protection; front and rear black bumpers; black fender flares; monotone paint with bodyside accent stripe; sealed beam halogen headlamps; additional exterior lights include center high mounted stop light; driver and passenger manual black folding outside mirrors; front and rear 15" x 6" silver styled steel wheels, hub wheel covers; P205/75SR15 BSW AT front and rear tires; outside rear mounted compact steel spare wheel; fixed antenna; 1 power accessory outlet; analog instrumentation display includes tachometer gauge, oil pressure gauge, water temp gauge, volt gauge, trip odometer; warning indicators include battery, key in ignition; dual airbags; tinted windows, manual rear windows; fixed interval front windshield wipers; seating capacity of 2, front bucket seats with fixed adjustable headrests, driver seat includes 4-way direction control, passenger seat includes 4-way direction control; easy entry front height-adjustable seatbelts; vinyl seats, front carpet floor covering ; day-night rearview mirror; partial floor console, locking glovebox, front cupholder, dashboard storage, driver and passenger door bins; cargo tie-downs; body-colored grille, black door handles.

SPORT (in addition to or instead of SE): 4L I-6 OHV SMPI 12-valve engine; 3.07 axle ratio; front and rear 15" x 7" silver steel wheels, hub wheel covers; P215/75SR15 BSW AT front and rear tires; AM/FM stereo with clock, seek-scan, 2 speakers; seating capacity of 4; removeable full folding rear bench seat; full carpet floor covering; cargo net.

SAHARA (in addition to or instead of SPORT): 600-amp HD battery; 117-amp HD alternator; HD front shocks, HD rear shocks; 19 gal capacity fuel tank; running boards, skid plates; front black bumper with tow hook(s); body-colored fender flares; additional exterior lights include front fog/driving lights, center high mounted stop light, underhood light; front and rear silver alloy wheels, hub wheel covers; P225/75SR15 OWL AT front and rear tires; alloy spare wheel; AM/FM stereo with seek-scan, cassette, 4 speakers; variable intermittent front windshield wipers; driver seat includes 4-way direction control, easy entry; cloth seats, full carpet floor covering with carpeted floor mats; interior lights include dome light; leather-wrapped steering wheel with with tilt adjustment; full floor console, dashboard storage, 2 seat back storage pockets, driver and passenger door bins.

JEEP WRANGLER

CODE	DESCRIPTION	INVOICE	MSRP

Base Prices

TJJL77	SE	13504	14090
TJJL77	Sport	15804	17505
TJJL77	Sahara	17661	19615
Destination Charge:		525	525

Accessories

CODE	DESCRIPTION	INVOICE	MSRP
NF1	19 Gallon Fuel Tank (SE/Sport)	55	65
	Includes tethered cap.		
DGA	3-Speed Automatic Transmission	531	625
	NOT AVAILABLE with 23A, 23N, 25C, 25D, 25G.		
DME	3.73 Axle Ratio (Sport/Sahara)	NC	NC
	REQUIRES 25C or 24C or 25D or 24D or DSA.		
AAS	30" Tire & Wheel Package (Sahara)	306	360
	Includes 5 tires and wheels. 30 x 9.5R15 Wrangler GSA A/T OWL tires, 15" x 8" aluminum wheels, high pressure gas charged shocks, conventional spare tire.		
AAS	30" Tire & Wheel Package (Sport)	667	785
	Includes 5 tires and wheels. 30 x 9.5R15 Wrangler GSA A/T OWL tires, 15" x 8" aluminum wheels, conventional spare tire, high pressure gas charged shocks. REQUIRES 25C or 24C. NOT AVAILABLE with TMW, TRN, CSA, WJ1.		
AAS	30" Tire & Wheel Package (Sport)	570	670
	Includes 5 tires and wheels. 30 x 9.5R15 Wrangler GSA A/T OWL tires, 15" x 8" aluminum wheels, high pressure gas charged shocks. REQUIRES 25D or 24D. NOT AVAILABLE with TMW, TRN, CSA, WJ1.		
RCD	4 Speakers (Sport)	208	245
BGK	4-Wheel Antilock Brakes (Sport/Sahara)	510	600
	NOT AVAILABLE with (DRK) Dana 44 rear axle.		
JKC	Add-a-Trunk With Lockable Storage	106	125
	REQUIRES (J6) seats or (K5) seats.		
HAA	Air Conditioning	761	895
	NOT AVAILABLE with (4XA) air conditioning bypass.		
4XA	Air Conditioning Bypass	NC	NC
	NOT AVAILABLE with (HAA) air conditioning.		
RAL	AM/FM Stereo with 2 Speakers (SE)	230	270
	NOT AVAILABLE with (RAS).		
RAS	AM/FM Stereo with Cassette (SE)	378	445
	Includes 4 speakers. NOT AVAILABLE with AAX, RAL, 23A, 22A.		
RAS	AM/FM Stereo with Cassette (SE)	608	715
	Includes 4 speakers. NOT AVAILABLE with AAX, RAL, 23N, 22N.		
RAS	AM/FM Stereo with Cassette (Sport)	361	425
	Includes 4 speakers.		
6X7	Black CC with Black HT (Sahara)	986	1160
	Includes hard top, cargo light, rear window wiper/washer, rear quarter and liftgate glass, full metal doors with roll-up windows. REQUIRES (24G) quick order package 24G or (25G) quick order package 25G. NOT AVAILABLE with (AEM) dual top group with matching colors.		

WRANGLER — JEEP

CODE	DESCRIPTION	INVOICE	MSRP
6X7	Black CC with Black HT (SE/Sport)	642	755

Includes hard top, cargo light, rear window wiper/washer, rear quarter and liftgate glass, full metal doors with roll-up windows. REQUIRES 22A or 23A or 22N or 23N or 24C or 25C or 24D or 25D. NOT AVAILABLE with AEM.

6X9	Black CC with Spice HT (Sahara)	986	1160

Includes hard top, cargo light, rear window wiper/washer, rear quarter and liftgate glass, full metal doors with roll-up windows. REQUIRES (24G) quick order package 24G or (25G) quick order package 25G. NOT AVAILABLE with (AEM) dual top group with matching colors.

6X9	Black CC with Spice HT (SE/Sport)	642	755

Includes hard top, cargo light, rear window wiper/washer, rear quarter and liftgate glass, full metal doors with roll-up windows. REQUIRES 22A or 23A or 22N or 23N or 24C or 25C or 24D or 25D. NOT AVAILABLE with AEM.

6X6	Black CC with Stone White HT (SE/Sport)	642	755

Includes hard top, cargo light, rear window wiper/washer, rear quarter and liftgate glass, full metal doors with roll-up windows. REQUIRES 22A or 23A or 22N or 23N or 24C or 25C or 24D or 25D. NOT AVAILABLE with AEM.

MRJ	Bodyside Steps (SE/Sport)	64	75
YCF	Border State (California) Emissions	145	170

NOT AVAILABLE with (NAE) CA/CT/MA/NY Emissions.

6U7	Bright Jade SG with Black HT (SE/Sport)	642	755

Includes hard top, cargo light, rear window wiper/washer, rear quarter and liftgate glass, full metal doors with roll-up windows. REQUIRES 22A or 23A or 22N or 23N or 24C or 25C or 24D or 25D. NOT AVAILABLE with AEM.

6U9	Bright Jade SG with Spice HT (SE/Sport)	642	755

Includes hard top, cargo light, rear window wiper/washer, rear quarter and liftgate glass, full metal doors with roll-up windows. REQUIRES 22A or 23A or 22N or 23N or 24C or 25C or 24D or 25D. NOT AVAILABLE with AEM.

6U6	Bright Jade SG with Stone White HT (SE/Sport)	642	755

Includes hard top, cargo light, rear window wiper/washer, rear quarter and liftgate glass, full metal doors with roll-up windows. REQUIRES 22A or 23A or 22N or 23N or 24C or 25C or 24D or 25D. NOT AVAILABLE with AEM.

NAE	CA/CT/MA/NY Emissions	145	170

Automatically coded. NOT AVAILABLE with (YCF) border state emissions.

6H7	Chili Pepper Red PC with Black HT (SE/Sport)	642	755

Includes hard top, cargo light, rear window wiper/washer, rear quarter and liftgate glass, full metal doors with roll-up windows. REQUIRES 22A or 23A or 22N or 23N or 24C or 25C or 24D or 25D. NOT AVAILABLE with AEM.

6H9	Chili Pepper Red PC with Spice HT (SE/Sport)	642	755

Includes hard top, cargo light, rear window wiper/washer, rear quarter and liftgate glass, full metal doors with roll-up windows. REQUIRES 22A or 23A or 22N or 23N or 24C or 25C or 24D or 25D. NOT AVAILABLE with AEM.

6H6	Chili Pepper Red PC with Stone White HT (SE/Sport)	642	755

Includes hard top, cargo light, rear window wiper/washer, rear quarter and liftgate glass, full metal doors with roll-up windows. REQUIRES 22A or 23A or 22N or 23N or 24C or 25C or 24D or 25D. NOT AVAILABLE with AEM.

JEEP WRANGLER

CODE	DESCRIPTION	INVOICE	MSRP
K5	Cloth High-Back Bucket Seats (SE)	633	745
	Includes rear seat. REQUIRES (23A) quick order package 23A or (22A) quick order package 22A. NOT AVAILABLE with (J6) seats.		
K5	Cloth High-Back Bucket Seats (SE/Sport)	128	150
	Includes rear seat. REQUIRES (23N) quick order package 23N or (22N) quick order package 22N.		
ADC	Convenience Group (SE/Sport)	140	165
	Includes underhood light, floor console with storage.		
TBB	Conventional Spare Tire (Sahara)	183	215
DRK	Dana 44 Rear Axle (Sport/Sahara)	506	595
	Includes trac-lok differential, 3.73 axle ratio. REQUIRES (TBB) conventional spare tire. NOT AVAILABLE with (BGK) 4-wheel antilock brakes.		
6Z7	Deep Amethyst PC with Black HT (SE/Sport)	642	755
	Includes hard top, cargo light, rear window wiper/washer, rear quarter and liftgate glass, full metal doors with roll-up windows. REQUIRES 22A or 23A or 22N or 23N or 24C or 25C or 24D or 25D. NOT AVAILABLE with AEM.		
6Z9	Deep Amethyst PC with Spice HT (SE/Sport)	642	755
	Includes hard top, cargo light, rear window wiper/washer, rear quarter and liftgate glass, full metal doors with roll-up windows. REQUIRES 22A or 23A or 22N or 23N or 24C or 25C or 24D or 25D. NOT AVAILABLE with AEM.		
6Z6	Deep Amethyst PC with Stone White HT (SE/Sport)	642	755
	Includes hard top, cargo light, rear window wiper/washer, rear quarter and liftgate glass, full metal doors with roll-up windows. REQUIRES 22A or 23A or 22N or 23N or 24C or 25C or 24D or 25D. NOT AVAILABLE with AEM.		
AEM	Dual Top Group with Matching Colors (Sahara)	1530	1800
	Includes easy folding soft top with soft windows. NOT AVAILABLE with 6X5, 6X2, 6J5, 6W1, 6W5.		
AEM	Dual Top Group with Matching Colors (SE/Sport)	1186	1395
	Includes easy folding soft top with soft windows. NOT AVAILABLE with 6X1, 6X5, 6X2, 6U1, 6U5, 6U2, 6H1, 6H5, 6H2, 6Z1, 6Z5, 6Z2, 6Y1, 6Y5, 6Y2, 6R1, 6R5, 6R2, 6A1, 6A2, 6K1, 6K2, 6J1, 6J5, 6J2, 6W1, 6W5, 6W2.		
6Y7	Emerald Green PC with Black HT (SE/Sport)	642	755
	Includes hard top, cargo light, rear window wiper/washer, rear quarter and liftgate glass, full metal doors with roll-up windows. REQUIRES 22A or 23A or 22N or 23N or 24C or 25C or 24D or 25D. NOT AVAILABLE with AEM.		
6Y9	Emerald Green PC with Spice HT (SE/Sport)	642	755
	Includes hard top, cargo light, rear window wiper/washer, rear quarter and liftgate glass, full metal doors with roll-up windows. REQUIRES 22A or 23A or 22N or 23N or 24C or 25C or 24D or 25D. NOT AVAILABLE with AEM.		
6Y6	Emerald Green PC with Stone White HT (SE/Sport)	642	755
	Includes hard top, cargo light, rear window wiper/washer, rear quarter and liftgate glass, full metal doors with roll-up windows. REQUIRES 22A or 23A or 22N or 23N or 24C or 25C or 24D or 25D. NOT AVAILABLE with AEM.		
NHK	Engine Block Heater	30	35

WRANGLER JEEP

CODE	DESCRIPTION	INVOICE	MSRP
6R7	**Flame Red CC with Black HT (SE/Sport)**	642	755
	Includes hard top, cargo light, rear window wiper/washer, rear quarter and liftgate glass, full metal doors with roll-up windows. REQUIRES 22A or 23A or 22N or 23N or 24C or 25C or 24D or 25D. NOT AVAILABLE with AEM.		
6R9	**Flame Red CC with Spice HT (SE/Sport)**	642	755
	Includes hard top, cargo light, rear window wiper/washer, rear quarter and liftgate glass, full metal doors with roll-up windows. REQUIRES 22A or 23A or 22N or 23N or 24C or 25C or 24D or 25D. NOT AVAILABLE with AEM.		
6R6	**Flame Red CC with Stone White HT (SE/Sport)**	642	755
	Includes hard top, cargo light, rear window wiper/washer, rear quarter and liftgate glass, full metal doors with roll-up windows. REQUIRES 22A or 23A or 22N or 23N or 24C or 25C or 24D or 25D. NOT AVAILABLE with AEM.		
LNJ	**Fog Lamps (Sport)**	102	120
	REQUIRES (HAA) air conditioning or (ADH) HD electrical group.		
CLC	**Front Floor Mats (SE/Sport)**	26	30
GCF	**Full Metal Doors with Roll-Up Windows**	106	125
6A7	**Gunmetal PC with Black HT (SE/Sport)**	642	755
	Includes hard top, cargo light, rear window wiper/washer, rear quarter and liftgate glass, full metal doors with roll-up windows. REQUIRES 22A or 23A or 22N or 23N or 24C or 25C or 24D or 25D. NOT AVAILABLE with AEM.		
6A6	**Gunmetal PC with Stone White HT (SE/Sport)**	642	755
	Includes hard top, cargo light, rear window wiper/washer, rear quarter and liftgate glass, full metal doors with roll-up windows. REQUIRES 22A or 23A or 22N or 23N or 24C or 25C or 24D or 25D. NOT AVAILABLE with AEM.		
GCD	**Hard Top Deep Tint Glass (SE/Sport)**	344	405
	Includes rear window defroster.		
ADH	**HD Electrical Group (SE/Sport)**	115	135
	Includes HD 117-amp alternator, HD 600-amp battery.		
SDU	**High Pressure Gas Charged Shocks (SE/Sport)**	77	90
	REQUIRES (TMW) tires or (TRN) tires.		
6K7	**Lapis Blue CC with Black HT (SE/Sport)**	642	755
	Includes hard top, cargo light, rear window wiper/washer, rear quarter and liftgate glass, full metal doors with roll-up windows. REQUIRES 22A or 23A or 22N or 23N or 24C or 25C or 24D or 25D. NOT AVAILABLE with AEM.		
6K6	**Lapis Blue CC with Stone White HT (SE/Sport)**	642	755
	Includes hard top, cargo light, rear window wiper/washer, rear quarter and liftgate glass, full metal doors with roll-up windows. REQUIRES 22A or 23A or 22N or 23N or 24C or 25C or 24D or 25D. NOT AVAILABLE with AEM.		
SCG	**Leather Wrapped Steering Wheel (SE/Sport)**	43	50
6J7	**Moss Green PC with Black HT (SE/Sport)**	642	755
	Includes hard top, cargo light, rear window wiper/washer, rear quarter and liftgate glass, full metal doors with roll-up windows. REQUIRES 22A or 23A or 22N or 23N or 24C or 25C or 24D or 25D. NOT AVAILABLE with AEM.		

JEEP WRANGLER

CODE	DESCRIPTION	INVOICE	MSRP
6J9	**Moss Green PC with Spice HT (Sahara)**	986	1160
	Includes hard top, cargo light, rear window wiper/washer, rear quarter and liftgate glass, full metal doors with roll-up windows. REQUIRES (24G) quick order package 24G or (25G) quick order package 25G. NOT AVAILABLE with (AEM) dual top group with matching colors.		
6J9	**Moss Green PC with Spice HT (SE/Sport)**	642	755
	Includes hard top, cargo light, rear window wiper/washer, rear quarter and liftgate glass, full metal doors with roll-up windows. REQUIRES 22A or 23A or 22N or 23N or 24C or 25C or 24D or 25D. NOT AVAILABLE with AEM.		
6J6	**Moss Green PC with Stone White HT (SE/Sport)**	642	755
	Includes hard top, cargo light, rear window wiper/washer, rear quarter and liftgate glass, full metal doors with roll-up windows. REQUIRES 22A or 23A or 22N or 23N or 24C or 25C or 24D or 25D. NOT AVAILABLE with AEM.		
22A	**Quick Order Package 22A (SE)**	NC	NC
	Includes vehicle with standard equipment. REQUIRES (HAA or 4XA) and EPE and DGA. NOT AVAILABLE with DSA, RAS, AAX, DDQ.		
22N	**Quick Order Package 22N (SE)**	735	865
	Includes AM/FM stereo with 2 speakers, vinyl high-back bucket seats. REQUIRES (HAA or 4XA) and EPE and DGA. NOT AVAILABLE with DSA, RAS, AAX, DDQ.		
23A	**Quick Order Package 23A (SE)**	NC	NC
	Includes vehicle with standard equipment. REQUIRES (HAA or 4XA) and EPE and DDQ. NOT AVAILABLE with RAS, AAX, DGA.		
23N	**Quick Order Package 23N (SE)**	735	865
	Includes AM/FM stereo with 2 speakers, vinyl high-back bucket seats. REQUIRES (HAA or 4XA) and EPE and DDQ. NOT AVAILABLE with RAS, AAX, DGA.		
24C	**Quick Order Package 24C (Sport)**	NC	NC
	Includes vehicle with standard equipment. REQUIRES (HAA or 4XA) and ERH and DGA. NOT AVAILABLE with DDQ.		
24D	**Quick Order Package 24D (Sport)**	459	540
	Includes Convenience Group: underhood light, floor console with storage, 19 gallon fuel tank, conventional spare tire, tilt steering column, intermittent wipers. REQUIRES (HAA or 4XA) and ERH and DGA. NOT AVAILABLE with DDQ.		
24G	**Quick Order Package 24G (Sahara)**	NC	NC
	Includes vehicle with standard equipment. REQUIRES (HAA or 4XA) and ERH and DGA. NOT AVAILABLE with DDQ.		
25C	**Quick Order Package 25C (Sport)**	NC	NC
	Includes vehicle with standard equipment. REQUIRES (HAA or 4XA) and ERH and DDQ. NOT AVAILABLE with DGA.		
25D	**Quick Order Package 25D (Sport)**	459	540
	Includes Convenience Group: underhood light, floor console with storage, 19 gallon fuel tank, conventional spare tire, tilt steering column, intermittent wipers. REQUIRES (HAA or 4XA) and ERH and DDQ. NOT AVAILABLE with DGA.		
25G	**Quick Order Package 25G (Sahara)**	NC	NC
	Includes vehicle with standard equipment. REQUIRES (HAA or 4XA) and ERH and DDQ. NOT AVAILABLE with DGA.		
GFA	**Rear Window Defroster (SE/Sport)**	140	165
	REQUIRES ADH or HAA.		

WRANGLER — JEEP

CODE	DESCRIPTION	INVOICE	MSRP
AAX	**Sound Group (SE)**	455	535
	Includes rear soundbar with padding, AM/FM stereo. NOT AVAILABLE with RAS, 22N, 23N, AAX.		
AAX	**Sound Group with 22N or 23N (SE)**	225	265
	Includes AM/FM radio and rear soundbar with padding, 4 speakers. NOT AVAILABLE with RAS, AAX, 22A, 23A.		
CSA	**Spare Tire Cover (SE/Sport)**	43	50
	NOT AVAILABLE with (AAS) 30" tire and wheel package.		
NHM	**Speed Control (Sahara)**	213	250
	Includes leather wrapped steering wheel.		
NHM	**Speed Control (SE/Sport)**	255	300
	Includes leather wrapped steering wheel.		
6W7	**Stone White CC with Black HT (SE/Sport)**	642	755
	Includes hard top, cargo light, rear window wiper/washer, rear quarter and liftgate glass, full metal doors with roll-up windows. REQUIRES 22A or 23A or 22N or 23N or 24C or 25C or 24D or 25D. NOT AVAILABLE with AEM.		
6W9	**Stone White CC with Spice HT (Sahara)**	986	1160
	Includes hard top, cargo light, rear window wiper/washer, rear quarter and liftgate glass, full metal doors with roll-up windows. REQUIRES (24G) quick order package 24G or (25G) Quick Order Package 25G. NOT AVAILABLE with (AEM) dual top group with matching colors.		
6W9	**Stone White CC with Spice HT (SE/Sport)**	642	755
	Includes hard top, cargo light, rear window wiper/washer, rear quarter and liftgate glass, full metal doors with roll-up windows. REQUIRES 22A or 23A or 22N or 23N or 24C or 25C or 24D or 25D. NOT AVAILABLE with AEM.		
6W6	**Stone White CC with Stone White HT (Sahara)**	986	1160
	Includes hard top, cargo light, rear window wiper/washer, rear quarter and liftgate glass, full metal doors with roll-up windows. REQUIRES (24G) quick order package 24G or (25G) Quick Order Package 25G. NOT AVAILABLE with (AEM) dual top group with matching colors.		
6W6	**Stone White CC with Stone White HT (SE/Sport)**	642	755
	Includes hard top, cargo light, rear window wiper/washer, rear quarter and liftgate glass, full metal doors with roll-up windows. REQUIRES 22A or 23A or 22N or 23N or 24C or 25C or 24D or 25D. NOT AVAILABLE with AEM.		
GXX	**Theft Deterrent System**	64	75
	Includes 2 keys.		
SUA	**Tilt Steering Column (SE/Sport)**	166	195
	Includes intermittent wipers.		
TBB	**Tire: Conventional Spare (SE/Sport)**	98	115
TMW	**Tires: P215/75R15 AT OWL (SE)**	238	280
	Includes 5 tires; conventional spare tire. REQUIRES (WJ5) wheels. NOT AVAILABLE with (TRN) tires.		
TMW	**Tires: P215/75R15 AT OWL (Sport)**	200	235
	Includes 5 tires; conventional spare tire. REQUIRES 25C or 24C. NOT AVAILABLE with TRN, AAS.		
TMW	**Tires: P215/75R15 AT OWL (Sport)**	102	120
	Includes 5 tires. REQUIRES 25D or 24D. NOT AVAILABLE with TRN, AAS.		

JEEP WRANGLER

CODE	DESCRIPTION	INVOICE	MSRP
TRN	Tires: P225/75R15 Wrangler AT OWL (SE) .... Includes 5 tires; conventional spare tire. REQUIRES (WJ5) wheels. NOT AVAILABLE with (TMW) tires.	400	470
TRN	Tires: P225/75R15 Wrangler AT OWL (Sport) .... Includes 5 tires. REQUIRES 25D or 24D. NOT AVAILABLE with TMW, AAS.	264	310
TRN	Tires: P225/75R15 Wrangler AT OWL (Sport) .... Includes 5 tires; conventional spare tire. REQUIRES 25C or 24C. NOT AVAILABLE with TMW, AAS.	361	425
XEA	Tow Hooks (2 Front) (SE/Sport)	34	40
DSA	Trac-Lok Differential .... REQUIRES (TBB) conventional spare. NOT AVAILABLE with (22A) quick order package 22A, (22N) quick order package 22N.	242	285
J6	Vinyl High-Back Bucket Seats (SE) .... Includes rear seat. NOT AVAILABLE with (K5) seats.	506	595
WJ1	Wheels: 15" X 7" Grizzly Aluminum (Sport) .... Includes 5 wheels. REQUIRES (TBB) conventional spare tire. NOT AVAILABLE with (AAS) 30" tire and wheel package.	225	265
WJ5	Wheels: 15"x 7" Full Face Argent Steel (SE) .... Includes 5 wheels.	196	230

Don't forget to swing by the Townhall when you visit Edmund's website at http://www.edmunds.com. Talk to our editors and compare notes on your favorite cars and trucks. Join others to scope out smart shopping stategies, get answers to your questions, or share your expertise. To get to the Townhall, just click on the link on the homepage or go directly to http://www.edmunds.com/edweb/townhall/welcomeconflist.html.

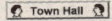

One 15-minute call could save you 15% or more on car insurance.

America's 6th Largest Automobile Insurance Company

1-800-555-2758

SPORTAGE   KIA

CODE   DESCRIPTION   INVOICE   MSRP

1997 SPORTAGE

1997 Kia Sportage

What's New?

An automatic transmission is offered on 2WD models, and the EX trim level is available in 2WD for the first time. Power door locks, a theft deterrent system, and a spare tire carrier are all standard on all Sportages for 1997. A new option is a CD player. Sportage gets a new grille. A tan interior can be combined with black paint for the first time. Base 2WD models lose their standard alloy wheels.

Review

Many residents of the Midwest and along the East Coast don't know what the heck a Kia is. Kia's are built near Seoul, South Korea, and are currently sold in western and southeastern U.S. markets. The company builds an inexpensive compact sedan, called the Sephia, and a wonderfully affordable sport utility called the Sportage.

Part-owned by Ford and Mazda, Kia relies heavily on resources from both companies as it struggles to its feet in a tough marketplace. The Sportage is the product of a collaboration between Kia, Ford, Mazda and suspension-tuning guru Lotus. Designed from the start as a sport utility, the Sportage sports tough ladder frame construction, shift-on-the-fly four-wheel-drive, and a Mazda-based powerplant.

Two trim levels are available: base and EX. Base models are well-trimmed, including power windows, tinted glass, split-folding seats, a remote fuel door release, power mirrors and a rear defroster. Power door locks, a theft deterrent system, and a spare tire carrier are newly standard for 1997. The EX adds cruise control, rear wiper and a remote liftgate release. Optional are a roof rack, air conditioning, premium stereo, CD player, leather interior, an automatic transmission and a limited slip differential.

A wide variety of colors are available on the Sportage's smoothly-styled flanks; few of which appear to have originated from the minds of the folks currently in charge of painting Matchbox cars. The look is rugged yet cute; perfect for family duty in the 'burbs. Off-road, we found the Sportage confidence-inspiring, but it didn't feel as tight as a Toyota RAV4.

For most owners, that won't matter. Few SUV's actually leave the pavement, and on the pavement is where the Sportage shines. Lotus engineers worked wonders here, and the

SPORTAGE

Sportage is stable and comfortable. The seating position is high and upright, visibility is outstanding, and the layout of the dashboard and controls is top-notch. Rear seat riders enjoy lots of room and support, afforded by "stadium style" elevated seating. From the driver's seat, the Sportage looks and feels much more substantial than its low price would lead you to believe. Our only quibble with the Sportage's interior is the lack of storage space, though this year's standard spare tire carrier certainly helps.

Kia hopes the younger families and active singles that will be buying the Sportage will find its affordability a welcome trade for some cargo room. With a loaded 4WD EX topping out at around $21,000, we think they've got little to worry about.

Safety Data

Driver Airbag: *Standard*
Side Airbag: *Not Available*
Traction Control: *Not Available*
Driver Crash Test Grade: *Average*

Passenger Airbag: *Not Available*
4-Wheel ABS: *Not Available*
Integrated Child Seat(s): *Not Available*
Passenger Crash Test Grade: *Average*

Standard Equipment

SPORTAGE: 2.0-liter DOHC 16-valve inline 4-cylinder engine, power ball-and-nut steering, power front disc/rear drum brakes with rear anti-lock, alloy wheels (4WD), body-color bumpers, dual black power exterior mirrors, intermittent windshield wipers, tinted glass, full-size spare tire carrier, cloth reclining front bucket seats with adjustable headrests and driver's manually-adjustable lumbar support, split folding rear seatback, rear seat headrests, front door map pockets, dual cupholders, digital clock, tachometer, passenger visor vanity mirror, theft deterrent system, power windows, power door locks, remote fuel filler door release, rear window defroster, driver airbag, driver knee airbag, steel side door guard beams (do not meet 1999 truck standard), child-safe rear door locks, day/night rearview mirror, part-time 4WD with automatic locking hubs (4WD models).

EX (in addition to or instead of BASE equipment): Cruise control, body-color exterior mirrors, alloy wheels, rear window wiper/washer, roof rack.

Base Prices

Code	Description	Invoice	MSRP
42221	4-door 2WD (5-spd.)	13177	14495
42222	4-door 2WD (auto.)	14087	15495
42421	4-door 4WD (5-spd.)	14410	15995
42422	4-door 4WD (auto.)	15320	16995
42241	4-door 2WD EX (5-spd.)	13865	15390
42242	4-door EX 2WD (auto.)	14775	16390
42441	4-door EX 4WD (5-spd.)	14835	16615
42442	4-door EX 4WD (auto.)	15745	17615
Destination Charge:		425	425

Accessories

Code	Description	Invoice	MSRP
AC	Air Conditioning	763	900
AW	Alloy Wheels (Base 2WD)	242	340
CA	California Emissions	70	70

SPORTAGE — KIA

CODE	DESCRIPTION	INVOICE	MSRP
CF	Carpeted Floor Mats	45	64
LE	Leather Package (EX)	865	1000
	Includes leather seats, leather door inserts, and leather-wrapped steering wheel		
SP	Rear Spoiler	143	189
RR	Roof Rack (Base)	142	185
SG	Sport Appearance Graphic	60	95
RP	Stereo: Premium with cassette	305	400
CD	Stereo: Premium with CD player	430	545

One 15-minute call could save you 15% or more on car insurance.

America's 6th Largest Automobile Insurance Company

1-800-555-2758

For expert advice in selecting/buying/leasing a new car, call

1-900-AUTOPRO

($2.00 per minute)

LAND ROVER — DEFENDER 90

CODE DESCRIPTION   INVOICE   MSRP

1997 DEFENDER 90

1997 Defender 90

What's New?

After a one year hiatus, Defender 90 returns in convertible and hardtop bodystyles. A 4.0-liter V-8 engine is standard, mated to a ZF 4-speed automatic transmission. A redesigned center console includes cupholders, and hardtops have new interior trim. Convertibles get improved top sealing, while all Defender 90s are treated to fresh paint colors.

Review

When launched as a 1994 model, the Defender 90 was the only convertible-topped sport-utility vehicle with a V-8 engine. Macho, go-anywhere looks aren't an illusion, as the off-road talents of this high-priced fantasy machine, operating with permanent four-wheel drive, rank among the finest. Occupants are surrounded by a "Safari" roll cage setup, over a spartan and uncomfortable interior. Don't try to roll down the soft-top's windows, which slide open for ventilation and can be removed if desired.

In late 1995, a limited production run of hardtop Defender 90s debuted, able to seat six passengers in slightly more sophisticated interior fittings. No 1996 models were produced, thanks to emissions regulations and the limited production nature of the Defender 90. With the transplantation of the powertrain from the Discovery, the Defender 90 returns for an encore performance for 1997, in both convertible and hardtop bodystyles.

Long-travel coil springs front and rear help produce an acceptable ride over a variety of terrain. A removable fastback soft top is standard on the convertible. Optional configurations include a Bimini half-top and surrey-style roof—or no top at all. Hardtops feature an aluminum roof and four center-facing rear jump seats. Convertibles come with a rear bench seat. A swing-away spare tire adds to interior space, and passengers ride on weather-resistant twill-effect upholstery.

Propulsion comes from a 4.0-liter aluminum V-8 that yields 182 horsepower, driving a ZF 4-speed automatic transmission. Riding a compact 92.9-inch wheelbase, the Defender wears aluminum body panels with minimal front and rear overhangs. Neither airbags nor anti-lock brakes are available, and the brief option list only includes a CD changer and special Beluga Black paint.

DEFENDER 90 — LAND ROVER

| CODE | DESCRIPTION | INVOICE | MSRP |

Land Rovers aren't known for silence or for sedate behavior, on or off the road. Gears are noisy, and road sounds are likely to assault passenger ears. Standing more than 6-1/2 feet tall, the sharply-profiled body can't help but lean over when undertaking sharp curves and corners.

High price means the Defender 90 cannot qualify as a value leader among sport-utilities, but you do get the heritage that comes from the company that built the first jungle-trotting Land Rovers, nearly half a century ago.

Safety Data

Driver Airbag: *Not Available*
Side Airbag: *Not Available*
Traction Control: *Not Available*
Driver Crash Test Grade: *Not Available*

Passenger Airbag: *Not Available*
4-Wheel ABS: *Not Available*
Integrated Child Seat(s): *Not Available*
Passenger Crash Test Grade: *Not Available*

Standard Equipment

DEFENDER 90 CONVERTIBLE: 4.0-liter aluminum V-8 engine, permanent 4WD, 2-speed transfer case with manual locking center differential, ZF 4-speed automatic transmission, 4-wheel long-travel coil spring suspension, front/rear sway bars, 4-wheel power disc brakes, internal/external custome Safari Cage system, P265/75R16 B.F. Goodrich all-season tires, 5-spoke alloy wheels with bright silver finish, element-repellent Tweed vinyl upholstery, reclining front bucket seats with integrated headrests, removable rear bench seat, lockable center cubby bin with integral audio system and cupholders, premium high-powered AM/FM cassette audio system with 4 weather-resistant speakers, mast-mounted antenna, swing-away rear-mounted spare tire carrier, half doors with removable sliding windows, door and seatback storage pockets, dual exterior mirrors, 2-speed intermittent front wipers, quartz halogen headlights, tachometer, class III trailer tow hitch receiver, flexible black wheel flares with integrated black bumpers.

HARDTOP (in addition to or instead of CONVERTIBLE equipment): Aluminum top with roll-up front and sliding rear windows, one-piece side and rear doors, pop-up sunroof, four inward facing rear seats, full carpeting, full interior trim.

Base Prices

—	Convertible	28700	32000
—	Hardtop	30300	34000
	Destination Charge:	625	625

Accessories

—	Air Conditioning	1050	1200
—	California Emissions	100	100
—	Paint: Beluga Black	250	300

LAND ROVER DISCOVERY

1997 DISCOVERY

1997 Land Rover Discovery

What's New?

A diversity antenna is added, and all interiors are trimmed with polished burled walnut. The sunroof has darker tinting, the airbag system benefits from simplified operation, and engine management is improved. Three new exterior colors debut: Oxford Blue; Roja Red; Charleston Green.

Review

Introduced in April 1994, this compact 4X4 builds on a couple of Land Rover legends. Designed for go-anywhere capability, the Discovery exhibits excellent off-road ability. Built in England, the Discovery also exhibits a distressing tendency toward reliability problems. We receive lots of horror stories regarding Discovery reliability via e-mail, and *Automobile* magazine wrapped up a long-term test with a very troublesome 1995 model recently. Just one body style is available: a five-door wagon with permanent four-wheel-drive. An automatic transmission is optional. This year, three trim levels are available; the SD, SE and SE7.

Beneath the hood of all models sits an aluminum 4.0-liter, 182-horsepower V-8 engine. Acceleration isn't bad, but is accompanied by gear noise and other aural annoyances. Worse, this powerplant is rated for 13 mpg city/17 mpg highway, and that's with a light foot. Sizable ground clearance (8.1 inches) is a bonus while off-roading, but contributes to the Discovery's tendency to lean through curves and corners, and also makes it harder to climb inside. Though firm, the sport-utility's suspension delivers a suitable ride, via 16-inch Michelin or Goodyear tires. New exterior colors help differentiate the 1997 Discovery from those that preceded it.

The driver sits high — three feet above the road surface. Rear passengers sit higher still, for a superior view. Seating is available for seven, in the form of center-facing, stowable rear seats that come standard on the SE7, but this is a five-passenger vehicle in SD and SE trim. Though roomy enough, the Discovery holds fewer luxury fittings than might be expected in this price league. Only a handful of options are available, including leather upholstery. The spare tire resides outside. The driver and front passenger have adjustable lumbar supports, and enjoy the benefits of dual-temperature control air conditioning. A full-size glovebox and four cupholders are included.

DISCOVERY LAND ROVER

Changes for 1997 are minimal. A diversity antenna is added, and all interiors are trimmed with polished burled walnut. The sunroof has darker tinting, the airbag system benefits from simplified operation, and engine management is improved.

Legendary off-road capabilities help make the aluminum-bodied Discovery an attractive choice, augmented by safety equipment. If you expect to drive mainly around the suburbs rather than through the woods, the Discovery's high center of gravity and short wheelbase could be a drawback. The fact that a Discovery can ford a stream up to 19.7 inches deep isn't exactly a benefit when its primary duties involve driving to the office or the mall. In urban America, the Discovery is all about prestige, and it doesn't come cheaply or conveniently. We recommend the Discovery for off-road use, but most consumers will want a different truck to haul the Little Leaguers in.

Safety Data

Driver Airbag: *Standard*
Side Airbag: *Not Available*
Traction Control: *Not Available*
Driver Crash Test Grade: *Good*

Passenger Airbag: *Standard*
4-Wheel ABS: *Standard*
Integrated Child Seat(s): *Not Available*
Passenger Crash Test Grade: *Good*

Standard Equipment

DISCOVERY SD: 4.0-liter aluminum V-8 engine, permanent 4WD, 2-speed transfer gearbox with manually locking center differential, long-travel single-rate front and dual-rate rear coil-spring suspension, dual-acting hydraulic dampers front and rear, front/rear sway bars, cloth upholstery, reclining front bucket seats with integrated adjustable lumbar support, cruise control, dual-zone climate control system, leather-wrapped steering wheel, burled walnut wood trim on dashboard, dual front airbags, four-wheel anti-lock disc brakes, remote keyless entry, security system featuring engine immobilization, illuminated entry, cargo cover, rear door child safety locks, power window and sunroof lockout switch, locking fuel cap, power windows with one-touch down feature on front windows, power-off delay logic for windows and sunroof, central locking, dual cupholders, center console storage bin, front/rear door map pockets, overhead net storage, roof-mounted storage bins, front seatback storage pockets, illuminated driver/passenger visor vanity mirrors, auto-dimming rearview mirror, 60/40 split-folding rear seat, dual power heated exterior mirrors, rear window defroster, variable intermittent wipers, rear window wiper/washer, quartz halogen headlights with power washers, tachometer, class III trailer tow hitch receiver, P235/70HR16 Michelin or Goodyear all-season tires, alloy wheels, full-size spare tire mounted on rear door, premium audio system with four speakers, amplified subwoofer system, and A-pillar tweeters; CD changer prewiring, diversity power antenna.

SE (in addition to or instead of SD equipment): Heated power leather seats, burled walnut trim on door panels and gear shift, unique alloy wheels, dual sunroofs, front fog lights, HomeLink transmitter.

SE7 (in addition to or instead of SE equipment): Rear jump seats, rear air conditioning, hydraulic rear step.

Base Prices

Code	Description	Invoice	MSRP
SDVZ	SD w/Cloth Interior (5-spd)	28480	32000
SDVZ	SD w/Cloth Interior (auto)	28480	32000
SDVZ	SD w/Leather Interior (auto)	30260	34000

LAND ROVER DISCOVERY / RANGE ROVER

CODE	DESCRIPTION	INVOICE	MSRP
SDVZ	SE (auto)	32040	36000
SDVZ	SE7 (5-spd)	34265	38500
SDVZ	SE7 (auto)	34265	38500
Destination Charge:		625	625

Accessories

—	California Emissions	100	100
—	CD Changer w/6 disc capacity	525	625
—	Leather Power Seat Package (SD w/Cloth (auto))	1780	2000
—	Paint — Beluga Black Clearcoat	250	300
—	Rear Jump Seats — Cloth (SD w/Cloth)	735	875
—	Rear Jump Seats — Leather (SD w/Leather & SE)	819	975

1997 RANGE ROVER

1997 Land Rover Range Rover 4.6 HSE

What's New?

4.0 SE gets three new exterior colors (Oxford Blue, Roja Red, and White Gold, all matched to Saddle leather interior), a HomeLink transmitter, and jeweled wheel center caps. The 4.6 HSE gets three new exterior colors (British Racing Green, Monza Red, AA Yellow), one new interior color (Lightstone with contrasting piping), and a leather shift handle.

Review

Virtually unbeatable in both snob appeal and off-road talent, the Range Rover comes in two trim levels: 4.0 SE and 4.6 HSE. Both are the benefactors of new colors and fresh finishing touches for 1997.

In the 4.0 SE, an update of Land Rover's 4.0-liter aluminum V-8 engine works in concert with a ZF four-speed automatic transmission, offering normal, sport, and manual shift programs.

RANGE ROVER — LAND ROVER

CODE   DESCRIPTION   INVOICE   MSRP

The 4.6 HSE comes equipped with a significantly stronger 4.6-liter V-8 engine. Electronic traction control augments the permanent four-wheel-drive system. All-disc, all-terrain anti-lock braking is standard. So is a CD changer. This Range Rover 4.0 SE can tow 6,500 pounds on the highway, or 7,700 pounds in low range. Under the sheetmetal is a ladder-type chassis, plus an electronic air suspension system and beam axles. Rear trailing arms are made of lightweight composite material.

The Range Rover is loaded with standard equipment. That means leather and burled walnut in the interior, automatic climate control for the driver and front passenger (with micro-pollen filtration), 10-way adjustable heated front seats with memory preset, sunroof, 120-watt stereo—well, you get the idea. Dual airbags protect driver and passenger.

In addition to a stronger engine, the 4.6 HSE adds Pirelli 255/55HR18 tires, five-spoke 18-inch alloy wheels, mud flaps, a leather shifter, and a chrome exhaust.

With a 4.0 SE priced well past fifty thou', the Range Rover obviously isn't for everyone. The Land Rover company calls it the "world's most advanced sport utility," aimed at "discerning drivers and sportsmen." We won't argue with that description. Given a choice, we'd prefer something on the order of a Lexus LS400 for ordinary highway driving. Still, if a taste of off-roading lies in your future, and a run-of-the-mill sport-utility vehicle doesn't turn you on, what better way to blast into the bush than in a Range Rover? It's not a drive, it's an experience.

Safety Data

Driver Airbag: *Standard*
Side Airbag: *Not Available*
Traction Control: *Standard*
Driver Crash Test Grade: *Not Available*

Passenger Airbag: *Standard*
4-Wheel ABS: *Standard*
Integrated Child Seat(s): *Not Available*
Passenger Crash Test Grade: *Not Available*

Standard Equipment

4.0 SE: 4.0-liter aluminum V-8 engine, one-piece serpentine belt system, permanent 4WD, viscous coupling unit on center differential, 2-speed transfer gearbox with electronically-controlled range change, ZF 4-speed electronic automatic transmission with Normal, Sport, and Manual shift programs; electronic air suspension system with air springs, shock absorbers, and height sensors at each wheel; front sway bar, P225/65HR16 Michelin tires, 5-spoke 16"x 8" alloy wheels with sparkle silver finish and jeweled center caps, full-size spare tire, cruise control, tilt and slide glass sunroof, 10-way power adjustable heated front seats with headrests and lumbar support, 2-position preset memory feature for front seats, remote-activated memory for seats and mirrors when unlocking vehicle, one-touch open and close for windows and sunroof, automatic dual-zone climate control system with micro-pollen air filtration system, programmable defrost function with ice warning indicator, premium 120-watt audio system with 11 active speakers and 6-disc CD changer, steering wheel stereo controls, weatherband radio, dual glass-mounted diversity antenna system, HomeLink remote transmitter, security system with perimetric and volumetric functions, engine immobilization feature, key-activated all-colse feature for windows and sunroof, cargo cover, dual front airbags, electronic traction control, four-wheel anti-lock disc brakes, anti-submarining seat frames, inertia switch to unlock doors, activate flashers, and interupt fuel flow in case of an accident, automatic dimming rearview mirror, tilt and telescopic steering wheel, integrated computer message center and vehicle condition displays, ignition-off delay logic for window and sunroof operation, front and rear puddle lamps, power windows with one-touch up and down feature, dual illuminated visor vanity mirrors, remote central locking, center console with cubby box and cupholders, remote fuel door release, dual power heated mirrors with right side dip feature when reversing, heated windshield and rear window, variable front wipers with heated washer jets, rear window wiper/washer with automatic activation when reversing with front wipers on, quartz halogen headlights with heated power washers and wipers, class III trailer tow hitch receiver and wiring harness, front spoiler with integrated fog lights, rear fog lights, leather-wrapped steering wheel, burled walnut interior trim, leather upholstery, polished aluminum sill plates.

LAND ROVER — RANGE ROVER

CODE	DESCRIPTION	INVOICE	MSRP

4.6 HSE (in addition to or instead of 4.0 SE equipment): 4.6-liter aluminum V-8 engine, P255/55HR18 Pirelli tires, five-spoke 18"x 8" alloy wheels with jeweled Land Rover badge, leather shift handle, body-flush mud flaps, chrome exhaust tip.

Base Prices

Code	Description	Invoice	MSRP
SXLA	4.0 SE	49125	55500
SXLA	4.6 HSE	55750	63000
	Destination Charge:	625	625

Accessories

Code	Description	Invoice	MSRP
416	Beluga Black Paint (4.0 SE)	250	300
—	California Emissions	100	100
—	Kensington Interior Package (4.6 HSE)	2675	3000

Don't forget to swing by the Townhall when you visit Edmund's website at http://www.edmunds.com. Talk to our editors and compare notes on your favorite cars and trucks. Join others to scope out smart shopping stategies, get answers to your questions, or share your expertise. To get to the Townhall, just click on the link on the homepage or go directly to http://www.edmunds.com/edweb/townhall/welcomeconflist.html.

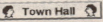
Town Hall

Save hundreds, even thousands, off the sticker price of the new car *you* want.

Call Autovantage®
your FREE auto-buying service
1-800-201-7703

No purchase required. No fees.

LX 450

LEXUS

1997 LX450

1997 Lexus LX450

What's New?

There are no changes to the 1997 LX450.

Review

Japanese automakers are being very cautious these days. High production costs are softening sales across the board, and executives across the Pacific are frantically searching for ways to cut costs. Decontenting is one way to do this. Badge engineering is the other. Lexus chose the latter method when making the decision to offer a sport utility vehicle.

The Toyota Land Cruiser, legendary desert runner and jungle jumper, was donated to the Lexus team of plastic surgeons. They grafted a new grille, new headlamps, new alloy wheels, and bodyside cladding onto Toyota's big SUV. Inside, they added leather and wood. Underneath the sheetmetal, suspension tuning was reworked to provide a better ride on the pavement. Standard equipment levels were raised to include automatic climate controls, rear seat heater, and an amazing 195-watt audio system powering seven loudspeakers. Topping things off, a LX450 badge was added to the tailgate.

The rest of Land Cruiser remains intact on the LX450. The familiar 4.5-liter inline six produces 212 horsepower and 275 lb-ft. of torque. Four-wheel anti-lock disc brakes are standard, and the LX450 can tow 5,000 pounds when properly equipped. All-wheel drive is permanently engaged, and an optional manual differential lock system provides outstanding traction, for the two LX450 owners who will actually go way off-road in truly lousy weather. Dual airbags and adjustable front seat belts come standard, as well as a handy first-aid kit.

You'll pay a $7,000 premium over the Land Cruiser to get into a LX450, which is less than you'd spend optioning the Toyota up to Lexus standards. Factory options on the LX450 include a CD changer, moonroof, and differential locks. Incredibly, floor mats and wheel locks are optional. Talk about nickel-and-diming; these items should be included as standard equipment.

LEXUS — LX 450

| CODE | DESCRIPTION | INVOICE | MSRP |

Land Rover sales have been skyrocketing, and luxury marques from the United States and Japan have definitely noticed. However, at $47,000, the only reason to purchase a LX450 is for status value, or to save a few thousand over the cost of a Range Rover 4.0 SE. Most luxury SUV intenders will find the value inherent in the GMC Yukon SLE, Chevy Suburban LT, and upcoming Ford Expedition and Lincoln Navigator twins more attractive than nice leather and wood inserted into a tough Toyota.

Safety Data

Driver Airbag: *Standard*
Side Airbag: *Not Available*
Traction Control: *Not Available*
Driver Crash Test Grade: *Not Available*

Passenger Airbag: *Standard*
4-Wheel ABS: *Standard*
Integrated Child Seat(s): *Not Available*
Passenger Crash Test Grade: *Not Available*

Standard Equipment

LX450: 4.5 liter 24-valve EFI inline 6 cylinder engine, 4-speed ECT automatic transmission with overdrive, power steering, anti-lock power 4-wheel disc brakes, power door locks, tachometer, cruise control, leather-wrapped tilt steering wheel, electric rear window defroster, power windows with driver's side express down feature, driver and front passenger air bags, front and rear stabilizer bars, P275/70R16 SBR tires, conventional spare tire, alloy wheels, console, tool kit, automatic air conditioning, variable intermittent windshield wipers, intermittent rear window wiper/washer, privacy glass, anti-theft system, keyless remote entry system, voltmeter, oil pressure gauge, remote fuel filler door release, skid plates (transfer case, fuel tank), dual power mirrors, illuminated passenger visor vanity mirror, lower bodyside moldings, AM/FM ETR stereo radio with cassette and 7 speakers, front and rear tow hooks, power reclining front bucket seats, fold-down middle seat, split fold-down removable rear seat, leather seating and door trim panels, full-time 4WD with locking center differential, 25 gallon fuel tank, color keyed bumpers.

Base Prices

9600	LX450	41595	48450
	Destination Charge:	495	495

Accessories

DC	CD Auto Changer	840	1050
2D	Convenience Package A	646	1039
	Includes running boards, luggage rack, trailer towing hitch, and cargo mat.		
CF	Front/Rear Carpeted Floor Mats	68	112
DL	Front/Rear Locking Differentials	720	900
SR	Power Glass Moonroof	1040	1300
	Includes tilt, slide and shade		
WL	Wheel Locks	35	50

CarFinance.com — Instant Lease & Loan Quotes for New & Used Vehicles!
www.CarFinance.com/edmunds

NAVIGATOR

LINCOLN

1998 NAVIGATOR

1998 Lincoln Navigator

What's New?

This all-new entrant into the competitive luxury SUV market is the first truck ever sold by Lincoln. Based on the highly-acclaimed Ford Expedition, this truck is powered by a 5.4-liter SOHV V-8 engine, and has standard goodies that include illuminated running boards, a load-leveling air suspension and standard anti-lock brakes. This truck also features one of the largest grilles this side of the Lincoln Town Car.

Review

Long-suffering Lincoln has been steadily losing sales ever since the luxury SUV boom took off. As customers have flocked to Land Rover, Jeep, and Ford dealerships to snap up Discoveries, Grand Cherokees and Explorers, Lincoln has been left sitting with sales lots full of slow-selling Town Cars, Continentals, and Mark VIIIs. Understandably frustrated with the status quo, Lincoln dealers lobbied to get a luxury version of one of Ford's SUVs. Mercury received the Mountaineer last year based on the sales-leading Explorer, so that model was out of the question. Turns out that good things come to those who wait. The first truck ever sold at a Lincoln dealership will be one based on the all-new Ford Expedition.

The Expedition is an outstanding truck, which fortunately meshes well with the image that people already have of Lincoln products. People don't walk into a Lincoln dealership trying to find small, fuel-efficient, econoboxes. Rather, they frequent Lincoln to buy big, luxurious, chrome-laden, gadget-riddled, road hogs. As we've noted before, the Expedition itself is a colossal vehicle; second in size only to the Chevrolet/GMC Suburbans. Add a big chrome grille, some luxury doo-dads, and a few Lincoln exclusive items to that truck, and you've got yourself a Navigator.

Lest we sound like we're disparaging this truck, let us quickly say that it is indeed a serious workhorse. The Navigator is equipped with a sophisticated SOHC V-8 engine that produces 230 horsepower and 325 pound-feet of torque. It has a payload capacity of nearly two tons, can hold 116.4 cubic feet of flotsam and jetsam, and can tow 8,000 pounds right out of the box.

LINCOLN NAVIGATOR

When equipped with 4WD, the Navigator can pound through the forest faster than Paul Bunyon on Babe the blue ox. Its interior will comfortably hold eight passengers, and the second row seats come standard as captain's chairs. As a Lincoln, it features all of the luxury conveniences that are normally reserved for passenger cars.

No, its not that the Navigator is a bad performer, merely that its styling is a tad overdoneParticularly displeasing to our eyes is the Navigator's obnoxious grille and overly-busy hood. Also, the side-cladding and integrated running boards conspire to make the truck look chubby; not that hard to do on a 5,500-pound vehicle.

Despite these quibbles, we think that Lincoln dealers will soon find themselves flush with cash. The base price of the Navigator is over $39,000 and ,according to *Automotive News*, Lincoln has already taken 6,000 pre-orders for their newest addition to the family. If you want one, march down to your local dealership with cash in hand and be ready to wait; there may be a backlog for this debutante of the national forest.

Safety Data

Driver Airbag: *Standard*
Side Airbag: *Not Available*
Traction Control: *Not Available*
Driver Crash Test Grade: *Good*

Passenger Airbag: *Standard*
4-Wheel ABS: *Standard*
Integrated Child Seat(s): *Not Available*
Passenger Crash Test Grade: *Excellent*

Standard Equipment

NAVIGATOR: 5.4-liter SOHC V-8 engine, 4-speed automatic transmission, recirculating ball speed-sensitive variable assist power steering, load leveling air suspension, front and rear anti-sway bars, heavy-duty Control Trac 4WD (4WD), 3.73 limited slip rear axle (4WD), heavy-duty class III tow package, 30 gallon fuel tank, front tow hooks (4WD), 16" aluminum wheels, P245/75R16 A/S tires, bright grille, wrap-around front bumper with accent colors, fog lamps, color-keyed bodyside cladding, illuminated running boards, privacy glass on liftgate and rear windows, bright luggage rack, beltline, and door handles; power heated outside mirrors, rear step bumper, LED high mounted stoplight, wood and leather-trimmed wheel, wood accents on dash, instrument panel, doors and console; power front seats, second row audio controls, second row climate controls, overhead console with map lights, power quarter window switches, mini computer, and compass; automatic climate control, second row bucket seats with console, removable third row bench seat, illuminated power window and lock switches, dual airbags, 4-wheel disc brakes with ABS, side-impact door beams, remote keyless entry with panic button, illuminated entry, child safety door locks, and speed sensitive windshield wipers.

Base Prices

Code	Description	Invoice	MSRP
U27	Navigator 2WD	34303	39310
U28	Navigator 4WD	37151	42660
	Destination Charge:	640	640

Accessories

Code	Description	Invoice	MSRP
64H	17" Cast Aluminum Wheels (4WD)	200	235
	REQUIRES P255/75R17 OWL tires.		
64C	17" Chrome Wheels (4WD)	808	950
	REQUIRES P255/75R17 OWL tires.		
91P	6-Disc CD Changer	506	595
575	Auxiliary Climate Controls	599	705
	NOT AVAILABLE with moonroof.		

NAVIGATOR — LINCOLN

CODE	DESCRIPTION	INVOICE	MSRP
422	California Emissions	144	170
59B	Electrochromic Rearview Mirror	94	110
41H	Engine Block Heater	30	35
16X	Floor Mat Delete	(42)	(50)
XH6	Limited Slip 3.73 Rear Axle (2WD) *STANDARD on 4WD models.*	217	255
T5P	P245/75R17 OWL Tires (4WD)	259	305
43M	Power Moonroof	1407	1655
916	Premium Stereo w/ Cassette	302	355
61D	Roof Rack Delete	(174)	(205)
21S	Second Row Bench Seat *REPLACES standard quad seating.*	NC	NC
413	Skid Plates (4WD)	89	105

Take Advantage of Warranty Gold!

Savings up to 50% off Dealer's Extended Warranty Prices. Protect and enhance YOUR investment with the best extended warranty available.

Call Toll Free 1-800-580-9889

One 15-minute call could save you 15% or more on car insurance.

GEICO DIRECT

America's 6th Largest Automobile Insurance Company

1-800-555-2758

MAZDA B-SERIES PICKUP

| CODE | DESCRIPTION | INVOICE | MSRP |

1998 B-SERIES

1998 Mazda B4000 SE 2WD

What's New?

Fresh styling, a revised front suspension, a larger regular cab, a more powerful 2.5-liter four-cylinder engine, a stiffer frame, and a new 4WD system ensure that Mazda's compact truck will remain competitive through the end of the century.

Review

Kinship of Mazda's B-Series with Ford's Ranger is evident both on the surface and beneath, but for 1998 the similarities are blurred more than ever. Both compact pickups are built at the same New Jersey factory, from the same design, and employ virtually identical powertrains and four-wheel-drive setups. Competent and attractive, the B-Series differs from the Ranger primarily in styling and pricing structure.

Mazda has substantially updated the B-Series for 1998. The most obvious change is easy to spot: the styling has been modified from front to rear, though the new look is still distinctively Mazda. Research indicated to stylists that import truck buyers prefer a lower, more horizontal look. To achieve such a stance, designers have blended the front grille and headlights into a single band across the front of the truck, serving as the starting point for a fender line that runs rearward. Blistered fenders accentuate the look and provide some muscularity to the design.

Regular cab models have been stretched three inches, resulting in some much-needed cab space. Otherwise, the interior is carried over from last year, but features standard de-powered front airbags. The passenger airbag can be switched off for those times when children must ride in front. Underneath, the forward section of the frame rails has been fully boxed, resulting in a 350 percent increase in frame stiffness. This has allowed for a re-tuning of the suspension for better ride and handling characteristics.

The front suspension is a new short-long arm independent design, and new rack-and-pinion steering provides more control and better feel. Order a B4000 model and you can opt for a rare five-speed automatic transmission. The new shift-on-the-fly four-wheel drive system features pulse vacuum hub-lock technology, allowing the driver to engage 4WD at speeds up to 70 mph. No stopping or backing up is required when shifting into or out of 4-Lo. This less expensive and complex system improves fuel economy and reduces maintenance requirements.

B-SERIES PICKUP — MAZDA

CODE	DESCRIPTION	INVOICE	MSRP

Available in SX or SE trim with a choice of three engines and several option packages, one interesting interior feature is the optional Radio Broadcast Data System (RBDS) stereo system. Normally available only on higher-end luxury cars like Audi, BMW, or Cadillac, RBDS allows the listener to search radio stations by program type and format, and displays the call letters of the station as well as the frequency. It can also be programmed to interrupt a cassette or CD with traffic alerts.

Select any Mazda truck, and you get rugged construction and good looks; and with the B4000, a spirited powertrain. Best of all, Mazda offers one of the best comprehensive truck warranties in the business. It's hard to go wrong with a Mazda B-Series pickup.

Safety Data

Driver Airbag: *Standard*
Side Airbag: *Not Available*
Traction Control: *Not Available*
Driver Crash Test Grade: *Not Available*

Passenger Airbag: *Standard*
4-Wheel ABS: *Opt. (B4000); N/A (B2500/B3000)*
Integrated Child Seat(s): *Not Available*
Passenger Crash Test Grade: *Not Available*

Standard Equipment

2WD B2500 SX REGULAR CAB: 2.5L I-4 SOHC MPI 8-valve engine; 5-speed overdrive manual transmission; 58-amp battery; 95-amp alternator; rear wheel drive, 3.45 axle ratio; steel exhaust; front independent double wishbone suspension with anti-roll bar, front coil springs, front shocks, rear suspension with rear leaf springs, rear shocks; power rack-and-pinion steering; front disc/rear drum brakes with rear wheel anti-lock braking system; 17 gal capacity fuel tank; front and rear mud flaps; front and rear black bumpers with rear step; monotone paint; aero-composite halogen headlamps; additional exterior lights include center high mounted stop light; driver and passenger manual black folding outside mirrors; front and rear 14" x 6" silver styled steel wheels with hub wheel covers; P205/70SR14 BSW AS front and rear tires; underbody mounted full-size conventional steel spare wheel; 2 power accessory outlets, driver foot rest; analog instrumentation display includes oil pressure gauge, water temp gauge, volt gauge, trip odometer; warning indicators include oil pressure, battery, lights on, key in ignition, door ajar; driver side airbag, passenger side cancellable airbag; tinted windows; variable intermittent front windshield wipers; seating capacity of 3, bench front seat with fixed adjustable headrests, driver seat includes 2-way direction control, passenger seat includes 2-way direction control; front height adjustable seatbelts; vinyl seats, full cloth headliner, full vinyl floor covering; interior lights include dome light, illuminated entry; day-night rearview mirror; glove box with light, instrument panel bin; black grille, black side window moldings, black front windshield molding, black rear window molding, black door handles.

2WD B2500 SE REGULAR CAB (in addition to or instead of 2WD B2500 SX REGULAR CAB equipment): 3.73 axle ratio; front and rear chrome bumpers with black rub strip; bodyside accent stripe; additional exterior lights include pickup cargo box light; AM/FM stereo with clock, seek-scan, 4 speakers and fixed antenna; tachometer gauge; 60-40 split-bench front seat and center armrest with storage, driver seat includes 4-way direction control, passenger seat includes 4-way direction control; cloth seats, vinyl door trim insert, carpet floor covering; interior lights; partial floor console, driver and passenger door bins.

2WD B2500 SE EXTENDED CAB (in addition to or instead of 2WD B2500 SE REGULAR CAB equipment): 20.5 gal capacity fuel tank; fixed rear windows; seating capacity of 5, driver seat includes easy entry feature, passenger seat includes easy entry feature; 50-50 folding rear jump seats; leather gear shift knob; passenger side vanity mirror; carpeted cargo floor, cargo net.

MAZDA B-SERIES PICKUP

| CODE | DESCRIPTION | INVOICE | MSRP |

4WD B3000 SX REGULAR CAB (in addition to or instead of 2WD B2500 SX REGULAR CAB equipment): 3.0L V-6 OHV MPI 24-valve engine; 72-amp battery; part-time 4 wheel drive, auto locking hub control and electronic shift, 3.27 axle ratio; front torsion springs, front torsion bar, skid plates; rear tow hooks; black fender flares; P215/75SR15 OWL AS front and rear tires; AM/FM stereo, clock, with seek-scan, 4 speakers and fixed antenna; tachometer gauge

2WD B3000 SE EXTENDED CAB (in addition to or instead of 2WD B2500 SE EXTENDED CAB equipment): 3.0L V-6 OHV MPI 24-valve engine.

4WD B3000 SE REGULAR CAB (in addition to or instead of 2WD B2500 2WD SE REGULAR CAB equipment): 3.0L V-6 OHV MPI 24-valve engine; 72-amp battery; part-time 4 wheel drive, auto locking hub control and electronic shift, 3.27 axle ratio; front torsion springs, front torsion bar, skid plates; rear tow hooks; black fender flares; P215/75SR15 OWL AS front and rear tires.

4WD B3000 SE EXTENDED CAB (in addition to or instead of 2WD B3000 SE EXTENDED CAB equipment): 72-amp battery; part-time 4 wheel drive, auto locking hub control and electronic shift, 3.27 axle ratio; front torsion springs, front torsion bar, skid plates; rear tow hooks; black fender flares; P215/75SR15 OWL AS front and rear tires; battery with run down protection; cabback insulator; illuminated entry; partial floor console.

2WD B4000 SE EXTENDED CAB (in addition to or instead of 2WD B3000 EXTENDED CAB equipment): 4.0L V-6 OHV MPI 24-valve engine; 72-amp battery with run down protection; 3.08 axle ratio; P225/70SR14 OWL AS front and rear tires; cabback insulator; illuminated entry; 2 seat back storage pockets.

4WD B4000 SE EXTENDED CAB (in addition to or instead of 2WD B4000 EXTENDED CAB equipment): Part-time 4 wheel drive, auto locking hub control and electronic shift, 3.27 axle ratio; front torsion springs, front torsion bar; skid plates; rear tow hooks; black fender flares.

Base Prices

Code	Description	Invoice	MSRP
B25SSX2P	B2500 SX 2WD Regular Cab	10102	10885
B25SSE2P	B2500 SE 2WD Regular Cab	11375	12705
B25CSE2P	B2500 SE 2WD Extended Cab	13286	14845
B30CSE2P	B3000 SE 2WD Extended Cab	14098	15795
B40CSE2P	B4000 SE 2WD Extended Cab	14498	16245
S3XSSXXP	B3000 SX 4WD Regular Cab	14377	15415
B3XSSEXP	B3000 SE 4WD Regular Cab	15116	16945
B3XCSEXP	B3000 SE 4WD Extended Cab	16445	18430
B4XCSEXP	B4000 SE 4WD Extended Cab	16846	18880
Destination Charge:		510	510

Accessories

Code	Description	Invoice	MSRP
AC1	Air Conditioning	660	805
1SE	Appearance Package (2WD B2500 SE Reg Cab)	902	1100
	Manufacturer Discount	(779)	(950)
	Net Price	123	150

Includes alloy wheels, P225/70R15 AS OWL tires, Bright Group, AM/FM stereo with cassette player and clock, sliding rear window, bedliner.

B-SERIES PICKUP — MAZDA

CODE	DESCRIPTION	INVOICE	MSRP
1SE	Appearance Package (2WD B2500 SE X-cab)	1046	1275
	Manufacturer Discount	(841)	(1025)
	Net Price	205	250
	Includes alloy wheels, P225/70R15 AS OWL tires, Bright Group, AM/FM stereo with cassette player and clock, sliding rear window, bedliner, pivoting quarter windows, privacy glass, cargo cover, payload package.		
1SE	Appearance Package (2WD B3000/B4000 SE X-cab)	1267	1545
	Manufacturer Discount	(939)	(1145)
	Net Price	328	400
	Includes alloy wheels, P225/70R15 AS OWL tires, Bright Group, AM/FM stereo with cassette player and clock, sliding rear window, bedliner, pivoting quarter windows, privacy glass, cargo cover, payload/performance package.		
1SE	Appearance Package (4WD B3000 SE Reg Cab)	902	1100
	Manufacturer Discount	(779)	(950)
	Net Price	123	150
	Includes alloy wheels, P225/70R15 AS OWL tires, Bright Group, AM/FM stereo with cassette player and clock, sliding rear window, bedliner.		
1SE	Appearance Package (4WD B3000/B4000 SE X-cab)	1267	1545
	Manufacturer Discount	(898)	(1095)
	Net Price	369	450
	Includes alloy wheels, P225/70R15 AS OWL tires, Bright Group, AM/FM stereo with cassette player and clock, sliding rear windows, bedliner, pivoting quarter windows, privacy glass, cargo cover, payload/performance package.		
AT1	Automatic Transmission (B2500 Reg Cab/B3000)	877	1070
AT1	Automatic Transmission (B4000)	906	1105
BLN	Bedliner	165	275
CE1	CA/CT/MA/NY Emissions	139	170
ORG	Cargo Organizer (SE X-cab)	36	60
3SE	Comfort Package (2WD B4000 SE X-cab)	4207	5130
	Manufacturer Discount	(1337)	(1630)
	Net Price	2870	3500
	Includes alloy wheels, P225/70R15 AS OWL tires, Bright Group, premium AM/FM stereo with CD player, cassette player, RBDS, and clock; sliding rear window, bedliner, pivoting quarter windows, privacy glass, cargo cover, payload/performance package, air conditioning, power door locks, power windows, power exterior mirrors, cruise control, tilt steering wheel, leather-wrapped steering wheel, sport bucket seats, four-wheel ABS, remote keyless entry.		
3SE	Comfort Package (4WD B4000 SE X-cab)	4358	5315
	Manufacturer Discount	(1365)	(1665)
	Net Price	2993	3650
	Includes alloy wheels, P225/70R15 AS OWL tires, Bright Group, premium AM/FM stereo with CD player, cassette player, RBDS, and clock; sliding rear windows, bedliner, pivoting quarter windows, privacy glass, cargo cover, payload/performance package, air conditioning, power door locks, power windows, power exterior mirrors, cruise control, tilt steering wheel, leather-wrapped steering wheel, sport bucket seats, four-wheel ABS, remote keyless entry, fog lights.		

MAZDA B-SERIES PICKUP

CODE	DESCRIPTION	INVOICE	MSRP
FLM	Floor Mats (SE)	56	80
JCP	Paint: Two-Tone (SE)	165	235
2SE	Power Package (2WD B2500 SE Reg Cab)	2517	3070
	Manufacturer Discount	(918)	(1120)
	Net Price	1599	1950

Includes alloy wheels, P225/70R15 AS OWL tires, Bright Group, AM/FM stereo with CD player and clock, sliding rear window, bedliner, air conditioning, power door locks, power windows, power exterior mirrors, cruise control, tilt steering wheel, leather-wrapped steering wheel.

2SE	Power Package (2WD B2500 SE X-cab)	2661	3245
	Manufacturer Discount	(939)	(1145)
	Net Price	1722	2100

Includes alloy wheels, P225/70R15 AS OWL tires, Bright Group, AM/FM stereo with CD player and clock, sliding rear window, bedliner, pivoting quarter windows, privacy glass, cargo cover, payload package, air conditioning, power door locks, power windows, power exterior mirrors, cruise control, tilt steering wheel, leather-wrapped steering wheel.

2SE	Power Package (2WD B3000/B4000 SE X-cab)	2882	3515
	Manufacturer Discount	(1037)	(1265)
	Net Price	1845	2250

Includes alloy wheels, P225/70R15 AS OWL tires, Bright Group, AM/FM stereo with CD player and clock, sliding rear window, bedliner, pivoting quarter windows, privacy glass, cargo cover, payload/performance package, air conditioning, power door locks, power windows, power exterior mirrors, cruise control, tilt steering wheel, leather-wrapped steering wheel.

2SE	Power Package (4WD B3000 SE Reg Cab)	2517	3070
	Manufacturer Discount	(1000)	(1095)
	Net Price	1517	1975

Includes alloy wheels, P225/70R15 AS OWL tires, Bright Group, AM/FM stereo with CD player and clock, sliding rear window, bedliner, air conditioning, power door locks, power windows, power exterior mirrors, cruise control, tilt steering wheel, leather-wrapped steering wheel.

2SE	Power Package (4WD B3000/B4000 SE X-cab)	2882	3515
	Manufacturer Discount	(1037)	(1265)
	Net Price	1845	2250

Includes alloy wheels, P225/70R15 AS OWL tires, Bright Group, AM/FM stereo with CD player and clock, sliding rear window, bedliner, pivoting quarter windows, privacy glass, cargo cover, payload/performance package, air conditioning, power door locks, power windows, power exterior mirrors, cruise control, tilt steering wheel, leather-wrapped steering wheel.

RA1	Radio: AM/FM Stereo (2WD B2500 SX)	148	180
	REQUIRES AT1.		
—	Security Package (SE)	28	45

Includes wheel and tailgate locks.

MPV — MAZDA

1998 MPV

1998 Mazda MPV All Sport

What's New?

A CD player is now standard.

Review

The MPV is getting old. Nearly a decade ago, the MPV arrived in the United States as one of the first car-like minivans from Japan, taking a cue from Chrysler's popular minis rather than the ungainly Toyota, Nissan, and Mitsubishi boxes-on-wheels that were on sale at the time. Truly, the MPV was a class-leader in the late '80s. Not so these days, when the only reason the MPV continues to exist is to fill a teensy tiny niche as a sport-utility minivan.

The MPV is the closest thing to an SUV that Mazda has to offer. The lineup consists of two trim levels: a well equipped LX, and luxury ES. All MPVs with the exception of the LX 2WD come with All Sport decor (a grille guard, fender flares, rear bumper guard, stone guard, roof rack, special graphics, and alloy wheels), which turns this Mom-mobile into a four-door van that looks like it can tackle any terrain. Combine this styling gimmick with shift-on-the-fly four-wheel-drive, and the MPV serves reasonably well as a pseudo-Explorer. Four-wheel disc anti-lock brakes are standard on all models. The ES edition contains such pleasantries as leather seating surfaces and automatic load leveling.

Like Honda's Odyssey, the longer-lived Mazda minivan does without sliding entry doors, matching the Odyssey by providing conventional rear doors on both sides. Mazda promises sedan-like comfort and ride qualities for up to eight passengers in the MPV. Front MacPherson struts and front/rear stabilizer bars help keep the minivan comfortable and on-course. Bucket seats hold the front occupants, while three each can fit on the middle and back seat. Optional on LX and standard on ES models are quad captain's chairs. Center-section legroom is less than great, but most riders aren't likely to complain. When fewer passengers are aboard, cargo space can reach 110 cubic feet.

Acceleration with the 155-horsepower, 18-valve, 3.0-liter V-6 engine is sufficient. Four-wheel drive cuts into potential performance, because of its sizable extra weight. Gas mileage also dips considerably with 4WD vans. A four-speed automatic, with electronic controls, is the sole transmission choice. With 4WD, a dashboard switch can lock the center differential, for peak low-speed traction.

MAZDA MPV

Inside and out—especially up front—MPVs offer a distinctive appearance, not quite like most minivans. Styling was revised for 1996, and the MPV now sports a protruding, ungainly countenance in an effort to make it look more like a sport utility. A contemporary instrument panel contains dual airbags. Visibility is terrific from the airy cabin.

The 1998 MPV is the equivalent of an Arch Deluxe that's been sitting under the heating lamp too long. There's more to it, but it's old, loaded with fat, and costs more than many competitors. We liked the older MPV plenty for its crisp, clean looks and fun rear-wheel drive personality. This heavier, bulbous, SUV-wannabe model leaves us cold. And with base stickers approaching $23,500 with destination charges, we can't recommend the MPV over most other minivans on the market.

Safety Data

Driver Airbag: *Standard*
Side Airbag: *Not Available*
Traction Control: *Not Available*
Driver Crash Test Grade: *Good*

Passenger Airbag: *Standard*
4-Wheel ABS: *Standard*
Integrated Child Seat(s): *Not Available*
Passenger Crash Test Grade: *Good*

Standard Equipment

MPV LX 2WD: 3.0-liter SOHC 16-valve V-6 engine, 4-speed electronically-controlled automatic transmission with overdrive, engine-rpm-sensing power rack and pinion steering, power 4-wheel disc anti-lock brakes, 15-inch steel wheels with full wheel covers, P195/75R15 tires, dual power exterior mirrors, variable intermittent windshield wipers, intermittent rear window wiper/washer, bodyside moldings, tinted glass, dual front airbags, 8-passenger seating, reclining front bucket seats with adjustable headrests, second row reclining seat with fore/aft adjustment, easy-fold flip forward and removable third row seat, velour upholstery, tilt steering wheel, rear window defogger, AM/FM stereo with CD player and four speakers, digital clock, power door locks, cruise control, power windows, map pockets on front door panels, child safety locks for rear doors, remote fuel door release, tachometer, rear heat vents.

LX 4WD (in addition to or instead of LX 2WD equipment): Multi-mode four-wheel drive system, lockable center differential, All-Sport Appearance Package (includes stone guard, grille guard, fender flares, rear bumper guard, roof rack, P225/70R15 tires, polished 5-spoke alloy wheels), special two-tone paint, 4-seasons Package (includes rear heater, large capacity windshield washer tank, heavy-duty battery), larger cooling fan, full-size spare tire.

ES 2WD (in addition to or instead of LX 2WD equipment): All-Sport Appearance Package (includes stone guard, grille guard, fender flares, rear bumper buard, roof roack, P215/65R15 tires, polished 5-spoke alloy wheels), special two-tone paint, Load leveling Package (includes automatic load leveling system, transmission oil cooler, larger cooling fan, full-size spare tire), 7-passenger seating with quad captain's chairs and 3 passenger third row seat, leather seating surfaces, leather-wrapped steering wheel.

ES 4WD (in addition to or instead of ES 2WD equipment): Multi-mode four-wheel drive system, lockable center differential, 4-seasons Package (includes rear heater, large capacity windshield washer tank, heavy-duty battery).

MPV — MAZDA

CODE	DESCRIPTION	INVOICE	MSRP

Base Prices

LV522	LX 2WD	20834	23095
LV523	LX 4WD	24258	26895
LV522	ES 2WD	23807	26395
LV523	ES 4WD	26060	28895
	Destination Charge:	480	480

Accessories

CODE	DESCRIPTION	INVOICE	MSRP
1AP	All-Sport Package (LX 2WD)	748	880
	Includes grille guard, stone guard, fender flares, rear bumper guard, roof rack, All-Sport graphics, polished alloy wheels, P215/65R15 all-season tires. REQUIRES JCP.		
CE1	CA/CT/MA/NY Emissions (2WD)	128	150
CAS	Cassette Player	213	250
1ES	ES Preferred Equipment Group 1 (ES)	1913	2250
	Manufacturer Discount	(642)	(755)
	Net Price	1271	1495
	Includes front and rear air conditioning, remote keyless entry, rear privacy glass, floor mats.		
1TP	Load Leveling Package (LX 2WD)	506	595
	Includes automatic load leveling, transmission oil cooler, high capacity cooling fan, and full-size spare tire.		
1TP	Load Leveling Package (LX 4WD)	421	495
	Includes automatic load leveling and transmission oil cooler.		
1LX	LX Preferred Equipment Group 1 (LX)	1318	1550
	Manufacturer Discount	(642)	(755)
	Net Price	676	795
	Includes air conditioning, remote keyless entry, rear privacy glass, floor mats.		
2LX	LX Preferred Equipment Group 2 (LX)	1913	2250
	Manufacturer Discount	(642)	(755)
	Net Price	1271	1495
	Includes front and rear air conditioning, remote keyless entry, rear privacy glass, floor mats.		
MR1	Power Sunroof (ES)	1020	1200
QC1	Quad Captain's Chairs (LX)	340	400
JCP	Two-Tone Paint (LX 2WD)	298	350

Don't forget to swing by the Townhall when you visit Edmund's website at http://www.edmunds.com. Talk to our editors and compare notes on your favorite cars and trucks. Join others to scope out smart shopping stategies, get answers to your questions, or share your expertise. To get to the Townhall, just click on the link on the homepage or go directly to http://www.edmunds.com/edweb/townhall/welcomeconflist.html.

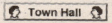
Town Hall

MERCEDES-BENZ ML320

1998 ML320

1998 Mercedes-Benz ML320

What's New?

Mercedes enters the sport/ute fray this fall with the introduction of the ML320. Designed from a clean sheet of paper, the ML320 offers the best of the car and truck worlds.

Review

Despite increased sales during the last few years, the good people at Mercedes recognized a gaping hole that has existed in their lineup since 1993. This was the last year that Mercedes offered any sort of AWD vehicle, and the cancellation of their 4Matic sedans and wagons for the 1994 model year left them rather vulnerable to attacks from Audi, Subaru, and Volvo. Recognizing this weakness, Mercedes has introduced AWD availability to the E-Class of sedans and wagons, and has gone one step further than the competition by developing a true sport-utility vehicle.

Unlike much of its competition, the ML320 is neither derived from an existing SUV, like the re-badged Lexus LX450, nor built on a hybrid car platform, like the Subaru Forester. Instead, the ML320 was designed from the ground up as a unique Mercedes, designed to take people off road or through poor weather, without sacrificing the luxury, safety, or performance that Mercedes' shoppers have come to expect.

This means that the ML320 combines many technologies that have heretofore been exclusively car or exclusively truck. Mercedes, for example, has decided use a separate frame for this vehicle, boxed at both ends, this frame gives the ML320 the sort of torsional rigidity that is necessary for serious off-road maneuvers. To this truck-tough frame, Mercedes has attached a 4-wheel independent double-wishbone suspension, the first ever application of double-wishbone suspension technology at all four wheels of a truck. The result is a fantastic on-road ride that enables this tall vehicle to hustle through the slalom at the same impressive speed as the E320 sedan.

This Mercedes SUV has all of the touches that we expect of a car that carries the three-pointed star on its hood. Interior materials, except for the plastic on the dashboard, are first rate, the chairs are comfortable for all-day driving, there are multiple cupholders for front and rear passengers, the stereo sounds great and the secondary controls are thankfully devoid of the confusing pictographs that have adorned many of M-B's previous efforts.

ML320 — MERCEDES-BENZ

Mercedes has priced the ML320 aggressively, making it, in fact, the second cheapest vehicle in their entire lineup. Compared to trucks like the Ford Explorer Limited and Jeep Grand Cherokee Limited, the ML320 is easily the superior vehicle in all but the most demanding of off-road challenges. On-road, these American contenders can't touch this Teutonic trailblazer. If your vehicle purchase is leading you to the 4-wheel drive neck-of-the-woods, not looking at the Mercedes-Benz ML320 is the biggest mistake you could make.

Safety Data

Driver Airbag: *Standard*
Side Airbag: *Standard*
Traction Control: *Standard*
Driver Crash Test Grade: *Not Available*

Passenger Airbag: *Standard*
4-Wheel ABS: *Standard*
Integrated Child Seat(s): *Not Available*
Passenger Crash Test Grade: *Not Available*

Standard Equipment

ML320: 3.2L V-6 SOHC SMPI 18-valve engine, requires premium unleaded fuel; 5-speed electronic overdrive automatic transmission with lock-up; engine oil cooler; full-time 4-wheel drive, traction control, 3.69 axle ratio; steel exhaust; front independent double-wishbone suspension with anti-roll bar, front torsion springs, front torsion bar, front shocks; rear independent double-wishbone suspension with anti-roll bar, rear coil springs, rear shocks; power rack-and-pinion steering; 4-wheel disc brakes with 4-wheel anti-lock braking system; 19 gal capacity fuel tank; liftback rear cargo door; roof rack; front and rear black bumpers; black bodyside molding, rocker panel extensions; monotone paint; aero-composite halogen headlamps with delay-off feature; additional exterior lights include center high mounted stop light; driver and passenger power remote black heated folding outside mirrors; front and rear 16" x 8" silver alloy wheels; inside under cargo mounted compact steel spare wheel; air conditioning, air filter, rear heat ducts; AM/FM stereo with seek-scan, cassette, CD pre-wiring, 4 speakers, amplifier, theft deterrent, and window grid diversity antenna; cruise control; power door locks with 2-stage unlock, remote keyless entry, child safety rear door locks, power remote hatch/trunk release, power remote fuel release; cell phone pre-wiring, 3 power accessory outlet, driver foot rest, retained accessory power; analog instrumentation display includes tachometer gauge, water temp gauge, in-dash clock, systems monitor, trip odometer; warning indicators include water temp warning, battery, low oil level, low coolant, lights-on, key-in-ignition, low fuel, low washer fluid, bulb failure, brake fluid; dual airbags, door mounted side airbag; ignition disable, panic alarm, security system; tinted windows, power front windows with driver and passenger 1-touch down, power rear windows, fixed 1/4- vent windows; variable intermittent front windshield wipers, fixed interval wiper, rear window defroster; seating capacity of 5, front bucket seats with adjustable headrests, center armrest with storage, driver seat includes 6-way direction control, passenger seat includes 6-way direction control; split-bench rear seat with tilt headrests; front and rear height adjustable seatbelts; cloth seats, leatherette door trim insert, full cloth headliner, full carpet floor covering with carpeted floor mats; interior lights include dome light with fade, front and rear reading lights, illuminated entry; steering wheel with tilt adjustment; dual illuminated vanity mirrors; day-night rearview mirror; full floor console, glove box, front and rear cupholders, instrument panel bin, driver and passenger door bins, rear door bins; carpeted cargo floor, cargo cover, cargo tie downs, cargo light; black grille, and black door handles.

Base Prices

Code	Description	Invoice	MSRP
ML320	ML320	30558	33950
	Destination Charge:	595	595

MERCEDES-BENZ ML320

CODE	DESCRIPTION	INVOICE	MSRP

Accessories

Code	Description	Invoice	MSRP
259	Bose Premium Sound System	942	1050
	Includes 6-disc CD changer. REQUIRES (136) Option Package M1.		
—	Metallic Paint	424	475
136	Option Package M1	2658	2950
	Includes leather shift knob, leather-wrapped steering wheel, outside temperature display, rear privacy glass, auto-dimming rearview mirror, underseat storage, power heated seats, leather seating surface trim, trip computer, burl walnut wood trim. REQUIRES (414) power tilt/sliding sunroof with tinted glass. NOT AVAILABLE with (151) Option Package M7 with cloth.		
137	Option Package M4	1438	1595
	Includes dual stainless steel side runners, spare tire carrier, wheel, spare alloy, front and rear mud guards. REQUIRES (414) power tilt/sliding sunroof with tinted glass.		
151	Option Package M7 with Cloth	807	900
	NOTE: Third row seat material will be determined by front seat material selection. Includes dual forward facing 3rd row seats and power flip-open rear quarter windows. REQUIRES (414) power tilt/sliding sunroof with tinted glass. NOT AVAILABLE with (136) Option Package M1 or (152) Option Package M7 with Leather.		
152	Option Package M7 with Leather	942	1050
	NOTE: Third row seat material will be determined by front seat material selection. Includes dual forward facing 3rd row seats and power flip-open rear quarter windows. REQUIRES (136) Option Package M1 and (414) power tilt/sliding sunroof with tinted glass. NOT AVAILABLE with (151) Option Package M7 with Cloth.		
414	Power Tilt/Sliding Sunroof with Tinted Glass	983	1095

One 15-minute call could save you 15% or more on car insurance.

GEICO DIRECT

America's 6th Largest Automobile Insurance Company

1-800-555-2758

MOUNTAINEER — MERCURY

| CODE | DESCRIPTION | INVOICE | MSRP |

1998 MOUNTAINEER

1998 Mercury Mountaineer

What's New?

The Mountaineer gets minor front and rear styling tweaks as it enters its second year of production. In addition, a new model with full-time four-wheel drive receives the SOHC V-6 and 5-speed automatic transmission that became available on the Explorer last year.

Review

Mercury's second year with the Mountaineer proves that you don't want to mess around too much with a sure thing. Minor exterior changes show that Mercury is unwilling to roll the dice with a dramatic departure in styling from the best-selling Ford Explorer (on which the Mountaineer is based). Under the hood, however, some good things happen, as the 1998 Mountaineer is now available with the powerful and less thirsty SOHC V-6 engine and 5-speed transmission combo that was previously only available on the Explorer.

With half the world already owning Explorers, to whom does Mercury intend to sell this truck? Well, it appears that they have their sights set on women and upscale families. Jim Engelhardt, vice-president of Mercury light-truck development, says, "We know that women are particularly concerned about safety and security, so the Mountaineer includes many important features that are not always found on compact sport/utility vehicles." These features include dual airbags, anti-lock brakes, fog lamps, and tailgate reflectors. For those living in inclement climates, or those who actually intend to make use of the vehicle's off-road capabilities, there is a full-time all-wheel drive model available, and a new for 1998 four-wheel drive model that features an SOHC V-6 engine and Command Trac four-wheel drive. Families with children will be happy to know that they can order a Mountaineer with an integrated child seat. However, to get the child seat they must also order the leather interior. Does that make sense? Who wants kids climbing all over their leather interior? I bet the designer who came up with that option requirement never had to pick up four toddlers in cleats after a pee-wee soccer match.

The Mountaineer has been a hit at Lincoln-Mercury dealers. Like the Explorer it is based on, the Mountaineer has plenty of space for hauling people and their stuff through the suburban jungle. The Mercury SUV's abundant standard features provide a great deal of comfort, and the strong engine choices are a bonus when passing at freeway speeds. We laughed the Mountaineer off last year as a sport-ute pretender, nothing for the people at Jeep or GMC to

MERCURY MOUNTAINEER

take seriously. With the addition of the new engine and Control Trac four-wheel drive system the Mountaineer has gotten more serious, and we've stopped laughing. We are still not sold on the look-at-me nature of the Mountaineer, but if you want your SUV to stand out in the parking lot, this may be the one for you.

Safety Data

Driver Airbag: *Standard*
Side Airbag: *Not Available*
Traction Control: *Not Available*
Driver Crash Test Grade: *Good*

Passenger Airbag: *Standard*
4-Wheel ABS: *Standard*
Integrated Child Seat(s): *Optional*
Passenger Crash Test Grade: *Good*

Standard Equipment

2WD: V-6 SOHC SMPI 12-valve engine; 5-speed electronic overdrive automatic transmission; 72-amp battery with run down protection; engine oil cooler, HD radiator; 95-amp alternator; rear-wheel drive, viscous limited slip differential, 3.73 axle ratio; steel exhaust; front independent suspension with anti-roll bar, front coil springs, front torsion bar, HD front shocks, rear suspension with anti-roll bar, rear leaf springs, HD rear shocks; power rack-and-pinion steering; 4-wheel disc brakes with 4-wheel anti-lock braking system; 21 gal capacity fuel tank; liftback rear cargo door; front and rear body-colored bumpers with colored rub strip, rear step; colored bodyside molding; two-tone paint; aero-composite halogen headlamps; additional exterior lights include front fog/driving lights, center high mounted stop light; driver and passenger power remote black folding outside mirrors; front and rear 15" x 7" silver alloy wheels with hub wheel covers; P235/75SR15 OWL AT front and rear tires; underbody mounted full-size temporary steel spare wheel; air conditioning, rear heat ducts; premium AM/FM stereo, clock, seek-scan, cassette, 4 speakers and fixed antenna; cruise control with steering wheel controls; power door locks with 2 stage unlock, child safety rear door locks; 2 power accessory outlets, retained accessory power; analog instrumentation display includes tachometer gauge, water temp gauge, trip odometer; warning indicators include oil pressure, battery, lights-on, key-in-ignition; dual airbags; ignition disable; deep tinted windows, power front windows with driver 1-touch down, power rear windows; variable intermittent front windshield wipers, flip-up rear window, fixed interval rear wiper rear window defroster; seating capacity of 5, front bucket seats with fixed adjustable headrests, center armrest with storage, driver seat includes 4-way direction control, passenger seat includes 4-way direction control; 60-40 folding rear bench seat with adjustable rear headrest; front height adjustable seatbelts; cloth-leather seats, vinyl door trim insert, full cloth headliner, full carpet floor covering, deluxe sound insulation; interior lights include dome light with fade, front reading lights, 2 door curb lights, illuminated entry; leather-wrapped steering wheel with tilt adjustment; dual illuminated vanity mirrors, dual auxiliary visors; day-night rearview mirror; full floor console, glove box with light, front and rear cupholders, driver and passenger door bins; carpeted cargo floor, vinyl trunk lid, cargo tie downs, cargo light; chrome grille, black side windows moldings, black front windshield molding, black rear window molding, body-colored door handles.

4WD (in addition to or instead of 2WD equipment): Part-time 4-wheel drive, auto locking hub control and electronic shift, 3.55 axle ratio; skid plates.

AWD (in addition to or instead of 4WD equipment): 5L V-8 OHV engine; 4-speed automatic transmission with lock-up; and 3.73 axle ratio.

MOUNTAINEER — MERCURY

CODE	DESCRIPTION	INVOICE	MSRP

Base Prices

Code	Description	Invoice	MSRP
U52	2WD	24118	26680
U54	4WD	25878	28680
U55	AWD	25878	28680
	Destination Charge:	525	525

Accessories

Code	Description	Invoice	MSRP
44U	4-Speed Automatic Transmission With OD (2WD/AWD)	NC	NC
558	Appearance Group	421	495
	Includes two tone paint, chrome wheels, paint stripe. NOT AVAILABLE with (650A) Preferred Equipment Package 650A or (660A) Preferred Equipment Package 660A.		
422	California Emissions	144	170
	Required on units for California/Massachusetts/New York/Connecticut registration. NOT AVAILABLE with (428) high altitude principle use.		
Z	Cloth Sport Bucket Seats	553	650
	Includes 6-way power driver's seat and dual power lumbar supports. NOT AVAILABLE with (660A) Preferred Equipment Package 660A.		
59B	Electrochromic Rearview Mirror	158	185
	Includes automatic on/off headlamps. NOT AVAILABLE with (650A) Preferred Equipment Package 650A.		
151	Electronics Group	348	410
	Includes puddle lamps on exterior mirrors, remote keyless entry, and security alarm. REQUIRES (Z) seats or (F) seats.		
41H	Engine Block Heater	30	35
99P	Engine: 5.0L EFI V8 (2WD)	395	465
	REQUIRES (T7R) tires and (XD4) limited slip performance axle, and (44U) transmission.		
428	High Altitude Principle Use	NC	NC
87C	Integrated Child Seat	170	200
	REQUIRES (F) seats. NOT AVAILABLE with (650A) Preferred Equipment Package 650A.		
F	Leather Sport Bucket Seats	557	655
	Includes 6-way power driver's seat and dual power lumbar supports. NOT AVAILABLE with (650A) Preferred Equipment Package 650A.		
XD4	Limited Slip Performance Axle (2WD/4WD)	302	355
	Includes trailer tow package.		
91P	Multi Disc CD Changer	314	370
	NOT AVAILABLE with (650A) Preferred Equipment Package 650A.		
439	Power Moonroof	680	800
	Includes overhead storage, shade, outside temperature and compass display, and reading lights. NOT AVAILABLE with (650A) Preferred Equipment Package 650A.		

MERCURY MOUNTAINEER

CODE	DESCRIPTION	INVOICE	MSRP
650A	Preferred Equipment Package 650A	527	620
	Manufacturer Discount	(429)	(505)
	Net Price	98	115

Includes floor mats, luggage rack, running boards, 4.0L SOHC V-6 engine (2WD), 5-speed automatic transmission (2WD), P225/70R15 BSW tires, cloth captain's seats. NOT AVAILABLE with F, 87C, 59B, 439, 91P, or 558.

655A	Preferred Equipment Package 655A (2WD/4WD)	2253	2650
	Manufacturer Discount	(1148)	(1350)
	Net Price	1105	1300

Includes floor mats, luggage rack, running boards, retractable cargo cover, cloth sport bucket seats, overhead console with outside temperature and compass display and reading lights, Electronics Group with remote keyless entry and security alarm, high series floor console with rear audio controls and rear heater, premium AM/FM dual media radio, 4.0L SOHC V-6, 5-speed automatic transmission, and P225/70R15 BSW tires. NOT AVAILABLE with (582) radio.

655A	Preferred Equipment Package 655A (AWD)	2253	2650
	Manufacturer Discount	(1148)	(1350)
	Net Price	1105	1300

Includes floor mats, luggage rack, running boards, retractable cargo cover, cloth sport bucket seats, overhead console with outside temperature and compass display and reading lights, Electronics Group with remote keyless entry and security alarm, high series floor console with rear audio controls and rear heater, premium AM/FM dual media radio, P235/75R15SL AT OWL tires, limited slip performance axle. NOT AVAILABLE with (582) radio.

660A	Preferred Equipment Package 660A (2WD/4WD)	3634	4275
	Manufacturer Discount	(1488)	(1750)
	Net Price	2146	2525

Includes floor mats, luggage rack, running boards, retractable cargo cover, overhead console with outside temperature and compass display and reading lights, Electronics Group with remote keyless entry and security alarm, high series floor console with rear audio controls and rear heater, Appearance Group with paint stripe, leather sport bucket seats, Mach AM/FM dual media stereo, chrome wheels, 4.0L SOHC V-6 engine (2WD), 5-speed automatic transmission (2WD), and P225/70R15 AT OWL tires. NOT AVAILABLE with Z, 58K, 582, 558.

660A	Preferred Equipment Package 660A (AWD)	3634	4275
	Manufacturer Discount	(1488)	(1750)
	Net Price	2146	2525

Includes floor mats, luggage rack, running boards, retractable cargo cover, overhead console with outside temperature and compass display and reading lights, Electronics Group with remote keyless entry and security alarm, high series floor console with rear audio controls and rear heater, Appearance Group with paint stripe, leather sport bucket seats, Mach AM/FM dual media stereo, chrome wheels, P235/75R15SL AT OWL tires, and limited slip performance axle. NOT AVAILABLE with Z, 58K, 582, or 558.

MOUNTAINEER / VILLAGER — MERCURY

CODE	DESCRIPTION	INVOICE	MSRP
916	Radio: Mach AM/FM Dual Media	403	475
	Includes clock, sub-woofer, amp, digital signal processor and power antenna. NOT AVAILABLE with (650A) Preferred Equipment Package 650A, (91P) Multi Disc CD Changer, or (660A) Preferred Equipment Package 660A.		
58K	Radio: Premium AM/FM Dual Media	277	325
	NOT AVAILABLE with (582) radio or (660A) Preferred Equipment Package 660A.		
582	Radio: Premium AM/FM Stereo with CD	128	150
	NOT AVAILABLE with (655A) Preferred Equipment Package 655A, (58K) radio, or (660A) Preferred Equipment Package 660A.		
655	Retractable Cargo Cover	68	80
T7R	Tires: P235/75R15SL AT OWL (2WD/4WD)	196	230

1998 VILLAGER

1998 Mercury Villager Nautica

What's New?

A brand new Villager debuts in 1999, so don't waste your time buying one this year. Next year's model will have a driver's side sliding door, longer wheelbase and a better ride.

Review

Mercury entered the minivan market in 1993 as part of a joint venture with Nissan. Designed in California and built at the same factory in Ohio, Mercury Villagers and Nissan Quests share plenty of sleek styling touches and on-the-road traits. Wheelbases are similar to the first-generation, short-bodied Dodge Caravan, but the Villager measures nearly a foot longer overall. Four models grace showrooms: GS and LS wagons, a glitzy Nautica edition (attractively trimmed to remind occupants of the sea, or overpriced clothing, depending on your orientation), plus a lower-cost cargo van.

MERCURY VILLAGER

CODE	DESCRIPTION	INVOICE	MSRP

Car-like characteristics were a priority when the Villager and Quest were created, and the result is impressive. Even though you're sitting taller than in a passenger car, behind a rather high steering wheel, it's easy enough to forget that this is a minivan. The driver's seat is supportive and comfortable, and there's plenty of space up front. Standard gauges are smallish but easy to read (optional digital instruments are not). You get fairly nimble handling, plus a smooth, quiet ride from the absorbent suspension. Only one powertrain is available—Nissan's 151-horsepower, 3.0-liter V-6 hooked to a four-speed automatic transmission—but that's a smoothie, too.

Four-wheel anti-lock braking is standard on the LS and Nautica models; optional on the GS. Villagers offer ample space for five, and many are fitted to seat seven, in a flexible interior configuration. The far rear seat on seven-passenger models slides forward and back on a set of tracks, and center seats lift out. Be warned, though: those "removable" seats aren't lightweights. A full load of storage bins and cubbyholes augments the Villager's practical appeal.

Villager blends comfort and convenience into one tidy package, and while we have been cheerleaders for this van in the past, it doesn't look like a smart buy when compared to what next year's Villager promises to be. If a driver's side sliding door and more refinement are on your list, you should definitely wait.

Safety Data

Driver Airbag: *Standard*
Side Airbag: *Not Available*
Traction Control: *Not Available*
Driver Crash Test Grade: *Good*

Passenger Airbag: *Standard*
4-Wheel ABS: *Standard LS, Nautica; Optional GS*
Integrated Child Seat(s): *Optional GS, LS*
Passenger Crash Test Grade: *Average*

Standard Equipment

GS CARGO VAN: 3L V-6 SOHC SMPI 24-valve engine; 4-speed electronic overdrive automatic transmission with lock-up; 60-amp battery with run down protection; HD radiator; 110-amp alternator; front wheel drive; front strut suspension with anti-roll bar, front strut springs, brand name front shocks, rear suspension rear shocks; power rack-and-pinion steering; front disc/rear drum brakes with 4-wheel anti-lock braking system; 20 gal capacity fuel tank; 3 doors with sliding right rear passenger door, liftback rear cargo door; front and rear body-colored bumpers; body-colored bodyside molding; monotone paint; aero-composite halogen headlamps; additional exterior lights include cornering lights, center high mounted stop light, underhood light; driver folding outside mirror; underbody mounted full-size conventional spare wheel; AM/FM stereo, with cassette, 4 speakers; child safety rear door locks; includes tachometer gauge, water temp gauge, trip odometer; warning indicators include lights-on, key-in-ignition, low fuel, low washer fluid, door ajar; dual airbags; deep tinted windows; fixed interval front windshield wipers, rear window wiper, rear window defroster; front bucket seats with tilt adjustable headrests; front height adjustable seatbelts; cloth seats, cloth door trim insert, front cloth headliner, front carpet floor covering; interior lights include dome light with fade, 3 door curb lights; vanity mirrors; day-night rearview mirror; glove box with light, front cupholder, interior concealed storage, driver and passenger door bins; vinyl cargo floor; chrome grille, black front windshield molding, and body-colored door handles.

GS PASSENGER VAN (in addition to or instead of GS CARGO VAN equipment): 3.86 axle ratio; partial stainless steel exhaust; front independent suspension front coil springs, front shocks, rear strut suspension with rear leaf springs; passenger folding outside mirror; front and rear 15" x 5.5" wheels; full-size temporary steel spare wheel; stereo wih clock, seek-scan, and fixed antenna; 1 power accessory outlet; analog instrumentation display PRNDL in instrument panel; warning indicators include water temp warning, battery; tinted windows, vented rear

VILLAGER MERCURY

CODE	DESCRIPTION	INVOICE	MSRP

windows, manual 1/4 vent windows; variable intermittent front windshield wipers; seating capacity of 5, front captain seats driver seat includes 4-way direction control, passenger seat includes 4-way direction control; full folding bench with reclining adjustable rear headrest, full headliner, full floor covering with carpeted floor mats; interior lights include dome light; dashboard storage; carpeted cargo floor; black side windows moldings, and black rear window molding.

LS (in addition to or instead of GS equipment): 4-wheel anti-lock braking system; roof rack; chrome bodyside insert; two-tone paint; air conditioning; 2 power accessory outlets, retained accessory power; deep tinted windows, power front windows, power 1/4 vent windows; rear window defroster; seating capacity of 7; removeable 2nd row seat; 3rd row seat removeable full folding bench, 3rd row headrest, interior lights include front and rear reading lights; 2 seat back storage pockets; and cargo light.

NAUTICA (in addition to or instead of LS equipment): Firm ride suspension, rear independent suspension with anti-roll bar, premium rear shocks; black bodyside molding with colored bodyside insert; deluxe paint; rear heat ducts; leather captain's chairs; and body-colored grille.

Base Prices

Code	Description	Invoice	MSRP
V14	GS Cargo	18444	20350
V11	GS Passenger	18755	20705
V11	LS Passenger	22513	24975
V11	Nautica Passenger	24123	26805
	Destination Charge:	580	580

Accessories

Code	Description	Invoice	MSRP
55G	"Gold" Sport Package (GS Passenger)	251	295
	Available only with Deep Forest Green, Black, White or Cabernet monotone exterior. Includes color keyed grille, heated side-view mirrors, deluxe aluminum wheels, and gold badging. NOT AVAILABLE with (691A) Preferred Equipment Package 691A, (684) suspension handling, or (952) paint.		
55G	"Gold" Sport Package (LS)	NC	NC
	Includes two-tone delete credit. Available only with Deep Forest Green, Black, White or Cabernet monotone exterior. Two-tone paint must be deleted when ordering an LS. Includes color keyed grille, heated side-view mirrors, deluxe aluminum wheels, and body side molding. NOT AVAILABLE with (684) suspension handling.		
67B	4-Wheel Antilock Brakes (GS Passenger)	502	590
90P	6-Way Power Driver's Seat (GS Passenger)	336	395
	Includes power lumbar.		
21A	7 Passenger Seating with Cloth Trim (GS Passenger/LS)	NC	NC
572	Air Conditioning (GS Cargo)	727	855
904	Anti-Theft Security System (GS Passenger/LS/Nautica)	85	100
	Includes blinking security light. REQUIRES (67B) 4-wheel antilock brakes.		
422	California Emissions	144	170
	Required on all units for California/Massachusetts/New York/Connecticut (if specified) registration. NOT AVAILABLE with (428) high altitude principal use.		
18N	Cargo Net (GS Passenger/LS Nautica)	26	30
573	Dual Zone Automatic Climate Control (LS)	153	180
574	Dual Zone Climate Control (GS Passenger)	395	465

MERCURY VILLAGER

CODE	DESCRIPTION	INVOICE	MSRP
15A	Electronic Instrument Cluster (LS)	208	245

Includes outside temperature reading with digital speedometer, odometer, dual trip odometers, tachometer, trip computer with instantaneous fuel economy, average fuel economy and distance-to-empty.

543	Exterior Mirrors: Dual Power (GS Cargo)	85	100
17F	Flip Open Liftgate Window (GS Passenger)	97	115
428	High Altitude Principal Use	NC	NC
L	Leather Seat Trim Delete (LS)	(735)	(865)

REQUIRES (21A) 7 Passenger Seating with Cloth Trim or (87C) 2 integrated child seats.

593	Light Group and Power Rear Vent Windows (GS Passenger)	140	165

Includes driver side single liftgate lamp, lamps with time delay and front door step lamps. Requires (57Q) electric rear window defroster, front and rear reading lights, and power rear vent windows. NOT AVAILABLE with (691A) Preferred Equipment Package 691A.

615	Luggage Rack (GS Passenger)	149	175
951	Monotone Paint (LS)	(115)	(135)
943	Power Convenience Group (GS Cargo)	484	570

Includes power door locks and power front door windows.

439	Power Moonroof (LS/Nautica)	659	775

Includes sliding sunshade and fixed air deflector.

680A	Preferred Equipment Package (GS Cargo Van)	NC	NC

Includes vehicles with standard equipment.

691A	Preferred Equipment Package 691A (GS Passenger)	2515	2960
	Manufacturer Discount	(1156)	(1360)
	Net Price	1359	1600

Includes air conditioning, electric rear window defogger, quad captain's chairs, speed control, Power Group: power front door windows, power door locks, and dual power mirrors. NOT AVAILABLE with 64J, 55G, 593, 684, 91P, or 91X.

692A	Preferred Equipment Package 692A (GS Passenger)	4858	5715
	Manufacturer Discount	(1967)	(2315)
	Net Price	2891	3400

Includes electric rear window defogger, quad captain's chairs, speed control, Power Group: power front door windows, power door locks, dual power mirrors, 4-wheel antilock brakes, privacy glass, luggage rack, underseat storage, remote keyless entry with panic alarm, security panic alarm, illuminated entry, 6-way power driver's seat, aluminum wheels, flip open liftgate window, rear auxiliary air conditioning and heater, and 72-amp battery.

696A	Preferred Equipment Package 696A (LS)	3343	3935
	Manufacturer Discount	(1704)	(2005)
	Net Price	1639	1930

Includes Light Group and Power Rear Vent Windows: front and rear reading lights, power rear vent windows, leather quad captain's chairs, speed control, remote keyless entry with panic alarm: security panic alarm, illuminated entry, 6-way power

VILLAGER — MERCURY

CODE	DESCRIPTION	INVOICE	MSRP
	driver's seat, flip open liftgate window, rear auxiliary air conditioning and heater: 72 amp. battery, Leather Wrapped Steering Wheel: speed control, dual heated power mirrors, premium sound AM/FM cassette stereo, dual illuminated visor mirrors, 4-way power passenger's seat, leather seat trim, autolamp on/off delay system, and deluxe aluminum wheels.		
697A	Preferred Equipment Package 697A (Nautica)	2439	2870
	Manufacturer Discount	(1164)	(1370)
	Net Price	1275	1500
	Includes deluxe aluminum wheels, Light Group and Power Rear Vent Windows: front and rear reading lights, power rear vent windows, Nautica Appearance Package: 5 unique paint combinations, captain's chairs package, floor mats, color keyed body side moldings, color keyed grille, suspension handling: P215/70R15 Eagle GA BSW tires, firm ride suspension, white painted aluminum wheels, 4-way power passenger's seat, 6-way power driver's seat, flip open liftgate window, electronic instrument cluster, autolamp on/off delay system, remote keyless entry with panic alarm: illuminated entry, rear auxiliary air conditioning and heater: automatic climate controls, 72-amp battery, premium AM/FM cassette stereo, leather-wrapped steering wheel; speed control, dual heated power mirrors, and dual illuminated visor mirrors.		
924	Privacy Glass (GS Passenger)	352	415
91P	Radio: Premium AM/FM Stereo Cassette with CD (GS Passenger)	578	680
	Includes 6-disc CD changer. NOT AVAILABLE with (691A) Preferred Equipment Package 691A, or (91X) radio.		
91P	Radio: Premium AM/FM Stereo Cassette with CD Changer (LS/Nauica)	314	370
	Includes 6-disc CD changer.		
91X	Radio: Premium Sound AM/FM Cassette (GS Passenger)	263	310
	Includes rear seat volume and tuning controls with front seat lockout, dual 'mini' headphone jacks, cassette/CD storage console, 80 total watts RMS, and CD compatibility. NOT AVAILABLE with (691A) Preferred Equipment Package 691A, or (91P) radio.		
588	Radio: Supersound AM/FM with Cassette and CD (LS/Nautica)	735	865
	Includes 114 total watts RMS and subwoofer speaker.		
948	Remote Keyless Entry with Panic Alarm (GS Passenger)	149	175
	Includes 2 keyfobs with security panic alarm.		
684	Handling Suspension (GS Passenger/LS)	73	85
	Includes rear stabilizer bars, P215/70R15 Eagle GA BSW tires, and firm ride suspension. REQUIRES (64J) wheels. NOT AVAILABLE with (691A) Preferred Equipment Package 691A or (55G) "Gold" Sport Package.		
534	Trailer Towing Package (GS Passenger/LS/Nautica)	213	250
	Includes trailer towing module and harness, HD battery, and full-size spare tire.		
87C	Two Integrated Child Seats (GS Passenger/LS)	204	240
	REQUIRES (21A) 7 Passenger Seating with Cloth Trim.		
952	Two-Tone Paint (GS Passenger)	251	295
	NOT AVAILABLE with (55G) "Gold" Sport Package.		
64J	Wheels: Deluxe Aluminum (GS Passenger)	34	40
	REQUIRES (692A) Preferred Equipment Package 692A. NOT AVAILABLE with (691A) Preferred Equipment Package 691A.		

MITSUBISHI MONTERO

1997 MONTERO

1997 Mitsubishi Montero SR

What's New?

This year sees the deletion of the LS w/manual transmission, and the addition of a more powerful V-6 engine. Leather seats are now available on the LS as well as the SR.

Review

Marketed since 1983, Mitsubishi's 7-passneger sport-utility ranks as an old-timer in its field, though the current four-door version has only been around since '89. This year, Mitsubishi updates its veteran mountain machine with a 3.5-liter V-6 that makes 200-horsepower and 228 lbs./ft. of torque.

Mitsubishi has seen fit to make some substantial refinements to its premium SUV. New features this year are an optional Infinity sound system, an all-weather package, leather seats on the LS model, and tinted privacy glass. Sure, these changes push the Montero into competition with the Toyota Land Cruiser, Acura SLX, and Land Rover Discovery, but that's OK. The new Montero Sport will keep Mitsubishi competitive with the Ford Explorer and Honda Passport.

Active Trac four-wheel-drive can be shifted "on the fly," or set up to operate all the time. All-disc brakes are standard, but only the SR has Multi-Mode anti-lock braking (optional in the LS version). A power sunroof is either standard or optional, depending on the model. Prior Monteros could tow as much as 4,000 pounds, but the current peak rating is 5,000. A variable shock-absorber system, optional on the SR, has three settings: hard, medium, and soft.

The Montero is an interesting blend of gee-whiz gadgetry, luxurious conveniences, go-anywhere capability, and unique styling. While it is true that all this cool stuff comes at a premium, buyers considering other luxury sport utility vehicles will want to drop by the Mitsubishi dealer and consider this one as well.

MONTERO — MITSUBISHI

CODE	DESCRIPTION	INVOICE	MSRP

Safety Data

Driver Airbag: *Standard*
Side Airbag: *Optional*
Traction Control: *Optional*
Driver Crash Test Grade: *Good*

Passenger Airbag: *Standard*
4-Wheel ABS: *Optional*
Integrated Child Seat(s): *Standard*
Passenger Crash Test Grade: *Average*

Standard Equipment

LS: 3.5-liter SOHC V-6 engine, 4-speed automatic transmission, shift-on-the-fly 4WD, power steering, 4-wheel disc brakes, double wishbone front suspension, 3-link coil spring rear suspension, front and rear stabilizer bars, front and rear tow hooks, skid plates, 24.3 gallon fuel tank, mud guards, tinted glass, 2-speed windshield wipers, rear window wiper/washer, 15" aluminum wheels, P235/75R15 A/S tires, rear mounted spare tire carrier, dual air bags, dual visor vanity mirror, tilt steering column, leather-wrapped steering column, rear window defroster, power windows, power door locks, AM/FM stereo with cassette and 6 speakers, power antenna, rear seat heater ducts, center console with storage and cupholders, cruise control, full carpeting, and cargo tie-down hooks.

SR (in addition to or instead of LS): Locking rear differential, engine oil cooler, widebody fender flares, headlight washer system, power sunroof, P265/70R15 tires, multimeter with compass, driver's illuminated vanity mirror, air conditioning, power driver's seat, premium stereo with CD player and diversity antenna, leather upholstery, and third row folding seats.

Base Prices

Code	Description	Invoice	MSRP
MP45-N	LS	25028	29290
MP45-W	SR	30436	36460
	Destination Charge:	445	445

Accessories

Code	Description	Invoice	MSRP
C4	10-Disc Compact Disc Changer (LS)	465	675
	INCLUDED in V1 and V2 value packages.		
AA	Air Conditioning (LS)	1070	1305
	INCLUDED in V1 value package.		
P4	All Weather Package (LS)	1150	1420
	Includes anti-lock brakes and heated leather seats.		
P6	All Weather Package (SR)	1300	1585
	Includes anti-lock brakes, heated front seats and adjustable shock absorbers.		
KD	Cargo Storage Kit (LS)	153	235
	INCLUDED in V1 value package.		
C3	CD Player (LS)	299	399
CW	Chrome Wheels (SR)	760	927
FM	Floor Mats (LS)	40	70
	Included in V1 value package.		
FK	Fog Light Kit	152	230
P3	Luxury Package (LS)	1585	1933
	Includes premium stereo with cassette, leather front and second row seats, and power driver's seat.		

EDMUND'S 1998 NEW TRUCKS

MITSUBISHI MONTERO

CODE	DESCRIPTION	INVOICE	MSRP
P1	Preferred Equipment Package 1 (LS)	1160	1422
	Includes third row rear seat, multimeter with compass, power sunroof, and sliding rear quarter windows.		
P2	Preferred Equipment Package 2 (LS)	1356	1640
	Includes third row rear seat, multimeter with compass, power sunroof, privacy glass, and sliding rear quarter windows.		
KE	Remote Keyless Entry (LS)	150	216
	INCLUDED in V1 value package.		
RR	Roof Rack (LS)	160	246
	NOT AVAILABLE with sunroof.		
SE	Security System (LS)	224	345
	INCLUDED in V1 value package.		
RB	Side Steps (LS)	247	367
	INCLUDED in V1 value package.		
TC	Spare Tire Carrier (LS)	123	189
	INCLUDED in V1 value package.		
HI	Trailer Hitch with Wiring Harness	164	252
V1	Value Package 1 (LS)	2515	3480
	Manufacturer Discount	(628)	(1525)
	Net Price	1887	1955
	Includes air conditioning, 10-Disc CD changer, remote keyless entry, security system, alloy wheels, wheel locks, spare tire carrier, cargo cover, cargo area mat, cargo net, and roof rack.		
V2	Value Package 2 (SR)	2530	3585
	Manufacturer Discount	(674)	(1663)
	Net Price	1856	1922
	Includes 10-Disc CD changer, remote keyless entry, security system, wood interior trim, cargo mat, cargo net, cargo cover, floor mats, side steps, spare tire carrier, roof rack, and wheel locks.		
TL	Wheel Locks (LS)	33	48

Save hundreds, even thousands, off the sticker price of the new car you want.

Call Autovantage®
your FREE auto-buying service
1-800-201-7703

No purchase required. No fees.

MONTERO SPORT — MITSUBISHI

| CODE | DESCRIPTION | INVOICE | MSRP |

1998 MONTERO SPORT

1998 Mitsubishi Montero Sport LS 4WD

What's New?

The Montero Sport gets plenty of added features to option packages, and 4WD models now come with standard ABS.

Review

Mitsubishi was in the vanguard at the beginning of the sport-utility boom. Way back in 1989, when the Explorer had yet to be introduced and the Grand Cherokee was little more than scribblings in a designer's notebook, the Montero had already evolved into a wonderfully practical 4-door design that offered excellent utility and go-anywhere capability. As the years passed, however, the Montero moved further and further up-market as Mitsubishi lavished their only sport-ute with additional equipment and expensive gee-whiz components. Today the price of the Montero starts at just under $30,000 and doesn't include options such as a roof rack, air conditioning, anti-lock brakes, or floor mats.

Realizing that they were losing sales as a result of this steep price, last year Mitsubishi penned a new shape, placed it on a proven platform, and came up with a not-very-original name for a smaller, less-expensive SUV. The Montero Sport shares a frame with the larger Montero, which is a good thing for those seeking off-road capability, but is shorter overall due to decreased front and rear overhangs. The Montero Sport's cabin holds five passengers instead of the Montero's seven-passenger capability. Interesting, however, is the fact that the Montero Sport's cargo space actually surpasses that of the full-size Montero.

The Montero Sport is available in three trim levels: ES, LS, and XLS. The ES is powered by a 4-cylinder 134-horsepower engine. Not many people opt for this value leader, due to its weak engine and sparse equipment. It's in the lineup merely as a customer-grabber in the Sunday new car ads. The most popular model is the LS 4WD automatic. The base price of this truck is over $24,000 (including destination charges), and includes a more powerful V-6 engine. Add preferred packages #3 and #4 and the price climbs to over $26,000. If you want power door locks, windows, and mirrors, you're looking at an expensive truck; and the Montero's alleged value is diminishing quickly.

MITSUBISHI MONTERO SPORT

| CODE | DESCRIPTION | INVOICE | MSRP |

Nevertheless, it is possible to get a well-optioned Montero Sport for right around $30,000. We think that by staying under that magic number, the Montero Sport has a chance for survival in the SUV sales battle. Be sure to check out the Montero Sport's rear seat, however; we were disappointed by the short seat cushion and lack of leg room. If you've got lanky teenagers to cart around, this may not be the right truck.

Safety Data

Driver Airbag: *Standard*
Side Airbag: *Not Available*
Traction Control: *Not Available*
Driver Crash Test Grade: *Average*

Passenger Airbag: *Standard*
4-Wheel ABS: *N/A (ES/LS 2WD); Std. (LS 4WD/XLS)*
Integrated Child Seat(s): *Not Available*
Passenger Crash Test Grade: *Average*

Standard Equipment

2WD ES: 2.4L I-4 SOHC MPI 16-valve engine; 5-speed overdrive manual transmission; 50-amp alternator; rear wheel drive, 4.22 axle ratio; stainless steel exhaust; front independent suspension with anti-roll bar, front coil springs, front shocks, rear suspension with anti-roll bar, rear leaf springs, rear shocks; power re-circulating ball steering; front disc/rear drum brakes; 19.5 gal capacity fuel tank; front and rear mud flaps, skid plates; tailgate rear cargo door; front and rear body-colored bumpers with front and rear tow hooks, rear step bumper; monotone paint; aero-composite halogen headlamps; additional exterior lights include center high mounted stop light; folding passenger convex outside mirror; front and rear 15" x 6" silver styled steel wheels; P225/75SR15 BSW M&S front and rear tires; underbody mounted full-size conventional steel spare wheel; AM/FM stereo with clock, seek-scan, single CD player, 4 speakers and fixed antenna; remote fuel release; 2 power accessory outlets, driver foot rest; analog instrumentation display includes tachometer gauge, water temp gauge, trip odometer; warning indicators include oil pressure, battery, door ajar, brake fluid; dual airbags; tinted windows; manual rear windows, fixed 1/4 vent windows; fixed interval front windshield wipers, flip-up rear window, rear window defroster; seating capacity of 5, front bucket seats with tilt adjustable headrests, center armrest with storage, driver seat includes 6-way direction control, passenger seat includes 4-way direction control; full folding rear bench seat with adjustable rear headrests, rear center armrest with storage; front height adjustable seatbelts; cloth seats, cloth door trim insert, full cloth headliner, full carpet floor covering; interior lights include dome light, front reading lights, 2 door curb lights; steering wheel with tilt adjustment; vanity mirrors; day-night rearview mirror; full floor console, locking glove box, front cupholder, interior concealed storage; carpeted cargo floor, plastic trunk lid, cargo tie downs, cargo light, cargo concealed storage; black grille, black side window moldings, black front windshield molding, black rear window molding, black door handles.

LS 2WD (in addition to or instead of 2WD ES equipment): 3L V-6 SOHC MPI 24-valve engine; 4-speed electronic automatic transmission with lock-up; 90-amp alternator; 4.27 axle ratio; cassette player, 6 speakers and power retractable antenna; deep tinted windows; variable intermittent front windshield wipers rear window wiper; 60-40 folding rear bench seat.

LS 4WD (in addition to or instead of 2WD LS equipment): Part-time 4 wheel drive, auto locking hub control and manual shift; 4 wheel disc brakes.

XLS 2WD (in addition to or instead of LS 2WD): 4.63 axle ratio; running boards; front electric sliding and tilting glass sunroof; body-colored fender flares; two-tone paint; front and rear 15" x 7" silver alloy wheels; P265/75SR15 BSW M&S front and rear tires; underbody mounted full-size conventional alloy spare wheel; air conditioning; 8 Infinity speakers; cruise control; power door locks; deep tinted windows, power front windows manual rear windows; variable intermittent front windshield wipers, rear window wiper; leather seats, leatherette door trim insert; leather-wrapped steering wheel with tilt adjustment; rear cupholders; chrome grille.

MONTERO SPORT — MITSUBISHI

CODE	DESCRIPTION	INVOICE	MSRP

Base Prices

CODE	DESCRIPTION	INVOICE	MSRP
MT45B	ES 2WD (5-speed)	16580	18030
MT45G	LS 2WD (automatic)	19806	22260
MT45P	XLS 2WD (automatic)	25237	28360
MT45K	LS 4WD (5-speed)	21288	23920
MT45K-A	LS 4WD (automatic)	22048	24780
MT45X	XLS 4WD (automatic)	28695	32250
	Destination Charge:	445	445

Accessories

CODE	DESCRIPTION	INVOICE	MSRP
C4	10 Disc CD Changer (LS/XLS)	478	675
TR	15" Trim Rings (ES/2WD LS)	46	70
P8	Accessory Package #1 (LS/XLS)	417	612
	Includes roof rack with sunroof wind deflector, rear floor mats, cargo area cover, cargo net.		
P9	Accessory Package #2 (ES/LS)	520	755
	Includes roof rack and rear side steps.		
AC	Air Conditioning (ES/LS)	768	915
	NOT AVAILABLE with (AC) air conditioning.		
P2	Appearance Package (LS)	1524	1815
	Includes fender flares, P265/70R15 tires, leather-wrapped steering wheel, chrome grille, side steps, 7" x 15" alloy wheels, two-tone paint.		
KV	Cargo Area Cover	71	100
CN	Cargo Net	25	37
KC	Cargo Storage Kit	135	200
	Includes floor mats, cargo area cover, cargo net.		
P1	Convenience Package (LS)	697	829
	Includes power mirrors, power windows, power door locks, cruise control.		
—	Destination Surcharge: Alaska	120	120
FM	Floor Mats	53	85
P3	Limited Slip Axle Package (LS 4WD)	625	744
	Includes rear heater, multi-meter, limited slip rear differential.		
LD	Limited Slip Rear Differential (LS/XLS 2WD)	307	366
P6	Luxury Package (LS)	1020	1220
	Includes Infinity AM/FM cassette with 8 speakers, power sunroof.		
P4	Off-Road Package (LS 4WD)	983	1171
	Includes Limited Slip Axle Package: rear heater, multi-meter, limited slip rear differential; tire carrier, cargo net, wheel locks, tire cover.		
RO	Roof Rack (ES/LS)	170	260
	NOT AVAILABLE with (P6) Luxury Package.		
RR	Roof Rack with Sunroof (LS/XLS)	170	260
	REQUIRES (P6) Luxury Package.		
SE	Security System (LS/XLS)	231	345
	Includes keyless entry.		

MITSUBISHI MONTERO SPORT

CODE	DESCRIPTION	INVOICE	MSRP
SS	Side Steps (ES/LS)	252	350
C3	Single Disc CD Player (LS/XLS)	307	399
HI	Trailer Hitch With Harness	169	252
WL	Wheel Locks (LS/XLS) *NOT AVAILABLE with (P4) Off-Road Package.*	34	50
W2	Wheels: 6" x 15" Alloy (LS 4WD) *Includes P225 tires.*	359	427
RD	Wind Deflector: Rear	98	145

Take Advantage of Warranty Gold!

Savings up to 50% off Dealer's Extended Warranty Prices. Protect and enhance YOUR investment with the best extended warranty available.

Call Toll Free   1-800-580-9889

Don't forget to swing by the Townhall when you visit Edmund's website at http://www.edmunds.com. Talk to our editors and compare notes on your favorite cars and trucks. Join others to scope out smart shopping stategies, get answers to your questions, or share your expertise. To get to the Townhall, just click on the link on the homepage or go directly to http://www.edmunds.com/edweb/townhall/welcomeconflist.html.

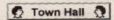

PATHFINDER — NISSAN

1998 PATHFINDER

1998 Nissan Pathfinder LE

What's New?

The only changes to the 1998 Pathfinder include chrome bumpers for the XE model, the addition of air conditioning to XE and SE models' standard equipment lists, and additions to the XE Sport Package equipment.

Review

The recently redesigned Toyota 4Runner has largely overshadowed the Nissan Pathfinder. We think that's too bad. Yes, the 4Runner is a good truck, but it is certainly not the only import SUV on the market. By taking a long, hard look at the Pathfinder, some buyers may be rewarded with a truck that is better than most of the others on the road.

The Pathfinder sports one of the friendliest interiors of any SUV that we've tested in recent years. Ample passenger space fore and aft, a large cargo area with convenient tie-down hooks, standard dual air bags, a killer sound system, comfortable seats, and a great view are just a few of the reasons we like this truck so much. A few things we don't like, however, are the too narrow rear doors, and tubular running boards. This poorly planned combination means that passengers exiting from the rear of the truck will undoubtedly have their pants scuffed by the ineffectual running board as they try to squeeze through the small door.

With Nissan's 1996 redesign came a gutsier version of their familiar V-6 engine. Though not the engine of choice for speed freaks, it moves the Pathfinder along highways and two-track roads with ease. Speaking of two-track roads, the Nissan has lost none of its sporting personality when it acquired its much-heralded car-like ride. Just ask our editor-in-chief, who took the Pathfinder on a daylong jaunt along the Continental Divide and managed to squeeze the truck through some nasty Jeep trails without scratching the paint.

The Nissan Pathfinder gives a competent on and off-road ride, while surrounding its passengers in surprising comfort and luxury. Our favorite model is the rugged SE 5-speed equipped with the Off-Road Package and Bose Audio/Sunroof Package. If you require a rugged yet sophisticated vehicle for hauling your tribe around the town and over the hills, the Pathfinder deserves your attention.

NISSAN PATHFINDER

| CODE | DESCRIPTION | INVOICE | MSRP |

Safety Data

Driver Airbag: *Standard*
Side Airbag: *Not Available*
Traction Control: *Not Available*
Driver Crash Test Grade: *Average*

Passenger Airbag: *Standard*
4-Wheel ABS: *Standard*
Integrated Child Seat(s): *Not Available*
Passenger Crash Test Grade: *Average*

Standard Equipment

XE: 3.3-liter SOHC V6 engine, power assisted rack-and-pinion steering, power front disc/rear drum anti-lock brakes, independent front suspension with stabilizer bar, 5-link coil rear suspension with stabilizer bar, fuel tank skid plate, black grille, chrome bumpers, halogen headlamps, front and rear towing hooks, front and rear splash guards, tinted glass, variable intermittent windshield wipers, dual outside mirrors, rear window wiper washer, P235/70R15 tires, 15" chrome wheels, dual air bags, rear window defroster with timer, tilt steering column, cargo tie down hooks, cargo area lights, full carpeting, overhead storage compartment, map lamps, passenger vanity mirror, CFC-free air conditioning, AM/FM stereo with CD player and 6 speakers, digital quartz clock, cloth interior, front bucket seats, and child safety rear door locks.

SE (in addition to or instead of XE): P265/70R15 M/S tires, 15" aluminum wheels, power antenna, chrome grille and bumpers, fog lamps, upgraded seat trim, dual heated front seats, black fender flares, tubular step rails, luggage rack, air deflector, dual illuminated vanity mirrors, cruise control, power windows, power door locks, vehicle security system, remote keyless entry, power driver's seat, rear seat center armrest, cargo net, and retractable cargo area cover.

LE (in addition to or instead of SE): 4-speed automatic transmission, limited-slip differential, body color bodyside molding, pin striping, chrome running boards, 15" luxury aluminum wheels, leather seats, leather-wrapped steering wheel, simulated wood interior trim, HomeLink transmitter, automatic temperature control, and digital compass with outside temperature gauge.

Base Prices

Code	Description	Invoice	MSRP
09258	XE 2WD (5-spd)	21610	23999
09218	XE 2WD (auto)	22510	24999
09658	XE 4WD (5-spd)	23410	25999
09618	XE 4WD (auto)	24311	26999
09758	SE 4WD (5-spd)	26202	29099
09718	SE 4WD (auto)	27103	30099
19318	LE 2WD (auto)	27418	30449
19818	LE 4WD (auto)	29580	32849
	Destination Charge:	490	490

Accessories

Code	Description	Invoice	MSRP
J02	Bose Audio/Sunroof Package (SE)	1331	1549
	Includes Bose AM/FM stereo with cassette and CD player, dual sun visors, integrated HomeLink transmitter, and power antenna.		
P92	Class III Trailer Hitch	292	389

PATHFINDER — NISSAN

CODE	DESCRIPTION	INVOICE	MSRP
G02	Convenience Package	1245	1449
	Includes power windows with driver's side 1-touch down, power door locks, large door armrests, vehicle security system, remote keyless entry, cruise control, retractable cargo area cover, cargo net, roof-mounted luggage rack, and power mirrors.		
F92	Floor Mats	52	79
L95	Genuine Burlwood Woodtrim (XE/SE)	252	349
	REQUIRES (G02) Convenience Package on XE.		
X03	Leather Package (SE)	1201	1399
	Inludes leather seats, leather-wrapped steering wheel, simulated leather door trim, and heated front seats.		
S09	Luxury Package (LE)	1116	1299
	Includes power sunroof and power front seats.		
T07	Off-Road Package (SE)	214	249
	Includes limited slip rear differential, and black bumpers. REQUIRES (J02) Bose Audio/Sunroof Package.		
U06	Spare Tire Carrier (XE/SE)	257	299
	REQUIRES (V01) Sport Package or (T07) Off-Road Package.		
V01	Sport Package 2WD (XE 2WD)	944	1099
	Includes 6-spoke alloy wheels, P265/70R15 mud and snow tires, roof-mounted luggage rack, step rails, black fender flares, halogen fog lamps, and rear window air deflector. REQUIRES (G02) Convenience Package.		
V01	Sport Package 4WD (XE 4WD)	248	499
	Includes roof-mounted luggage rack, halogen fog lamps, rear window air deflector, and limited slip differential. REQUIRES (G02) Convenience Package.		
M92	Wheels: Alloy (XE 2WD)	588	849

One 15-minute call could save you 15% or more on car insurance.

America's 6th Largest Automobile Insurance Company

1-800-555-2758

NISSAN QUEST

| CODE | DESCRIPTION | INVOICE | MSRP |

1997 QUEST

1997 Nissan Quest XE

What's New?

A few new colors are the only changes to the 1997 Quest.

Review

Nissan claims that its Quest is the top-selling import-brand minivan. Actually, they're made in Ohio, in XE and luxury GXE trim, along with the closely related—but not identical—Mercury Villager. After last year's makeover, the Quest receives few changes for 1997.

Versatile passenger space is the Quest's stock in trade. With seven-passenger Quest Trac Flexible Seating in an XE model, you can get 20 different combinations. In a GXE with captain's chairs, the total possibilities reach an even two dozen. Second row seats can fold down into a table, or be removed completely. The third-row seat also folds into a table, folds further for more cargo space, or slides forward on integrated tracks—all the way to the driver's seat.

Exceptionally smooth and quiet on the road, the Quest delivers more than adequate acceleration when merging or passing, courtesy of the 151-horsepower, 3.0-liter V-6 engine. The column-shifted four-speed automatic transmission changes gears neatly, without a hint of harshness, helped by electronic controls. You also get a smooth, comfortable highway ride and undeniably car-like handling—more so than most. Visibility is great, too, from upright but comfortable seating that's tempting for a long trek. Gauges are small, but acceptable, and controls are pleasing to operate.

Air conditioning and a tachometer are standard fare, while the GXE adds anti-lock braking (including rear disc brakes), a roof rack, and a host of powered conveniences. Distinctive in shape, enjoyable on the road, Quests are solidly assembled and perform admirably. Except for the upright seating position, it's easy to forget that you're inside a minivan, not a plain sedan.

QUEST

Safety Data

Driver Airbag: *Standard*
Side Airbag: *Not Available*
Traction Control: *Not Available*
Driver Crash Test Grade: *Good*

Passenger Airbag: *Standard*
4-Wheel ABS: *Standard (GXE); Optional (XE)*
Integrated Child Seat(s): *Optional*
Passenger Crash Test Grade: *Average*

Standard Equipment

XE: 3.0-liter V-6 engine, 4-speed electronically controlled transmission, power rack-and-pinion steering, front disc/rear drum brakes, independent front suspension, leaf spring rear suspension, front stabilizer bar, 15" wheel covers, P205/75R15 tires, 20 gallon fuel tank, halogen headlamps, cornering lamps, variable intermittent winshield wipers, tinted glass, manual outside mirrors, rear window defroster, rear window wiper/washer, front door map pockets, dual vanity mirrors, tilt steering column, tachometer, trip odometer, air conditioning, stereo with cassette, digital clock, cloth seats with reclining seatbacks, full carpeting, and color-keyed floor mats.

GXE (in addition to or instead of XE): 4-wheel anti-lock brakes, privacy glass, luggage rack, heated outside mirrors, 15" aluminum wheels, power windows and door locks, remote keyless entry, retained accessory power, cruise control with steering wheel mounted buttons, leather-wrapped steering wheel with stereo buttons, illuminated vanity mirrors, rear climate controls, power antenna, power driver's seat, upgraded cloth interior, lockable underseat storage compartment, 2nd row captain's chairs, cargo net, and opening liftgate glass.

Base Prices

Code	Description	Invoice	MSRP
10317	XE	18913	21249
10417	GXE	23186	26049
	Destination Charge:	470	470

Accessories

Code	Description	Invoice	MSRP
B07	Anti-Lock Brakes (XE)	428	499
G06	Captain's Chairs (XE)	514	599
	REQUIRES A04, F05, and S02.		
F05	Convenience Package (XE)	558	649
	Includes cargo net, cruise control, luggage rack, rear audio controls, lockable underseat storage, dual illuminated vanity mirrors, and remote keyless entry system.		
R03	Handling Package (GXE)	472	549
	Includes 21/50R15 tires, full-size spare tire, and rear stabilizer bar. REQUIRES V01.		
K06	Integrated Child Seat	170	199
	REQUIRES A04, F05, S02, and B07 on XE. NOT AVAILABLE with X03 on GXE.		
X03	Leather Package (GXE)	1116	1299
	Includes leather seats and power passenger seats. REQUIRES V01.		
V01	Luxury Package (GXE)	1074	1249
	Includes automatic temperature control, moonroof, and in-dash CD changer.		
S02	Power & Glass Package (XE)	1074	1249
	Includes power front windows, power door locks, power heated outside mirrors, retained accessory power, and tinted glass.		
A04	Rear Air Conditioning (XE)	558	649
	REQUIRES F05 and S02.		

NISSAN QUEST / TRUCK

CODE	DESCRIPTION	INVOICE	MSRP
T09	Touring Package (XE)	858	999
	Includes 5-spoke alloy wheels, full-size spare tire, leather-wrapped steering wheel, in-dash CD changer, and steering wheel mounted audio controls.		
E10	Two-Tone Paint	257	299

1997 TRUCK

1997 Nissan Truck 2WD XE

What's New?

No changes in light of an upcoming redesign.

Review

While other makes play games with names, Nissan calls its compact truck exactly what it is: a Truck. Nothing fancy here, just good dollars-and-cents value and a down-to-business demeanor. A new two-wheel-drive SE edition rounds out the seven model lineup. XE Trucks continue to rank as one of the best values on the compact truck market.

Rear-wheel anti-lock braking is included on all models, but four-wheel ABS is not available. A standard airbag should improve the Truck's average crash test score for the driver. Pasengers still ride without airbag protection. Front suspensions contain torsion bar springs and a stabilizer, while back ends hold traditional leaf springs.

Acceleration is acceptable with manual shift and the 2.4-liter four-cylinder engine. The four is somewhat coarse, and the din easily finds its way inside the cab. Either five-speed manual shift or an electronically controlled automatic transmission is available. Five-speed 4x4s have a clutch interlock "cancel" control, letting you start off in first gear without pushing down the clutch—a feature that can keep the truck from rolling back down a slope.

Payload and towing capacities lag some compact-pickup rivals, and the lack of car-like qualities puts Nissan a step behind the leaders. Even so, these solid machines aren't lacking

WE'VE GOT WHAT IT TAKES TO MAKE YOUR 1998 TRUCK LOOK & PERFORM BETTER THAN EVER!

JC Whitney — ESTABLISHED 1915
EVERYTHING AUTOMOTIVE

(TEAR HERE)

THE #1 AUTOMOTIVE ACCESSORIES & PARTS SOURCE

JC Whitney — EVERYTHING AUTOMOTIVE

(TEAR HERE)

CALL TO ORDER FREE CATALOGS
312-431-6102
ANYTIME

FREE

JC Whitney Catalogs for Everything Automotive

SAVE UP TO 50%

Shop from the world's largest, most complete selection of accessories & parts for:

American Cars • Imported Cars • Pickups
Vans • Offroad Vehicles

Mail this card today and you'll receive our newest catalogs absolutely **FREE**. On your **FIRST** order from our General 200pg. Catalog— **RECEIVE A 10% DISCOUNT**.

"Your Vehicle Data Enables Us to Serve You Better"

Make of VEHICLE	Model	Year

Name _____
(Please Print)

Address _____

City _____ State _____ Zip _____

Do you have:
☐ Mastercard ☐ Visa ☐ Discover ☐ American Express

CODE H302

JC Whitney — EVERYTHING AUTOMOTIVE
AMERICA'S ACCESSORIES AND PARTS SOURCE FOR
PICKUPS
1000's of ACCESSORIES & PARTS for **1998 MODELS**
CALL ROUND THE CLOCK **312-431-6102**

SOME 100 BRAND NAMES

Featuring...Low Prices
• Newest Products
• Hard-To-Find Items
• Custom-Fit Accessories
• Parts Advantage

IN A HURRY?
CALL (312) 431-6102
MENTION CODE **H302**

Please send me the following catalogs (please limit your selections to 3):
☐ PICKUP ☐ MOTORCYCLE
☐ GENERAL CATALOG
☐ VOLKSWAGEN ☐ JEEP®

MAKE YOUR TRUCK A REAL STANDOUT WITH ACCESSORIES & PARTS FROM THE LOW PRICE LEADER!

(TEAR HERE)

THE **#1** AUTOMOTIVE ACCESSORIES & PARTS SOURCE

(TEAR HERE)

FREE JC WHITNEY CATALOGS

BUSINESS REPLY MAIL

FIRST-CLASS MAIL PERMIT NO. 9315 CHICAGO IL

POSTAGE WILL BE PAID BY ADDRESSEE

1 JC Whitney Way
P.O. Box 3000
La Salle, IL 61301-9927

CALL TO ORDER
FREE CATALOGS
312-431-6102
ANYTIME

NO POSTAGE
NECESSARY
IF MAILED
IN THE
UNITED STATES

TRUCK

| CODE | DESCRIPTION | INVOICE | MSRP |

in temptations—especially when considering the starting price for the Standard model. Moving up to an SE King Cab boosts the ante considerably. The Truck has been carried over unchanged from 1996. 1998 will bring us an all-new model that will replace the current hard-body platform.

Safety Data

Driver Airbag: *Standard*
Side Airbag: *Not Available*
Traction Control: *Not Available*
Driver Crash Test Grade: *Not Available*

Passenger Airbag: *Not Available*
4-Wheel ABS: *Not Available*
Integrated Child Seat(s): *Not Available*
Passenger Crash Test Grade: *Not Available*

Standard Equipment

STANDARD: 2.4-liter 4-cylinder engine, 5-speed manual transmission, (4-speed automatic transmission), power front disc/rear drum brakes, rear-wheel anti-lock brakes, recirculating ball power steering, independent front suspsension, solid rear axle with leaf springs, P195/75R15 tires, driver's air bag, vinyl bench seat, vinyl floor covering, removable tailgate, and halogen headlamps.

XE (in addition to or instead of STANDARD): Power steering, manual locking front hubs (4WD), front and rear mud guards (4WD), P235/75R15 tires (4WD), dual outside mirrors, rear bumper, sport steering wheel, center console with dual cup holders (King Cab), skid plates (4WD), tow hooks (4WD), fender flares (4WD), titanium finish wheels (4WD), sliding rear window, full carpeting, cloth seats, reclining bucket seats (King Cab), and rear jump seats (King Cab).

SE (in addition to or instead of XE): Alloy wheels, limited slip differential, P215/75R14 tires, automatic-locking front hubs, under rail bedliner, chrome grille, chrome bumpers, chrome outside mirrors, SE decals, power windows, power mirrors, power door locks, privacy glass, leather-wrapped steering wheel, cut-pile carpeting, front and rear passenger assist grips, and air conditioning.

Base Prices

Code	Description	Invoice	MSRP
33057	2WD Standard Regular Cab (5-spd)	10587	10999
33556	2WD XE Regular Cab (5-speed)	11772	12499
33517	2WD XE Regular Cab (auto)	13330	13999
53557	2WD XE King Cab (5-spd)	13495	14649
53517	2WD XE King Cab (auto)	14416	15649
33757	4WD XE Regular Cab (5-spd)	14921	16199
53757	4WD XE King Cab (5-spd)	16439	18049
53257	2WD SE King Cab (5-speed)	15528	17049
53217	2WD SE King Cab (auto)	16439	18049
53357	4WD SE King Cab (5-spd)	18008	19999
Destination Charge:		470	470

Accessories

Code	Description	Invoice	MSRP
A01	Air Conditioning (XE)	858	999
U07	Alloy Wheels (XE)	428	499
H92	CD Player	349	469

EDMUND'S 1998 NEW TRUCKS

NISSAN TRUCK

CODE	DESCRIPTION	INVOICE	MSRP
W0	Chrome Package (XE)	351	399
G01	Convenience Package (XE)	256	298
	Includes power mirrors, variable intermittent windshield wipers, locking glove box, visor vanity mirror, low fuel warning lamp, front tow hooks, center console with dual cupholders (King Cab), and full-size spare tire (4WD).		
N05	Driver Comfort Package (XE/SE)	343	399
	Includes tilt steering and cruise control.		
F92	Floor Mats	43	59
H93	In-Dash 3-Disc CD Changer (XE/SE)	511	669
L94	Over Rail Bedliner (Standard/XE)	140	299
P06	Power Steering (Standard)	274	319
J08	Privacy Glass	85	99
X10	Standard Delete Package (XE Reg Cab 4WD)	(968)	(1700)
	DELETES rear step runner, sliding rear window, titanium wheels, right hand outside mirror, and cloth interior.		
H01	Stereo with Cassette	428	499
L93	Under Rail Bedliner (Standard/XE)	140	299

Take Advantage of Warranty Gold!

Savings up to 50% off Dealer's Extended Warranty Prices. Protect and enhance YOUR investment with the best extended warranty available.

Call Toll Free 1-800-580-9889

Don't forget to swing by the Townhall when you visit Edmund's website at http://www.edmunds.com. Talk to our editors and compare notes on your favorite cars and trucks. Join others to scope out smart shopping stategies, get answers to your questions, or share your expertise. To get to the Townhall, just click on the link on the homepage or go directly to http://www.edmunds.com/edweb/townhall/welcomeconflist.html.

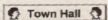

BRAVADA — OLDSMOBILE

1998 BRAVADA

1998 Oldsmobile Bravada

What's New?

Front styling is revised, and new body side cladding alters the Bravada's profile. Inside, dual second generation airbags are housed in a new dashboard. A heated driver's side exterior mirror is newly standard, while heated front seats have been added to the options roster. Battery rundown protection and a theft deterrent system are new standard features.

Review

After a one year hiatus, the Oldsmobile Bravada returned for the 1996 model year, based on the same platform that serves as the basis for the Chevrolet Blazer and the GMC Jimmy. We said we doubted Oldsmobile would find buyers for the Bravada, partly because of myriad choices in the luxo-SUV market, and partly because we didn't think the Bravada was worth the price of admission over similarly equipped Chevy Blazers and GMC Jimmys. Sales didn't meet expectations that first year, but climbed slightly during 1997. Still, Oldsmobile would like to be moving twice as many Bravadas.

They ought to be able to, because the Bravada is a great truck. No tacky fender flares and no dopey two-tone paint schemes here. The interior is swathed in leather, and offers one of the most comfortable driver's seats we've encountered in an SUV. The sound system is outstanding. Controls are easy to see and use, though they look and feel somewhat cheap. Bravada's Smart-Trak all-wheel drive system makes off-roading carefree. Last year, the split rear tailgate was replaced by a liftgate with separately opening rear glass. Best of all, this is one speedy, fun-to-drive truck that can easily swallow a full-size dryer. Truly, the Bravada is what a luxury sport/utility is all about.

The Bravada comes loaded with nearly every conceivable luxury option; appropriate since this is Oldsmobile's entry into the expanding luxury sport ute arena. This market niche is quickly filling to capacity, with luxury SUV's from Lincoln and Infiniti reaching showrooms recently.

Is the Bravada worth the price of admission over the Blazer and the Jimmy? Well, the front seats are exclusive to Oldsmobile, and the Smart-Trak all-wheel drive system is standard on the Olds (it's optional on the Chevy and GMC). In fact, most of the standard equipment on the Bravada is available on the Chevy or the GMC, with an end result that is less expensive than the Oldsmobile.

OLDSMOBILE BRAVADA

| CODE | DESCRIPTION | INVOICE | MSRP |

Few options are available on the Bravada. Buyers can order a heavy-duty 5000-pound towing package, an engine block heater, a CD player that replaces the cassette deck, white-letter tires, a gold-trim package, and a power tilt and slide sunroof. New this year are heated seats, but only with leather upholstery. Cloth seats are a no-charge replacement for the standard leather hides. Olds says the Bravada has a "two-fold mission: keep the driver moving in the face of adverse weather or road conditions and deliver all occupants in comfort and style to the destination of their choice."

Styling is pretty much identical to the Chevy Blazer and GMC Jimmy. The Bravada gets a unique grille and headlamp treatment, bumper trim, and body cladding. The overall effect distances the Olds far enough away from its corporate siblings to make it look and feel unique in a world populated by look-alike Jeep Grand Cherokees and Ford Explorers. A 4.3-liter Vortec V6 engine that makes 190 horsepower propels the Bravada's four wheels. Though strong, we find the V6 a strange choice when the Jeep and the Ford can be equipped with a V8 engine. The Explorer-based Mercury Mountaineer also has all-wheel drive, like the Bravada, along with standard V8 power. Four-wheel disc brakes provide very good stopping ability, though we could do without the mushy brake pedal.

The original Bravada, which competed in a market populated by few luxury-oriented SUV's, never sold very well. It was based on ancient technology, and buyers saw through the first-generation Bravada quicker than they did the ill-fated Cadillac Cimarron. Oldsmobile has come up with quite an enticing package with the second-generation Bravada. However, the luxury market is becoming saturated with very good trucks, which will inevitably push demand for any particular model down. We also think that aging, affluent Boomers are going to tire of climbing in and out of these things in time, depositing their aching legs and backs into the seats of the Cadillacs, BMWs and Acuras that they're currently trading like baseball cards for the more rugged, outdoorsy, SUV image.

Safety Data

Driver Airbag: *Standard*
Side Airbag: *Not Available*
Traction Control: *Not Available*
Driver Crash Test Grade: *Not Available*

Passenger Airbag: *Standard*
4-Wheel ABS: *Standard*
Integrated Child Seat(s): *Not Available*
Passenger Crash Test Grade: *Not Available*

Standard Equipment

BRAVADA: 4.3L V-6 OHV SMPI 12-valve engine; 4-speed electronic overdrive automatic transmission with lock-up; battery with run down protection; engine oil cooler; 525-amp alternator; full-time 4 wheel drive, limited slip differential, 3.73 axle ratio; stainless steel exhaust; front independent suspension with anti-roll bar, front torsion springs, front torsion bar, front shocks, rear suspension with anti-roll bar, rear leaf springs, rear shocks; power re-circulating ball steering with engine speed-sensing assist; 4 wheel disc brakes with 4 wheel anti-lock braking system; 18 gal capacity fuel tank; front license plate bracket; liftback rear cargo door; roof rack; front and rear body-colored bumpers with tow hooks, rear step bumper; body-colored bodyside cladding, body-colored wheel well molding; monotone paint with bodyside accent stripe; aero-composite halogen fully automatic headlamps with daytime running lights and delay-off feature; additional exterior lights include front fog/driving lights, center high mounted stop light, underhood light; driver side folding heated outside mirror; front and rear 15" x 7" silver alloy wheels; P235/70SR15 BSW AS front and rear tires; underbody mounted full-size temporary steel spare wheel; air conditioning with climate control, rear heat ducts; AM/FM stereo with clock, seek-scan, cassette, 6 speakers, graphic equalizer, and fixed antenna; cruise control; power door locks with remote keyless entry, child safety rear door locks, power remote hatch release; 3 power accessory outlets, retained accessory power, garage door opener; analog instrumentation display includes tachometer gauge, oil pressure gauge, water temp gauge, volt gauge, compass, exterior temp, trip computer, trip odometer; warning indicators include battery, lights on, key in ignition; dual airbags; ignition disable; deep tinted windows, power front windows with driver

BRAVADA — OLDSMOBILE

CODE	DESCRIPTION	INVOICE	MSRP

1-touch down, power rear windows, fixed 1/4 vent windows; variable intermittent front windshield wipers, flip-up rear window, fixed interval rear wiper, rear window defroster; seating capacity of 5, front bucket seats with tilt adjustable headrests, center armrest with storage, driver seat includes 6-way power seat with power lumbar support, passenger seat includes 4-way direction control with power lumbar support; 60-40 folding rear split-bench seat with adjustable rear headrest; leather seats, leatherette door trim insert, full cloth headliner, full carpet floor covering with carpeted floor mats, leather gear shift knob; interior lights include dome light, front and rear reading lights, illuminated entry; leather-wrapped steering wheel with tilt adjustment; dual illuminated vanity mirrors; auto-dimming day-night rearview mirror; partial floor console, full overhead console with storage, glove box with light, front cupholder, 2 seat back storage pockets, driver and passenger door bins, rear door bins; carpeted cargo floor, carpeted trunk lid, cargo cover, cargo net, cargo tie downs, cargo light, cargo concealed storage; body-colored grille, black side window moldings, black front windshield molding, black rear window molding, black door handles.

Base Prices

Code	Description	Invoice	MSRP
V06TV-R7A	Base	27734	30645
	Destination Charge:	515	515

Accessories

Code	Description	Invoice	MSRP
YF5	California Emissions	146	170
	Automatically added to vehicles shipped to and/or sold to retailers in California. Out-of-state retailers must order on vehicles to be registered or leased in California. NOT AVAILABLE with (NG1) NY/MA/CT Emissions.		
**C	Cloth Seat Trim	NC	NC
	Replaces standard leather seat trim.		
K05	Engine Block Heater	28	33
KA1	Heated Front Seats	194	225
NG1	NY/MA/CT Emissions	146	170
	Automatically added to vehicles shipped to and/or sold to retailers in Massachusetts/New York/Connecticut. Out-of-state retailers must order on vehicles to be registered or leased in Massachusetts/New York/Connecticut. NOT AVAILABLE with (YF5) California Emissions.		
1SA	Option Package 1SA	NC	NC
	Includes vehicle with standard equipment.		
CF5	Power Sunroof	598	695
UP0	Radio: AM/FM Stereo with CD & Cassette	172	200
QBG	Tires: P235/70R15 AS WOL SBR	116	135
Z82	Trailer Towing Package	181	210
R9B	Value Option Package	60	770
	Includes heated front seats, AM/FM stereo with CD and cassette, P235/70R15 AS WOL SBR tires, trailer towing package.		

OLDSMOBILE SILHOUETTE

1998 SILHOUETTE

1998 Oldsmobile Silhouette

What's New?

Side-impact airbags are standard for front seat passengers, and Oldsmobile is building more short-wheelbase vans with dual sliding doors. Front airbags get second generation technology, which results in slower deployment speeds.

Review

After years of unsuccessfully peddling a plastic four-wheeled version of the Dustbuster found in your hall closet, Oldsmobile went back to the drawing board and introduced a fresh, conservative, steel-bodied, fun-to-drive minivan to market. Available in three trim levels and three body styles, the new Silhouette is indeed one minivan consumers need to consider.

Why is this Oldsmobile so good? You name the convenience, and Olds has thought of it. Want a sliding driver's side door? You can get one here. Wish that passenger's side sliding door was power operated? Oldsmobile has you covered. Want leather? A CD player? Separate audio controls for rear passengers? Traction control? A powerful V6 engine? Easy to unload seats that can be configured in a variety of ways? It's all here, depending on the body style and trim level you select.

Silhouette is available in three flavors; regular length 3-door and extended length 3- or 4-door equipped in GS, GL, and GLS trim levels. All Silhouettes are front-wheel drive, and are powered by a 180-horsepower 3.4-liter V6 mated to an electronically controlled 4-speed automatic transmission. Dual airbags and anti-lock brakes are standard.

GS models come with air conditioning, tilt steering wheel, cruise control, power door locks, power windows, and fog lights. Optionally available are traction control, alloy wheels, integrated child seats, leather upholstery, and 8-passenger seating.

The GL trim level adds remote keyless entry, a theft deterrent system, power sliding right side door, power seats, and deep tinted glass to the base model's equipment list. Next up is the GLS, which adds a touring suspension package, rear climate controls, alloy wheels, and rear audio controls to the GL standard equipment roster.

We've driven the Silhouette and came away from our ride quite impressed. The van is smooth, powerful, and fun-to-drive with excellent road feel provided by sharp steering and

SILHOUETTE — OLDSMOBILE

easily modulated brakes. Our complaints are limited to uncomfortable rear seating and a noticeable amount of cheap-looking plastic inside the cabin.

Some of you may have seen the Dateline NBC expose in which several minivans were crashed into a deformable offset barrier at 40 mph. While there is no standard regarding offset crash protection in the United States, and the Silhouette does meet all current federal safety standards, this test showed that GM's new minivans did not do a good job of protecting the driver in such an accident. General Motors responded that the test represented a tiny percentage of real world crashes. Later in the year, the National Highway and Traffic Safety Administration (NHTSA) ran a new GM minivan into a fixed barrier at 35 mph during official crash testing, and the van scored very well for both front seat occupants. If GM's contention is correct, and head-on crashes are more common, the Silhouette should protect passengers adequately. But here's the Catch 22; after several GM vehicles performed poorly in NHTSA's side-impact testing in 1997, the company denounced NHTSA's procedure, claiming it did not adequately correlate with real world crashes. Go figure.

While we like the new Oldsmobile Silhouette, and find its exterior styling to be the most attractive of the three new GM minivans, we can't help but wonder just how crashworthy this model really is. Maybe the new-for-1998 side-impact airbags will help.

Safety Data

Driver Airbag: *Standard*
Side Airbag: *Standard*
Traction Control: *Optional*
Driver Crash Test Grade: *Good*

Passenger Airbag: *Standard*
4-Wheel ABS: *Standard*
Integrated Child Seat(s): *Not Available*
Passenger Crash Test Grade: *Good*

Standard Equipment

GL EXTENDED: 3.4L V-6 OHV SMPI 12-valve engine; 4-speed electronic overdrive automatic transmission with lock-up; battery with run down protection; front wheel drive, 3.29 axle ratio; stainless steel exhaust; front independent strut suspension with anti-roll bar, front coil springs, front shocks, rear non-independent suspension with rear coil springs, rear shocks; power rack-and-pinion steering; front disc/rear drum brakes with 4 wheel anti-lock braking system; 25 gal capacity fuel tank; body-colored front and rear mud flaps, side impact bars; 4 doors with sliding left rear passenger door and sliding right rear passenger door, liftback rear cargo door; roof rack; front and rear body-colored bumpers with rear step; body-colored bodyside molding, rocker panel extensions; monotone paint; aero-composite halogen headlamps with daytime running lights; additional exterior lights include front fog/driving lights, center high mounted stop light, underhood light; driver and passenger power remote black folding outside mirrors; front and rear 15" x 6" steel wheels with full wheel covers; P215/70SR15 BSW AS front and rear tires; underbody mounted compact steel spare wheel; air conditioning, air filter; AM/FM stereo with clock, seek-scan, cassette, 4 speakers, automatic equalizer, and window grid antenna; cruise control; power door locks with remote keyless entry, child safety rear door locks; 3 power accessory outlets; analog instrumentation display includes tachometer gauge, water temp gauge, compass, exterior temp, PRNDL in instrument panel, trip computer, trip odometer; warning indicators include battery, low oil level, low coolant, lights on, key in ignition; dual airbags, seat mounted side airbags for front passengers; panic alarm; deep tinted windows, power front windows with driver 1-touch down, power rear 1/4 vent windows; variable intermittent front windshield wipers, fixed interval rear wiper, rear window defroster; seating capacity of 7, front bucket seats with tilt adjustable headrests and inboard armrests, driver seat includes 4-way power seat with 8-way direction control and lumbar support, passenger seat includes 4-way power seat with 8-way direction control and lumbar support; removeable 60-40 folding split-bench 2nd row seat with adjustable rear headrest; removeable 50-50 folding split-bench 3rd row seat; front height adjustable seatbelts; cloth seats, cloth door trim insert, full cloth headliner, full carpet floor covering with carpeted floor mats; interior lights include dome light, front and rear reading lights, illuminated entry; steering wheel with tilt adjustment; dual illuminated vanity mirrors; day-night rearview mirror; full overhead console with storage, engine cover console with

OLDSMOBILE SILHOUETTE

storage, locking glove box with light, front and rear cupholders, instrument panel bin, dashboard storage, 2 seat back storage pockets, driver and passenger door bins; carpeted cargo floor, plastic trunk lid, cargo net, cargo light; body-colored grille, black side window moldings, black front windshield molding, black rear window molding, body-colored door handles.

GS REGULAR LENGTH (in addition to or instead of GL EXTENDED equipment): 20 gal capacity fuel tank; tinted windows; driver seat includes 6-way direction control, passenger seat includes 4-way direction control; mini overhead console.

GLS EXTENDED (in addition to or instead of GS REGULAR): Touring ride suspension with auto-levelling; 25 gal capacity fuel tank; steering wheel radio controls, rear radio controls; remote keyless entry, power remote hatch release; compass, exterior temp readout; panic alarm; deep tinted windows; seating capacity of 6, driver seat includes 4-way power seat, passenger seat includes 4-way power seat; leatherette seats, leatherette door trim insert; interior lights include illuminated entry; leather-wrapped steering wheel; full overhead console with storage.

Base Prices

Code	Description	Invoice	MSRP
3UN16	GS 4-door	22109	24430
3UM16	GL 4-door Extended	21688	23965
3UM16	GLS 4-door Extended	24584	27165
	Destination Charge:	570	570

Accessories

Code	Description	Invoice	MSRP
AG9	6-Way Power Front Seats (GL)	494	575
YF5	California Emissions	146	170
	Automatically added to vehicles shipped to and/or sold to retailers in California. Out-of-state retailers must order on vehicles to be registered or leased in California. NOT AVAILABLE with (NG1) MA/NY/CT Emissions.		
ABD	Captains Chairs (Second Row) (GS/GL)	215	250
	NOT AVAILABLE with (ZP8) seats.		
R8P	Convenience Package (GL)	464	540
	Includes rear heater and ventilation system, rear seat audio controls.		
WJ7	Custom Leather Seat Trim (GS)	748	870
AN5	Dual Integrated Child Safety Seats (GS/GL)	194	225
	NOT AVAILABLE with (AN2) seats.		
ZP8	Eight Passenger Seating (GS/GL)	202	235
	NOT AVAILABLE with (ABD) seats.		
K05	Engine Block Heater	17	20
AN2	Integral Child Safety Seat (GS/GL)	108	125
	NOT AVAILABLE with (AN5) seats.		
NG1	MA/NY/CT Emissions	146	170
	Automatically added to vehicles shipped to and/or sold to retailers in Massachusetts/New York/Connecticut. Out-of-state retailers must order on vehicles to be registered or leased in Massachusetts/New York/Connecticut. NOT AVAILABLE with (YF5) California Emissions.		
1SA	Option Package 1SA (GL)	NC	NC
	Includes vehicle with standard equipment.		

SILHOUETTE — OLDSMOBILE

CODE	DESCRIPTION	INVOICE	MSRP
1SB	Option Package 1SB (GS)	NC	NC
	Includes vehicle with standard equipment.		
1SC	Option Package 1SC (GLS)	NC	NC
	Includes vehicle with standard equipment.		
R8U	Personal Attention Package (GS)	1320	1535
	Includes touch control steering wheel, rear seat audio controls, AM/FM stereo with CD and cassette, captains chairs (second row), custom leather seat trim. NOT AVAILABLE with (UN0) radio.		
R8Q	Personal Convenience Package (GL)	1010	1175
	Includes captains chairs (second row), AM/FM stereo with CD and cassette, 6-way power front seats, remote keyless entry and theft deterrent. NOT AVAILABLE with (UN0) radio.		
E58	Power Sliding Passenger's Side Door (GL)	340	395
UN0	Radio: AM/FM Audio System with CD	86	100
	NOT AVAILABLE with (UN7) radio, (R8U) Personal Attention Package, (R8Q) Personal Convenience Package.		
UN7	Radio: AM/FM Stereo with CD & Cassette	172	200
	NOT AVAILABLE with (UN0) radio.		
C34	Rear Air Conditioning & Heater (GLS)	387	450
UK6	Rear Seat Audio Controls (GS/GL)	77	90
UA6	Remote Keyless Entry & Theft Deterrent (GL)	129	150
UK3	Touch Control Steering Wheel (GS)	108	125
	Includes radio controls on steering wheel.		
FE3	Touring Suspension Group (GS/GL)	232	270
	Package includes an air inflation kit, automatic load leveling.		
NW9	Traction Control	168	195
V92	Trailer Towing Package (GLS)	73	85
V92	Trailer Towing Package (GS/GL)	305	355
	Includes engine oil cooler, transmission oil cooler, 5 wire trailer wiring harness, Touring Suspension Group with automatic load leveling and HD radiator.		
PH3	Wheels: Aluminium (GS/GL)	245	285

For expert advice in selecting/buying/leasing a new car, call
1-900-AUTOPRO
($2.00 per minute)

PLYMOUTH GRAND VOYAGER

| CODE | DESCRIPTION | INVOICE | MSRP |

1998 GRAND VOYAGER

1998 Plymouth Grand Voyager

What's New?

The Voyager SE now comes with a standard 3.0-liter V6. An "Expresso" package adds to appearance, not performance, in both the Voyager and Grand Voyager. And for convenience, the Voyager comes with rear-seat mounted grocery bag hooks and driver's-side easy-entry Quad seat. All Chrysler products are equipped with "Next Generation" depowered airbags.

Review

In the past, Plymouth renderings of Chrysler Corporation's popular front-drive minivans have been virtual clones of the Dodge Caravan. In engineering and design, that's also true of this latest iteration, the Voyager, introduced as an early '96 model. In an assertive marketing move, however, Plymouth is pushing value pricing, aiming squarely at entry-level buyers who are shopping for their first minivans. Instead of the three-model lineup that Dodge shoppers face, Plymouth offers only two short-wheelbase Voyagers: the base model and a step-up SE.

Even a base-model Voyager is loaded with style and features, though anti-lock braking is an option here, unlike the other Chrysler minis. Sleek, lengthened, freshly-rounded bodies surround roomier-than-ever interiors, claiming more cargo space than the competition. Views to the ground and all around have improved, as a result of increasing the minivan's glass area by 30 percent and lowering the cowl. An "Easy Out" roller rear seat makes it easier to modify the passenger/cargo layout to suit specific needs.

Leading the list of appealing innovations is the optional driver-side sliding door--a boon to suburbanites who might want to load their minivans from either side. Two out of three buyers are expected to choose this option. Snowbelt-dwellers who've endured frosted windshields might also like the new optional electric windshield-wiper de-icer.

Anyone who appreciated the prior Voyager's car-like characteristics will be even more pleased by the latest edition, with its light steering response and super-smooth ride. This is an easy minivan to control, with a body that stays reasonably flat through curves, but threatens to lean just a little too much if pushed overly hard.

GRAND VOYAGER — PLYMOUTH

| CODE | DESCRIPTION | INVOICE | MSRP |

Base engine is a new 16-valve dual-cam four, whipping out 50 more horsepower than the prior four-cylinder. That's an impressive output hike, but many buyers are likely to choose the 3.0- or 3.3-liter V-6 anyway.

Soft seats are amply supportive, and cupholders "ratchet down" to smaller size. Climate controls are a little too complex, and the column-mounted gearshift is oddly-shaped, but the dashboard exhibits an alluring curvature. Inside and out, the latest Voyager and Caravan look poised to retain their league-leading position in the minivan race.

Safety Data

Driver Airbag: *Standard*
Side Airbag: *Not Available*
Traction Control: *Not Available*
Driver Crash Test Grade: *Average*

Passenger Airbag: *Standard*
4-Wheel ABS: *Opt. (Base); Std. (SE)*
Integrated Child Seat(s): *Opt. (SE); N/A (Base)*
Passenger Crash Test Grade: *Good*

Standard Equipment

GRAND VOYAGER BASE: 3.0L V-6 SOHC 12-valve engine; 3-speed automatic transmission; 500-amp battery; 90-amp alternator; front wheel drive, 3.19 axle ratio; stainless steel exhaust; comfort ride suspension, front independent strut suspension with anti-roll bar, front coil springs, front shocks, rear non-independent suspension with rear leaf springs, rear shocks; power rack-and-pinion steering; front disc/rear drum brakes; 20 gal capacity fuel tank; rear lip spoiler; 4 doors with sliding left rear passenger door, sliding right rear passenger door, liftback rear cargo door; front and rear colored bumpers, rear step bumper; colored bodyside molding; monotone paint; aero-composite halogen headlamps; additional exterior lights include center high mounted stop light; driver and passenger manual black folding outside mirrors; front and rear 14" x 6" steel wheels with full wheel covers; P205/75SR14 BSW AS front and rear tires; underbody mounted compact steel spare wheel; AM/FM stereo with clock, seek-scan, 4 speakers and fixed antenna; child safety rear door locks; 2 power accessory outlets, driver foot rest; analog instrumentation display includes water temp gauge, PRNDL in instrument panel, trip odometer; warning indicators include oil pressure, water temp warning, battery, lights on, key in ignition, low fuel, low washer fluid, door ajar, trunk ajar; dual airbags; tinted windows, fixed rear windows, manual 1/4 vent windows; variable intermittent front windshield wipers, variable intermittent rear wiper; seating capacity of 7, front bucket seats with fixed adjustable headrests, driver and passenger armrests, driver seat includes 4-way direction control, passenger seat includes 4-way direction control; removeable full folding 2nd row bench seat; 3rd row removeable full folding bench seat; front and rear height adjustable seatbelts; cloth seats, vinyl door trim insert, full cloth headliner, full carpet floor covering; interior lights include dome light, front reading lights; vanity mirrors; day-night rearview mirror; glove box, front and rear cupholders, instrument panel bin, interior concealed storage; carpeted cargo floor, vinyl trunk lid, cargo light; colored grille, black side window moldings, black front windshield molding, black rear window molding, black door handles.

SE (in addition to or instead of BASE equipment): 4-speed electronic overdrive automatic transmission with lock-up; 3.9 axle ratio; wide bodyside moldings; 4 wheel anti-lock braking system; front and rear 15" x 6.5" wheels; cassette player; cruise control with steering wheel controls; tilt steering wheel; rear heat ducts; tachometer gauge; cloth door trim insert, passenger seatback assist strap; folding middle bench seat, folding 3rd row bench seat; deluxe sound insulation; cargo net.

PLYMOUTH GRAND VOYAGER

CODE	DESCRIPTION	INVOICE	MSRP

Base Prices

NSHL53	Base	18270	20125
NSHH53	SE	20171	22285
	Destination Charge:	580	580

Accessories

Code	Description	Invoice	MSRP
DGA	3-Speed Automatic Transmission (Base)	NC	NC
DGB	4-Speed Automatic Transmission (Base)	213	250
DGB	4-Speed Automatic Transmission (SE)	NC	NC
BGF	4-Wheel Antilock Brakes (Base)	480	565
CYR	7 Passenger Deluxe Seating with 2 Child Seats (SE)	191	225

Includes front reclining buckets with armrests, middle 2 passenger reclining and folding bench with headrests and armrests, and rear 3 passenger reclining and folding bench with headrests and adjustable track. Child seats are located in middle bench. NOT AVAILABLE with CYS, 26A, 28A, 25L, 28L, 25N, 28N.

CYK	7 Passenger Seating with 2 Child Seats (Base)	242	285

Includes front reclining buckets, middle 2 passenger bench with headrests, and rear 3 passenger bench with headrests and adjustable track. Child seats are located in middle bench. NOT AVAILABLE with 24S, 28S.

CYS	7 Passenger Seating with Quad Buckets (SE)	553	650

Includes front reclining buckets with armrests and driver manual lumbar, 2 middle reclining and folding buckets with armrests, and rear 3 passenger reclining and folding bench with headrests and adjustable track. NOT AVAILABLE with CYR, 28B, 26A, 28A, 25B, 26B, 25L, 28L, 25C, 28C, 25N, 28N.

HAA	Air Conditioning	731	860

NOT AVAILABLE with 4XA, 24T, 28T, 26B, 25B, 28B, 26D, 25D, 28D, 25L, 28L, 25C, 28C, 25E, 28E, 25N, 28N.

4XA	Air Conditioning Bypass	NC	NC

NOT AVAILABLE with HAA, 24T, 28T, 25B, 26B, 28B, 25D, 26D, 28D, 25L, 28L, 25C, 28C, 25E, 28E, 25N, 28N.

YCF	Border State (California) Emissions	145	170

NOT AVAILABLE with (NAE) CA/CT/MA/NY Emissions.

NAE	CA/CT/MA/NY Emissions	145	170

NOT AVAILABLE with (YCF) Border State Emissions.

AAA	Climate Group II	383	450

Includes air conditioning, sunscreen glass, windshield wiper de-icer. NOT AVAILABLE with 4XN, 24S, 28S, 26A, 28A, 25C, 28C, 25E, 28E, 25N, 28N.

AAB	Climate Group III (SE)	578	680

Includes air conditioning with dual zone temperature control, sunscreen glass, rear air conditioning and heater. REQUIRES 25C or 28C. NOT AVAILABLE with 4XN.

AAB	Climate Group III (SE)	485	570

Includes air conditioning with dual zone temperature control, sunscreen glass, rear air conditioning and heater. REQUIRES 25E or 28E. NOT AVAILABLE with 4XN.

AAB	Climate Group III (SE)	417	490

Includes air conditioning with dual zone temperature control, sunscreen glass, rear air conditioning and heater. REQUIRES 25N or 28N. NOT AVAILABLE with 4XN.

GRAND VOYAGER — PLYMOUTH

CODE	DESCRIPTION	INVOICE	MSRP
AAB	**Climate Group III (SE)**	961	1130
	Includes air conditioning with dual zone temperature control, sunscreen glass, rear air conditioning and heater. REQUIRES 25B or 26B or 28B. NOT AVAILABLE with 4XN.		
AAB	**Climate Group III (SE)**	867	1020
	Includes air conditioning with dual zone temperature control, sunscreen glass, rear air conditioning and heater. REQUIRES 25D or 26D or 28D. NOT AVAILABLE with 4XN.		
AAB	**Climate Group III (SE)**	799	940
	Includes air conditioning with dual zone temperature control, sunscreen glass, rear air conditioning and heater. REQUIRES 25L or 28L. NOT AVAILABLE with 4XN.		
AAC	**Convenience Group I (Base)**	370	435
	Includes dual power fold-away mirrors, speed control, tilt steering column. REQUIRES 24T or 28T.		
AAE	**Convenience Group II (Base)**	638	750
	Includes Convenience Group I: dual power fold-away mirrors, speed control, tilt steering column; power door locks. REQUIRES 24T or 28T.		
AAE	**Convenience Group II (SE)**	268	315
	Includes Convenience Group I: dual power fold-away mirrors, speed control, tilt steering column; power door locks (some items may be standard on SE models). REQUIRES 25B or 26B or 28B or 25C or 28C.		
AAF	**Convenience Group III (SE)**	582	685
	Includes Convenience Group II: dual power fold-away mirrors, speed control, tilt steering column, power door locks; power quarter vent windows, power windows with driver's one touch down (some items may be standard on SE models). REQUIRES 25B or 26B or 28B or 25C or 28C.		
AAG	**Convenience Group IV (SE)**	200	235
	Includes Convenience Group III: dual power fold-away mirrors, speed control, tilt steering column, power door locks, power quarter vent windows, power windows with driver's one touch down; headlight off time delay, illuminated entry, remote keyless entry (some items may be standard on SE models). NOT AVAILABLE with 26A, 28A, 25B, 26B, 28B, 25C, 28C.		
AAH	**Convenience Group V (SE)**	327	385
	Includes Convenience Group IV: dual power fold-away mirrors, speed control, tilt steering column, power door locks, power quarter vent windows, power windows with driver's one touch down, headlight off time delay, illuminated entry, remote keyless entry; security alarm (some items may be standard on SE models). NOT AVAILABLE with 26A, 28A, 25B, 26B, 28B, 25C, 28C.		
NHK	Engine Block Heater	30	35
EFA	Engine: 3.0L V6 MPI	NC	NC
EGA	Engine: 3.3L MPI V6	170	200
EGM	Engine: 3.3L V6 FFV (SE)	170	200
	Operates on ethanol (E85) or unleaded fuel.		
RCE	**Infinity Sound System (SE)**	336	395
	Includes 10 speakers. REQUIRES RAZ. NOT AVAILABLE with 26A, 28A, 25B, 26B, 28B, 25C, 28C.		
SER	**Load Leveling & Height Control (SE)**	247	290
	NOT AVAILABLE with 26A, 28A, 25B, 26B, 28B, 25C, 28C.		

PLYMOUTH GRAND VOYAGER

CODE	DESCRIPTION	INVOICE	MSRP
AAP	Loading & Towing Group II (SE)	153	180
	Includes HD suspension, P215/70R15 AS touring tires, 15" wheels with full covers, full-size spare tire. NOT AVAILABLE with 26A, 28A.		
AAR	Loading/Towing Group III (SE)	378	445
	Includes Loading and Towing Group II: HD suspension, P215/70R15 AS touring tires, 15" wheels with full covers, full-size spare tire; 120-amp alternator, 685-amp battery, HD brakes. NOT AVAILABLE with 26A, 28A, 26B, 28B, 25B, 25C, 28C.		
AAR	Loading/Towing Group III (SE)	323	380
	Includes Loading and Towing Group II: HD suspension, P215/70R15 AS touring tires, 15" wheels with full covers, full-size spare tire; 120-amp alternator, 685-amp battery, HD brakes. REQUIRES AAB. NOT AVAILABLE with 26A, 28A, 26B, 28B, 25B, 25C, 28C.		
—	Low Back Bucket Seats (SE)	NC	NC
24S	Quick Order Package 24S (Base)	NC	NC
	Includes vehicle with standard equipment. REQUIRES HAA or 4XA and EFA and DGA. NOT AVAILABLE with RAS, RBR, AAE, MWG.		
24T	Quick Order Package 24T (Base)	752	885
	Manufacturer Discount	(731)	(860)
	Net Price	21	25
	Includes air conditioning, rear floor silencer pad, under seat lockable drawer. REQUIRES EFA and DGA. NOT AVAILABLE with NAE, 4XA, AAA.		
25B	Quick Order Package 25B (SE)	1024	1205
	Manufacturer Discount	(859)	(1010)
	Net Price	165	195
	Includes air conditioning, 7 passenger seating. REQUIRES EGM and DGB. NOT AVAILABLE with AAA, AAR, RCE, CYS, SER.		
25C	Quick Order Package 25C (SE)	1768	2080
	Manufacturer Discount	(1016)	(1195)
	Net Price	752	885
	Includes air conditioning, rear window defroster, AM/FM stereo with CD player, 7-passenger seating with recline and fold 2nd row and 3rd row bench seats, Expresso Decor: body-color door handles, sunscreen glass, remote keyless entry, illuminated entry, headlamp time delay, tape stripe, side window outline, special wheel covers. REQUIRES EGM and DGB. NOT AVAILABLE with NAE, HAA, 4XA.		
25D	Quick Order Package 25D (SE)	1904	2240
	Manufacturer Discount	(1114)	(1310)
	Net Price	790	930
	Includes air conditioning, deluxe sound insulation, light group, Convenience Group III: dual power fold-away mirrors, speed control, tilt steering column, power door locks, power quarter vent windows, power windows with driver's one touch down (some items may be standard on SE; dual illuminated visor vanity mirrors, 7 passenger seating. REQUIRES (EGM) engine and (DGB) transmission. NOT AVAILABLE with (AAA) Climate Group II.		
25E	Quick Order Package 25E (SE)	2648	3115
	Manufacturer Discount	(1271)	(1495)
	Net Price	1377	1620
	Includes air conditioning, rear window defroster, AM/FM stereo with CD player,		

GRAND VOYAGER — PLYMOUTH

CODE	DESCRIPTION	INVOICE	MSRP

7-passenger seating with recline and fold 2nd row and 3rd row bench seats, front and rear floor mats, light group, power door locks, illuminated visor vanity mirrors, power windows with driver's one-touch down, power quarter vent windows, Expresso Decor: body-color door handles, sunscreen glass, remote keyless entry, illuminated entry, headlamp time delay, tape stripe, side window outline, special wheel covers. REQUIRES EGM and DGB. NOT AVAILABLE with NAE, HAA, 4XA, AAE, AAF.

25L   Quick Order Package 25L (SE) 3013   3545
       Manufacturer Discount .... (1114)   (1310)
       Net Price 1899   2235

Includes air conditioning, overhead console with trip computer, deluxe sound insulation, light group, Convenience Group III: dual power fold-away mirrors, speed control, tilt steering column, power door locks, power quarter vent windows, power windows with driver's one touch down (some items may be standard on SE), dual illuminated visor vanity mirrors, 8-way power driver's seat, 7 passenger seating with quad buckets, low back bucket seats. REQUIRES EGM and DGB. NOT AVAILABLE with AAA, CYR.

25N   Quick Order Package 25N (SE) 3757   4420
       Manufacturer Discount .... (1271)   (1495)
       Net Price 2486   2925

Includes air conditioning, rear window defroster, AM/FM stereo with CD player, 7-passenger seating with quad low back bucket seats, recline and fold 3rd row bench seat, front and rear floor mats, light group, power door locks, illuminated visor vanity mirrors, power windows with driver's one-touch down, power quarter vent windows, overhead console with trip computer, 8-way power driver's seat with manual lumbar support, Expresso Decor: body-color door handles, sunscreen glass, remote keyless entry, illuminated entry, headlamp time delay, tape stripe, side window outline, special wheel covers. REQUIRES EGM and DGB. NOT AVAILABLE with NAE, HAA, 4XA, AAE, AAF, CYS.

26A   Quick Order Package 26A (SE) .... NC   NC

Includes vehicle with standard equipment. REQUIRES HAA or 4XA and EFA and DGB. NOT AVAILABLE with AAB, AAR, MWG, RCE, RAZ, CYR, CYS, AAG, AAH, SER.

26B   Quick Order Package 26B (SE) 1024   1205
       Manufacturer Discount .... (859)   (1010)
       Net Price 165   195

Includes air conditioning, 7 passenger seating. REQUIRES EFA and DGB. NOT AVAILABLE with AAA, AAR, RCE, CYS, SER.

26D   Quick Order Package 26D (SE) 1904   2240
       Manufacturer Discount .... (1114)   (1310)
       Net Price 790   930

Includes air conditioning, deluxe sound insulation, light group, Convenience Group III: dual power fold-away mirrors, speed control, tilt steering column, power door locks, power quarter vent windows, power windows with driver's one touch down (some items may be standard on SE), dual illuminated visor vanity mirrors, 7 passenger seating. REQUIRES (EFA) engine and (DGB) transmission. NOT AVAILABLE with (AAA) Climate Group II.

PLYMOUTH GRAND VOYAGER

CODE	DESCRIPTION	INVOICE	MSRP
28A	Quick Order Package 28A (SE)	NC	NC

Includes vehicle with standard equipment. REQUIRES EGA and DGB and NAE. NOT AVAILABLE with AAB, AAR, MWG, RCE, RAZ, CYR, CYS, AAG, AAH, SER.

28B	Quick Order Package 28B (SE)	1024	1205
	Manufacturer Discount	(859)	(1010)
	Net Price	165	195

Includes air conditioning, 7 passenger seating. REQUIRES EGA and DGB and NAE. NOT AVAILABLE with CYS, AAG, AAH, AAR, 4XA, SER, AAA, RCE.

28C	Quick Order Package 28C (SE)	1768	2080
	Manufacturer Discount	(1016)	(1195)
	Net Price	752	885

Includes air conditioning, rear window defroster, AM/FM stereo with CD player, 7-passenger seating with recline and fold 2nd row and 3rd row bench seats, Expresso Decor: body-color door handles, sunscreen glass, remote keyless entry, illuminated entry, headlamp time delay, tape stripe, side window outline, special wheel covers. REQUIRES EGM and DGB and NAE. NOT AVAILABLE with HAA, 4XA.

28D	Quick Order Package 28D (SE)	1904	2240
	Manufacturer Discount	(1114)	(1310)
	Net Price	790	930

Includes air conditioning, deluxe sound insulation, light group, Convenience Group III: dual power fold-away mirrors, speed control, tilt steering column, power door locks, power quarter vent windows, power windows with driver's one touch down (some items may be standard on SE), dual illuminated visor vanity mirrors, 7 passenger seating. REQUIRES EGA and DGB and NAE. NOT AVAILABLE with 4XA, AAA.

28E	Quick Order Package 28E (SE)	2648	3115
	Manufacturer Discount	(1271)	(1495)
	Net Price	1377	1620

Includes air conditioning, rear window defroster, AM/FM stereo with CD player, 7-passenger seating with recline and fold 2nd row and 3rd row bench seats, front and rear floor mats, light group, power door locks, illuminated visor vanity mirrors, power windows with driver's one-touch-down, power quarter vent windows, Expresso Decor: body-color door handles, sunscreen glass, remote keyless entry, illuminated entry, headlamp time delay, tape stripe, side window outline, special wheel covers. REQUIRES EGM and DGB and NAE. NOT AVAILABLE with HAA, 4XA, AAE, AAF.

28L	Quick Order Package 28L (SE)	3013	3545
	Manufacturer Discount	(1114)	(1310)
	Net Price	1899	2235

Includes air conditioning, overhead console with trip computer, deluxe sound insulation, light group, Convenience Group III: dual power fold-away mirrors, speed control, tilt steering column, power door locks, power quarter vent windows, power windows with driver's one touch down (some items may be standard on SE), dual illuminated visor vanity mirrors, 8-way power driver's seat, 7 passenger seating with quad buckets, low back bucket seats. REQUIRES EGA and DGB and NAE. NOT AVAILABLE with 4XA, AAA, CYR.

GRAND VOYAGER — PLYMOUTH

CODE	DESCRIPTION	INVOICE	MSRP
28N	Quick Order Package 28N (SE)	3757	4420
	Manufacturer Discount	(1271)	(1495)
	Net Price	2486	2925

Includes air conditioning, rear window defroster, AM/FM stereo with CD player, 7-passenger seating with quad low back bucket seats, recline and fold 3rd row bench seat, front and rear floor mats, light group, power door locks, illuminated visor vanity mirrors, power windows with driver's one-touch down, power quarter vent windows, overhead console with trip computer, 8-way power driver's seat with manual lumbar support, Expresso Decor: body-color door handles, sunscreen glass, remote keyless entry, illuminated entry, headlamp time delay, tape stripe, side window outline, special wheel covers. REQUIRES EGM and DGB and HAA. NOT AVAILABLE with HAA, 4XA, AAE, AAF, CYS.

28S	Quick Order Package 28S (Base)	NC	NC

Includes vehicle with standard equipment. REQUIRES HAA or 4XA and EGA and DGB. NOT AVAILABLE with AAE, RAS, RBR, MWG.

28T	Quick Order Package 28T (Base)	752	885
	Manufacturer Discount	(731)	(860)
	Net Price	21	25

Includes air conditioning, rear floor silencer pad, under seat lockable drawer. REQUIRES NAE and EGA and DGB. NOT AVAILABLE with 4XA, AAA.

RAS	Radio: AM/FM Stereo with Cassette (Base)	153	180

Includes 4 speakers. NOT AVAILABLE with 24S, 28S, RBR.

RAZ	Radio: AM/FM Stereo with Cassette & CD (SE)	276	325

Includes 3 band equalizer and 10 Infinity speakers in 8 locations. NOT AVAILABLE with 26A, 28A, 25C, 28C, 25E, 28E, 25N, 28N.

RAZ	Radio: AM/FM Stereo with Cassette & CD (SE)	153	180

Includes 3 band equalizer and 10 Infinity speakers in 8 locations. REQUIRES 25C or 28C or 25E or 28E or 25N or 28N.

RBR	Radio: AM/FM Stereo with CD (Base)	276	325

Includes 5 band equalizer, CD changer controls, and 10 Infinity speakers in 8 locations. NOT AVAILABLE with 24S, 28S, RAS.

4XN	Rear Air Conditioning Bypass (SE)	NC	NC

NOT AVAILABLE with (AAB) Climate Group III, (AAA) Climate Group II.

GFA	Rear Window Defroster	196	230

Includes heated exterior mirrors, windshield wiper de-icer. REQUIRES (24T or 28T) and (AAA or AAC or AAE) on Base models. NOT AVAILABLE with 26B, 25B, 28B, 26D, 25D, 28D, 25L, 28L, 25C, 28C, 25E, 28E, 25N, 28N.

GFA	Rear Window Defroster (Base)	166	195

Includes heated exterior mirrors, windshield wiper de-icer.

MWG	Roof Rack	149	175

NOT AVAILABLE with 24S, 28S, 26A, 28A.

AWS	Smokers Group	17	20

Includes cigar lighter and 3 ash receiver inserts (front, intermediate, and rear).

PLYMOUTH   VOYAGER

| CODE | DESCRIPTION | INVOICE | MSRP |

1998 VOYAGER

1998 Plymouth Voyager

Safety Data

Driver Airbag: *Standard*
Side Airbag: *Not Available*
Traction Control: *Not Available*
Driver Crash Test Grade: *Good*

Passenger Airbag: *Standard*
4-Wheel ABS: *Opt. (Base); Std. (SE)*
Integrated Child Seat(s): *Optional*
Passenger Crash Test Grade: *Good*

Standard Equipment

VOYAGER BASE: 2.4L I-4 DOHC SMPI 16-valve engine; 3-speed automatic transmission; 600-amp battery; 90-amp alternator; front wheel drive, 3.19 axle ratio; stainless steel exhaust; front independent strut suspension with anti-roll bar, front coil springs, front shocks, rear non-independent suspension with rear leaf springs, rear shocks; power rack-and-pinion steering; front disc/rear drum brakes; 20 gal capacity fuel tank; front mud flaps, rear lip spoiler; 3 doors with sliding right rear passenger door, liftback rear cargo door; front and rear colored bumpers, rear step bumper; colored bodyside molding; monotone paint; aero-composite halogen headlamps; additional exterior lights include center high mounted stop light; driver and passenger manual black folding outside mirrors; front and rear 14" x 6" steel wheels with full wheel covers; P205/75SR14 BSW AS front and rear tires; underbody mounted compact steel spare wheel; AM/FM stereo with clock, seek-scan, 4 speakers and fixed antenna; child safety rear door locks; 2 power accessory outlets, driver foot rest; analog instrumentation display includes water temp gauge, PRNDL in instrument panel, trip odometer; warning indicators include oil pressure, water temp warning, battery, lights on, key in ignition, low fuel, low washer fluid, door ajar, trunk ajar; dual airbags; tinted windows, fixed rear windows, manual 1/4 vent windows; variable intermittent front windshield wipers, variable intermittent rear wiper; seating capacity of 5, front bucket seats with fixed adjustable headrests, driver and passenger armrests, driver seat includes 4-way direction control, passenger seat includes 4-way direction control; removeable 2nd row bench seat; front and rear height adjustable seatbelts; cloth seats, vinyl door trim insert, full cloth headliner, full carpet floor covering; interior lights include dome light, front reading lights; vanity mirrors; day-night rearview mirror; glove box, front and rear cupholders,

VOYAGER — PLYMOUTH

| CODE | DESCRIPTION | INVOICE | MSRP |

instrument panel bin, interior concealed storage; carpeted cargo floor, vinyl trunk lid, cargo light; colored grille, black side window moldings, black front windshield molding, black rear window molding, black door handles.

SE (in addition to or instead of BASE equipment): 3L V-6 SOHC 12-valve engine; 4-speed electronic overdrive with lock-up; 500-amp battery; 3.9 axle ratio; wide bodyside moldings; deluxe sound insulation; 4 wheel anti-lock braking system; front and rear 15" x 6.5" wheels; rear heat ducts; cassette player; cruise control with steering wheel controls; tachometer gauge; seating capacity of 7; full folding 2nd row bench seat; 3rd row removable full folding bench seat; cloth door trim insert; passenger seatback assist strap; steering wheel with tilt adjustment; cargo net.

Base Prices

Code	Description	Invoice	MSRP
NSHL52	Base	15845	17415
NSHH52	SE	19255	21290
	Destination Charge:	580	580

Accessories

Code	Description	Invoice	MSRP
DGA	3-Speed Automatic Transmission (Base)	NC	NC
DGB	4-Speed Automatic Transmission (Base)	213	250
DGB	4-Speed Automatic Transmission (SE)	NC	NC
BGF	4-Wheel Anti-lock Brakes (Base)	480	565
HAA	Air Conditioning	731	860
	REQUIRES 22S or 26A, or 28A. NOT AVAILABLE with (4XA) air conditioning bypass, (AAA) Climate Group II.		
4XA	Air Conditioning Bypass	NC	NC
	NOT AVAILABLE with 25C, 28C, 25E, 28E, 25N, 28N, 22T, 25B, 26B, 28B, 25D, 26D, 28D, 25L, 28L, AAA, HAA.		
YCF	Border State (Non-Federal) Emissions	145	170
	NOT AVAILABLE with (NAE) CA/CT/MA/NY Emissions.		
NAE	CA/CT/MA/NY Emissions	145	170
	NOT AVAILABLE with (YCF) Border State Emissions.		
AAA	Climate Group II	383	450
	Includes air conditioning and sunscreen glass. NOT AVAILABLE with 22S, 26A, 28A, 25E, 28E, 25N, 28N, 28E, 4XA, HAA.		
AAC	Convenience Group I (Base)	370	435
	Includes speed control, tilt steering column, power exterior mirrors. NOT AVAILABLE with (22S) Quick Order Package 22S.		
AAE	Convenience Group II (Base)	638	750
	Includes Convenience Group I: speed control, tilt steering column, power exterior mirrors; power door locks. NOT AVAILABLE with (22S) Quick Order Package 22S.		
AAE	Convenience Group II (SE)	268	315
	Includes Convenience Group I: power exterior mirrors, cruise control, tilt steering wheel; power door locks (some items may be standard on SE models). NOT AVAILABLE with 26A, 28A, 25E, 28E, 25N, 28N.		

PLYMOUTH VOYAGER

CODE	DESCRIPTION	INVOICE	MSRP
AAF	**Convenience Group III (SE)**	582	685

Includes Convenience Group II: power exterior mirrors, cruise control, tilt steering wheel, power door locks; power rear quarter windows, power windows with driver's one-touch down (some items may be standard on SE models). NOT AVAILABLE with 25E, 28E, 25N, 28N, 26A, 28A, 25D, 26D, 28D, 25L, 28L, AAE, AAG, AAH.

AAG	**Convenience Group IV (SE)**	200	235

Includes Convenience Group III: power exterior mirrors, cruise control, tilt steering wheel, power quarter vent windows, power windows with driver's one-touch down; remote keyless entry, illuminated entry, headlight off time delay (some items may be standard on SE models). NOT AVAILABLE with 26A, 28A, 26B, 25B, 28B, 25C, 28C, AAE, AAF.

AAH	**Convenience Group V (SE)**	327	385

Includes Convenience Group IV: power exterior mirrors, cruise control, tilt steering wheel, power quarter vent windows, power windows with driver's one-touch down; remote keyless entry, illuminated entry, headlight off time delay; security alarm (some items may be standard on SE models). NOT AVAILABLE with 26A, 28A, 26B, 25B, 28B, 25C, 28C, AAE, AAF.

TBB	**Conventional Spare Tire**	94	110

NOT AVAILABLE with 22S, 26A, 28A, AAP.

GKD	**Driver's Side Sliding Door (Base)**	506	595

NOT AVAILABLE with (22S) Quick Order Package 22S.

NHK	**Engine Block Heater**	30	35
EDZ	**Engine: 2.4L DOHC 16V I-4 (Base)**	NC	NC
EFA	**Engine: 3.0L MPI V6 (Base)**	655	770
EFA	**Engine: 3.0L MPI V6 (SE)**	NC	NC
EGA	**Engine: 3.3L MPI V6 (Base)**	825	970
EGA	**Engine: 3.3L MPI V6 (SE)**	170	200
EGM	**Engine: 3.3L V6 FFV (SE)**	170	200

Operates on ethanol (E85) or unleaded gasoline.

RCE	**Infinity Sound System (SE)**	336	395

200 watts through 10 speakers. NOT AVAILABLE with 26A, 28A, 26B, 25B, 28B, 25C, 28C.

AAP	**Loading & Towing Group II (SE)**	153	180

Includes HD suspension, conventional spare tire, P215/65R15 BSW AS tires, 15" wheel covers. NOT AVAILABLE with TBB, 26A, 28A.

MWG	**Luggage Rack**	149	175

NOT AVAILABLE with 22S, 26A, 28A.

22S	**Quick Order Package 22S (Base)**	NC	NC

Includes vehicle with standard equipment. REQUIRES (HAA or 4XA) and EDZ and DGA. NOT AVAILABLE with RBR, CYK, AAE, TBB, RAS, GKD, MWG, GFA.

22T	**Quick Order Package 22T (Base)**	1050	1235
	Manufacturer Discount	(1050)	(1235)
	Net Price	NC	NC

Includes air conditioning, 7 passenger seating group, rear floor silencer pad, under seat lockable drawer. REQUIRES EDZ and DGA. NOT AVAILABLE with 4XA, AAA, TBB.

VOYAGER — PLYMOUTH

CODE	DESCRIPTION	INVOICE	MSRP
25B	Quick Order Package 25B (SE)	1024	1205
	Manufacturer Discount	(859)	(1010)
	Net Price	165	195

Includes air conditioning, rear window defroster, heated exterior mirrors, 7 passenger deluxe seating. REQUIRES EGM and DGB. NOT AVAILABLE with RAZ, CYS, 4XA, AAG, AAH, AAE, AAF, AAP, AAA, TBB, NAE.

25C	Quick Order Package 25C (SE)	1768	2080
	Manufacturer Discount	(1016)	(1195)
	Net Price	752	885

Includes air conditioning, rear window defroster, heated exterior mirrors, 7 passenger deluxe seating, Expresso Group: body-color door handles, sunscreen glass, remote keyless entry, illuminated entry, headlamp time delay, tape stripe, side window outline, unique 15" full wheel covers, AM/FM stereo with CD player. REQUIRES EGM and DGB. NOT AVAILABLE with RAZ, 4XA, AAA, AAP, AAE, AAF, NAE.

25D	Quick Order Package 25D (SE)	1904	2240
	Manufacturer Discount	(1114)	(1310)
	Net Price	790	930

Includes air conditioning, 7 passenger deluxe seating, light group, dual illuminated visor vanity mirrors, deluxe sound insulation, Convenience Group III: power exterior mirrors, cruise control, tilt steering wheel, power door locks, power rear quarter windows, power windows with driver's one-touch down (some items may be standard on SE models); rear window defroster, heated exterior mirrors. REQUIRES (EGM) engine and (DGB) transmission. NOT AVAILABLE with (RAZ) radio, (NAE) emissions.

25E	Quick Order Package 25E (SE)	2648	3115
	Manufacturer Discount	(1271)	(1495)
	Net Price	1377	1620

Includes air conditioning, rear window defroster, heated exterior mirrors, deluxe sound insulation, light group, power door locks, dual illuminated visor vanity mirrors, 7 passenger deluxe seating, power rear quarter windows, Expresso Group: body-color door handles, sunscreen glass, remote keyless entry, illuminated entry, headlamp time delay, tape stripe, side window outline, unique 15" full wheel covers, AM/FM stereo with CD player. REQUIRES EGM and DGB. NOT AVAILABLE with RAZ, 4XA, AAA, AAP, AAE, AAF, NAE.

25L	Quick Order Package 25L (SE)	3013	3545
	Manufacturer Discount	(1114)	(1310)
	Net Price	1899	2235

Includes air conditioning, light group, dual illuminated visor vanity mirrors, deluxe sound insulation, Convenience Group III: power exterior mirrors, cruise control, tilt steering wheel, power door locks, power rear quarter windows, power windows with driver's one-touch down (some items may be standard on SE models); rear window defroster, heated exterior mirrors, overhead console with mini trip computer, 8-way power driver's seat, 7 passenger deluxe quad bucket seats, premium cloth highback bucket seats. REQUIRES (EGM) engine and (DGB) transmission. NOT AVAILABLE with (RAZ) radio, (NAE) emissions.

PLYMOUTH VOYAGER

CODE	DESCRIPTION	INVOICE	MSRP
25N	Quick Order Package 25N (SE)	3757	4420
	Manufacturer Discount	(1271)	(1495)
	Net Price	2486	2925

Includes air conditioning, overhead console with mini trip computer, rear window defroster, heated exterior mirrors, deluxe sound insulation, light group, power door locks, dual illuminated visor vanity mirrors, 8-way power driver's seat, 7 passenger deluxe quad bucket seats, premium cloth highback bucket seats, power rear quarter windows, Expresso Group: body-color door handles, sunscreen glass, remote keyless entry, illuminated entry, headlamp time delay, tape stripe, side window outline, unique 15" full wheel covers, AM/FM stereo with CD player. REQUIRES EGM and DGB. NOT AVAILABLE with RAZ, 4XA, AAA, AAP, AAE, AAF, NAE.

26A	Quick Order Package 26A (SE)	NC	NC

Includes vehicle with standard equipment. REQUIRES HAA or 4XA and EFA and DGB. NOT AVAILABLE with CYR, CYS, AAE, AAF, AAG, AAH, TBB, AAP, RAZ, MWG, NAE.

26B	Quick Order Package 26B (SE)	1024	1205
	Manufacturer Discount	(859)	(1010)
	Net Price	165	195

Includes air conditioning, rear window defroster, heated exterior mirrors, 7 passenger deluxe seating. REQUIRES EFA and DGB. NOT AVAILABLE with CYS, 4XA, AAG, AAH, RAZ, AAE, AAF, AAP, AAA, TBB, NAE.

26D	Quick Order Package 26D (SE)	1904	2240
	Manufacturer Discount	(1114)	(1310)
	Net Price	790	930

Includes air conditioning, rear window defroster, heated exterior mirrors, 7 passenger deluxe seats, light group, dual illuminated visor vanity mirrors, deluxe sound insulation, Convenience Group III: power exterior mirrors, cruise control, tilt steering wheel, power door locks, power rear quarter windows, power windows with driver's one-touch down (some items may be standard on SE models). REQUIRES EFA and DGB. NOT AVAILABLE with RAZ, 4XA, AAE, AAF, AAA, TBB, AAP, NAE.

28A	Quick Order Package 28A (SE)	NC	NC

Includes vehicle with standard equipment. REQUIRES HAA or 4XA and EGA and DGB and NAE. NOT AVAILABLE with CYR, CYS, AAE, AAF, AAG, AAH, TBB, AAP, RAZ, MWG.

28B	Quick Order Package 28B (SE)	1024	1205
	Manufacturer Discount	(859)	(1010)
	Net Price	165	195

Includes air conditioning, rear window defroster, heated exterior mirrors, 7 passenger deluxe seating. REQUIRES NAE and EGA and DGB. NOT AVAILABLE with CYS, 4XA, AAG, AAH, RAZ, AAA, AAE, AAF, AAP, TBB, YCF.

28C	Quick Order Package 28C (SE)	1768	2080
	Manufacturer Discount	(1016)	(1195)
	Net Price	752	885

Includes air conditioning, rear window defroster, heated exterior mirrors, 7 passenger deluxe seating, Expresso Group: body-color door handles, sunscreen glass, remote keyless entry, illuminated entry, headlamp time delay, tape stripe, side window outline, unique 15" full wheel covers, AM/FM stereo with CD player,. REQUIRES EGA and DGB and NAE. NOT AVAILABLE with RAZ, CYS, AAG, AAH, 4XA, AAA, AAP, AAE, AAF.

VOYAGER — PLYMOUTH

CODE	DESCRIPTION	INVOICE	MSRP
28D	Quick Order Package 28D (SE)	1904	2240
	Manufacturer Discount	(1114)	(1310)
	Net Price	790	930

Includes air conditioning, rear window defroster, heated exterior mirrors, 7 passenger deluxe seating, light group, dual illuminated visor vanity mirrors, deluxe sound insulation, Convenience Group III: power exterior mirrors, cruise control, tilt steering wheel, power door locks, power rear quarter windows, power windows with driver's one-touch down (some items may be standard on SE models). REQUIRES NAE and EGA and DGB. NOT AVAILABLE with RAZ, 4XA, AAA, AAE, AAF, TBB, AAP, YCF.

28E	Quick Order Package 28E (SE)	2648	3115
	Manufacturer Discount	(1271)	(1495)
	Net Price	1377	1620

Includes air conditioning, rear window defroster, heated exterior mirrors, deluxe sound insulation, light group, power door locks, dual illuminated visor vanity mirrors, 7 passenger deluxe seating, power rear quarter windows, Expresso Group: body-color door handles, sunscreen glass, remote keyless entry, illuminated entry, headlamp time delay, tape stripe, side window outline, unique 15" full wheel covers, AM/FM stereo with CD player. REQUIRES EGA and DGB and NAE. NOT AVAILABLE with RAZ, 4XA, AAA, AAP, AAE, AAF.

28L	Quick Order Package 28L (SE)	3013	3545
	Manufacturer Discount	(1114)	(1310)
	Net Price	1899	2235

Includes air conditioning, rear window defroster, heated exterior mirrors, light group, dual illuminated visor vanity mirrors, deluxe sound insulation, Convenience Group III: power exterior mirrors, cruise control, tilt steering wheel, power door locks, power rear quarter windows, power windows with driver's one-touch down (some items may be standard on SE models); overhead console with mini trip computer, 8-way power driver's seat, 7 passenger deluxe quad bucket seats, premium cloth highback bucket seats. REQUIRES EGA and DGB and NAE. NOT AVAILABLE with RAZ, CYR, 4XA, AAA, AAE, AAF, TBB, AAP, CYS.

28N	Quick Order Package 28N (SE)	3757	4420
	Manufacturer Discount	(1271)	(1495)
	Net Price	2486	2925

Includes air conditioning, overhead console with mini trip computer, rear window defroster, heated exterior mirrors, deluxe sound insulation, light group, power door locks, dual illuminated visor vanity mirrors, 8-way power driver's seat, 7 passenger deluxe quad bucket seats, premium cloth highback bucket seats, power flip-open rear quarter windows, Expresso Group: body-color door handles, sunscreen glass, remote keyless entry, illuminated entry, headlamp time delay, tape stripe, side window outline, unique 15" full wheel covers, AM/FM stereo with CD player. REQUIRES EGA and DGB and NAE. NOT AVAILABLE with RAZ, CYR, CYS, 4XA, AAA, AAP, AAE, AAF.

RAS	Radio: AM/FM Stereo with Cassette (Base)	153	180

NOT AVAILABLE with (22S) Quick Order Package 22S, (RBR) radio.

RBR	Radio: AM/FM Stereo with CD (Base)	276	325

NOT AVAILABLE with (22S) Quick Order Package 22S, (RAS) radio.

PLYMOUTH VOYAGER

CODE	DESCRIPTION	INVOICE	MSRP
RAZ	Radio: AM/FM Stereo with CD & Cassette (SE)	276	325
	Includes graphic equalizer and 10 Infinity speakers in 8 locations. NOT AVAILABLE with 26A, 28A, 25C, 28C, 25E, 28E, 25N, 28N.		
RAZ	Radio: AM/FM Stereo with CD & Cassette (SE)	153	180
	Includes graphic equalizer and 10 Infinity speakers in 8 locations. NOT AVAILABLE with 26A, 26B, 26D, 28A, 28B, 28D, 28L, 25B, 25D, 25L.		
GFA	Rear Window Defroster	196	230
	Includes windshield de-icer, heated exterior mirrors. REQUIRES AAE or AAA or AAC and 22T on Base models. NOT AVAILABLE with 25B, 26B, 28B, 25D, 26D, 28D, 25L, 28L, 25C, 28C, 25E, 28E, 25N, 28N.		
GFA	Rear Window Defroster (Base)	166	195
	Includes windshield de-icer, heated exterior mirrors.		
CYE	Seats: 7 Passenger (Base)	298	350
	Includes front reclining buckets with armrests; middle 2 passenger fixed bench with armrest and easy out roller system; rear 3 passenger folding bench with adjustable track and easy out roller system. NOT AVAILABLE with CYK, 22T.		
CYS	Seats: 7 Passenger Deluxe Quad Buckets (SE)	553	650
	Includes front reclining buckets with armrests, middle reclining and folding buckets with armrests, and rear 3 passenger reclining and folding bench with adjustable headrests, adjustable track and easy out roller system. NOT AVAILABLE with CYR, 26A, 28A, 25B, 26B, 28B, 25L, 28L, 25C, 28C, 25N, 28N.		
CYR	Seats: 7 Passenger Deluxe with Child Seats (SE)	191	225
	Includes front reclining buckets with armrests, middle 2 passenger reclining and folding bench seat with 2 integrated child seats and easy out roller system, and rear 3 passenger reclining and folding bench with adjustable headrests and easy out roller system. NOT AVAILABLE with CYS, 26A, 28A, 25L, 28L, 25N, 28N.		
CYK	Seats: 7 Passenger with Integrated Child Seat (Base)	242	285
	Includes front reclining buckets with armrests, middle 2 passenger reclining and folding bench seat with 2 integrated child seats and easy out roller system, and rear 3 passenger folding bench with adjustable track and easy out roller system. NOT AVAILABLE with (22S) Quick Order Package 22S, (CYE) seating group: 7 passenger.		
AWS	Smokers Group	17	20
	Includes cigar lighter and ashtrays.		

Don't forget to swing by the Townhall when you visit Edmund's website at http://www.edmunds.com. Talk to our editors and compare notes on your favorite cars and trucks. Join others to scope out smart shopping stategies, get answers to your questions, or share your expertise. To get to the Townhall, just click on the link on the homepage or go directly to http://www.edmunds.com/edweb/townhall/welcomeconflist.html.

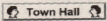

TRANS SPORT — PONTIAC

| CODE | DESCRIPTION | INVOICE | MSRP |

1998 TRANS SPORT

1998 Pontiac Trans Sport Montana

What's New?

Short-wheelbase models get the dual sliding doors and power sliding door options. Side-impact airbags are standard, and a white two-tone paint job is new. Second generation airbags are standard for front seat occupants.

Review

The difference is like night and day. Pontiac's new Trans Sport is so much better than the previous version that there really is no comparison. So forget about the bullet-nosed, plastic-bodied, Dustbuster Trans Sport of yesteryear. Pontiac is rewriting Chrysler's book on minivans.

How so? For starters, the Trans Sport features a standard 3.4-liter, 180-horsepower V6 engine. That's substantially more power than Chrysler offers with its top-of-the-line motor. Available, just like on the Chrysler vans, is a driver's-side sliding door. Buyers needing eight-passenger seating can select the Trans Sport, the only minivan on the market offering this configuration. Chrysler vans feature roll-away bench seats, but they're heavy suckers to unload. The Trans Sport can be equipped with modular seats that weight just 38 pounds each, and are a breeze to remove.

This is one safe van, on paper. Traction control is optional, while dual airbags and anti-lock brakes are standard. For 1998, side airbags are also part of the standard equipment list. Daytime running lights operate the parking lamps rather than the headlights. If GM provided a similar arrangement on all DRL-equipped models, we bet the negative criticism for them wouldn't be nearly as severe or widespread. The new Trans Sport meets current side impact standards, too. Be warned, however, that the Trans Sport fared very poorly in offset crash testing conducted by the Insurance Institute for Highway Safety, but peformed remarkably well during federal head-on crush runs. There are no federal standards governing offset crashworthiness.

The sliding door on the right side of the van can be equipped to open automatically with the push of a button. The ventilation system features a replaceable pollen filter, which is good news for allergy sufferers. Optional rear audio controls allow rear passengers to listen to a CD, cassette, or stereo via headphones while front passengers listen to their choice of any of the three mediums simultaneously.

PONTIAC TRANS SPORT

| CODE | DESCRIPTION | INVOICE | MSRP |

Around town, the Trans Sport feels downright spunky, with good throttle response and car-like handling. Braking is excellent for a 4,000-pound vehicle. Visibility is uncompromised, thanks in part to the huge exterior mirrors that effectively eliminate blind spots. Front seats are quite comfortable, and most controls are easy to see and use. If it weren't for the expansive windshield and high driving position, drivers might not realize the Trans Sport was a van.

Pontiac is pushing the Montana package, making Trans Sports so equipped the focal point of the lineup. Product planners claim that the Montana bridges the gap between sport utility and minivan. Ummm, we don't think so. It takes more than body-cladding, white-letter tires, alloy wheels, fog lights, and traction control to match an SUV when it comes to capability. Heck, the press kit conveniently left out ground clearance in the specification table. Image is another matter, and the Montana does blur the line between minivan and sport/utility in terms of styling, but nobody will mistake this Pontiac for a Jeep Grand Cherokee.

Sounds good, for a minivan. There are problems, however. Chief among them are seriously uncomfortable modular seats that provide little in the way of thigh and leg support. When sitting in one of the rear chairs, adult passengers will grow cranky quickly. The automatic sliding door is designed to reverse direction when it determines that an object is blocking its closure path. Be warned; the door doesn't behave like an elevator door. It can almost knock unsuspecting adults over before reversing. Teach children that they are strong enough to push the door back, and not to be afraid of getting closed in if the door doesn't stop immediately. Other flaws include difficult-to-reach center console storage, lack of a power lock switch in the cargo area, and excessive amounts of cheap-looking plastic inside.

Basically, we like the Trans Sport for its standard and optional features, combined with a pleasantly surprising fun-to-drive demeanor. So long as adult passengers drive or call shotgun, Pontiac's people mover makes perfect sense.

Safety Data

Driver Airbag: *Standard*
Side Airbag: *Standard*
Traction Control: *Optional*
Driver Crash Test Grade: *Good*

Passenger Airbag: *Standard*
4-Wheel ABS: *Standard*
Integrated Child Seat(s): *Optional*
Passenger Crash Test Grade: *Good*

Standard Equipment

SE 3-DOOR REGULAR LENGTH: 3.4L V-6 OHV SMPI 12-valve engine; 4-speed electronic overdrive automatic transmission with lock-up; 600-amp battery with run down protection; 105-amp alternator; front wheel drive, 3.29 axle ratio; stainless steel exhaust; front independent strut suspension with anti-roll bar, front coil springs, front shocks, rear non-independent suspension with anti-roll bar, rear coil springs, rear shocks; power rack-and-pinion steering; front disc/rear drum brakes with 4 wheel anti-lock braking system; 20 gal capacity fuel tank; 3 doors with sliding right rear passenger door, liftback rear cargo door; front and rear body-colored bumpers with rear step pad; body-colored bodyside molding, body-colored bodyside cladding, rocker panel extensions; monotone paint; aero-composite halogen fully automatic headlamps with daytime running lights; additional exterior lights include front fog/driving lights, center high mounted stop light, underhood light; driver and passenger power remote black folding outside mirrors; front and rear 15" x 6" steel wheels with full wheel covers; P205/70SR15 BSW AS front and rear tires; inside under cargo mounted compact steel spare wheel; air conditioning, air filter; AM/FM stereo with clock, seek-scan, 4 speakers and window grid antenna; power door locks, child safety rear door locks, power remote hatch release; 2 power accessory outlets, driver foot rest; analog instrumentation display includes tachometer gauge, water temp gauge, PRNDL in instrument panel, trip odometer; warning indicators include oil pressure, water temp warning, battery, low oil level, low coolant, lights on, key in ignition, low fuel, door ajar; dual airbags, seat mounted side airbags; tinted windows, vented rear windows, manual 1/4 vent windows; variable intermittent front windshield wipers, fixed interval rear wiper; seating capacity of 7, front bucket seats with adjustable headrests, driver and passenger armrests, driver seat includes 6-way

TRANS SPORT — PONTIAC

CODE	DESCRIPTION	INVOICE	MSRP

direction control with lumbar support and easy entry feature, passenger seat includes 4-way direction control with lumbar support; removeable full folding 2nd row bench seat with fixed rear outboard headrests, 3rd row removeable full folding bench seat with fixed headrests; front height adjustable seatbelts; cloth seats, cloth door trim insert, full cloth headliner, full carpet floor covering with carpeted floor mats; interior lights include dome light with fade, front reading lights; sport steering wheel with tilt adjustment; vanity mirrors; day-night rearview mirror; engine cover console with storage, locking glove box with light, front and rear cupholders, instrument panel covered bin, interior concealed storage, 2 seat back storage pockets, driver and passenger door bins, rear door bins, front underseat tray; carpeted cargo floor, plastic trunk lid, cargo light; body-colored grille, black side window moldings, black front windshield molding, black rear window molding, body-colored door handles.

4-DOOR REGULAR LENGTH (in addition to or instead of 3-DOOR REGULAR LENGTH equipment): Body-colored bodyside insert; cassette stereo with theft deterrent; cruise control; 40-60 folding 2nd row split-bench seat; 3rd row 50-50 folding split-bench seat; cargo net.

4-DOOR EXTENDED LENGTH (in addition to or instead of 4-DOOR REGULAR LENGTH equipment): 25 gal capacity fuel tank.

Base Prices

Code	Description	Invoice	MSRP
2UN06	3-door Regular Length	18860	20840
2UN16	4-door Regular Length	20254	22380
2UM16	4-door Extended Length	20896	23090
	Destination Charge:	570	570

Accessories

Code	Description	Invoice	MSRP
AG1	6-Way Power Driver's Seat	240	270
	NOT AVAILABLE with (1SA) Option Package 1SA, (1SB) Option Package 1SB.		
AG9	6-Way Power Passenger's Seat	271	305
	REQUIRES ABB or ABD or ZP8. NOT AVAILABLE with 1SA, 1SB, 1SC.		
ABD	7 Passenger Seating with 2nd Row Captains Chairs	236	265
	Includes 50/50 modular split bench. REQUIRES 1SD on 3-door. NOT AVAILABLE with ABB, ZP8, 1SA, 1SB, AN2, AN5.		
ABD	7 Passenger Seating with 2nd Row Captains Chairs (3-door)	534	600
	Includes 50/50 modular split bench. REQUIRES 1SC and ABA. NOT AVAILABLE with ABB, ZP8, 1SA, 1SB, AN2, AN5.		
ABB	7 Passenger Seating with Rear Buckets	102	115
	REQUIRES 1SD.		
ABB	7 Passenger Seating with Rear Buckets (3-door)	400	450
	REQUIRES 1SB or 1SC. NOT AVAILABLE with 1SA.		
ABA	7 Passenger Seating with Split-Back Rear (3-door)	298	335
	Includes 40/60 split and 50/50 modular split bench. REQUIRES 1SB or 1SC. NOT AVAILABLE with 1SA.		
ZP8	8 Passenger Seating	236	265
	Includes bucket/split bench seating. REQUIRES 1SD. NOT AVAILABLE with 1SA.		
ZP8	8 Passenger Seating (3-door)	534	600
	Includes bucket/split bench seating. REQUIRES 1SB or 1SC. NOT AVAILABLE with 1SA.		

PONTIAC TRANS SPORT

CODE	DESCRIPTION	INVOICE	MSRP
G67	Automatic Level Control	178	200
	Includes saddle bag storage. REQUIRES (XPU) tires. NOT AVAILABLE with (1SA) Option Package 1SA.		
YF5	California Emissions	151	170
	AVAILABLE with (NG1) MA/NY Emissions.		
AJ1	Deep Tinted Glass (3-door)	245	275
	REQUIRES 1SA or 1SB.		
AN5	Dual Integrated Child Safety Seats	200	225
	REQUIRES ABA or ABB or ZP8. NOT AVAILABLE with 1SA, ABD, AN2.		
C49	Electric Rear Window Defogger (3-door)	160	180
	REQUIRES 1SA or 1SB.		
K05	Engine Block Heater	18	20
UZ5	Extended Range Coaxial Speakers	44	50
	REQUIRES (U1C) radio. NOT AVAILABLE with (1SA) Option Package 1SA.		
C34	Front & Rear Air Conditioning (Extended 4-door)	400	450
	Includes deep tinted glass and saddle bag storage. REQUIRES (WX4) Montana Package or (G67) automatic level control.		
C34	Front & Rear Air Conditioning (Extended 4-door)	409	460
	Includes deep tinted glass and saddle bag storage.		
AN2	Integrated Child Safety Seat	111	125
	REQUIRES ABA or ABB or ZP8. NOT AVAILABLE with 1SA, ABD, AN5.		
WJ7	Leather Seating Area Trim	939	1055
	Includes leather-wrapped steering wheel with steering wheel mounted radio controls. REQUIRES AG1 and UT6 or U1C or UP3 or UM1. NOT AVAILABLE with 1SA, 1SB.		
UK3	Leather-Wrapped Steering Wheel	165	185
	Includes steering wheel mounted radio controls. NOT AVAILABLE with (1SA) Option Package 1SA.		
V54	Luggage Rack	156	175
NG1	MA/NY Emissions	151	170
	NOT AVAILABLE with (YF5)		
WX4	Montana Package with 1SC (Extended 4-door)	1055	1185
	Includes 'Montana' identification, luggage rack, 15" aluminum wheels, self sealing tires, traction control, automatic level control, saddle bag storage, charcoal accent lower body cladding, touring suspension package, P215/70R15 WOL tires. REQUIRES (1SC) Option Package 1SC.		
WX4	Montana Package with 1SC (Regular 4-door)	1090	1225
	Includes 'Montana' identification, luggage rack, 15" aluminum wheels, self sealing tires, traction control, automatic level control, saddle bag storage, charcoal accent lower body cladding, touring suspension package, P215/70R15 WOL tires. REQUIRES (1SC) Option Package 1SC.		
WX4	Montana Package with 1SD (Extended 4-door)	899	1010
	Includes 'Montana' identification, luggage rack, 15" aluminum wheels, self sealing tires, traction control, automatic level control, saddle bag storage, charcoal accent lower body cladding, touring suspension package, P215/70R15 WOL tires. REQUIRES (1SD) Option Package 1SD.		

TRANS SPORT — PONTIAC

CODE	DESCRIPTION	INVOICE	MSRP
WX4	**Montana Package with 1SD (Regular 4-door)**	934	1050
	Includes 'Montana' identification, luggage rack, 15" aluminum wheels, self sealing tires, traction control, automatic level control, saddle bag storage, charcoal accent lower body cladding, touring suspension package, P215/70R15 WOL tires. REQUIRES (1SD) Option Package 1SD.		
1SA	**Option Package 1SA (3-door)**	NC	NC
	Includes vehicle with standard equipment. NOT AVAILABLE with E58, DK6, R6A, ABA, ABB, ABD, ZP8, WJ7, AN2, AN5, AG1, AG9, UT6, U1C, UP3, UM1, UK3, UZ5, G67, NW9, V92.		
1SB	**Option Package 1SB (3-door)**	409	460
	Includes cargo net, cruise control, AM/FM stereo with cassette and 4 speakers. NOT AVAILABLE with DK6, R6A, ABD, WJ7, AG1, AG9, UT6, UP3, UM1, NW9, V92.		
1SB	**Option Package 1SB (4-door)**	NC	NC
	Includes vehicle with standard equipment. NOT AVAILABLE with R6A, DK6, ABD, WJ7, AG1, AG9, UT6, UP3, UM1, NW9, V92.		
1SC	**Option Package 1SC (3-door)**	1290	1450
	Includes cruise control, cargo net, AM/FM stereo with cassette and 4 speakers, perimeter lighting, power door locks, power windows with driver's side express down, rear power vent window, electric rear window defogger, deep tinted glass, remote keyless entry. NOT AVAILABLE with (R6A) Safety and Security Package, (AG9) 6-way power passenger's seat.		
1SC	**Option Package 1SC (4-door)**	828	930
	Includes perimeter lighting, power door locks, power windows with driver's side express down, rear power vent window, electric rear window defogger, deep tinted glass, remote keyless entry. NOT AVAILABLE with (AG9) 6-way power passenger's seat.		
1SD	**Option Package 1SD (3-door)**	2221	2495
	Includes cruise control, cargo net, AM/FM stereo with cassette and 4 speakers, perimeter lighting, power door locks, power windows with driver's side express down, rear power vent window, electric rear window defogger, deep tinted glass, remote keyless entry, 6-way power driver's seat, roof console with compass/temperature display, dual illuminated visor vanity mirrors, luggage rack, 7 passenger seating with split-back rear bench.		
1SD	**Option Package 1SD (4-door)**	1460	1640
	Includes perimeter lighting, power door locks, power windows with driver's side express down, rear power vent window, electric rear window defogger, deep tinted glass, remote keyless entry, 6-way power driver's seat, roof console with compass/temperature display, dual illuminated visor vanity mirrors, luggage rack.		
E58	**Power Sliding Door**	343	385
	Includes rear power vent window. NOT AVAILABLE with (1SA) Option Package 1SA.		
A31	**Power Windows with Driver's Side Express Down (3-door)**	289	325
	NOT AVAILABLE with (1SA) Option Package 1SA.		
UT6	**Radio: AM/FM Stereo with Cassette**	147	165
	Includes rear seat audio controls, seek-scan, equalizer, auto reverse cassette player, digital clock, leather-wrapped steering wheel, steering wheel mounted radio controls, extended range coaxial speakers. REQUIRES WJ7. NOT AVAILABLE with U1C, UP3, UM1, 1SA, 1SB.		

PONTIAC TRANS SPORT

CODE	DESCRIPTION	INVOICE	MSRP
UT6	**Radio: AM/FM Stereo with Cassette**	312	350
	Includes rear seat audio controls, seek-scan, equalizer, auto reverse cassette player, digital clock, leather-wrapped steering wheel with steering wheel mounted radio controls, extended range coaxial speakers. REQUIRES 1SC or 1SD. NOT AVAILABLE with 1SA, 1SB.		
UN6	**Radio: AM/FM Stereo with Cassette (3-door)**	174	195
	Includes 4 speakers. REQUIRES 1SA.		
U1C	**Radio: AM/FM Stereo with CD**	89	100
	Includes 4 speakers and digital clock. REQUIRES 1SB or 1SC or 1SD. NOT AVAILABLE with 1SA.		
UP3	**Radio: AM/FM Stereo with CD**	400	450
	Includes seek-scan, equalizer, digital clock, leather-wrapped steering wheel with steering wheel mounted radio controls, rear seat radio controls with jack, extended range coaxial speakers. REQUIRES 1SC or 1SD. NOT AVAILABLE with 1SA, 1SB.		
UP3	**Radio: AM/FM Stereo with CD**	236	265
	Includes seek-scan, equalizer, digital clock, leather-wrapped steering wheel, steering wheel mounted radio controls, rear seat radio controls with jack, extended range coaxial speakers. REQUIRES WJ7. NOT AVAILABLE with UT6, U1C, UM1, 1SA, 1SB.		
UM1	**Radio: AM/FM Stereo with CD & Cassette**	325	365
	Includes rear seat audio controls, dual playback, seek-scan, digital clock, leather-wrapped steering wheel with steering wheel mounted radio controls, extended range coaxial speakers. REQUIRES WJ7. NOT AVAILABLE with UT6, U1C, UP3, 1SA, 1SB.		
UM1	**Radio: AM/FM Stereo with CD & Cassette**	490	550
	Includes dual playback, seek-scan, digital clock, leather-wrapped steering wheel with steering wheel mounted radio controls, extended range coaxial speakers. REQUIRES 1SC or 1SD. NOT AVAILABLE with 1SA, 1SB.		
AU0	**Remote Keyless Entry (3-door)**	134	150
	NOT AVAILABLE with (1SA) Option Package 1SA.		
DK6	**Roof Console**	156	175
	Includes storage and driver's information center with compass and temperature display; dual illuminated visor vanity mirrors. REQUIRES (1SC) Option Package 1SC.		
R6A	**Safety & Security Package**	187	210
	Includes theft deterrence, remote keyless entry, self sealing tires. NOT AVAILABLE with 1SA, 1SB, 1SC.		
R6A	**Safety & Security Package with WX4 (4-door)**	53	60
	Includes theft deterrence, remote keyless entry, self sealing tires. REQUIRES (WX4) Montana Package. NOT AVAILABLE with (1SB) Option Package 1SB.		
XPU	**Tires: P215/70R15 Touring SBR (Extended 4-door)**	31	35
XPU	**Tires: P215/70R15 Touring SBR (Regular)**	67	75
P42	**Tires: Self Sealing**	134	150
	REQUIRES XPU or WX4.		
NW9	**Traction Control**	174	195
	REQUIRES (G67) automatic level control. NOT AVAILABLE with (1SA) Option Package 1SA, (1SB) Option Package 1SB.		

TRANS SPORT — PONTIAC

CODE	DESCRIPTION	INVOICE	MSRP
V92	Trailer Towing Package .... *Includes heavy duty flasher, wiring provisions, HD radiator cooler; HD transmission oil cooler, automatic level control, saddle bag storage, engine oil cooler, 3,500-lb. rating. NOT AVAILABLE with (1SA) Option Package 1SA, (1SB) Option Package 1SB.*	134	150
D84	Two-Tone Paint .... *Includes light taupe lower accent color.*	111	125
PH3	Wheels: 15" Painted Aluminum .... *REQUIRES (XPU) tires or (P42) tires.*	249	280

Take Advantage of Warranty Gold!

Savings up to 50% off Dealer's Extended Warranty Prices. Protect and enhance YOUR investment with the best extended warranty available.

Call Toll Free 1-800-580-9889

Save hundreds, even thousands, off the sticker price of the new car _you_ want.

**Call Autovantage®
your FREE auto-buying service**

1-800-201-7703

No purchase required. No fees.

SUBARU FORESTER

| CODE | DESCRIPTION | INVOICE | MSRP |

1998 FORESTER

1998 Subaru Forester

What's New?

Subaru attacks the mini-SUV market head-on with the Forester, which actually consists of an SUV body on an Impreza platform with a Legacy engine under the hood. The most car-like of the mini-utes, Forester is also the most powerful. Airbags remain the full power variety, despite new rules allowing lower deployment speeds.

Review

What do you do when sport-utility buyers won't drive home in your all-wheel drive station wagon, which is dressed up like an SUV, because it's too "wagony" in appearance? If you're gutsy like Subaru, you put a taller, more squared-off body on your wagon chassis, and call it good. The new Forester is a Subaru parts bin exercise, and since the parts bin is rather small at Fuji Heavy Industries, which owns the upstart all-wheel drive automaker, the car is cobbled together from a mixture of Impreza and Legacy bits.

Based on the rally-proven Impreza platform, the Forester uses the same AWD system found in other Subaru models. The 2.5-liter boxer engine comes from the Legacy Outback, and makes 165-horsepower in the Forester. This means the Forester has gobs more power than its primary competitors.

Also, thanks to its hunkered-down stance, low center of gravity, and car-based foundation, the Forester handles better than the Chevrolet Tracker, Honda CR-V, Suzuki Sidekick, and Toyota RAV4. The trade-off is lower ground clearance and less capable off-road ability, but you weren't going to go too far off the beaten path anyway, were you? (Wink, wink, nudge, nudge.)

Inside is generous room for four adults, with a rear center position marked off for a fifth rider in a pinch. Cargo space is equivalent to what you'd find in the RAV4 or Tracker, and storage room abounds.

Three Forester models are available; the base, the mid-level L, and the high-end S. Air conditioning, roof rack, rear defogger, tachometer, power windows, tilt steering, rear wiper/washer, and an 80-watt cassette stereo are standard on the base model. The L adds anti-lock brakes, power door locks, and cosmetic goodies. With a base price barely over $20,000, we believe the

FORESTER  SUBARU

| CODE | DESCRIPTION | INVOICE | MSRP |

L will be Subaru's volume seller. The uplevel S gets a toothy chrome grille, alloy wheels, bigger tires, rear disc brakes, cruise control, and upgraded interior trimmings. Remote keyless entry is optional on the L and S, while leather can be added to the S only. Options include CD player, alloy wheels, cruise control, trailer hitch, and a variety of cosmetic upgrades.

While we are partial to the Impreza Outback Sport and Legacy Outback models, the Forester will attract buyers who want an inexpensive, functional, all-wheel drive vehicle that looks like a truck and drives like a car. As long as Subaru can keep a lid on pricing, the Forester should pick right up where the Outback wagons leave off.

Safety Data

Driver Airbag: *Standard*
Side Airbag: *Not Available*
Traction Control: *Not Available*
Driver Crash Test Grade: *Not Available*

Passenger Airbag: *Standard*
4-Wheel ABS: *Standard*
Integrated Child Seat(s): *Not Available*
Passenger Crash Test Grade: *Not Available*

Standard Equipment

FORESTER BASE: 2.5L H-4 DOHC SMPI 16-valve engine; 5-speed overdrive manual transmission; full-time 4 wheel drive, 4.44 axle ratio; steel exhaust; HD ride suspension, front independent strut suspension with anti-roll bar, front coil springs, front shocks, rear independent strut suspension with anti-roll bar, rear coil springs, rear shocks; power rack-and-pinion steering with engine speed-sensing assist; front disc/rear drum brakes with 4 wheel anti-lock braking system; 15.9 gal capacity fuel tank; liftback rear cargo door; trailer harness; roof rack; front and rear body-colored bumpers; body-colored bodyside cladding, rocker panel extensions; two-tone paint; aero-composite halogen auto off headlamps; additional exterior lights include front fog/driving lights, center high mounted stop light; driver and passenger manual black folding outside mirrors; front and rear 15" x 6" silver styled steel wheels; P205/70SR15 OWL AS front and rear tires; inside under cargo mounted full-size conventional steel spare wheel; air conditioning, rear heat ducts; AM/FM stereo with clock, seek-scan, cassette, 4 speakers and fixed antenna; child safety rear door locks; 2 power accessory outlets, driver foot rest; analog instrumentation display includes tachometer gauge, water temp gauge, trip odometer; warning indicators include oil pressure, battery, key in ignition, low fuel, door ajar, trunk ajar; dual airbags; tinted windows, power front windows with driver 1-touch down, power rear windows, fixed 1/4 vent windows; fixed interval front windshield wipers, rear window wiper, rear window defroster; seating capacity of 5, front bucket seats with tilt adjustable headrests, driver seat includes 6-way direction control with lumbar support, passenger seat includes 4-way direction control; 50-50 folding rear bench seat with reclining adjustable rear headrest; front height adjustable seatbelts; cloth seats, cloth door trim insert, full cloth headliner, full carpet floor covering; interior lights include dome light, front reading lights; steering wheel with tilt adjustment; day-night rearview mirror; full floor console, mini overhead console with storage, locking glove box with light, front and rear cupholders, instrument panel bin, driver and passenger door bins; carpeted cargo floor, plastic trunk lid, cargo tie downs, cargo light, cargo concealed storage; black grille, black side window moldings, black front windshield molding, black rear window molding, black door handles.

L (in addition to or instead of BASE equipment): Front and rear mud flaps; rear step bumper; front and rear 16" x 6.5" alloy wheels; full-size temporary spare wheel; cargo cover; 4-speed electronic automatic transmission with lock-up (on automatic models).

S (in addition to or instead of L equipment): 4 wheel disc brakes; cruise control; center armrest with storage; carpeted floor mats; vanity mirrors; 2 seat back storage pockets; chrome grille, driver and passenger power remote black folding outside mirrors; front bucket seats.

S with COLD PACKAGE (in addition to or instead of S equipment): Heated side view mirrors; heated driver and passenger seats.

SUBARU FORESTER

CODE	DESCRIPTION	INVOICE	MSRP

Base Prices

CODE	DESCRIPTION	INVOICE	MSRP
WCA	Base (5-speed)	17454	18695
WCB	L (5-speed)	18034	19995
WCC	L (automatic)	18745	20795
WCD	S (5-speed)	19925	22195
WCE	S (automatic)	20636	22995
WCF	S with Cold Package (5-speed)	20191	22495
WCG	S with Cold Package (automatic)	20902	23295
	Destination Charge:	495	495

Accessories

CODE	DESCRIPTION	INVOICE	MSRP
KWA	Air Filter	56	85
KWB	Beige Armrest Extension (L/S)	58	89
PWF	Bumper Cover (Base)	40	61
EWC	CD Auto Changer	517	689
EWB	CD Player	315	420
CWB	Cruise Control (5-speed) (Base/L)	221	340
CWA	Cruise Control (automatic) (L)	221	340
LWB	Custom Tail Pipe Cover	26	39
PWA	Differential Protector	104	159
NWE	Dual Power Outlet	58	88
LWE	Forester Decal	13	20
NWC	Gauge Pack — Beige Housing (L/S)	296	395
NWD	Gauge Pack — Gray Housing	296	395
KWC	Gray Armrest Extension	58	89
BWB	Gray Carpet Floor Covers (Base)	49	75
PWE	Grille Guard	282	375
PWB	Hood Deflector	48	73
RWA	Keyless Entry System (L/S)	146	225
IWE	Leather Seats — Beige (L/S)	975	1295
IWF	Leather Seats — Gray	975	1295
IWC	Leather Shift Knob (5-speed)	30	45
IWD	Leather Shift Knob (automatic) (L/S)	49	75
OWA	Luggage Compartment Cover — Beige (L/S)	80	122
OWB	Luggage Compartment Cover — Gray	80	122
MWA	Rear Cargo Net	27	41
MWD	Rear Cargo Tray (Base)	47	73
LWC	Rear Window Dust Deflector	72	110
RWB	Security System Upgrade Kit (L/S)	82	125
PWD	Side Underguard Bar	228	350
LWD	Splash Guards (Base)	64	98
DWB	Subwoofer/Amplifier	202	310
LWG	Trailer Hitch	192	295
DWC	Tweeter Kit	65	100
DWA	Upgraded Speaker Kit	127	195

FORESTER   SUBARU

CODE	DESCRIPTION	INVOICE	MSRP
MSV	Wheel Locks	18	34
HWA	Wheels: 15" Aluminum (Base/L)	447	595
IWH	Woodgrain Kit (5-speed) (L/S)	130	199
IWG	Woodgrain Kit (automatic) (L/S)	130	199

Take Advantage of Warranty Gold!

Savings up to 50% off Dealer's Extended Warranty Prices. Protect and enhance YOUR investment with the best extended warranty available.

Call Toll Free 1-800-580-9889

Don't forget to swing by the Townhall when you visit Edmund's website at http://www.edmunds.com. Talk to our editors and compare notes on your favorite cars and trucks. Join others to scope out smart shopping stategies, get answers to your questions, or share your expertise. To get to the Townhall, just click on the link on the homepage or go directly to http://www.edmunds.com/edweb/townhall/welcomeconflist.html.

Town Hall

One 15-minute call could save you 15% or more on car insurance.

GEICO DIRECT

America's 6th Largest Automobile Insurance Company

1-800-555-2758

SUZUKI SIDEKICK

| CODE | DESCRIPTION | INVOICE | MSRP |

1997 SIDEKICK

1997 Suzuki Sidekick Convertible

What's New?

A JS Sport 2WD model is added to the Sidekick lineup. It has a DOHC engine that makes 120-horsepower at 6500 rpm. There are no changes to the rest of the Sidekick line.

Review

Even folks who find it easy to fault small sport-utes run the risk of falling for a Sidekick—especially the convertible model. Neither a true truck nor a car, this mini SUV has created a niche that other manufacturers are rushing to capitalize on. The Geo Tracker that's sold by Chevrolet dealers is basically identical, and the Kia Sportage is a new competitor. Toyota introduced the RAV4 to do battle with the Sidekick, and Honda is rushing to bring their CRV over from Japan to do the same. Suzuki aims the Sidekick squarely at teens and twenty-somethings, but older adventurers are likely to find it irresistible, too.

The Sidekick is available in two body styles and two series totaling three trim levels. Basic Sidekicks come with a frisky 16-valve, 95-horsepower engine in JS or JX trim. The JS is a two-wheel drive runabout; the JX is a four-wheel drive mountain goat. Convertible and four-door hardtop models are available. New for 1996 is a Sport model, which is offered only with the four-door body style in JX, JS and JLX trim. Hallmarks of the Sport include a larger, more powerful twin-cam engine good for 120 horsepower, and a track that has been increased by two inches for increased stability and response. Sixteen-inch tires and wheels, a shiny grille, and a two-tone paint scheme set the Sport model even further apart from garden-variety Sidekicks.

Four-wheel anti-lock brakes are optional on Sidekick; standard on Sidekick Sport. Exclusive to the Sport is a 100-watt Alpine stereo system, cruise control (on the JLX only), security alarm system, power windows and locks, split-fold rear seat, remote fuel door release, cloth door trim, power remote mirrors, rear window wiper/washer and overhead map lights. The Sport also gets unique paint colors from which to select.

Frankly, we think that the base Sidekick is the best looking vehicle. The Sport's two-tone paint and chrome-ringed grille make the Sidekick look like a little freckle-faced kid wearing an Armani suit. The monochromatic look of the base model, combined with the Sport's engine and track width, would be a hot setup — too bad Suzuki doesn't see it that way.

SIDEKICK

| CODE | DESCRIPTION | INVOICE | MSRP |

Safety Data

Driver Airbag: *Standard*
Side Airbag: *Not Available*
Traction Control: *Not Available*
Driver Crash Test Grade: *Poor*

Passenger Airbag: *Standard*
4-Wheel ABS: *Optional*
Integrated Child Seat(s): *Not Available*
Passenger Crash Test Grade: *Average*

Standard Equipment

JS: 1.6-liter SOHC 16-valve 4-cylinder engine, recirculating ball steering, power front disc/rear drum brakes, fuel tank skid plate, halogen headlamps, swing-open rear gate with spare tire carrier, P195/75R15 A/S tires (2WD), P205/75R15 tires (4WD), 15" styled wheels, dual airbags, full carpeting, tinted glass, 2-speed intermittent windshield wipers, dual outside mirrors, side window de-misters, DRLS, reclining cloth front seats, fold down rear bench seat, center console, dual cup holders, tachometer, and trip meter.

JX (in addition to or instead of JS): 2-speed transfer case (4WD), manual locking hubs (4WD), and rear skid plate (4WD).

SPORT JX (in addition to or instead of JX): 1.8-liter DOHC engine, 4-wheel disc brakes, 18.5 gallon fuel tank, 4WD indicator lamp, P215/65R16 A/S tires, full size spare tire, passenger vanity mirror, power exterior mirrors, power windows with driver's express down, power locks, air conditioning, map lights, and rear window defogger.

SPORT JLX (in addition to or instead of SPORT JX): 4-wheel anti-lock brakes, automatic locking hubs, spare tire cover, rear window wiper/washer, 16" 5-spoke alloy wheels, cloth door trim, and cruise control.

Base Prices

Code	Description	Invoice	MSRP
FCE623V	2WD JS Convertible (5-spd)	12254	12899
LTL663V	2WD JS 4-Door (5-spd)	13391	14399
LTL693V	2WD JS 4-Door (auto)	14274	15349
FCE653V	2WD JS Convertible (auto)	12824	13499
FAE623V	4WD JX Convertible (5-spd)	13642	14669
LPL663V	4WD JX 4-Door (5-spd)	14559	15999
LPL693V	4WD JX 4-Door (auto)	15423	16949
FAE653V	4WD JX Convertible (auto)	14200	15269
LRL77SV	4WD JX Sport 4-Door (5-spd)	16106	17699
LRL78SV	4WD JX Sport 4-Door (auto)	17016	18699
LRL77TV	4WD JLX Sport 4-Door (5-spd)	17471	19199
LRL78TV	4WD JLX Sport 4-Door (auto)	18381	20199
Destination Charge:		420	420

Accessories

—	4-wheel Anti-lock Brakes (JS/JX/JLX) *Standard on Sport models.*	540	600

SUZUKI X-90

| CODE | DESCRIPTION | INVOICE | MSRP |

1997 X-90

1997 Suzuki X-90

What's New?

No changes to Suzuki's interesting alternative to AWD vehicles.

Review

Suzuki's cool new X-90 sport ute takes the place of the now defunct Samurai in the maker's lineup. Larger, more powerful, and more sophisticated than the Samurai ever dreamed of being, the X-90 is aimed squarely at young singles with disposable income and no responsibilities.

The X-90 is an amalgam of two-seater sports coupe, convertible and four-wheel drive sport utility. The two-seat cockpit sits beneath a T-top roof, just forward of an 8.4 cubic foot conventional trunk, and on top of a two- or four-wheel drive chassis. Body on frame construction is motivated by a 95-horsepower four cylinder engine. An automatic transmission is available in place of the standard five-speed manual gear changer.

The only part of this formula that seems wrong is the 1.6-liter engine. Its power output seems to be a bit on the meager side for a vehicle with such sporting pretensions. The Sidekick Sport's 120-horsepower, 1.8-liter engine should at least be an option on the heavier four-wheel drive model.

Dual airbags, four-wheel anti-lock brakes and daytime running lights are standard. All X-90's come equipped with power windows and locks, power steering, alloy wheels, and intermittent wipers. Order four-wheel drive and you'll get cruise control, a security alarm and an Alpine stereo.

Suzuki's taking a chance here, creating a new niche in the SUV market. We think that the X-90 will find limited success in climates and terrains where its four-wheel drive will have some relevancy, and in places where style-conscious buyers don't find what they want in the slightly more versatile Geo Tracker, Jeep Wrangler, and Suzuki's own Sidekick convertible. The X-90's T-top roof is easier to operate than the soft tops of any of those vehicles, but this new Suzuki won't carry more than two people; the others will carry four. Us? We'd rather have a used two-year old Miata for the same price, and forget about traversing tough mountain trails in favor of twisty two-lane highways.

X-90

| CODE | DESCRIPTION | | INVOICE | MSRP |

Safety Data

Driver Airbag: *Standard*
Side Airbag: *Not Available*
Traction Control: *Not Available*
Driver Crash Test Grade: *Not Available*

Passenger Airbag: *Standard*
4-Wheel ABS: *Optional*
Integrated Child Seat(s): *Not Available*
Passenger Crash Test Grade: *Not Available*

Standard Equipment

2WD: 1.6-liter SOHC 4-cylinder engine, power recirculating ball steering, power assist front disc/rear drum brakes, MacPherson strut, coil spring front suspension; coil spring, wishbone, trailing link rear suspension; 11.1 gallon fuel tank, daytime running lights, halogen headlamps, tinted glass, intermittent windshield wipers, dual outside mirrors, lockable fuel filler door, remvable T-top, 15" spoke alloy wheels, dual airbags, power windows, power door locks, cloth interior, tachometer, center console, and rear window defogger.

4WD (in addition to or instead of 2WD): 2-speed transfer case, automatic locking hubs, 5-spoke alloy wheels, remote keyless security system, AM/FM stereo with 4 speakers.

Base Prices

Code	Description	Invoice	MSRP
LCC66TV	2WD (5-spd)	12407	13199
LCC694V	2WD (auto)	13300	14149
LAC66TV	4WD (5-spd)	13577	14599
LAC69TV	4WD (auto)	14460	15549
Destination Charge:		420	420

Accessories

Code	Description	Invoice	MSRP
ABS	Anti-Lock Brakes (2WD)	540	600
ABS	Anti-Lock Brakes (4WD) *Includes cruise control.*	700	800

Take Advantage of Warranty Gold! Savings up to 50% off Dealer's Extended Warranty Prices. Protect and enhance YOUR investment with the best extended warranty available. Call Toll Free 1-800-580-9889

TOYOTA 4RUNNER

1998 4RUNNER

1998 Toyota 4Runner 4WD Limited V6

What's New?

For 1998, the Toyota 4Runner gets rotary HVAC controls, a new 4-spoke steering wheel, and revised audio control head units.

Review

In 1996, Toyota separated this high-volume SUV from its pickup truck roots. Thus, the current 4Runner shares little with the Tacoma pickup. As a result, engineers have created a refined vehicle without sacrificing tough off-road ability. Generous suspension travel and tread width provide capable off-road ability, ride, and handling. The interior is quite roomy, thanks to a wheelbase that is two inches longer than the previous version. A low floor and wide doors make getting into and out of the 4Runner less of a exercise in contortionism than those riding in Jeep Cherokees or Nissan Pathfinders are likely to experience.

Two engines are available on the 4Runner: a 2.7-liter inline four cylinder that makes 150 horsepower at 4800 rpm and 177 pounds-feet of torque at 4000 rpm, and a 3.4-liter V-6 producing 183 horsepower at 4800 rpm and 217 pounds-feet of torque at 3600 rpm. These figures represent a substantial improvement over the old anemic four cylinder and wheezy V-6. In fact, the new 2.7-liter four is more powerful than the 1995 model's 3.0-liter six, and is nearly as powerful as the base engine found in the Ford Explorer XL.

Needless to say, all of this adds up to a very competitive sport-ute. Safety isn't ignored in the revamped 4Runner, either, which sports dual airbags and standard anti-lock brakes on V-6 models. (Anti-lock brakes are optional on four cylinder models.)

Overall, the 4Runner is a very nice truck, which provides the sophistication that we have come to expect from Toyota products with the overall ruggedness more often associated with Jeeps. Prices are high, however, running from $20,500 for a 2WD four cylinder Base model to over $36,000 for a fully loaded Limited. This lands the 4Runner right smack dab in the Mercedes-Benz ML320, Nissan Pathfinder LE, and Ford Explorer Limited territory. The competition in this segment is getting fierce and there are plenty of good choices for your money, definitely something worth considering when shelling out such a large chunk of change.

4RUNNER — TOYOTA

| CODE | DESCRIPTION | INVOICE | MSRP |

Safety Data

Driver Airbag: *Standard*
Side Airbag: *Not Available*
Traction Control: *Not Available*
Driver Crash Test Grade: *Average*

Passenger Airbag: *Standard*
4-Wheel ABS: *Optional (4-Cyl), Standard (V6)*
Integrated Child Seat(s): *Not Available*
Passenger Crash Test Grade: *Average*

Standard Equipment

BASE: 2.7-liter DOHC 4-cylinder engine, power rack-and-pinion steering, power front disc/rear drum brakes, shift-on-the-fly 4WD (4WD), double wishbone front suspension with coil springs and gas shocks, 4-link coil spring rear suspension, front and rear stabilizer bar, 2-speed transfer case (4WD), front and rear mud flaps, tinted glass, halogen headlamps, argent front and rear bumpers, skid plates, windshield wiper with mist cycle, black exterior mirrors, 15" styled steel wheels, P225/75R15 tires, dual air bags, passenger side vanity mirror, stereo with 4 speakers, front bucket seats, center console with storage, front and rear cup holders, full carpeting, split-fold rear bench seat, power rear window, and front and rear grab handles.

SR5 (in addition to or instead of BASE equipment): 3.4-liter DOHC V-6 engine, 4-wheel anti-lock brakes, chrome bumpers, chrome grille, power color-keyed exterior mirrors, privacy glass, variable intermittent windshield wipers, rear window wiper/washer, front map lights, tilt steering wheel, power door locks, digital clock, and upgraded stereo with cassette.

LIMITED (in addition to or instead of SR5 equipment): All-Weather Package, color-keyed fender flares, P265/70R16 tires, 16" aluminum wheels, cruise control, power windows, premium stereo with cassette, 6 speakers, and power antenna, one-touch 4WD selector (4WD), leather interior, and floor mats.

Base Prices

Code	Description	Invoice	MSRP
8641	2WD (5-spd)	17997	20558
8640	2WD (auto)	18785	21458
8657	4WD (5-spd)	19881	22708
8658	4WD (auto)	20668	23608
8642	SR5 V-6 2WD (auto)	21990	25118
8665	SR5 V-6 4WD (5-spd)	22997	26268
8664	SR5 V-6 4WD (auto)	23784	27168
8648	Limited 2WD	28233	32248
8668	Limited 4WD	30307	34618
	Destination Charge:	420	420

Accessories

Code	Description	Invoice	MSRP
AC	Air Conditioner (Base)	788	985
	NOT AVAILABLE with (UP) Base Upgrade Package.		
AC	Air Conditioner (SR5)	788	985
CK	All Weather Guard Package (Base/SR5/Limited 2WD)	59	70

Includes heavy duty battery, heavy duty starter, heavy duty window wiper reservoir. NOT AVAILABLE with (CQ) Convenience Package. REQUIRES (RH) rear heater and rear intermittent wiper defogger or (RH) rear heater and (CQ) Convenience Package #2.

TOYOTA 4RUNNER

CODE	DESCRIPTION	INVOICE	MSRP
AB	Anti-lock Brake System (Base)	507	590
CA	California Emissions (Base)	NC	NC
CA	California Emissions (SR5/Limited)	29	34
CF	Carpeted Floor Mats	48	80
CQ	Convenience Package (Base)	577	705
	Includes tilt wheel, variable intermittent wipers, dual rear cupholders, digital clock, intermittent rear wiper, rear window defogger, map light.		
CL	Cruise Control Package (Base/SR5)	232	290
DL	Differential Locks (Base 4WD)	268	325
	Includes locking rear differential. REQUIRES (SV) 16-inch steel wheels with P265 tires.		
DL	Differential Locks (SR5 4WD)	268	325
	Includes locking rear differential; requires (AW) aluminum wheels with 31-inch tires and (SP) Sports Package. NOT AVAILABLE with (SX) Sports Package and differential locks.		
LA	Leather Trim Package (SR5)	1228	1535
	Includes leather sport seats with 4-way adjustable headrests, leather door trim, leather-wrapped steering wheel and shift knob (5-spd 4WD only), and cruise control. NOT AVAILABLE with (FS) sport seats.		
PX	Metallic Paint	NC	NC
SR	Power Moonroof (SR5/Limited)	732	915
PO	Power Package (Base)	648	810
	Includes power locks, black outside mirrors, and lighting package. INCLUDED in (UP) Upgrade Package.		
PP	Power Windows (SR5)	404	505
AG	Preferred Equipment Group 2 (SR5)	1673	2105
	Includes air conditioning, aluminum wheels with P255/75R15 tires, power windows, stereo with cassette, 6 speakers and power antenna.		
AI	Preferred Equipment Package (SR5)	2190	2750
	Includes air conditioning, aluminum wheels with 31" tires, power windows, AM/FM stereo with cassette and 6 speakers, and power antenna.		
PG	Privacy Glass (Base)	236	295
EV	Radio: AM/FM Stereo with CD Player (Base/SR5)	75	100
	Includes deluxe ETR AM/FM Stereo with CD player and 4 speakers.		
CE	Radio: Premium Stereo with Cassette (SR5)	165	220
	Includes premium ETR AM/FM radio with cassette and 6 speakers.		
DC	Radio: Premium Stereo with cassette and CD player (Limited)	135	180
	Includes premium 3-in-1 combo AM/FM radio with cassette, CD player, and 6 speakers.		
DC	Radio: Premium Stereo with cassette and CD player (SR5)	375	500
	Includes premium 3-in-1 combo AM/FM radio with cassette, CD player, and 6 speakers.		
RH	Rear Heater	132	165
RW	Rear Wiper and Defogger (Base)	292	365

4RUNNER — TOYOTA

CODE	DESCRIPTION	INVOICE	MSRP
SP	Sports Package (SR5 4WD)	1422	1760
	Includes aluminum wheels, P265/70R16 tires, sport seat package, fender flares, and large wheel arch molding. NOT AVAILALBE with (FS) sports seats.		
SX	Sports Package and Differential Locks (SR5 4WD AT)	1690	2085
	Includes (SP) sports package and locking rear differential.		
FS	Sports Seat (SR5)	548	685
	Includes cloth sports seat with 4-way adjustable headrests, fabric door trim, leather shift knob (SR5 V-6 5-spd), cruise control with leather wrapped steering wheel. NOT AVAILABLE with (LA) leather trim package.		
SV	Steel Wheels with P265 Tires (Base)	480	600
	Includes 16-inch steel wheels with P265/70R16 tires and large wheel arch moldings.		
TW	Tilt Wheel (Base)	201	235
	Includes variable intermittent wipers.		
CD	Tonneau Cargo Cover (Base/SR5)	68	85
UP	Upgrade Package (Base)	1805	2275
	Includes air conditioner, power locks, power outside mirrors, deluxe ETR AM/FM radio with cassette and 4 speakers, cruise control, and carpeted floor mats.		
AA	Wheels: 16-inch Aluminum (SR5 AT)	1092	1355
	Includes 16-inch aluminum wheels with P265/70R16 tires, large wheel arch molding, locking rear differential; NOT AVAILABLE with (SP) or (SX) Sports Packages		
AY	Wheels: Aluminum (Base/SR5)	332	415
	Includes aluminum wheels with P225/75R15 tires. NOT AVAILABLE with (SX) Sport Package.		
AW	Wheels: Aluminum with 31-inch Tires (Base/SR5)	824	1030
	Includes aluminum wheels with P265/70R16 tires and large wheel arch molding. NOT AVAILABLE with (SP) Sport Package.		

One 15-minute call could save you 15% or more on car insurance.

GEICO DIRECT

America's 6th Largest Automobile Insurance Company

1-800-555-2758

TOYOTA LAND CRUISER

| CODE | DESCRIPTION | INVOICE | MSRP |

1997 LAND CRUISER

1997 Land Cruiser

What's New?

What's New for Toyota Land Cruiser in 1997 — The Black Package is discontinued, but black paint becomes an available color choice. A 40th Anniversary Package lets buyers slather their cruiser in leather and choose one of two unique paint schemes.

Review

Long before Explorers and Troopers—and years ahead of the first Blazers and Broncos—Toyota joined the slowly-blossoming sport-utility arena with the first Land Cruiser, rival mainly to Jeeps and Land Rovers. That was 1960, when the first canvas-topped "Landcruisers" cost less than $3000. Today, Toyota offers a descendant of that vehicle under the same name that is more powerful and a lot more expensive.

Only one model is for sale, a four-wheel-drive wagon powered by a 4.5-liter, 24-valve six-cylinder engine that cranks out 212 horsepower. Revamping for 1995 added airbags for both the driver and front passenger. Those front occupants also enjoy the benefit of height-adjustable seatbelts. Four-wheel anti-lock braking is installed on all Land Cruisers, working with all-disc binders. The Black Package is dropped for 1997, but vampires and other creatures of the night can still opt for black paint.

For peak traction in difficult spots at low speeds, an exclusive front and rear locking differential is available. That makes Land Cruiser the only sport-utility on sale in the U.S. with three locking units, to amplify the effect of the standard permanent four-wheel-drive system. In fully-locked mode, all four wheels are driven in unison, with equal torque distribution. A second-gear-start feature boosts traction on slippery surfaces. Land Cruisers seat seven and can tow a 5,000-pound trailer.

For its stout sticker price, at least you get a lot of equipment, including air conditioning, power locks and windows, cruise control, and more. Traditionally, potential shoppers have faced long waiting lists to get a Land Cruiser, undaunted by the prospect of a stiff ride or quickly-depleting fuel tank. These capable machines attract the kind of customer who might otherwise pay big bucks for a Land Rover or Range Rover, whether or not any plans for off-roading lay ahead. Any of them would look good decorating a driveway in an affluent neighborhood—especially to passersby who can appreciate the heritage that accompanies such a purchase.

LAND CRUISER   TOYOTA

| CODE | DESCRIPTION | INVOICE | MSRP |

Safety Data

Driver Airbag: *Standard*
Side Airbag: *Not Available*
Traction Control: *Not Available*
Driver Crash Test Grade: *Not Available*

Passenger Airbag: *Standard*
4-Wheel ABS: *Standard*
Integrated Child Seat(s): *Not Available*
Passenger Crash Test Grade: *Not Available*

Standard Equipment

LAND CRUISER: 4.5-liter 6-cylinder engine, 4-speed automatic transmission, full-time 4WD, front disc/rear drum anti-lock brakes, power steering, coil spring front suspension, 4-link coil spring rear suspension, front and rear stabilizer bars, locking center differential, front and rear tow hooks, towing package, weather guard package, fender flares, front and rear mud guards, chrome front bumper trim, chrome grille, halogen headlamps with auto-off, tinted glass, color-keyed outside mirrors, variable intermittent windshield wipers, rear window wiper, 16" styled wheels, P275/70R16 tires, full-size spare tire, tilt steering wheel, cruise control, power windows, power door locks, air conditioning, front and rear heater vents, stereo with cassette and 9 speakers, cloth seats, full carpeting, rear window defroster, digital clock, and reclining front bucket seats.

Base Prices

Code	Description	Invoice	MSRP
6154	4WD Wagon	35319	41068
	Destination Charge:	420	420

Accessories

Code	Description	Invoice	MSRP
SE/SN	40th Anniversary Limited Edition Package	4471	5549
	Includes automatic air conditioning, leather seats, leather-wrapped steering wheel, leather-wrapped transmission lever, third seat package, power driver's seat, power passenger's seat, alloy wheels, and special paint.		
AW	Aluminum Alloy Wheels	420	525
BX	Black Paint	NC	NC
LA	Leather Package	3455	4280
	Includes cowhides on all visible surfaces and a power driver and passenger seat.		
DL	Locking Front and Rear Differential	681	825
SR	Moonroof	948	1185
DC	Stereo with CD Player & Cassette	709	945
TX	Third Row Seat	1212	1515
	Includes sliding rear windows, passenger assist handles, and privacy glass.		

Don't forget to swing by the Townhall when you visit Edmund's website at http://www.edmunds.com. Talk to our editors and compare notes on your favorite cars and trucks. Join others to scope out smart shopping stategies, get answers to your questions, or share your expertise. To get to the Townhall, just click on the link on the homepage or go directly to http://www.edmunds.com/edweb/townhall/welcomeconflist.html.

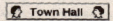

TOYOTA — RAV4

1998 RAV4

1998 Toyota RAV4

What's New?

Toyota's jellybean enters its third year of production with minor changes to the grille, headlights, taillamps, and interior. Four door RAV4s get new seat fabric.

Review

The mini-SUV business is booming. Introductions of fresh models by Honda, Kia, and Subaru indicate that there continues to be a large market for those who want the security of an AWD truck without the punishing ride and gas mileage that goes with it. Largely comprised of car-based AWD vehicles, this new market will gain even more entrants over the next few years as Land Rover, BMW, and Mercedes introduce small trucklets to the US. One of the early players in the game was Toyota, which saw this potential boom early on and jumped into the fray with the RAV4 in 1996.

A 2.0-liter, 120-horsepower engine hooked to either a five-speed manual or four-speed automatic transmission powers the front or all wheels of the different RAV4 models. This makes the RAV4 the first sport utility available with front-wheel drive. All-wheel drive models use powertrain components from the now-defunct Celica All-Trac. Four-wheel anti-lock brakes are optional on all RAV4s. Minimum ground clearance is 7.5-inches on the four-door model; two-door RAV4s get .2 additional inches of clearance.

The RAV4 is a pretty decent around-town driver, handling more like the car that its platform comes from than a traditional SUV. Power is on the low side, however; the 120-horsepower engine works hard to drag this mini-ute up even small hills. The interior is not a bad place to spend time, offering fairly comfortable seating for four adults in the four-door models. The cargo area of the four-door is larger than one would expect too, offering more room behind the rear seat than a Ford Crown Victoria. Two-door models are fine for singles or couples without children. The rear seat is tiny, and less than 10 cubic feet of cargo volume is available with the back seat up.

The Toyota RAV4 is a convincing package. Its eye-grabbing looks appeal to those who are young or just young at heart. Around college campuses the RAV4 litters the streets in front of Greek Row more than smashed bottles of Boone's Farm. Surprisingly, however, we have also

RAV4

TOYOTA

| CODE | DESCRIPTION | INVOICE | MSRP |

seen the RAV4 towed behind a large number of motor homes that swoop into Arizona, Texas, and California every winter, leading us to believe that they are a hit with the more mature crowd, too. We are fond of the RAV4, but there are a number of choices in this growing segment and we can't help but think that the more refined and powerful Honda CR-V might offer shoppers more of what they are looking for in a small truck — power, utility, and value.

Safety Data

Driver Airbag: *Standard*
Side Airbag: *Not Available*
Traction Control: *Not Available*
Driver Crash Test Grade: *Not Available*

Passenger Airbag: *Standard*
4-Wheel ABS: *Standard*
Integrated Child Seat(s): *Not Available*
Passenger Crash Test Grade: *Not Available*

Standard Equipment

RAV4: 2.0-liter 16-valve DOHC 4-cylinder engine, power assisted rack-and-pinion steering, power assisted front disc/rear drum brakes, independent MacPherson strut front suspension, double wishbone rear suspension, full-time AWD (AWD), locking center differential (AWD), halogen headlamps, black outside mirrors, intermittent front windshield wipers, rear window wiper, rear window defogger, P215/70R16 A/S tires, passenger's vanity mirror, front bucket seats, cloth interior trim, reclining split-bench seat, cup holders, and dual airbags.

Base Prices

Code	Description	Invoice	MSRP
4413	2WD 2-Door (5-spd)	14026	15388
4412	2WD 2-Door (auto)	14983	16438
4417	2WD 4-Door (5-spd)	14809	16248
4416	2WD 4-Door (auto)	15768	17298
4423	4WD 2-Door (5-spd)	15052	16798
4427	4WD 4-Door (5-spd)	15882	17658
4426	4WD 4-Door (auto)	16763	18708
Destination Charge:		420	420

Accessories

Code	Description	Invoice	MSRP
AC	Air Conditioner	788	985
CK	All Weather Guard Package	59	70
	Includes rear heater ducts, HD battery, HD washer tank, and HD starter motor.		
AB	Anti-lock Brakes	507	590
CA	California Emissions	54	63
CL	Cruise Control	232	290
LD	Limited Slip Differential (4WD)	309	375
SR	Moonroof (4-Door)	732	915
PG	Privacy Glass (2-Door)	176	220
PG	Privacy Glass (4-Door)	236	295
RR	Radio Prep Package	NC	NC
EX	Radio: Stereo with Cassette and 4 Speakers	263	350
EV	Radio: Stereo with CD Player and 4 Speakers	338	40
TW	Tilt Wheel	145	170

TOYOTA RAV4 / SIENNA

CODE	DESCRIPTION	INVOICE	MSRP
SR	Twin Sunroof (2-Door)	480	600
UT	Upgrade Package with Tilt Wheel (4-Door)	744	930
	Includes power windows, power door locks, power mirrors, deluxe AM/FM radio with cassette and 4 speakers, digital clock, and tilt wheel.		
VP	Value Package 1 (4-Door)	1505	1672
	Includes air conditioner, stereo with cassette, tilt wheel, cruise control, power windows, power locks, power mirrors, carpeted floor mats, and trunk mat.		
VK	Value Package 2 (4-Door)	1595	1772
	Includes air conditioning, premium stereo, tilt steering wheel, cruise control, power windows, power door locks, power mirrors, cloth front headrests, soft spare tire cover, cladding graphic, carpeted floor mats, and trunk mat.		
AW	Wheels: Aluminum	548	685
	Includes aluminum wheels, 215/70R16 tires, and center wheel cap ornament.		
AL	Wheels: Aluminum with Fender Flares (4WD)	912	1140

1998 SIENNA

1998 Toyota Sienna

What's New?

A new minivan from Toyota brings some innovation to the family truckster market. A powerful 194-horsepower V-6 engine rests under the hood of all models. Safety equipment includes standard anti-lock brakes, low tire pressure warning systems, and 5 mph front and rear bumpers.

Review

Just when you thought it was safe to call the minivan market dead, Toyota does the unthinkable and makes this typically boring corner of automobilia interesting. Toyota's new minivan sits in sharp contrast to the one it replaces. Whereas the Previa was a study in minivan abnormalities, with rear-wheel drive, a midship-mounted supercharged engine, and a shape that looked like the droid escape pod from the first *Star Wars* movie, the new Sienna is a model of suburban respectability.

SIENNA

That doesn't, however, mean that the new minivan is boring. Resting under the hood is a powerful 3.0-liter V-6 engine that was stolen from the Camry parts bin. The engine isn't the only piece of equipment pilfered from the Camry; the Sienna rides on a stretched and modified Camry platform and uses much of the Camry's interior switchgear. Referred to internally as "The Camry of minivans," we can only assume that Toyota expects this new creation to be as popular as their recently redesigned sedan.

In order to harness the 194-horses at work under the hood, Sienna engineers put anti-lock brakes at all four wheels of every Camry. While we have not yet conducted a road test of this model, we doubt that we will have anything to complain about in the stopping and going departments. Other safety equipment includes dual airbags, side-impact protection that meets future federal standards, and seatbelt pretensioners for both front seats. Toyota is so confident in this vehicle's crashworthiness, that they proclaim in their press kit that it will deliver "best-in-class" in tests administrated by third parties.

Interestingly, Toyota was able to talk rivals General Motors and Chrysler into lending a hand on the Sienna's manufacturing process. Not used to making such a large vehicle, Toyota had questions about how to deal with interior assembly on this van that has well over 130 cubic feet of cargo space.

In the end, General Motors and Chrysler may be sorry that they offered to help Toyota figure out some of their manufacturing logistics. Toyota is expecting to sell 70,000 of these minvans this year alone. If they increase capacity, they could become a real thorn in the side of the Big Three that has heretofore dominated the minivan industry. Whatever the case may be, we have no hesitation about recommending this outstanding, if somewhat homely, minivan.

Safety Data

Driver Airbag: *Standard*
Side Airbag: *Not Available*
Traction Control: *Not Available*
Driver Crash Test Grade: *Not Available*

Passenger Airbag: *Standard*
4-Wheel ABS: *Standard*
Integrated Child Seat(s): *Optional*
Passenger Crash Test Grade: *Not Available*

Standard Equipment

NOTE: Standard equipment information was unavailable at the time of publication.

Base Prices

Code	Description	Invoice	MSRP
5322	CE 4-Door	21140	18724
5332	LE 4-Door	20573	23500
5334	LE 5-Door	20989	23975
5344	XLE 5-Door	23514	27100
	Destination Charge:	420	420

Accessories

Code	Description	Invoice	MSRP
AC	Air Conditioner (CE)	360	450
	NOT AVAILABLE with (TO) or (UV).		
CA	California Emissions	NC	NC
CC	Cloth Captain's Chairs (LE)	520	650
	NOT AVAILABLE with (KS) or (UR).		
TF	Full-size Spare Tire (CE/LE)	68	85
	NOT AVAILABLE with (AW) or (UR).		
EH	Heated Power Outside Mirrors (CE)	144	180
	NOT AVAILABLE with (EM).		

TOYOTA SIENNA

CODE	DESCRIPTION	INVOICE	MSRP
EH	Heated Power Outside Mirrors (LE)	24	30
	NOT AVAILABLE with (EH).		
KS	Integrated Child Seat (CE/LE)	200	250
	NOT AVAILABLE with (CC) or (UR) on LE.		
LA	Leather Seats with Captain's Chairs (XLE)	1128	1410
	NOT AVAILABLE with (XE).		
UP	Package 1 (LE)	333	430
	Includes (CE) premium stereo with cassette, privacy glass, and roof rack.		
UR	Package 2 (LE)	1341	1690
	Includes (AW) alloy wheels, (CE) premium stereo with cassette, (PG) privacy glass, (DR) roof rack, and (CC) cloth captain's chairs.		
XE	Package 3 (XLE)	1912	2390
	Includes (LA) leather package and (SR) power moonroof.		
SR	Power Moonroof (XLE)	784	980
	NOT AVAILABLE with (XE).		
EM	Power Outside Mirrors (CE)	120	150
PO	Power Package (CE)	716	895
AJ	Power Sliding Door (LE 5-Door)	300	375
	REQUIRES (PN).		
CE	Radio: Premium Stereo with Cassette (LE)	165	220
	NOT AVAILABLE with (EV), (DC), (DV), (UP), or (UR).		
DC	Radio: Premium Stereo with Cassette and CD Player (LE)	375	500
DC	Radio: Premium Stereo with Cassette and CD Player (XLE)	135	180
	NOT AVAILABLE with (EV), (DC), (DV), (UP), or (UR).		
DV	Radio: Premium Stereo with CD Player (LE)	240	320
EV	Radio: Stereo with CD Player (CE/LE)	75	100
PG	Rear Quarter Privacy Glass (CE)	288	360
DF	Rear Window Defroster (CE)	168	210
PN	Security Package (LE/XLE)	352	440
TO	Towing Package (CE)	480	600
TO	Towing Package (LE/XLE)	120	150
	NOT AVAILABLE with (AC) or (UV). REQUIRES (TF) and (UR) on LE.		
UV	Towing Package 2 (CE)	120	150
AW	Wheels: Alloy with Full Size Spare (LE)	488	610
	NOT AVAILABLE with (TF) or (UR).		

T100 PICKUP — TOYOTA

| CODE | DESCRIPTION | INVOICE | MSRP |

1997 T100

1997 Toyota T100

What's New?

Two new colors debut this year and the optional wheel and tire packages are larger this year. Standard models get radio pre-wiring, mid-level models get fabric door trim panels, and SR5 models get chrome wheel arches.

Review

When launched as a 1993 model, Toyota's larger-than-before pickup came only with a regular cab that seated three—and that center person suffered a shortage of usable space. During 1995, an extended Xtracab version joined the T100 line, in either DX or SR5 trim. So did a new, more powerful 3.4-liter V-6 engine that yielded 190 horsepower, bringing towing capacity up to 5,200 pounds.

Cargo space is minimal in a regular-cab T100, but much more practical in the Xtracab, which measures 21.7 inches longer and includes forward-facing 50/50 rear jump seats for three. Unlike some extended-cab trucks whose auxiliary seats are bolt-upright, the T100's recline 15 degrees.

Toyota claims that its biggest pickup can beat some full-size domestic rivals with V-8 engines in the acceleration department. Even before the arrival of the more powerful engine, a V-6 pickup moved out quickly enough with manual shift, though an automatic sapped its vigor somewhat. As expected, 4x4s are slower, due largely to their increased weight. Two-wheel-drive models ride more comfortably, too, but any T100 with an empty cargo bed can turn into a unwieldy handful on the highway, its rear axle unable to remain planted in place. Only the standard 2WD, regular cab half-ton pickup comes with a 2.7-liter four-cylinder engine, which delivers 150 horsepower and 177 lbs.-ft. of torque.

Ranking in size between Dodge's mid-size Dakota and any of the domestically built full-size pickups, the T100 can be ordered in two trim levels: Standard, or SR5 with chrome trim, sliding rear window, tilt steering, and a tachometer. SR5 is available only on Xtracab models. This year the T100 gets higher standard equipment content and a few new colors. A driver's airbag is installed in all models, but four-wheel anti-lock braking is optional only with the V-6 engine. Naturally, T100 owners get the benefit of Toyota's reputation for refinement and excellent assembly quality, as well as high levels of customer satisfaction.

TOYOTA T100 PICKUP

| CODE | DESCRIPTION | INVOICE | MSRP |

Safety Data

Driver Airbag: *Standard*
Side Airbag: *Not Available*
Traction Control: *Not Available*
Driver Crash Test Grade: *Not Available*

Passenger Airbag: *Not Available*
4-Wheel ABS: *Optional (V-6)*
Integrated Child Seat(s): *Not Available*
Passenger Crash Test Grade: *Not Available*

Standard Equipment

T100 STANDARD: 2.7-liter DOHC 4 cylinder engine, power rack-and-pinion steering, power front disc/rear drum brakes, P215/75R15 tires, independent front suspension, leaf spring rear suspension, halogen headlamps, tinted glass, driver's side outside mirror, locking fuel filler door, 15" steel wheels, driver's side airbag, door map pockets, vinyl bench seat, and radio prep package.

T100 DX (in addition to or instead of T100 STANDARD): 3.4-liter V-6 engine, recirculating-ball power steering, H/D battery, starter, wiper motor, and distributor; on demand 4WD (4WD models), Hi-Trac Suspension (4WD), skid plates (4WD), front tow hooks (4WD), styled steel wheels (4WD), full wheel covers (2WD), front and rear mud guards, trip meter, tachometer, fabric seats, P235/75R15 tires, and full carpeting.

T100 SR5 (in addition to or instead of T100 DX): Chrome package, variable intermittent windshield wipers, rear sliding window, tilt steering, map lights, passenger visor mirror, and AM/FM stereo with 4 speakers.

Base Prices

Code	Description	Invoice	MSRP
8723	2WD Standard Xtracab (5-spd)	16620	18548
8711	2WD Standard Regular Cab (5-spd)	13568	14638
8722	2WD Standard Xtracab (auto)	17427	19448
8710	2WD Standard Regular Cab (auto)	14402	15538
8823	4WD Standard Xtracab (5-spd)	19795	22348
8822	4WD Standard Xtracab (auto)	20591	23248
8725	2WD SR5 Xtracab (5-spd)	17826	20008
8724	2WD SR5 Xtracab (auto)	18626	20908
8825	4WD SR5 Xtracab (5-spd)	21071	23928
8824	4WD SR5 Xtracab (auto)	21866	24828
Destination Charge:		420	420

Accessories

Code	Description	Invoice	MSRP
AC	Air Conditioning	NC	NC
	NOTE: prices are not currently available for this option.		
CK	All-Weather Package (4-Cyl)	110	130
	Includes anti-chip paint and H/D battery.		
AL	Aluminum Wheels (2WD DX)	428	535
AL	Aluminum Wheels (2WD SR5)	484	605
AW	Aluminum Wheels (4WD SR5)	660	825
AW	Aluminum Wheels (DX 4WD)	572	715
RA	AM/FM Radio (Std/DX)	184	245

T100 PICKUP — TOYOTA

CODE	DESCRIPTION	INVOICE	MSRP
AB	Anti-Lock Brakes (V-6)	507	590
CA	California Emissions (V-6)	29	34
CH	Chrome Package (DX)	128	160
CW	Chrome Wheels (DX 4WD)	264	330
CQ	Convenience Package (Std/DX Xtracab)	414	505
	Includes tilt steering, tachometer, sliding rear window, variable intermittent windshield wipers, and privacy glass.		
CL	Cruise Control (DX)	248	310
CL	Cruise Control (SR-5)	316	395
ER	Deluxe Stereo w/4 Speakers (Std/Base)	285	380
EX	Deluxe Stereo w/Cassette (DX)	454	605
EX	Deluxe Stereo w/Cassette (SR5)	169	225
FW	Full Wheel Covers (4-Cyl.)	72	90
PO	Power Package (V6)	528	660
	Includes power door locks, power windows, power antenna, deluxe stereo and power outside mirrors.		
CE	Premium AM/FM Stereo w/Cassette & 6 Speakers (SR5)	315	420
WR	Sliding Rear Window (4-Cyl.)	120	150
WR	Sliding Rear Window (DX Xtracab)	216	270
FS	Sport Seats (SR5)	264	330
ST	Styled Steel Wheels (4WD SR5)	228	285
ST	Styled Steel Wheels (DX 2WD)	88	110
ST	Styled Steel Wheels (DX 4WD)	260	325
TW	Tilt Steering (DX)	198	235
	Includes variable intermittent windshield wipers.		
TU	Tire Upgrade (Standard)	100	125
	Includes P235/75R15 tires.		
TT	Two-Tone Paint	292	365
BG	Upgrade Package (4-Cyl.)	530	650
	Includes tilt steering wheel, variable intermittent windshield wipers, full wheel covers, fabric bench seat, digital clock, and dual outside mirrors.		

For expert advice in selecting/buying/leasing a new car, call

1-900-AUTOPRO

($2.00 per minute)

TOYOTA TACOMA

1998 TACOMA

1998 Toyota Tacoma

What's New?

The 1998 four-wheel drive Tacomas receive fresh front-end styling that makes them more closely resemble their two-wheel drive brothers. A new option package appears for 1998 as well, a TRD Off-Road Package for extended cab models is designed to make the Tacoma appeal to would-be Baja 1000 racers. On the safety front, Toyota introduces a passenger's side airbag that can be deactivated with a cut-off switch, making the Tacoma somewhat safer for children and short adults.

Review

Toyota's sixth-generation compact pickup debuted in April, as a 1995.5 model, with an actual model name: Tacoma. It's supposed to suggest the rugged outdoors, as well as strength and adventure. Any of three potent new engines goes under the hood, and the pickup rides an all-new chassis. Toyota aimed for aggressive styling, inside and out, and Tacomas sport an excellent selection of interior fittings. Regular and extended cab bodies are available, with either two- or four-wheel drive. A freshening of the front end occurred on the 1997 two-wheel drive Tacoma and the 1998 four-wheel models follow this year. Swoopy fenders, a larger bumper, aero-style headlamps, and a new grille set this truck apart from its forebears.

Two-wheel-drive Tacomas get a 2.4-liter four-cylinder base engine, rated 142 horsepower. Tacoma 4x4s earn a 150-horsepower, 2.7-liter four. Toyota claims that its four-cylinder engines are comparable to V-6s from competitors. If those won't suffice, however, consider the V-6 option: a dual-overhead-cam, 24-valve unit that whips out 190 horses and 220 pound-feet of torque. With V-6 power, borrowed from the bigger T100, this compact pickup can tow up to 5,000 pounds and soundly trounce any factory sport truck in the stoplight dragrace. In contrast, the V-6 engine available in the prior-generation pickup delivered only 150 horsepower and 180 pound-feet.

All Tacomas have front coil springs instead of the former torsion bars, but 4x4s feature longer suspension travel to improve ride/handling qualities. Manual-shift trucks feature reverse-gear synchronization, to reduce gear noise when shifting into reverse. Four-wheel anti-lock braking

TACOMA   TOYOTA

is optional on all Tacomas, and all pickups contain dual airbags with a shut-off switch for the passenger's side. In top-of-the-line Limited pickups, a One-Touch Hi-4 switch is available for easy, pushbutton engagement of four-wheel-drive.

Tacomas are produced at the NUMMI joint-venture facility in Fremont, California, having been designed in that state. Options include cruise control, air conditioning, a sliding rear window, tilt steering wheel, and moonroof. We like the Tacoma, but question the value it represents. These new Toyota trucks don't come cheap. Guess that's the price you pay for the peace of mind a Toyota provides.

Safety Data

Driver Airbag: *Standard*
Side Airbag: *Not Available*
Traction Control: *Not Available*
Driver Crash Test Grade: *Very Poor*

Passenger Airbag: *Standard*
4-Wheel ABS: *Optional*
Integrated Child Seat(s): *Not Available*
Passenger Crash Test Grade: *Average*

Standard Equipment

BASE STANDARD CAB 2WD: 2.4L I-4 DOHC MPI 16-valve engine; 5-speed overdrive manual transmission or 4-speed electronic automatic transmission with lock-up; HD battery; rear-wheel drive, 3.42 axle ratio; stainless steel exhaust; front independent double wishbone suspension with anti-roll bar, front coil springs, front shocks, rear suspension with rear leaf springs, rear shocks; manual rack-and-pinion steering; front disc/rear drum brakes; 15.1 gal capacity fuel tank; regular pick-up box; black bumper; monotone paint; aero-composite halogen headlamps; additional exterior lights include center high mounted stop light; folding passenger convex outside mirror; front and rear 14" x 5" steel wheels with full wheel covers; P195/75SR14 BSW AS front and rear tires; underbody mounted full-size conventional steel spare wheel; fuel filler door; 3 power accessory outlets, driver foot rest; analog instrumentation display includes water temp gauge; warning indicators include battery, lights-on, key-in-ignition, low washer fluid; driver side airbag, passenger side cancellable airbag; tinted windows; seating capacity of 3, bench front seat with adjustable headrests, driver seat includes 2-way direction control, passenger seat includes 2-way direction control; front height adjustable seatbelts; cloth seats, cloth door trim insert, full vinyl headliner, full carpet floor covering; interior lights include dome light; day-night rearview mirror; glove box, front cupholder, instrument panel bin, driver and passenger door bins; black grille, black side window moldings, black front windshield molding, black rear window molding, and black door handles.

BASE EXTENDED CAB 2WD (in addition to or instead of BASE STANDARD CAB 2WD equipment): rear black step bumper; vented rear windows; seating capacity of 5, 60-40 split-bench front seat with tilt adjustable headrests, driver seat includes 4-way direction control, passenger seat includes 4-way direction control with easy entry; 50-50 folding rear jump seat; interior concealed storage; and carpeted cargo floor.

BASE EXTENDED CAB V-6 2WD (in addition to or instead of BASE EXTENDED CAB 2WD equipment): 3.4L V-6 SMPI engine, 3.15 axle ratio, and power steering.

BASE STANDARD CAB 4WD (in addition to or instead of BASE STANDARD CAB 2WD equipment): 2.7L I-4 MPI engine; part-time 4 wheel drive, manual locking hub control and manual shift transfer case, 3.42 axle ratio; 18 gal capacity fuel tank; front and rear mud flaps, skid plates; tow hooks; warning indicators includes oil pressure.

TOYOTA TACOMA

| CODE | DESCRIPTION | INVOICE | MSRP |

BASE EXTENDED CAB 4WD (in addition to or instead of BASE STANDARD CAB 4WD equipment): Vented rear windows; seating capacity of 5, 60-40 split-bench front seat with tilt adjustable headrests, driver seat includes 4-way direction control passenger seat includes 4-way direction control with easy entry; 50-50 folding rear jump seat; interior concealed storage; and carpeted cargo floor.

BASE EXTENDED CAB V-6 4WD (in addition to or instead of BASE EXTENDED CAB 4WD equipment): 3.4L V-6 SMPI engine; engine oil cooler; and 3.91 axle ratio.

LIMITED EXTENDED CAB V-6 4WD (in addition to or instead of EXTENDED CAB V-6 4WD equipment): Front and rear chrome bumpers; chrome wheel well molding; AM/FM stereo with seek-scan, cassette, 4 speakers and fixed antenna; cruise control; tachometer gauge, in-dash clock, trip odometer; warning indicators include low fuel; power front windows with driver 1-touch down; variable intermittent front windshield wipers, sliding rear window; seating capacity of 4, front sports seats, driver seat includes 6-way direction control with lumbar support; premium cloth seats; interior lights include; steering wheel with; passenger side vanity mirror; partial floor console, with light; chrome grille, and chrome door handles.

Base Prices

Code	Description	Invoice	MSRP
7103	Base Standard Cab 2WD (5-spd)	11493	12538
7104	Base Standard Cab 2WD (auto)	12154	13258
7113	Base Extended Cab 2WD (5-spd)	13330	14708
7114	Base Extended Cab 2WD (auto)	13983	15428
7503	Base Standard Cab 4WD (5-spd)	15616	17428
7504	Base Standard Cab 4WD (auto)	16422	18328
7513	Base Extended Cab 4WD (5-spd)	16916	18878
7514	Base Extended Cab 4WD (auto)	17723	19778
7153	Extended Cab V-6 2WD (5-spd)	14545	16048
7154	Extended Cab V6 2WD (auto)	15361	16948
7553	Extended Cab V-6 4WD (5-spd)	17892	19968
7554	Extended Cab V-6 4WD (auto)	18699	20868
7557	Limited Extended Cab V-6 4WD (5-spd)	21531	24028
7558	Limited Extended Cab V-6 4WD (auto)	22336	24928
Destination Charge:		420	420

Accessories

Code	Description	Invoice	MSRP
FB	4-WD Selector Switch (Limited 4WD)	107	130
AB	4-Wheel Antilock Brakes	507	590
FD	4-Wheel Demand (Base 4WD)	190	230
	NNOT AVAILABLE with (DL) Differential Locks.		
AC	Air Conditioning	788	985
CK	All Weather Guard Package	59	70
	Includes HD starter, HD windshield wiper motor, and rain channeled windshield moulding.		
CA	California Emissions	29	34

TACOMA — TOYOTA

CODE	DESCRIPTION	INVOICE	MSRP
CH	**Chrome Package (Base)**	188	235
	Includes chrome front bumper, chrome grille, and chrome door handles. NOT AVAILABLE with (LX) SR5 Package, (IX) SR5 Package, or (KP) Color Key Package.		
CH	**Chrome Package (Base)**	304	380
	Includes chrome front bumper, chrome grille, chrome door handles, and chrome rear step bumper. NOT AVAILABLE with (PQ) Value Edition Package, or (QY) Value Edition Plus Package with (KP) Color Key Package.		
BU	**Cloth Bucket Seats (Base)**	48	60
	Includes headrests and center console box.		
BU	**Cloth Bucket Seats (Base)**	232	290
	Includes headrests and center console box.		
KP	**Color Key Package (Base 2WD)**	72	90
	Includes valance panel and grille. REQUIRES PQ or PX. NOT AVAILABLE with PY, CH, or LX.		
KP	**Color Key Package (Base 4WD)**	132	165
	REQUIRES PX. NOT AVAILABLE with (SX), CH, or LX.		
CQ	**Convenience Package (Base)**	581	710
	Includes glove box/ignition key cylinder/ashtray lights, cruise control, tachometer, trip meter, digital clock, tilt wheel, and variable intermittent windshield wipers.		
CL	**Cruise Control (Base)**	232	290
DL	**Differential Locks (4WD)**	268	325
	REQUIRES (AA and TA) or ((SX) and TA) or (AA and (CQ)) or ((SX) and (CQ)). NOT AVAILABLE with OF.		
PX	**Metallic Paint**	NC	NC
SR	**Pop-Up Moonroof (Extended Cab)**	312	390
PO	**Power Package (Base)**	376	470
	Includes power windows and power door locks. REQUIRES (CL) cruise control or (CQ) Convenience Package.		
PS	**Power Steering (Base 2WD 4-cyl)**	257	300
RR	**Radio Prep Package (Base Extended Cab)**	173	230
	Includes antenna, wiring harness and 4 speakers. NOT AVAILABLE with (LX) SR5 Package, (IX) SR5 Package with (KP), or (EX) radio.		
RA	**Radio: AM/FM Stereo with 2 Speakers (Base Standard Cab)**	203	270
	Includes antenna. NOT AVAILABLE with (EU) radio or (PV) Value Edition Plus Package.		
EU	**Radio: AM/FM Stereo with Cassette (Base Standard Cab)**	278	370
	Includes 2 speakers and antenna. NOT AVAILABLE with (RA) radio.		
EX	**Radio: AM/FM Stereo with Cassette and 4 Speakers (Base Extended)**	435	580
	NOT AVAILABLE with (RR) Radio Prep Package.		
WR	**Sliding Rear Window (Base Extended Cab)**	216	270
	Incudes privacy glass.		
WR	**Sliding Rear Window (Base Standard Cab)**	120	150
SX	**Sport Value Package (Base 4WD Standard Cab)**	882	980
	Includes cloth bucket seats, Chrome Package with chrome front bumper, chrome grille, and chrome door handles, sliding rear window, and aluminum wheels with 265/75R15 tires. NOT AVAILABLE with (AL) wheels, (KP) Color Key Package.		

TOYOTA — TACOMA

CODE	DESCRIPTION	INVOICE	MSRP
LX	**SR5 Package (Base Extended 4WD)**	1152	1280
	Includes Chrome Package with chrome front bumper, chrome grille, and chrome door handles, AM/FM stereo with cassette and 4 speakers, air conditioning, and sliding rear window. NOT AVAILABLE with KP, RR, IX, or CH.		
LX	**SR5 Package (Base Extended V-6 2WD)**	702	780
	Includes Chrome Package with chrome front bumper, chrome grille, and chrome door handles; power steering, AM/FM stereo with cassette and 4 speakers, air conditioning, and sliding rear window. NOT AVAILABLE with KP, RR, IX, or CH.		
LX	**SR5 Package (Extended Cab 2WD)**	837	930
	Includes Chrome Package with chrome front bumper, chrome grille, and chrome door handles; power steering, AM/FM stereo with cassette and 4 speakers, air conditioning, sliding rear window. NOT AVAILABLE with KP, RR, IX, or CH.		
IX	**SR5 Package with KP (Extended Cab 2WD)**	639	710
	Includes Color Key Package, power steering, AM/FM stereo with cassette and 4 speakers, air conditioning, and sliding rear window. REQUIRES PX. NOT AVAILABLE with CH, RR, or LX.		
IX	**SR5 Package with KP (Extended Cab 2WD)**	819	910
	Includes Color Key Package, power steering, AM/FM stereo with cassette and 4 speakers, air conditioning, and sliding rear window. REQUIRES PX. NOT AVAILABLE with CH, RR, or LX.		
IX	**SR5 Package With KP (Extended Cab 4WD)**	1089	1210
	Includes Color-Key Package, AM/FM stereo with cassette and 4 speakers, air conditioning, sliding rear window. REQUIRES PX. NOT AVAILABLE with CH, RR, or LX.		
TA	**Tachometer (Base)**	72	90
TW	**Tilt Wheel (Base)**	201	235
	Includes variable intermittent windshield wipers.		
TU	**Tires: 215/70R14 (Base Standard Cab 2WD)**	144	180
	Includes full wheel covers. NOT AVAILABLE with (AW) wheels.		
OF	**TRD Off-Road Package (Limited 4WD)**	654	805
	Includes tachometer and color-keyed overfenders, unique aluminum wheels, off-road suspension, and tripmeter.		
OF	**TRD Offroad Package (Extended Cab 4WD)**	1362	1690
	Includes black overfenders, unique aluminum wheels, off-road suspension, tachometer, trip meter, differential locks. NOT AVAILABLE with (AA) wheels, (AL) wheels, or (DL) differential locks.		
PQ	**Value Edition Package (2WD)**	238	265
	Includes power steering, painted rear step bumper, AM/FM stereo, carpet floor mats. NOT AVAILABLE with (CH) Chrome Package, (PY) Value Edition Plus Package, or (QY) Value Edition Plus Package with (KP).		
PY	**Value Edition Plus Package (Standard Cab 2WD)**	751	835
	Includes air conditioning, power steering, Chrome Package with chrome front bumper, chrome grille, and chrome door handles; AM/FM stereo with cassette, and carpet floor mats. NOT AVAILABLE with (KP) Color Key Package, (PQ) Value Edition Package, or (QY) Value Edition Plus Package with (KP).		
PV	**Value Edition Plus Package (Standard Cab 4WD)**	499	555
	Includes air conditioning, AM/FM stereo with cassette, carpet floor mats. NOT AVAILABLE with (RA) radio.		

TACOMA — TOYOTA

CODE	DESCRIPTION	INVOICE	MSRP
QY	Value Edition Plus Package with KP (Base Standard Cab 2WD) ..... Includes Color-Key Package, air conditioning, power steering, chrome rear step bumper, AM/FM stereo with cassette, and carpet floor mats. REQUIRES PX. NOT AVAILABLE with PQ, PY, or CH.	733	815
AW	Wheels: Aluminum (Base 2WD) ..... Includes 215/70R14 tires. NOT AVAILABLE with (TU) tires.	480	600
AW	Wheels: Aluminum (Base 2WD)	336	420
AL	Wheels: Aluminum with 225/75R15 Tires (Base 4WD) ..... NOT AVAILABLE with (AA) Wheels, (SX) Sport Value Package, or (OF) TRD Off-Road Package.	364	455
AA	Wheels: Aluminum with 265/75R15 Tires (Base 4WD) ..... Includes wheel arch molding. NOT AVAILABLE with (AL) wheels, (OF) TRD Off-Road Package.	796	995
AA	Wheels: Aluminum with 265/75R15 Tires (Limited 4WD)	320	400

Don't forget to swing by the Townhall when you visit Edmund's website at http://www.edmunds.com. Talk to our editors and compare notes on your favorite cars and trucks. Join others to scope out smart shopping stategies, get answers to your questions, or share your expertise. To get to the Townhall, just click on the link on the homepage or go directly to http://www.edmunds.com/edweb/townhall/welcomeconflist.html.

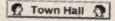

One 15-minute call could save you 15% or more on car insurance.

America's 6th Largest Automobile Insurance Company

1-800-555-2758

Specifications and EPA Mileage Ratings

1997 / 1998 New Trucks

Contents

Acura	477		Lexus	502
Chevrolet	477		Mazda	503
Chrysler	483		Mercedes-Benz	504
Dodge	484		Mercury	504
Ford	488		Mitsubishi	505
GMC	492		Nissan	506
Honda	497		Oldsmobile	507
Infiniti	498		Plymouth	507
Isuzu	498		Pontiac	508
Jeep	500		Subaru	508
Kia	501		Suzuki	508
Land Rover	502		Toyota	509
Lincoln	503			

1998 Pontiac Trans Sport Montana

SPECIFICATIONS & EPA MILEAGE RATINGS

	ACURA SLX	ACURA SLX Premium	CHEVROLET Astro 2WD	Astro AWD	Blazer 2WD 2-Door	Blazer 2WD 4-Door	Blazer 4WD 2-Door	Blazer 4WD 4-Door
Acceleration (0-60/sec)	12	12	10.1	10.4	NA	NA	9.1	9.3
Braking Dist. (60-0/ft)	144	144	148	151	147	147	147	147
Turning Circle (in.)	38.1	38.1	39.5	40.5	36.6	38.5	36.9	39.5
Length (in.)	183.5	183.5	189.8	189.8	174.7	181.2	174.7	181.2
Width (in.)	72.4	72.4	77.5	77.5	67.8	67.8	67.8	67.8
Height (in.)	72.2	72.2	76	76	66	65.9	66.9	66.9
Curb Weight (lbs.)	3946	4640	4197	NA	3515	3685	3874	4046
Wheelbase (in.)	108.7	108.7	111	111	100.5	107	100.5	107
Front Head Room (in.)	39.4	39.4	39.2	39.2	39.6	39.6	39.6	39.6
Rear Head Room (in.)	39.8	39.8	38.7	NA	38.2	38.2	38.2	38.2
Front Leg Room (in.)	40.8	40.8	41.6	41.6	42.4	42.4	42.4	42.4
Rear Leg Room (in.)	39.1	39.1	38.5	NA	36.3	36.3	36.3	36.3
Maximum Seating	5	5	8	2	5	6	5	6
Max Cargo Capacity (cu ft.)	85.3	85.3	170.4	170.4	66.9	74.1	66.9	74.1
Maximum Payload (lbs.)	870	870	1753	1673	935	1165	911	1254
Number of Cylinders	6	6	6	6	6	6	6	6
Displacement (liters)	3.2	3.2	4.3	4.3	4.3	4.3	4.3	4.3
Horsepower @ RPM	200@5000	200@5000	190@4400	190@4400	190@4400	190@4400	190@4400	190@4400
Torque @ RPM	228@3500	228@3500	250@2800	250@2800	250@2800	250@2800	250@2800	250@2800
Fuel Capacity	24	24	25	25	19	18	19	18
Towing Capacity	5000	5000	5500	5000	5500	5500	5000	5000
EPA City (mpg) - Manual	NA	NA	NA	NA	18	NA	18	NA
EPA Hwy (mpg) - Manual	NA	NA	NA	NA	24	NA	24	NA
EPA City (mpg) - Auto	16	15	16	15	17	17	17	17
EPA Hwy (mpg) - Auto	19	18	20	19	22	22	22	22

SPECIFICATIONS & EPA MILEAGE RATINGS

	C/K 1500 Series Pickup 2WD Reg Cab SB	C/K 1500 Series Pickup 2WD Reg Cab LB	C/K 1500 Series Pickup 2WD X-cab SB	C/K 1500 Series Pickup 2WD X-cab LB	C/K 1500 Series Pickup 4WD Reg Cab SB	C/K 1500 Series Pickup 4WD Reg Cab LB	C/K 1500 Series Pickup 4WD X-cab SB	C/K 1500 Series Pickup 4WD X-cab LB	C/K 2500 Series Pickup 2WD Reg Cab LB	C/K 2500 Series Pickup 2WD HD Reg Cab LB
Acceleration (0-60/sec)	NA	NA	9.3	9.3	NA	NA	NA	NA	NA	NA
Braking Dist. (60-0/ft)	144	144	147	147	NA	NA	NA	NA	NA	NA
Turning Circle (in.)	39.8	39.8	46.6	46.6	40.7	40.7	47.6	47.6	43.7	43.4
Length (in.)	194.5	213.4	217.5	236.6	194.5	213.4	218	236.6	213.4	213.4
Width (in.)	76.8	76.8	76.8	76.8	76.8	76.8	76.8	76.8	76.8	76.8
Height (in.)	70.8	70	70.6	70.1	72.7	72.5	72.6	73.2	75.5	75.5
Curb Weight (lbs.)	3869	4021	4160	4407	4275	4426	4533	4825	4269	4269
Wheelbase (in.)	117.5	131.5	141.5	155.5	117.5	131.5	141.5	155.5	131.5	131.5
Front Head Room (in.)	39.9	39.9	39.9	39.9	39.9	39.9	39.9	39.9	39.9	39.9
Rear Head Room (in.)	NA	NA	37.5	37.5	NA	NA	37.5	37.5	NA	NA
Front Leg Room (in.)	41.7	41.7	41.7	41.7	41.7	41.7	41.7	41.7	41.7	41.7
Rear Leg Room (in.)	NA	NA	34.8	34.8	NA	NA	34.8	34.8	NA	NA
Maximum Seating	3	3	6	6	3	3	6	6	3	3
Max Cargo Capacity (cu ft.)	NA	NA	NA	NA	NA	NA	NA	NA	NA	NA
Maximum Payload (lbs.)	2231	2079	2040	1793	1825	1674	2067	1975	2931	4331
Number of Cylinders	6	6	6	8	6	6	6	8	8	8
Displacement (liters)	4.3	4.3	4.3	5	4.3	4.3	4.3	5	5	5
Horsepower @ RPM	200@4400	200@4400	200@4400	230@4600	200@4400	200@4400	200@4400	230@4600	230@4600	230@4600
Torque @ RPM	255@2800	255@2800	255@2800	285@2800	255@2800	255@2800	255@2800	285@2800	285@2800	285@2800
Fuel Capacity	25	34	25	34	25	34	25	34	34	34
Towing Capacity	7500	7500	7500	7500	7500	7500	7500	7500	8500	8500
EPA City (mpg) - Manual	NA	NA	NA	NA	NA	NA	NA	NA	NA	NA
EPA Hwy (mpg) - Manual	NA	NA	NA	NA	NA	NA	NA	NA	NA	NA
EPA City (mpg) - Auto	NA	NA	NA	NA	NA	NA	NA	NA	NA	NA
EPA Hwy (mpg) - Auto	NA	NA	NA	NA	NA	NA	NA	NA	NA	NA

SPECIFICATIONS & EPA MILEAGE RATINGS

	C/K 2500 Series Pickup 2WD X-cab SB	C/K 2500 Series Pickup 2WD HD X-cab LB	C/K 2500 Series Pickup 4WD Reg Cab LB	C/K 2500 Series Pickup 4WD X-cab SB	C/K 2500 Series Pickup 4WD X-cab LB	C/K 3500 Series Pickup 2WD Reg Cab LB	C/K 3500 Series Pickup 2WD X-cab LB	C/K 3500 Series Pickup 4WD Reg Cab LB	C/K 3500 Series Pickup 2WD Crew Cab	C/K 3500 Series Pickup 4WD Reg Cab LB	C/K 3500 Series Pickup 4WD X-cab LB
Acceleration (0-60/sec)	NA	NA	NA	NA	NA	NA	NA	NA	NA	NA	NA
Braking Dist. (60-0/ft)	NA	NA	NA	NA	NA	NA	NA	NA	173	NA	NA
Turning Circle (in.)	46.6	50.5	44.7	48.5	51.9	43.4	50.2	53.8	44.7	51.9	
Length (in.)	217.9	236.6	213.4	217.9	236.6	213.4	236.6	250.9	213.4	236.6	
Width (in.)	76.8	76.8	76.8	76.8	76.8	76.8	76.8	76.8	76.8	76.8	
Height (in.)	71.2	75.5	75.8	74.3	75.8	72.6	72.6	73.9	74	74	
Curb Weight (lbs.)	4400	4961	4640	5339	5339	4798	5338	5475	5181	5778	
Wheelbase (in.)	141.5	155.5	131.5	141.5	155.5	131.5	155.5	168.5	131.5	155.5	
Front Head Room (in.)	39.9	39.9	39.9	39.9	39.9	39.9	39.9	39.9	39.9	39.9	
Rear Head Room (in.)	37.5	37.5	NA	37.5	37.5	NA	37.5	40.8	NA	37.5	
Front Leg Room (in.)	41.7	41.7	41.7	41.7	41.7	41.7	41.7	41.7	41.7	41.7	
Rear Leg Room (in.)	34.8	34.8	NA	34.8	34.8	NA	34.8	37.9	NA	34.8	
Maximum Seating	6	6	3	6	6	3	6	6	3	6	
Max Cargo Capacity (cu ft.)	NA	NA	NA	NA	NA	NA	NA	NA	NA	NA	
Maximum Payload (lbs.)	2800	3639	3960	3261	3261	4202	4662	3525	4019	4222	
Number of Cylinders	8	8	8	8	8	8	8	8	8	8	
Displacement (liters)	5	5.7	5	5	5.7	5.7	5.7	5.7	5.7	5.7	
Horsepower @ RPM	230@4600	255@4600	230@4600	230@4600	255@4600	255@4600	255@4600	255@4600	255@4600	255@4600	
Torque @ RPM	285@2800	330@2800	285@2800	285@2800	330@2800	330@2800	330@2800	330@2800	330@2800	330@2800	
Fuel Capacity	25	34	34	25	34	34	34	34	34	34	
Towing Capacity	8500	8500	8000	8000	8000	10000	10000	10000	10000	10000	
EPA City (mpg) - Manual	NA	NA	NA	NA	NA	NA	NA	NA	NA	NA	NA
EPA Hwy (mpg) - Manual	NA	NA	NA	NA	NA	NA	NA	NA	NA	NA	NA
EPA City (mpg) - Auto	NA	NA	NA	NA	NA	NA	NA	NA	NA	NA	NA
EPA Hwy (mpg) - Auto	NA	NA	NA	NA	NA	NA	NA	NA	NA	NA	NA

SPECIFICATIONS & EPA MILEAGE RATINGS

	C/K 3500 Series Pickup 4WD Crew Cab	Chevy Van 1500	Chevy Van 2500	Chevy Van 2500 Extended	Chevy Van 3500	Chevy Van 3500 Extended	Express G1500	Express G2500	Express G2500 Extended	Express G3500
Acceleration (0-60/sec)	NA	NA	NA	NA	NA	NA	NA	NA	NA	NA
Braking Dist. (60-0/ft)	173	NA	NA	NA	NA	NA	NA	NA	NA	NA
Turning Circle (in.)	55.7	45.1	47.4	53.4	47.5	53.5	45.1	47.4	53.4	47.5
Length (in.)	250.9	218.7	218.7	238.7	218.7	238.7	218.7	218.7	238.7	218.7
Width (in.)	76.8	79.2	79.2	79.2	79.2	79.2	79.2	79.2	79.2	79.2
Height (in.)	74.5	80.7	82.7	81.3	83.3	82.1	80.7	82.7	81.3	83.3
Curb Weight (lbs.)	5827	4654	4829	4983	5434	5609	5075	5803	6008	5937
Wheelbase (in.)	168.5	135	135	155	135	155	135	135	155	135
Front Head Room (in.)	39.9	39	40.6	40.6	40.6	40.6	40.6	40.6	40.6	40.6
Rear Head Room (in.)	40.8	NA	NA	NA	NA	NA	38.2	38.2	38.2	38.2
Front Leg Room (in.)	41.7	41.2	41.2	41.2	41.2	41.2	41.2	41.2	41.2	41.2
Rear Leg Room (in.)	37.9	NA	NA	NA	NA	NA	38.5	35.4	36.2	35.4
Maximum Seating	6	2	2	2	2	2	8	12	12	12
Max Cargo Capacity (cu ft.)	NA	267	267	317	267	317	267	267	317	267
Maximum Payload (lbs.)	3373	1446	2471	2317	4066	3891	2025	2798	2592	3563
Number of Cylinders	8	6	6	6	8	8	6	8	8	8
Displacement (liters)	5.7	4.3	4.3	5.7	5.7	5.7	4.3	5.7	5.7	5.7
Horsepower @ RPM	255@4600	200@4400	200@4400	200@4400	250@4600	250@4600	200@4400	250@4600	250@4600	250@4600
Torque @ RPM	330@2800	250@2800	250@2800	250@2800	330@2800	330@2800	250@2800	330@2800	330@2800	330@2800
Fuel Capacity	34	31	31	31	31	31	31	31	31	31
Towing Capacity	10000	6000	8000	8000	10000	10000	6000	8000	8000	10000
EPA City (mpg) - Manual	NA	NA	NA	NA	NA	NA	NA	NA	NA	NA
EPA Hwy (mpg) - Manual	NA	NA	NA	NA	NA	NA	NA	NA	NA	NA
EPA City (mpg) - Auto	NA	15	15	15	13	13	15	13	13	13
EPA Hwy (mpg) - Auto	NA	19	19	19	18	18	19	18	18	18

SPECIFICATIONS & EPA MILEAGE RATINGS

	Express G3500 Extended	S-10 2WD Reg Cab SB	S-10 2WD Reg Cab LB	S-10 2WD X-cab	S-10 4WD Reg Cab SB	S-10 4WD Reg Cab LB	S-10 4WD X-cab	Suburban C1500	Suburban C2500	Suburban K1500
Acceleration (0-60/sec)	NA	NA	NA	NA	9.2	9.3	9.3	9.9	NA	NA	10.3
Braking Dist. (60-0/ft)	NA	NA	NA	NA	160	NA	NA	NA	157	157	165
Turning Circle (in.)	53.5	NA	NA	NA	NA	NA	NA	NA	43.7	43.4	44.7
Length (in.)	238.7	188.6	204.6	203.3	188.6	204.6	203.3	219.5	219.5	219.5
Width (in.)	79.2	67.9	67.9	67.9	67.9	67.9	67.9	76.7	76.7	76.7
Height (in.)	82.1	63.2	63.2	63.3	63.9	65	63.9	71.3	73.6	73
Curb Weight (lbs.)	6142	NA	NA	NA	NA	NA	NA	4802	5243	5234
Wheelbase (in.)	155	108.3	117.9	122.9	108.3	117.9	122.9	131.5	131.5	131.5
Front Head Room (in.)	40.6	39.5	39.5	39.6	39.5	39.5	39.6	39.9	39.9	39.9
Rear Head Room (in.)	38.2	NA	NA	NA	NA	NA	NA	37.9	37.9	37.9
Front Leg Room (in.)	41.2	42.4	42.4	42.4	42.4	42.4	42.4	41.3	41.3	41.3
Rear Leg Room (in.)	36.2	NA	NA	NA	NA	NA	NA	27.1	27.1	27.1
Maximum Seating	15	3	3	5	3	3	5	9	9	9
Max Cargo Capacity (cu ft.)	317	NA	NA	NA	NA	NA	NA	149.5	149.5	149.5
Maximum Payload (lbs.)	3358	NA	NA	NA	NA	NA	NA	2898	3357	2816
Number of Cylinders	8	4	4	4	6	6	6	8	8	8
Displacement (liters)	5.7	2.2	2.2	2.2	4.3	4.3	4.3	5.7	5.7	5.7
Horsepower @ RPM	250@4600	118@5200	118@5200	118@5200	180@4400	180@4400	180@4400	255@4600	255@4600	255@4600
Torque @ RPM	330@2800	130@2800	130@2800	130@2800	240@2800	240@2800	240@2800	330@2800	330@2800	330@2800
Fuel Capacity	31	19	19	19	19	19	19	42	42	42
Towing Capacity	10000	6000	6000	6000	5500	5500	5500	6500	10000	6000
EPA City (mpg) - Manual	NA	23	23	23	17	17	17	NA	NA	NA
EPA Hwy (mpg) - Manual	NA	30	30	30	22	22	22	NA	NA	NA
EPA City (mpg) - Auto	13	20	20	20	16	16	16	13	13	13
EPA Hwy (mpg) - Auto	18	27	27	27	21	21	21	18	17	18

SPECIFICATIONS & EPA MILEAGE RATINGS

	Suburban K2500	Tahoe 2-Door 2WD	Tahoe 2-Door 4WD	Tahoe 4-Door 2WD	Tahoe 4-Door 4WD	Tracker 2WD Convertible	Tracker 2WD 4-door	Tracker 4WD Convertible	Tracker 4WD 4-door	Venture 3-Door Reg Length
Acceleration (0-60/sec)	9.9	NA	9.5	8.7	9.6	11.6	12.1	13.6	13	9.9
Braking Dist. (60-0/ft)	157	NA	156	153	166	139	133	153	142	143
Turning Circle (in.)	45	38.1	39.8	39.8	40.7	32.2	35.4	32.9	35.4	37.4
Length (in.)	219.5	188	188	199.6	199.6	143.7	158.7	143.7	158.7	186.9
Width (in.)	76.7	77.1	77.1	76.8	76.8	64.2	64.4	64.2	64.4	72
Height (in.)	74.6	71.4	73	72.8	75	64.3	65.7	65.1	66.5	67.4
Curb Weight (lbs.)	5687	4453	4807	4423	4807	2339	2619	NA	NA	3671
Wheelbase (in.)	131.5	111.5	111.5	117.5	117.5	86.6	97.6	86.6	97.6	112
Front Head Room (in.)	39.9	39.9	39.9	39.9	39.9	39.5	40.6	39.5	40.6	39.9
Rear Head Room (in.)	37.9	37.8	37.8	38.9	38.9	39	40	39	40	38.8
Front Leg Room (in.)	41.3	41.7	41.7	41.7	41.7	42.1	42.1	42.1	42.1	39.9
Rear Leg Room (in.)	27.1	36.4	36.4	36.7	36.7	31.7	32.7	31.7	32.7	34
Maximum Seating	9	6	6	6	6	4	4	4	4	7
Max Cargo Capacity (cu ft.)	149.5	99.4	99.4	124.5	124.5	32.9	45	32.9	45	126.6
Maximum Payload (lbs.)	2913	1647	1443	1877	1993	NA	NA	NA	NA	1422
Number of Cylinders	8	8	8	8	8	4	4	4	4	6
Displacement (liters)	5.7	5.7	5.7	5.7	5.7	1.6	1.6	1.6	1.6	3.4
Horsepower @ RPM	255@4600	255@4600	255@4600	255@4600	255@4600	95@5600	95@5600	95@5600	95@5600	180@5200
Torque @ RPM	330@2800	330@2800	330@2800	330@2800	330@2800	98@4000	98@4000	98@4000	98@4000	205@4000
Fuel Capacity	42	30	30	30	30	11.1	14.5	11.1	14.5	20
Towing Capacity	10000	7000	7000	7000	7000	1000	1500	1000	1500	3500
EPA City (mpg) - Manual	NA	NA	NA	NA	NA	24	24	24	24	NA
EPA Hwy (mpg) - Manual	NA	NA	NA	NA	NA	26	26	26	26	NA
EPA City (mpg) - Auto	13	14	14	14	14	23	22	23	22	NA
EPA Hwy (mpg) - Auto	17	17	17	17	17	24	25	24	25	NA

SPECIFICATIONS & EPA MILEAGE RATINGS

	Venture 4-Door Reg Length	Venture 3-Door Ext Length	Venture 4-Door Ext Length	CHRYSLER	Town & Country SX	Town & Country LX AWD	Town & Country LX	Town & Country LXi AWD	Town & Country LXi
Acceleration (0-60/sec)	9.9	9.9	10.9		NA	NA	NA	NA	NA
Braking Dist. (60-0/ft)	143	143	143		NA	NA	NA	NA	NA
Turning Circle (in.)	37.4	39.7	39.7		37.7	39.4	39.5	39.4	39.5
Length (in.)	186.9	200.9	200.9		186.3	199.6	199.6	199.6	199.6
Width (in.)	72	72	72		75	75	75	75	75
Height (in.)	67.4	68.1	68.1		68.5	68.5	68.5	68.5	68.5
Curb Weight (lbs.)	3671	3792	3792		NA	NA	NA	NA	NA
Wheelbase (in.)	112	120	120		113.3	119.3	119.3	119.3	119.3
Front Head Room (in.)	39.9	39.9	39.9		39.8	39.8	39.8	39.8	39.8
Rear Head Room (in.)	38.8	38.9	38.9		40.1	40	40	40	40
Front Leg Room (in.)	39.9	39.9	39.9		41.2	41.2	41.1	41.2	41.1
Rear Leg Room (in.)	34	36.7	36.7		36.6	39.6	39.6	39.6	39.6
Maximum Seating	7	7	7		7	7	7	7	7
Max Cargo Capacity (cu ft.)	126.6	148.3	155.9		142.9	168.5	168.5	168.5	168.5
Maximum Payload (lbs.)	1422	1301	1301		NA	NA	NA	NA	NA
Number of Cylinders	6	6	6		6	6	6	6	6
Displacement (liters)	3.4	3.4	3.4		3.3	3.3	3.8	3.8	3.8
Horsepower @ RPM	180@5200	180@5200	180@5200		158@4850	158@4850	180@4300	180@4300	180@4300
Torque @ RPM	205@4000	205@4000	205@4000		203@3250	203@3250	227@3100	227@3100	227@3100
Fuel Capacity	20	25	25		20	20	20	20	20
Towing Capacity	3500	3500	3500		2000	2000	2000	2000	2000
EPA City (mpg) - Manual	NA	NA	NA		NA	NA	NA	NA	NA
EPA Hwy (mpg) - Manual	NA	NA	NA		NA	NA	NA	NA	NA
EPA City (mpg) - Auto	17	NA	NA		NA	NA	NA	NA	NA
EPA Hwy (mpg) - Auto	24	NA	NA		NA	NA	NA	NA	NA

SPECIFICATIONS & EPA MILEAGE RATINGS — DODGE

	Caravan 3L V-6	Caravan 3.3L V-6	Dakota 2WD Reg Cab SB	Dakota 2WD Reg Cab LB	Dakota 4WD Reg Cab SB	Dakota 2WD Club Cab	Dakota 4WD Club Cab	Durango	Grand Caravan 3.0L V-6
Acceleration (0-60/sec)	NA	NA	8.4	8.4	NA	9	12.6	NA	NA
Braking Dist. (60-0/ft)	NA	NA	149	149	NA	154	165	NA	NA
Turning Circle (in.)	37.6	37.6	36	39.4	35.8	41.2	41	NA	39.5
Length (in.)	186.3	186.3	195.8	215.1	195.8	214.8	214.8	193.3	199.6
Width (in.)	75	75	71.5	71.5	71.5	71.5	71.5	71.5	75.6
Height (in.)	68.5	68.5	65.6	65.3	68	65.6	68.5	72.9	68.5
Curb Weight (lbs.)	NA	NA	3273	3353	3767	3762	4018	NA	NA
Wheelbase (in.)	113.3	113.3	111.9	123.9	112	131	131	115.9	119.3
Front Head Room (in.)	39.8	39.8	40	40	40	40	40	39.8	39.8
Rear Head Room (in.)	40.1	40.1	NA	NA	NA	38	38	40.6	40
Front Leg Room (in.)	41.2	41.2	41.9	41.9	41.9	41.9	41.9	41.9	41.1
Rear Leg Room (in.)	36.6	36.6	NA	NA	NA	22.1	22.1	35.4	39.6
Maximum Seating	7	7	3	3	3	6	6	5	7
Max Cargo Capacity (cu ft.)	142.9	142.9	NA	NA	NA	NA	NA	88	168.5
Maximum Payload (lbs.)	NA	NA	2600	2600	2000	2000	1800	1450	NA
Number of Cylinders	6	6	4	4	6	6	6	6	6
Displacement (liters)	3	3.3	2.5	2.5	3.9	3.9	3.9	3.9	3
Horsepower @ RPM	150@5200	158@4850	120@5200	120@5200	175@4800	175@4800	175@4800	175@	150@5200
Torque @ RPM	176@4000	203@3250	145@3250	145@3250	225@3200	225@3200	225@3200	225@	176@4000
Fuel Capacity	20	20	15	15	15	15	15	25	20
Towing Capacity	2000	2000	6700	6700	6500	6400	6200	4100	2000
EPA City (mpg) - Manual	NA	NA	21	21	15	16	15	NA	NA
EPA Hwy (mpg) - Manual	NA	NA	25	25	19	22	19	NA	NA
EPA City (mpg) - Auto	19	18	NA	NA	18	16	15	NA	NA
EPA Hwy (mpg) - Auto	24	24	NA	NA	18	20	18	NA	NA

SPECIFICATIONS & EPA MILEAGE RATINGS

	Grand Caravan 3.8L V-6	Grand Caravan 3.3L V-6	Ram 1500 WS 2WD Reg Cab SB	Ram 1500 WS 2WD Reg Cab LB	Ram 1500 LT 2WD Reg Cab SB	Ram 1500 LT 2WD Reg Cab LB	Ram 1500 ST 2WD Club Cab SB	Ram 1500 ST 2WD Club Cab LB	Ram 1500 LT 4WD Reg Cab SB	Ram 1500 LT 4WD Reg Cab LB
Acceleration (0-60/sec)	NA	NA	NA	10.6	10.6	9	9	10	10	NA	NA
Braking Dist. (60-0/ft)	NA	NA	NA	145	145	148	148	152	152	NA	NA
Turning Circle (in.)	NA	39.5	40.6	45.2	40.6	45.2	46.9	51.6	40.6	45.2
Length (in.)	199.6	199.6	204.1	224.1	204.1	224.1	224	244	204.1	224.1
Width (in.)	75.6	75.6	79.4	79.4	79.4	79.4	79.4	79.4	79.4	79.4
Height (in.)	68.5	68.5	71.9	71.8	71.9	71.8	71.6	71.5	74.7	74.6
Curb Weight (lbs.)	NA	NA	4009	4132	4028	4339	4575	4658	4525	4682
Wheelbase (in.)	119.3	119.3	118.7	134.7	118.7	134.7	138.7	154.7	118.7	134.7
Front Head Room (in.)	39.8	39.8	40.2	40.2	40.2	40.2	40.2	40.2	40.2	40.2
Rear Head Room (in.)	40	40	NA	NA	NA	NA	39.4	39.4	NA	NA
Front Leg Room (in.)	41.1	41.1	41	41	41	41	41	41	41	41
Rear Leg Room (in.)	39.6	39.6	NA	NA	NA	NA	31.6	31.6	NA	NA
Maximum Seating	7	7	3	3	3	3	6	6	3	3
Max Cargo Capacity (cu ft.)	168.5	168.5	NA	NA	NA	NA	NA	NA	NA	NA
Maximum Payload (lbs.)	NA	NA	2001	1698	2372	2069	1825	1742	1875	1712
Number of Cylinders	6	6	6	6	6	6	8	8	8	8
Displacement (liters)	3.8	3.3	3.9	3.9	3.9	3.9	5.2	5.2	5.2	5.2
Horsepower @ RPM	180@4300	158@4850	175@	175@4800	175@4800	175@4800	220@4400	220@4400	220@4400	220@4400
Torque @ RPM	240@3100	203@3250	230@	230@3200	230@3200	230@3200	300@3200	300@3200	300@3200	300@3200
Fuel Capacity	20	20	26	35	26	35	26	35	26	35
Towing Capacity	2000	2000	3600	3600	8100	8100	8100	8100	7800	7800
EPA City (mpg) - Manual	NA	NA	16	16	16	16	14	14	13	13
EPA Hwy (mpg) - Manual	NA	NA	20	20	20	20	19	19	17	17
EPA City (mpg) - Auto	NA	NA	14	14	14	14	13	13	12	12
EPA Hwy (mpg) - Auto	NA	NA	18	18	18	18	17	17	16	16

	Ram 1500 ST 4WD Club Cab SB	Ram 1500 ST 4WD Club Cab LB	Ram 2500 2WD HD Reg Cab	Ram 2500 2WD Club Cab SB	Ram 2500 2WD Club Cab LB	Ram 2500 4WD HD Reg Cab	Ram 2500 4WD Club Cab SB	Ram 2500 4WD Club Cab LB	Ram 3500 2WD Reg Cab DRW	Ram 3500 2WD Club Cab DRW
Acceleration (0-60/sec)	10.2	10.2	NA	NA	NA	NA	8.2	NA	NA	NA
Braking Dist. (60-0/ft)	178	178	NA	NA	NA	NA	168	NA	NA	NA
Turning Circle (in.)	46.3	51	45.4	46.9	51.8	45	46.7	51.3	46.4	51.9
Length (in.)	224	244	224.1	224	244	224.1	224	244	224.1	244
Width (in.)	79.4	79.4	79.4	79.4	79.4	79.4	79.4	79.4	93.5	93.5
Height (in.)	74.6	74.5	72.1	72.9	72.8	75.1	77.2	77.1	73	72.8
Curb Weight (lbs.)	4960	5039	4765	4983	5103	5219	5239	5359	5254	5583
Wheelbase (in.)	138.7	154.7	134.7	138.7	154.7	134.7	138.7	154.7	134.7	154.7
Front Head Room (in.)	40.2	40.2	40.2	40.2	40.2	40.2	40.2	40.2	40.2	40.2
Rear Head Room (in.)	39.4	39.4	NA	39.4	39.4	NA	39.4	39.4	NA	39.4
Front Leg Room (in.)	41	41	41	41	41	41	41	41	41	41
Rear Leg Room (in.)	31.6	31.6	NA	31.6	31.6	NA	31.6	31.6	NA	31.6
Maximum Seating	6	6	3	6	6	3	6	6	3	6
Max Cargo Capacity (cu ft.)	NA	NA	NA	NA	NA	NA	NA	NA	NA	NA
Maximum Payload (lbs.)	1440	1361	4043	3817	3697	3581	3561	3441	5246	4917
Number of Cylinders	8	8	8	8	8	8	8	8	8	8
Displacement (liters)	5.2	5.2	5.9	5.9	5.9	5.9	5.9	5.9	5.9	5.9
Horsepower @ RPM	220@4400	220@4400	235@4000	235@4000	235@4000	235@4000	235@4000	235@4000	235@4000	235@4000
Torque @ RPM	300@3200	300@3200	330@3000	330@3000	330@3000	330@3000	330@3000	330@3000	330@3000	330@3000
Fuel Capacity	26	35	35	26	35	35	26	35	35	35
Towing Capacity	7800	7800	13600	13600	13600	13200	13200	13200	13200	13200
EPA City (mpg) - Manual	13	13	NA	NA	NA	NA	NA	NA	NA	NA
EPA Hwy (mpg) - Manual	17	17	NA	NA	NA	NA	NA	NA	NA	NA
EPA City (mpg) - Auto	12	12	NA	NA	NA	NA	NA	NA	NA	NA
EPA Hwy (mpg) - Auto	16	16	NA	NA	NA	NA	NA	NA	NA	NA

SPECIFICATIONS & EPA MILEAGE RATINGS

SPECIFICATIONS & EPA MILEAGE RATINGS

	Ram 3500 4WD Reg Cab DRW	Ram 3500 4WD Club Cab DRW	Ram Van 1500 SWB	Ram Van 1500 LWB	Ram Van 2500 SWB	Ram Van 2500 LWB	Ram Van 2500 Maxivan	Ram Van 3500 LWB	Ram Van 3500 Maxivan
Acceleration (0-60/sec)	NA	NA	9.7	9.7	9.7	9.7	NA	NA	NA
Braking Dist. (60-0/ft)	NA	NA	167	167	167	167	NA	NA	NA
Turning Circle (in.)	46.4	51.3	40.5	46.2	40.5	46.2	46.2	52.4	52.4
Length (in.)	224.1	244	187.2	205.2	187.2	205.2	231.2	205.2	231.2
Width (in.)	93.5	93.5	79.8	79.8	79.8	79.8	79.8	79.8	79.8
Height (in.)	77.4	77.2	79.5	79.9	79.9	79.9	79.9	79.9	79.9
Curb Weight (lbs.)	5612	5940	3799	3992	3829	4082	4234	4414	4633
Wheelbase (in.)	134.7	154.7	109.6	127.6	109.6	127.6	127.6	127.6	127.6
Front Head Room (in.)	40.2	40.2	40.5	40.5	40.5	40.5	40.5	40.5	40.5
Rear Head Room (in.)	NA	39.4	NA	NA	NA	NA	NA	NA	NA
Front Leg Room (in.)	41	41	39	39	39	39	39	39	39
Rear Leg Room (in.)	NA	31.6	NA	NA	NA	NA	NA	NA	NA
Maximum Seating	3	6	2	2	2	2	2	2	2
Max Cargo Capacity (cu ft.)	NA	NA	206.6	247	206.6	246.7	304.5	246.7	304.5
Maximum Payload (lbs.)	4888	5060	2211	2018	2517	2368	2166	3186	3877
Number of Cylinders	8	8	6	6	6	6	6	8	8
Displacement (liters)	5.9	5.9	3.9	3.9	3.9	3.9	3.9	5.2	5.2
Horsepower @ RPM	235@4000	235@4000	175@4800	175@4800	175@4800	175@4800	175@4800	225@4400	225@4400
Torque @ RPM	330@3000	330@3000	225@3200	225@3200	225@3200	225@3200	225@3200	295@3200	295@3200
Fuel Capacity	35	35	35	35	35	35	35	35	35
Towing Capacity	12800	12800	NA	NA	NA	NA	NA	NA	NA
EPA City (mpg) - Manual	NA	NA	NA	NA	NA	NA	NA	NA	NA
EPA Hwy (mpg) - Manual	NA	NA	NA	NA	NA	NA	NA	NA	NA
EPA City (mpg) - Auto	NA	NA	15	15	15	15	15	13	13
EPA Hwy (mpg) - Auto	NA	NA	17	17	17	17	17	17	17

SPECIFICATIONS & EPA MILEAGE RATINGS

	Ram Wagon 1500 SWB	Ram Wagon 2500 LWB	Ram Wagon 3500 LWB	Ram Wagon 3500 Maxiwagon	**FORD**	Club Wagon Super	Econoline E150 Regular	Econoline E250 Regular	Econoline E250 Regular HD	Econoline E350 Regular
Acceleration (0-60/sec)	9.7	9.7	NA	NA		NA	11.1	11.1	11.1	NA
Braking Dist. (60-0/ft)	167	167	NA	NA		162	162	162	162	162
Turning Circle (in.)	40.5	46.2	52.4	52.4		47.8	46.7	45.6	46.5	46.5
Length (in.)	187.2	205.2	205.2	231.2		231.8	211.8	211.8	211.8	211.8
Width (in.)	79.8	79.8	79.8	79.8		79.5	79.3	79.3	79.3	79.3
Height (in.)	79.5	79.5	79.5	79.9		83.4	80.7	83.4	83.4	84.1
Curb Weight (lbs.)	4339	4790	5047	5247		4972	4680	5076	5080	5215
Wheelbase (in.)	109.6	127.6	127.6	127.6		138	138	138	138	138
Front Head Room (in.)	40.5	40.5	40.5	40.5		41.5	41.5	41.5	41.5	41.5
Rear Head Room (in.)	37	36.7	36.7	36.4		NA	NA	NA	NA	NA
Front Leg Room (in.)	39	39	39	39		39.5	39.5	39.5	39.5	39.5
Rear Leg Room (in.)	40.5	40.3	40.3	40.4		NA	NA	NA	NA	NA
Maximum Seating	8	12	12	15		15	2	2	2	2
Max Cargo Capacity (cu ft.)	206.6	246.7	246.7	304.5		299.8	260.8	260.8	260.8	260.8
Maximum Payload (lbs.)	1611	1610	2453	3263		3920	2140	1240	3470	4185
Number of Cylinders	6	8	8	8		8	6	8	8	8
Displacement (liters)	3.9	5.2	5.2	5.2		5.4	4.2	5.4	5.4	5.4
Horsepower @ RPM	175@4800	225@4400	225@4400	225@4400		235@4250	200@4800	235@4250	235@4250	235@4250
Torque @ RPM	225@3200	295@3200	295@3200	295@3200		335@3000	250@2800	335@3000	335@3000	335@3000
Fuel Capacity	35	35	35	35		35	35	35	35	35
Towing Capacity	NA	NA	NA	NA		10000	10000	10000	10000	10000
EPA City (mpg) - Manual	NA	NA	NA	NA		NA	NA	NA	NA	NA
EPA Hwy (mpg) - Manual	NA	NA	NA	NA		NA	NA	NA	16	14
EPA City (mpg) - Auto	15	12	12	12		14	14	14	14	14
EPA Hwy (mpg) - Auto	17	14	16	16		18	18	18	18	18

SPECIFICATIONS & EPA MILEAGE RATINGS

	Econoline E350 Super	Expedition 2WD	Expedition 4WD	Explorer 2WD 2-Door	Explorer 4WD 2-Door	Explorer 2WD 4-Door	Explorer 4WD 4-Door	Explorer AWD 4-Door	F-Series 2WD X-cab SWB	F-Series 2WD Reg Cab SWB
Acceleration (0-60/sec)	NA	NA	NA	NA	10.6	10.6	9.5	10.6	NA	10	NA
Braking Dist. (60-0/ft)	162	NA	NA	NA	146	146	146	146	NA	149	NA
Turning Circle (in.)	48	40.4	40.5	34.6	34.6	37.3	37.3	37.3	45.9	40.5
Length (in.)	231.8	204.6	204.6	178.6	178.6	188.5	188.5	188.5	220.8	202.2
Width (in.)	79.3	78.6	78.6	70.2	70.2	70.2	70.2	70.2	78.4	78.4
Height (in.)	84.1	74.4	76.4	67.8	67.8	67.5	66.8	67.5	72.8	72.7
Curb Weight (lbs.)	5380	4850	4850	3981	3981	4189	4189	NA	4045	3850
Wheelbase (in.)	138	119	119	101.7	101.7	111.5	111.5	111.5	138.5	119.9
Front Head Room (in.)	41.5	39.8	39.8	39.9	39.9	39.9	39.9	39.8	40.8	40.8
Rear Head Room (in.)	NA	39.8	39.8	39.1	39.1	39.3	39.3	39.9	37.8	NA
Front Leg Room (in.)	39.5	40.9	40.9	42.4	42.4	42.4	42.4	39.3	40.9	40.9
Rear Leg Room (in.)	NA	38.9	38.9	36.5	36.6	37.7	37.7	37.7	32.2	NA
Maximum Seating	2	9	9	4	4	6	6	5	6	3
Max Cargo Capacity (cu ft.)	299.8	NA	NA	69.4	69.4	81.6	81.6	81.6	39.2	NA
Maximum Payload (lbs.)	4185	2000	2000	750	750	900	900	82	1955	1700
Number of Cylinders	8	8	8	6	6	6	6	8	6	6
Displacement (liters)	5.4	4.6	4.6	4	4	4	4	5	4.2	4.2
Horsepower @ RPM	235@4250	215@4400	215@4400	160@4400	160@4400	160@4400	160@4400	NA@	210@	210@
Torque @ RPM	335@3000	290@3250	290@3250	225@2800	225@2800	225@2800	225@2800	NA@	255@	255@
Fuel Capacity	35	26	30	17.5	17.5	21	21	21	25	25
Towing Capacity	10000	8000	8000	5100	5100	6700	5100	6500	7000	7200
EPA City (mpg) - Manual	14	NA	NA	18	17	17	17	NA	NA	NA
EPA Hwy (mpg) - Manual	16	NA	NA	21	21	21	21	NA	NA	NA
EPA City (mpg) - Auto	14	14	14	17	15	15	15	NA	NA	NA
EPA Hwy (mpg) - Auto	18	20	18	20	20	20	20	NA	NA	NA

SPECIFICATIONS & EPA MILEAGE RATINGS

	F-Series 2WD X-cab LWB	F-Series 2WD Reg Cab LWB	F-Series 4WD X-cab SWB	F-Series 4WD Reg Cab SWB	F-Series 4WD X-cab LWB	F-Series 4WD Reg Cab LWB	F-Series 2WD X-cab Flareside	F-Series 2WD Reg Cab Flare	F-Series 4WD Reg Cab Flare	F-Series 4WD X-cab Flareside
Acceleration (0-60/sec)	10	NA	NA	NA	NA	NA	10	NA	9	NA
Braking Dist. (60-0/ft)	149	NA	NA	NA	NA	NA	148	NA	162	NA
Turning Circle (in.)	51.3	45.9	45.8	40.4	51.2	40.4	45.9	40.5	40.4	45.8
Length (in.)	239.4	220.8	222.3	203.7	240.9	222.3	239.4	205.9	207.4	226
Width (in.)	78.4	78.4	79.5	79.5	79.5	79.5	79.1	79.1	79.5	79.5
Height (in.)	72.5	72.4	75.4	75.4	75.1	75.1	72.8	72.7	75.4	75.5
Curb Weight (lbs.)	4200	3960	4478	4235	4606	4339	4196	3922	4308	4624
Wheelbase (in.)	157.1	138.5	138.8	120.2	157.4	138.8	138.5	119.9	120.2	138.8
Front Head Room (in.)	40.8	40.8	40.8	40.8	40.8	40.8	40.8	40.8	40.8	40.8
Rear Head Room (in.)	37.8	NA	37.8	NA	37.8	NA	37.8	NA	NA	37.8
Front Leg Room (in.)	40.9	40.9	40.9	40.9	40.9	40.9	40.9	40.9	40.9	40.9
Rear Leg Room (in.)	32.2	NA	32.2	NA	32.2	NA	32.2	NA	NA	32.2
Maximum Seating	6	3	6	3	6	3	6	3	3	6
Max Cargo Capacity (cu ft.)	39.2	NA	39.2	NA	39.2	NA	32.2	NA	NA	39.2
Maximum Payload (lbs.)	1800	2435	1520	1765	1390	1660	1795	1620	1690	1365
Number of Cylinders	6	6	8	6	8	6	6	6	6	8
Displacement (liters)	4.2	4.2	4.6	4.2	4.6	4.2	4.2	4.2	4.2	4.6
Horsepower @ RPM	210@	210@	210@	210@	210@	210@	210@	210@	210@	210@
Torque @ RPM	255@	255@	290@	255@	290@	255@	255@	255@	255@	290@
Fuel Capacity	30	30	24.5	24.5	30	30	25	25	24.5	24.5
Towing Capacity	7200	7200	6600	6800	6600	6800	7000	7200	6800	6600
EPA City (mpg) - Manual	NA	NA	NA	NA	NA	NA	NA	NA	NA	NA
EPA Hwy (mpg) - Manual	NA	NA	NA	NA	NA	NA	NA	NA	NA	NA
EPA City (mpg) - Auto	NA	NA	NA	NA	NA	NA	NA	NA	NA	NA
EPA Hwy (mpg) - Auto	NA	NA	NA	NA	NA	NA	NA	NA	NA	NA

SPECIFICATIONS & EPA MILEAGE RATINGS

	F350 Pickup 2WD Crew Cab	F350 Pickup 4WD Crew Cab	F350 Pickup 2WD Crew Cab DRW	F350 Pickup 4WD Crew Cab DRW	F350 Pickup 2WD Ext Cab DRW	F350 Pickup 2WD Reg Cab	F350 Pickup 2WD Reg Cab DRW	F350 Pickup 4WD Reg Cab	Ranger Reg Cab 2WD LB	Ranger Reg Cab 4WD LB	Ranger Ext Cab 4WD
Acceleration (0-60/sec)	NA	NA	NA	NA	NA	NA	NA	NA	NA	NA	NA
Braking Dist. (60-0/ft)	NA	NA	NA	NA	NA	NA	NA	NA	NA	NA	NA
Turning Circle (in.)	NA	59	59	50.4	43.9	43.9	43.9	36.7	37.4	39.4	
Length (in.)	248.7	248.7	248.7	235.3	213.3	213.3	213.3	200.7	200.7	202.9	
Width (in.)	79	79	94.5	95.4	79	95.4	79	69.4	69.4	69.4	
Height (in.)	71	74	71	74	71	71	71	63.8	67.4	67.5	
Curb Weight (lbs.)	5215	5660	5380	5345	4480	4900	5135	NA	NA	NA	
Wheelbase (in.)	168.4	168.4	168.4	155	133	133	133	118	118	126	
Front Head Room (in.)	40.2	40.2	39.9	39.9	40.3	40.3	40.3	39.2	39.2	39.3	
Rear Head Room (in.)	39.6	39.6	39.6	37.6	NA	NA	NA	NA	NA	NA	
Front Leg Room (in.)	41.1	41.1	41.1	41	41.1	41.1	41.1	42.2	42.2	42.2	
Rear Leg Room (in.)	37.9	37.9	37.9	28.8	NA	NA	NA	NA	NA	NA	
Maximum Seating	6	6	6	6	3	3	3	3	3	5	
Max Cargo Capacity (cu ft.)	NA	NA	NA	NA	NA	NA	NA	43.5	43.5	37.4	
Maximum Payload (lbs.)	3985	3540	4620	4655	4305	6595	4030	1260	1260	1260	
Number of Cylinders	8	8	8	8	8	8	8	4	6	6	
Displacement (liters)	5.8	5.8	5.8	7.5	5.8	5.8	5.8	2.5	3	3	
Horsepower @ RPM	210@3600	210@3600	210@3600	245@4000	210@3600	210@3600	210@3600	119@4800	150@5000	150@5000	
Torque @ RPM	325@2800	325@2800	325@2800	400@2400	325@2800	325@2800	325@2800	146@2400	185@3250	185@3250	
Fuel Capacity	37	37	37	37	37	37	37	20	20	20	
Towing Capacity	12500	12500	12500	12500	12500	12500	10000	1600	2300	2100	
EPA City (mpg) - Manual	NA	NA	NA	NA	NA	NA	NA	NA	NA	NA	
EPA Hwy (mpg) - Manual	NA	NA	NA	NA	NA	NA	NA	NA	NA	NA	
EPA City (mpg) - Auto	NA	NA	NA	NA	NA	NA	NA	NA	NA	NA	
EPA Hwy (mpg) - Auto	NA	NA	NA	NA	NA	NA	NA	NA	NA	NA	

SPECIFICATIONS & EPA MILEAGE RATINGS

	Ranger Ext Cab 2WD	Ranger Reg Cab 4WD SB	Windstar 3.0L	Windstar 3.8L	**GMC** Jimmy 2WD 2-door	Jimmy 2WD 4-door	Jimmy 4WD 2-door	Jimmy 4WD 4-door	Safari 2WD
Acceleration (0-60/sec)	NA	NA	10.3	10.3	NA	NA	9	9.4	10.3
Braking Dist. (60-0/ft)	NA	NA	139	139	NA	NA	147	155	151
Turning Circle (in.)	39.4	37.4	40.7	40.7	34.8	36.6	36.9	41.2	39.5
Length (in.)	202.9	187.5	201.2	201.2	175	181.2	175.1	181.1	189.8
Width (in.)	69.4	69.4	74.3	74.3	67.8	67.8	67.8	67.8	77.5
Height (in.)	67.5	66.7	68	68	66	64.8	66.9	64.8	76
Curb Weight (lbs.)	NA	NA	3800	3800	3535	3692	3814	4023	4197
Wheelbase (in.)	126	112	120.7	120.7	100.5	107	100.5	107	111
Front Head Room (in.)	39.3	39.2	39.3	39.3	39.5	39.5	39.5	39.5	39.1
Rear Head Room (in.)	NA	NA	38.1	38.1	38.1	38.1	38.1	38.1	38.7
Front Leg Room (in.)	42.2	42.2	41.8	41.8	42.4	42.4	42.4	42.4	41.6
Rear Leg Room (in.)	NA	NA	35.3	35.3	36.3	36.3	36.3	36.3	38.5
Maximum Seating	5	3	7	7	4	6	4	6	8
Max Cargo Capacity (cu ft.)	37.4	37.4	144	144	66.9	74.1	66.9	74.1	170.4
Maximum Payload (lbs.)	1260	1260	1800	1800	914	1158	971	1277	1753
Number of Cylinders	6	6	6	6	6	6	6	6	6
Displacement (liters)	3	3	3	3.8	4.3	4.3	4.3	4.3	4.3
Horsepower @ RPM	150@5000	150@5000	150@5000	200@4000	190@4400	190@4400	190@4400	190@4400	190@4400
Torque @ RPM	185@3250	185@3250	170@3000	230@3000	250@2800	250@2800	250@2800	250@2800	250@2800
Fuel Capacity	20	17	20	25	19	18	19	18	25
Towing Capacity	2100	2300	3500	3500	5500	5500	5000	5000	5500
EPA City (mpg) - Manual	NA	NA	NA	NA	NA	NA	NA	NA	NA
EPA Hwy (mpg) - Manual	NA	NA	NA	NA	NA	NA	NA	NA	NA
EPA City (mpg) - Auto	NA	17	NA	NA	NA	NA	NA	NA	NA
EPA Hwy (mpg) - Auto	NA	24	NA	NA	NA	NA	NA	NA	NA

SPECIFICATIONS & EPA MILEAGE RATINGS

	Safari AWD	Savana 1500 SWB Cargo	Savana 1500 SWB Passenger	Savana 2500 SWB Cargo	Savana 2500 LWB Cargo	Savana 2500 SWB Passenger	Savana 2500 LWB Passenger	Savana 3500 SWB Cargo	Savana 3500 LWB Cargo	Savana 3500 SWB Passenger
Acceleration (0-60/sec)	12.7	NA	NA	NA	NA	NA	NA	NA	NA	NA
Braking Dist. (60-0/ft)	151	NA	NA	NA	NA	NA	NA	NA	NA	NA
Turning Circle (in.)	40.5	45.1	45.1	45.1	53.4	47.4	53.4	47.4	53.4	47.4
Length (in.)	189.8	218.8	218.8	218.8	238.8	218.8	238.8	218.8	238.8	218.8
Width (in.)	77.5	79.2	79.2	79.2	79.2	79.2	79.2	79.2	79.2	79.2
Height (in.)	76	80.7	80.7	82.7	81.3	82.7	81.3	83.3	82.1	83.3
Curb Weight (lbs.)	4427	4654	5075	4829	4983	5803	6008	5434	5609	5937
Wheelbase (in.)	111	135	135	135	155	135	155	135	155	135
Front Head Room (in.)	39.1	40.6	40.6	40.6	40.6	40.6	40.6	40.6	40.6	40.6
Rear Head Room (in.)	38.7	NA	39.1	NA	NA	39.1	39.1	NA	39.1	39.1
Front Leg Room (in.)	41.6	41.1	41.1	41.1	41.1	41.1	41.1	41.1	41.1	41.1
Rear Leg Room (in.)	38.5	NA	38.6	NA	NA	38.6	38.6	NA	NA	38.6
Maximum Seating	8	2	12	2	2	12	12	2	2	12
Max Cargo Capacity (cu ft.)	170.4	267.3	267.3	267.3	316.8	267.3	316.8	267.3	316.8	267.3
Maximum Payload (lbs.)	1673	1446	2025	2471	2317	2798	2592	4066	3891	3563
Number of Cylinders	6	6	6	6	6	8	8	8	8	8
Displacement (liters)	4.3	4.3	4.3	4.3	4.3	5.7	5.7	5.7	5.7	5.7
Horsepower @ RPM	190@4400	200@4400	200@4400	200@4400	200@4400	250@4600	250@4600	250@4600	250@4600	250@4600
Torque @ RPM	250@2800	250@2800	250@2800	250@2800	250@2800	330@2800	330@2800	330@2800	330@2800	330@2800
Fuel Capacity	25	31	31	31	31	31	31	31	31	31
Towing Capacity	5000	6000	6000	8000	8000	8000	8000	10000	10000	10000
EPA City (mpg) - Manual	NA	NA	NA	NA	NA	NA	NA	NA	NA	NA
EPA Hwy (mpg) - Manual	NA	NA	NA	NA	NA	NA	NA	NA	NA	NA
EPA City (mpg) - Auto	NA	NA	NA	NA	NA	NA	NA	NA	NA	NA
EPA Hwy (mpg) - Auto	NA	NA	NA	NA	NA	NA	NA	NA	NA	NA

SPECIFICATIONS & EPA MILEAGE RATINGS

	Savana 3500 LWB Passenger	Sierra 1500 2WD Reg Cab SB	Sierra 1500 2WD Reg Cab LB	Sierra 1500 2WD X-cab SB	Sierra 1500 2WD X-cab LB	Sierra 1500 4WD Reg Cab SB	Sierra 1500 4WD Reg Cab LB	Sierra 1500 4WD X-cab SB	Sierra 1500 4WD X-cab LB	Sierra 2500 2WD Reg Cab LD
Acceleration (0-60/sec)	NA	NA	NA	NA	9.2	9.2	NA	NA	NA	NA
Braking Dist. (60-0/ft)	NA	144	144	147	147	NA	NA	NA	NA	144
Turning Circle (in.)	53.5	39.8	39.8	46.6	46.6	40.7	40.7	47.6	47.6	43.4
Length (in.)	238.8	194.5	213.4	217.5	236.6	194.5	213.4	218	236.6	213.1
Width (in.)	79.2	76.8	76.8	76.8	76.8	76.8	76.8	76.8	76.8	76.8
Height (in.)	82.1	70.8	70	70.6	70.1	72.7	72.5	72.6	73.2	NA
Curb Weight (lbs.)	6142	3869	4021	4160	4407	4275	4426	4533	4825	4293
Wheelbase (in.)	155	117.5	131.5	141.5	155.5	117.5	131.5	141.5	155.5	131.5
Front Head Room (in.)	40.6	39.9	39.9	39.9	39.9	39.9	39.9	39.9	39.9	39.9
Rear Head Room (in.)	38.4	NA	NA	37.5	37.5	NA	NA	37.5	37.5	NA
Front Leg Room (in.)	41.1	41.7	41.7	41.7	41.7	41.7	41.7	41.7	41.7	41.7
Rear Leg Room (in.)	38.4	NA	NA	34.8	34.8	NA	NA	34.8	34.8	NA
Maximum Seating	15	3	3	6	6	3	3	6	6	3
Max Cargo Capacity (cu ft.)	316.8	NA	NA	NA	NA	NA	NA	NA	NA	NA
Maximum Payload (lbs.)	3358	2231	2079	2040	1793	1825	1674	2067	1975	2907
Number of Cylinders	8	6	6	6	8	6	6	6	8	8
Displacement (liters)	5.7	4.3	4.3	4.3	5	4.3	4.3	4.3	5	4.3
Horsepower @ RPM	250@4600	200@4400	200@4400	200@4400	230@4600	200@4400	200@4400	200@4400	230@4600	230@4600
Torque @ RPM	330@2800	255@2800	255@2800	255@2800	285@2800	255@2800	255@2800	255@2800	285@2800	285@2800
Fuel Capacity	31	25	34	25	34	25	34	25	34	34
Towing Capacity	10000	7000	7000	7000	7000	6500	6500	6500	6500	8500
EPA City (mpg) - Manual	NA	NA	NA	NA	NA	NA	NA	NA	NA	NA
EPA Hwy (mpg) - Manual	NA	NA	NA	NA	NA	NA	NA	NA	NA	NA
EPA City (mpg) - Auto	NA	NA	NA	NA	NA	NA	NA	NA	NA	NA
EPA Hwy (mpg) - Auto	NA	NA	NA	NA	NA	NA	NA	NA	NA	NA

SPECIFICATIONS & EPA MILEAGE RATINGS

	Sierra 2500 2WD Reg Cab HD	Sierra 2500 2WD X-cab SB	Sierra 2500 2WD X-cab LB	Sierra 2500 4WD Reg Cab HD	Sierra 2500 4WD X-cab SB	Sierra 2500 4WD X-cab LB	Sierra 3500 2WD Reg Cab	Sierra 3500 2WD X-cab Dualie	Sierra 3500 4WD Reg Cab	Sierra 3500 2WD Crew Cab
Acceleration (0-60/sec)	NA	NA	NA	NA	NA	NA	NA	NA	NA	NA
Braking Dist. (60-0/ft)	144	NA	NA	NA	NA	NA	NA	NA	NA	173
Turning Circle (in.)	43.4	NA	51.9	NA	NA	51.9	43.4	NA	NA	53.8
Length (in.)	213.1	217.9	236.6	213.1	217.9	236.6	213.1	236.6	213.1	250.9
Width (in.)	76.8	76.8	76.8	76.8	76.8	76.8	76.8	94.3	76.8	76.8
Height (in.)	NA	NA	NA	71.2	76	NA	NA	NA	72.6	73.9
Curb Weight (lbs.)	4293	NA	NA	5013	5154	NA	5442	4474	5395	5201	5169
Wheelbase (in.)	131.5	141.5	155.5	131.5	141.5	155.5	131.5	155.5	131.5	168.5
Front Head Room (in.)	39.9	39.9	39.9	39.9	39.9	39.9	39.9	39.9	39.9	39.9
Rear Head Room (in.)	NA	37.5	37.5	NA	37.5	37.5	NA	37.5	NA	40.8
Front Leg Room (in.)	41.7	41.7	41.7	41.7	41.7	41.7	41.7	41.7	41.7	41.7
Rear Leg Room (in.)	NA	34.8	34.8	NA	34.8	34.8	NA	34.8	NA	37.9
Maximum Seating	3	6	6	3	6	6	3	6	3	6
Max Cargo Capacity (cu ft.)	NA	NA	NA	NA	NA	NA	NA	NA	NA	NA
Maximum Payload (lbs.)	4307	NA	3587	NA	3446	NA	3158	4126	3205	4316	3431
Number of Cylinders	8	8	8	8	8	8	8	8	8	8
Displacement (liters)	5.7	5	5.7	5.7	5.7	5.7	5.7	5.7	5.7	5.7
Horsepower @ RPM	255@4600	230@4600	255@4600	255@4600	255@4600	255@4600	255@4600	255@4600	255@4600	255@4600
Torque @ RPM	330@2800	285@2800	330@2800	330@2800	330@2800	330@2800	330@2800	330@2800	330@2800	330@2800
Fuel Capacity	34	25	34	34	25	34	34	34	34	34
Towing Capacity	8500	8500	8500	8000	8000	8000	10000	10000	10000	10000
EPA City (mpg) - Manual	NA	NA	NA	NA	NA	NA	NA	NA	NA	NA
EPA Hwy (mpg) - Manual	NA	NA	NA	NA	NA	NA	NA	NA	NA	NA
EPA City (mpg) - Auto	NA	NA	NA	NA	NA	NA	NA	NA	NA	NA
EPA Hwy (mpg) - Auto	NA	NA	NA	NA	NA	NA	NA	NA	NA	NA

SPECIFICATIONS & EPA MILEAGE RATINGS

	Sierra 3500 4WD X-cab Dually	Sierra 3500 4WD Crew Cab	Sonoma 2WD Reg Cab SB	Sonoma 2WD Reg Cab LB	Sonoma 2WD X-cab	Sonoma 4WD Reg Cab SB	Sonoma 4WD Reg Cab LB	Sonoma 4WD X-cab	Suburban C1500	Suburban C2500
Acceleration (0-60/sec)	NA	NA	NA	NA	9.4	9.3	9.3	10.1	NA	13.7
Braking Dist. (60-0/ft)	NA	NA	NA	NA	155	NA	NA	131	150	157
Turning Circle (in.)	51.9	55.7	36.9	36.9	41.3	37.3	37.3	41.6	43.7	43.4
Length (in.)	236.6	250.9	189	205	203.7	189	205	203.7	219.5	219.5
Width (in.)	94.3	76.8	67.9	67.9	67.9	67.9	67.9	67.9	76.7	76.7
Height (in.)	74	74.5	63.2	62.1	63.3	65.4	65.4	63.9	71.3	73
Curb Weight (lbs.)	5778	5527	2930	2983	3168	3469	3565	3717	4802	5243
Wheelbase (in.)	155.5	168.5	108.3	117.9	122.9	108.3	117.9	122.9	131.5	131.5
Front Head Room (in.)	39.9	39.9	39.5	39.5	39.5	39.5	39.5	39.5	39.9	39.9
Rear Head Room (in.)	37.5	40.8	NA	NA	NA	NA	NA	NA	37.9	37.9
Front Leg Room (in.)	41.7	41.7	42.4	42.4	42.4	42.4	42.4	42.4	41.3	41.3
Rear Leg Room (in.)	34.8	37.9	NA	NA	NA	NA	NA	26.2	27.1	NA
Maximum Seating	6	6	3	3	5	3	3	5	9	9
Max Cargo Capacity (cu ft.)	NA	NA	NA	NA	NA	NA	NA	NA	149.5	149.5
Maximum Payload (lbs.)	2822	3073	1200	1547	1195	1132	1537	909	1998	3357
Number of Cylinders	8	8	4	4	4	6	6	6	8	8
Displacement (liters)	5.7	5.7	2.2	2.2	2.2	4.3	4.3	4.3	5.7	5.7
Horsepower @ RPM	255@4600	255@4600	118@5200	118@5200	118@5200	180@4400	180@4400	180@4400	255@4600	255@4600
Torque @ RPM	330@2800	330@2800	130@2800	130@2800	130@2800	240@2400	240@2800	240@2800	330@2800	330@2800
Fuel Capacity	34	34	19	19	19	19	19	19	42	42
Towing Capacity	10000	10000	6000	6000	6000	5500	5500	5500	6500	10000
EPA City (mpg) - Manual	NA	NA	NA	NA	NA	NA	NA	NA	NA	NA
EPA Hwy (mpg) - Manual	NA	NA	NA	NA	NA	NA	NA	NA	NA	NA
EPA City (mpg) - Auto	NA	NA	NA	NA	NA	NA	NA	NA	NA	NA
EPA Hwy (mpg) - Auto	NA	NA	NA	NA	NA	NA	NA	NA	NA	NA

SPECIFICATIONS & EPA MILEAGE RATINGS

	Suburban K1500	Suburban K2500	Yukon 2WD 2-door	Yukon 4WD 2-door	Yukon 2WD 4-door	Yukon 4WD 4-door	HONDA	CR-V	Odyssey LX
Acceleration (0-60/sec)	10.1	9.9	9.5	NA	8.7	9.6		NA	11.7
Braking Dist. (60-0/ft)	162	157	169	NA	154	159		NA	139
Turning Circle (in.)	44.7	44.7	38.1	39	39.8	40.7		34.8	37.6
Length (in.)	219.5	219.5	188	188	199.6	199.6		177.6	187.2
Width (in.)	76.7	76.7	77.1	77.1	76.8	76.8		68.9	70.6
Height (in.)	73.6	74.6	71.4	71.4	72.8	75		65.9	64.6
Curb Weight (lbs.)	5235	5687	4471	4827	4816	5225		3164	3472
Wheelbase (in.)	131.5	131.5	111.5	111.5	117.5	117.5		103.2	111.4
Front Head Room (in.)	39.9	39.9	39.9	39.9	39.9	39.9		40.5	40.1
Rear Head Room (in.)	37.9	37.9	37.8	37.8	38.9	38.9		39.2	39.3
Front Leg Room (in.)	41.3	41.3	41.7	41.7	41.7	41.7		41.5	40.7
Rear Leg Room (in.)	27.1	27.1	36.4	36.4	36.7	36.7		36.7	40.2
Maximum Seating	9	9	6	6	6	6		4	7
Max Cargo Capacity (cu ft.)	149.5	149.5	99.4	99.4	118.2	118.2		67.2	93.5
Maximum Payload (lbs.)	1965	2914	1629	1423	1484	1575		NA	1257
Number of Cylinders	8	8	8	8	8	8		4	4
Displacement (liters)	5.7	5.7	5.7	5.7	5.7	5.7		2.0	2.2
Horsepower @ RPM	255@4600	255@4600	255@4600	255@4600	255@4600	255@4600		126@5400	140@5600
Torque @ RPM	330@2800	330@2800	330@2800	330@2800	330@2800	330@2800		133@4300	145@4500
Fuel Capacity	42	42	30	30	30	30		15.3	17.2
Towing Capacity	6000	10000	7000	6500	7000	7000		1000	1000
EPA City (mpg) - Manual	NA	NA	NA	NA	NA	NA		NA	NA
EPA Hwy (mpg) - Manual	NA	NA	NA	NA	NA	NA		NA	NA
EPA City (mpg) - Auto	NA	NA	NA	NA	NA	NA		22	20
EPA Hwy (mpg) - Auto	NA	NA	NA	NA	NA	NA		25	24

SPECIFICATIONS & EPA MILEAGE RATINGS

	Odyssey EX	Passport EX/LX 2WD 5M	Passport EX/LX 2WD AT	Passport EX/LX 4WD 5M	Passport EX/LX 4WD AT	**INFINITI** QX4	**ISUZU** Hombre S/XS Regular Cab
Acceleration (0-60/sec)	11.2	10	10.9	10	10.9	11.2	12.6
Braking Dist. (60-0/ft)	141	139	139	139	139	146	149
Turning Circle (in.)	37.6	37.7	37.7	37.7	37.7	NA	36.9
Length (in.)	187.2	176.5	176.5	176.5	176.5	178.3	188.9
Width (in.)	70.6	66.5	66.5	66.5	66.5	68.7	67.9
Height (in.)	64.6	66.5	66.5	66.5	66.5	67.1	62.1
Curb Weight (lbs.)	3483	3848	3883	4078	4133	NA	3125
Wheelbase (in.)	111.4	108.5	108.5	108.5	108.5	106.3	108.3
Front Head Room (in.)	38.9	38.5	38.5	38.5	38.5	39.5	39.5
Rear Head Room (in.)	39.3	38	38	38	38	37.5	NA
Front Leg Room (in.)	40.7	41	41	41	41	41.7	42.4
Rear Leg Room (in.)	40.2	34.5	34.5	34.5	34.5	31.8	NA
Maximum Seating	6	5	5	5	5	5	3
Max Cargo Capacity (cu ft.)	102.5	74.9	74.9	74.9	74.9	85	NA
Maximum Payload (lbs.)	1257	NA	NA	NA	NA	NA	1138
Number of Cylinders	4	6	6	6	6	6	4
Displacement (liters)	2.2	3.2	3.2	3.2	3.2	3.3	2.2
Horsepower @ RPM	140@5600	190@5600	190@5600	190@5600	190@5600	168@4800	118@5200
Torque @ RPM	145@4500	188@4000	188@4000	188@4000	188@4000	196@2800	130@2800
Fuel Capacity	17.2	21.9	21.9	21.9	21.9	21.1	18.5
Towing Capacity	1000	4500	4500	4500	4500	5000	2000
EPA City (mpg) - Manual	NA	16	NA	16	NA	NA	23
EPA Hwy (mpg) - Manual	NA	19	NA	19	NA	NA	30
EPA City (mpg) - Auto	20	NA	15	NA	15	15	NA
EPA Hwy (mpg) - Auto	24	NA	18	NA	18	19	NA

SPECIFICATIONS & EPA MILEAGE RATINGS

	Hombre XS Spacecab 4 cyl.	Hombre XS Spacecab V-6	Oasis	Oasis LS	Rodeo V-6 (A4)	Rodeo V-6 (M5)	Rodeo S 2.2L (M5)	Trooper S 5M	Trooper S AT	Trooper LS
Acceleration (0-60/sec)	NA	NA	NA	12.4	12.4	NA	NA	NA	NA	11.2	11.2
Braking Dist. (60-0/ft)	NA	NA	NA	141	141	NA	NA	NA	143	143	143
Turning Circle (in.)	41.3	41.3	37.6	37.6	38.4	38.4	38.4	38.1	38.1	38.1
Length (in.)	203.5	203.5	187.2	187.2	176.7	183.4	176.7	183.5	183.5	183.5
Width (in.)	67.9	67.9	70.6	70.6	70.4	70.4	70.4	69.5	69.5	72.2
Height (in.)	62.2	62.2	64.6	64.6	65.6	68.1	65.6	72.2	72.2	72.2
Curb Weight (lbs.)	3305	3500	3473	3483	NA	NA	NA	4275	4315	4315
Wheelbase (in.)	122.9	122.9	111.4	111.4	106.4	106.4	106.4	108.7	108.7	108.7
Front Head Room (in.)	39.5	39.5	40.1	38.9	38.9	38.9	38.9	39.8	39.8	39.8
Rear Head Room (in.)	NA	NA	37.5	37.5	38.3	38.3	38.3	39.8	39.8	39.8
Front Leg Room (in.)	42.4	42.4	40.7	40.7	42.1	42.1	42.1	40.8	40.8	40.8
Rear Leg Room (in.)	NA	NA	34	34	35	35	35	39.1	39.1	39.1
Maximum Seating	5	5	7	6	5	5	5	5	5	5
Max Cargo Capacity (cu ft.)	NA	NA	93.5	102.5	81.1	81.1	81.1	90.2	90.2	90.2
Maximum Payload (lbs.)	1154	1154	1267	1257	NA	NA	NA	1235	1195	1195
Number of Cylinders	4	6	4	4	6	6	4	6	6	6
Displacement (liters)	2.2	4.3	2.2	2.2	3.2	3.2	2.2	3.2	3.2	3.2
Horsepower @ RPM	118@5200	175@4400	140@NA	140@NA	205@5400	205@NA	130@5200	190@5600	190@5600	190@5600
Torque @ RPM	130@2800	240@2800	145@NA	145@NA	214@3000	214@NA	144@4000	188@4000	188@4000	188@4000
Fuel Capacity	18.5	18.5	17.2	17.2	21.1	21.1	21.1	22.5	22.5	22.5
Towing Capacity	5500	5500	840	1000	4500	4500	2500	5000	5000	5000
EPA City (mpg) - Manual	23	NA	NA	NA	NA	NA	NA	NA	NA	NA
EPA Hwy (mpg) - Manual	30	NA	NA	NA	NA	NA	NA	NA	NA	NA
EPA City (mpg) - Auto	NA	20	20	20	NA	NA	NA	NA	NA	NA
EPA Hwy (mpg) - Auto	NA	24	24	24	NA	NA	NA	NA	NA	NA

SPECIFICATIONS & EPA MILEAGE RATINGS

	Trooper Limited	JEEP	Cherokee SE 2WD 2-Door	Cherokee SE 2WD 4-Door	Cherokee SE 4WD 2-Door	Cherokee SE 4WD 4-Door	Cherokee Spt/Cntry 2WD 2-Dr	Cherokee Spt/Cntry 2WD 4-Dr	Cherokee Spt/Cntry 4WD 2-Dr	Cherokee Spt/Cntry 4WD 4-Dr
Acceleration (0-60/sec)	11.2		NA	NA	8.4	8.4	NA	NA	8.4	8.4
Braking Dist. (60-0/ft)	143		146	146	146	146	146	146	146	146
Turning Circle (in.)	38.1		35.9	35.9	35.9	35.9	35.9	35.9	35.9	35.9
Length (in.)	183.5		167.5	167.5	167.5	167.5	167.5	167.5	167.5	167.5
Width (in.)	72.2		67.9	67.9	67.9	67.9	67.9	67.9	67.9	67.9
Height (in.)	72.2		63.9	63.9	64	64	63.9	63.9	64	64
Curb Weight (lbs.)	4640		2947	2993	3111	3153	2947	2993	3111	3153
Wheelbase (in.)	108.7		101.4	101.4	101.4	101.4	101.4	101.4	101.4	101.4
Front Head Room (in.)	39.4		37.8	37.8	37.8	37.8	37.8	37.8	37.8	37.8
Rear Head Room (in.)	37.8		38.5	38.5	38.5	38.5	38.5	38.5	38.5	38.5
Front Leg Room (in.)	40.8		41.4	41.4	41.4	41.4	41.4	41.4	41.4	41.4
Rear Leg Room (in.)	39.1		35	35	35	35	35	35	35	35
Maximum Seating	5		5	5	5	5	5	5	5	5
Max Cargo Capacity (cu ft.)	85.3		71	71	71	71	71	71	71	71
Maximum Payload (lbs.)	870		1150	1150	1150	1150	1150	1150	1150	1150
Number of Cylinders	6		4	4	4	4	6	6	6	6
Displacement (liters)	3.2		2.5	2.5	2.5	2.5	4	4	4	4
Horsepower @ RPM	190@5600		125@5400	125@5400	125@5400	125@5400	190@4600	190@4600	190@4600	190@4600
Torque @ RPM	188@4000		150@3250	150@3250	150@3250	150@3250	225@3000	225@3000	225@3000	225@3000
Fuel Capacity	22.5		20	20	20	20	20	20	20	20
Towing Capacity	5000		5000	5000	5000	5000	5000	5000	5000	5000
EPA City (mpg) - Manual	NA		19	19	18	18	17	17	17	17
EPA Hwy (mpg) - Manual	NA		23	23	22	22	23	23	21	21
EPA City (mpg) - Auto	NA		NA	NA	NA	NA	15	15	15	15
EPA Hwy (mpg) - Auto	NA		NA	NA	NA	NA	21	21	19	19

SPECIFICATIONS & EPA MILEAGE RATINGS

	Grand Cherokee 2WD	Grand Cherokee 4WD	Grand Cherokee Limited 5.9	Wrangler SE	Wrangler Sport/Sahara	KIA	Sportage 4-dr 2WD 5M	Sportage 4-dr 2WD AT	Sportage 4-dr 4WD 5M	Sportage 4-dr 4WD AT
Acceleration (0-60/sec)	NA	8.6	NA	NA	8.8		NA	NA	12	NA
Braking Dist. (60-0/ft)	138	138	NA	132	132		167	167	167	167
Turning Circle (in.)	37.5	37.5	37.5	33.6	33.6		34.8	34.8	34.8	34.8
Length (in.)	177.2	177.2	176.3	151.8	151.8		167.1	167.1	167.1	167.1
Width (in.)	69.3	69.3	69.3	66.7	66.7		68.1	68.1	68.1	68.1
Height (in.)	64.9	64.9	64.8	70.2	70.2		65	65	65	65
Curb Weight (lbs.)	3609	3785	NA	3092	3229		3170	3214	3314	3358
Wheelbase (in.)	105.9	105.9	105.9	93.4	93.4		104.3	104.3	104.3	104.3
Front Head Room (in.)	38.9	38.9	39	42.3	42.3		39.6	39.6	39.6	39.6
Rear Head Room (in.)	39	39	39	40.6	40.6		37.8	37.8	37.8	37.8
Front Leg Room (in.)	40.9	40.9	40.9	41.1	41.1		44.5	44.5	44.5	44.5
Rear Leg Room (in.)	35.7	35.7	35.7	34.9	34.9		31.1	31.1	31.1	31.1
Maximum Seating	5	5	5	4	4		5	5	5	5
Max Cargo Capacity (cu ft.)	79.3	79.3	79.3	55.7	55.7		55.4	55.4	55.4	55.4
Maximum Payload (lbs.)	1150	1150	1150	800	800		838	838	838	838
Number of Cylinders	6	6	8	4	6		4	4	4	4
Displacement (liters)	4	4	5.9	2.5	4		2	2	2	2
Horsepower @ RPM	185@4600	185@4600	250@4000	120@5400	181@4600		130@5500	130@5500	130@5000	130@5000
Torque @ RPM	220@2400	220@2400	335@3200	140@3500	222@2800		127@4000	127@4000	127@4000	127@4000
Fuel Capacity	23	23	23	15	15		15.8	15.8	15.8	15.8
Towing Capacity	6700	6500	5000	2000	2000		2000	2000	2000	2000
EPA City (mpg) - Manual	NA	NA	NA	19	17		19	NA	19	NA
EPA Hwy (mpg) - Manual	NA	NA	NA	21	21		22	NA	23	NA
EPA City (mpg) - Auto	15	15	NA	17	15		NA	19	NA	19
EPA Hwy (mpg) - Auto	21	20	NA	19	18		21	NA	22	NA

SPECIFICATIONS & EPA MILEAGE RATINGS

	LAND ROVER						LEXUS	
	Defender 90 Convertible	Defender 90 Hardtop	Discovery 5M	Discovery AT	Range Rover 4.0 SE	Range Rover 4.6 HSE	LX 450	
Acceleration (0-60/sec)	10.5	10.5	11	11.7	11.2	9.6	11.6	
Braking Dist. (60-0/ft)	169	169	146	146	143	141	132	
Turning Circle (in.)	40	40	39.4	39.4	39	39	40.4	
Length (in.)	157.1	157.1	178.7	178.7	185.5	185.5	189.8	
Width (in.)	70.5	70.5	70.6	70.6	74.4	74.4	76	
Height (in.)	80.2	80.2	77.4	77.4	71.6	71.6	73.6	
Curb Weight (lbs.)	3913	3913	4465	4465	4960	4960	4977	
Wheelbase (in.)	92.9	92.9	100	100	108.1	108.1	112.2	
Front Head Room (in.)	57	57	37.4	37.4	38.1	38.1	40.3	
Rear Head Room (in.)	NA	NA	39.2	39.2	38.2	38.2	36.7	
Front Leg Room (in.)	NA	NA	38.5	38.5	42.6	42.6	41.7	
Rear Leg Room (in.)	NA	NA	36.3	36.3	36.5	36.5	28.5	
Maximum Seating	4	6	7	7	5	5	7	
Max Cargo Capacity (cu ft.)	NA	NA	69.8	69.8	58	58	90.9	
Maximum Payload (lbs.)	NA	NA	NA	NA	NA	NA	NA	
Number of Cylinders	8	8	8	8	8	8	6	
Displacement (liters)	3.9	3.9	3.9	3.9	4	4.6	4.5	
Horsepower @ RPM	182@4750	182@4750	182@4750	182@4750	190@4750	225@4750	212@4600	
Torque @ RPM	233@3000	233@3000	233@3000	233@3000	236@3000	280@3000	275@3200	
Fuel Capacity	15.6	15.6	23.4	23.4	24.6	24.6	25	
Towing Capacity	5000	5000	7700	7700	7700	7700	5000	
EPA City (mpg) - Manual	NA	NA	13	NA	NA	NA	NA	
EPA Hwy (mpg) - Manual	NA	NA	17	NA	NA	NA	NA	
EPA City (mpg) - Auto	NA	NA	NA	14	13	12	13	
EPA Hwy (mpg) - Auto	NA	NA	NA	17	17	16	15	

SPECIFICATIONS & EPA MILEAGE RATINGS

	LINCOLN Navigator 2WD	LINCOLN Navigator 4WD	MAZDA B-Series B2500 SX 2WD Regular Cab	B-Series B2500 SE 2WD Regular Cab	B-Series B2500 SE 2WD Extended Cab	B-Series B3000 SE 2WD Extended Cab	B-Series B4000 SE 2WD Extended Cab	B-Series B3000 SX 4WD Regular Cab
Acceleration (0-60/sec)	NA	NA	NA	NA	NA	NA	9.2	8.7	10.5
Braking Dist. (60-0/ft)	NA	NA	NA	NA	NA	147	147	147
Turning Circle (in.)	NA	NA	36.4	36.4	41.6	41.6	41.6	37
Length (in.)	204.8	204.8	187.5	187.5	202.9	202.9	202.9	187.7
Width (in.)	79.9	79.9	69.4	69.4	69.4	67.4	69.4	70.3
Height (in.)	76.7	76.7	64.9	64.9	64.7	64.7	64.7	67.5
Curb Weight (lbs.)	NA	NA	3025	3025	3237	3237	3237	3433
Wheelbase (in.)	119	119	111.6	111.6	125.7	125.7	125.7	111.6
Front Head Room (in.)	NA	NA	39.2	39.2	39.2	39.2	39.2	39.2
Rear Head Room (in.)	NA	NA	NA	NA	35.6	35.6	35.6	NA
Front Leg Room (in.)	NA	NA	42.4	42.4	42.2	42.2	42.2	42.4
Rear Leg Room (in.)	NA	NA	NA	NA	40.3	40.3	40.3	NA
Maximum Seating	7	7	3	3	5	5	5	3
Max Cargo Capacity (cu ft.)	116.4	116.4	NA	NA	NA	NA	NA	NA
Maximum Payload (lbs.)	NA	NA	1260	1260	1260	1620	1620	1260
Number of Cylinders	8	8	4	4	4	6	6	6
Displacement (liters)	5.4	5.4	2.5	2.5	2.5	3	4	3
Horsepower @ RPM	230@4250	230@4250	119@5000	119@5000	119@5000	150@5000	160@4200	150@5000
Torque @ RPM	325@3000	325@3000	146@3000	146@3000	146@3000	185@3750	225@3000	185@3750
Fuel Capacity	30	30	17	17	20.5	20.5	20.5	17
Towing Capacity	8000	8000	1580	1580	1380	2500	3420	2380
EPA City (mpg) - Manual	NA	NA	23	23	23	18	18	17
EPA Hwy (mpg) - Manual	NA	NA	27	27	27	24	23	22
EPA City (mpg) - Auto	NA	NA	21	21	21	17	16	16
EPA Hwy (mpg) - Auto	NA	NA	25	25	25	23	22	22

SPECIFICATIONS & EPA MILEAGE RATINGS

	B-Series B3000 SE 4WD Regular Cab	B-Series B3000 SE 4WD Extended Cab	B-Series B4000 SE 4WD Extended Cab	MPV	ML320	Mountaineer AWD	Mountaineer 2WD V-6	Mountaineer 4WD V-6
Acceleration (0-60/sec)	10.5	NA	1	12.1	NA	NA	NA	NA
Braking Dist. (60-0/ft)	147	NA	147	158	NA	NA	NA	NA
Turning Circle (in.)	37	41.6	41.6	39.6	37.1	37.3	37.3	37.3
Length (in.)	187.7	201.7	201.7	183.5	180.6	188.5	188.5	188.5
Width (in.)	70.3	70.3	70.3	71.9	72.2	70.2	70.2	70.2
Height (in.)	67.5	67.5	67.5	71.5	69.9	66.7	66.7	66.8
Curb Weight (lbs.)	3433	3625	3625	4105	NA	NA	NA	NA
Wheelbase (in.)	111.6	125.8	125.9	110.4	111	111.5	111.5	111.5
Front Head Room (in.)	39.2	39.2	39.2	40	39.8	39.8	39.9	39.9
Rear Head Room (in.)	NA	35.6	35.6	36.9	39.7	39.3	39.3	39.3
Front Leg Room (in.)	42.4	42.2	42.2	40.4	44.3	42.4	42.4	42.4
Rear Leg Room (in.)	NA	40.3	40.3	32.5	38	37.7	37.7	37.7
Maximum Seating	3	5	5	8	5	5	5	5
Max Cargo Capacity (cu ft.)	NA	NA	NA	110	85.4	81.6	81.6	81.6
Maximum Payload (lbs.)	1260	1260	1500	NA	1684	NA	NA	NA
Number of Cylinders	6	6	6	6	6	8	6	6
Displacement (liters)	3	3	4	3	3.2	5	4	4
Horsepower @ RPM	150@5000	150@5000	160@4200	155@5000	215@5500	210@4600	205@5000	205@5000
Torque @ RPM	185@3750	185@3750	225@3000	169@4000	233@3000	275@3200	250@3000	250@3000
Fuel Capacity	17	20.5	20.5	19.8	19	21	21	21
Towing Capacity	2380	2200	3180	NA	5000	6500	NA	NA
EPA City (mpg) - Manual	17	17	16	NA	NA	NA	NA	NA
EPA Hwy (mpg) - Manual	22	22	20	NA	NA	NA	NA	NA
EPA City (mpg) - Auto	16	16	16	NA	15	NA	NA	NA
EPA Hwy (mpg) - Auto	22	20	20	19	NA	NA	NA	NA

MERCEDES-BENZ
MERCURY

SPECIFICATIONS & EPA MILEAGE RATINGS

	Villager	MITSUBISHI	Montero LS	Montero SR	Montero Sport LS (A4)	Montero Sport XLS (A4)	Montero Sport LS (M5)	Montero Sport LS (A4)	Montero Sport ES (M5)	Montero Sport XLS (A4)
Acceleration (0-60/sec)	12.3		13.4	10.4	NA	NA	NA	NA	NA	NA
Braking Dist. (60-0/ft)	141		144	137	NA	NA	NA	NA	NA	NA
Turning Circle (in.)	39.9		38.7	38.7	38.8	38.8	38.8	38.8	38.8	38.8
Length (in.)	190.2		185.2	186.6	178.3	178.3	178.3	178.3	178.3	178.3
Width (in.)	73.8		66.7	70.3	66.7	66.7	66.7	66.7	66.7	66.7
Height (in.)	65.9		73.8	74.6	67.3	67.3	67.3	67.3	67.3	67.3
Curb Weight (lbs.)	3990		4300	4465	NA	NA	NA	NA	NA	NA
Wheelbase (in.)	112.2		107.3	107.3	107.3	107.3	107.3	107.3	107.3	107.3
Front Head Room (in.)	39.4		40.9	40.9	38.9	38.9	38.9	38.9	38.9	38.9
Rear Head Room (in.)	39.7		40	40	37.3	37.3	37.3	37.3	37.3	37.3
Front Leg Room (in.)	39.9		40.3	40.3	42.8	42.8	42.8	42.8	42.8	42.8
Rear Leg Room (in.)	34.8		37.6	37.6	33.5	33.5	33.5	33.5	33.5	33.5
Maximum Seating	7		7	7	5	5	5	5	5	5
Max Cargo Capacity (cu ft.)	126		72.7	72.7	79.3	79.3	79.3	79.3	79.3	79.3
Maximum Payload (lbs.)	1200		1406	1381	NA	NA	NA	NA	NA	NA
Number of Cylinders	6		6	6	6	6	6	NA	4	6
Displacement (liters)	3		3	3.5	3	3	3	NA	2.4	3
Horsepower @ RPM	151@4800		177@5500	215@5000	173@5250	173@5250	173@5250	NA@NA	134@5500	173@5250
Torque @ RPM	174@4400		188@4500	228@3000	188@4000	188@4000	188@4000	NA@NA	148@2750	188@4000
Fuel Capacity	20		24.3	24.3	19.5	19.5	19.5	19.5	19.5	19.5
Towing Capacity	3500		5000	5000	5000	5000	5000	5000	2300	5000
EPA City (mpg) - Manual	NA		NA	NA	NA	NA	NA	NA	NA	NA
EPA Hwy (mpg) - Manual	NA		NA	NA	NA	NA	NA	NA	NA	NA
EPA City (mpg) - Auto	17		15	14	NA	NA	NA	NA	NA	NA
EPA Hwy (mpg) - Auto	23		18	18	NA	NA	NA	NA	NA	NA

SPECIFICATIONS & EPA MILEAGE RATINGS — NISSAN

	Pathfinder 2WD 5M	Pathfinder 2WD AT	Pathfinder 4WD 5M	Pathfinder 4WD AT	Quest XE/GXE	Truck - 2WD Reg Cab SB 5M	Truck - 2WD Reg Cab SB AT	Truck - 2WD X-cab 5M	Truck - 2WD X-cab AT
Acceleration (0-60/sec)	10.4	10.5	11.2	11.3	12.1	NA	NA	NA	NA
Braking Dist. (60-0/ft)	148	148	148	148	142	NA	NA	NA	NA
Turning Circle (in.)	35.4	35.4	35.4	35.4	39.9	33.5	33.5	36.7	36.7
Length (in.)	178.3	178.3	178.3	178.3	189.9	174.6	174.6	190	190
Width (in.)	68.7	68.7	68.7	68.7	73.7	65	65	65	65
Height (in.)	67.1	67.1	67.1	67.1	65.6	62	62	62	62
Curb Weight (lbs.)	3675	3695	3920	3945	3876	2805	2805	2900	2900
Wheelbase (in.)	106.3	106.3	106.3	106.3	112.2	104.3	104.3	116.1	116.1
Front Head Room (in.)	39.5	39.5	39.5	39.5	39.5	39.3	39.3	39.3	39.3
Rear Head Room (in.)	37.5	37.5	37.5	37.5	39.7	NA	NA	NA	NA
Front Leg Room (in.)	41.7	41.7	41.7	41.7	39.9	42.2	42.2	42.6	42.6
Rear Leg Room (in.)	31.8	31.8	31.8	31.8	36.3	NA	NA	NA	NA
Maximum Seating	5	5	5	5	7	3	3	4	4
Max Cargo Capacity (cu ft.)	85	85	85	85	114.8	NA	NA	NA	NA
Maximum Payload (lbs.)	NA	1155	NA	NA	NA	1400	1400	1400	1400
Number of Cylinders	6	6	6	6	6	4	4	4	4
Displacement (liters)	3.3	3.3	3.3	3.3	3	2.4	2.4	2.4	2.4
Horsepower @ RPM	168@4800	168@4800	168@4800	168@4800	151@4800	134@5200	134@5200	134@5200	134@5200
Torque @ RPM	196@4000	196@4000	196@4000	196@4000	174@4400	154@3600	154@3600	154@3600	154@3600
Fuel Capacity	21	21	21	21	20	15.9	15.9	15.9	15.9
Towing Capacity	3500	5000	3500	5000	3500	3500	3500	3500	3500
EPA City (mpg) - Manual	17	NA	16	NA	NA	22	NA	22	NA
EPA Hwy (mpg) - Manual	20	NA	18	NA	NA	26	NA	26	NA
EPA City (mpg) - Auto	NA	16	NA	15	17	NA	21	NA	21
EPA Hwy (mpg) - Auto	NA	20	NA	19	23	NA	26	NA	25

SPECIFICATIONS & EPA MILEAGE RATINGS

	Truck - 4WD Reg Cab 5M	Truck - 4WD X-cab AT	Truck - 4WD X-cab 5M	**OLDSMOBILE**	Bravada	Silhouette 3-door Reg Length	Silhouette 3-door Ext. Length	Silhouette 4-door Ext Length	**PLYMOUTH**	Grand Voyager
Acceleration (0-60/sec)	NA	NA	NA		10.2	9.9	10.9	10.9		13.5
Braking Dist. (60-0/ft)	151	151	151		143	143	143	143		140
Turning Circle (in.)	36.7	36.7	36.7		39.5	37.4	39.7	39.7		37.6
Length (in.)	190	190	190		180.9	187.4	201.4	201.4		196.6
Width (in.)	65	65	65		66.5	72.2	72.2	72.2		76.8
Height (in.)	67.1	67.1	67.1		63.2	67.4	68.1	68.1		68.5
Curb Weight (lbs.)	2900	2900	2900		4023	3721	3843	3942		3700
Wheelbase (in.)	116.1	116.1	116.1		107	112	120	120		119.3
Front Head Room (in.)	39.3	39.3	39.3		39.7	39.9	39.9	39.9		39.8
Rear Head Room (in.)	NA	NA	NA		38.6	38.8	38.8	38.8		40
Front Leg Room (in.)	42.6	42.6	42.6		42.4	39.9	39.9	39.9		41.2
Rear Leg Room (in.)	NA	NA	NA		36.1	34	36.7	36.7		39.6
Maximum Seating	4	4	4		5	7	7	7		7
Max Cargo Capacity (cu ft.)	NA	NA	NA		74.1	126.6	148.3	155.9		168.5
Maximum Payload (lbs.)	1400	1400	1400		1277	NA	NA	NA		NA
Number of Cylinders	4	4	4		6	6	6	6		4
Displacement (liters)	2.4	2.4	2.4		4.3	3.4	3.4	3.4		2.4
Horsepower @ RPM	134@5200	134@5200	134@5200		190@4400	180@5200	180@5200	180@5200		150@5200
Torque @ RPM	154@3600	154@3600	154@3600		250@2800	205@4000	205@4000	205@4000		167@4000
Fuel Capacity	15.9	15.9	15.9		18	20	25	25		20
Towing Capacity	3500	3500	3500		5000	2000	3500	3500		3500
EPA City (mpg) - Manual	18	18	18		NA	NA	NA	NA		NA
EPA Hwy (mpg) - Manual	20	20	20		NA	NA	NA	NA		NA
EPA City (mpg) - Auto	NA	NA	NA		16	18	18	18		NA
EPA Hwy (mpg) - Auto	NA	NA	NA		21	25	25	25		NA

SPECIFICATIONS & EPA MILEAGE RATINGS

	Voyager	**PONTIAC** Trans Sport SWB 3-door	Trans Sport Ext. 3-door	Trans Sport Ext. 4-door	**SUBARU** Forester (A4)	Forester (M5)	**SUZUKI** Sidekick 4WD Sport 4-Dr 5M
Acceleration (0-60/sec)	NA	9.9	10.9	10.9	NA	NA	NA
Braking Dist. (60-0/ft)	NA	143	143	143	NA	NA	NA
Turning Circle (in.)	37.6	37.4	39.7	39.7	35.4	35.4	36.1
Length (in.)	186.3	187.3	201.3	201.3	175.2	175.2	162.4
Width (in.)	76.8	72.7	72.7	72.7	68.3	68.3	66.7
Height (in.)	68.5	67.4	68.1	68.1	62.8	62.8	66.3
Curb Weight (lbs.)	3533	3702	3825	3920	NA	NA	2917
Wheelbase (in.)	113.3	112	120	120	99.4	99.4	97.6
Front Head Room (in.)	39.8	39.9	39.9	39.9	40.6	40.6	40.6
Rear Head Room (in.)	40.1	38.8	38.9	38.9	39.6	39.6	38.6
Front Leg Room (in.)	41.2	39.9	39.9	39.9	43	43	42.1
Rear Leg Room (in.)	36.6	34	36.7	36.7	33.4	33.4	32.7
Maximum Seating	7	8	8	8	5	5	4
Max Cargo Capacity (cu ft.)	146.2	126.6	155.9	155.9	64.6	64.6	45
Maximum Payload (lbs.)	NA	1655	1532	1437	NA	NA	765
Number of Cylinders	4	6	6	6	4	4	4
Displacement (liters)	2.4	3.4	3.4	3.4	2.5	2.5	1.6
Horsepower @ RPM	150@4800	180@5200	180@5200	180@5200	165@5600	165@5600	120@6500
Torque @ RPM	167@2800	205@4000	205@4000	205@4000	162@4000	162@4000	114@3500
Fuel Capacity	20	20	25	25	15.9	15.9	18.5
Towing Capacity	3500	3500	3500	3500	2000	2000	1500
EPA City (mpg) - Manual	NA	NA	NA	NA	21	21	23
EPA Hwy (mpg) - Manual	NA	NA	NA	NA	29	29	25
EPA City (mpg) - Auto	20	18	18	18	21	21	NA
EPA Hwy (mpg) - Auto	25	25	25	25	28	28	NA

SPECIFICATIONS & EPA MILEAGE RATINGS

	Sidekick 4WD Sport 4-Dr AT	X-90 2WD 5M	X-90 4WD 5M	X-90 4WD AT	4Runner 2WD 5M	4Runner 2WD AT	4Runner 4WD 5M	4Runner 4WD AT	4Runner 2WD V6 AT
Acceleration (0-60/sec)	NA	NA	NA	NA	NA	NA	NA	NA	NA
Braking Dist. (60-0/ft)	NA	NA	NA	NA	NA	NA	NA	NA	10.1
Turning Circle (in.)	36.1	32.2	32.2	32.2	37.4	37.4	37.4	37.4	37.4
Length (in.)	162.4	146.1	146.1	146.1	178.7	178.7	178.7	178.7	178.7
Width (in.)	66.7	66.7	66.7	66.7	66.5	66.5	66.5	66.5	66.5
Height (in.)	66.3	60.5	60.5	60.5	66.5	66.5	66.5	66.5	66.5
Curb Weight (lbs.)	2950	2321	2493	2542	3340	3355	3690	3735	3565
Wheelbase (in.)	97.6	86.6	86.6	86.6	105.3	105.3	105.3	105.3	105.3
Front Head Room (in.)	40.6	34.2	34.2	34.2	39.2	39.2	39.2	39.2	39.2
Rear Head Room (in.)	38.6	NA	NA	NA	38.7	38.7	38.7	38.7	38.7
Front Leg Room (in.)	42.1	41.5	41.5	41.5	43.1	43.1	43.1	43.1	43.1
Rear Leg Room (in.)	32.7	NA	NA	NA	34.9	34.9	34.9	34.9	34.9
Maximum Seating	4	2	2	2	5	5	5	5	5
Max Cargo Capacity (cu ft.)	45	8.4	8.4	8.4	79.7	79.7	79.7	79.7	79.7
Maximum Payload (lbs.)	732	413	461	412	1810	1795	1560	1515	1685
Number of Cylinders	4	4	4	4	4	4	4	4	6
Displacement (liters)	1.6	1.6	1.6	1.6	2.7	2.7	2.7	2.7	3.4
Horsepower @ RPM	120@6500	95@5600	95@5600	95@5600	150@4800	150@4800	150@4800	150@4800	183@4800
Torque @ RPM	114@3500	98@4000	98@4000	98@4000	177@4000	177@4000	177@4000	177@4000	217@3400
Fuel Capacity	18.5	11	11.1	11.1	18.5	18.5	18.5	18.5	18.5
Towing Capacity	1500	1000	1000	1000	3500	3500	3500	3500	5000
EPA City (mpg) - Manual	NA	25	25	NA	20	NA	17	NA	NA
EPA Hwy (mpg) - Manual	NA	28	28	NA	25	NA	21	NA	NA
EPA City (mpg) - Auto	21	NA	NA	23	NA	20	NA	19	18
EPA Hwy (mpg) - Auto	24	NA	NA	27	NA	24	NA	22	21

TOYOTA

SPECIFICATIONS & EPA MILEAGE RATINGS

	4Runner 4WD V6 5M	4Runner 4WD V6 AT	Land Cruiser	RAV4 2-Door 2WD 5M	RAV4 2-Door 2WD AT	RAV4 4-Door 2WD 5M	RAV4 4-Door 2WD AT	RAV4 2-Door 4WD 5M	RAV4 2-Door 4WD AT	RAV4 4-Door 4WD 5M	RAV4 4-Door 4WD AT
Acceleration (0-60/sec)	NA	10.1	11.6	9.8	NA	10.1	NA	NA	NA	NA	NA
Braking Dist. (60-0/ft)	NA	NA	131	NA	NA	NA	NA	NA	NA	NA	NA
Turning Circle (in.)	37.4	37.4	40.4	33.5	33.5	36.1	36.1	33.5	36.1	36.1	36.1
Length (in.)	178.7	178.7	189.8	147.2	147.2	163.4	163.4	147.2	162	162	162
Width (in.)	66.5	66.5	76	66.7	66.7	66.7	66.7	66.7	66.7	66.7	66.7
Height (in.)	66.5	68.7	93.6	64.8	65.2	65.4	65	65.2	65.4	65.4	65.4
Curb Weight (lbs.)	3850	3925	4834	2496	2513	2612	2844	2646	2789	2844	2844
Wheelbase (in.)	105.3	105.3	112.2	86.6	86.6	94.9	94.9	86.6	94.9	94.9	94.9
Front Head Room (in.)	39.2	39.2	40.3	40	40	40.3	40.3	40	40.3	40.3	40.3
Rear Head Room (in.)	38.7	38.7	39.7	38.6	38.6	39	39	38.6	39	39	39
Front Leg Room (in.)	43.1	43.1	42.2	39.5	39.5	40.4	40.4	40.4	40.4	40.4	40.4
Rear Leg Room (in.)	34.9	34.9	33.6	33.9	33.9	30.1	30.1	30.1	30.1	30.1	30.1
Maximum Seating	5	5	7	4	4	5	5	4	5	5	5
Max Cargo Capacity (cu ft.)	79.7	79.7	90.9	34.3	34.3	57.9	57.9	34.3	57.9	57.9	57.9
Maximum Payload (lbs.)	1400	1310	1636	1003	821	1246	1201	859	1102	1036	1036
Number of Cylinders	6	6	6	4	4	4	4	4	4	4	4
Displacement (liters)	3.4	3.4	4.5	2	2	2	2	2	2	2	2
Horsepower @ RPM	183@4800	183@4800	212@4600	120@5400	120@5400	120@5400	120@5400	120@5400	120@5400	120@5400	120@5400
Torque @ RPM	217@3400	217@3600	275@3200	125@4600	125@4600	125@4600	125@4600	125@4600	125@4600	125@4600	125@4600
Fuel Capacity	18.5	18.5	25.1	15	15	15	15	15	15	15	15
Towing Capacity	5000	5000	5000	1500	1500	1500	1500	1500	1500	1500	1500
EPA City (mpg) - Manual	17	NA	NA	24	NA	24	NA	22	22	NA	NA
EPA Hwy (mpg) - Manual	20	NA	NA	30	NA	30	NA	27	27	NA	NA
EPA City (mpg) - Auto	NA	17	12	NA	24	NA	24	NA	NA	NA	22
EPA Hwy (mpg) - Auto	NA	19	15	NA	29	NA	29	NA	NA	NA	27

SPECIFICATIONS & EPA MILEAGE RATINGS

	T100 2WD Reg Cab 5M	T100 2WD Reg Cab AT	T100 2WD Xtracab 5M	T100 2WD Xtracab AT	T100 4WD Xtracab 5M	T100 4WD Xtracab AT	Tacoma 2WD Reg Cab 5M	Tacoma 2WD Reg Cab AT	Tacoma 2WD Xtracab 5M	Tacoma 2WD Xtracab AT
Acceleration (0-60/sec)	NA	NA	NA	8.6	NA	8.9	NA	8.3	NA	NA
Braking Dist. (60-0/ft)	NA	NA	NA	169	NA	169	143	143	142	133
Turning Circle (in.)	37.7	37.7	37.7	37.7	43.3	43.3	35.4	41.3	35.4	41.3
Length (in.)	209.1	209.1	209.1	209.1	209.1	209.1	180.5	199	180.5	199
Width (in.)	75.2	75.2	75.2	75.2	75.2	75.2	66.5	66.5	66.5	66.5
Height (in.)	67.2	67.2	68.6	68.6	71.6	71.6	61.8	62	61.8	62
Curb Weight (lbs.)	3320	3350	3580	3600	4040	4110	2560	2745	2580	2765
Wheelbase (in.)	121.8	121.8	121.8	121.8	121.8	121.8	103.3	121.9	103.3	121.9
Front Head Room (in.)	39.6	39.6	39.6	39.6	39.6	39.6	38.2	38.4	38.2	38.4
Rear Head Room (in.)	NA	NA	37.8	37.8	37.8	37.8	NA	35.5	NA	35.5
Front Leg Room (in.)	42.9	42.9	42.9	42.9	42.9	42.9	41.7	42.8	41.7	41.7
Rear Leg Room (in.)	NA	NA	29.6	29.6	29.6	29.6	NA	NA	NA	NA
Maximum Seating	3	3	6	6	6	6	3	5	3	5
Max Cargo Capacity (cu ft.)	NA	NA	NA	NA	NA	NA	NA	NA	NA	NA
Maximum Payload (lbs.)	1680	1650	2120	2070	1960	2070	1684	1752	1664	1732
Number of Cylinders	4	4	6	6	6	6	4	4	4	4
Displacement (liters)	2.7	2.7	3.4	3.4	3.4	3.4	2.4	2.4	2.4	2.4
Horsepower @ RPM	150@4800	150@4800	190@4800	190@4800	190@4800	190@4800	142@5000	142@5000	142@5000	142@5000
Torque @ RPM	177@4000	177@4000	220@3600	220@3600	220@3600	220@3600	160@4000	160@4000	160@4000	160@4000
Fuel Capacity	24	24	24	24	24	24	15	15	15	15
Towing Capacity	4000	4000	5200	5200	5000	5000	5000	5000	5000	5000
EPA City (mpg) - Manual	20	NA	17	NA	17	NA	22	NA	22	NA
EPA Hwy (mpg) - Manual	24	NA	21	NA	19	NA	28	NA	28	NA
EPA City (mpg) - Auto	NA	19	NA	17	NA	16	NA	22	NA	22
EPA Hwy (mpg) - Auto	NA	22	NA	20	NA	18	NA	25	NA	25

SPECIFICATIONS & EPA MILEAGE RATINGS

	Tacoma 4WD Xtracab 5M	Tacoma 4WD Reg Cab 5M	Tacoma 4WD Xtracab AT	Tacoma 4WD Reg Cab AT	Tacoma 4WD Reg Cab V6 5M	Tacoma 2WD Xtracab V6 5M	Tacoma 2WD Xtracab V6 AT	Tacoma 4WD Xtracab V6 5M	Tacoma 4WD Xtracab V6 AT
Acceleration (0-60/sec)	NA	NA	NA	NA	9	7.1	8.5	9.1	9.5
Braking Dist. (60-0/ft)	144	NA	144	NA	NA	133	133	144	144
Turning Circle (in.)	41.3	35.4	41.3	35.4	35.4	41.3	41.3	41.3	41.3
Length (in.)	199	180.5	199	180.5	180.5	199	199	199	199
Width (in.)	66.5	66.5	66.5	66.5	66.5	66.5	66.5	66.5	66.5
Height (in.)	68.3	68.5	68.3	68.5	68.5	62	62	68.3	68.3
Curb Weight (lbs.)	3345	3190	3375	3220	3245	2895	2915	3410	2740
Wheelbase (in.)	121.9	103.3	121.9	103.3	103.3	121.9	121.9	121.9	121.9
Front Head Room (in.)	38.2	38.2	38.4	38.2	38.4	38.4	38.4	38.4	38.4
Rear Head Room (in.)	35.3	NA	35.3	NA	NA	35.5	35.5	35.3	35.3
Front Leg Room (in.)	43.7	41.7	43.7	41.7	41.7	42.8	42.8	42.8	42.8
Rear Leg Room (in.)	NA	NA	NA	NA	NA	NA	NA	NA	NA
Maximum Seating	5	3	5	3	3	5	5	5	5
Max Cargo Capacity (cu ft.)	NA	NA	NA	NA	NA	NA	NA	NA	NA
Maximum Payload (lbs.)	1884	1914	1729	1860	1859	1602	1582	1694	1664
Number of Cylinders	4	4	4	4	6	6	6	6	6
Displacement (liters)	2.7	2.7	2.7	2.7	3.4	3.4	3.4	3.4	3.4
Horsepower @ RPM	150@4800	150@4800	150@4800	150@4800	190@4800	190@4800	190@4800	190@4800	190@4800
Torque @ RPM	177@4000	177@4000	177@4000	177@4000	220@3600	220@3600	220@3600	220@3600	220@3600
Fuel Capacity	18	15	18	15	15.1	15	15.1	18	18
Towing Capacity	5000	5000	5000	5000	5000	5000	5000	5000	5000
EPA City (mpg) - Manual	18	18	NA	NA	18	19	NA	17	NA
EPA Hwy (mpg) - Manual	22	22	NA	NA	22	23	NA	19	NA
EPA City (mpg) - Auto	NA	NA	18	18	NA	NA	19	NA	17
EPA Hwy (mpg) - Auto	NA	NA	21	21	NA	NA	22	NA	19

We don't have hoists and grease pits, but we give incredible service!

"Your Detroit Car and Truck Connection."

Our auto dealership doesn't have a service department but our customers keep coming back, time after time. Why? Because we give them the best prices, support and product knowledge of any dealer in the country!

We're NATIONWIDE AUTO BROKERS. For nearly thirty years, we have provided our customers with the lowest vehicle prices and best service because *we do the shopping for them*! Once you approve our low, low price (as little as $50-$125 over dealer invoice*) on the domestic or import vehicle of your choice, **NATIONWIDE** can order your domestic vehicle and have it delivered direct to a dealership near you. Factory-authorized service is then handled by the local dealership, and you rest easy knowing you've received a truly remarkable deal!

VISIT OUR INTERNET WEB SITE AT http://www.car-connect.com

These two numbers could SAVE YOU THOUSANDS OF DOLLARS the next time you BUY A NEW CAR OR TRUCK!

Auto Quote line: 1-800-521-7257

9 am - 7 pm EST Mon.-Fri.

Obtain a printed computer quote on the make and model of your choice. Your quote contains all factory equipment available in an easy to read format. Instructions and pricing (both "**MSRP**" and dealer "**INVOICE**") make it simple to price your own vehicle.
First Quote $11.95, each additional quote $9.95. Add $6.95 for faxes.

Auto Hot Line: 1-900-884-6800

9 am - 5 pm EST Mon.-Fri.

Talk live to one of our sales staff for information on an "**IMMEDIATE QUOTE**", options, rebates, dealer incentives, used vehicle fair market value and plain old good advice!
*$2.00 per minute. 6-10 min. avg. per call.
You must be 18 or older to use this service.*

*Some vehicles may be higher. Some specialty imports and limited production models and vehicles may not be available for delivery to your area or through our pricing service. A message on your printout will advise you of this. You will still be able to use the printout in negotiating the best deal with the dealer of your choice. New car pricing and purchasing services not available where prohibited by law.

NATIONWIDE Auto Brokers
29623 Northwestern Hwy., Southfield, MI 48034 • (810) 354-3400 • FAX (810) 223-1770

CRASH TEST DATA

In 1994, the National Highway and Traffic Safety Administration (NHTSA) changed the way they rate frontal crash test performances of the cars and trucks they run into a fixed barrier at 35 mph. Instead of the confusing numerical scale that had been in place for years, NHTSA decided to make the data more user-friendly for interested consumers by converting to a five star rating system, just like that used by the movie reviewer in your local paper and the lucky folks AAA employs to travel around the world eating and sleeping in the best restaurants and hotels. Boy, they've got it rough, don't they?

The scale is as follows:

1 Star	Better than a 45% chance of life-threatening injury
2 Stars	A 35-45% chance of life-threatening injury
3 Stars	A 20-35% chance of life-threatening injury
4 Stars	A 10-20% chance of life-threatening injury
5 Stars	Less than a 10% chance of life-threatening injury

The Insurance Institute for Highway Safety (IIHS) began conducting offset frontal crash tests in 1995. The offset test is conducted at 40 mph, and vehicles crash into a fixed barrier just like in the NHTSA testing, but only half of the front end of the vehicle contacts the barrier. The IIHS claims this test, at this speed, more accurately reflects the most deadly real-world crash situations. Offset crash tests do not conform to the scale listed above.

In 1997, NHTSA began testing side impact protection as well as frontal impact protection. For side impact testing, NHTSA runs a deformable barrier into the side of a car twice, once at the front passenger's level and once at the rear passenger's level. As with frontal impact testing, the side impact test is conducted at 5 mph above the federal standard, which means the deformable barrier hits the car at 38 mph. Side impact test results conform to the scale listed above. NHTSA will begin side-impact testing trucks in 1999.

Here are the results of crash testing conducted since 1994. All test results are applicable to the 1998 equivalent of the listed model, with one caveat. Many of the listed models come equipped with de-powered airbags this year, and until the vehicle is re-tested by NHTSA, it is unknown how the presence of a de-powered airbag will affect occupant safety.

CRASH TEST DATA

Crash Test Data 1994 (frontal impact):

Chevrolet Camaro	Driver: 5 Stars	Passenger: 5 Stars
Mercedes C-Class	Driver: 4 Stars	Passenger: 4 Stars
Toyota T100	Driver: 4 Stars	Passenger: 4 Stars

Crash Test Data 1995 (frontal impact):

Acura Integra	Driver: 4 Stars	Passenger: 3 Stars
Audi A6 Wagon	Driver: 5 Stars	Passenger: 5 Stars
BMW 3-Series	Driver: 4 Stars	Passenger: 4 Stars
Cadillac Eldorado	Driver: 4 Stars	Passenger: 4 Stars
Chevrolet Lumina	Driver: 5 Stars	Passenger: 4 Stars
Chevrolet Monte Carlo	Driver: 4 Stars	Passenger: 4 Stars
Chrysler Cirrus	Driver: 3 Stars	Passenger: No Data
Chrysler Sebring Coupe	Driver: 5 Stars	Passenger: 5 Stars
Dodge Avenger	Driver: 5 Stars	Passenger: 5 Stars
Dodge Stratus	Driver: 3 Stars	Passenger: No Data
Eagle Talon	Driver: 4 Stars	Passenger: 4 Stars
Ford Contour	Driver: 5 Stars	Passenger: 4 Stars
Ford Explorer	Driver: 4 Stars	Passenger: 4 Stars
Honda Odyssey	Driver: 4 Stars	Passenger: 4 Stars
Hyundai Sonata	Driver: 3 Stars	Passenger: 4 Stars
Isuzu Trooper	Driver: 3 Stars	Passenger: 3 Stars
Mazda Millenia	Driver: 4 Stars	Passenger: 5 Stars
Mazda Protege	Driver: 3 Stars	Passenger: No Data
Mercury Mystique	Driver: 5 Stars	Passenger: 4 Stars
Mitsubishi Eclipse	Driver: 4 Stars	Passenger: 4 Stars
Nissan Maxima	Driver: 4 Stars	Passenger: 3 Stars
Oldsmobile 88	Driver: 5 Stars	Passenger: 3 Stars
Oldsmobile Aurora	Driver: 3 Stars	Passenger: 3 Stars
Pontiac Bonneville	Driver: 5 Stars	Passenger: 3 Stars
Pontiac Firebird	Driver: 5 Stars	Passenger: 5 Stars
Saab 900	Driver: 4 Stars	Passenger: 4 Stars
Subaru Legacy	Driver: 4 Stars	Passenger: 4 Stars
Volkswagen Golf	Driver: 3 Stars	Passenger: 3 Stars
Volkswagen Jetta	Driver: 3 Stars	Passenger: 3 Stars

CRASH TEST DATA

Crash Test Data 1996 (frontal impact):

Acura SLX	Driver: 3 Stars	Passenger: 3 Stars
Acura TL Series	Driver: 4 Stars	Passenger: 4 Stars
Audi A4	Driver: 5 Stars	Passenger: 4 Stars
Chevrolet Astro	Driver: 3 Stars	Passenger: 3 Stars
Chevrolet C/K Pickup	Driver: 5 Stars	Passenger: No Data
Chevrolet Tracker Convertible	Driver: 2 Stars	Passenger: 3 Stars
Chrysler Town & Country LWB	Driver: 3 Stars	Passenger: 4 Stars
Dodge Grand Caravan	Driver: 3 Stars	Passenger: 4 Stars
Dodge Neon	Driver: 4 Stars	Passenger: 4 Stars
Ford Crown Victoria	Driver: 5 Stars	Passenger: 5 Stars
Ford Mustang Convertible	Driver: 5 Stars	Passenger: 5 Stars
Ford Taurus	Driver: 4 Stars	Passenger: 4 Stars
GMC Safari	Driver: 3 Stars	Passenger: 3 Stars
GMC Sierra	Driver: 5 Stars	Passenger: No Data
Honda Civic Coupe	Driver: 4 Stars	Passenger: 4 Stars
Honda Civic Sedan	Driver: 4 Stars	Passenger: 5 Stars
Hyundai Elantra	Driver: 3 Stars	Passenger: 3 Stars
Infiniti I30	Driver: 4 Stars	Passenger: 3 Stars
Jeep Grand Cherokee	Driver: 3 Stars	Passenger: 4 Stars
Land Rover Discovery	Driver: 3 Stars	Passenger: 3 Stars
Mazda Miata	Driver: 4 Stars	Passenger: 3 Stars
Mazda MPV	Driver: 4 Stars	Passenger: 4 Stars
Mercury Grand Marquis	Driver: 5 Stars	Passenger: 5 Stars
Mercury Sable	Driver: 4 Stars	Passenger: 4 Stars
Mercury Villager	Driver: 4 Stars	Passenger: 3 Stars
Nissan Quest	Driver: 4 Stars	Passenger: 3 Stars
Nissan Sentra	Driver: 4 Stars	Passenger: 4 Stars
Plymouth Neon	Driver: 4 Stars	Passenger: 4 Stars
Plymouth Grand Voyager	Driver: 3 Stars	Passenger: 4 Stars
Subaru Impreza	Driver: 4 Stars	Passenger: 4 Stars
Suzuki Sidekick Convertible	Driver: 2 Stars	Passenger: 3 Stars
Toyota 4Runner	Driver: 3 Stars	Passenger: 3 Stars
Toyota Avalon	Driver: 4 Stars	Passenger: 5 Stars
Toyota Tacoma Regular Cab	Driver: 2 Stars	Passenger: 3 Stars

Crash Test Data 1997 (frontal impact):

Buick LeSabre	Driver: 4 Stars	Passenger: 4 Stars
Cadillac DeVille	Driver: 4 Stars	Passenger: 4 Stars
Chevrolet Cavalier Coupe	Driver: 4 Stars	Passenger: 4 Stars

CRASH TEST DATA

Vehicle	Driver	Passenger
Chevrolet Cavalier Sedan	Driver: 4 Stars	Passenger: 3 Stars
Chevrolet C/K Pickup	Driver: 5 Stars	Passenger: 4 Stars
Chevrolet Malibu	Driver: 4 Stars	Passenger: 4 Stars
Chevrolet Metro	Driver: 4 Stars	Passenger: 4 Stars
Chevrolet Tahoe	Driver: 4 Stars	Passenger: 4 Stars
Chevrolet Venture	Driver: 4 Stars	Passenger: 4 Stars
Chrysler Sebring Convertible	Driver: 4 Stars	Passenger: 4 Stars
Chrysler Town & Country SWB	Driver: 4 Stars	Passenger: 4 Stars
Dodge Caravan	Driver: 4 Stars	Passenger: 4 Stars
Dodge Dakota	Driver: 4 Stars	Passenger: 4 Stars
Ford Club Wagon	Driver: 3 Stars	Passenger: 4 Stars
Ford Econoline	Driver: 3 Stars	Passenger: 4 Stars
Ford Escort	Driver: 3 Stars	Passenger: 4 Stars
Ford Expedition	Driver: 4 Stars	Passenger: 5 Stars
Ford F-150 Pickup	Driver: 4 Stars	Passenger: 5 Stars
Ford Mustang Coupe	Driver: 4 Stars	Passenger: 4 Stars
GMC Sierra	Driver: 5 Stars	Passenger: 4 Stars
GMC Yukon	Driver: 4 Stars	Passenger: 4 Stars
Hyundai Accent	Driver: 3 Stars	Passenger: 4 Stars
Infiniti QX4	Driver: 3 Stars	Passenger: 3 Stars
Isuzu Oasis	Driver: 4 Stars	Passenger: 4 Stars
Jeep Cherokee	Driver: 3 Stars	Passenger: 3 Stars
Jeep Wrangler	Driver: 4 Stars	Passenger: 5 Stars
Kia Sportage	Driver: 3 Stars	Passenger: 3 Stars
Mercury Tracer	Driver: 3 Stars	Passenger: 4 Stars
Mitsubishi Galant	Driver: 4 Stars	Passenger: 4 Stars
Mitsubishi Montero Sport	Driver: 3 Stars	Passenger: 3 Stars
Nissan 200SX	Driver: 5 Stars	Passenger: 4 Stars
Nissan 240SX	Driver: 3 Stars	Passenger: 4 Stars
Nissan Pathfinder	Driver: 3 Stars	Passenger: 3 Stars
Oldsmobile Cutlass	Driver: 4 Stars	Passenger: 4 Stars
Oldsmobile Regency	Driver: 5 Stars	Passenger: 3 Stars
Oldsmobile Silhouette	Driver: 4 Stars	Passenger: 4 Stars
Plymouth Breeze	Driver: 3 Stars	Passenger: No Data
Plymouth Voyager	Driver: 4 Stars	Passenger: 4 Stars
Pontiac Grand Am Coupe	Driver: 4 Stars	Passenger: 5 Stars
Pontiac Grand Am Sedan	Driver: 5 Stars	Passenger: 4 Stars
Pontiac Grand Prix	Driver: 4 Stars	Passenger: 4 Stars
Pontiac Sunfire Coupe	Driver: 4 Stars	Passenger: 4 Stars
Pontiac Sunfire Sedan	Driver: 4 Stars	Passenger: 3 Stars
Pontiac Trans Sport	Driver: 4 Stars	Passenger: 4 Stars
Saturn SL	Driver: 4 Stars	Passenger: 4 Stars

CRASH TEST DATA

Toyota Camry	Driver: 4 Stars	Passenger: 4 Stars
Toyota Paseo	Driver: 4 Stars	Passenger: 4 Stars
Toyota Tacoma XtraCab	Driver: 1 Star	Passenger: 3 Stars
Toyota Tercel	Driver: 4 Stars	Passenger: 4 Stars
Volvo S90	Driver: 4 Stars	Passenger: 4 Stars

Crash Test Data 1997 (side impact):

Cadillac DeVille	Front: 4 Stars	Rear: 4 Stars
Chevrolet Camaro	Front: 3 Stars	Rear: 4 Stars
Chevrolet Cavalier Coupe	Front: 1 Star	Rear: 2 Stars
Chevrolet Lumina	Front: 4 Stars	Rear: 3 Stars
Chevrolet Malibu	Front: 1 Star	Rear: 3 Stars
Chrysler Cirrus	Front: 3 Stars	Rear: 2 Stars
Dodge Stratus	Front: 3 Stars	Rear: 2 Stars
Ford Contour	Front: 3 Stars	Rear: 4 Stars
Ford Crown Victoria	Front: 4 Stars	Rear: 4 Stars
Ford Escort	Front: 3 Stars	Rear: 3 Stars
Ford Taurus	Front: 3 Stars	Rear: 3 Stars
Honda Civic Sedan	Front: 3 Stars	Rear: 3 Stars
Hyundai Sonata	Front: 1 Star	Rear: 2 Stars
Mercury Grand Marquis	Front: 4 Stars	Rear: 4 Stars
Mercury Sable	Front: 3 Stars	Rear: 3 Stars
Mercury Tracer	Front: 3 Stars	Rear: 3 Stars
Mitsubishi Galant	Front: 3 Stars	Rear: 2 Stars
Nissan Maxima	Front: 4 Stars	Rear: 3 Stars
Oldsmobile Cutlass	Front: 1 Star	Rear: 3 Stars
Plymouth Breeze	Front: 3 Stars	Rear: 2 Stars
Pontiac Firebird	Front: 3 Stars	Rear: 4 Stars
Pontiac Grand Am Sedan	Front: 1 Star	Rear: 3 Stars
Pontiac Sunfire Coupe	Front: 1 Star	Rear: 2 Stars
Saturn SL	Front: 3 Stars	Rear: 3 Stars
Toyota Camry	Front: 3 Stars	Rear: 3 Stars
Toyota Tercel Coupe	Front: 3 Stars	Rear: 4 Stars

Crash Test Data 1998 (frontal impact):

Ford Windstar	Driver: 5 Stars	Passenger: 5 Stars
Lincoln Navigator	Driver: 4 Stars	Passenger: 5 Stars

CRASH TEST DATA

40 mph offset frontal crash tests:

1997 BMW 5-series	Good
1997 Chevrolet Astro	Poor
1995 Chevrolet Cavalier	Poor
1995 Chevrolet Lumina	Good
1997 Chevrolet Venture	Poor
1995 Chrysler Cirrus	Poor
1997 Chrysler Town & Country	Marginal
1997 Dodge Grand Caravan	Marginal
1995 Dodge Stratus	Poor
1995 Ford Contour	Poor
1996 Ford Explorer	Acceptable
1997 Ford Windstar	Good
1997 GMC Safari	Poor
1997 Honda Odyssey	Marginal
1996 Infiniti I30	Poor
1997 Infiniti Q45	Marginal
1997 Isuzu Oasis	Marginal
1996 Land Rover Discovery	Acceptable
1997 Lexus LS400	Good
1995 Mazda Millenia	Acceptable
1997 Mazda MPV	Marginal
1997 Mercedes-Benz E-Class	Acceptable
1996 Mercury Mountaineer	Acceptable
1995 Mercury Mystique	Poor
1997 Mercury Villager	Marginal
1995 Mitsubishi Galant	Poor
1995 Nissan Maxima	Poor
1997 Nissan Quest	Marginal
1997 Oldsmobile Silhouette	Poor
1997 Plymouth Grand Voyager	Marginal
1997 Pontiac Trans Sport	Poor
1995 Saab 900	Poor
1995 Subaru Legacy	Acceptable
1996 Toyota 4Runner	Acceptable

LEASING TIPS

You've seen the ads: Mazda Miata for $199 a month. Nissan Altima for $269 a month. Jeep Grand Cherokee for $319 a month. Zowie! Visions of new golf clubs in your trunk, a big-screen TV in your living room and two weeks of prime vacationing in Vail release endorphins at twice the Surgeon General's recommended level. Hold on a sec. Read the fine print. See where it says *"Capitalized Cost Reduction"*? That's lease-speak for down payment. See where it says "30,000 miles over three-year term"? That's lease-speak for "You're going to the Safeway and back—and that's all folks." Want the car for zero down? That's gonna cost you. You drive someplace more than twice a month? That's gonna cost you too.

Like most consumers, you want to know how to buy or lease the car of your choice for the best possible price. Buyers are attracted to leasing by low payments and the prospect of driving a new car every two or three years. Many people figure that a car payment is an unavoidable fact of budgetary life, and they might as well drive 'new' rather than 'old.' True, leasing is an attractive alternative, but there are some things you need to understand about leasing before jumping in feet first without a paddle. Whatever. You know what we mean.

1.) How to Lease

Never walk into a dealership and announce that you want to lease a car. Don't talk payment either. Concentrate on finding a car you like, and know before you go into the dealership what you can afford. Lease payments are based on something called a *capitalized cost,* which is the selling price of the car. The *residual value* is usually the predicted value of the vehicle at the end of the lease term, and can be expressed as a percentage of the MSRP. Sometimes, the residual value is not the predicted value of the car at the end of the lease, but a number that allows the leasing company to lower the cost of the lease as much as possible without incurring excessive risk. A *money factor*, which is lease-speak for 'interest rate,' is also involved in the calculation of a lease payment. If the money factor is expressed as a percentage, convert the percentage to the money factor by dividing the number by 24 (yes, it's 24 regardless of the term of the lease). For example, a 7% (.07) interest rate converts to a .0029 money factor. Then, of course, there are associated taxes and fees that are added. Accept the fact that if the car you want to lease is not a popular model, your lease may be a bit higher than you anticipated.

Calculating an actual lease payment is nearly impossible, particularly when the lease is subsidized by the automaker, but you can arrive at an approximate ball-park figure by using the following formula, which we will illustrate using a 1998 Toyota Camry as an example. Remember, if you put any money down, or trade in your old car, you must deduct this amount from the capitalized cost. This deduction is called the *capitalized cost reduction.*

LEASING TIPS

We recommend paying the destination charge, the acquisition fee, the security deposit, and any taxes up front. Don't roll them into the lease.

1998 Toyota Camry LE V6 (MSRP)	**$22,558**
Capitalized Cost	**$22,558**
Destination Charge	**$420**
Acquisition Fee	**$450**
Security Deposit	**$450**
Capitalized Cost Reduction	**$1,320**
Residual Value after 3 years	55% of MSRP in this example) $22,558 x .55 = **$12,406.90**
Term Depreciation	(Capitalized Cost - Residual Value) $22,558 - $12,406.90 = **$10,151.10**
Money Factor	(Interest Rate divided by 24) 7.5% divided by 24 = **.0031**
Monthly Lease Rate	Capitalized Cost + Residual Value x .0031) $22,558 + $10,151.10 x .0031 = **$101.38**
Monthly Depreciation	(Term Depreciation divided by Lease Term) $11,151.10 divided by 36 = **$281.98**
State Sales Tax	(Monthly Depreciation + Monthly Lease Rate x Sales Tax Rate [6.5% in this ex.) $281.98 + $101.38 x .065 = **$24.92**
Monthly Payment	(Monthly Depreciation + Monthly Lease Rate + Sales Tax) $281.98 + $101.38 + $24.92 = **$408.28**

Keep in mind that every vehicle will have a unique residual value, and that the above formula doesn't take into consideration delivery and handling fees (D&H fees), documentation fees, the cost of license plates, city or county sales tax (if applicable in your part of the country), or trade-in values. Deduct the trade-in value from the Capitalized Cost before calculating the lease. If you're *upside down* on your trade, which means the car is worth less than you owe on the loan, then you'll need to add the difference between the balance due on the loan and the trade in value to the Capitalized Cost. Also, deduct the amount of any cash down payment from the Capitalized Cost before calculating the lease.

The example we illustrated is a straightforward lease with no factory subsidy. This formula will not account for *subsidized leases*. Subsidized leases allow dealers to lower payments by artificially raising residual values

LEASING TIPS

or lowering the capitalized cost through dealer incentives. You can recognize a subsidized lease easily. Any nationally or regionally advertised lease is generally subsidized by the manufacturer to keep lease payments low. The $199 per month Mazda Miata and $319 per month Jeep Grand Cherokee are examples of subsidized leases.

Computing a lease payment can be frustrating. Ford Motor Company has developed special calculators for the sole purpose of computing lease payments because their method is not nearly as simplistic as the one above. However, a buyer interested in a Ford can use the formula to calculate a ball-park figure and find out whether or not the lease fits their budget. This figure can also be compared with similar calculations for competing models whose manufacturer may or may not be offering subsidized leases.

Actual lease payments are affected by negotiation of the sticker price on the vehicle, term of the lease, available incentives, residual values, and layers of financial wizardry that even sales managers can't interpret without divine intervention. Once you find a car you can afford, negotiate the sticker price and then explore leasing based on the negotiated price. Ask what the residual value is and subtract any rebates or incentives from the Capitalized Cost. Use the formula above to calculate a ball-park figure, and if the dealer balks at your conclusion, ask them to explain the error of your ways.

Your best bet when leasing is to choose a model with a subsidized lease. Payments are very low, terms are simple to understand, and they are the only true bargain in the world of leasing.

2.) Low Payments

Low payments aren't a fallacy with leasing, when taken in proper context. For example, a well-equipped Ford Ranger XLT SuperCab stickers for about $21,000, give or take. To lease for two years with no *capitalized cost reduction* (down payment); it'll cost you about $415 per month (plus tax). To lease for three years; about $360 per month (plus tax). Assume that a single payment of $900 was made up front to cover the acquisition fee and the security deposit. Generally, Ford allows 15,000 miles per year and charges 11 cents per mile for each one over the term limit. To buy that Ranger, financed for 24 months at 10% APR with no money down, you would pay about $967 per month (plus tax). For three years at 10%, the payment would be around $678 per month (plus tax). So you see, leasing is cheaper on a monthly basis when compared to financing *for the same term*.

There are two flaws here. First, 60-month financing is now the standard, and 72-month financing is becoming more popular. The Ranger will cost right around $446 per month (plus tax) for five years, at 10% APR with zero down, and still be worth a good chunk of change at the end of the loan if cared for properly. Second, ownership is far less restrictive, even if the bank holds the title until 2003. You can drive as far as you want, paint the

LEASING TIPS

thing glow-in-the-dark orange with magenta stripes, and spill coffee on the seats without sweating a big wear-and-tear bill down the road. Leasing for two years costs about $10,410 (assuming you get the entire security deposit back), and you don't own the truck at lease-end. Financing for two years costs about $23,210, but you own a truck worth about $13,650 when the payment book is empty (unless, of course, you've actually painted it orange with magenta stripes and spilled coffee all over the interior), which makes your actual cost a tad over $9,560. Is leasing cheaper? Monthly payments, when compared to financing over the same term, are lower. But in many cases, leasing is actually more expensive.

Let's compare the longer-term effects of leasing vs. buying, over the same term and under identical conditions. By leasing the Ranger in this example for two years, and then buying the truck for its $13,650 residual value with financing at a slightly higher interest rate than you would have paid new (interest rates rise as the vehicle gets older), you pay hundreds less than if you had financed for 60 months at a lower rate when the truck was new. Assume the interest rate for 36 months on a two-year-old truck is 12%. Payments for the loan would total about $455 per month, or just over $16,380 for the life of the loan. Added to the cost of the two-year lease, the $21,000 Ranger has cost you $26,390 (plus tax). Had you bought the Ranger outright, financing for 60 months at 10% interest, the Ranger would have cost $26,775 (plus tax).

In our hypothetical example, the lease customer comes out ahead by nearly $950 once the security deposit has been returned. But there are several factors that should be kept in mind. When leasing, tax is calculated on the payment; when buying, tax is calculated on the selling price of the truck. At a 6.5% sales tax rate, the Ranger costs the buyer using conventional 60-month financing $169.65 less in sales tax than the buyer who leases and then purchases the truck at the residual value. Other factors, like fluctuating interest rates, down payments, and contractual obligations can also affect the lease vs. loan scenario. Additionally, vehicle condition can have a tremendous affect on value. A few dents, dings, or scratches could easily make a lease the more expensive proposition. When trying to determine if it is less expensive to lease and buy for the residual or finance outright, carefully weigh all the factors that can affect payments over the term of the lease or loan, including the way you drive and maintain a vehicle.

3.) Restrictions

Leasing severely restricts your use of a vehicle. Mileage allowances are limited, modifications to the vehicle can result in hefty fines at the end of the lease, and if the vehicle is not in top condition when it is returned, excessive wear-and-tear charges may be levied. Many dealers will be more lenient if you buy or lease another vehicle from them at the end of your

LEASING TIPS

term, but if you drop off the car and walk, prepare yourself for some lease-end misery.

Be sure to define these limitations at the beginning of the lease so that you know what you're getting yourself into. Find out what will be considered excessive in the wear-and-tear department and try to negotiate a higher mileage limit.

4.) Benefits

By leasing, you always get to drive a new vehicle every two or three years. This also means that, in most cases, the only time the car will be in the shop is for routine maintenance. And, as long as you lease only for the term of the original manufacturer's warranty, you're not liable for catastrophic repair bills. Additionally, leasing can allow a buyer to make that dream car fit the budget when conventional financing will not. Finally, and perhaps for some people this is the most important benefit, you're never again upside-down on a car loan, unless you try to end the lease early.

5.) Lease-end

Studies show that consumers generally like leases, right up until they end. The reason for their apprehension is rooted in the dark days of *open-end leasing*, when Joe Lessee was dealt a sucker punch by the lessor on the day Joe returned the car to the leasing agent. Back then, residual values were established at the beginning of the lease, but the lessee was responsible for the difference between the residual value and the fair market value at the end of the lease. The resulting lease-end charges maxxed out credit cards and dealers laughed all the way to the bank.

Leasing has evolved, and with today's *closed-end leases* (the only type of lease you should consider), the lease-end fees are quite minimal, unless the car has 100,000 miles on it, a busted-up grille and melted chocolate smeared into the upholstery. Dealers want you to buy or lease another car from them, and can be rather lenient regarding excess mileage and abnormal wear. After all, if they hit you with a bunch of trumped up charges you're not going to remain a loyal customer, are you?

Additionally, closed-end leasing establishes a set, non-negotiable residual value for the car in advance, at the beginning of the lease. Also, any fees or charges you may incur at the lease-end are spelled out in detail before you sign the lease. All the worry is removed by the existence of concrete figures.

Another leasing benefit is the myriad of choices you have at the end of the term. Well, maybe not a myriad, but there are four, which is more than you have after two or three years of financing. They are:

LEASING TIPS

* **Return the car to the dealer and walk away from it** after paying any applicable charges like a termination fee, wear-and-tear repairs, or excessive mileage bills. Of course, if you don't plan to buy or lease another car from the dealer, you may get hit for every minor thing, but those are the risks.

* **Buy the car** from the dealer for the residual value established at the beginning of the lease. If the car is in good shape, the residual value is probably lower than the true value of the car, making it a bargain, and many leasing companies will guarantee financing at the lowest interest rate available at the time your lease ends. If you've trashed the lease car, compare the lease-end wear-and-tear charges to the devaluation in worth the vehicle has suffered while in your care. You might be surprised to find that it's easier and less expensive to just give the car back and pay the fines.

* **Use any equity in the car as leverage in a new deal** with the dealer. Since residual values are generally set artificially high, the car is not likely to be worth more than the residual value at lease-end. However, a well-maintained, low mileage lease car might allow the dealer to knock up to a couple of thousand bucks off your next deal.

* **Sell the car** yourself and pay off the residual value, pocketing whatever profit you make.

Closed-end leasing is a win-win situation for everybody. The manufacturer sells more cars, the dealer sells more cars, and you get low payments and a new car every couple of years. However, it is important to stress that you never own the car and leasing can be quite restrictive. If you're a low mileage driver who maintains cars in perfect condition, don't like tying up capital in down payments and don't mind never-ending car payments, leasing is probably just right for you. If you're on the road all day every day, beat the stuffing out of your wheels, enjoy a 'customized' look or drive your cars until the wheels fall off, buy whatever it is you're considering, or plan to buy the leased car at the end of the term.

* *Thanks to Tim O'Connor of Centennial Leasing in Lakewood, Colorado, for sharing his insight.*

WARRANTIES & ROADSIDE ASSISTANCE

All new vehicles sold in America come with at least two warranties, and many include roadside assistance. Described below are the major types of warranties and assistance provided to consumers.

Basic. Your basic warranty covers everything except items subject to wear and tear, such as oil filters, wiper blades, and the like. Tires and batteries often have their own warranty coverages, which will be outlined in your owner's manual. Emission equipment is required to be covered for five years or 50,000 miles by the federal government.

Drivetrain. Drivetrain coverage takes care of most of the parts that make the car move, like the engine, transmission, drive axles and driveshaft. Like the basic warranty, parts subject to wear and tear like hoses and belts are not covered. However, most of the internal parts of the engine, such as the pistons and bearings, which are subject to wear and tear are covered by the drivetrain warranty. See your owner's manual or local dealer for specific coverages.

Rust. This warranty protects you from rust-through problems with the sheetmetal. Surface rust doesn't count. The rust must make a hole to be covered. Keep your car washed and waxed, and rust shouldn't be a problem.

Roadside Assistance. Most manufacturers provide a service that will rescue you if your car leaves you stranded, even if it's your fault. Lock yourself out of the car? Somebody will come and open it up. Run out of gas? Somebody will deliver some fuel. Flat tire? Somebody will change it for you. See your owner's manual for details, or ask the dealer about the specifics, and don't pay for extended coverage if your insurance company already provides this type of assistance.

WARRANTIES & ROADSIDE ASSISTANCE

Make	Basic (yrs/mi)	Drivetrain (yrs/mi)	Rust (yrs/mi)	Roadside Assistance (yrs/mi)
Acura	4/50,000	4/50,000	4/Unlimited	4/50,0000
Audi	3/50,000	3/50,000	10/Unlimited	3/Unlimited
BMW	4/50,000	4/50,000	6/Unlimited	4/50,000
Buick	3/36,000	3/36,000	6/100,000	3/36,000
Cadillac	4/50,000	4/50,000	6/100,000	4/50,000
Chevrolet	3/36,000	3/36,000	6/100,000	3/36,000
Chrysler	3/36,000	3/36,000	5/100,000	3/36,000
Dodge	3/36,000	3/36,000	5/100,000	3/36,000
Eagle	3/36,000	3/36,000	5/100,000	3/36,000
Ford	3/36,000	3/36,000	5/Unlimited	3/36,000
Geo	3/36,000	3/36,000	6/100,000	3/36,000
GMC	3/36,000	3/36,000	6/100,000	3/36,000
Honda	3/36,000	3/36,000	5/60,000	None Available
Hyundai	3/36,000	5/60,000	5/100,000	3/36,000
Infiniti	4/60,000	5/70,000	7/Unlimited	4/60,000
Isuzu	3/50,000	5/60,000	6/100,000	5/60,000
Jaguar	4/50,000	4/50,000	6/Unlimited	4/50,000
Kia	3/36,000	5/60,000	5/100,000	3/36,000
Jeep	3/36,000	3/36,000	5/100,000	3/36,000
Land Rover	3/42,000	3/42,000	6/Unlimited	3/42,000
Lexus	4/50,000	6/70,000	6/Unlimited	4/Unlimited
Lincoln	4/50,000	4/50,000	5/Unlimited	4/50,000
Mazda	3/50,000	3/50,000	5/Unlimited	3/50,000
Mercedes	4/50,000	4/50,000	4/50,000	3/50,000 (Millenia only)
Mercury	3/36,000	3/36,000	5/Unlimited	Unlimited
Mitsubishi	3/36,000	5/60,000	7/100,000	3/36,000
Nissan	3/36,000	5/60,000	5/Unlimited	5/60,000
Oldsmobile	3/36,000	3/36,000	6/100,000	None Available
Plymouth	3/36,000	3/36,000	5/100,000	3/36,000
Pontiac	3/36,000	3/36,000	6/100,000	3/36,000
Porsche	2/Unlimited	2/Unlimited	10/Unlimited	2/Unlimited
Saab	4/50,000	N/A	6/Unlimited	4/50,000
Saturn	3/36,000	3/36,000	6/100,000	3/36,000
Subaru	3/36,000	5/60,000	5/Unlimited	None Available
Suzuki	3/36,000	3/36,000	3/Unlimited	None Available
Toyota	3/36,000	5/60,000	5/Unlimited	None Available
Volkswagen	2/24,000	10/100,000	6/Unlimited	2/24,000
Volvo	4/50,000	4/50,000	8/Unlimited	4/Unlimited

DEALER HOLDBACKS

Dealer holdback is built-in profit to the dealer. It comes in the form of a quarterly kickback for every vehicle the dealer sold during the previous quarter. Think of it as a dealer credit, paid by the manufacturer as a reward for selling a car.

For example, let's say you're interested in a Ford with a Manufacturer's Suggested Retail Price (MSRP) of $20,000, including optional equipment. Dealer invoice on this hypothetical Ford is $18,000, including optional equipment. The invoice includes a dealer holdback that, in the case of all Ford vehicles, amounts to 3% of the total MSRP. The destination charge should not be included when figuring the holdback. So, on this particular Ford, the true dealer cost is actually $17,400, plus destination charges. Even if the dealer sells you the car for invoice, which is highly unlikely, he would still be making $600 on the deal when his quarterly check arrived. That $600 is profit to the dealer only; the sales staff doesn't see any of it.

Does the dealer need to use holdback money to pay the bills? That depends on how long the car has been sitting on the lot. Holdback money is an incentive from the manufacturer to the dealer to entice the dealer to stock vehicles on the lot. Dealers pay a monthly floorplanning fee for each vehicle in stock. If the Ford used in the example above arrived on the lot in December, and you bought it in July, chances are very good that floorplanning fees for this particular car have eaten up most, if not all, of the holdback money. However, the dealer is more than making up for this loss with sales of cars that have been in stock for only a month or two.

To determine a fair price for the car illustrated above, you would add 5% to the true dealer cost. Edmund's recommends 5% because it will allow the dealer to cover costs involved with selling the car, and it will provide the salesperson, who likely makes a meager commission, with a paycheck. In this example, add a fair profit of $870, for a target price of $18,270. Remember, this price doesn't include destination charges, the dealer's D&H (Delivery & Handling) fee, advertising charges, tax, license plates, or any fees associated with processing paperwork.

Dealer holdback allows dealers to advertise big sales. Often, ads promise that your new car will cost you just "$1 over/under invoice!" Additionally, the dealer stands to reap further benefits if there is some sort of dealer incentive or customer rebate on the car. Generally, sale prices stipulate that all rebates and incentives go to the dealer. Using the example above, let's see what happens when there is a rebate.

DEALER HOLDBACKS

Suppose the car described above has a $1,000 rebate in effect. You need to subtract that $1,000 rebate (remember, the dealer is keeping the rebate) from the true dealer cost of $17,400, which results in a new dealer cost of just $16,400. Now, you must calculate a fair price. In this example, 5% of true dealer cost of $16,400 is $820, which means that the price you should try to buy the car for is $17,220, plus destination, advertising, tax, and fees.

Your best strategy is to avoid mentioning that you know the holdback amount and what it is during negotiations. Dealers absolutely will not give away this money! Only explain how you arrived at your offer if prodded, and be prepared to throw in a few hundred more dollars to make the deal happen.

Domestic manufacturers (Chrysler, Ford, and GM) generally offer dealers a holdback equaling 3% of the total sticker price, or MSRP, of the car. Import manufacturers (Honda, Nissan, Toyota, etc.) provide holdback amounts that are equal to a percentage of total MSRP, base MSRP, or base invoice. Following is a current list of makes and the amount of the 1998 dealer holdback.

Make	Holdback
Acura	2% of the Base MSRP
Audi	No Holdback
BMW	2% of the Base MSRP
Buick	3% of the Total MSRP
Cadillac	3% of the Total MSRP
Chevrolet	3% of the Total MSRP
Chrysler	3% of the Total MSRP
Dodge	3% of the Total MSRP
Eagle	3% of the Total MSRP
Ford	3% of the Total MSRP
GMC	3% of the Total MSRP
Honda	2% of the Base MSRP (except Prelude, which has no holdback.)
Hyundai	2% of the Total Invoice
Infiniti	1% of the Total MSRP + 1% of the Total Invoice
Isuzu	3% of the Total MSRP
Jaguar	2% of the Base Invoice
Jeep	3% of the Total MSRP
Kia	No Holdback

DEALER HOLDBACKS

Land Rover	No Holdback
Lexus	No Holdback
Lincoln	3% of the Total MSRP
Mazda	2% of the Base Invoice
Mercedes-Benz	3% of the Total MSRP
Mercury	3% of the Total MSRP
Mitsubishi	2% of the Total MSRP
Nissan	3% of the Total Invoice
Oldsmobile	3% of the Total MSRP
Plymouth	3% of the Total MSRP
Pontiac	3% of the Total MSRP
Porsche	No Holdback
Saab	3% of the Base MSRP
Saturn	One-price sales. Customer pays MSRP.
Subaru	2% of the Total MSRP
Suzuki	2% of the Base MSRP
Toyota	2% of the Base Invoice (Amount may differ in Southeastern U.S.)
Volkswagen	2% of Total MSRP
Volvo	$300 Flat Amount

1998 GMC Yukon

PAYMENT TABLE

*Depicts monthly payment per $1,000 borrowed**

		TERM (length of loan)				
		12	24	36	48	60
I	4%	85.15	43.40	29.50	22.55	18.45
N	5%	85.60	43.85	29.95	23.00	18.90
T	6%	86.05	44.30	30.40	23.50	19.35
E	7%	86.55	44.75	30.90	23.95	19.80
R	8%	87.00	45.25	31.35	24.40	20.30
E	9%	87.45	45.70	31.80	24.90	20.75
S	10%	87.90	46.15	32.25	25.35	21.25
T	11%	88.40	46.60	32.75	25.85	21.75
	12%	88.85	47.05	33.20	26.35	22.25
R	13%	89.30	47.55	33.70	26.85	22.75
A	14%	89.80	48.00	34.20	27.35	23.25
T	15%	90.25	48.50	34.65	27.85	23.80
E	16%	90.75	48.95	35.15	28.35	24.30

*rounded to nearest nickel

Automobile Manufacturers
Customer Assistance Numbers

Acura	1-800-382-2238
Chevrolet	1-800-222-1020
Chrysler	1-800-992-1997
Dodge	1-800-992-1997
Ford	1-800-392-3673
GMC	1-800-462-8782
Honda	1-800-999-1009
Infiniti	1-800-662-6200
Kia	1-800-333-4542
Land Rover	1-800-637-6837
Lexus	1-800-255-3987
Lincoln	1-800-392-3673
Mazda	1-800-222-5500
Mercedes-Benz	1-800-222-0100
Mercury	1-800-392-3673
Mitsubishi	1-800-222-0037
Nissan	1-800-647-7261
Oldsmobile	1-800-442-6537
Plymouth	1-800-992-1997
Pontiac	1-800-762-2737
Subaru	1-800-782-2783
Suzuki	1-800-934-0934
Toyota	1-800-331-4331

FREE for Edmund's readers!

Take the *haggling* out of New Truck buying!

Call 1-800-201-7703 now and save hundreds, even thousands, off the sticker price!

❶ It's easy. Simply provide the make, model, and year of the New Truck or Car you want.

❷ We'll tell you the "Preferred Price" and the dealer nearest you who will honor it!

❸ The "Preferred Price" means you save hundreds, even thousands, off the sticker price without the *hassle of negotiating!*

AutoVantage

Call AutoVantage now
1-800-201-7703
(Please refer to Free offer #99940142.)

"Great service saved us $4,000!"
Robert Wilson — Forked River, NJ

Please note: This is a Free consumer service. You are not obligated to visit the dealer or make a purchase.

AutoVantage is a service provided by CUC International Inc., which may modify and improve any part of the service at any time and without prior notice.

© 1997, CUC International Inc.

FREQUENTLY ASKED QUESTIONS

Edmund's solicits e-mail from consumers who visit our website at http://www.edmund.com. Below are 22 commonly asked questions regarding new cars and the buying process.

1. How soon after a price increase does Edmund's modify its data?

This depends on how soon our sources are notified. Sometimes, it's a matter of days; other times, it can take longer. Rest assured that we painstakingly attempt to maintain the most up-to-date pricing. If a dealer disputes the accuracy of our pricing, ask them to prove it by showing you the invoice so that you can compare. If prices have indeed increased, the amount will not be very substantial, and the new figures should easily be within a few percentage points of those published in this guide.

2. Do factory orders cost more than buying from dealer stock?

All things considered equal, ordered vehicles cost no more than vehicles in dealer stock and, in some cases, may actually cost less. When you buy from dealer stock, you may have to settle for a vehicle with either more or less equipment or your second or third color choice. Moreover, the dealership pays interest on stocked vehicles at a predetermined monthly rate to the manufacturer. This interest is called floor plan, and is subsidized by the dealer holdback. When you factory order, you get exactly what you want, in the color you want, and the dealer eliminates the floor plan. In most cases, the dealer passes the savings on to the customer, and the savings could amount to several hundred dollars.

The downside to ordering is that incentives and rebates are only good on the day of delivery. If an incentive or rebate plan was in effect when the vehicle was ordered, but not in effect the day of delivery, the customer is not eligible for the incentive or rebate. If you order a vehicle, and the delivery date is very close to the expiration date of a rebate or incentive program, beware that the dealer may try to delay delivery until after the rebate or incentive has expired.

FREQUENTLY ASKED QUESTIONS

From a negotiation standpoint, dealers may be more likely to offer a better price on a vehicle in stock, particularly if the monthly floor plan payments have exceeded the holdback amount and are now chewing into the dealer's profit.

3. Can I order a car directly from the factory without going through a dealer?

No, you cannot. Direct factory ordering is a hoax concocted by Zeke and Butherus over their nightly Jack Daniels' pow-wow at Hic a Billies. Dealers are franchisees of the manufacturer, and are protected as such.

4. Why is the car I'm looking at on the West Coast priced differently than what's listed in this guide?

California, Oregon, Washington and Idaho are the testing grounds for different pricing and option schemes. Because of the popularity of imported makes in this market, domestic manufacturers will often slash dealer profit margins and offer better-equipped cars at lower prices than those available in other parts of the country. This is why some dealer incentives and customer rebates do not apply on the West Coast, and why some option packages available in those states may not be listed in this guide.

5. When should a car be considered used?

Technically, a vehicle is considered used if it has been titled. However, some dealers can rack up hundreds or thousands of miles on a new car without titling it. In these cases, the ethical definition of a used car should include any car used for extensive demonstration or personal use by dealership staff members. The only miles a new car should have on the odometer when purchased are those put on during previous test drives by prospective buyers (at dealerships where demonstrators are not used), and any miles driven during a dealer trade, within a reasonable limit. If the new car you're considering has more than 300 miles on the odometer, you should question how the car accumulated so many miles, and request a discount for the excessive mileage. We think a discount amounting to a dime a mile is a fair charge for wear and tear inflicted by the dealership.

FREQUENTLY ASKED QUESTIONS

A car should not be considered used if it is a brand-new leftover from a previous model year. However, it should be discounted, because many manufacturers offer dealers incentives designed to help the dealer lower prices and clear out old stock.

6. Why doesn't Edmund's list option prices for some makes and models?

Almost all Acura, Honda, and Suzuki options are dealer installed. Some manufacturers, like Nissan, Subaru, and Volvo, will offer both factory- and dealer-installed options. Pricing for these items can vary depending on region and dealer. Therefore, it is impossible for Edmund's to list an accurate price for these items. Our experience shows that these items often carry a 100% mark up in dealer profit. We recommend that you avoid buying dealer-installed options if you can help it.

7. How can a dealer sell a new car for much less than the invoice price Edmund's publishes?

Auto manufacturers will often subsidize volume-sellers to keep sales and production up by offering car dealers hefty cash rewards for meeting monthly or quarterly sales goals. In other words, the dealer will take a slight loss on the car in anticipation of larger cash rewards if sales goals are met. It has been our experience that when a dealer sells a vehicle for less than invoice, the deal is always being subsidized by the manufacturer in one form or another. In print ads, always look for phrases such as "all incentives and/or rebates assigned to dealer."

Also, since profit can be made on other parts of the deal, a dealer may be willing to take a loss on the price of the car in exchange for profit gleaned from a low-ball trade-in value, financing, rustproofing, an extended warranty, and aftermarket or dealer-installed accessories. We once met a Plymouth salesman who bragged that he sold a Neon for invoice, but with the undervalued trade-in, high-interest financing and dealer-installed items factored into the deal, the buyer actually paid more than $20,000 for the car. Keep in mind that there is more to a good deal than a low price.

FREQUENTLY ASKED QUESTIONS

8. How much does an extended warranty cost the warranty company?

The cost of an extended warranty is based upon the degree of probability that any given vehicle will require repairs during the extended warranty period. Reliability records and repair cost information for a vehicle are evaluated to forecast potential future repair costs, and the extended warranty company will then charge a premium adequate enough to cover the potential cost of repairing the vehicle during the warranty period, while still making a profit. It is important to note that the cost of an extended warranty includes administrative costs for handling paperwork and claims, and insurance to guarantee that claims will be paid.

Extended warranty costs are based on averages, so the cost of applying an extended warranty to any given make and model of car can vary from consumer to consumer. Let's say you bought a $1,000 extended warranty for two identical Brand X vehicles; Car A and Car B. During the extended warranty period, Car A never breaks, so the extended warranty is never used. At the same time, Car B suffers bills amounting to $1,200 for transmission and valve problems. Profit on the warranty sold for Car A will counterbalance the loss suffered on Car B. Extended warranty companies sell thousands of warranties annually, and are able to make a profit when the actual loss experience is lower than the forecast potential for future repair. In other words, when sales exceed overhead, the company makes money.

You can purchase an extended warranty several ways, and we recommend shopping around for the best price. Start with the warranty providers, such as Warranty Gold, and then compare to what the dealer can offer. The majority of the time, the dealer cannot beat your best price from a warranty provider because of the markup a dealer must charge to make a profit on the extended warranty offered. Also, when shopping extended warranties, be sure the policies are comparable in terms of deductible costs, covered parts and the amount of labor that will be paid for.

FREQUENTLY ASKED QUESTIONS

9. Why won't the dealer accept my offer of 5% over true dealer cost?

The dealer doesn't have to sell you a car. If demand for the model is high, or if supplies are short, or if the dealer enjoys making a healthy profit, you won't be able to buy the car for a fair price. Don't argue the point, just find another dealer. If all the dealers you contact refuse to sell the car at this price, then your offer is too low, and you must start over at a higher value.

10. How do I figure a fair deal?

Use this formula: Dealer Invoice of car and options - Dealer Holdback - Rebates/Incentives + 5% Fair Profit + Destination Charge + Advertising Fees + Tax = Fair Deal

11. Why should I pay advertising fees?

The auto manufacturer charges the car dealer an advertising fee roughly equivalent to 1% of the sticker price. The car dealer passes this cost on to the consumer. Additionally, regional and local advertising pools exist in most medium to large metropolitan areas. Participation by the car dealer in these regional and local advertising pools is voluntary, but the auto manufacturer may ensure that a dealer join a local advertising pool by withholding stock, sending less popular rather than hot-selling models to the dealer, and cutting incentive money. Essentially, the factory is blackmailing the dealer, forcing the dealer to join regional and local advertising pools in an effort to make its models more visible to the consumer. Regional advertising fees should never be more than 2% of the sticker price. If you're paying more than 3% of the sticker price in advertising fees, find another dealership.

12. Can I negotiate the price of a new Saturn?

No, you cannot. All Saturn dealers post the same non-negotiable price for identical cars. This way, a buyer cannot shop down the street for a better deal, because the deal will be the same. You can, however, demand top dollar for your trade and/or a lower interest rate to lower the overall cost of the deal.

FREQUENTLY ASKED QUESTIONS

13. How can I find out what customer rebates or dealer incentives are currently available?

Rebates to customers are clearly announced in advertising. Incentives to dealers, commonly known as "back-end monies," are not. Edmunds publishes current national and large regional rebate and incentive programs online at http://www.edmund.com. Local rebate and incentive programs also exist on occasion, but Edmund's doesn't have access to this information. Ask your dealer if the local automobile dealer association or advertising association is sponsoring any rebates or incentives in your metropolitan area.

14. Why do some dealer incentives on specific models have a range of values?

Sometimes, the manufacturer will tell the dealer that he must sell a certain number of cars to qualify for an incentive. For example, let's say Nissan offered dealers an incentive of $100-1,000 on the Altima. This a quota-based incentive. It means that to get the $100 per car, the dealer might have to sell 10 cars before a certain date. To get $500 per car, the dealer might have to sell 50 cars before a certain date. To get $1,000 per car, the dealer might have to sell 100 cars before a certain date. The more cars the dealer sells, the more money he makes, because quota-based rebates are retroactive.

With these types of quota-based incentives, you have leverage. With your sale, the dealer is one more car closer to clearing the next hurdle and making more money. We recommend that you request half of the maximum quota-based incentive while negotiating your deal, unless the dealer or salesperson bungles and admits that your sale will put them into the next tier of incentive qualification. In this case, demand the maximum incentive.

15. When I use Edmund's formula to calculate a lease, I get a payment that is substantially higher than what the dealer quoted me. Why is this?

Most nationally advertised leases are subsidized by the manufacturer. This means that the manufacturer gives the dealer incentive money to lower the capitalized cost (selling price) listed on the lease,

FREQUENTLY ASKED QUESTIONS

or that the financing institution owned by the manufacturer has artificially inflated the residual value to lower the monthly payment, or both. Dealers may not inform you of these adjustments in the numbers.

Another problem with advertised lease payments seen in newspapers and on television is that consumers don't read the terms of the lease carefully. Sometimes, a substantial capitalized cost reduction (down payment) is required. Sometimes hefty deposits and other drive-off fees are involved. Mileage limits may be ridiculously low. Payments may be required for 48 or 60 months rather than the conventional 24- or 36-month term. Read the fine print carefully!

Also, keep in mind that there are more than 250 different lending institutions across the country, and each one sets its own residual values for lease contracts. Don't be surprised if you go to three different dealers and get three different lease payments for the same vehicle over the same term.

16. Why are destination charges the same for every dealer around the country?

Auto manufacturers will average the cost to ship a car from the factory to the furthest dealership with the cost to ship a car from the factory to the closest dealership. Some manufacturers do this for each model, others average costs across an entire make. Sometimes, shipping costs to Hawaii and Alaska may be higher than the averaged amount for the contiguous 48 states.

17. Can I avoid paying the destination charge by picking up a car at the factory?

Currently, the only North American factories that allow customers to take delivery the minute a car rolls off the assembly line are the Corvette plant in Bowling Green, Kentucky, and the Dodge Viper plant in Detroit. Buyers who opt to travel to the Bluegrass or Great Lakes states to pick up their new Corvette or Viper still pay the dealer they bought it from the destination charge. We don't know if you can avoid paying destination charges on European models by ordering and taking delivery of a car in Europe, but that's an expensive proposition to avoid paying a few hundred bucks.

FREQUENTLY ASKED QUESTIONS

18. What is a carryover allowance?

At the beginning of a new model year, some manufacturers provide dealers with a carryover allowance in addition to the dealer holdback. The carryover allowance is applied to cars from the previous model year, and is designed to assist dealers in lowering prices and clearing out old stock. Currently, the only domestic automaker that gives its dealers a carryover allowance is Ford Motor Company. The amounts can vary, but they average five percent of the MSRP. General Motors and Chrysler target slow sellers with heavy incentives and rebates. Most import manufacturers subscribe to the incentive and rebate philosophy as well.

19. Should I buy rustproofing, fabric protection packages, paint sealant, and other dealer-installed items?

Of course not. Most new cars are covered against rust perforation for several years and up to 100,000 miles. Want to protect your fabric? Go to an auto parts store and buy a can or two of Scotchgard. New cars have clearcoat paint, which offers protection from the elements. A little elbow grease and a jar of carnauba wax will keep the finish protected and looking great. By investing a little time and effort into your automobile, you can save hundreds on these highly profitable dealer protection packages.

20. Who sets the residual value for a lease?

The financing institution that is handling the lease for the dealership sets the residual value, which can be affected by market forces and vehicle popularity. When shopping leases, it is important to shop different financing institutions for the highest residual value and the lowest interest rate.

21. I want to pay cash for my new car. Do I have an advantage?

Not necessarily. You must remember that no matter how you pay for your car, it's all cash to the dealer. In the old days when dealers carried your note, you could save money by paying cash because there was no risk to the dealer. Today, dealerships finance through one of several lending institutions (banks, credit unions, or the

FREQUENTLY ASKED QUESTIONS

automaker's captive financing division) who pay them cash when the contract is presented. In fact, if dealerships do the financing on your behalf, they tend to make more money on your contract in the form of a reserve; anywhere from ½ to 1 point spread on the interest. For example, if the published rate is 8.75%, the lender to dealer rate may be discounted to 8%; the .75% being the reserve held by the dealer as additional profit. This may not sound like much, but it adds up to hundreds of thousands of dollars a year at larger dealerships. This is the reason you should always arrange financing before going to the dealership, and then ask the dealer if they can beat your pre-approved rate. In most cases, they cannot, because of the reserve.

Paying cash is an advantage if you suffer from poor credit or bankruptcy, because it allows you to avoid the higher interest rates charged on loans to people with past credit problems.

22. *When is the best time to purchase a car from a dealer?*

The absolute best day to buy a car is December 31, particularly if it is raining or snowing. If you can't wait that long, try the day before Christmas or Thanksgiving. If that doesn't work out for you, any day the last week of any given month is a great time, and the nastier the weather, the better. Make the deal near closing time, when the sales staff is eager to go home for the night, but not so eager that they're willing to throw away a deal that could make them a few bucks. To ensure success, go into the dealership a few days beforehand and make sure they know you want to do the deal, but don't commit on that day. They'll call you back before quota time is up at the end of the month.

Why is this the best time to buy? Sales people are given quotas and incentives to reach X sales for the month. It is not uncommon for a salesperson to let a car go at invoice during the last week of the month to hit their goal, which results in a monetary or other tangible reward.

Get The Best Price On Your New Or Used Vehicle With Financing Pre-Arranged...
ON THE INTERNET!

visit us at http://www.CarFinance.com/edmunds

Surf your way to great rates and terms that give you extremely low payments...

It's Easy!

1. Tell us about the vehicle you may be interested in

2. Review our financing products at your own pace & with no sales pressure— 24 hours a day. (Be sure to check out our newest products including balloon loans and used car leasing— all designed to lower your monthly payments!)

3. Get pre-qualified - instantly and completely anonymously

4. Apply using our "3 minute" application and get a credit decision within 48 hours

5. Approved applicants can visit their dealer of choice and finish negotiating with confidence

NEGOTIATE YOUR BEST PRICE WITH PRE-APPROVED FINANCING!

It's Convenient and It's Confidential!
We use a secure system. Your personal information is held in confidence.

www.CarFinance.com/edmunds

ROAD TEST: Mercedes-Benz ML320

Better Than It Looks, Much Better

by B. Grant Whitmore
Managing Editor

1998 Mercedes-Benz ML320

When we got the first pictures of Mercedes' new AAV last year we were thrilled. A muscular shape, aggressive stance, and purposeful Mercedes-Benz elegance defined this vehicle that we prayed would enter production. As the year dragged on, spy shots informed us that the vehicle was indeed slated for production, and that it looked like the basic shape would at least make it to the showroom floor. Well, this vehicle, now dubbed the ML320, hits dealerships on September 21, and we're sorry to say that it looks nothing like the fluidly strong truck that we first saw pictures of over one year ago. Looking like the bastard offspring of the prototype and a Mercury Villager minivan, the ML320's outward visage has left many of Edmund's staff members scratching their heads wondering, "What happened to that beautiful truck we saw last summer?"

Seldom do prototype dreams enter production reality, though, so it's of little use to us to ponder what might have been. No, the ML320 isn't going to win any beauty pageants, but its shortcomings in the swimsuit competition are far overshadowed by its outstanding performance in the talent and congeniality contests.

ROAD TEST: Mercedes-Benz ML320

Designed from the ground up as a unique Mercedes product, the ML320 is a fantastic example of out-of-the-box thinking. Unconstrained by an existing idea of what a sport-ute should be, Mercedes decided to give it many of the best characteristics of both cars and trucks. This means a unique assemblage of technologies not normally seen together, such as: body-on-frame construction with a 4-wheel independent double-wishbone suspension, all-wheel drive that includes a low range, side-impact air bags and a 5,000-lb. towing capacity. No other vehicle, whether car or truck, features such diversity of concept or design.

There are so many features unique to this vehicle that touching on all of them in one road test would be nearly impossible. We will, however, attempt to highlight some of the more important ones. The ML320 is Mercedes' first recipient of its new family of V-type engines. Powered by a 3.2-liter V-6 engine that makes 215 horsepower and 233 lbs./ft. of torque, the ML320 is capable of accelerating from 0-60 mph in 9 seconds. A 5-speed automatic transmission is borrowed from the Mercedes-Benz parts bin, and does the work of rowing the truck's gears. This powerful engine is able to report best-in-class fuel economy numbers at 17 mpg city/21 mpg highway. Nothing to write home about, to be sure, but a darn sight better than the 13.5 mpg that a recent Lincoln Navigator test truck turned in *on the freeway!* The ML320 uses a three valves (two intake/one exhaust), twin-sparkplug cylinder head design, thus reducing cold start emissions by nearly 40%. This allows the ML320 to be classified as a Low Emissions Vehicle in all 50 states.

In addition to its all-new engine, the ML320 has chassis and suspension innovations that are not often seen in the sport-ute arena. To provide the strength demanded of SUVs, Mercedes has designed the ML320 with a separate frame that is boxed at both ends to provide strength and torsional rigidity. Seemingly anachronistic in a company that so often loads its vehicles with technology, this body-on-frame construction allows the ML320 to tow 5,000 lbs., and it keeps body panels from rubbing during off-road maneuvers. In order that the ML320 posses the ride and handling characteristics demanded by Mercedes customers, the designers in Stuttgart fitted this truck with an aluminum double-wishbone suspension front and rear. Allowing surprisingly quick turn-in and deceptively easy direction changes, this suspension concept

ROAD TEST: Mercedes-Benz ML320

will undoubtedly make its way to competing SUVs as customers continue to demand increasingly car-like performance from their 4-wheel drive vehicles.

Mercedes has never been a company to scrimp on safety and their efforts with the ML320 are no exception. Possessing dual front airbags, side-impact airbags (the first-ever application of such technology in an SUV), crumple zones, and adjustable headrests at each seating position, the ML320 is loaded with passive safety equipment. Strangely, though, the rear middle passenger's seat is missing a shoulder belt and has to get by with only a lap belt. Equally important in our opinion is the ML320's full complement of active safety features. Anti-lock brakes stop this truck in a hurry, and precise rack-and-pinion steering lets the driver steer out of harm's way.

Enough with the technical stuff. What you probably want to know is how this thing handles on and off the road. In other words, how does it compare in a market that is saturated with excellent vehicles? The answer, quite simply, is that this is probably the best all-around SUV in the sub-$40,000 price class. It goes faster than any sport-ute except a V-8-equipped Jeep Grand Cherokee, it turns better than anything this side of a Nissan Maxima, it stops with the authority that we have come to expect of German sport sedans, and it has more cargo capacity than the voluminous Ford Explorer. Off-road is another story. Although the ML320 is competent in the muck, nobody is going to mistake it for a boulder-crawling Jeep Wrangler. The main problem facing the ML320's off road abilities is the truck's limited ground clearance. At 8.4 inches at its lowest point, the ML320 is far lower to the ground than the towering 4Runner or Jeep Grand Cherokee. The ML320 also has tires that are biased toward a comfortable on-road ride; the result off-road is somewhat limited traction on mossy rocks and muddy trails. Never fear, however, most people would not think of taking their $35,000 SUV on a trail half as treacherous as the one Mercedes had us successfully negotiate during the introduction of the ML320 in Portland, Oregon. We say without hesitation that it will successfully handle 99.9% of the bad weather/off-road duties thrown at it by its owners.

One of our favorite things about this remarkable vehicle is its well-planned interior. Cupholders that hold more than a 12 oz. can of soda abound, as do handy storage cubbies, map pockets, and a deep center

ROAD TEST: Mercedes-Benz ML320

console. Comfortable chairs offer enough leg, shoulder, and headroom to accommodate five large people, and the cargo area will hold an entire week's worth of camping gear without any trouble. The controls for operating the ML320's myriad systems are all within easy reach of the driver, and are thankfully devoid of the pictographic icons that are so prevalent in the design of German interiors. Despite its considerable size, it is easy to pilot the ML320 in a crowded parking lot thanks to the copious amounts of glass that wrap around all sides of this truck. Our main complaint about the interior of the ML320 is the less-than-expected quality of the dashboard plastic and the overly confusing operation required to fold the rear seats down. Other than that, it's hard to tell that you aren't sitting in a tall E-Class sedan.

Mercedes did the unexpected when designing this vehicle. They didn't badge-engineer like Infiniti or Acura, nor did they go after the high side of the market against the likes of Land Rover or Lexus. Instead, they made a novel, competent vehicle that is neither car nor truck that competes directly against the best-selling vehicles in the class like the Jeep Grand Cherokee, Ford Explorer and Toyota 4Runner. Plant capacity is limited to 60,000 units per year, a good thing for the ML320's competitors, because there is nothing besides this truck's somewhat homely looks that should keep it from becoming the most desired SUV on the market.

Save hundreds, even thousands, off the sticker price of the new car _you_ want.

**Call Autovantage®
your FREE auto-buying service
1-800-201-7703**

No purchase required. No fees.

ROAD TEST: Isuzu Rodeo

EE-soo-zoo Roh-dee-oh

by Christian J. Wardlaw
Editor-in-Chief

1998 Isuzu Rodeo

Vehicle Tested: 1998 Isuzu Rodeo LS 4WD

Base Price of Vehicle: $29,355 (includes destination charge)

Options on Test Vehicle: Rear Spare Tire Carrier with Cover, Limited Slip Differential, Leather Seating Surfaces, Power Moonroof, California Emissions

Price of Vehicle as Tested: $31,480 (Includes destination charge)

Isuzu. Funny name, isn't it? Listen to it roll off the tongue: ee-soo-zoo. Looks funny too. But there's nothing funny looking, or funny sounding, about the all new Rodeo, the company's bread-and-butter best selling sport utility. This is a serious competitor in the popular mid-size SUV class.

Years ago, Isuzu sold both cars and trucks in the U.S. They too, had funny names like I-Mark and Impulse. But unlike the brand moniker, I-Mark was forgettable and nobody bought the idea that a company

ROAD TEST: Isuzu Rodeo

with a funny name could offer the Impulse sports car. Cut to a scene in a singles bar, where an attractive member of the opposite sex sidles up to an Impulse driver for some light conversation. "So good looking, what do you drive?" "An Isuzu." Hasta la vista, baby.

Perhaps the best-known Isuzu car was the Geo Storm, sold by Chevrolet dealers between 1990 and 1993. A sporty 2+2 hatchback that looked just like a miniature Camaro Z28, the Storm was a big hit with young singles looking for racy transportation and a low insurance rate. While the Storm was a success under the Geo umbrella of captive imports at Chevy stores, the Isuzu-badged Impulse and Stylus sedan were wheezing along the lower fringes of the sales charts like a Suzuki Esteem loaded with linebackers. In 1993, Isuzu decided to quit building cars, and concentrate on trucks.

The Storm wasn't the first collaboration between General Motors and Isuzu. Remember the Chevrolet LUV, one of the mini-pickups from the 1970s that started the compact truck trend? It was a rebadged Isuzu. These days, the tables have turned. General Motors began sending the Chevrolet S-10 compact pickup to Isuzu when the trusty Half Ton pickup was retired in 1994. Isuzu gives the S-10 a light makeover and the Hombre nameplate. One staff member owned a bulletproof (so he claims) 1992 Isuzu pickup, and thinks the Hombre is a weak effort in comparison. Isuzu can be thankful they decided to revamp the Rodeo themselves, instead of asking GM for the Blazer.

If the opportunity arose, GM would do well to consider badge engineering a Rodeo to replace the rapidly aging Chevrolet Blazer/GMC Jimmy/Oldsmobile Bravada. The 1998 Isuzu Rodeo is without a doubt one of the best sport utility vehicles you can buy for less than $30,000. True, our fully-loaded LS test model ran a smidge higher than this tally, but dropping the leather upholstery and the power sunroof brings the price right back into line. We found our test truck to be powerful, comfortable, and tastefully designed. Off the beaten path, you'll lose your nerve before the Rodeo runs out of talent.

ROAD TEST: Isuzu Rodeo

We headed southwest from Denver for an afternoon of mud-bogging the Rodeo in the mountains, as the commercials for the truck encourage. Forecasters predicted rain and gloom; what better time to put a new 4WD through its paces? Well, as usual, the forecasters were wrong; at least for the portion of Colorado's Front Range that spans the distance between the U.S. Air Force Academy and suburban Denver. There, the sun was shining. As we climbed in elevation, the rolling plains unfolding below to the east, we noticed that clouds ringed our location in all directions. We drove skyward as if through the eye of a hurricane.

Nevertheless, we subjected the Rodeo to our usual rutted, rock-strewn, two-track trail through the foothills of central Colorado. The Rodeo managed the path with ease, maneuvering between pine trees and over jagged escarpments with confidence. A new push-button four-wheel drive system comes in handy when the going gets tough, shifting into 4-Hi at speeds up to ??? mph. A floor-mounted lever will produce 4-Lo when conditions warrant. The Rodeo's new rack-and-pinion steering gear is nicely weighted but slow to respond to directional changes, which is less than ideal on pavement but is comforting when a large rock jolts the steering wheel from the driver's grip, threatening to send the vehicle into the woods. Kickback is also severe, making the steering feel as though a bolt has loosened somewhere between the tie rods and the leather-wrapped wheel rim. We found that the Rodeo's suspension wasn't up to the task of absorbing deep dips and sharp bumps at speeds much above a trot, but keep the Rodeo crawling through the back country and almost nothing will be able to impede its progress.

The Rodeo's old drop-down tailgate has been replaced by something Isuzu calls a hatchgate (more funny names), which features a rear window that lifts up to drop small items into the cargo area, and a door that swings from right to left in order to accept bulkier items. The hatchgate chattered incessantly on bad surfaces, and after our dirty off-road excursion, we found a fine layer of pure Rocky Mountain dust coating the inside of the hatchgate and much of the plastic trim lining the cargo area. Other bad things about the hatchgate include inaccessibility when parallel parked in tight quarters, and the

ROAD TEST: Isuzu Rodeo

fact that people can't stand on both sides of the truck to lift large items inside. Good things about the hatchgate include an optional gate-mounted spare tire, and a lock that keeps the gate from swinging closed on an incline. Damn the utility! Shallow journalists that we are, we like the hatchgate because it's unique, and allows for a rugged looking gate-mounted spare tire.

Around town, the Rodeo is a real treat. A 3.2-liter V6 makes 205 horsepower at 5,400 rpm and 214 ft.-lbs. of torque at 3,000 rpm. This means a Rodeo driver can make Mitsubishi Montero Sport, Nissan Pathfinder and Toyota 4Runner drivers eat dust from a stoplight, while keeping pace with GMC Jimmys and Jeep Cherokees. The smooth overhead cam engine is a treat to run hard, but the penalty is abysmal fuel economy. The light-foots at the EPA could only wring 20 mpg from the Rodeo on the highway, and got a paltry 16 mpg in the city, so you can imagine how often we visited the local Conoco station during our week with the truck.

While the Rodeo can't hang with Jeeps in terms of handling on the road or off, it takes corners about as well as could be expected of a high-centered all-terrain-tired SUV and provides a smooth ride. A wider track for 1998 helps improve overall stability. The slow steering that helps directional stability so nicely when the pavement ends is a royal pain in the butt in parking lots, where the driver saws at the wheel for what seems like eternity to point the Rodeo toward the exit. Front disc/rear drum brakes stop the Rodeo short, and the pedal provides very good modulation feel. Throttle response is excellent, revving the engine as soon as the accelerator is depressed.

Despite a shorter wheelbase than the old Rodeo, the new truck has retained its large rear seat, and interior accommodations have actually grown in size. Leg room, shoulder room, and head room figures are all up for 1998, and Isuzu claims that cargo room has increased 8.3%, though space for luggage still looks rather tight to our eyes. A low step-in height makes getting into the Rodeo simple, but exiting from the rear seat requires some concentration due to an

ROAD TEST: Isuzu Rodeo

intrusive rear wheel well. Seat comfort is excellent front and rear, but one editor complained that the driver's seat was mounted too low to the floor. The driver faces a thick four-spoke steering wheel, flanked by secondary control buttons mounted on the dash. Stalks for turn signals and wipers feel solid, yet fluid, in operation. The simple climate controls are a model of ergonomic efficiency. Interior materials look and feel substantial, and the fake wood in our test truck added some needed warmth to the otherwise industrial gray atmosphere. Our LS was equipped with the optional power sunroof, and it featured one-touch opening. A Power/Winter mode is available with the automatic transmission. The hatchgate door has a very handy storage bin and cargo net built into the inside trim panel.

While the interior designers did a great job of creating a comfortable and attractive interior, we found some ergonomic glitches. Perhaps most notable was the placement of the 4WD engagement button right next to the cruise control engagement button on the dashboard to the left of the steering wheel. The buttons are the same size, the same color, and have nearly identical lettering. At night, they are poorly lit. We called Isuzu and found out that 4-Hi can be engaged at speeds up to 65 mph. "So," we asked, "what if somebody is cruising across Nebraska at 80 mph one sunny summer day, and accidentally hits the 4WD button instead of the cruise control button?" The Isuzu spokesman we talked to claimed that, unofficially, the system was designed to refuse such a request, and 4WD would not engage if vehicle speed was determined to be higher than 65 mph. Unofficially, we wonder when the first warranty claim will be made.

Another issue we took with the interior involved small lettering and symbols on the stereo buttons. Also worthy of mention is the lack of power window and power lock switch illumination at night, though a tiny indicator does help guide your finger to the driver's window button in the dark. We were put off by the disorganized appearance of the center console area, which is home to the automatic transmission shifter, the 4-Hi shifter, exposed dual cupholders, the Power/Winter transmission mode selectors, and a virtually useless coin storage slot. We didn't like the fact that to close the door of the hatchgate, you've got to use two hands; one to release the lock that

ROAD TEST: Isuzu Rodeo

holds the door open on an incline and one to swing the door closed. Finally, and parents take note, there are no rear seat cupholders.

With the exception of the placement of the 4WD engagement button, these are relatively minor issues. The Isuzu Rodeo is a great looking, great driving sport utility. Honda will again be offering a rebadged version of the Rodeo called the Passport, but we'd skip it. Yes, the Passport is the same truck with a more socially acceptable chrome H in the center of the grille, but the Isuzu's superior warranty is worthwhile. Honda gives the Passport 3-year/36,000-mile basic and powertrain coverage, and 5-year/60,000-mile rust protection. Roadside assistance is not available. In contrast, Isuzu provides buyers with a 3-year/50,000-mile basic limited warranty, a 5-year/60,000-mile powertrain warranty, a 6-year/72,000-mile rust through guarantee, and 24-hour roadside assistance for five years or 60,000 miles. So, by selecting the Isuzu over the Honda you're getting what amounts to a free extended warranty.

Accounting for 85 percent of all Isuzu sales, the first-generation Rodeo enjoyed a brief run as the best-selling imported sport utility in the U.S. until 1994, when the Toyota 4Runner and Nissan Pathfinder alternately began finding their way into more American driveways. The current Nissan Pathfinder is very car-like in terms of interior accommodations and ride. From the driver's seat, it's hard to tell you're in a truck capable of taking you just about anywhere you might reasonably want to go. Today's Toyota 4Runner makes no such attempt, with a broad-shouldered look, cramped interior, and trucky ride. Under the Toyota's hood resides a powerful and smooth overhead cam V6 engine, and off-road the 4Runner does a reasonably fair impression of a mountain goat. To try and recapture best-seller status, Isuzu has infused the 1998 Rodeo with the best elements of the Pathfinder and 4Runner: rugged styling, a powerful overhead cam V6, competent off-road ability, a smooth highway ride, and an inviting car-like interior. We think they have a good shot at regaining the title.

Notes

Notes

Notes

Notes

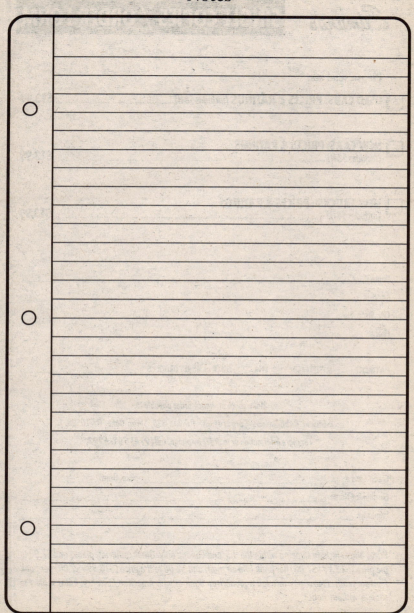

Edmund's SINGLE COPIES / ORDER FORM

Please send me:

☐ **USED CARS: PRICES & RATINGS** *(includes S&H)* **$13.99**

☐ **NEW CARS: PRICES & RATINGS**
(includes S&H) **$13.99**

☐ **NEW TRUCKS : PRICES & RATINGS**
(includes S&H) **$13.99**

Name _____
Address _____
City, State, Zip _____
Phone _____

PAYMENT: ___ MASTERCARD   ___ VISA   ___ CHECK or MONEY ORDER $ _____

Make check or money order payable to:
Edmund Publications Corporation P.O. Box 338, Shrub Oaks, NY 10588
For more information or to order by phone, call **(914) 962-6297**

Credit Card # _____ Exp. Date: _____
Cardholder Name: _____
Signature _____

Prices above include shipping within the U.S. and Canada only. Other countries, please add $7.00 to the price ($13.99+$7.00) per book (via air mail) and $2.00 to the price ($13.99+$2.00) per book (surface mail). Please pay through an American Bank or with American Currency. Rates subject to change without notice.

Edmund's SUBSCRIPTIONS / ORDER FORM
BUYER'S PRICE GUIDES

Please send me a one year subscription for:

☐ **USED CAR PRICES & RATINGS**
(package price includes $10.00 S&H) **$34.00**
Canada $40.00/Foreign Countries $48.00 (includes air mail S&H)
<u>4 issues/yr</u>

☐ **NEW CARS PRICES & RATINGS**
(package price includes $7.50 S&H) **$25.50**
Canada $30.00/Foreign Countries $36.00 (includes air mail S&H)
<u>3 issues/yr</u>

☐ **NEW TRUCKS PRICES & RATINGS**
(package price includes $7.50 S&H) **$25.50**
Canada $30.00/Foreign Countries $36.00 (includes air mail S&H)
<u>3 issues/yr</u>

☐ **NEW VEHICLE PRICES**
(package price includes $15.00 S&H) **$51.00**
Canada $60.00/Foreign Countries $72.00 (includes air mail S&H)
<u>6 issues/yr:</u>
3 NEW CARS PRICES & REVIEWS
3 NEW TRUCKS PRICES & REVIEWS

☐ **PREMIUM PLAN**
(package price includes $25.00 S&H) **$85.00**
Canada $100.00/Foreign Countries $120.00 (includes air mail S&H)
<u>10 issues/yr:</u>
4 USED CARS PRICES & REVIEWS
3 NEW CARS PRICES & REVIEWS
3 NEW TRUCKS PRICES & REVIEWS

Name _____

Address _____

City, State, Zip _____

PAYMENT: ___ MC ___ VISA ___ Check or Money Order-Amount $_____   Rates subject to change without notice

Make check or money order payable to:
Edmund Publications Corporation P.O.Box 338, Shrub Oaks, NY 10588
For more information or to order by phone, call **(914) 962-6297**

Credit Card # _____ Exp. Date: _____
Cardholder Name: _____
Signature _____

Edmund's

BUYER'S DECISION GUIDES
SCHEDULED RELEASE DATES FOR 1997/8*

VOL. 31/32		RELEASE DATE	COVER DATE
U3201	USED CARS: Prices & Ratings	JAN 98	SPRING 98
N3201	NEW CARS: Prices & Reviews [American & Import]	MAR 98	SPRING 98
S3201	NEW TRUCKS: Prices & Reviews [American & Import]	MAR 98	SPRING 98
U3202	USED CARS: Prices & Ratings	APR 98	SUMMER 98
N3202	NEW CARS: Prices & Reviews [American & Import]	JUN 98	SUMMER/FALL 98
S3202	NEW TRUCKS: Prices & Reviews [American & Import]	JUN 98	SUMMER/FALL 98
U3203	USED CARS: Prices & Ratings	JUL 98	FALL 98
U3204	USED CARS: Prices & Ratings	OCT 98	WINTER 98
N3203	NEW CARS: Prices & Reviews [American & Import]	DEC 98	WINTER 99
S3203	NEW TRUCKS: Prices & Reviews [American & Import]	DEC 98	WINTER 99

*Subject to Change